# THE VIVA List LATIN AMERICA

333 PLACES AND EXPERIENCES THAT PEOPLE LOVE

By the Vivatravelguides.com Online Community

Edited by Paula Newton, Michelle Hopey and Crit Minster, PhD

Visit www.vivatravelguides.com to learn more

# Credits:

**Managing Editor:** Paula Newton
**Executive Editor and Writer:** Michelle Hopey
**Head Writer and Content Editor:** Dr. Crit Minster
**Assistant Editor:** Katie Hale
**Editorial Assistant:** Katie Tibbetts
**Editorial Interns:** Mariana Cotlear, Leigh Gower
**Publisher:** Viva Publishing Network

**Cover Design:** Jose Padilla
**Cover Photos provided by:** Caroline Bennett, Craig Gibson, Michelle Hopey, Cat Hartwell, JenFu Cheng
**Designers:** Michelle Hopey, Paula Newton
**Assisting Layout Designers:** Mariana Cotlear, Leigh Gower, Katie Hale, Dr. Crit Minster

**Distributed by:** Independent Publishers Group

# Many Thanks To:

**Ries van Twisk, Gerard Setho and Tania Morales,** the programming masterminds who keep our parent website www.vivatravelguides.com running smoothly and always lend a hand to the not-always-computer-savvy staff. Also, **Santiago Rivera** and the whole Metamorf team, especially **Jose Padilla** for designing our maps and **Jorge Vintimilla** for painstakingly creating them all.

A very big thank you to the **V!VA Travel Guides community** who contributed so much towards this book, and without whom, this book would not be possible. Special thanks to those who contributed numerous great photos, especially **Maximilian Hirschfeld, Freyja Ellis, Stephany Slaughter, Caroline Bennett** and **Will Gray**. Thanks to Will and Freyja for also providing passport stamps. Thanks to those who agreed to give up their valuable time to proof read sections of the book: **Lorraine Caputo, Will Gray, Freyja Ellis, Allison Korn, Katie Hale** and **Kelley Coyner**. Our special thanks to Kelley Coyner, our honorary staff member, for all her support in helping us promote our community. Last, but by no means least, thank you to **Ricardo Segreda** for proofreading and to our interns, **Leigh Gower, Mariana Cotlear and Erin Helland** who worked hard to help us in the preparation of this book.

Published by Viva Publishing Network S.A.
ISBN-10: 0-9791264-0-1
ISBN-13: 978-0-9791264-0-6

Copyright © 2007, Viva Publishing Network.
Voice: (970) 744-4244
Fax: (612) 605-5720
Website: www.vivatravelguides.com
Information: info@vivatravelguides.com

Copyright © 2007, Viva Publishing Network.
All rights reserved. No part of this book may be reproduced, stored in a retrieval system, or transmitted in any form or by any means, electronic, mechanical, photocopying, recording in any format, including video and audiotape or otherwise, without the prior written consent of the Publisher.

Some articles may be available for reprint by attributing both the author, and the vivatravelguides.com website. Please contact info@vivatravelguides.com for reprint permission.

Each author is responsible for the choice and presentation of the facts contained in this book and for the opinions expressed therein, which are not necessarily those of Viva Publishing Network S.A. and do not commit the Organization. The publisher and authors assume noresponsibility for errors or omissions. Nor is any liability assumed for damages resulting from the use of the information contained.

Travel is inherently dangerous, Viva Publishing Network, its owners, members, employees, contributors, and the authors cannot be held liable for events outside of their control and we make no guarantee as to the accuracy of published information. Please travel safely, be alert, and let us know how your vacation went.

For bulk orders please contact:
Independent Publishers Group
orders@ipgbook.com
Phone USA: 312.337.0747 or 800.888.4741

www.vivatravelguides.com

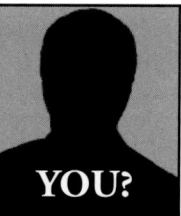

# *Have you had a V!VA List Experience?*

# Tell the world about it by sharing your story with V!VA World!

Submissions are now being accepted for the V!VA List World book, due to be published in April 2008. Go to **www.vivatravelguides.com** to find out more!

- Share your experience with the world and be published
- Earn royalties on contributed texts and photos, or have your royalties donated to charity
- Contribute to an innovative, community-created travel guide
- Pride! Fame! Glory!

### *Is it V!VA List worthy?*

Had an experience so exhilarating that, if given the opportunity again, you'd conceivably plan your entire trip around it? Have you traveled to a known hotspot like the Taj Mahal in a way no one else has? Discovered an unknown treasure? Can you tell your story such that it takes other travelers there without ever leaving their chairs? If so, your piece is V!VA List worthy!

# CONTENTS

- Mexico p. 106
- Cuba p. 100
- Dominican Republic p. 97
- Puerto Rico p. 94
- Belize p. 164
- Guatemala p. 144
- Honduras p. 174
- El Salvador p. 180
- Bonaire p. 93
- Nicaragua p. 182
- Venezuela p. 78
- Costa Rica p. 192
- Guyana p. 76
- Panama p. 214
- Suriname p. 76
- French Guiana p. 76
- Colombia p. 224
- Brazil p. 56
- Ecuador p. 236
- Peru p. 270
- Bolivia p. 300
- Paraguay p. 48
- Chile p. 322
- Uruguay p. 40
- Argentina p. 2

All Latin p. 344
Index p. 352

# V!VA LIST: HOW IT BEGAN...

Creating this book was a fascinating project. As a traveler, I was delighted to read about all the most amazing places to go all over Latin America and look at the spectacular photographs. It was my privilege to see professional writers and photographers and non-professionals writing so passionately about everything Latin.

V!VA List grew from a spark of an idea in October 2005, through to launch of the V!VA List section of our website in February 2006. The idea developed and flourished with ideas from the team, into the book that you have in front of you now. The site was designed and built for writers and photographers to either just nominate places for inclusion in the book, or let us know of their intention to write a piece about the place. Photographs and pieces of writing could also be submitted via the site. On February 3rd, 2006, the V!VA List site was launched and an email was sent to community members with a plea to spread the word about the book and kick off the project. Immediately, my mailbox was overwhelmed with responses from talented writers and photographers with questions about the project and ideas that they had for contributions. Later, once all the contributions were in, we also requested they go to the website to vote for the best of the best, of ruins, hikes, colonial plazas, markets and more.

## Who are the writers and photographers?

V!VA List is compiled from submissions sent online from writers located all over the globe, from six of the seven continents and as far afield as Australia, Malaysia, South Africa, Finland, the UK, France, Canada, the US, and (of course) Latin America itself.

Diversity was not just limited to geographical location however. Within the book, there are pieces written by an adventurous 57-year old grandmother, a college student, a jilted ex-girlfriend, a semi-retired radio announcer, and several who were on trips throughout the Latin world on career breaks, gap years or sabbaticals. Some are professional writers, some are professional travel writers, some want to be professional writers, but they all had one thing in common: they were so enthusiastic about the places that they had visited, that they wanted to share their love with the world.

Some had been on a short trip that they loved, some were traveling on extensive trips through Latin America, but many had lived and worked or volunteered in the countries and places that they wanted to share with us. Living and working in Latin America gave them the opportunity to ex-

*"It is a great idea you have had to ask travelers to write, and really nice for us to have a chance to write about real experience!"*
*Claire Peltier, contributor for Caraz, Peru.*

plore those off-the-beaten-path places that true travelers just adore. And while we're on the subject of diversity, you will note that writers dialects' have been kept—for example, British English has been kept in pieces by British writers, while North American English has been kept for those contributors from the U.S.A. and Canada.

## What motivated the contributors?

V!VA List contributors submitted more for love than money. Sure, everyone that made it in the book will get royalties, but it was obvious from the start that their true purpose was to share their experiences, not fill their pockets. When we launched, some "star" travel writers contacted us and demanded $1 per word or more to participate: they were quickly put off by the idea of equitable profit sharing. We didn't think that writers who saw the world from a perspective of dollars-per-word would provide the best travel writing. We found that the best writers are the passionate ones, those who, once they understood the desire to share the Latin America we all know and love, said "count me in."

We received daily comments such as, *"Thank you for the opportunity to write about these wonderful places, I'm very excited to get started!"*, (Albert Garcia, contributor to Guatemala and Peru), and *"this is a wonderful idea"*, (Terence Baker, contributor to Colombia and Guatemala). Many were driven by an inner motivation to write. Judging by the diversity of origin of the contributors, it seems that people everywhere have the universal desire to write and be heard.

Aspiring writers were keen to get published. Established writers from other fields were keen to break into the travel writing field. Nearly all could be said to be either writers who loved to travel, or travelers who loved to write.

A large number of the contributors were eager to share with the world their most amazing and bizarre experiences, to help others experience what they had. Sharing experience was a very important motivator: *"I would love to contribute something to your book from the wealth of travel experiences I've had around Latin America and the Caribbean,"* (David Vincent, contributor to Brazil, Chile and Cuba). And everyone wanted to know when the book would be published and how to help promote it, for example, Bonnie Jernigan, contributor for Peru, *"I'm delighted that you are using my contributions, and I would certainly like to know how I can be involved in promotional opportunities."*

Sharing experience was an especially important factor for those who had lived and worked in one of the featured countries and therefore had reached a level of cultural comfort and understanding not available to the regular tourist who is just passing through.

Other writers still had a great desire to be inspirational to others. To return momentarily to the 57-year old grandmother, her drive came from a need to encourage others in her position to do what she had done. In some of the pieces, there were signs of this type of motivation, for example, Martin Crossland, writing of a bicycling trip around the Antigua area with a group of younger participants, *"Too difficult? Not really! If I can do it, anyone can!"*

With so much passion that had been expressed within every single piece submitted, deciding which pieces to use for the book was enormously challenging. The aim was to produce a book with widespread appeal for those who love everything Latin: ruins, markets, scenery, bizarre festivals, hikes, rafting and even eating lemon ants. True to its origins, all the stories can also be read online—just follow the links at the bottom of each page. This book is shared with you from those who traveled, lived and worked in Latin America, and is meant to be shared with others. Enjoy!

*Paula Newton*
*Managing Editor, V!VA List*

Left page from top: Maya women dressed in traditional woven *huipiles* in Antigua, Guatamala. As is true in much of rural Latin America, unique pattern and color schemes on fabric are symbolic of different regions. A Maya shaman healer outside of the temple of *San Simón* in San Andres Iztapa, Guatemala. Photos by Caroline Bennett. This page: photo of the Argentinean side of the Iguazú Falls in Misiones, Argentina. Photo by Christian Denes.

# V!VA LIST: COMMON THREADS

## What is Latin America?

In asking for and accepting submissions for this book, we had to agree on a definition of "Latin America." If we went with a strict definition—any nation whose language is derived from Latin—we'd have included French-speaking Haiti (which we did not include) and kicked out English-speaking Belize (which we did include). If we included only sovereign nations, Puerto Rico would be ineligible. Some people's definition of Latin America does not include Brazil (ours does).

Eventually, we decided that we needed to define "Latin America" more in terms of attitude and flavor than geography. Latin America is not about Spanish, it's about meringue. It's not about national exports, it's about national dishes. The essence of Latin America is not found in the presidential palaces, the posh resorts, or in the fancy restaurants: it's in the streets of Guadalajara, Santo Domingo, Caracas, Quito and Rio de Janeiro.

You don't have to be born in Costa Rica, Paraguay, Venezuela or the Dominican Republic to have a bit of Latin America in your soul. Latin Americans believe that football is more important than work, today is more important than tomorrow and family is more important than anything else. The frenzied pace of life in Europe or North America has made many of us forget about these priorities, but Latin America is a part of the world that has never forgotten to put its soul before its bank account.

We love Latin America. We love the food, the people, the sights, the sounds and even the smells (most of the time). When we set out to create this book, we wanted to bring Latin America into the homes and hearts of readers everywhere, who unfortunately seem to get too much of their information about this part of the world from bad Hollywood movies (fact: most countries in Latin America are not actually controlled by drug barons or villainous colonels).

In this book, we have tried to include a variety of pieces, written in different styles and concerning diverse subjects. We tried to divide the pieces we included between the well-known places that everyone has heard of—Machu Picchu, Iguazú Falls—and totally unknown places and activities (Vapor Cué, Paraguay, is about as far off the "Gringo Trail" as you can get). Our purpose in deliberately diversifying our topics was simple: we wanted to reflect the reality of this part of the world. After all, you can't write about the best places in Latin America and not include the Galápagos Islands (the very notion is heresy). But by the same token, Latin America does not begin and end with the big tourist sites: there is much, much more to see and do once you've finished hiking the Inca Trail and danced until dawn at Rio's famous Carnaval.

This book was an experiment of sorts: we wanted to collect pieces of travel writing that reflected the Latin America we know and love, not simply the Latin America of Club Med, crowded beaches and ruins mobbed by tourists. We believe that we've succeeded, and the result is in your hands right now.

## The other side of the lake

The magnificent Llao Llao resort on Lake Perito Moreno, Argentina, is one of South America's top destinations, an internationally renowned five-star resort that draws people from all walks of life and all corners of the earth. They come to relax in the spa, enjoy the unparalleled beauty of Argentina's lake district, and enjoy the food and service that inevitably come with famous five star resorts. Ask any travel agent, anywhere, about the Llao Llao and they'll know what you're talking about: ask anyone who has ever stayed there and they'll recall it fondly, with a big smile. Search for it on the internet and you'll get thousands of results.

On the other side of Lake Perito Moreno, a narrow road winds through the hills, which gets ever steeper until you come across a dirt driveway that leads to "a green clearing with a dusting of purple along the top," according to Ellery Biddle, an adventurous young woman from Philadelphia, Pennsylvania, U.S.A. who spent one sunny afternoon exploring with a friend. They found the Meli Hue Lavender Farm, which no doubt came as a surprise to them, as they were not looking for it. The Meli Hue Lavender farm is not famous. No American travel agent has ever heard of it. An internet search for it yields less than 150 results (of which the only two in English are the result of Ellery submitting her piece to us here at Viva Travel Guides). Ellery and her friend had a great visit: the farm was fascinating, they had tea outside with a stunning view of the lake (and of the Llao Llao as well), and they bought some fine lavender products to take home.

The Meli Hue Lavender farm and the Llao Llao hotel and resort share a breathtaking lake in Argentina, and they share a page in this book (p. 16). It's fitting, because Latin America isn't just about the huge Llao Llaos, nor is it about the little lavender farms. It's about both, about world-famous tourist attractions and off-the-beaten-path discoveries that are equally unforgettable. For every Galapagos Islands (p. 264), there is an Ometepe Island (p. 190).

> *Latin Americans believe that football is more important than work, today is more important than tomorrow and family is more important than anything else.*

For every Machu Picchu (p. 285), there is a Caracol ruins (p. 165).

Our book starts in Ushuaia, Argentina and ends in Puerto Williams, Chile. If you draw a direct line from one of these towns to the other, both of which incidentally claim to be the southernmost city in the world, you'll realize that they're only a few miles apart. But that's as the condor flies, and we prefer to take a different route from Ushuaia to Puerto Williams. Our route has, I suppose you could say, a few little detours: we go up one side of South America, hop over to the Caribbean, take a U-turn in Mexico, go through Central America and come back down the other side of South America. Sure, we admit it's not a terribly efficient way to get from one city to the other, but our way is more fun.

Along the way, you'll shop in the fish markets of coastal Chile, hike the Inca Trail to Machu Picchu, stay as a guest in a Cuban home and sleep in the same room where Simón Bolívar did almost two hundred years ago. You'll swim with sea lions, visit an underground salt mine which has been carved into a cathedral, visit the grave of the most notorious American filibuster in history and watch a game at Brazil's most storied football stadium.

## What sets us apart?

The last few years have seen the release of several books by talented writers and established travel guide publishers, all of which will tell you all about the places and things you must see and do, given your limited time on this lovely blue marble we affectionately refer to as "earth." Like those books, the volume you are currently holding will tell you about places, people, cultures and sights and how and why you should go about visiting them.

The similarities end there, though. We decided early on to focus less on fancy hotels and restaurants and more on real experiences. We prefer to let our writers speak for themselves, believing that you don't need us to tell you where to stay and what to do. The other books did rely on multiple writers and sources, but the editors chopped their stories into bite-sized chunks, distilling these raw experiences into collections of lists, must-sees and must-dos, and bits of semi-relevant information. We give it to you straight, right from our writers to our readers, person to person, traveler to traveler.

Although it was not our intention, our stories tend to fall into certain categories. Many of our writers enjoy adventure travel, and they'll take you hang gliding in Rio (p. 63) or climbing majestic Cotopaxi, an active volcano in Ecuador (p. 248). Still other writers prefer cultural experiences, such as the offerings to Pachamama on Bolivia's Sun Island (p. 302) or volunteering in Costa Rica (p. 205). Eco-tourism is a hot topic: check out the pieces on Ecuador's Black Sheep Inn (p. 250) or the Sian Ka'an Biosphere Reserve in Mexico (p. 143). Many of our writers are interested in food, and in the cultural bridges it can create: check out Kelley Coyner's piece on beef in Paraguay (p. 53) or Jenna Mahoney's fascinating narrative about Santa Teresa's soda in Costa Rica (p. 201).

Many of our writers enjoyed telling us about special, magical moments they had while traveling, such as Amanda Kass, whose experience in the Dominican Republic (p. 99) is best left in her own words: "As darkness falls, you join the locals as they make their way from their homes to the local *colmado*, which must be Spanish for "battered mini-mart," and settle in for a friendly night of chatting, watching TV and gossiping. If you're lucky, someone will bring a guitar and treat everyone to a little bit of live music."

So pour yourself a cup of coffee or hot chocolate or even a Caipirinha—the signature drinks of our favorite part of the world—sit back, and prepare to be transported to a land of emerald jungles, golden beaches, icy mountains, booming volcanoes and modern cities. Along the way, you'll come to know the unforgettable lands and friendly people of Latin America … from both sides of the lake.

*Dr Christopher "Crit" Minster*
*Head Writer and Content Editor, V!VA List*

Left page: Volcán de Agua towers over the colorful streets of Antigua, Guatemala. Photo by Caroline Bennett. This page from top: A Whitetip Shark at Cocos Island, Costa Rica. Photo by Jenfu Cheng. "Hay tiempo" in rural San Lucas Tolimán, Guatemala, looking out from a streetside window. Photo by Caroline Bennett.

*From outdoor adventures to bustling market stalls, Latin America is a place for all tastes...*

*A vibrant tapestry hangs in a shop doorway in highland Guatemala, just a glimpse of the myriad of colors symbolic of the region.*

Clockwise from top left: Three indigenous women donning brightly colored outfits at a market in Ecuador. Photo by Maximilian Hirschfeld; Two Grey-Crowned Cranes at Foz do Iguaçu Bird Park in Brazil. Photo by Freyja Ellis. A mother and child watch passersby in Santiago Atitlan, Guatemala. Photo by Caroline Bennett.

This page, clockwise from top left: Colorful Sally Lightfoot crabs scatter the beach on an island in the Galápagos in Ecuador. Photo by Caroline Bennett. A multi-colored house in the iconic neighborhood of La Boca in Buenos Aires, Argentina. Photo by Christian Denes. Carnaval in Rio de Janeiro, Brazil. Photo by Freyja Ellis.

*A festive float at Rio Carnaval in Brazil, one of the countless fiestas to be experienced in a region that truly knows how to let go and celebrate…*

Clockwise from top: Laguna Verde, the green lagoon in the Uyuni Desert in Bolivia. Photo by Maximilian Hirschfeld. A rendition of the famous Argentine tango singer Carlos Gardel, painted on a garage door on Anchorena Street in Buenos Aires, Argentina. Photo by Christian Denes. A woman sits on the shore of Lake Titicaca in Puno, Peru. Photo by Maximilian Hirschfeld.

# ARGENTINA

**Argentina: Just the name conjures up drama and romance.**

The tango. The lambada. Evita. Gauchos. Wine. Champion fútbol teams. Perhaps the single best word to capture its essence is passion.

Argentines are passionate about everything, from their culture to their food to their land. With a strong European heritage, this Latin American country embraces sophistication and modernity with a bohemian, colorful flair.

Buenos Aires, proudly claimed by Argentineans as "the Paris of South America," is a study in contrasts; Latin America's most sophisticated capital, an ultra-modern city surrounded by deserted, primeval grassy plains. It is a city of ghosts and although Ché Guevara, Evita Perón and tango icon Carlos Gardel are long gone, their spirits linger in cafés and government halls, and street vendors hawking t-shirts. It is a city with a long rich history as well as a bright future, a city of friendly people which nethertheless has the most psychoanalysts per capita in the world. The city that gave rise to the notoriously suggestive lambada was also home to one of literature's most brilliantly cerebral writers, Jorge Luis Borges.

Beyond Buenos Aires, the famous Patagonia mountain range inspires and challenges hikers and climbers the world over. The Perito Moreno Glacier is part of the dramatic South Patagonian Icefield and the Gauchos are still a tradition rather than a tale from the past. Along the border with Brazil, the Iguazú waterfall never fails to dazzle visitors.

At the southernmost tip of Argentina you'll find the bracingly beautiful Tierra del Fuego and the hardy town of Ushuaia. It's your gateway to Antarctica, or you can just visit and enjoy the coldly majestic scenery.

So, if you're lacking passion in your life, head south to Argentina, where they have enough to share.

# USHUAIA

*By Will Gray, Kettering, England*

Down at the foot of South America, beyond the wilds of Patagonia and across the treacherous Straits of Magellan, lies the vibrant outpost of Ushuaia, the self-proclaimed southernmost city in the world. Simply getting to this remote outpost of civilisation is an experience in itself.

If you choose to take the ground route from Punta Arenas, the bus will take you alongside the Straits of Magellan, one of the world's most famous waterways, then onto a ferry for the 25-minute crossing, a bumpy ride at the best of times that is often cancelled due to the rough waters that splash over onto the unprotected cars on the deck.

Landing on Tierra del Fuego, the journey continues across barren lands where icy winds blow with gale-force ferocity as you cross from Chile into Argentina. The mountains begin to rise again as the coast road winds its way along to the city of Ushuaia, snugly set into the hills beside the Beagle Channel.

This rugged port town functions primarily as the gateway to Antarctica. It is a rare day when there is not at least one ship in the docks being filled with passengers or goods to sail away around Cape Horn and into the fearsome, iceberg-filled Southern Ocean, and that is what gives the place its buzz.

Typically cold for most of the year, the place has the feel of a ski town, clinging on to the slippery snow-covered slopes yet offering a warm and welcome hospitality, with restaurants a-plenty and cosy hotels to keep you comfortable for your stay. On the waterfront, a poignant statue stands at attention, in silent tribute to those Argentines killed on the Malvinas (Falklands) Islands.

A trip out into the calm bay area, protected from the rough seas, is essential to view the picturesque city and the snow-capped mountains. 11 km from the city lies the Tierra del Fuego national park, a bracken-covered tundra with trails leading to Lago Roca, where you can hike along the Lapataia River while staring at the sight of Cerro Cóndor before reaching the turnaround point at the borderline with Chile. You can take the "end of the world" train. On the other side of the Park, best seen with a tour outfit, lies Lapataia Bay, where you can see Laguna Verde and Laguna Negra before heading back out.

It is possible, but not easy or cheap, to book onto a scenic flight over the infamous Cape Horn or get passage on a vessel to the ice continent of Antarctica further south, but if you do not have the time the transfixing experience of visiting Ushuaia once will make you want to return for that trip of a lifetime in the future.

Will Gray grew up in Northamptonshire, England. He currently lives in London. He studied aeronautical engineering at Southampton University, but switched to journalism soon after graduation and has worked and travelled as a sports journalist for the last five years.

The craziest cultural experience he encountered was with the Karbalah Martyrs in Bahrain. Men marched through the streets cutting their heads with swords while the black cloaked women watched from the pavements.

### USHUAIA TRAVEL TIPS:

• If interested in area history, stop by the *Museo Marítimo de Ushuaia*. This museum tells Ushuaia's early history when the city was a penal colony for local citizens and military officers. Open daily, this destination offers a plethora of area information, perhaps tempting the tourist back for more than one visit.

• For more area history, check out the *Museo del Fin de Mundo* housed in the historical building, Casa Fernández Valdés, built in 1903. The museum does a thorough job of covering the history of the area's indigenous population.

• Take the chair lift from behind the Hotel del Glaciar up to Glaciar Martial for stunning views of the Beagle Channel.

Ushuaia Signpost. Photo by Freyja Ellis.

# SAILING THE BEAGLE CHANNEL

## By Will Gray, Kettering, England

Way down at the bottom of the South American continent, the Beagle Channel is a treacherous body of icy water that flows out into the Antarctic Ocean. A trip across it to the southernmost habitation in Chile's Puerto Williams is an unforgettable journey.

Ushuaia's yacht harbour is an exciting place to visit as the boats are moored inside and the sailors around them are certain to have some stories to tell, many having made the ambitious journey across the Atlantic and a good number either planning to go to Antarctica or buzzing from their recent visit to the icy continent at the bottom of the world. If you are lucky, you can catch a lift.

With a lack of organised trips across the Beagle Channel, that is exactly what you have to do to secure passage to Puerto Williams, and it will usually take a day or two of asking the harbourmaster before you find someone who is heading off in that direction and can give you the lift of a lifetime over the choppy waters between the mountainous and glacier-fed deep south.

With passports stamped, the boat can break away from its moorings and motor out of the protected harbour. The departure offers beautiful views of Ushuaia and the surrounding snow-capped mountains, but you are soon hard at work hauling up the headsail and mainsail ready to cut the noise of the engine and experience the tranquillity of the wild surroundings.

Tough weather conditions are sometimes not worth risking but even on the calmest of days this area is windy and the boat will soon get up a good speed as it sails out of the protected harbour area and into the deep. The waves rise up to four feet even when it is "flat" but they are still not a patch on the conditions found at the infamous Cape Horn just a few kilometres south of the passage.

The scenery becomes bleaker as the boat heads along its journey, which takes between five and ten hours depending on the wind conditions. You can feel as if you are heading to the end of the earth as the fog rolls over the icy mountains before the welcome sight of the Puerto Williams community appears on the horizon. The journey is completed by a bizarre and informal border crossing, where an immigrations officer will board the vessel before you disembark.

Puerto Williams, made up mostly of a Chilean naval base, claims to be the southernmost town in the world and has a pleasant little community with the hub of the town in a small central square, where convenience stores and sweet shops double as airline booking offices and hairdressers. Down by the sea, the beach provides the perfect venue to watch the sun set over the mountains.

Despite its small size, a population totaling around 1,800, Puerto Williams offers several interesting activities to follow on from the exciting arrival. One popular option is to hire one of the little local nine-seater propeller planes for a sightseeing flight over Cape Horn, which sits in the archipelago of islands beneath the tiny Isla Navarino on which Puerto Williams is located.

This flight, a bumpy ride over a mountainous region where uplifts and downdrafts throw the little plane around like a toy, is not for the fainthearted or those with limited funds but it offers a great way to see the Horn without experiencing its fearsome waves and provides an opportunity to get to the absolute base of the continent for those with little time to do so.

There is also a magnificent walk up to a viewpoint over the Beagle Channel. This begins with a trail heading west to a small waterfall before a steep climb through a forest, where the route is marked by red dots, to a huge mossy hilltop that offers a spectacular panorama of views, from the mountains behind Ushuaia and the city itself out toward the route you have sailed to the ocean in the distance, with rugged mountains at your back.

But you cannot stay in Puerto Williams forever, and the best way to leave is to take a flight over the craggy mountain scenery back to Punta Arenas. This route flies west along the Beagle Channel, to keep in Chilean airspace and offers views of Cape Horn if you are lucky, then banks hard right over the glaciated lake-filled part of Tierra del Fuego and over the Magellan Straits to complete a fantastic scenic trip.

*"One man shouting makes more noise than 100,000 in silence."*
*-José de San Martin, Argentine Revolutionary (1778-1850)*

## TOP LIST: WICKED WATERFALLS

Iguazú falls may be one of the most visited waterfalls in Latin America, but it far from the only one. There are dozens more which are worth a look. Here's what our readers recommend:

**1. Iguazú Falls, Brazil and Argentina (see p. 59 and p. 28).**
"Better to go out of season when there aren't so many tourists—despite the numbers of people it's still worth a visit!" Carol Ann, Scotland.
"Experience both sides!" Sandra Scott, Mexico, New York. U.S.A.
"The falls with the most individual falls in the world," Teresa Colomer, Spain.

**2. Angel Falls, Venezuela (see p. 80).**
"When I saw the Angel Falls—I knew that God existed." Donna, South Africa.
"The tallest falls in the world." Teresa Colomer, Spain.

**3. Aguas Azules, Palenque, Mexico.**
"Just fun to lie around in ... and they go on forever." Cynthia Winn, California, U.S.A.

# TOLHUIN, TIERRA DEL FUEGO

By John Polga-Hecimovich, Burnsville, Minnesota, U.S.A.

Tolhuin is an ideal off-the-beaten-path destination whose charm resides in its small-town feel and breathtaking natural surroundings. It is also a welcome relief from the monotony of sheep ranches that dominate the rolling hills and plains of northern Tierra del Fuego.

Located between the Strait of Magellan and the Beagle Channel, the town offers rugged mountain scenery without Ushuaia's tourists, as well as one of the most well-known bakeries in the world, La Unión Panadería. From here it is two hours by car to either of Tierra del Fuego's cities, Río Grande in the north, or Ushuaia in the south, and most visitors are Argentine truckers en route to other places, or residents of La Isla (Tierra del Fuego). In fact, the town is well-removed from the tourist circuit, and its few dirt-road streets are lined by low-slung houses and wood cabins.

Tolhuin gives the visitor a chance to experience being in one of the southernmost regions of the world, without feeling like just another tourist. Here, in what E. Lucas Bridges deemed the Uttermost Part of the Earth, the sun no longer rises in the east and sets in the west, but hovers longingly in the north. At night, the stars of the Southern Hemisphere emerge luminous in the obsidian skies, and the Southern Cross wordlessly points the way to Antarctica. The wind howls and shrieks, penetrates clothing, bends trees, and sways signposts.

Nature dominates.

In fact, the raw power of the gale-force winds of Tierra del Fuego that howl in from the South Pacific cannot be over exaggerated. Birds flap their wings in the air yet move in reverse. Small sheep tumble over on the hills. Exposed trees are gnarled and deformed, one side absent of branches and leaves, while the other side reaches towards the heavens in supplication.

This region of Tierra del Fuego is the Andes' last hurrah, their final majestic stand before sinking into the frigid Sea of Argentina and the South Atlantic in a tangled maze of rock and glacier. The unbroken white of the southern Andean Cordillera spreads from west to east here, just south of Tolhuin, and morphs into geologically young, sharp white peaks. To the north of the Cordillera lies Tolkien-esque forests of lenga and beech, innumerable routes to Mordor, which come to a dead end at sheer vertical cliffs which dramatically and precipitously drop off into the shimmering aqua waters of the 100-kilometer long Lago Fagnano.

One draw for interested travelers is fishing in Fagnano's glacial waters or hiking the marvelous and (mostly) uninhabited surrounding mountains. Of course, empanadas and cappuccino at La Unión must top-off any visit; the bakery is known for its delicious European-style pastries, inexpensive Argentine delicacies—such as the lamb empanadas—and coffees. Tolhuin is the perfect destination for those looking to experience the mountains and scenery of southern Tierra del Fuego without the tourist traps of often visited Ushuaia.

Born and raised in Minnesota, John Polga-Hecimovich attended Dartmouth College in New Hampshire for an undergraduate degree in Government. Traveling with his family has given way to stints in Latin America, and he is currently working on his Master's degree in Latin American Studies in Quito, Ecuador. His hobbies include photography and travel writing, and he is convinced that responsible tourism is the key to development in many Latin American countries.

His dream excursion is to retrace the Amazon source-to-sea expedition described by Joe Kane in *Running the Amazon*, from Arequipa, Peru to Belém, Brazil. He never leaves home without his Uruguayan yerba mate paraphernalia and thermos—they have visited mountains, rainforests, and tundra along side him.

## LATIN REVOLUTIONARIES # 5: JOSÉ DE SAN MARTÍN

(1778-1850)

José de San Martín was born in Argentina in 1778, the son of a Spanish military official. He followed his father into the armed forces, attending military school in Madrid as a young man. He was a skilled officer and had reached the rank of Lieutenant Colonel by the age of 30. He fought for Spain in wars in Africa and against Portugal. When Napoleon's forces invaded Spain in 1812, he fought against them. Napoleon's troops were victorious, and San Martín returned to Argentina, where he joined the independence movement and was given the rank of general.

Over the next few years, San Martín was the driving force of southern South American independence from Spain. Argentina was liberated in 1816, followed by Chile in 1818. San Martín turned his sights on Peru, which proved to be a tougher nut to crack. He invaded Peru in 1820 and fought several important battles against Spanish and loyalist forces and winning the decisive battle of Pisco on December 6, 1820. By 1821, Peru had been temporarily liberated: it was truly liberated in 1824.

After the wars of independence, San Martín settled down in Argentina and stayed out of politics. After his wife died in 1824, he moved to France where he lived in peaceful seclusion. He died in 1850, and in 1880, his remains were transferred to the Buenos Aires Cathedral.

ARGENTINA

# PERITO MORENO GLACIER

## By Dr. Crit Minster, Rochester, New York, U.S.A.

Originally from Rochester, New York, Dr. Christopher "Crit" Minster is a graduate of Penn State, The University of Montana and Ohio State. He holds a doctorate from Ohio State in Spanish Literature, with an emphasis on the literature from the Spanish colonial era in Latin America. He is the resident V!VA Travel Guides expert on ruins, history and culture, as well as spooky things like haunted museums. He worked for the U.S. Peace Corps in Guatemala as a volunteer from 1991 to 1994 and has traveled extensively in Latin America, including Argentina, Peru, Bolivia, Brazil, Chile, Ecuador, Costa Rica, El Salvador, Honduras and Mexico. He currently resides in Quito.

His craziest cultural experience was in Brazil when they won the 2002 World Cup: "It was better than carnival—carnival happens every year, but Brazil only has five World Cup titles."

Once every few years, the water pressure in the Brazo Rico sector of Lake Argentino becomes too intense for the Perito Moreno Glacier to contain. The forward edge of the glacier builds up over time, connecting the ageless mountain rock to the massive South Patagonian Icefield, severing the Brazo Rico from the rest of the lake. The trapped water can rise 30 meters (about 90 feet) over the course of several years before the ice gives way in an awesome display of nature's might, bursting in a spectacular thunderclap of massive chunks of ice, roaring water, rocks and debris. If you're lucky enough to witness this awe-inspiring natural wonder, you'll never forget it.

The Perito Moreno Glacier is located in Los Glaciares National Park in the southwestern part of Santa Cruz province, Argentina. When it snows high in the Patagonian Andes, the snow and ice does not melt. Rather, it accumulates, forming the massive South Patagonian Icefield, a glacier system that straddles Argentina and Chile. The enormous pressure of tons of snow and ice compresses the existing ice and gives it a distinctive bluish tint. At such great pressures, the frozen water actually flows, inching out of the Andes and into the valleys where it melts, forming lakes and rivers. The Perito Moreno Glacier is one of 48 such outlets for the South Patagonian Icefield.

This hulking hunk of ice is named for Dr. Francisco Pascasio "Perito" Moreno, an Argentine explorer who traveled through much of his nation's rugged wilderness in the late 19th century. In 1903, he donated some land to the Argentine government that would later form the nucleus of Nahuel Huapi National Park. Naming the majestic glacier after him was a fitting tribute to the man who spent a lifetime exploring Argentina's interior and preserving it for future generations.

Visitors who are not fortunate enough to see the great wall of ice give way need not fret: the glacier is advancing into Lake Argentino at an approximate speed of two meters (six feet) per day. Believe it or not, however, this massive ice bed never really progresses forward; huge slabs of ice break off at more or less the same rate as the glacier creeps into the lake. Every few minutes great chunks of ice, some weighing as much as several tons, crack off the glacial face and tumble into the lake with a roar. These massive frozen blocks bob around in the lake as icebergs for a while, slowly melting.

There are observation platforms to watch this process, and many visitors take tour boats into the lake. The boats keep a respectful distance—you never know when a mini iceberg is going to break off—but the views are spectacular. Like watching rain on a lake or a brightly burning bonfire, witnessing the glacier groan, creak and crumble into the lake is very hypnotic. Perito himself would be pleased to see the looks of awe and fascination on the faces of those lucky enough to experience the natural wonder that bears his name.

FACTOID:

The glacier is one of only three Patagonian glaciers that are not retreating.

Moreno Glacier. Photo by Dr. Crit Minster.

# EL CHALTEN AND CERRO TORRE

By Will Gray, Kettering, Enlgand

In the wilds of Argentine Patagonia, over the border from the Torres del Paine National Park, lies the less visited area of El Chalten, a truly rugged mountain escape.

Continually changing weather systems that feed off the surrounding ice fields make it difficult to catch a golden glimpse of this park's two main attractions: the icicle-sharp finger of rock that is Cerro Torre, one of the toughest ascents in the world, and its more bulky, but equally intimidating neighbour, Mount Fitzroy. Just being in the park is a fantastically bleak and unique experience.

Substantial beauty and immense technical challenges make these two mountains a climber's dream, capped off with nightmarish ascents. Some climbers wait months for one brief shot at climbing these monsters; others slog along the painstaking route day-by-day, slaves to the whims of the weather gods. But the two towers are merely the jewels in a range equal to that found in Torres del Paine, in a park that offers exciting hiking on low or high ground, whether you can see the mountains or not.

It is easy to set up base in the town, as there are plenty of comfortable hotels, but out in the mountains is the place to be. Torre and Fitzroy rise up from two different mountain chains, separated by glaciers. Two main treks cut through the park, one to Lago Torre, where on a good day you can see

> *Substantial beauty and immense technical challenges make these two mountains a climber's dream, capped off with nightmarish ascents.*

Cerro Torre, and the other to Lago de Los Tres, where you can see Fitzroy when the clouds steer clear.

The first route begins close to the YHA's Rio Grande hostel, climbing through fields and forests with resident woodpeckers to a clearing with awesome views of the mighty mountains. From here, the trail drops into a river valley and heads towards a distant glacier. A short scramble up the loose moraine brings you to an awe-inspiring view of the iceberg-filled lake, the path of the glacier and the rising pointed fingers of Cerro Torre. A long circular route can then take you past a waterfall and through rocky terrace-like fields back to town.

The second walk begins with a viewpoint over the river valley in front of El Chalten, before climbing an open hill with clear views of Fitzroy. From there the trek again heads along a river where it is possible to make a detour to Lake Capri before continuing on down the windy valley, where two steep climbs make the going difficult. Icy wind and snow often make the path punishing, but be persistent and if you're lucky you'll be rewarded with a fantastic view of the deep blue ice lake, the face of the glacier and a close-up of the towering Fitzroy.

There is no doubt that a fair helping of good fortune is needed to see this area with clear skies; but it is the bleakness of the mountains and the many stories of weather-torn climbing failures that add to the area's mystique. Seeing snow-shrouded Cerro Torre and Fitzroy with an icy wind nipping at your face is all part of the real experience.

## TOP LIST: STAIRWAY TO HEAVEN HIKES AND TREKS

**1. The Inca Trail to Machu Picchu, Peru (p. 284).**
"Is the most amazing hike trip in the world." Hernan Soto, Peru
"Grueling but awesome." Sadie, Winchester, U.K.
"Heck of a climb." Mark Mellander, California, U.S.A.

**2. Hiking in Torres del Paine, Chile (p. 341).**
"Stunning mountain scenery, cool blue lakes. If you are a beginner, get hooked here." Chris Hurling, U.K.

**3. Hiking to the Lost City, Colombia (p. 228).**
"A challenging jungle hike, especially if you take the little used 'alternative' route." Chris Hurling, U.K.

**4. Hiking in the Atacama Desert, Chile (p. 325).**
Atacama Desert, Chile, "Magnificent landscapes, great for walking, biking and 4x4." Carol Ann, Scotland

**5. The Inca Trail to Ingapirca, Ecuador.**
"Starts in Achupallas, climbs through spectacular páramo and ends at Ingapirca ruins." Jason, Colorado, U.S.A.

**6. Hiking in the Cajas National Park, Ecuador. (p. 258).** "Spectacular scenery, beautiful blue lakes, llamas, what more could you want from a hike?" Paula Newton, Seaton, Devon, England.

**Runners up:**

Papallacta Trail, Ecuador (p. 244)
"Not far from the lodge, trail goes along a creek, really neat. Easy." Gideon Welles, Scottsville, New York, U.S.A.

Ausangate, Peru. Rick McCharles, Canada

Huayhuash, Peru. Rick McCharles, Canada

# VALDEZ PENINSULA

By Kelley Coyner, Texas, U.S.A.

Based in La Paz, Bolivia, Kelley Coyner works as an advisor to non-profits by day and writes by night. Being a lawyer and ex-CEO, she craves any opportunity that gets her of the office and brings her together with what may seem an odd combination of elements—wildlife, trekking and her kids, Sarah 10, Claire, 7 and Andrew 2. She attended the Georgetown University School of Foreign Service, Law School at the University of Virginia, and Laredo Junior College (where after 20 years of study, she finally began to learn to speak Spanish). Her secret qualification is that her daughters keep her honest in her travel reporting and her husband Tim keeps her laughing through the drafts (when she would rather be hiking in the Andes, which she can see outside her office window).

Coyner has no one dream destination in particular—she said she has been fortunate enough to travel extensively, and she believes what makes an ordinary trip a dream excursion is the company you keep. Her best trips have been with her immediate and extended family.

Wildlife and wild beaches await those who adventure to the austere, windswept land jutting out into the fierce Atlantic Ocean. The untamed beauty of Valdez Peninsula is sure to awe and inspire animal aficionados and nature enthusiasts alike.

From November to March, a menagerie of migratory birds and sea mammals decorate the otherwise barren coast, while whales and dolphins play in the frigid waters offshore. From Puerto Pirámide, slightly reminiscent of a Mediterranean resort town, visitors can hop on a boat headed to out to observe whales. For "guaranteed" whale and dolphin spotting, head to Puerto Madryn, just south of the peninsula.

Slightly furrier friends can be spotted lounging along the peninsula's shores from September to March, when sea lions, seals, and penguins arrive to mate beneath the towering white cliffs. On the roadside stretching away from the beach one can spot pups frolicking about, but be wary of these burly beasts (and their slightly larger guardians); male elephant seals can weigh as much as 4000 kilograms and their aggressive tendencies are best observed from a distance. A dominant male readily picks off weaker members of his sex, chasing "intruders" both on land and in the sea.

Feathered friends congregate at the aptly named *Isla de los Pájaros* (Island of Birds) located in the Golfo San José. Unless you're prepared for a hefty swim, however, the birds are best viewed from observation stations mounted with telescopes at the neck of the peninsula.

On the peninsula and further south along the road weaving through Puerto Madryn toward Trelew, guanaco graze and rhea bound. Found across Chile and Argentina, guanaco entertain with their elegant appearance and ambling gait, the result of double jointed knees. Easily startled, these camel-cousins are a bit camera shy, so be ready.

A couple of hours south of Península Valdés at Punto Tumbo is the world's largest hatchery for Magellanic penguins. The birds arrive in November and by February the reserve is brimming with the million or so hatchery residents. There are other reserves in South American for the Magellanic, but none can top Punto Tumbo's for sheer numbers. From the fenced-in observation area, one can observe hundreds of Magellanic penguin standing stoically, gazing towards the surrounding hills. Below the viewpoint, adults and youths (we're talking penguins, of course) waddle to the surf to dive for food.

Signs forbidding visitors to leave the observation area are ignored by the penguins. Claire, then four and a half, discovered this when she found herself eye-to-eye with a half dozen tuxedo-clad birds This was perhaps the wildest encounter yet. What else to do but flash a smile and introduce yourself?

Sealions. Photo by Freyja Ellis.

# SAN ANTONIO OESTE

By Lorraine Caputo, Columbia, Missouri, U.S.A.

In the late afternoon, scores of birds fly along the narrow arm of the gulf. Sunlight dapples the slow waters. Sea lions frolic in the evening surf as the first of the fishing boats comes in.

Located on the Gulf of San Matías in northern Patagonia, San Antonio Oeste is a South American birdwatching Mecca. These wetlands are a critical stopping point for countless species of migratory birds which make their annual journeys up and down South America's eastern coast. There are six endemic species: the Sandy Gallito, White-throated Cachalote, Rusty-backed Monjita, Cinnamon Warbling-Finch, the Burrowing Parrot and the endangered Yellow Cardinal. Other birds that can be seen are the Chimango, Hudson's Black Tyrant, and several types of gulls and egrets. Birds aren't the only local resident: sea lions have established colonies nearby and they can frequently be seen basking on the banks of the gulf near town.

Only 17 kilometers (10 miles) to the south is the popular Las Grutas, or "the grottoes," named for a series of water-carved caves, and 17 kilometers (10 miles) in the direction of Punta Delgada is Mar Grande, with isolated stretches of sand swarming with bird and sea mammal life. On the way to San Antonio Este, the main port, Saco Viejo, features deserted beaches rich in clams, mussels and other seafood. San Antonio Oeste is a good base from which to make boating and scuba excursions to these and other, more remote areas.

Also, don't miss Salina de Gualicho, 45 Kilometers (27 miles) to the south, a blinding white salt flat set in depression 70 meters (229 feet) below sea level.

In the town of San Antonio Oeste itself, a number of early 20th century buildings are preserved: some are now museums. "Nahuel Huasi," the house of Ingeniero Jacobacci, the man who was responsible for the construction of the Viedma-Bariloche line and that of The Old Patagonia Express, is presently being restored. The municipal museum has interesting displays and the administrator is happy to chat about the region's history.

Hotels are open year-round, and in summer there are full-service camp sites. Las Grutas is closed during the off-season months.

The train to Bariloche and Viedma still passes through San Antonio Oeste; connecting service to Buenos Aires may be made once a week from Carmen de Patagones, across the river from Viedma. There is also a frequent bus service

San Antonio Oeste and its environs offer opportunities to see abundant birdlife, take excursions, fish or scuba dive, or swim in one of the town's balnearios. Stop for a few days: walk along the estuary, take a boat ride along the gulf coast, listen for the songs of birds, or camp beneath the Southern Cross, and listen to the choruses of the night. The austral summer is the best time to visit northern Patagonia.

Upon re-declaring her independence at age 29, Lorraine Caputo packed her trusty Rocinante (so her knapsack's called) and began traipsing throughout the Americas, from Alaska to Patagonia. When this native-born United Statien is not travelling and writing, she works as a freelance researcher, editor, translator and radio programmer—as well as the occasional odd hotel chambermaid and dishwasher. Her works have been published in almost 50 journals, 14 books, an anthology of women's travel writings and three recordings in the US, Canada and Latin America, and she has done over 200 poetry readings from Denali to Buenos Aires. Lorraine and Rocinante have been living and working in Latin America for over three years. After over three years of traveling, she is looking for someplace to settle down for a while, to work and to finish editing a project of many, many years: a collection of poems and stories of train journeys from Alaska to Patagonia.

## MARTÍN FIERRO By Dr. Crit Minster

*Aquí me pongo a cantar*
*Al compás de la vigüela...*

*Here I sit down to sing*
*To the rhythm of the guitar...*

So begins *El Gaucho Martín Fierro* ("The Gaucho, Martín Fierro"), the classic Argentine epic poem written in 1872 by José Hernández. He followed it up with *La Vuelta de Martín Fierro* ("The Return of Martín Fierro") in 1879 and the two are generally considered to be parts of the same work.

The epic tells the tale of a gaucho—sort of an Argentine cowboy—and his life on the rugged pampas. Fierro is drafted to fight the Indians on the frontier, but soon deserts to return home. Finding his home destroyed and his family gone, Fierro sets out across the desolate plains. After he kills a rival in a knife fight, he is hunted as a murderer and deserter. Martín Fierro is a fictional character, but the gauchos were very real, and Hernandez' poem decries the loss of the culture of these rugged men of the plains, living in freedom under their own brutal code. By the end of the nineteenth century, the gauchos were a dying breed.

The two parts of the poem were immediately huge successes in Argentina, and by the 1920's they were considered by important Argentine writers such as Ricardo Güiraldes and Jorge Luis Borges to be the definitive work of Argentinian literature, a bit like *Don Quixote* is in Spain. Today, the poems have been translated into dozens of languages and made into movies, and although the gauchos are long gone, Martín Fierro has secured a place in the hearts of the people of Argentina.

# WELSH TEA IN PATAGONIA

By Fiona Leslie, Chester, England

They say that today's descendants of the "Little Wales Beyond Wales" are more Welsh than the Welsh. The quaint streets bear names like E. Morgan, Lewis Jones and E. M. Thomas: they are lined with 19th century Welsh cottages. As you wander these streets, you're sure to feel as if you've somehow transported yourself across the ocean from Argentina to Wales. Sitting at the southern tip of a country known for its succulent steak and swaggering gauchos, Welsh Patagonia is somewhat of a cultural aberration, but certainly one worth experiencing.

After more than 20 years of studying Western Art and Design History and working in national decorative art museums in the UK and New York, Fiona Leslie wrote *Designs for 20th-Century Interiors* (1999, V&A) and co-authored *Contemporary Rugs: Art and Design* (2001, Merrell). Her long-term South American interests took over, and in 2004 she decided to leave London for a change of scene.

She participated on a scientific expedition in Bolivia with the SES, navigating the unexplored Rio Grande and carrying out archaeology along the way, followed by some voluntary teaching in remote Bolivian schools and then set off to see the rest of South America. She currently resides in Cusco, Peru, where she is designing textiles and developing weaving projects with remote Andean communities where she is also learning Quechua.

The first Welsh settlers landed at Puerto Madryn in July 1865. They soon pushed across the Chubut Valley to the foothills of the Andes and founded Esquel, located 272 kilometers south of Bariloche. As they pressed across country in search of more cultivatable land, this hardy bunch left an indelible mark on the landscape in the form of Welsh-style windmills, school houses and chapels. Although Spanish is now the most commonly spoken language in the region, the concentration of Welsh architecture and culture is astonishing. Perhaps the coziest way to experience Welsh Patagonia is to spend an afternoon sipping tea and sampling freshly-baked treats at one of the local tea houses.

In Gaiman, a small Welsh village situated in the Lower Valley of the Chubut River, taking tea is a serious business. With quintessential Welsh names such as Ty Nain, Nain Maggie and Plas Y Coed, these tea houses offer more than just a tourist-friendly slice of transplanted Welsh culture: prepare yourself for an authentic taste of life in Welsh Patagonia.

Most tea houses open after three, which affords plenty of time to wander the tree-lined streets and admire the architectural throwbacks to Europe's Wales. The atmosphere is noticeably relaxed: locals chat on street corners, the sound of their conversations (in Welsh) set to the musical backdrop of trickling streams.

A visit to one of the local history museums provides a fascinating glimpse into the lives of the first settlers: survival stories of tumultuous ship-crossings from Liverpool to Argentina, followed by harrowing tales of scraping out lives as farmers in the Indian-inhabited and arid Patagonia.

Complementing these astounding stories are displays filled with Welsh hats, lace costumes, domestic paraphernalia and fading photographs. Wedding photos of Mary Jones and Pedro Meschio highlight the cultural fusion that characterized unions among Welsh immigrants, Argentines and other European settlers, largely from Spain, Italy and Germany. These colonial Welsh leftovers and the stories that accompany them provide poignant insight into the new Argentine identity carved out of this solitary spot in the Southern Hemisphere.

When you've finished the local historical walkabout, head to Casa de Té, one of the best tea houses in Gaiman. As you pass through the front door you'll be greeted by all the trappings of traditional Welsh domesticity: dressers appointed with traditional ceramic ornaments, fireplaces flanked by colorful tapestries, and walls decorated with framed prints and paintings of Wales. A hostess leads you to a simple wooden table draped with a gingham table cloth, and once seated, you can await your Welsh tea experience while listening to the harmonious vocals of an all-male choir. The welcome tea arrives, warmed by a crocheted cozy, and with it a myriad of plates piled high with buttered sliced bread as well as fresh scones, served with butter and homemade fruit jam. To ensure you don't leave hungry, another round of plates arrives with slices of piping hot apple pie, egg custard tart, a local variation of dulce de leche crumble, and—last but not least—a seemingly infinite array of the most scrumptious traditional Welsh cakes, from black cake with sultanas to an iced madeira and chocolate sandwich sponge.

To work off your meal, take a wander through the rose-filled gardens located behind the house. Brightly-colored wooden carts lie scattered across the lawn, and in the background broad snow-capped mountains sweep into expansive sun-stroked valleys. The intoxicating scenery is the perfect complement to such a culinary spread, and whether taken as a night-cap or aperitif it is sure to please.

*"My biggest fear in life is to be forgotten."*
-Evita Perón, Argentine First Lady (1919-1952)

# LA TROCHITA

By John Ciullo, San Diego, California, U.S.A.

Infamous for its relentless winds and endless wide-open terrain, Patagonia is a land where only the hardiest of things—both natural and man-made—can survive. The Patagonian resilience is best personified by La Trochita, Argentina's only fully-functioning steam engine train and one of the few remaining narrow-gauge steam train lines in the world. An opportunity to ride behind the old engine and see its billowing smoke rise through the pale blue Patagonian sky is an experience for all ages.

The adventure begins as the train climbs out of the amphitheatre-shaped Esquel valley. The snow-capped Andean mountains loom on the western horizon as the train travels eastward through the Chubut foothills. Chilean flamingos congregate in the fertile marshlands below.

Before long, the train turns north and enters the moisture-deprived region called the Patagonian steppe. These arid, wind-swept plains extend eastward as far as the eye can see, barren and stark yet fascinatingly beautiful. To the west, the mountains stand like ancient sentinels looking over this unforgiving terrain. Signs of life are limited to an occasional herd of guanacos grazing on pampas grass. Not intimidated by its surroundings, La Trochita forges on.

The story of La Trochita is one of starts and stops, much just like the original 402-kilometer (250 mile) route through the Rio Negro and Chubut provinces. The state-run rail project was a high-risk proposal when it began in 1906. The Argentine government proposed building a series of railways that would connect the inaccessible central region of Patagonia to Atlantic ports. The complex plan languished due to the financial constraints of World War I, but in the early 1920s work began on the narrow-gauge-section.

From the original go-forward decision, the .75-meter (2.5 feet) gauge tracks took nearly 40 years to reach the town of El Maitén in the province of Chubut. The final tracks did not reach the terminal station of Esquel until 1945, with service beginning that same year.

Despite reaching top speeds of around 20 miles per hour, the train experienced dozens of mishaps. Mostly derailments, the accidents have resulted from inclimate weather of high winds and ice, to more bizarre collisions: running into a cow.

But La Trochita's most difficult struggles were yet to come. The national decline of Patagonia rail lines began in the 1970s due to their inability to compete with alternative modes of transportation. By the 1990s, most trains were all but abandoned. But La Trochita, special in the hearts and minds of those who traveled its steely rails, continued to operate. Her following grew with the publication of Paul Theroux's 1980 book entitled, The Old Patagonian Express. Public outcries against ceasing train operations prompted local governments to swallow their threats and keep it rolling for future generations.

Today the steam engines, Philadelphia-made Balwins and German-made Henschel & Sohn, as well as the Belgium-made passenger coaches, are all painstakingly refurbished and maintained in local workshops.

La Trochita now departs with its coaches teeming with travelers eager to ride the nostalgic 25-mile, three-hour round trip from Esquel to Nahuel Pan (a similar trip is offered from the other terminal station in El Maitén). For those with time and a superhuman tolerance for back-breaking wooden seats, the train also travels the entire six and one-half hour route from Esquel to El Maitén during the annual train festival in mid-February.

The Argentine Patagonia is not short on stories of struggle and survival but some are naturally more endearing than others. A passage through Patagonia would not be complete without a passage on-board Argentina's loveable legend, La Trochita.

John Ciullo is a freelance writer and has worked in the travel industry for over ten years, including guiding through dozens of national parks in Canada and the United States. He owns and operates an eco-tourism company called Parallel 41 Patagonia. He currently resides in Bariloche, Argentina, with his wife and seven-year-old son.

He dreams of visiting Antarctica and never travels without Glide dental floss.

> TRAVEL TIP:
> A winter ride on the train is especially romantic. The landscape seems more dramatic dusted in white and passengers can throw logs into the train furnace to keep warm. Aim for June to hit mid-winter. If around for longer than a day there are many other types of activity available in Esquel, including hiking, fishing and skiing.

La Trochita arrives at station. Photo by John Ciullo.

# EL BOLSÓN

### By Louise Hannah, Ledbury, Herefordshire, England

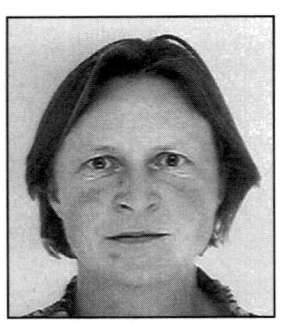

Lousie Hannah was brought up in Ledbury in Herefordshire, then went to Scotland to study Archaelogy at Edinburgh University. She has worked as a carpenter and more recently as a Housing Association Development Manager in London.

Her dream destination is Afghanistan 40 years ago and she plans on visiting either Central America or China during her next adventure.

---

**EL BOLSÓN TRAVEL TIPS:**
This city is the location for the National Hops Festival. During February, a celebration ensues for the locally grown plant which is the main beer-making ingredient. The growing of hops brings in a fair amount of agricultural income for El Bolsón.

---

How could you resist staying in a place whose name roughly translates to "The Sack?" El Bolsón, so called because it lies in a bag-shaped valley between snow capped peaks, has a magnetic charm that makes you want to stay forever.

In the 1970s, as part of an international movement to abandon city life for simple rural pleasures, young urbanites fled to El Bolsón, where they could spoil themselves in the warm microclimate favourable to growing soft fruit, or venture into the spectacular mountain scenery and rich forest environment—which they promptly set about saving from the logging agreements issued by the government.

Today, as in the 70s, you can enjoy walks from El Bolsón up into the stunning and well-preserved forest environment where 400 year old coihue and 1000 year old alcerce trees still stand. Follow the trails that wind towards grand waterfalls or alongside trout-filled rivers brimming with crisp blue water, fed by glaciers beyond the snow line.

Plan on staying a few days, but if you only have one day, walk up to Cerro Piltriquitrón via the Bosque de Tallado, where a tree sculpture park stands on a slope once ravaged by a forest fire. Local artists decided to turn the remaining trunks into highly individual pieces—the giant hand is my personal favourite. A little further up is the Club Andino refugio (mountain hut), at the base of Cerro Piltiquitrón where you can stay overnight for a small fee. The view from up here is spectacular: Lago Puelo dominates the immediate landscape, while El Bolsón and the snowy peaks of Chile unfold in the distance. One glimpse of the intoxicating beauty, coupled with the pure mountain air, will leave you reeling and you may even resolve to book a tandem paragliding flight over the valley from the jump-off point just below you.

High altitude adventures aside, a more placid pleasure comes with discovering that the refugio managers are also accomplished brewers and bread makers. Up here they bake bread every day in little wood ovens. This home-baked treat is perfect for sandwiches, ideally washed down with a crisp homemade beer. For an experience of a lifetime walk up to Canyon Azul and stay in what must surely rank among the best refugios in Argentina. Rickety swing bridges set amid remote and unspoiled scenery, coupled with the chance to see modern-day gauchos on horseback, are part of the rustic, but relaxing, experience.

Fear not if mountains are not your thing, for Bolsón has another gem in its bag—Jauja. Right in the heart of Bolsón, just a stone's throw from the market and tourist information centre, Jauja is a *heladeria* (ice cream parlour) unparalleled in South America. Over 70 flavours of ice cream are made on the premises, and perhaps as important is that its doors remain open during the siesta period. Jauja prides itself on the quality of its organic ingredients, most of which are sourced locally with the exception of the organic sugar, which comes from the Misiones region. Try the distinctly Argentinian Yerba Mate (tea) flavour, or the fabulous calafate (blueberry) made with organic sheep milk from the local chakra (farm). With all the flavors glistening in their steel containers, you may find it hard to choose which to try first. Apparently others have had difficulty deciding too; you can get your treats to go in insulated tubs.

The craft fair takes place three times a week just behind the tourist information centre. It's well worth a look even if you don't intend to buy. Wood-based crafts dominate the market, but you can also find exquisite silverwork, knives and woolen scarves, in addition to hand made clothes. The daring can purchase a bag of morels (edible fungi) gathered from the nearby forest or settle for yet more home brewed beer.

Stunning scenery, lively markets, and the best ice cream in South America add to the allure of this already-attractive destination. But this place offers more than just things to see and do. On the road towards town a modest sign declares, "La vida vale más del oro." *Life is worth more than gold.* The message is telling: beyond activities and attractions, it is the laid-back atmosphere of the town that is the most appealing.

---

## FACTOIDS ABOUT ARGENTINA

Argentinian director Luis Puenzo won a 1985 Oscar for *La Historia Oficial* (*The Official Story*), an intensely dramatic movie about an affluent Buenos Aires couple who realize that their adopted daughter is the child of a woman who "disappeared" (and was therefore most likely executed) during Argentina's "Dirty War" of the 1970s.

The Teatro Colón in Buenos Aires is one of the world's premier opera houses, regularly staging operas, concerts and visiting orchestras.

Argentina's signature dance/music, the tango, is a fusion of European music, African rhythms and the South American Milonga.

# SAN CARLOS DE BARILOCHE

## By Dr. Crit Minster, Rochester, New York, U.S.A.

Picture yourself meandering down a cobblestone street, admiring the sloped roofs and gingerbread look of the homes around you. You've just finished a day of skiing, and you're looking forward to a great meal in one of the cozy local restaurants. Before passing a chocolate shop you peer through its window. Chocolate tree branches and boxes of treats make up the tempting display. All around you, snippets of languages from around the world can be heard: English, Italian, Spanish, German. Are you in Bavaria? Switzerland? Northern Italy, perhaps?

Nope. You're in South America, Argentina to be precise. The confusion is understandable: The city of San Carlos de Bariloche was settled in the late 1800s by Austrians and Germans looking for economic opportunity in Argentina, which at the time welcomed thousands of Europeans. Naturally, these immigrants sought out a countryside that reminded them of their Alpine home, and they found it in a fertile, breathtakingly beautiful valley deep in the Andes.

They were not the first ones in the area, however. The rugged, formidable Andes were home to various native groups for centuries before the arrival of the Spanish. The Mapuche Indians of Central Chile—also known as the Araucanians—valiantly fought off all attempts at Spanish domination for centuries before they finally signed treaties in the 1880s.

Today, the city is a world-famous travel destination, offering a host of activities year-round. The skiing is top-notch at Cerro Catedral, probably South America's largest ski resort, and the city itself is located within the borders of Nahuel Huapi National Park, which is known for world class hiking, wildlife and lakes. Ranging in altitude from 700 to 3,000 meters, the park is one of the most diverse regions in the world, and home to both rainforests and glaciers.

Visitors to Bariloche will surely want to visit some of the park's highlights, such as the Arrayanes forest, which boasts one hundred-year-old trees, or the majestic Cántaros waterfall. Once you've had your fill of nature, take a stroll down Mitre Street, where you can shop for some of Bariloche's famous chocolate. Try a typical "ramita" or "little branch"—a treat that looks like a branch broken off a chocolate tree.

Bariloche is also a jumping off point for the spectacular lakes crossing to Chile. The crossing takes visitors from Bariloche to Puerto Montt, Chile or vice-versa. The crossing usually takes one to two days and involves a combination of buses and boats. The scenery is fantastic: breathtaking mountains, pristine lakes and inspiring pine forests abound. If you're lucky you may even catch a glimpse of the rare Andean condor. Eye-captivating landscapes and mouth-watering handmade chocolate—what more could you ask for?

---

**BARILOCHE FACTOID:**
The chocolate for which Bariloche is famous was brought by the Europeans after World War II. The immigrants began making chocolates at home but these days, the chocolates are mainly produced in factories. Chocoholics should check out Mamushka, Rapa Nui or Fenoglio for some of the best.

---

Bariloche. Photo by Christian Denes.

ARGENTINA

www.vivatravelguides.com/103446    V!VA List    13

# LAKE CROSSING INTO CHILE

By Dr. Crit Minster, Rochester, New York, U.S.A.

The Araucanians, a proud South American tribe also known as the Mapuche, knew there was a pass through the rugged mountains, but they never revealed its location, especially to the despised Spanish.

For centuries, these doughty natives of southern Chile and Argentina held off the invaders, clinging to their independence long after the mighty Inca Empire to the north had fallen. The pass, which consisted of a network of trails, and lakes that could be crossed by small boat, was one of their best kept secrets.

Time and intrepid explorers eventually uncovered this hidden travel network, and by the 1930s it was possible to cross the 70 miles from Bariloche, Argentina, to Puerto Montt, Chile, in a combination of small lake boats and oxcarts. Although airplanes have made the pass irrelevant, thousands of people still make the lake crossing through the mountains every month.

Anyone who has visited this lake region, nestled between Argentina and Chile, knows why travelers would trade a 40 minute flight for a two-day excursion. Seeped in history, the region boasts some of the most breathtaking scenery on earth, and the crossing overwhelms the eye with one gorgeous view after another. Modern day transport enables visitors to enjoy such dazzling views in relative comfort: buses have replaced the oxen, and boats with large motors can cross the lakes in a fraction of the time it used to take to paddle across.

Most visitors make the crossing between Bariloche and Puerto Montt (or vice versa) in one to two days, taking a series of four buses and three boats. The route cuts through two national parks, wraps around four lakes, and features stops in the picturesque towns of Bariloche, Puerto Montt and Puerto Varas, which is known for its roses. Bariloche is a world class visitor destination known for adrenaline-pumping outdoor sports, such as skiing and hiking, and for its mouth-watering handmade chocolate.

Highlights of the route include a magnificent view of Tronador Mountain, whose name means "Thunderer," and stops at the Petrohue and Helechos waterfalls. Petrohue is a series of scenic falls that wend their way through ancient volcanic rock. Helechos is remote, inspirational waterfall reached by horseback from the town of Peulla. Travelers taking the two day trip can also enjoy an overnight stop at the historic Peulla Hotel, a Swiss-style mountain lodge constructed in 1896. A variety of activities, from fishing and horseback riding, to whitewater rafting and hiking, offer outdoor enthusiasts the opportunity to get out and rub elbows with Nature.

The secret is out. The locals couldn't keep this much natural beauty hidden forever.

FACTOID: So why was Tronador Mountain named by the locals for loud sounds? Its name refers to the sounds of falling seracs atop the giant. Seracs are blocks of ice formed by intersecting crevasses on a glacier that can fall with little warning, and "thunder" when they hit the ground, or other nearby ice formations.

Lake Crossing into Chile. Photo by Christian Denes.

*"Latins are tenderly enthusiastic. In Brazil they throw flowers at you. In Argentina they throw themselves."*
-Marlene Dietrich, German Actress (1901-1992)

# BARILOCHE TO PUERTO VARAS

### By Will Gray, Kettering, England

This spectacular cross-border trip, called Cruce de Lagos, is an epic journey made up of four bus rides and three ferry trips that steer through the Andes from the picturesque town of Bariloche, in Argentina, to Puerto Varas, in Chile.

The lake district crossing follows a route that the original German settlers used to export their goods through the port town of Puerto Montt, Chile. The adventure begins with a lakeside drive beside the massive Nahuel Huapi Lake which, like the lakes in Switzerland, can look either serene and inviting or rough and menacing, depending on the weather.

Don't fret if you encounter cloudy skies; the massive mountain range rising between the departure and destination towns works as a weather system-stopper, so wet and windy on one side might mean stunning sunny scenery on the other.

After an hour the route reaches the set-off point for the first boat. A large catamaran takes you onto the lake for the hour-long ride to Puerto Blest, a trip that offers pleasant scenes of the surrounding mountains and a wonderful wide view of Bariloche disappearing into the distance. Once off the boat, a rickety bus heads out onto the dirt roads for a bouncy 15 minute jaunt to Puerto Alegra, sitting on the next of this chain of lakes.

This is where it gets a bit more rustic, with a single jetty out to a boat with wooden benches. The second lake, Lake Frias, is set in a deep crater-like bowl of mountains and is much narrower than the first. Flowing through lush green surroundings, it takes you right up to the border between Argentina and Chile, and some unusual emigration controls, where you can warm your feet up beside a log fire as you sign out of the country.

It is then a two-hour bus ride, breaking the back of the Andes, to the Chilean border post, which lies right on the edge of the tiny town of Peulla. From here, travelers have a number of options - you can take advantage of the long break before the next bus and stop for a hearty lunch, or explore one of the steep trails winding through the forest and into the mountains towards a spectacular three-tier, 100 metre-high waterfall and a viewpoint over the lake. Or, if you have the funds, you could break the journey with an overnight stay in the heart of nature at the luxurious Peulla Hotel then catch the next ferry out.

The final boat then heads out onto Lago Todos los Santos, where on a good day the water is mirror-still and the awesome pointy ice-covered top of Puntiagudo and perfect dome-shaped Osorno volcanoes are reflected on the water as they appear miraculously from around the corner. A jaw-dropping beautiful journey of one-and-a-half hours then follows until the boat moors up in Petrohue.

The last bus ride heads from there to Puerto Varas, but the one-and-three-quarter hours journey is broken up by a highly-recommended stop at Saltas de Petrohue, where the water rolls down ancient lava floes in a wide and very photogenic waterfall, before the journey arrives at its final destination and it is time to sample one of the local restaurants as the sun sets behind the shore.

Bariloche to Puerto Varas. Photo by Will Gray.

## PATO

### By Dr. Crit Minster

Pato, Spanish for "duck," is the official national game of Argentina. Sort of a cross between basketball and polo, pato is played by two, four-player teams on horseback who attempt to score by throwing the ball (which has six handles) through a vertical net and into a hoop. Originally, the game was played by gauchos who used an actual duck as the "ball."

**ARGENTINA**

# LAVENDER FARM

By Ellery Biddle, Philadelphia, Pennsylvania, U.S.A.

We walked along, looking down at the north shore of the Lago Perito Moreno in Argentina's lake district. The road first descended and then rose between two mountains and as the hills grew steeper, we caught sight of a small, open space—a green clearing with a dusting of purple along the top. A sign by the road read, "Meli Hue Finca Lavanda" in small, purple letters. It was a lavender farm. Intrigued and curious, my friend and I decided to explore this mysterious farm in the middle of the mountains.

Ellery Biddle was born and raised in Philadelphia, PA. She graduated from Kenyon College in 2005, where she studied creative writing and Spanish-American literature. She also traveled to Cuba in the spring of 2005 to study sociology and public health at la Universidad de la Habana. After performing in the Philly Fringe Festival in September of 2005, Ellery moved to Buenos Aires, Argentina, to write, dance and officially begin her exploration of South America.

She dreams of traveling to Easter Island, but the most strange destination she has seen is Havana's malecón, where she watched transvestites stroll.

A narrow, dirt driveway divided the field in two, the wind making purple waves as it blew through rows and rows of lavender bushes. As the drive began to curve, the purple fields gave way to a large stone house. A girl appeared at the door and led us into the small, sweet-smelling shop where the wooden shelves were stocked with lavender oils, soaps and candles. As she put a droplet of oil on each of our wrists, she explained that the farm was run by a retired couple, as a sort of hobby and a way to make some extra money. She told us to rub the oil in slowly I held my wrist to my nose and took a deep breath, feeling my face relax as the essence fell deep into my lungs. We each bought a small bottle for the road.

Next to the shop, there was a small tea room. It had sturdy-looking wooden chairs and tables, a fireplace and a big bay window looking out onto the wildflower garden set against an unforgettable view of the lake. We walked outside and sat among the flowers in two Adirondack chairs at a small wicker table. Across the glassy blue water, the Hotel Llao Llao beamed back at us: a large, elegant old estate that sat between two of the seven lakes that surround Bariloche and that is said to be Argentina's most luxurious hotel. A few minutes later, the young girl returned with a steaming pot of lavender tea, a basket of tiny but hearty scones and two ramekins of homemade jam. She told us that the jams were made of local raspberries and guinda, a berry that is native to Patagonia and similar to a cherry. I took a scone and spread a thin layer of guinda jam on top. The scone was buttery and the jam tasted tart and sweet. The tea steeped a minute longer and then we poured and sat, breathing in the steam off the tops of our little cups and enjoying a perfect moment of release before we began our big hike through Patagonia for the day.

## THE LLAO LLAO HOTEL AND RESORT

By Dr. Crit Minster

On the shores of Lake Nahuel Huapi and Lake Moreno, the sprawling Llao Llao Hotel and Resort boasts what is arguably the most beautiful views of any hotel in the world. The 360 degree panorama features stunning blue lakes, majestic white-capped mountains, green islands and rolling hills. This internationally renowned 5 star resort features a world-class spa, golf course, pool, archery range and much, much more.

Built in 1940 to service the increasing tourism traffic to Argentina's jaw-droppingly beautiful lake district, the Llao Llao was completely refurbished in 1993. It has hosted numerous international celebrities including former US president Bill Clinton. The Llao Llao has won numerous awards, including making Travel and Leisure Magazine's list of the top ten hotels in Mexico, Central America and South America. The on-site restaurants are outstanding and a destination in their own right.

The Llao Llao is not for everyone—the price tag will make all but the most well-heeled travelers cringe—but there is no arguing that it is one of the best, and the most beautiful, hotels in the world. If you're visiting Argentina's lake district, you may want to consider splurging for a night or two, or perhaps enjoying a fine meal at this unique hotel and resort.

# JURASSIC PARK—NEUQUÉN

By Kelley Coyner, Texas, U.S.A.

In the last year, Neuquén Basin in northern Argentine Patagonia was the site of internationally acclaimed fossil finds. (*dakosaurus andenisis*, and *nequenraptor argentinus*). At one site near Lago Barreallos, investigators have made more than 60 significant finds in recent years. Whether you're a scientist, archeologist, or just a dinosaur enthusiast, these discoveries mean a visit to Argentine Patagonia can be a visit to a real Jurassic Park (or Cretaceous Park).

If you like to see Guinness World Record holders with your own eyes, visit the small museum in Villa El Chocón, where you will find the fossilized skeletons of the world's largest herbivores and carnivores (dinosaurs of course!). The fossilized remains of *giganotosaurus carolinii*, the largest carnivore, was found near Villa El Chocón in an area that had been a lagoon. *Argentinosaurus*, the largest herbivore and largest known dinosaur, was located by staff of the Carmen Funes Musuem. While you are in El Chocón, visit Cretaceous Valley or take a short drive to see dino footprints alongside Lake Mexia.

Neuquén also harbors hundreds of long-since abandoned dino-egg clusters. Discovered by Rodolfo Coria and his team, the find marks a number of firsts: the first dinosaur embryos to show fossilized skin, the first known embryos of the giant plant-eating sauropod dinosaurs, the first dinosaur embryos found in the southern hemisphere, and the largest dinosaur nesting site ever discovered. You can view an exhibit on the eggs at the Carmen Funes Municipal Museum in the capital of the province at the Centro Cultural Plaza Huincul.

At one site in Lago Barreales, investigators made so many finds they moved the museum lock, stock and barrel to the site. Guests can observe the work at the site, where they can learn about preservation and investigation techniques inside the center, and even sign up for a short work trip in the field. Look for the Dino Project at Centro Paleontológico, Lago Barreales.

If you cannot make it to the more remote Neuquén, visit the Museo Egidio Feruglio in Trelew or the Museo de Ciencias Naturales de La Plata in the city of the same name, or head to the Museo Argentino de Ciencias Naturales, Buenos Aires. Any one of these collections gives a taste of why paleontologist James Kirkland says that Argentina is one of the top three most important *dinolandias* in the world.

*"For the Argentine, friendship is a passion and the police a mafia."*
*-Jorge Luís Borges, Argentine Poet and Writer (1899-1986)*

## YERBA MATE

By Michelle Hopey

To western folks it looks illegal and possibly dangerous, and if you're not familiar with specifics of drug paraphernalia, you're likely to think it's a bong or pipe for smoking marijuana.

But no worries, those men and women sitting in cafes, restaurants and parks, and on the ranch, bus and train sucking in on that long metal straw that juts out of the hollowed bowl sending an airy smell of strong, woody herbs, are completely legit. In fact, as locals sit in a circle and pass the strange pipe device around, you still might not believe its legality. Have no doubt, these common folk are engaging in one of the most culturally historic traditions of South America, a ritual that has transitioned flawlessly into modern-day life—perhaps more than most Latin traditions—drinking the natural, non-hallucinogenic beverage, Yerba Mate.

Yerba Mate (pronounced Year-BA, MA-TAY) is a highly caffeinated beverage that is made by steeping dried, ground Yerba leaves in hot water. With origins dating back to the Guarani Indians, Yerba Mate, a perennial plant, is native to subtropical highlands of South America. It is a small evergreen tree belonging to the Holly family and because of this, straight Yerba Mate tastes bitter with a strong wood-like, vegetable, herbal flavor.

To sip Yerba Mate, start by sucking on the straw or *bombilla* which is typically made of a metal or copper. The bombilla serves two purposes: straw and filter. Much like a loose tea infuser, the bottom end of the bombilla has small holes that let the brewed liquid in, but that is designed to block the large chunks of sticks and stems of the leaves. The actual bowl that the Yerba mixture is packed into, and which one drinks from, is called the gourd, mate or guampa, depending upon your location. In Brazil, it's called the *cuia*. Drinking mate is primarily a pastime in Argentina, southern regions of Brazil and Bolivia, Paraguay, and Uruguay. Rarely will you find it north of Peru. Not only is Yerba Mate a way of life, but it is a strong social connection. So, if any locals pass you the infamous gourd, don't be alarmed. Take a sip and enjoy this South American drink.

ARGENTINA

# RUTA NACIONAL 3, PATAGONIA

By John Polga-Hecimovich, Burnsville, Minnesota, U.S.A.

Patagonia is as much a real land as it is a myth. It captured the imagination of its explorers and wanderers, from Ferdinand Magellan and Pedro Sarmiento de Gamboa to Sir Francis Drake and Charles Darwin, despite, or perhaps because of, its unforgiving weather and hostile geography. It remains a wild and untamed land to this day. The enormous region is generally considered to begin south of the Río Colorado in Argentina and extend to Tierra del Fuego, comprising roughly a third of the country (as well as parts of Chile), although only 5% of Argentines call it home. The best way to experience Patagonia is on the road, eating its meat, drinking its wine, and living its solitude.

Ruta Nacional 3 traces the eastern border of the region, beginning in Buenos Aires, winding its way down through the Pampas and terminating just west of Ushuaia, the southernmost city in the world. It is the primary artery of terrestrial traffic through Patagonia, and unlike Route 40, its western counterpart, the majority of Route 3 fails to offer mountain views, skiing lodges, cave paintings or glaciers. It does, however, offer a raw view of Patagonia, capturing the essence of its people, its towns, and its open spaces. Seemingly endless stretches of barbed wire scar the rugged landscape, punctuating man's presence in an otherwise wild land. Against its sheer size and seemingly endless expanse of land, Texas would pale in comparison. The road cuts through small towns and large cities, past the wild, windy monotony of sheep ranches and oil pumps, and into the heart of the lonely desert that stretches from Viedma to Río Gallegos, near the Strait of Magellan.

Aside from the remoteness of the cities it links, the most astounding aspect of this road is the uninterrupted vastness and flatness of the terrain it bisects. The endless steppe is in places nearly featureless, and the tedium of the roadside topography is broken only by scattered sheep, guanaco, rhea, cows, and, incredibly, the flaming pink of the occasional flock of flamingos. At dusk, the vast sea of earth fades into the horizon until the blues and pinks and purples turn to a firm black, and the stars finally come out. Most towns fail to offer any particularly unique views, landscape, or sights; just basic food and lodging, and the ubiquitous little Argentine children playing soccer in the wind.

Ushuaia is the southernmost city in the world, if you don't count the small naval base of Puerto Williams, Chile (Argentines don't). The town lies on the shimmering turquoise waters of the Beagle Channel, protected on three sides by hulking snow-capped peaks. Besides its breathtaking views, the town provides a point of departure for expeditions to Cape Horn, the Drake Passage and Antarctica. It is here in Lapataia Bay, after 3,062 kilometers, that Route 3 finally draws to a halt. A road sign with a map of Tierra del Fuego indicates—with little pomp—that the traveler has reached the end of the road, here in Argentina's 24th district. The pavement, beginning in one of the world's largest cities, now ends here, so abruptly, that one truly feels they have reached the end of the earth.

Of course, it is the journey, and not the destination, that counts. A plane flight from Buenos Aires to Ushuaia might be easier, or even cheaper, but it certainly doesn't have the character of dusty Route 3, with its solitary towns and wild landscapes, infused with the rich flavor of the real Patagonia.

Wind swept tree. Photo by John Polga-Hecimovich.

# MOUNTAIN BIKING AND TEA IN THE ANDES

By Will Bennett, London, England

The approaching valley is combed with vineyards stretching deep green and purple towards the horizon. Behind me a bleeding sun tints the snow-capped peak of Mt. Aconcagua, its warmth belying the gelid wind that has been with us all day. Save for sudden gusts that stir the thick arrangements of wild lavender, there is complete silence. Below, the foothill city of Mendoza glows in the growing dark. After an adventure-packed day of mountain biking and white water rafting, the city looks diminutive and deserted.

Pulling away from the view, I head back towards the rest of the cycling party, which has congregated on the last plateau overlooking our final descent. Awaiting us at the bottom is a much-anticipated calabash of mate (pronounced maté), an Argentinean herbal tea drink, forest green in colour, thick, sweet, and most importantly warm. Pressed forward by the thought of something warm in our stomachs, we imitate Gabriel, our fearless guide, and push our front wheels over the edge and begin our descent.

The Andes rise in the distance, stunning and coarse, growing higher as we thump down the pitted terrain. From the west, the last remnants of sun streak through the serrated peaks, casting a kaleidoscope-vision of color and light on the unfolding landscape. A cold wind nips at my nose and ears, stinging my eyes and blurring my vision. Through frozen tears, I make out a hut next to the lonely dirt road. Sticking out like a sore thumb is the minibus, our chariot to Mendoza. A row of now-abandoned bicycles lean against the whitewash stone-walled hut; their riders eagerly tossed them aside as they strode towards the hut's light and the promise of a warm drink.

By the look on his face, I could tell that Gabriel had been waiting a while: he must have downed a few liters of mate before I arrived. Cautiously I sip the murky brew through the ornate silver straw, not wanting to burn my mouth. The drink has a potent taste, like a cross between green tea and coffee, infused with flavors of tobacco and oak. Despite its foreign taste, it is pleasantly sweet and offers welcome warmth. A wry smile spreads across Gabriel's face as he watches us sample this foreign substance—a benchmark of Argentinean culture. Nodding towards his cup he says flatly, "mate dulce." Sweet Mate. I learned later that this is the preference in the Mendoza Province.

I sip and chew my way to the end, trying to imitate the plump bus driver drinking on a stool in the corner. Feeling full and warm, I return the pot to Gabriel with a nod and a sincere *gracias*. As others continue sipping, we pass around anecdotes from the day, recollecting the frenzied paddling through the white water rapids and recalling the rugged and remote landscape through which we rode. When the driver finishes he beckons us to the bus and we head back to Mendoza and our varying standards of accommodation; although tonight, hostel and hotel dwellers alike are guaranteed a deep and unbroken sleep.

Will Bennett just completed a History degree at Bristol University. He is currently an English teacher and freelance travel writer and photographer.

One of his strangest experiences abroad was being cleaned with sand-papered mittens in a Syrian hamam. He also found it peculiar being asked to pose for family photographs and sign autographs in Beijing, simply because he was western. He loves imagining that somewhere in China his confused face is in a frame on the mantelpiece.

# TOP LIST: BICYCLE TRIPS TO BRAG ABOUT

Some parts of the world were simply made to be seen from two wheels. Latin America, with its hills, mountains and valleys, is a cyclist's dream! Constantly changing scenery, friendly people, and the toughest workout your lungs have ever had are all guaranteed!

1. Biking the World's Most Dangerous Road, La Paz, Bolivia (p. 305). "Downhill all the way but challenging and exceptionally beautiful." Cynthia Winn, California, U.S.A.

2. Cycling in the Argentinian Andes, near Mendoza. Mat Crompton, England.

3. Mountain biking down Cotopaxi (p. 248). "Spectacular scenery, a bit scary but lots of fun!" Lucy Whitehead, Scotland.

4. Biking Tours around Buenos Aires (p. 32). "On this tour you are privy to secrets only known to locals; you become porteño for a day." Michelle, New Hampshire, U.S.A.

**ARGENTINA**

# MENDOZA

By Michelle Hopey, New Hampshire, U.S.A.

Michelle Hopey has worked as a journalist for seven years, writing and researching for a number of magazines and newspapers all over the United States. For two years before embarking on her graduate degree in investigative journalism at Boston University, Hopey worked as a market researcher for a San Francisco-based consumer research firm.

After graduating, her wanderlust carried her to South America, where she dogged her way up Machu Picchu and café-hopped through Buenos Aires, finally landing in Quito, Ecuador, with V!VA Travel Guides.

Adventure sports in the snow capped Andes, lazy days in the Maipu valley, a growing gastronomic scene, artistically rich culture, and of course, fine wine, all make Mendoza, Argentina one of the top travel destinations in South America.

Nestled in the western Cuyo region, just 1,000 kilometers (620 miles) west of Buenos Aires and only 340 kilometers (211 miles) from Santiago de Chile, Mendoza is surrounded by picture-perfect mountains, lush green valleys, and seemingly endless tracts of dense forest.

Home to several universities, the city is shaped by its artistic culture. Museums, such as the *Museo Municipal de Arte Moderno* located underneath the main Plaza Independencia host monthly exhibits from the country's top painters. Dance, music and live performances all serve important roles in Mendocino life. On weekends, parks, including Plaza Independencia, Plaza San Martin, Plaza España and Plaza Pellegrini and Parque San Martin host a variety of cultural events. From musicians, antique and artisan markets and occasional dance troupes, they have it all covered. Cleaner and safer than most parks in North America or Europe, gathering in parks is a staple of Mendoza life.

It's a common joke in these parts that you'll come to Mendoza for a few days, and end up staying several weeks. Thanks to the 110, 000 Mendocinos who call this place home, the relaxing atmosphere is no mistake. A laid-back bunch, the Mendocinos cater to the loafing lifestyle that so often lulls visitors into lingering a bit longer than planned. With the vast topographic area surrounding, this town has something for just about everyone.

Besides its inescapable magnetism, Mendoza is best known for its vineyards and the grapes that are grown in them. In particular, its region-specific *vino*, Malbec, and the hundreds of wineries (or *bodegas* as they are called in these parts) are what draw travelers to Mendoza—and rightfully so. Older than its relatives in California's Napa Valley, and less commercialized than its cousins in France, the Mendoza wine region is raw and real. While the more serious "winos" dedicate a week or more to bodega hopping, other not so wine-savvy travelers may want to set aside a day or two to develop their sipping skills. Not only are the wine and olive oil samplings palate pleasers, but the historic buildings and exquisite vineyards are all photograph-worthy as well.

Sound too relaxing? Craving more of an outdoor adventure? No fear, Mendoza is situated on the eastern Andean piedmont at 761 meters (2,496 feet) above sea level, and provides endless opportunity for mountain biking, skiing, snowboarding, hiking, horseback riding, along with kayaking and white-water rafting.

Mendoza is also famous for its close proximity to *Cerro Aconcagua*, the highest peak in all of South America at 6,962 meters (22,835 feet). Nicknamed the "Roof of the Americas," only experienced mountaineers attempt the summit, but hiking to base camp and the surrounding area is a popular option—and an unforgettable one at that. Because of the diverse geographic area, the Diamante, Atuel and Upper Rio Mendoza rivers also provide some of the best white-water rafting in the country.

Whether you go to catch some culture, sip wine or take to the slopes, you're likely to be happy you strolled through Mendoza, especially if you end up staying a bit longer than planned.

## CUEVA DE LAS MANOS

By Mariana Cotlear

Within the cavernous walls of the Pinturas River in the Santa Cruz province is *Cueva de las Manos*, or Cave of the Hands. A UNESCO World Heritage Site since 1999, this cave is covered in drawings of hands (thus its name), as well as animals, plants, hunting scenes and geometric designs. Possibly made by the *Tehuelches* civilization, who roamed this part of the Patagonia, archaeologists have dated the cave drawings at somewhere between 13,000 and 9,500 years old. The hands have been stenciled onto the rocks with red, white, black and yellow mineral-based pigments to create an impressive overlapping design, a visual testament to humanity that seems to have withstood geological time.

ARGENTINA

# CARO PEPE

### By Michelle Hopey, New Hampshire, U.S.A.

You've probably heard that Argentina is famous for its tender, juicy cuts of beef, but what you might not know, is that when it comes to food, Argentines love their buffets. And these buffets are not simply a few dishes thrown out for the taking. These are gourmet meals delicately prepared to satisfy palates of carnivores and vegetarians alike.

Nestled between Chile Street and Mendoza's bustling avenue Las Heras, Caro Pepe is the premiere buffet bistro in Mendoza. A favorite restaurant among locals, Caro Pepe is also a true Argentine experience—hospitable waiters, mouth-watering food, and a complete wine bar offering over 100 different wines birthed and aged in the Mendoza province itself.

A large open space with minimal décor—which attracts large Argentine families on the weekends—the restaurant boasts a barbeque pit that grills up marinated and smoked beef, chicken, pork—and don't forget the blood sausage. All chef-carved to your liking, the meats alone could be enough to fill you up. But rarely can one turn to leave the BBQ station, without stopping by the two large buffet islands, which boast an array of culinary creations, from paella to gourmet quiches, special chicken entrees to vegetable curries, and a complete salad bar to boot.

And before you even begin to think about dessert, it's worth a stroll on over to the cook's station where you can choose your own pasta and sauces, and have the chef mix it up before your eyes.

You may as well ignore those signs of satiety because a third buffet island includes fresh fruit salads and a variety of postres, including rich chocolate mousse and to-die-for cakes. If your pants aren't too tight yet, you might want to swing by the make-your-own crepe station, where you can choose between a chocolate or apple crepe topped with chocolate sauce, whisky, or caramel, and if you can manage it, try it alamode—it's a guaranteed sweet tooth finale.

Mendoza. Photo by Michelle Hopey.

# WINE COUNTRY

### By Michelle Hopey, New Hampshire, U.S.A.

Napa and Loire Valley take note: It's only a matter of time until the next bubbling wine country, Mendoza Argentina, pops the cork off your local variety.

Wine novices, lovers and aficionados listen up: Better get a move on south before Mendoza's popularity garners so much attention that there are new hotels, shopping malls and wider highways which inevitably will be needed to accommodate the herds of aspiring winos descending upon the small, quaint valleys of Mendoza.

But if you get there soon, within the next five years, you'll get the chance to mosey along the quiet, charming, green tree-lined streets by bike or car and tour Mendoza's valleys just the way it is today: with beautiful landscapes including Cerro Aconcagua, (6962 meters, 22,841 feet) and white-water rafting paradise, Río Mendoza not to mention all the peaks for skiing, quaint family-run wineries and a number of unique tasting opportunities, including artesian olive oil spreads, and dark chocolate liquor filled truffles.

Currently producing 70 percent of all the wine made in Argentina, (Argentina is also the fifth largest wine producer in the world), Mendoza province sees little rainfall through out the year, and remains mostly hot and dry. Such a climate is perfect for visiting, not to mention, excellent growing conditions for red grapes. While Malbec is the true bottle of choice in these parts, Pinot Noir is on the rise as well, thanks in part to the popularity of the 2004 independent flick, Sideways. White wines are not a specialty of Mendoza province.

The two main wine regions close to Mendoza city are Luján de Cuyo, 19km south of Mendoza and Maipú 16 km from the city. Each area contains a concentrated number of wineries that are open to the public for touring and tastings. While all winery tours and tastings are free, some of the high-end varieties will cost to taste.

Olive trees are also heavily grown in this region and several wineries also produce olive oils and specialty spreads for crackers and breads, and are also available for tastings. Since homemade chocolate is another delicacy in Argentina, along the wine trail you'll come across several chocolate shops where you can nibble on chocolates and other candies.

Wine making here is still an art but the sophistication level is not as high as Napa or Loire. Wine culture is still being born in Mendoza and there is still very much a artesian flavor to Argentina's wine country, but that is exactly what makes touring here different, exciting and Argentinean.

From Mendoza City it's not difficult to sign-up for a wine tour. In fact, walk along Avenida Las Heras or along the pedestrian mall, Avineda Sarmiento and you'll come across countless tour operators. Most of these companies offer a one-day tour, with the chance to visit three wineries and then a chocolate artesian too. Sometimes the tour includes lunch at a winery or famed restaurants in town. Tour guides and vineyard guides typically speak English, as well as Spanish.

With so many tour companies in town, marketing to certain demographics is common. For example, Campo Base Adventures, a tour operator, affiliated with Hostelling International offers a great, basic one-day wine tour, but since this is marketed towards a young backpacker crowd (and HI guests can sign-up in the lobby of their hostel), you are likely to be tasting wine alongside other backpackers.

Sometimes tours like these do not cut it if you are a connoisseur of wine and want to visit the fancy high-end vineyards. If you want to skip Introduction to Wine 101, with the basics of a tour, there are some upper-end tour companies beginning to establish themselves, and they are easily booked ahead of time through the web. Many of these operators will let you customize your itinerary, and of course this option will be on the pricier side. It might cost you more, but those who have done it, say it's worth it.

It is also possible to rent a car or hire a taxi (if you want to do some care free tasting) Taxis for long term rent are called telephone taxis. With wine maps readily available from the tourist office, you can plan your own trip around town and hit certain wineries that a tour doesn't necessarily visit. This is the best economic option for making sure you reach the popular wineries, without worrying about missing any. Another option is to hop on the bus going either to Maipú or south to Luján de Cuyo and see what you can find.

And finally, if you don't plan to drink or buy too much wine on your day of tasting, renting a bike (available nearly everywhere from hostels to bike rental shops) is a beautiful way to see the area and tour around, especially Maipú, which has a reputation for being the rider's route. Stunning scenery mixed with flat valley roads for riding and warm weather make for a spectacular bike ride. Of course, getting back on the bike after having one too many is always an issue as is strapping bottles of wine to your back, but if you are just out for a romantic adventure, rent some bikes and head off into the vineyards.

## STAYING AT AN ESTANCIA

### By Leigh Gower

Argentina's world-famous estancias, traditional ranches whose primary residences have been converted into luxurious guest houses, offer a perfect escape after visiting some of the country's bustling cities and other tourist attractions.

Covering one-fifth of the country, the grassy Pampas region of Argentina is home to a large proportion of these estancias. Here visitors can unwind by taking part in traditional Argentinean field activities including horse riding, fishing and hunting. One can also observe the traditional work of the Gauchos. These Argentinean cowboys continue to manage the land, drive cattle and shear sheep as they have done since the seventeenth century, when the estancias were established by a number of prominent Creole families.

Although relatively expensive, a stay at one of these traditional homesteads promises to be a unique cultural experience. Guests receive a high level of personal attention and insight into the living customs of the Argentinean countryside, amid stunning colonial architecture and friendly people. Just make sure to avoid interfering in the preparation of the roast—that role is solely in the hands of the "expert."

# MALBEC WINE

### By Peter Anderson, Christchurch, New Zealand

**M**albec has become the emblematic grape of Argentina. Known as *Auxerrois* in Cahors and *Cot* in the Loire, this grape has undergone a mini-renaissance in the last decade, largely fuelled by its success in South America. The Malbec grape is widely grown in Argentina and produces deep coloured wines with generous black fruit characteristics, balanced acidity and smooth tannins. It is either bottled on its own or as part of a Bordeaux blend.

Argentina is the fifth largest wine producer in the world and the sixth ranked per capita, even though consumption has dropped from 90 litres per capita in the 70s to 38 litres today (that's per year, of course). This drop is attributed to the aggressive marketing of beer, which is becoming increasingly popular in Argentina. Argentina had three wines in *Wine Spectator's* Top 100, 2004, all with 91 points: Bodegas Terrazas de Los Andes' Malbec Mendoza Reserva 2002, (53rd), Bodega Catena Zapata's Malbec Mendoza 2002 (67th) and Valentín Bianchi's Cabernet Sauvignon San Rafael Famiglia 2002, (which contains 7% Malbec) finished 78th. The price of Malbec varies considerably, from US$7 to US$85 and this price range covers 12 Malbecs, all with 89 points or more from *Wine Spectator's* list.

Not even Cahors, Malbec's motherland, in the South of France, produces wines as exciting as those made in Argentina. Notable areas of Argentine production are Luján de Cuyo and Tupungato in the Province of Mendoza. Wines made with 100% Malbec are richest in personality: they also have very exuberant aromas, with ripe, fruity overtones and a full body, which in the best wines can almost be chewed.

Argentina grows over 42,000 acres of Malbec. One advantage of the Malbec business in this region is lack of competition with other countries. While California must contend with Bordeaux, Argentina pretty much stands alone in its field. Unfettered by the standards or recognizable flavours set by other regions, Argentina and its Malbecs are making quite an impact.

Outstanding vintages include Angélica Zapata Malbec Alta (1995, 1997), Achával Ferrer Gran Malbec Finca Altamira (1999, 2000), la Celia Malbec Reserva 2000 and Terrazas Gran Malbec 1999.

Wines from Argentina received a huge boost in 1995, when their exports skyrocketed, thanks mainly to Mother Nature. Frost and droughts devastated the top European wine-producing countries that year and consequently there was a shortage of wines from the regular producers. Since then Argentine wine is making inroads into the international wine market (albeit slowly).

Besides its budding wine industry, Argentine also produces some of the best beef in the world and for steak lovers, what could be more appetizing than a well-cooked Argentine steak served with a glass or two—maybe even three—of Malbec wine?

Peter Anderson is a New Zealander who has been based in Malaysia since 1984. Educated at Canterbury University, he is a travel photojournalist by profession. He has published over 100 travel articles in 12 countries in English, Malay, Chinese and Arabic and authored or photographed 10 travel books.

His dream trip is to drive the length of South America, but next he is embarking on a trip to Slovenia and Croatia.

Malbec barrels. Photo by Michelle Hopey.

# WINDING YOUR WAY THROUGH THE ANDES

By Sarah Tonner, Tampa, Florida, U.S.A.

In stark contrast to Buenos Aires, the peace and serenity of the Andes, on the border between Argentina and Chile, is a tranquil journey.

Sarah Tonner was born in Tampa, Florida, but moved to England when she was four years old. She attended the University of Sheffield where she studied Hispanic Studies. Following a period working for a Marketing and Promotions company in Houston, Texas, she is now studying for a Master's at Texas A&M University in College Station in Comparative Literature and Culture. She lives in College Station with her boyfriend and they are hoping to move to Europe when they graduate in 2008. When not studying, Tonner loves to ski and travel.

The craziest place she has traveled to is Baku, Azerbaijan, in 1996, soon after the Russians retreated back across the border and no longer had control of the state.

Tonner hopes to visit Cuba next, but also wouldn't mind a 5-star luxury trip to Fiji.

Whether you choose to rent a car, take a local bus, or join a tour to wind your way through the Andes, the scenery of this geographic Mecca is simply breathtaking. From dry, enticing vineyards to the perilous terrain of snow-capped Aconcagua, it's a perfect way to see all you can of the countryside and the small villages that are common to this region.

Heading northwest from Mendoza, your first stop should be the snow-capped, Aconcagua, at 6,962 meters (22,841 feet) the highest peak in South America. The apparent brown of the mountains shrouds an array of color; purples, maroons, iridescent greens and yellows are visible to the roving eye, bouncing off the bright blue, cloudless backdrop. You may wish to pinch yourself just to make sure it is real.

A trip to Villavicencio, the source of the national bottled water, begins by winding through the Pampas and then up into the Pre-Cordillera, the lower-lying part of the Andes that precedes the Cordillera. Hotel Termas is an Alpine style chalet nestled in a 7000 hectare nature reserve full of native flora and fauna. Although no longer a working hotel, it is the well-preserved symbol of the popular *eau minerale* that is bottled nearby from Aconcagua's streams. The hot springs are a product of the same water, which enters the heart of the mountain and re-emerges at only 1,700 meters (5,577 feet), driven by pressure and high temperatures, forming springs. A meander around the hotel's grounds is enjoyable and tranquil at any time of the year.

Journeying onward through the barren landscape brings you to Ciudad Fantasmal, an abandoned Jesuit mining village. Ghost-like and silent, all you can hear is the echo of the Cordillera. A wander around the ruins leads you to an odd looking cross adorned with all sorts of goodies, from plastic flowers to tin pots. It is a shrine to Gaucho Cubillos, "Don Quixote of the Andes," a well-known bandit who was known to have a weakness for the local ladies.

Nearby, find a local guide and explore the dark tunnels of the inconspicuous mines of Paramillos, originally carved out by the monks who lived in Ciudad Fantasmal. They were later mined by the English, who abandoned them after the invasion of the Falkland Islands. They are fascinating if not a little eerie, as you cautiously negotiate the old train tracks and remnants of hand-chipped mineral that carpet the floor. Make sure that you ask your tour guide, with the all-essential phrase-book in hand, to take you to eat *asado*, beautifully grilled beef and lots of it, at the only restaurant for miles around. It is a raw and rustic dining experience, but the food and family service are first class. Make sure you get a glimpse of the local farm animals huddling nearby, especially the guanacos. They're similar to their cousins the llamas, and spit just as well.

Head up Cordillera, for it truly should not to be missed. A brief stop at Penitentes, the popular ski-station, allows you to take the chair-lift to the top of the mountain, even in summer, to take in the extraordinary views. Bundle up, because the snow may well fall at your next stop, which is Cristo Redentor, a bronze figure that was erected in 1886 to promote peaceful relations between Argentina and Chile. It marks the *frontera* between these two feuding countries and the statue is made out of the melted down cannons that were used to defend national pride on both sides. A visit to the Thermal Baths on the road home will warm you up and the natural salts in the water will address your ailments. The hot chocolates are absolutely delicious and the local craft stalls are worth a peek, or even forking out a few pesos for a hand-made textile.

There are many organized tours in this area that are great value for money and they are the best way to discover the secrets of this unspoiled, largely unknown terrain. They are also a great way to immerse oneself in Argentine culture; locals fill the tour bus, passing around the mate (local tea), as is the social norm throughout this country and with spontaneous clapping, cheering and singing there is never a dull moment as the wheels navigate another hairpin bend. The linguistic benefits are second to none as English is, refreshingly, broken and sparse.

One final thing—make sure you go white-water rafting down the Río Mendoza. Take the day trip and you will enjoy four hours of rafting, including a leisurely lunch stop, on this river that is accommodating for the beginner and challenging for the expert.

# SALTA

*By Brian Hagenbuch, Methow Valley, Washington, U.S.A.*

Home to delicious regional cuisine, a wealth of historical sites and a thriving arts scene, Salta City is a vibrant, provincial capital of 500,000 inhabitants. Sitting high in the rolling Andean foothills in northern Argentina, locals claim the city has a "perfect" climate.

Sight-seeing is concentrated around the recently restored, well-lit Plaza 9 de Julio, where new walking streets have cut traffic noise.

On the plaza are the imposing facades of the Catedral Basilica, dating from 1858, and the asymmetrical Cabildo, the old city hall. Three blocks away is Iglesia San Francisco; painted a rusty red with white pillars and gilt trim, the striking church is Salta's most emblematic building. Downtown museums are numerous, highlighted by the new Museo de Arqueología de Alta Montana. Opened two years ago, the museum contains the three astonishingly well-preserved corpses unearthed by archeologists in 1999 on the heights of the Volcano Llullaillaco.

The Mercado Artesanal—founded in 1968, making it Argentina's oldest handicraft market—is a sprawling display of local basket and textile weaving, silver, metal and leather work; also available are handcrafted musical instruments and wines and cheeses.

To get a bird's eye view of the city, take the gondola from Parque San Martín to the summit of Cerro San Bernardino and enjoy the sunset. Back in the city, nightfall brings another round of delights. Abundant restaurants offer affordable and delicious dishes, while local favorites like *empanadas* are sold in streets filled with the sounds of local folk rhythms. Musical roots run deep in Salta, and its rich tradition has produced some of the country's most notable folk musicians.

*Zamba* and *chacarera*, lively folk sub-genres based on traditional dance steps, are native to the province of Salta, and the city's *peñas*, bars where traditional music and dance are performed, are some of the best folk music venues in the country. A dense concentration of *peñas* and bars—many tending more toward the modern with dance music replacing guitars and *Mojitos* substituting wine jugs—can be found around the train station. Find the corner of Balcarce and Necochea, and follow your ears, or ask around for the two classic *peñas*: Boliche Balderrama and La Vieja Estación.

Another source of pride for *salteños* is the Symphonic Orchestra of Salta, a select group of classical musicians from all over the country that plays regularly in the city.

Unfortunately, administrative disputes have closed the spectacular Tren de las Nubes, once Salta's most popular tourist attraction. Truck trips paralleling the tracks can be arranged to observe the engineering marvels of the train.

Salta City is a culinary and cultural haven, and it's also a great base to explore the endless attractions of northern Argentina—from charming rural vineyards to isolated red-rock canyons to small town carnivals.

Brian Hagenbuch hails from the Methow Valley in north central Washington state. He graduated from Western Washington University with a B.A. in literature in 1999. Since then he traveled from Alaska to Argentina, working a number of different jobs, while writing on the side.

The craziest place Hagenbuch has ever visited is the Greyhound Station in downtown L.A. and his most bizarre cultural experience involved Bolivian karaoke.

Iglesia San Francisco, Salta. Photo by Scott Ferree.

### SALTA TRAVEL TIPS:

• Long-distance buses can be taken to Salta Capital from Buenos Aires, and there are regular flights into Aeropuerto Internacional Martín Miguel de Guemes.

• If you're in the city beforehand, stop by the provincial tourist office at Av. R. Saénz Peña 933 (4326-1314).

• For complete information on Salta, check www.turismo-salta.gov.ar.

**ARGENTINA**

# QUEBRADA DE HUMAHUACA

By Marc Sehrt, New York City, U.S.A.

High up in the Andean north of Argentina, a traveller can experience it all: colourful canyons, colonial cities and a thriving indigenous culture. The area is not only blessed with a temperate climate and awesome beauty, but with one of the friendliest local cultures of the region. It is easy to see why Argentineans love the region of Salta: its beauty, its preservation of indigenous traditions and heritage, its affordable prices, and its proximity.

Born in New York City, Marc Sehrt, a German national, began his travels at a very young age. By age seven he had already moved to Europe where Zurich, Milan, Marseilles, Paris and Madrid all became home.

A trained journalist, Marc has a master's degree in Media Science form the University of Cologne (Germany), a postgraduate degree in Journalism from the German Broadcasting Academy (DHA) in Dortmund, and a master's in International Business from the French Business School ESCI Fontainbleau, Paris XII.

Marc has worked as a freelance journalist for many years and is currently a public information officer at the United Nations, New York, where he has been living for the past four years.

His first five favorite travel destinations that come to mind are Berlin, New York, Buenos Aires, British Columbia, and Andalusia, but the list is definitely not exclusive!

Only an hour by plane from Buenos Aires, the regional capital of Salta is an old Spanish settlement filled with great restaurants and known for its bustling nightlife.

This popular city is also a perfect hub for either independent trips or guided tours of the region. Possibility abounds, giving adventure-hungry travelers plenty of worthwhile options.

By far the most rewarding trip is that of the North Circuit. A focal part of this route is Quebrada de Humahuaca, a narrow valley stretching 155 kilometers across the province of Jujuy. This rugged tear in the earth is flanked by equally dynamic scenery: Altiplano to the west and north, sub-Andean hills to the east, and warm valleys to the south.

Since the first hunter-gatherer society unpacked and settled down in the region 10,000 years ago, Quebrada de Humahuaca has served as an economic, social, and cultural crossroads: it was a caravan road for the Inca Empire in the 15th century, an important link between the Viceroyalty of Río de la Plata and the Viceroyalty of Peru, and more recently a battleground during the Argentine War of Independence. The area also boasts a network of prehistoric remains. Given its historical and cultural significance, it is no surprise that Quebrada de Humahuaca has been declared a UNESCO World Heritage Site.

At the mouth of the canyon is the tiny village of Purmamarca, surrounded by the polychrome Cerro de los Siete Colores (the hills of the seven colours). A short hike up to one of the hills will reward one with a splendid view of the village and the valley. For those who want to see a salina, (an enormous salt lake) it's only a one-hour trip easily done in a local taxi.

The next village in the Humahuaca valley is the ancient Tilcara, situated on the Río Grande river. Above the modern village is the reconstructed pre-Columbian city of Pucará with its intriguing pyramid. Little is known about the inhabitants who erected the fortified town. The Incas, who ruled the region for only for 50 years before the Spanish Conquistadores arrived, destroyed most of the site.

Further down the canyon is Humahuaca, a small town filled with delicate colonial details; cobblestone-paved streets, white Spanish-style houses and lively plazas. There is a large indigenous Quechua population, whose fine quality handicrafts and sonorous traditional music add to the town's popularity. Some restaurants even offer live traditional folklore music, often starting late—nothing before 10 p.m.!

Three hours north, near the Bolivian border, is yet another historic pearl, the village of Iruya, population 300. The lack of traffic (barring the occasional public bus which only arrives twice a day) in this three street village truly takes you back in time. Iruya hangs on a cliff so no matter where you are, a breathtaking view is sure to accompany you. This village is an ideal setting for a break; enjoy a range of activities and non-activities, from hardy day treks to appreciation of the simple.

The return trip to Salta will not disappoint as, once again, the unforgettable landscape of Quebrada de Humahuaca is ever-present. Regardless of how you choose to spend it, a trip along the North Circuit offers breathtaking beauty for a price that won't leave you gasping for air.

---

QUEBRADA DE HUMAHUACA TRAVEL TIPS:

• Temperate weather abounds here year round. There is some snow and rain in late July and early August, but daytime temperature still hovers in the 10/15 C range. Summer temperatures in January and February are around 30 C.

• There are many great outdoor activities in this area: white-water river rafting, paragliding, canopy, and horseback riding—all for very little money. There are no entrance fees for the national parks. The region is also known for its excellent birdwatching.

# CASABINDO

### By John Ciullo, San Diego, California, U.S.A.

North of the Tropic of Capricorn, in the northernmost Argentine province of Jujuy, the intrepid traveler can experience the fury of a two-ton bull while savoring the flavor of a centuries-old festival, all in one afternoon. The multi-day religious celebration culminates annually with the The Feast of the Asunción of the Virgin María Santísima, on August 15, in the small town of Casabindo, Argentina.

Located in the Puna, the high desert east of the Andean mountain range, at nearly 12,000 feet above sea level, Casabindo is a desolate yet provocative place. Unlike the Argentina of travel brochures, Casabindo does not feature infinite green pampas or glacier-carved crystalline lakes.

Nonetheless, once a year the population swells from 150 permanent residents, primarily herders of llama and sheep, to well over 4,000. Locals, religious pilgrims and tourists alike descend on the town to celebrate the ascension of the Blessed Virgin Mary, to partake in the primitive ceremonies and to witness the last remaining bullfight in Argentina.

Approaching the town via a bone-rattling, dusty road, one can spot a speck of white against the rust-colored hills. La Iglesia de la Asunción, a classic 18th century church, is Casabindo's most defining feature, and marks your arrival into town. The pueblo is steeped in history. A branch of the Inca road passed through this region. The first missionary arrived as early as the 1590s, defying ancient earth rituals with European Catholicism, a unique blending which survives in today's customs.

Locals perform ceremonies such as the blowing of the *erque*, a long Alpine-like horn, and the Danza del Samilantes that mimics the sacred suri (ostrich), one of many symbols of Mother Earth. The morning's events climax with the Procession of the Virgin.

Adjacent to the church stands a wall enclosing a rectangular "ring" about half the size of an American football field. This is the site for the afternoon's bullfight, known as El Toreo de la Vincha (bullfight of the ribbon), and the most popular part of the festival. Each year dozens of young men vie for the coveted torero (bullfighter) spots. They are not professionals, but boys full of pride and honor. The role requires physical quickness, mental fortitude and a great faith in the Virgin.

In this version of a Spanish bullfight, brought to South American centuries earlier, the goal is to remove the coins and ribbons taped between the bull's horns. The prize is later returned as an offering to the Virgin. Unlike the Spanish version, the Casabindo bullfight ends without the brutal killing of the animal. In fact, the bull is rarely harmed; the same cannot be said for the defenseless toreros. It is not uncommon for some of the bulls to leap up and over the five-foot wall surrounding the ring and into the unsuspecting crowd of spectators.

The annual Casabindo festival will not disappoint anyone who makes this remarkable journey through the Argentine Puna. Just remember to wear a sun hat and take caution when choosing your seats for the bullfight.

Man fighting bull. Photo by John Ciullo.

# IGUAZÚ FALLS

## By Dr. Crit Minster, Rochester, New York, U.S.A.

Stretching 82 feet by 50 yards, and varying from five to 13 feet deep, the 800,000 gallon, multi-purpose swimming pool at the William Woollett Jr. Aquatic complex in Irvine, California is one of the largest pools in the Unites States. Using a standard garden hose, it would take more than three weeks to fill. If you could somehow channel the torrent of water that passes over the massive Iguazú Falls on an average day, it would fill the swimming pool in just over three minutes. During the rainy season, the volume of water tumbling over the falls can exceed 450,000 cubic feet per second. At this rate, it would fill the swimming pool in roughly one quarter of one second.

The richness of life rising up from the mists of Iguazú Falls is a far cry from the bleak slabs of concrete overlooking the famous Niagara Falls. While the latter is infested with gawking tourists and noisy seagulls that fight over scraps of cold McDonald's French Fries, the former exudes nature-in-the-raw. The water that feeds these falls passes through more than 250 separate waterfalls before plunging more than 170 to 350 feet and crashing to the rocks below. The thunderous rush can be heard for miles. Out of the deafening roar, a fine spray rises in a cool plume, dampening the miles of inconspicuous trails lining both sides of Brazil and Argentina.

To the local Guaraní people, the falls area was a spiritual place, and it was they who named it Iguazú, or "Great Water." Time seems to stand still at this sacred spot, blatantly ignoring the rushing Iguazú River as it cuts through the verdant Argentine and Brazilian rainforest and out to sea. Birds and insects flitter among the trees that thrive in this unique ecosystem, fortified by the constant mist projected from falls. Nowhere is the delicate balance between brute force and sheer beauty more apparent than at "The Devil's Throat," where water cascades over 14 different falls, drops more than 350 feet, and finally disappears into a cloud of mist that rises more than 100 feet above the falls.

The souvenir vendors who hawk t-shirts and post cards keep a respectful difference, and the nearest Big Mac is in Buenos Aires. Small motorboats take visitors right to the roaring base of the falls, where they joyously shout to one another before returning to shore as soaked if they had followed the falls into the river. During the rainy season, between January and March, the falls swell with water, offering even more impressive views. Once you've finished your jaw-dropping gaze at the falls (and this may take a while), adventure into the surrounding park, where a variety of animal and bird species flourish.

Established in 1934, Argentina's Iguazú National Park spreads out across 67,620 hectares. On the Brazilian side, the government has set aside 170,000 hectares of protected land. Its remarkable beauty and abundant biodiversity earned this park the title of a UNESCO World Heritage site in 1984. A host of mammals call this place home, including five species of giant cat. Not to be outdone by their four-legged friends, more than 450 species of birds—including parrots, toucans and the rare great dusky swift—soar beneath the thick jungle canopy. Like the delicate mist rising from the rocky base of Iguazú Falls, beauty seems to blanket this enchanting jungle world, delighting and surprising visitors and every turn.

## IGUAZÚ GRAND HOTEL By Sandra Scott

Everyone is a winner at Iguazú Grand Hotel in Argentina, where naturalists, gamblers, and hedonists alike go to kick back and relax. Located near one of Mother Nature's greatest achievements, Iguazú Falls, the hotel is a perfect point from which to explore the area. Spend a day wandering the paths that wind towards the falls and through the nearby Parque Nacional Iguazú, or pass the time gazing into the thunderous waters of the falls. Regardless of how they spend their day, guests return to the luxury of the Grand Hotel where they enjoy the night rejuvenating at the spa, relaxing at the three-tiered pool, and trying their luck at the hotel's casino.

The spa includes Chocolate Therapy, wraps, thalassotherapy, a variety of massages including Thai massage, a steam room and Jacuzzi. A beauty salon is also available. The hotel is set up so that the casino and the spa do not invade guest accommodations; the same is true of the Le Bistro cabaret theater where live tango and other shows are held.

Besides the casino and spa there is a gift shop, fitness center, tennis courts and a nature trail. The multi-lingual staff attend to every need.

Iguazú Falls. Photo by Freyja Ellis.

# ESTEROS DEL IBERÁ

## By Brian Hagenbuch, Pateros, Washington, U.S.A.

Often over-shadowed by nearby Iguazú Falls, the provincial park of Esteros del Iberá is quickly becoming a top-flight destination for eco-travelers, especially birdwatchers looking for a more intimate, remote outing.

Occupying 13,000 square kilometers in the province of Corrientes, the park uniquely blends rural charm with rich biodiversity. The 118 kilometer dirt road from Corrientes' capital city, Mercedes, leads to the tranquil, 500 person town of Colonia Carlos Pellegrini, and the gateway to the park.

The park was once the floor of the Paraná River and slow drainage has allowed for most of the water to be recycled by the vegetation. Deeper lagoons (two meters at the deepest), marshy fields of aquatic plants, and stands of subtropical trees spread across the flat horizon, housing Iberá's main attraction: the flora and fauna.

Outings arranged with the various lodges by boat or on horseback are the best way to take in the astounding natural beauty of Iberá. Flat-bottomed aluminum boats power visitors across deeper waters and pole through shallow canals while docile horses plod through the marshlands amongst the park's many wonders.

With its abundance of water and convergence of three distinct climatic zones, Iberá is perfect for ornithologists. Counts vary from 350 to 400 species, including large populations of lapwings, egrets, storks, ducks, herons and a number of endangered species. Among signature species are the olive cormorant, jabiru, horned screamer (chajá) and the nearly extinct yellow cardinal.

Basking broad-nosed caiman (yacaré) are common, and glimpses can be caught of more furtive species such as marsh deer, bracket deer and grey wolves. Also among park residents are howler monkeys, otters, curiyus (yellow anaconda), skunks, tegu lizards, and the ubiquitous carpincho, a large rodent that acts as a lawn mower on the park's drier, grassy stands. Multi-colored and abundant butterfly populations are bountiful, as are a long list of tree species, aquatic plants and flowers, including orchids.

Beyond the typical tours, some lodges, such as Rincón del Socorro, provide fly-fishing, canoeing, and mountain biking excursions. The friendly, colorful locals combine with natural beauty and a wealth of activities to make Iberá a true paradise for outdoor enthusiasts.

---

ESTEROS DEL IBERÁ TRAVEL TIP: Take a night tour—many of the species that inhabit the wetlands are nocturnal and there is no better time to view them than during a warm, moonlit evening in a kayak or canoe.

---

Esteros del Iberá. Photo by Brian Hagenbuch.

# BUENOS AIRES

## By Dr. Crit Minster, Rochester, New York, U.S.A.

It was tango singer Carlos Gardel who said it best, in his immortal tango classic "Mi Buenos Aires Querido" ("My Beloved Buenos Aires"):

*Mi Buenos Aires querido,*
*cuando yo te vuelva a ver*
*no habrá más pena ni olvido.*

*Hoy que la suerte quiere que te vuelva a ver,*
*ciudad porteña de mi único querer,*
*y oigo la queja de un bandoneón*
*dentro del pecho pide rienda el corazón.*

*My beloved Buenos Aires,*
*When I see you again,*
*There will be no more sorrow and forgetfulness.*

*Today, good fortune wills that I see you again,*
*Port city of my only love*
*I hear the sad song of the accordion*
*And in my chest, my heart yearns to be set free.*

It is fitting that the signature dance of the city is the tango, a series of dramatic swings, erotic dips and prolonged eye contact. The tango is a dance of unadulterated desire, translated into motion and set to music. It is impossible to dance the tango in a half-assed way: it has to be done right or not at all. The tango is more than a dance to porteños: it is a reflection of how they live. Buenos Aires has many faces: it is a city of superlatives. It has the most stunning architecture in South America. Some of the best restaurants are there, and the most charming and picturesque neighborhoods.

It also features the most popular dead woman. The body of Eva Perón —Evita to you Broadway theater-goers—rests eternally at the Cemetery of La Recoleta, the hallowed burial ground of Argentine nobility. Despite the fact that she died in 1952, mourners still bring a steady supply of flowers to her tomb, which is as important a visitor attraction as anything else in the city. Although she shares the cemetery with a host of other notables, including past presidents of Argentina and José Hernández, author of the definitive Argentine epic poem, *Martín Fierro*, she is the one they all come to see.

Buenos Aires does not begin and end with Evita and the tango, however. The Plaza de Mayo, which is named for the date of the beginning of Argentina's independence, today is more famous as a place for political protest. It is here that the mothers of *los desaparecidos* ("the disappeared ones"), thousands of citizens who vanished without a trace during the military dictatorship of the late 1970s and early 1980s, hold a demonstration every Thursday to ask—in vain—for information about the fate of their loved ones. The neighborhood of San Telmo was often the first stop for immigrant Italian families in the latter half of the nineteenth century. Today, it is a maze of colorful streets, cozy restaurants, cafes and shops.

Outsiders have always had a profound impact on Buenos Aires. Evita was born in nearby Los Toldos; she arrived in the city as a teenager. Ernesto "Ché" Guevara was from the town of Rosario, but his uncompromising revolutionary idealism was forged as a medical student in the city. Carlos Gardel was born in Uruguay, but rose to fame in Buenos Aires: he's now a cultural icon, an Argentine Elvis Presley. Their images are everywhere you look: Buenos Aires does not forget its dead. Their footsteps echo in the streets.

If you visit the city, you'll learn what the millions of immigrants did more than a century ago: it's hard to leave once you're there. Even the ghosts of Buenos Aires are unwilling to leave their beloved city after death. They still whisper through the narrow avenues, along the waterfront and in the halls of power. Evita. Carlos Gardel. Los Desaparecidos. Ché Guevara. The immigrants. You can hear them if you listen.

Tango in the street. Photo by Michelle Hopey.

# SAN TELMO

## By Michelle Hopey, New Hampshire, U.S.A.

There is smell of fresh pastries swirled with the smoke wafting up from cigarette-touting gentlemen drinking coffee and sipping wine. Young designers, dancers and artists sit on a door step chugging beer, laughing and discussing their latest inspirations and aspirations.

Side-walk cafes, cobblestone streets, old mansions, tango dancers, live violinists, and street-side flower venders. Alone, San Telmo square with its Plaza Dorrego is enough to be the Paris of South America. It is vintage Parisian romance mixed with that dash of relaxed, bohemian flair—a defining characteristic of South America. It's a seductive vortex that could sweep you away. It has a similar feel to that city across the Atlantic, but with a much more liberal appeal.

Rich, like its original inhabitants, so is the history of San Telmo. Once home to Buenos Aires' aristocrats, it was the yellow fever epidemic of 1871 which propelled the elitists to flee this southern quarter and relocate to the north-central neighborhood of Recoleta. This move left San Telmo with empty mansions and a lost innocence. But, to the fresh immigrants just off the boats from Italy and Spain, the architecturally astute facades were more than appealing. The old homes were renovated into "conventillo," hosting hundreds of newcomers, transforming this once-affluent-only district into a dazzling mosaic of diversity and culture.

Nowadays, the neighborhood has been beautifully restored, fusing the old with the new, and making it a microcosm of true porteño culture.

Sundays are perhaps the most exciting time to experience this unique and alluring ambiance. From 10 a.m. to 5 p.m. people of all colors, sizes and nationalities flock to Plaza Dorrego for the weekly antique fair, Feria de San Pedro Telmos. Defensa Street between Avenida San Juan and Avenida Independencia is blocked off to motorists while travelers and locals alike, stroll through the marketplace discovering the assortment of antiques available: dinnerware, old cowboy get-up, colored soda siphons, and costume jewelry.

To off-set the old, a group of modern designers congregate in the northwest corner of Plaza Dorrego in what seems like a warehouse, or small one-level parking garage. After entering (there is no sign), you'll come upon a small market brimming with contemporary fashion designers. From avant-garde evening dresses to handmade suede shoes, leather handbags and modern jewelry designs, you are sure to feel as if you are truly in Paris—or London, or New York—sans the pretentious feel. Perhaps this is because of the affordability of the oh-so-creative items.

Outside in the open-air, painters, jewelers, and food artisans—including one man who makes a tasty dulce de leche liquor—set up shop along the side streets of Avenida Humberto 1 and Carlos Calvo. While popping in and out of Defensa's eclectic mix of shops, visitors are graced with live tango performances and other musical street troupes.

And if you get tired of strolling, tuck yourself into a chair at one of the many outdoor cafés where you can sip an espresso, nibble on a fresh pastry and people watch. Like the locals, you might just find yourself contemplating the crazy world and wondering why not everywhere can be this carefree and pleasant.

Shopping for pictures. Photo by Michelle Hopey.

# BIKE RIDING IN BUENOS AIRES

## By Michelle Hopey, New Hampshire, U.S.A.

The thick black tires of the 10-speed Beach Cruiser roll down the wide dirt path, kicking back pebbles and spraying sand dust into the air. The sunlight bounces off the pavement, its power reflecting onto your face. Tears of salty sweat roll down your cheeks, flowing across your skin, reviving the scent of the coconut sun lotion you smeared on earlier in efforts to protect yourself from that deep South American sun.

For $25, you assumed the four-hour jaunt with Lan and Krammer Bike tours would simply be a pleasant day trip around Buenos Aires. When you strapped on the helmet and put the rubber to the road you thought you were just a tourist, but you didn't know that you would be privy to secrets only known to locals; that you would become porteño for a day.

As your feet pedal in a two-beat rhythm, that long-buried carefree child-like spirit rises up from within and memories of childhood bike rides flash across your mind.

When you met the bilingual guides and fellow bikers at the Monument in Plaza San Martín, you were feeling a little nervous, especially when you didn't see any bicycles. You considered the possibility of fraud, but as the group walked together to the nearby parking garage, you were happy to find the fleet of 10-speed Beach Cruisers, bottles of water and helmets that awaited you, and like a child going on a bike journey with older siblings or parents, you felt taken care of.

You squeeze the brakes in efforts to come to a halt, and not collide with the other members of your bike tour. You count the parties accompanying you: two twenty-somethings from Brazil, a couple from Germany and three solo travelers from the States.

In the portside barrio of La Boca, you were told of the city's most loved soccer team, Club Atlético Boca Juniors (CABJ). As you looked around Estadio Doctor Camilo Cichero, or La Bombonera, it seemed oddly quiet. As you rode by, a handful of porteños sat on doorstep talking and looking fatigued. You felt as if you were disturbing a daily ritual of some sort, but you learned that despite the fanatical soccer lust and colorful homes, this barrio is home to tired, working-class porteños, and the ritual you disturbed was locals de-stressing from the workday and regaining gusto for the next.

Unlike the La Boca you heard about, as you continued to ride, in the distance you could hear tango music and people on the Caminito, a cobblestone walkway, once an old railway stop but now an area that holds a weekend art walk and live music.

As you continue to pedal along the perimeter of Buenos Aires, you realize she offers more than you'll ever possibly be able to see during a week or two vacation.

In San Telmo, the romantic renaissance sector of Buenos Aires, you passed antique stores, ice cream parlors, outdoor cafes and a number of inviting restaurants that you filed away in your brain for dinner later that night. You felt as if you belonged, and were just lofting around on a lazy Saturday with the rest of the city.

Looking behind in the distance you see the Buenos Aires you've come to explore, to understand, and be inspired by. Once nervous to ride in the city, you chuckle at how silly that thought was. You had no idea how large this city was, and that it is not all busy streets.

At Puerto Madero you saw wealthy porteños sipping wine and dining on steak at many of the outdoor restaurants. As you rode past, you were told that this sector was the modern seaport. Your guides explained that Puerto Madero, in recent history, was a well-used but run-down canal. From 1976 to 1983, during the military dictatorship, the entire port was off-limits. In the early 2000s, the city planned a facelift, which dramatically changed the area, and as you scanned the number of fancy restaurants and upscale clubs that lined the waterway, and the people strolling around watching the yachts rock back and forth, you understood what a clever idea this was.

The waters of the Río de la Plata crash gently against the tall grassy shores. Relaxed for a moment, your eyes close and for a second you forget you are in one of the world's largest metropolises.

Not far from barrio Puerto Madero, you rode through a series of dirt trails. You were amazed to be only blocks from the city center and in a quiet, peaceful nature reserve. When you rode into the Reserva Ecológica, which cut along the Río de la Plata, you watched carefully as the landscape changed from woods to fields to beach—all untouched. Oddly enough, this area was built over a landfill, but biology prevailed, and species of flora and fauna thrived, making it home to more than 400 species of birds and a place for porteños to play.

You navigate through the hidden roads, streets and parks watching porteños in action—sleeping in the park, drinking coffee, sipping wine, playing the guitar in city squares, jogging, and biking through the reserve, just like you.

## BUENOS AIRES AFTER DARK by Michelle Hopey

Typical early morning people need not apply: Buenos Aires is for night owls—all through the night owls. In a city that doesn't even serve-up its dinner until 10 p.m., the bars and lounges don't get pumping until at least 1 or 2 a.m., and some of the larger clubs don't buzz until 4 a.m. Whether you're looking for a cocktail or two, heavy debauchery or some late, late-night dancing, you can find it after dark in BA. Check out some of these hot spots to see for yourself:

Early evening drink-up spots include Farmacia, a former pharmacy in San Telmo. It is a casual, artsy place to grab an after dinner drink. While this gay friendly bar also offers a great dinner menu, a drink on the roof-top terrace is extra-special and a novelty in BA. Check it out at Bolivar 898. Cross Street: Estados Unidos. Open: 9 a.m. to 1:30 a.m., Tue-Thurs. & Sun. 9 a.m to 2:30 a.m. Sat.

Mid-night or midnight? Head on down to Gibraltar a dark, but classy watering-hole that serves-up pints of beers and fine whiskies to an array of tourists and even some locals. Check it out at Peru 895. Cross Street: Estados Unidos. Neighborhood: San Telmo. Open: 6 p.m. to 4 a.m. Mon-Sun.

Late Night Extremes: Niceto Club: Hot sweaty and wild, Niceto Club is famous for its Thursday night party—Club 69. While grinding to techno, house, hip-hop and funk, you'll also witness an elaborate theatrical performance something like the Rocky-Horror picture show. The show begins at 3 a.m. Check it out: Niceto Venga 5510. Cross Street: Humboldt. Neighborhood: Palermo Viejo. Open: 12:30 a.m. to dawn, Thurs & Fri. and 1 a.m. to dawn, Sat.

# MOTHERS OF THE DISAPPEARED

By Sarah Tonner, Tampa, Florida, U.S.A.

Perhaps the best part of traveling is the initial rush of optimism and excitement that precedes arriving to a new place. Perhaps it is the reassuring feeling of returning to a corner of the world you identified with. But how familiar does the average traveler become with the real workings of a country—the political and social issues, the internal strife, the daily struggles of its people—when she has precious few days to take in all the bright and buzzing attractions? Furthermore, does the average traveler wish to remain sheltered from the corruption and scandal lurking behind the must do's and can't-misses of a country?

Dictatorships and political scandals have plagued Argentina's history, rocking the country into a constant state of turmoil. Unfortunately, the darker side of Argentina remains hidden to those on the tourist circuit. A swift jaunt through any country does not allow for complete cultural immersion. The net result is a guidebook image of a country not necessarily in line with local perceptions. If you're in search of some perspective, then step outside Buenos Aires' comfy café culture and head to Plaza de Mayo.

Every Thursday afternoon at three thirty, the incorrectly named "Mothers of the Disappeared" (they are actually Grandmothers) walk silently around the Plaza de Mayo in front of the Presidential House, clinging to the hope that justice will be realized for their flesh and blood who simply "disappeared" twenty years earlier.

Between 1976 and 1983, during the so-called "National Reorganization Process," Argentina crumbled under a terrible campaign of ruthless state-sponsored violence. Spanning three dictatorships—Jorge Rafael Videla, Roberto Viola, and Leopoldo Galtieri—the Dirty War, as it became known, was marked by illegal arrests, torture, and executions or forced disappearance of supposed political dissidents. Children were tortured in front

> *Children were tortured in front of their parents, while countless innocents were drugged and their bodies dropped over the ocean during military "Death Flights."*

of their parents, while countless innocents were drugged and their bodies dropped over the ocean during military "Death Flights.". The period culminated with the unexplained disappearance of between 10,000 and 30,000 Argentineans. Sons and daughters, nieces and nephews and grandchildren, all loved dearly in one way or another, vanished in a gruesome, regretful heartbeat. The innocence of youth was quite literally slain.

It is probable that most of the victim's families have come to accept the cruel fate of their loved ones. No longer do they sit at kitchen tables, wringing hands and waiting for a long-awaited face to walk through the front door. Time has realized their worst fears. But the flame of hope burns eternal; hence the handful of Grandmothers who gather every Thursday at Plaza de Mayo. Some wear white headscarves, others have a well-worn photograph of their beloved, hanging from a withered cord, slung around their neck.

Does their presence really make the President and his cronies reflect on the atrocities that have been committed? Recent rulings suggest that their cries have not fallen on deaf ears. In June 2005, Argentina's Supreme Court upheld a congressional decision to abandon amnesty laws forbidding prosecution of military officers accused of human rights atrocities. At a ceremony commemorating the 30th anniversary of the Dirty War, President Nestor Kirchner unveiled a plaque bearing the words "Nunca Mas," or "Never Again." President Kirchner has since overturned laws granting amnesty to top officers, and cancelled presidential pardons granted to officers tried in 1985. Following on the heels of these announcements was a decision to open all military archives pertaining to the event.

While such actions will never bring back the dead, they do give hope that the children of the future will not suffer the same grim fate. The Mothers of the Disappeared have spoken for those who can no longer speak, and their voices have been heard. Time can only tell if their prayers for justice will be fully answered.

Mothers of the Disappeared. Photo by Sarah Tonner.

ARGENTINA

# PALERMO

By Jessica Bennett, Seattle, Washington, U.S.A.

Jessica Bennett is a 24-year-old struggling writer, living and working in New York City. A native of Seattle, Jessica graduated with a degree in Print Journalism and Anthropology from Boston University in 2004. Since then, she has spent time living in Buenos Aires, Argentina, travelling through South America, and working as a researcher and reporter for Newsweek.com and The Village Voice. She loves studying culture, progressive politics and Malbec.

Her most bizarre cultural experience? "Driving with a crazy Cuban cab-driver from Havana to Santiago in a car with a broken speedometer, whizzing down winding roads, while the cabby drank rum out of a bottle in the front seat and then dropped us off in the middle of town when we didn't want to rent a room at his mother's house."

The Palermo neighborhood of Buenos Aires will satisfy your desire for South American couture fashion. Divided into four districts—Viejo (old), Chico (small), Soho and Hollywood—Palermo boasts the trendiest and most diverse of Buenos Aires' boutiques, bars, restaurants and cafes.

When you arrive in Palermo, you'll need a map, though not of the city (you may need that too). What you really need is the special Palermo map (available on almost every corner), which pinpoints each of the neighborhood's most popular clothing stores, up and coming Argentine designers, fashion expos and galleries.

One thing's for sure about Palermo: You'll leave fashion forward. From neon spandex and metallics to punk-rock hairdos and mini-skirts, you can have first grabs at the goods by Argentine designers.

Feeling a little faint after your shopping spree? Palermo isn't just for the fashion savvy. If you're growing tired of the traditional steak and empañadas, Palermo offers a variety of chic restaurants covering a range of international cuisine—from Thai to Japanese to Mexican to American.

From its fashion centerfolds to its gastronomical spreads Palmero is sure to keep you busy. Part of Palmero's allure is the adventure of seeking out its hidden treasures, but just for kicks here's a rundown of each district:

Palermo Viejo (old Palermo) is an enchanting district has been home to famous figures like Che Guevara and Jorge Luis Borges. Spanish-style architecture dominates tiny streets packed with even tinier boutiques.

Palermo Chico (small Palermo). the wealthiest part of Palmero, is a predominantly residential area. If you're looking to stay (for a while) in style, check out apartments here. Palermo Hollywood (sometimes referred to as Palermo Soho) is—as you can gather from the title—the fashion and design district of the city. Cheaper than either Viejo or Chico, Hollywood also has tons of restaurants and is a popular draw for the young crowd.

Hit the pavement and dive into the latest fashion trends or head inside and dig into the trendiest culinary dish—whatever you do, don't pass up the chance to check out Buenos Aires' Palmero district.

## SPLURGING IN PALERMO

Compiled by Jessica Bennett

### SHOPPING

Mishka
Amazing selection of women's shoes
El Salvador 4673
Tel. 4834-6838

Rapsodia
Men and women's clothing boutique
Arguibel 2899
www.rapsodia.com.ar

María Cher
A unique women's boutique
El Salvador 4714
www.maria-cher.com.ar

Pri
Independent clothing boutique
Malabia 1833
www.priweb.com.ar

### RESTAURANTS

Pilares
An eclectic Italian restaurant
located in a charming two-storey house
Guatemala 4824, Phone: 4774-3559

Malas Artes
Restaurant, bar, nice outdoor seating
Honduras 4999

La Cabrera
Traditional and well-known parilla
On the corner of Cabrera and Thames
Phone: 4831-7002

Xalapa
Cute, tasty little Mexican restaurant
El Salvador 4800

# RECOLETA

### By Stephen Keeling, Southampton, England

Behind elegant neo-classical gates in a quiet corner of northern Buenos Aires lies a city in miniature. Avenues of cypress weave past stately yew lined mausoleums bearing ornate facades of granite and gleaming white marble. Silence hangs like mist in this quiet neighborhood where the dead slumber peacefully and the living tread softly.

Located in Recoleta, one of the city's most affluent suburbs, the grand Cemeterio Recoleta was created in 1822 for the wealthy, the powerful and occasionally, the famous. One of Argentina's architectural gems, this country club for the dead is crammed with exquisitely designed mausoleums and graceful monuments. Each of these stone shrines is embellished with lavish carvings of angels and images of the Holy Mother, and inscribed with the names of the country's most influential families—there are few individual tombs, tradition (and economics) dictating that families must be interred together. The departed slumber peacefully, lovingly wrapped in the same opulence and wealth that they were accustomed to while living. Of the cemetery's most famous residents, one in particular receives most of the attention.

Tucked away along one of La Recoleta's narrow, shaded alleys is the Duarte family tomb, a slab of smooth black marble marked by a series of bronze plaques and a heap of flowers. It was here, on October 22, 1976—24 years after she died—that María Eva Duarte Perón, the icon better known as Evita, was finally laid to rest with her family.

Besides the still-beloved Eva Perón, the cemetery is home to numerous Argentine luminaries of bygone eras: several presidents and generals, poet José Hernández, creator of the epic *Martín Fierro*, and Luis Leloir, the now largely forgotten winner of the Nobel Prize in Chemistry. Wander its tranquil aisles during the week and you'll see more cats than people, its grounds providing a haven for wild felines who sun themselves on the stone slabs.

The grounds are not vast, but contain around 4,700 tombs in various states of upkeep, from pristinely maintained mausoleums to sadly neglected ruins. Coffins are usually placed reverently inside in simple, multi-floored crypts—you can peek through the ornate windows of some and see freshly laid flowers offered in remembrance.

Beyond the cemetery gates, Recoleta forms part of the Barrio Norte, well worth a look for its well-appointed European-style homes and beautiful churches. The most famous is the Basílica Nuestra Señora del Pilar, the second oldest in the city and topped with distinctive cerulean-blue ceramic tiles. The highlight inside is the lavish silver altar, a masterpiece of Baroque art decorated with an Inca sun. The church is just north of the cemetery entrance, and only 500 m further is the Museo Nacional de Bellas Artes. The most important art gallery in Argentina, this grand edifice houses a significant collection of Argentine art.

Juan Perón never intended his wife should to be laid to rest in Recoleta, but it's hard to imagine a more stylish place to be buried; certainly it is one of the most wonderfully atmospheric and ornate corners of South America.

www.vivatravelguides.com/104024

Born in the UK and a Honors graduate from Oxford University with a B.A. in Modern History, Stephen Keeling has been working as a travel writer for the last two years, though his background is journalism. His first job was at the Baltic Observer in Riga, Latvia, before moving to Hong Kong in 1994 and working as a financial reporter for seven years. He has written the first *Rough Guide to Taiwan* for UK-based Rough Guides, due to publish in Spring 2007, and just updated the *Rough Guide to Spain*.

His dream destination is to Tristan Da Cunha, one the most isolated communities in the world, accessible by ship only.

# EVITA MUSEUM

### By Sandra Scott, Lowville, New York, U.S.A.

Eva "Evita" Duarte Perón, one of the most important women in Argentina's history and forever immortalized on stage and in film, has her own museum in Buenos Aires—Museo Evita. Built by the Carabassa family in the 1900s, the building originally served as a petit hotel. The original French architecture was later remodeled to incorporate Spanish and Italian Renaissance features, popular in the 1920s. Eventually, the house was purchased by the Eva Perón Social Aid Foundation and the museum was inaugurated in July 26, 2002, on the 50th anniversary of Eva's death.

Housing an assortment of film clips, pictures, speech recordings, and personal artifacts, the museum is a reverential shrine that pays homage to the late Mrs.Perón. Thirteen permanent exhibition rooms and one temporary display room trace the life of Eva, from her childhood through her youth as an actress, and then her most famous roles as social activist and the First Lady to Argentina president Juan Perón.

As figurehead to the Eva Perón Foundation, Eva Perón initiated countless crusades for social justice and equality. Impressive exhibits outline her relentless fight for causes including female civil rights and orphanages. She led the foundation until her resignation and death, when she was only in her early 30s; her body was kidnapped, interred in Italy, and finally returned to Argentina. For those lacking in Spanish skills, handy cards provide translations of the film clips in English. The museum showcases the macabre events that followed her untimely death. Perhaps the most bizarre piece in the collection is a replica of the original death mask featured in the memorial commissioned by her husband.

Not far away in Recoleta Cemetery you can join the daily procession of people who make the pilgrimage to the polished black granite Duarte family vault where Evita is interred. It is never without flowers left by her faithful admirers. To complete the homage to Eva, visit Casa Rosada in Plaza de Mayo Square, gaze at the balcony, and imagine the square packed with throngs of adoring worshipers listening, and crying, as she gave her farewell speech, "Don't Cry For Me Argentina." Before visiting Argentina, travelers should consider watching the 1997 film, *Evita*, in which Madonna played Evita, so they can compare the Hollywood version with the more factual Argentine version.

Sandra Scott is a retired history teacher and the co-author of two local history books. She is also the co-founder of the Mexico Historical Society, Mexico Point State Park, and Friends of Mexico Point Park. Scott has been traveling worldwide for over 20 years and writing about her travels since 1990. Her retired husband, John, is a traveling/writing partner. Their travels have taken them to over 100 countries, some several times. They have four children.

Her travel-related writing includes a weekly column in the *Syracuse Post Standard*, a syndicated monthly travel column for *Senior Wire Service*, and a column for www.cocktailatlas.com. She is a frequent contributor to *Copley News Service*, *Country Discoveries*, *Star Service Review*, *Inn Traveler*, *Trips and Journeys*, and several other travel magazines.

# A TASTE OF A SOCCER GAME

### By Maria Berns, Argentina

Maria Berns was born in Argentina where she worked as sociologist at urban marginal communities in Buenos Aires and at indigenous Mapuche community of Los Toldos. In Mexico City, she embraced film-making and scriptwriting and shot award winning Minimal Story of a Seduction and worked as the scriptwriter for the weekly news program and a special documentary series of Mexican television channel 11. In San Diego, she wrote and shot *Splendors, Diary of a Private Life*, and in Rochester, New York, where she was invited to teach scriptwriting and film production at Rochester Institute of Technology for two years; she shot *Winter in Jamaica* and *Black Ice*. At present, she is working on a non-fiction book about borders called *Chimera* and a feature length script, *Of Deers and Butterflies*.

She claims Tijuana as the craziest, and the best place she has ever visited.

Cowboy culture, mighty meat and toe-tapping tango all finish a distant second to Argentina's number one national pastime: fútbol (soccer). Don't shy away if someone invites you to a game, but bring a strong voice and your rally shoes. The national obsession, fútbol, is as much a part of Argentine life as eating, sleeping and breathing. It courses through conversations like blood through veins, and everybody—women and children included—is an expert in tactics and players. To attend a live game is to experience Argentinean culture in the raw. The event begins before the day of the game, at home and at the workplace, at the bus stop and in the café. Passionate discussions about fútbol culminate in flailing arms and flying insults. If you don't know about a team's history, it's better to sit back and listen to the experts: it is part of the pre-game training (and surely as exhausting as the players' professional training circuits).

On game day, hordes of fans swarm the streets, moving en masse like an army to the battlefield. Fútbol culture in Argentina has its own language, a collection of idioms, chants and hymns that accompany the trek to and from the stadium. These boisterous demonstrations of fútbol-piety echo through the streets, filling the air with an electric buzz. The atmosphere inside the stadium is no less charged. Once inside, don't be surprised to see wired fences separating the fans from the field; they are intended to protect players of rival players from the overzealous and sometimes violent advances of rabid hometown hinchadas (fans). While violence has been known to erupt at some matches, it is not the main event, nor is it the focus of the throngs of fans that descend on the stadium.

Most of the back-and-forth between rival fans is good natured, teetering between absolute hilarity and total absurdity. So don't be afraid: sit back, relax, and enjoy the dose of adrenaline administered at these tournaments. During some special games, the so called "Clasicos," such as Boca vs. River, Racing vs. Independiente or San Lorenzo vs. Huracán, you'll see incredible behaviors, such as fans throwing bags of sugar at the opposite team (an attempt to sweeten their sourness), or you may witness diapers sailing through the stands. The intended target: the *cobardes* (cowards) on the other side.

All the excitement may make you hungry. If your tummy starts to rumble, try the choripán, a sausage wedged between slices of fresh white bread. You can by it at the stadium entrance before or after the game.

For an insider's fútbol experience, go with a local fan who can debrief you on the teams, their records, the usual tricks and the prevailing mood in the stadium. It is not difficult to find such a mentor if you say that you love fútbol. Even the most timid of travelers will be swept away by the enthusiasm. When you find yourself spontaneously reacting as the crowd does, you will know that you are part of that collective body, and you will give your heart and your full voice, at least for that day, for the team of, yes, your love. Ultimately, fútbol is Argentina's number one passion: make it yours too.

www.vivatravelguides.com/104623

# BEEF IT UP IN BUENOS AIRES

### By Michelle Hopey, New Hampshire, U.S.A.

Just imagine sinking your teeth into a freshly-cut, plump, tender, juicy slab of grilled beef—everyday and not just once a day, but twice, and possibly even three times.

Even if you've never fancied beef before, you'll find yourself hankering for a large hunk of meat. It's as if the steak here is addictive. This meat eating culture is to blame for vegetarians who fall off the wagon while in the country. There is something about Argentine beef that lures the casual visitor, with its thick, meaty, charcoal-brazed waft. It's not uncommon for travelers to say that they "ate and drank their way through Buenos Aires." This is not an exaggeration.

It is said that the reason Argentine beef tastes so good is because the free-range organic Argentinean cattle feast on nutrient-filled pampas. They are also fed little to zero corn or corn feed and are not pumped with antibiotics and growth hormones like their American and European cattle cousins, making for thick and flavorful slabs of meat.

While the cuts of steak are worthy of awards itself, it is also the way Argentines cook the beef that really makes it so flavorful. Despite what you may think, only salt and sometimes lemon juice is added to the steak before throwing it on the grill (*a la parrilla*) or charcoal or wood. Traditional *gaucho* (cowboy) style (*asados*) barbecues use no marinades to grill the beef. The meat is slowly cooked as so to retain the natural juices and flavors.

Unless you meet a local who invites you to a family asado, or barbecue, you'll likely be seeking out restaurants on your own. Buenos Aires is filled with an abundance of five-star bistros and hole-in-the-wall parrilla joints.

Below are a few things you should keep in mind as you open the menu:

The finest cuts of beef have the highest price tags. The Argentine peso took a dive in 2001 and has been trying to reclaim itself ever since, because of this, the price is ridiculously low. The most popular cut is *bife de chorozo*, a steak cut off the rib and equivalent to rump or sirloin. *bife de lomo* is tenderloin, *bife de costilla* is similar to the T-bone and is the largest cut of beef. Unlike many other countries, cheaper cuts like shank and brisket are well-received by porteños. Called *churrasco*, these cuts are inexpensive, but full of flavor.

Oh and with beef such a serious business, servers will make sure to ask how you'd like the meat cooked—*poco hecho* (rare), *al punto* (medium) or *bien hecho* (well-done).

A grilled steak with a bottle of red wine only will cost you about 13 U.S. dollars. Of course it hasn't always been this way. Pre-2001, when bank scandals rattled all of Argentina, the price would have been double, if not more. To indulge your taste buds and body in a five-star meal worthy for a king, but economical enough for a backpacker, get to Buenos Aires as quick as you can.

# LA BOCA

## By Jessica Bennett, Seattle, Washington, U.S.A:

A word to the wise: be careful not to say "river" when you're in La Boca, despite the nearby port. That's not because La Boca isn't near the river, but rather because River is the barrio's oldest and most-despised soccer rival—and one whose name is likely to get you not-so-friendly stares. La Boca soccer fans of the neighborhood's famous Boca Juniors club, are as relentlessly zealous as they come. Boca (which once featured soccer legend Diego Maradona) is one of the top football clubs throughout all of South America. As a result, the neighborhood displays a lot of blue and gold (the Boca colors), everywhere from flags to team jerseys to, well, house-fronts.

But in Buenos Aires' most colorful neighborhood, the blue and gold blends in. La Boca's rainbow of brightly painted houses make this neighborhood one of the most fascinating, and memorable in all of Latin America. First settled by Italian immigrants who came to work in the port, La Boca (the mouth) is characterized by brightly painted wood and metal houses, artisan fairs, sidewalk cafes and street-side Tango performances. Its main street, Caminito, looks more like an open-air museum than an actual road with tourists flocking to the neighborhood each weekend to experience the street musicians, performers, Italian taverns and even drag shows. Also on the agenda for visitors is the neighborhood's famous soccer stadium, La Bombonera, which also provides daytime tours. The colorful houses that line the streets tell an interesting story: the neighborhood's first settlers who were port workers, built their homes out of leftover sheets of corrugated metal and other scraps from the nearby harbor and port. Due to the high price of paint, they actually used leftovers from ships to cover their houses—often switching colors numerous times throughout a paint job.

*"The Tango has an infamous origin, and it shows."*
*Jorge Luís Borges,*
*Argentine Poet and Writer*
*(1899-1986)*

La Boca. Photo by Michelle Hopey.

## TANGO By Katie Hale

Fixed in a tight embrace, the couple's eyes lock in a hypnotic gaze. The music starts with an enchanting beat and they begin to move—quick, quick, quick ...

Tracing its roots to the South American milonga, traditional African rhythms, and European folkloric dances, tango is both a social dance and musical genre that originated in one of 19th century Montevideo's lower-class neighborhoods. It later migrated to Argentina's cosmopolitan capital of Buenos Aires, where its unmistakable beat could be heard everywhere from brothels to opera houses.

To dance the tango is essentially to walk to music. Dancers keep their feet and knees very close together as they promenade. The Argentine tango, which contains deep stylistic differences to ballroom tango, consists of no basic steps itself, but certain moves that are often incorporated into the dance: cruzada, lapiz, salida cruzada, ocho, moliete, giro, sacada, and gancho. The moliente, or pinwheel, for example, is a move where the follower grapevines around the leader.

Tango music is usually played by an orchestra consisting of a violin, piano, guitar, flute, and most importantly, a bandoneon (an accordion-like instrument). A plethora of Argentine tango music is available due to the number of artists who have produced recordings over the last century.

Today, tango is more than a mere dance or musical genre — it represents the Argentine passion, energy and history. On any given day in the streets of Buenos Aires, high-heeled women can be seen bent over the arms of fedora-wearing men, proof that passion is alive and kicking every day here in the "Paris of South America."

# TOO TIRED TO TANGO
## By Kelley Coyner, Texas, U.S.A.

Known as nocturnal city, Buenos Aires could be a bit daunting for a baby boomer family with a brood of young children. With a bit of flexibility and a sprinkle of serendipity, however, BA's charms are accessible even for family travelers.

Too tired for late night tangos? If you and your family are usually tucked into bed before most porteños sit down for dinner—at 10 p.m. no less—look for daytime versions of late night traditions.

While evening tango shows might not be an option for the wee-ones, the café culture—a signature of Buenos Aires—is enough to captivate even the youngest travelers. The ultimate tea-party is available for all at Café Tortoni. As a traveling family, we found this cafe delightful for all. My daughters, Sarah and Claire, then four and seven, enjoyed *submarinos*—hot chocolate made with steamed milk and a chocolate bar—while the grown-ups sipped coffee and savored the ambience of the centuries old café. Señor Tortoni, known for his sumptuous ice cream, is no longer around, but his cafe remains as traditional as ever, and permeates old time Argentine flair with an accent of Italian and French culture. For a fee, Café Tortoni also puts on professional tango shows, however, the earliest show is at 8 p.m. Delicious petit fours and other tea time treats, from alfajors to cucumber sandwiches are all served in the same locale on Avenida de Mayo 825, where the Café opened its doors in the late 1800s. (It originally opened from the other side on Rivadavia.)

Step outside the café and go for a wander along one of Buenos Aires' many rambling streets, each seeped in history as rich as the Porteño culture itself. Kids and adults alike will love the scandalously and brightly painted colorful houses and parents can easily be swallowed up by one of the many flea and art markets. A city of spontaneity, Buenos Aires hosts many sidewalk shows and street performances, including a number of free tango shows. Kids and adults can become mesmerized by the eccentric dance, but it is also a chance for everyone to enjoy the music while swaying or dancing in the open-air.

Next, take a stroll through La Recoleta, a large well-kept grassy knoll park where kids can run and burn some energy. While in the area, pop into the famous La Recoleta Cemetery to visit the site of 1940s and 50s political diva, Eva "Evita" Peron's grave and afterwards liven things up with an excursion to the new modern art museum, the "monster" museum, also known as the MALBA (Museo de Arte Latinoamericano de Buenos Aires). The MALBA is a sure winner among both the young and old. The kids love the permanent exhibits of monsters made of recycled materials such as typewriter erasers, tooth brushes, steel wool and auto parts. Along the way, adults can take in the modern art exhibits. Be certain to head to the Sound Sculptures on the outdoor balcony where visitors can not only touch the art, but also pluck it, bang it, and stand in the middle of it—a sure kid-pleaser.

Another late-night delight that can also be enjoyed during is an elaborate meal. In many Latin American countries lunch is a major meal, and in Buenos Aires, this is no different. In fact, since dinner is late, lunch tends to be anywhere between 2 and 4 p.m. In fact, adults can indulge in local specialties without waiting for the 10 o'clock dinner bell. While adults sink their teeth into a gourmet tender cut of barbequed steak, (a staple and traditional Argentine dish) the young ones have an array of kid-friendly fare to choose from, including hamburgers, pasta and hot dogs.

The Buenos Aires Zoo is another good excursion. The animals, which appear to be well-treated, represent a cross section of species native to Argentina and from around the world. Botanical gardens across the street, with their flora and fauna, and smattering of 19th century architecture, make a great playground for adults.

For wildlife of another era, the Museum of Nature History has world class exhibits of dinosaurs and marine reptile fossils. The Nature Reserve, Reserva Ecologica, along the Rio Plata gives the whole family a break from the urban hustle and bustle and a chance to view the river environs in a more natural state.

Despite its reputation for early morning tangos and all-night parties, Buenos Aires boasts many family friendly alternatives. Towards the end of our first visit to Buenos Aires, my youngest, Sarah and I tucked into a café in the center of Buenos Aires to share a huge slice of lemon sponge cake and watch the people go by. Between bites, Sarah recounted our many adventures. After pausing to sip her submarino, she made my day saying, "This is the life. Where are we going next?"

## ICE CREAM By Michelle Hopey

Ice cream is not just an after dinner treat. In fact, in these parts, a line at the corner ice cream shop at 11 a.m. isn't out of the norm. Ice cream in Buenos Aires is a serious affair and porteños don't mess around with anything but the real thing. Over all of Argentina from Mendoza to Salta to Bariloche you can taste a variety of colorful flavors being scooped right out of the freezer, including the smooth exotic fruits of Latin America like mango, mora and coconut to the rich delights like dulce de leche, toffee, mint and café.

Although heladerias are blanketed on nearly every street corner, ice cream isn't said to be a national food of Argentina. Typically Argentina is known for its beef, dulce de leche, Yerba Mate and malbec and right next to these should sit ice cream. Since many Argentines hail from Italy, it is said the ice cream here is similar to the popular super creamy gelato. Some even say better. The Argentine ice cream is creamy like Gelato in texture and embraces strong natural flavors, usually only found in sorbets. Most parlors create icy treats that are made with chunks of real fruit and spices. Only the rawest and most natural of ingredients are used.

Large cities have their share of chain ice-cream shops, but the small, artisans tend to concoct more unique flavors. There are typically more than 20 choices offered, not to mention an elaborate spread of waffle cones. But, perhaps the most enchanting part of the Argentine ice cream experience is that you don't have to choose only one flavor if you want one scoop. It's a custom to choose two flavors to make up one scoop. So, get your creative juices flowing and order up a *banana con coconut* or whatever your taste buds are begging for and for the equivalent of one or two dollars U.S., who can blame Argentines for the daily indulge.

The Ranger, Patagonia. Photo by Christian Denes.

# URUGUAY

**The Oriental Republic**

Uruguay? Is that in Africa? Isn't that the capital of Paraguay? As the second smallest country in South America, the "Oriental Republic", or Uruguay, sometimes gets forgotten among its neighbors—alluring Argentina and vibrant Brazil. Uruguayans have perhaps kept their nation a secret for so long, because living there is so easy. Unlike many countries in South America that struggle with economics, education, and health care, Uruguay has the highest literacy rate in all of Latin America, an advanced social security system, and one of the highest standards of living at a very low cost.

Settled by the Portuguese and Spanish, today the remnants of the past can be seen in places like Colonia del Sacramento, an architectural pearl positioned on a peninsula, overlooking the Río de la Plata.

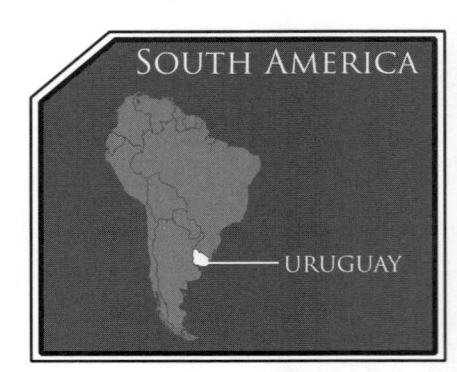

Over half of the nation's population resides in the hip, sophisticated capital of Montevideo. Only a short ferry ride from Buenos Aires, the city offers a respite for porteños during their summer. This capital is culturally rich with museums, theaters, plazas, and cathedrals, and casts an international flair to rival any metropolis.

For the non-city lover, Uruguay offers everything from estancias where real gauchos run the land to real live runway models basking in the sun on the beaches of Punta del Este.

Although tourism to Uruguay has jumped within the last few years, on the whole, the locals have done a pretty good job of keeping their land of rolling green hills, pristine white-sand beaches, and quiet colonial towns hush-hush. After you party in La Barra or relax in Carmelo, it's likely your lips too will be kept shut when Uruguay comes up as the topic of conversation.

# CARMELO

By Jenna Mahoney, New York City, New York, U.S.A.

The Four Seasons in Carmelo is the most romantic spot in the world. Outdoor showers, private casitas and sunsets over the estuary are only some of the features. This expansive hideaway sits on the clay banks of the Río de la Plata, just across the estuary from Argentina's capital, Buenos Aires. Once you check-in, you'll never have to (or want to) leave the eucalyptus and pine-forested property.

Guests at the upscale Four Seasons resort hotel stay in private individual *casitas*, or family friendly bi-level bungalows. Each of the structures has an expansive floor plan complete with fireplaces, deep soaking bathtubs and outdoor space. The hotel also has a pool, a spa, a casino and several restaurants, plus a nearby wine bodega and golf course. Needless to say, there are activities galore for romance-seeking couples, deep-relaxation pilgrims and fitness gurus.

Pick your poison: Golfing, horseback riding, swimming and yoga are just a few of the activities regularly offered at this exclusive hideaway. It's off-property, but the 72-par golf course is easily accessible via chauffeured antique cars. The clubhouse, with its sun-drenched porches overlooking the links and the water, has an excellent restaurant and lounge area.

During the summer months (December through April) the estuary also serves as a popular sports spot. Paddleboats, jet skis and swimmers abound. And the bi-level pool located at the center of the property is perfect for lounging or taking a dip. Equine explorers clop through the surrounding pine and eucalyptus trees and over the grassy knolls that lead down to the riverbank, while cyclists cruise around the property's packed dirt paths.

The Asian-inspired spa is located in its own building down the dirt path. Upon entering, guests are greeted by a statue of Shiva and a fountain in an open-air relaxation plaza. The treatment rooms are quiet and very private. And yes, that's a flower you see under your massage table. It is in this structure that the yoga classes are offered. The practice is slow, gentle and relaxing, just like its environment.

If you decide to explore outside the hotel complex, take a right onto the main paved street and you'll eventually bump into Carmelo, a small pueblo boasting a myriad of antique stores and yerba maté shops surrounding a plaza.

All of the quiet spaces, natural wonders and luxurious amenities make the Four Seasons Carmelo the perfect place for romance. The staff can arrange a private sunset dinner in a water front cabana, while the wooden structures overlooking the Río de la Plata are comfortably equipped for candlelit suppers and engagement proposals. The river's sandy shoals and grassy hills also invite an aura of romance. And in addition to stone fireplaces and oversized and ultra-comfortable beds, the private casitas have hidden outdoor showers surrounded by flora endemic to the property.

And if that's not decadent enough, there's always the option to order the spa treatments, food and champagne directly to your room.

As the daughter of an airline worker, Jenna Mahoney is a born traveler. She flew for the first time stand-by and she hasn't stopped hopping planes, trains and—yes—automobiles since. For the past four years, she has worked as a travel writer and editor at a national magazine based in New York City. She specializes in spa, active, and chic-on-the-cheap travel adventures.

Her dream trip is to surf down the Pacific coast, from Vancouver to Tierra del Fuego. Of course, she says her surfing skills will need to improve first.

## TOP LIST: TOUCHING DOWN WITH THE JETSETTERS

Latin America is full of world-class resorts and destinations! Splurge at any of the following and mingle with the A-List:

1. Hotel Monasterio, Cusco, Peru. "Converted colonial monastery is the ritziest place in Cusco." Frank Chambers, Baton Rouge, Louisiana, U.S.A.

2. Hotel Llao Llao, Bariloche, Argentina (p. 16). "Best view from their front lawn of any hotel, anywhere." Terry Guncie, Norfolk, Virginia, U.S.A.

3. La Mirage, Cotacachi, Ecuador. "Deluxe hotel and spa, very decadent." Priscilla Richards, Rochester, New York, U.S.A.

4. Miraflores Park, Lima, Peru. Jake Hastings, Tampa, Florida, U.S.A.

5. Anthony's Key Resort, Roatan, Honduras. "First-class dive resort." Lincoln Green, Toronto, Canada.

6. Copacabana Palace Hotel, Rio de Janeiro, Brazil. Samantha Davis, Chilicothe, Ohio, U.S.A.

URUGUAY

# COLONIA DEL SACRAMENTO

By Michelle Hopey, New Hampshire, U.S.A.

Paved with cobblestone roads aligned with 300-year-old stone houses overlooking the Río de La Plata, Colonia del Sacramento is a fine example of grace. Its youth was turbulent, the center of an extended custody battle between Spanish and Portuguese rulers. But Colonial del Sacramento, being the resilient city it is, evolved into an enchanting village even with the steady conflict it bore. Today this tranquil, down-to-earth town possesses authentically elegant grace. Remaining true to its small town roots, it is not an overdeveloped commercial Mecca, but rather a magnetic pull for those wishing to escape the hubbub of energetic Montevideo and sparkling Buenos Aires.

Colonia, as it is nicknamed, is one of the most charming destinations south of the equator. Situated 110 miles from Uruguay's capital city, Montevideo and two hours (via slow boat) across the river from Buenos Aires, Colonia del Sacramento is the calm between the two urban storms and is virtually a place to take a step back into time—as well as to retreat from hectic travel. You'll find an atmospheric town with history, delightful cafés, fine food, and a wealth of rentable motorbikes and beaches that fit Colonia's unpretentious, naturally picturesque image.

A point of contention between the Portuguese and the Spanish, Colonia del Sacramento was founded as *Nova Colonia del Sacramento* in 1680 by the Portuguese. Colonia del Sacramento's location on the Río de la Plata—with its direct access to the Atlantic Ocean—was prime real estate. The Spanish refuted Portuguese claims of sovereignty and shortly after its founding, they attacked. Battles ensued for the next hundred years, during which time control of Colonia shifted between both countries. Finally, with the San Ildefonso Treaty, Colonia del Sacramento was ceded to Spanish rule.

During the extended conflict, after each conquest, the victorious faction would build upon already existing infrastructures to mark their territory. The result: a distinctive architectural blend of Spanish and Portuguese culture. Ceramic tiles laced throughout the town remain from the Spanish conquest; Portuguese saddle roofs blanket homes.

This cultural and historic legacy becomes evident with a stroll through the historic district, *Barrio Histórico*. Named a UNESCO heritage site in 1995, the district is utterly charming—seemingly untouched, but observably well-maintained. The beautifully restored entrance to the old city, Puerta del Campo, continues to evoke a sense of awe. Built in 1745, the drawbridge, the only entrance to the city, was designed to safeguard it. Along the edge of the historic quarter, which juts out like a small peninsula, sits El Faro, literally, "the lighthouse." Built in 1857, this still active structure was constructed of stones from the Convento de San Francisco ruins. In present day, as visitors leave and depart Colonia by boat, the lighthouse has become the symbol of Colonia. To enjoy a spectacular sunset, for which Colonia is famous, the Calle de los Suspiros (Street of Sighs) is highly recommended.

History and architecture might be the obvious draws, but so are the peaceful and retreating beaches. Colonia del Sacramento's beaches, lined with soft crème sand and hardwood trees, are perfect for a day away. Rent a motorbike (or even cheaper, a golf cart) and cruise through the town to Playa de Ferrando. Off the beaten trail and a few miles from town, this is the perfect spot to picnic, play soccer or just sleep. The water is mild and soothing, like everything in this tiny town. In fact, any trip to Colonia del Sacramento plucks at one's heartstrings, making you relax and crave more of this hidden, gracefully aging treasure.

> *You'll find an atmospheric town with history, delightful cafés, fine food, and a wealth of rentable motorbikes and beaches that fit Colonia's unpretentious, naturally picturesque image.*

## PLAZA DE TOROS

By Leigh Gower

At Real de San Carlos you will encounter the ancient relic of Uruguay's only Plaza de Toros, or bullring. The 10,000 seater bullring was constructed at the turn of the 20th century after Don Nicolas Mihánovich, a Dalmatian-born businessman, thought that wealthy porteños would travel to Colonia to take advantage of Uruguay's liberal gambling laws at the time, if only an adequate arena was constructed. His elaborate plans included building a bullring, hippodrome and hotel-casino complex, among other edifices.

Unfortunately, the project turned out to be a total flop as the Uruguayan government outlawed *corridas*, or bullfighting, in 1912 after the Plaza de Toros had seen only eight fights. Today the complex is rather overgrown and crumbling but still worth a look (although the ring is fenced in so you are only able to take a look at it from the outside). The journey along the beach to reach the stadium is really pleasant, too. Of the original grand plan, only the racecourse is still in operation today. Visit the bullring at night for a more spectacular view of its stone remnants set against the starry sky. It is rather less impressive by daylight.

Nearby Colonia del Sacramento resembles old Lisbon and is the main waterway connecting visitors from Argentina who want to visit any part of Uruguay. It has an inviting selection of restaurants, museums, craft shops and a harbor packed with impressive yachts.

# MONTEVIDEO

By John Polga-Hecimovich, Burnsville, Minnesota, U.S.A.

Montevideo, the southernmost capital in the Americas, is the forgotten side of the Río de la Plata; according to official figures, only 45,000 Americans visit the whole of Uruguay each year. Those who skip over Montevideo for historic Colonia or the resort town of Punta del Este miss a relaxed city with delicious meat, sandy beaches, and a well-preserved culture.

The best way to see the whole city at once may be the winding, brick-lined Rambla, or boardwalk, that bends its way along the shoreline of the Río de la Plata where fishermen serenely cast from beachside rocks, couples stroll hand-in-hand alongside joggers and dog-walkers, and everyone from students to grandfathers sit on its brick rails as the sun sets, some drinking beer or mate, and other smoking cigarettes or both. Montevideo boasts 12 miles of white-sand beaches and a Mediterranean climate, but it is also a city filled with museums and architecture that fittingly reflect Uruguay's Italian and Spanish roots.

To best see Montevideo, start in the *Ciudadela* or Old City. The heart of the Ciudadela is in the Plaza de la Independencia, guarded by South America's first skyscraper, the 26-story Palacio Salvo, and the 30-ton monument commemorating independence hero José Artigas. North from here, through the giant colonial door, the Puerta de la Ciudadela is a wide pedestrian mall of museums, stores, and restaurants. The weekend is the most colorful time as musicians, tango dancers, and artists fill the space with their sounds and movements. The must-see portion of the walk is the Mercado del Puerto (Port Market). The portside building opened in 1868 and houses a throng of restaurants selling delicious Uruguayan beef, cut thick and piled high on iron grills. The best traditional way to top off a steak dinner here is with a glass of "medio y medio," a surprisingly tasty blend of sparkling and white wine.

The most distinctive aspects of Montevideo, however, go far beyond the Rambla and juicy steaks. One of the most defining characteristic of Uruguyans and Montevideo is their love of Yerba Mate (yer-ba mah-tay). "Mate," as it is also known, is an infusion similar to tea, but whose crushed leaves are sipped from a gourd via a silver straw, or "bombilla." An equally distinctive feature of Montevideo culture is *candombe* music. On Sunday nights, impromptu formations of candombe bands march through the streets, especially in the Barrio Sur, traditionally composed of many Afro-Uruguayans. Candombe is a uniquely Uruguayan musical rhythm based on Bantu tribal dances brought to the Americas by African slaves. It is played on three different pitched drums called *tambores* and is similar to Brazil's samba. In addition to candombe, Uruguay also has an important chapter in the history of tango; Carlos Gardel, the world's most famous tango singer, was born in Montevideo. Tango clubs dot the city to this day and fill up on the weekends with locals. Unlike Buenos Aires, Montevideo's clubs are inexpensive and almost totally devoid of tourists.

Uruguayans, especially middle- and upper-class Uruguayans, love to shop. One of the most controversial shopping centers in town is Punta Carretas Shopping, located between the Parque Rodó and Pocitos, which served as a prison up through the dictatorships of the 1970s and early 1980s. A visit to one or many of its 200 stores is a also a visit to the past.

Interesting sights also include the Parque Rodó, the Botanical Gardens, the wealthy suburb of Carrasco, and the weekend Tristan Narvaja Street Fair that stretches on for blocks and blocks in every direction and sells everything from mate paraphernalia and books to old license plates and hubcaps. El Cerro, an old fortress sitting atop Montevideo's only hill, is an interesting visit, and provides some great views of the Río de la Plata estuary and the city. The best museum in the Ciudadela is the Museo Joaquín Torres García. A friend and collaborator of Picasso and Gaudí in Spain, Torres García was a pioneering modernist artist. The Estadio Centenario, site of the first World Cup, plays host to soccer games and rock concerts throughout the year; the most anticipated game of the year is played between Nacional and Peñarol, the two Montevideo teams with the most history.

Montevideo. Photo by Amanda Massello.

## JOAQUÍN TORRES-GARCÍA

By Katie Hale

Born in Montevideo, Uruguay, in 1874, Torres-García would be a vital force in Latin American art. He moved to Spain with his family when he was a teenager and in 1926, met and befriended a number of avant-garde artists in France. This collaboration resulted in his experimentation with many modern artistic theories and movements.

Torres-García developed his own theory of art, which he called *Universalismo Constructivo* (Constructive Universalism). He believed that geometry was the most effective and universal art form in which to represent the human experience. Focusing on what he called "spiritual geometry," rather than strictly mathematic geometry, he created a system of abstraction that incorporated symbols filled with personal meaning and national history symbolism.

After 43 years of absence, he returned to Uruguay in 1934 and created a school to advance Constructive Universalism, El Taller Torres-García. Here, artists worked collectively on murals, architecture and sculpture often in conjunction with writers, musicians and performers.

# EL DRUGSTORE RESTAURANT

By Sandra Scott, Lowville, New York, U.S.A.

Wandering the cobbled streets of the historic district of Colonia del Sacramento, Uruguay, one senses that the past is tangibly present.

One of the most unique restaurants lining the tree-covered plazas is El Drugstore, easily recognizable by the yellow 1950s Morris car permanently parked under the trees. El Drugstore is located on a corner across from the Iglesia Matriz, near Plaza de Armas. The restaurant is a resting spot for several vintage automobiles. Along a side street sit a 1920s Ford and an antique Citroën, which sprouts trees through its decomposing shell. The Ford is set up as a private "dining" car with a small café table decked with a bright red tablecloth—its door has been removed for easy access. Both the Morris and the Ford still have their original motors.

The interior of the restaurant is a bit funky and reminiscent of San Francisco's Haight-Asbury district. It is a riot of color with bright blue, red, and yellow walls covered with eclectic posters and tables donning polka-dot cloths. Weather permitting, most guests choose to dine or share a bottle of wine under the trees. For dinner, beef barbecued on a traditional Uruguayan grill is a favorite. During lunch and dinner they offer live music, often a lady reprising Sinatra and other old-time American songs. El Drugstore is a place to enjoy the tranquility of Colonia on any afternoon or evening.

www.vivatravelguides.com/104174

# GRAF SPEE MUSEUM

By Kelley Coyner, Texas, U.S.A.

In August 1939, the German warship Graf Spee, a heavy, state-of-the-art cruiser with battleship-sized guns known as a "pocket battleship," passed north of Scotland before turning and sailing due south between Iceland and the British Isles, across the Equator and into the South Atlantic. For ten weeks, the Graf Spee ravaged merchant shipping in the South Atlantic, sending 50,000 tons of merchant ships to the bottom, mostly British vessels.

On December 13, a British South Atlantic Fleet force found the Graf Spee off the coast near the border between Argentina and Uruguay and immediately attacked. The Graf Spee sustained superficial damage but significant casualties and fled toward the neutral port of Montevideo, Uruguay. The Uruguayan government refused the Graf Spee's request for safe haven, but the ship remained in the harbor. The British used disinformation to make the Germans believe that they would soon be overwhelmed by a strong naval force. Fearful that his ship might be captured and knowing that it would not survive the midwinter trip home across the North Atlantic, the captain scuttled his ship on December 17 before committing suicide three days later.

The crew evacuated the Graf Spee. Maintaining neutrality, the Uruguayan government would neither repatriate the crew nor grant them asylum. For a short time, the German Legation housed them in Montevideo and then they sat out the war in an internment camp. After the war many of the German sailors elected to remain in Argentina.

Six decades later, the Graf Spee incident typically does not even merit a footnote in histories of World War II. The terror of Hitler's war on unarmed merchant shipping, the diplomatic crisis for Uruguay's government at the onset of the summer holidays, the people of Montevideo watching the burning ship from the city's beaches, the clever use of intelligence on the part of the British, and the fate of the ship's captain and its crew were emblematic of the impact of the war in South America.

The Museo Naval in Montevideo looks like someone's attic. It consists of a couple of large rooms filled with model ships, photographs, officers' mess silver, ships' nameplates, and the like displayed in rough chronological order without any attempt at historical interpretation. The most unusual item is "Foque," a stuffed spaniel who was ship's mascot on the ROU Capitán Miranda from 1987 to 1999. Why somebody back in 1999 decided to stuff poor Foque and place him in the Museo Naval is anyone's guess: perhaps the lack of historical interpretation should probably be counted as a piece of good luck

The Graf Spee exhibit runs floor to ceiling in a long, narrow room. It displays a ship's telephone, a stretcher used to evacuate a wounded sailor, the sword and scabbard that Captain Langsdorf surrendered to the Uruguayan navy and a large black medallion bearing Hitler's profile. A few photos memorialize the incident, the most interesting of which is the last photograph ever taken from the Graf Spee, a shot off the stern showing the Nazi naval ensign. Another photo shows the Graf Spee as it sank and burned, and there is even a signed photograph of captured British Merchant Marine officers, posing at a Christmas dinner that took place in the Graf Spee's officers' mess a few days before the ship's fateful encounter with the British. A souvenir program from the royal performance of a 1957 movie about the incident provides the only background in English.

# PUNTA DEL ESTE
### By Paola Singer, Montevideo, Uruguay

The sun rises on a soft summer morning in Punta del Este, Uruguay. Medialunas Calentitas, a casually hip pastry shop, fills with young men and women coming from late-night parties and clubs to quell after-party hunger pangs, not an uncommon sensation among revelers who descend on this South American beach town. A perfectly uncombed blonde wearing fuchsia pumps, a white strapless top and a pleated denim miniskirt tries unsuccessfully to snatch one of the coveted sofa seats on the outdoor patio.

Punta del Este is famous for its wild nightlife and limitless supply of chic youth. The bar-hopping crowds usually hit the La Barra neighborhood, where Medialunas Calentitas can be found.

For decades, Punta has been the vacation haven for upscale residents of Buenos Aires and wealthy Brazilians. Recently, however, its fame has spread, and North Americans and Europeans have been flocking there as well.

The South American summer runs from late December into February, transforming Punta del Este into a lively resort with reopened bars, restaurants, boutiques and a lengthy calendar of events. It can attract as many as 300,000 visitors during the season. For the rest of the year, Punta del Este is a tranquil coastal city.

The eastern coast, referred to as *Brava,* is popular with singles and surfers looking to ride the big ocean waves. Not far from the downtown area is Bikini, an ample white-sand beach that lives up to its name: the ladies sport tiny bathing suits. The calm-water beaches along the western shore, called *Mansa,* feature safer waters for families and are perfect for wind surfing, swimming, jet skiing and other water sports.

They typical party day includes a late wake-up call and a light breakfast followed by a few hours of sizzling on the beach. Later in the afternoon, an order of mussels at a beachside cafe is sure to put people in the mood for a very popular after-sunset activity: napping. The evening nap is sort of an art form in Punta, as it is difficult to party until dawn with the locals without one. The city awakens and goes into party mode at about 11 p.m.

Partiers will usually start the night with a dinner downtown before heading to La Barra for some *caipiroskas* at an outdoor pub. Afterwards, they may head to the famous Conrad casino for some gaming or to one of Punta's trendy nightclubs for a night of dancing and drinking until the sun comes up.

One favorite haunt is Tequila, a small club in La Barra's main street. Granted, the doormen can be unfriendly, sometimes even rude, but once you get past them the fun is almost guaranteed. While DJ's spin a catchy mix of techno and rock, the champagne flows, and partygoers get friendlier by the minute. ¡Viva Punta!

Paola Singer is a freelance journalist based in Brooklyn, New York. Her work has appeared in *The Wall Street Journal, Newsday,* and several New England newspapers. Most recently she worked as a translations editor for *The Wall Street Journal Americas,* and contributed regularly to the *Journal*'s main edition.

She was born in Montevideo, Uruguay, and has spent many memorable vacations in Punta del Este, the beach town she writes about in this guide. Singer would not leave for her travels without a pair of sneakers. While she'd like to visit the Aussies some day, her next trip will be back to Montevideo, to see her family.

## CARLOS GARDEL By Leigh Gower

Known as "The Magician," the Elvis of the tango world, and perhaps the greatest tango singer of all time, owning the right to claim his birth place still proves important for Uruguayans. They continue to contest against the French, until this very day, that Carlos Gardel is theirs.

Uruguay asserts that Gardel was born in the small town of Valle Edén, in their Tacuarembó region—the source of this claim being Gardel himself, who was quoted in newspaper interviews providing his origins as such. Photos and documents further attest to the singer's Uruguayan origins. However, since a French birth certificate for the him exists, skeptics insist that Gardel was born in Toulouse, France and that he was evasive about his place of birth in order to conceal embarrassment at having been born to a single mother. Of his origins, he was quoted saying: "I was born in Buenos Aires, at the age of 2 years and a half …" The controversy has spawned a plethora of books on Gardel's nationality, but one thing certainly remains true: Gardel has a godlike presence in the River Plate region.

Gardel was the first singer to create popular songs out of tango where it had previously been entirely instrumental dance music, considered inferior by the cultural elite for its common origins and earthy sensuality. He rose to fame in 1917 with the hit *Mi Noche Triste* which sold 100,000 copies and was celebrated throughout Latin America. Following tours across the continent, Gardel began to break into Europe and New York and was taken on by Paramount Pictures who saw him as the "Latin Lover" they needed to break into the Spanish-speaking movie market.

Flying out of Medellin, Colombia on June 24, 1935, Gardel's plane crashed and he was tragically killed together with his band. Fans mourned in throngs with many traveling to Montevideo to pay their respects to the singing legend. There he lay in state before being taken to La Chacarita cemetery in Buenos Aires where he was finally laid to rest. Reveled across the globe, you are likely to hear Gardel fans claim that "he sings better every day," while in the U.S. followers continue to petition for the idol to receive a star on Hollywood's "Walk of Fame."

# ROCHA

## By E. Elizabeth Sabatiuk, Baltimore, Maryland, U.S.A.

When people outside of Uruguay speak of Argentina and Brazil's pint-sized intermediary neighbor, the first thing to come to mind for most is Punta del Este, the exclusive international jet set resort. But rarely mentioned is the 180 kilometers (112 miles) of gorgeous white-sand beaches to "Punta's" east.

E. Elizabeth Sabatiuk grew up outside of Baltimore, Maryland, and received a degree in English Literature from Goucher College in Towson, Maryland. Since graduating she has worked as a face painter, a barista, a journalist on Capitol Hill, and a legal assistant. Currently, Sabatiuk lives in Montevideo, Uruguay, where she teaches English, and is improving her Spanish and tango skills.

At the moment she is fantasizing about a massive tour of Europe. She is dying to return to some of her favorite places from previous travels.

The shores of Rocha, the easternmost coastal province of Uruguay are studded with *balnearios*, (coastal towns), many of which are rich in history, culture, and beauty—perfect for any open-minded traveler who wants to take a bold step off the beaten path.

Each of Rocha's balnearios has its own unique character. Many have charming lighthouses, oceanic views, and colorful street-markets. The westernmost balneario of La Paloma is the largest and most touristy of the villages with a population that more than quadruples during the January high-season.

Located roughly 125 km (78 miles) east of Punta del Este, La Paloma is easily accessible from Montevideo or Punta, and has a number of restaurants and hotels, often with English-speaking personnel. Four kilometers (2.5 miles) east, a pot-hole freckled dirt road passes through the quaint fruit markets and modest restaurants of La Pedrera before ending at a steep, grassy hill overlooking the stunning beach below. You can take a crude staircase down to the shore, which is lined with sharp jutting rocks in varying shades of brown, slate and gold.

A twenty-minute drive down the road is Valizas, a balneario with a distinctly "hippie" flavor. Valizas is hiking distance from the remarkable small balneario, Cabo Polonio. Completely devoid of electricity and paved roads, the only way to reach Cabo Polonio is on foot, horseback, or in huge four-by-four dune buggies, which drive over hills, dunes and beach to reach the town center, a large dirt circle crowded with stands selling *chivitos* (a thin steak with egg, lettuce, tomato, mayonnaise and other optional accoutrements), chorizo sausages, funky jewelry, and other local specialties. East of the town, huge, golden sand dunes hulk. In the summertime, sea lions swim in droves to sun themselves on the smooth rocks near the lighthouse, and you can watch *toninas* (a type of dolphin) arcing through the peacock-hued water, while experiencing the laid-back, bohemian atmosphere of the waterfront restaurants and bars.

Further up the coast, the more established but still charmingly rustic Punto del Diablo offers great surf, food, and atmosphere. From Punto del Diablo you can easily visit Santa Teresa National Park, which features not only magnificent beaches, perfect for star-gazing or sun-bathing, but also gorgeous views of the green, gently undulating landscape, a fort from the mid-1700s, several eateries, a cactus garden, and a museum, to name a few of its many attractions. The majority of visitors camp, but there are cabañas available for rent as well.

It is not only the beautiful beaches and landscapes that make Rocha exceptional—it is a place to relax but also to experience another culture, another environment, and, sometimes, another way of life. Whether you're horseback riding on the beach, wandering the ombu forests, exploring lighthouses, observing wildlife, or watching the sun set over the water with a cold drink on the porch of a straw-roofed hut, anyone with an adventurous spirit, a love of nature, or both, will find themselves overwhelmed with possibilities in Rocha.

Cabo Polonia. Photo by E. Elizabeth Sabatiuk.

Private dining car, El Drugstore Restaurant, Colonia. Photo by Sandra Scott.

# PARAGUAY

## Small Country, Big History

Mention Paraguay to most Americans and Europeans, and you'll likely get one of two reactions: a blank look or the question "Paraguay…isn't that where all of the Nazi war criminals hid out after World War Two?"

Yes, Nazi war criminals did hide out there (and in Argentina and Brazil as well), but there is much, much more to Paraguay than this unfortunate and sordid bit of history.

One of the most heavily indigenous nations in South America, Paraguay was inhabited by the Guarani people for ages before the arrival of the Spanish. The early colonial period was marked by a great deal of mutual assimilation by the two peoples. It is also remembered for the Jesuit missions, remote outposts where the native people were protected and educated by missionaries.

After independence from Spain in 1814, the country was initially ruled by the maniacal Dr. José Gaspar Rodríguez de Francia, who treated the country like his own personal fiefdom. Paranoid and megalomaniacal, a 19th century forerunner of such twentieth century tyrants as Joseph Stalin and Pol Pot, Dr. Francia ruled supreme for 26 years, with no legislative or judicial institutions to speak of. Dissenters and criminals were tossed in dungeons or executed. He closed the borders and cut Paraguay off entirely from the outside world.

Paraguay was the loser in South America's bloodiest war, the War of the Triple Alliance (see box). Throughout the last two centuries, Paraguay has modernized, although it had always lagged behind its South American neighbors. Recently—from 1954 to 1989—the nation was home to another ruthless dictator, Alfredo Stroessner. He was overthrown by the people and today the country is a shaky democracy. Dissension is still frowned upon: community activists are regularly harassed and occasionally assassinated.

# ASUNCIÓN

By Wes Weston, Sarasota, Florida, U.S.A.

The streets are lined with aged buildings, some still showing evidence of a colonial style that is slightly dilapidated but not without a sense of timeless charm. A busy plaza hosts a multitude of daily routines where people-watching is often at its best.

Locals greet each other with a kiss on both cheeks whether they are longtime acquaintances or meeting for the first time. A group of friends passes around a cup of Yerba Mate (herbal tea typically shared in social settings) while conversing in a language that's not quite Spanish. Artisans have set out displays on the sidewalk, where they hawk pottery, necklaces, and other trinkets to the passersby. The scene is bustling with enough activity to overwhelm the senses with wonderful curiosity; however, it's just another day in Asunción, Paraguay.

Situated on the eastern bank of the Río Paraguay, Asunción is the country's only metropolitan city. Its establishment in 1537 by Juan de Salazar marked a blending of culture and customs between the Spanish and indigenous *Guaraní*. Both languages were preserved, with Guaraní more commonly being spoken in rural areas, and Spanish recognized as the country's official language.

Over time, Asunción boomed with commerce and trade. Today, it is an important port and home to more than 1.2 million people. The city has become a melting pot of economic prosperity and poverty, of strong social ties and cultural disillusionment, and of increasing nationalism and political instability.

Asunción has many renowned sights that capture the imagination. The *Museo de Bellas Artes* contains paintings and sculptures by Paraguayan artists while the *Cathedral Metropolitana* dates back to 1687 and is one of the city's oldest landmarks. The *Palacio de Gobierno* is an impressive structure that is not open to the public, but taking pictures of the building is now permitted. Dr. José de Francia's stringent rule in the early 19th century ordered that anyone caught so much as looking at the palace would be shot or arrested!

The road less traveled in Asunción leads to a variety of adventures. Luque, a suburb on the eastern outskirts of Asunción, is home to a sprawling marketplace spanning several blocks. Vendors sell jewelry, silver, ceramics, clothes and handmade artifacts at unbelievably low prices. National *fútbol* games are usually held in *Estadio de los Defensores del Chaco* and radiate with intense energy and emotion. Games are sporadic but the experience is a must. In June, the Festival de San Juan is fervently celebrated with food, games, contests, and fire walking. That's right...fire walking!

Asunción is one of the lesser known treasures of South America. Its value is defined not by a luxurious appearance, but by the wealth of its people's character and heart. The fact that it remains undiscovered by most tourists to this day is reason enough why one should go.

After graduating from the University of Colorado in 2002, the home that Wes Weston has been most familiar with is the one that he has carried on his back. With an insatiable thirst for traveling, he will always remember his first career being that of a professional nomad. The path has taken him on many twists and turns, highs and lows, to backpacking across Europe, working in the last frontier of Alaska to hiking the entirety of the Appalachian Trail: "The journey genuinely portrayed America's unique cultural values from the charm of southern hospitality up to the progressive liberalism of the north. It also made me appreciate the often forgotten about simplicity of life in small town America."

After spending a year in Costa Rica working with Habitat for Humanity International as the Volunteer Coordinator for Latin America, he now plans on pursuing one of his other passions ... teaching.

Asunción, Paraguay. Photo by Freyja Ellis.

# HERE'S THE BEEF: WHERE TO EAT TYPICAL/ATYPICAL CUISINE

By Kelley Coyner, Texas, U.S.A

Paraguay is cattle ranching country, the most agrarian country in all of South America. If you haven't been to Argentina, you can begin steak training here, or if you've just passed Buenos Aires, you'll be happy to know you can continue your carnivore diet here, where the most common menu is *parrillada*—a smorgasbord of grilled beef, sausage, organs and cuts that resemble slabs of brontosaurus meat. It sure makes for an easy wine selection.

Welcome to Asunción, a city blessed with a phenomenal restaurant scene. Not only do cooks here serve up typical Paraguayan food, but tasty Asian and European restaurants reflect the city's cultural fusion.

Before you bite into the world of Paraguayan food there are a few tips, or should I say, translations you should learn. First, the national starch is *sopa paraguaya*, not really soup at all, but a sort of coarse cornbread mixed in liberally with onions and cheese. Rice is plentiful, as is *cassava* (manioc), considered the poor man's starch. Mangos blanket the streets, sidewalks and yards, along with pretty much any tropical fruit in season. Curry and Mexican food lovers, be warned: Paraguayans aren't into any sort of spicy dishes.

Grab a *chipa*, a type of Paraguayan bread made from manioc flour. It is sold everywhere: supermarkets, the produce markets and by street vendors. The vendors hit the streets with fresh chipa around four or five in the afternoon and hawk it relentlessly for hours, so you really can't miss it. During Holy Week (usually in March or April) look for chipas shaped like animals native to the country.

The Holy Grail of beverages is *tereré*, a cold mate infusion served in the summer, which lasts nine months. In the cooler mornings, hot yerba mate is the preferred beverage. This tea-like beverage is imbibed from a *wampa*, or cow's horn and a silver *bombilla*, or metal straw. Sometimes special herbs are added for flavor or for their medicinal qualities. On the street you will see Paraguayans carrying tereré apparatus, including a thermos for hot or chilled water depending on the season. Even the police carry all their *terreré* accoutrement on the street and at their sentry points. If you are not similarly equipped, note that sipping tereré is considered a communal ritual and it is not socially acceptable to decline, save one reason. Simply insist "I just ate watermelon." Apparently the tea and melon just don't mix.

If you want to go international, check out Hiroshima, a great Japanese choice. However, you might want to hold on the sushi until Friday because the fish arrives from the Pacific coast of South America on the 8:00 p.m. flight on Thursday. There is a kebab and gyro sandwich place on San Martin with good cheap sandwiches, falafel and air conditioning. Casa Rica next door, a little German owned supermarket, has a great bakery with dark breads alongside more typical Latin pastries.

In fact, there are several German bakeries in Asunción that offer fresh brown bread and selections from the Central European pastry cart. People here eat fresh fruit for dessert or *dulce de leche*, a sort of caramel you can eat with a spoon. Dulce de leche finds its way into just about everything.

The stores carry good wine from Argentina and Chile. The lager is excellent—with such a large German community, what would you expect? From fresh grilled meats to chipa bread, no matter what your palette craves, you can find a world of food in Ascunción.

## CASABLANCA ON THE RÍO PARAGUAY

By Kelley Coyner

It is well known that over the years, Germany has provided Paraguay with some rather colorful characters who make up a large part of its fine and very productive immigrant community. But what of the French? Despite its dedication to "la mission civilisatrice," the French influence has only lurked in the background of Latin American culture, and Paraguay is no exception.

According to the French commercial attaché, that country's level of interest in Paraguay is "more than you would expect." Indeed, France has had a small yet significant amount of influence there for a long time: Paraguay's first constitution after independence from Spain was modeled on the French post-revolutionary *consulat*. The historical figure Dr. Francia, who attacked the Church and Paraguay's small population of land-owning elite, justified his actions by pointing to the intellectual basis of the French Revolution.

France has also provided a steady trickle of immigrants to Paraguay. One runs across the occasional French surname among Paraguayans, for example Graciela Courcelles, who works in the Embassy's procurement section. In addition, a number of "pieds-noirs," immigrants of European descent, have ended up here, as well as a small group of extremely right-wing Frenchmen who emigrated to Paraguay after Francois Mitterrand became President of France. In fact, the commercial attaché said one day in the Embassy that they did a count and discovered to their surprise that at least 10% of Paraguay's substantial cattle industry is in French hands. Who would have guessed it?

The downtown restaurant St. Tropez is a small dark refuge from the heat and traffic of midday Asuncion. It is run by some French immigrants who, interestingly, want nothing to do with the French Embassy (there seems to be a consensus that this is for the best). Though St. Tropez's name and management may be French, the kitchen is Paraguayan and serves local fare. The restaurant features a bar and a few yellowing posters advertising travel to the south of France. A boat with one of its gunwales cut away is filled with ice and serves as a salad bar.

In addition to escaping the intense midday sun under ceiling fans, you might catch a few conversations in French. A few Francophiles are typically in situ. The French in this country may be few, but they're certainly here, providing the visitor with another angle on the funky milieu that is Asunción.

# LAMBING AT THE ESTANCIA

## By Kelley Coyner, Texas, U.S.A

Two little girls decked out in fleece jackets and mud-covered, blue, rubber rain boots chase spring lambs for hours. The lambs skitter and bleat. The girls call out "That one's mine!" and "Come here little lamb." The lambs are largely impervious to the little girls' entreaties, and the girls retire to a pair of bedraggled lawn chairs. One girl holds a three week old lamb in her arms. The other one, the younger of the two, leans back, arms akimbo, feet tucked under, and studies the scene. Around the two girls, three dozen lambs aged from three days to six weeks run, jump, butt heads, and curl up to sleep in a warm spot of sun soaked grass. The locale is a small pasture adjacent to the barn. Later, a ranch hand invites the girls to watch an ewe give birth. He explains to the girls that the lambs are kept close at hand to keep them from becoming victims of the raptors in the area. He tells them their job is to keep the lambs safe. They nod their heads solemnly.

Cabanas San Francisco, about an hour and a half out of Route One from Asunción towards Ciudad del Este, is one tenth dude ranch, nine tenths Paraguayan sheep ranch. It really is a working ranch that happens to have a couple of rooms for weekend guests who stop over to get a glimpse of how the other four-fifths live: A fifth of the Paraguay's population lives in Asunción, the bulk of the rest live in the *campo* or countryside, and many of those are involved in ranching and farming. Paraguay is the most agrarian country in South America—agriculture makes up a quarter of the economy and figures prominently in the daily lives of the majority of the population.

There is a saying that for each 100 kilometers (60 miles) you travel from Asunción, you move ten years back in time. The little towns seem more rugged and more literary. The scene becomes more rustic and remote. Stop for gas or a soda, and you may not encounter many Spanish speakers. *Guaraní*—the other official language of Paraguay—quickly becomes the primary or only language spoken.

Increasingly, the scene becomes agrarian. Along the principal highway that runs eastward to Ciudad del Este, cattle or sheep crossing the road will interrupt most travelers at least once. Vendors sell produce and honey in small kiosks along the road. Occasionally, you'll pass a gaucho clad in chaps and cloaked in a woolen poncho riding on his blanket saddle.

At least two dozen *estancias* make the ranching life accessible by opening their doors to visitors. Some feature both ox cart rides and world class clay tennis courts. Others sport a bit of Paraguayan history. Most are a window into ranching life and a chance to relax in a hammock and perhaps take a swim. Cabanas San Francisco, just past the fishing mecca of Villa Florida, offers guests a view into a working sheep ranch.

The visitor's day follows the rhythm of ranch life. Though it is fine to decline, guests are invited to rise just before sunrise to help milk dairy cows—by hand—or search for fresh eggs. Breakfast follows as does a chance to let the sheep out to pasture. The day for a guest is low key: birdwatching, lamb watching, and walking are the main options. Horseback riding is available or you can back track to Villa Florida for a day on the river. At the end of the day, watch or lend a hand bringing in the flocks and feeding the chickens and their progeny.

When the day's work is done, (meaning after nine o'clock) a traditional dinner is served. It might be an undecipherable collection of sweet meats or very fresh lamb. On occasion, chicken might be served. The young guests who spent their day running with the animals surprise their parents by eating their lamb without batting an eye. Then they slurp down their rice pudding. And after a hard day on the ranch, the two young shepherds collapse into bed without protest.

Jesuit Mission Ruins, Trinidad. Photo by Freyja Ellis.

*"America's health care system is second only to Japan ... Canada, Sweden, Great Britain ... well, all of Europe. But you can thank your lucky stars we don't live in Paraguay!"*
-Homer Simpson,
American Nuclear Safety Inspector
(1956-)

### PARAGUAY FACTOIDS:

The country has two official languages: Spanish and Guaraní. The Guaraní culture has heavily influenced the nation, and even though only three percent of the population is of Guaraní heritage, approximately 90 percent of Paraguayans speak Guaraní fluently.

# VAPOR CUÉ

### By Kelley Coyner, Texas, U.S.A.

The resting place of a landlocked country's navy, from a forgotten war, the "town" of Vapor Cué has practically everything going for it: history, natural environment, a story too bizarre not to be true, and more than a touch of absurdity and sadness.

Vapor Cué was the end of the line in 1869, and 133 years later nothing much has changed. The asphalt road turns to gravel a couple kilometers before the site. There's no town at Vapor Cué; it's just a place where the remains of six boats were salvaged from the nearby river. The two large steamboats, the "Amambay" and the "Pirabebé" look as if they are ready to set sail. The exhibit does not describe the extent to which they have been reconstructed, but it must have been considerable. Only pieces remain of the four smaller steamboats; "Paraná," "Río Apa," "Ypora" and "Salto de Guairá."

The four smaller boats' wooden parts either burned or decayed in the river, so what remains is mostly cast iron. Massive furnaces and pressure tanks—labeled by boat—are mounted on concrete blocks and some of the power train and side wheels have also survived. None of the mechanisms are entirely preserved, but looking at all of them you can see how steam—the cutting edge of technology in the mid-19th century—powered these revolutionary vessels.

The remains of its wooden keel rests behind the salvaged "Salto de Guairá" and there is enough left of it to give a picture of what it must have been like: a wooden boat with a cast iron furnace powering two side wheels. Picture a large version of *The African Queen* without Humphrey Bogart and Katherine Hepburn. "Salto de Guairá" was built in Paraguay with British technical assistance and christened by Doña Rafaela López—sister of the President who precipitated the War of the Triple Alliance—on July 17, 1857, in the presence of her father, President Don Carlos Antonio López. (Doña Rafaela, along with her mother and sisters, snubbed Madame Lynch, their brother Francisco's mistress. When Francisco succeeded his father as President, Madame Lynch got her revenge by placing Doña Rafaela in a caged wagon.)

The larger boats were steam-powered but also had masts for sails and rigging. "Pirabebé" ("Flying Fish" in Guaraní) was propeller-driven. "Amhambay," a double side-wheeler, was captured from the Brazilians in one of the war's first actions. Marines from the "Ypora" and "Río Apa"—the remains of which now sit a few meters away from "Amhambay"—boarded and captured it. Four days later, on January 10, 1865, a gunpowder explosion killed 25 Paraguayan officers and men and sidelined the "Amhambay" for much of the war.

Vapor Cué is a Paraguayan national park developed with Spanish assistance. It is the fruit of the goodwill that existed between former Presidents Franco and Stroessner. The park is simple but nicely laid out. It has a monument to the sailors of the Paraguayan Navy and the remains of each boat are clearly labeled and displayed around a large dirt cul-de-sac.

Hardly anybody visits Vapor Cué. As a naval archaeological find, these boats are like fossils of the missing link, caught as they are right in the middle of the rapid transition from sail to steam. Clipper ships preceded these boats by a generation; dreadnoughts and ocean liners appeared just a generation later.

The War of the Triple Alliance destroyed Paraguay's national wealth and productive capacity for a generation and may have killed up to 20 percent of Paraguay's male population (demographic research has shown that it did not kill 80% of Paraguay's males, as is sometimes asserted). Their involvement in the war helped to consolidate the Brazilian and Argentine states and, ominously, made strong national institutions of their armed forces. And like the American Civil War, the War of the Triple Alliance held some important lessons about the future of warfare.

> **The War of the Triple Alliance destroyed Paraguay's national wealth and productive capacity for a generation and may have killed up to 20 percent of Paraguay's male population.**

---

## FANTASTIC FLORA

### By Kelley Coyner

The flowering lapacho trees are one of Asunción's pleasures. In August and September they adorn the city and countryside like giant pink bouquets. The lapacho tree (known as *tajy* in Guaraní) is a special joy because it produces its stunning flowers at a time when Asuncion is about as barren and brown as it gets. Another variety of lapacho blooms in September and October, and Paraguayans see its sulfur yellow blossoms as a harbinger of spring.

The lapacho tree is known as the *ipe roxo* or *pau d'arco* in Brazil, *lapacho tucumano* in Argentina and the *arbol de la trompeta* ("trumpet tree") in Mexico. The lapacho is more than just a pretty tree; it's a tree of great medicinal value, a *cúralo todo*, ("cure-all") as they say. Herbs and plants play an important role in people's daily lives here—medicinal herbs are on sale in the supermarkets and by women on the streets. People drink them daily with their mate or terere. For centuries the Guaraní have used a tea made from the heartwood of the lapacho tree as a cure for a gastrointestinal disorders and much more.

# MBARACAYÚ RESERVE

### By Kelley Coyner, Texas, U.S.A

Flying into Mbaracayú can feel like one is landing on a remote island. But, rather than surrounded by water, this nature reserve is enclosed by the trees of the Interior Atlantic Forest. Once spanning much of Brazil, Argentina and Paraguay, this forest formerly covered 300 million acres. Today only seven percent remains; the largest portion (3.2 million acres) of which is in Paraguay. About 150,000 acres are within the Mbaracayú Reserve, overseen by the Moisés Bertoni Foundation based in Paraguay's capital city, Asunción.

From the air, visitors are able to marvel at the size of the forest—an area only slightly smaller than the state of Connecticut—and bear witness to the tremendous threats to it. When established in the 1980s, the reserve blended into the rest of the forest. More recently, with land grabs for legal and illegal crops triggering deforestation and illegal logging, Mbaracayú's boundaries are now clear from the air. Jagged patches signal the presence of marijuana crops; roads in from Brazil provide easy access for illegal loggers, and the evenly spaced, well manicured fields of soy beans reveal the intense pressure to convert the forest into profitable farmland.

After touching down on a small dirt runaway, visitors are greeted by the beauty of both the forest and the grasslands. Known as *cerrado,* the grasslands spring from the deep red clay soil found in the area. The understory of the lowland forest is home to an incredible array of ferns that can reach the height of small trees.

The habitats of Mbaracayú are some of the most important in South America for the conservation of bird species threatened by extinction. According to The Nature Conservancy, it is one of only two sites in the world known to contain a population of the critically endangered White-Winged Nightjar *Caprimulgus candicans*. Other threatened species there include the Black-Fronted Piping-Guan, *Pipile jacutinga*, Vinaceous Amazon, *Amazona vinacea* and the Helmeted Woodpecker, *Dryocopus galeatus*. While these birds may be difficult to spot even within the reserve, your chances are better of seeing a Harpy Eagle or hearing a Bell Bird's distinct cry. Some describe it as three dissonant notes that sound like a clanging anvil.

As darkness falls on Mbaracayú, much that was hidden during the daytime emerges. The elusive nocturnal jaguar makes its home here: the reserve establishes a vital corridor for this majestic cat, which needs large, pristine areas in which to hunt. Far away from the cities, the night sky is a dazzling array of stars and planets, and although you're unlikely to actually spot a jaguar, you're at least almost guaranteed a good view of the Southern Cross. You'll also see the eternal cloudiness of the Milky Way and some shooting stars if you're patient. As the jungle insects sing you softly to sleep, you'll be thankful that you visited this emerald island amid a sea of greenery.

## MADAME LYNCH

### By Kelley Coyner

The lusty and vengeance-filled story of Madame Lynch, and her lover President Mariscal Francisco Solano López, has inspired numerous historical novels and biographies. Though both are colorful characters, it is the rags-to-riches and back-to-rags story of Eliza Lynch, a refugee from the Irish potato famine, that still captures the imagination more than one hundred years later.

The story begins when Paraguay's then-President Carlos Antonio López sent his son Francisco Solano to Europe for a grand tour. Franciso met Eliza Lynch there and the two fell hopelessly in love. She returned with him to Asuncíon, pregnant with the first of their five children. Due to prior commitments, the two never married. From the moment of her arrival on the docks of the Paraguay River, the "temptress" was greeted with scorn by the ladies of Paraguay's capital. Madame Lynch exacted her revenge on high society and on Paraguay's treasury. Eliza and Francisco went on a 15 year spending spree, buying and building all over Asunción. When money ran low in the national accounts, Eliza confiscated the jewels of high society women at costume balls styled as charity galas. Allegedly, the balls benefited Paraguay's armies during the doomed War of the Triple Alliance. Whether or not those on the front lines ever benefited from these crooked galas is still disputed. It is known, however, that Eliza reserved the least desirable ball costumes for Francisco's mother and sisters.

A traveler can still see many of the public works and private buildings attributed to Lynch and López. The white marbled Palacio de Gobierno commissioned by López took many years (and many lives) to complete. Today's Gran Hotel was originally Madame Lynch's home, and today it hosts a formal tea in Eliza's gilded salon. The 19th century train station, commissioned by López Sr., and recently reopened, stands on the Plaza Uraguaya. Lynch and López are said to have traveled from here to Piribebuey, the site of López Junior's military headquarters during the War of the Triple Alliance, and Lynch's country retreat.

Eliza died in obscurity in Paris some years after the war. Nevertheless, you can still visit Madame Lynch and her lover in Asunción. López's remains are now interred in the dubiously named Pantheon of Heroes, downtown, while Eliza rests at Cementerio Recoleta, the national cemetery. Longtime dictator, Gen. Stroessner, brought Eliza back and honored her with a stately mausoleum in this sprawling city of graves. Perhaps he sought to replicate Evita Peron's posthumous popular canonization. Perhaps he succeeded.

# CHACO ROAD WARRIOR

By Kelley Coyner, Texas, U.S.A

Some trips yield their pleasures like penny candy. You step aboard, look through a window, or walk through a museum, and beauty, intrigue and history overwhelm you. Paraguay's Gran Chaco however, the Mount Everest of road trips, makes you sweat for its rewards as you push forward attempting to conquer South America's last frontier. The 15 hour road trip across El Chaco from Asunción, Paraguay to Villa Montes, Bolivia boasts extreme conditions, both hot and desolate. It is a tough journey which is completely unforgettable.

Crossing the Río Paraguay, the road warrior leaves behind the muggy, overgrown landscape of eastern Paraguay and enters a browner scene that can be dry and dusty. Along the road is also the low slung dwelling of the Guaraní--an indigenous people displaced from other parts of Paraguay. During the rainy season, you may encounter shallow lakes populated with pink flamingos along the roadway. Pozo Colorado, an hour or so further down the road, is the last stop for gas or water for hours. From here there are several options.

Containing 60 percent of the country's landmass but less than 10 percent of its population, there is a lot of diverse territory to cover here. *Chaco Bajo* or Low Chaco offers palm trees and marshes. In the Middle Chaco, Mennonites inhabit a hub in Filadelfia—one of the alleged post-World War II retreats of Josef Mengele, the infamous death doctor of Auschwitz. In the Alto Chaco, there is the huge Parque Nacional Defensores. These three areas form the Paraguayan section of the Chaco, which also spans Argentina, Bolivia, and Brazil.

Taking a right at the Paraguayan military installation we fill up on gas and water before heading down a sandy road. It is five hours to the border of Bolivia and on a busy day, a solitary bus may pass showering anything and anyone in its way with fine sand. Tarps tightly pulled and gear double wrapped fail to keep the dust from penetrating duffels, backpacks and plastic-encased food stores.

There is no one out here. There are a few signs for ranches but no sign of ranchers. Even the ubiquitous road equipment has disappeared.

A few minutes before reaching the border there is a sign for Canada El Carmen and truck repairs. Destination reached. Workers at the truck stop will show you to the small metal cross honoring casualties of war. (Notably the trucks seem to enjoy better shelter than the humans here.) They will also hop aboard to help you find the reserve at Canada El Carmen as it is easy to miss.

A site of more than 40 battles during the Chaco War between 1932-1935, the area is valuable for a number of reasons; it is also the only place in the Gran Chaco where there is fresh water all year long. The *Palo Barrocho*—a water gorging tree whose trunk serves as its reservoir—is a further attraction. (The best specimen is just on the other side of the border in a neighboring park run by a Bolivian conservation organization.) Even during a daylight walk or drive you are likely to encounter trees filled with dozens of birds including parrots and some snakes. Mammals are trickier however, and you will most likely encounter only small rodents or, if you are lucky, a giant pig. Jaguars typically keep a night schedule, rendering only their footprints a reminder of their ethereal presence.

For the lucky few who manage to spot a rare daytime jaguar, it is hard to see how the see how the site could be "improved."

## BREAKING EGGS OR KNOCKING OVER CHAIRS

By Kelley Coyner

"Why is the chair turned over?" The tour guide didn't understand my question. The setting was the formal salon in the Palacio del Gobierno on a sweltering January morning. A painting depicting Paraguay's moment of independence occupies a prominent place in the room used when the President addresses the nation. In the painting, a chair is turned over.

The painting's historical explanation goes back to 1537, when the Spanish founded Asunción and made it the capital of this part of South America. Asunción remained the capital until the general administrative reorganization in 1776 when the Spanish created the Viceroyalty of La Plata, and with the stroke of a pen Paraguay was demoted to a province with a governor reporting to a Viceroy in Buenos Aires.

Spanish power in Europe collapsed when Napoleon invaded Spain, and Spain's civil and military apparatus in the Americas would soon fall bay the wayside as well. On May 25, 1810, a junta in Buenos Aires deposed the Viceroy and asserted its sovereignty over the entire Viceroyalty of La Plata. Asunción announced that it was not subject to the junta in Buenos Aires.

But a Spanish governor still ruled in Asunción, and everyone waited for the other shoe to drop. A group of Creole conspirators began meeting secretly in the Martinez Saenz house, now known as the Casa de la Independencia, a national monument and museum. On the night of May 14, 1811, the revolutionaries moved on the garrison. Governor Velazco's guards and emissaries stalled for time. Finally the conspirators called for church bells to be rung, bringing the city's population into the streets to assemble in front of the garrison. At three o'clock in the morning of May 15, 1811, Lieutenant Vincente Iturbe carried the revolutionaries' demands to the Governor. As Governor Velazco continued to stall, the revolutionaries moved two cannons and aimed them at the governor's residence. Seeing this, Velazco accepted the conditions imposed upon him by the revolutionaries, and Paraguay became a sovereign nation.

So why is the chair overturned in the painting? According to the tour guide, it is an allegory representing the overthrow of Spanish colonial power.

Jesuit Ruins, Trinidad. Photo by Freyja Ellis.

# BRAZIL

**The Land of Tomorrow**

In Brazil you will find great wealth and grinding poverty, beautiful beaches and filthy waterways fouled by industrial pollution, honest, open people and some of the most crooked politicians in Latin America. In a country where many of the national heroes are of African heritage—entertainers such as Gilberto Gil or soccer players such as Péle or Ronaldinho—racism is still a huge social problem. Some suburbs of Rio and Sao Paulo are as swank as any in the world, but the favelas, or slums, of those same cities are among the most dangerous anywhere. It is as rich in natural resources as any country in the world, yet it cannot seem to escape its status as an underdeveloped nation. "Brazil is the country of tomorrow" goes the famous quote "and it always will be."

Brazil's struggles with globalization, modernity, and its own identity should not prevent you from visiting. Despite all of its problems, Brazil will always have at least one thing going for it: its people. Brazilians are some of the friendliest, sensual, and most cheerful and most open people on the planet, and they like nothing better than sharing their country—which they all deeply love, warts and all—with guests and visitors.

Brazil has something for everyone. Nature buff? In addition to the Amazon River, the mightiest in the world, Brazil boasts thousands of miles of coastline and the Pantanal, a massive wetland home to jaguars, crocodiles, thousands of species of birds and more. Like to party? Brazil is, of course, home to the biggest one in the world: Carnaval. 'Nuff said. How about history? A Portuguese colony, Brazil was home to the Portuguese court and royal family for in the 19th century before Portugal was defeated and occupied by Napoleon's armies. Beach bum? If I need to tell you about Brazil's beaches—does the word Ipanema ring a bell?—you've been living on another planet.

Brazil is much, much more than Carnival and soccer. In the following pages, read what travelers like you have found among the cities, jungles and beaches of South America's largest country. Follow in their footsteps from the beaches to the cities, from the jungles to the islands, from the parties to the soccer stadiums.

# THE PANTANAL WETLANDS

By Sandy Guy, Ballarat, Australia

Think of Brazil and chances are you'll picture Rio de Janeiro's famous Carnival, glamorous Copacabana Beach, or the primordial Amazon rainforest. But this vast country, South America's largest, has a host of little-known yet fascinating destinations to explore.

I found one of them in remote Mato Grosso do Sul state in southwest Brazil. The Pantanal, an immense area of wetlands about half the size of France, stretches across this isolated part of Brazil and into nearby Bolivia and Paraguay. The sparsely-populated Pantanal—also known as Terra de Ninguem (No-man's Land)—contains wildlife in abundance: approximately 650 bird species, 50 reptile and 80 mammal species call it home.

From chaotic São Paulo our flight to the city of Campo Grande, the capital of Mato Grosso do Sul, took around one-and-a-half hours. From here we traveled by bus via the bitumen and gravel Transpantaneira, the only road through the southern Pantanal region, passing fields dotted with white Brahman cattle and dirt tracks leading to isolated cattle ranches along the way. Metre-high termite mounds dot the landscape and you can see giant emu-like birds running across the lush green landscape.

Five hours drive from Campo Grande, we turned off the Transpantaneira onto a rutted track towards Xaraés Ranch, 30 kilometres (18 miles) off the main road. Here Pousada Xaraés sits in grand isolation amid a 4,000-hectare property teeming with wildlife.

Recently refurbished, the pousada is a comfortable oasis in this remote location. Simple, but tastefully furnished, it has spacious lounge areas and modern conveniences such as air conditioning. After settling into one of 17 rustic rooms we enjoyed dinner featuring the Brazilian staple, beans and rice with farofa (manioc flour), along with vegetables, local beef, and piranha soup—a local delicacy. The coffee, of course, is excellent—this is Brazil after all.

During the rainy season (October to March), rivers in the Pantanal flood, inundating much of the low-lying area and creating patches of dry land thick with trees where cattle and native animals alike cluster together to escape the rising waters.

Horseback is the only way to see the Pantanal, and fortunately Pousada Xaraés has mild-mannered horses that can be ridden even by novices. Local cowboys with straw hats and spurs on their boots loaded the animals with thick woollen blankets and comfortable saddles as we prepared for a half-day trek across the property.

As our horses picked their way across tea-coloured waters we spied loads of exotic animals, including armadillos, black howler monkeys, iguanas, tapirs, giant anteaters, capybaras, and some of the more than 650 species of birds found here, including toucans with their huge multi-coloured beaks, Jabiru storks, and hyacinth macaws, one of the world's rarest birds.

Although huge anacondas measuring up to eight metres inhabit the surrounding marshes, our guide, Xaraés' owner João Cardadeiro, reassures us that they are shy around humans and rarely seen on the ranch. Caimans—a sort of small alligator—cruise through the waters of the river that winds through Xaraés Ranch, their snouts just poking above the surface. Although it looks inviting, it's not a good idea to swim here: the waters are infested with piranha. We took to canoes instead, spending many peaceful hours paddling along the silent, tranquil waterway.

From Xaraés it's a three-hour drive by dirt road to the small town of Bonito—meaning "beautiful"—in the south-west corner of Mato Grosso do Sul. Surrounding the town are cattle properties rich with pockets of lush jungle, extraordinarily clear rivers, cascading waterfalls, and subterranean caves with sapphire waters and ancient stalactites hanging from the ceiling. Bonito's beautiful rivers, which are thankfully piranha-free, are a natural freshwater aquarium teeming with multi-coloured fish. At Rio Sucuri, an 8000 hectare ranch 18 kilometres (11 miles) from Bonito, we donned wetsuits for a drift snorkel along the Sucuri River.

The river winds through a veritable Garden of Eden, luxuriant with ancient palms and thick foliage. But it is the super-transparent waters, up to six metres (19 feet) in depth that are so special. Drifting with the current you see scores of large, brilliantly coloured fish, some up to one-metre in length, swimming gracefully between water plants swaying in the current. You have a feeling of weightlessness and utter tranquility as you float along the river, which is silent but for the squeals of monkeys darting amidst the verdant canopy of trees overhead.

In the balmy evening we returned to Bonito and our simple but pleasant pousada, one of several on offer in the town. Later, we joined locals in one of Bonito's many outdoor cafés to enjoy an icy Caipirinha, Brazil's national drink—a knock-your-socks-off blend of cachaça (sugar cane brandy), crushed lime and sugar—as we planned another day drifting along the stunningly beautiful rivers of this isolated, yet captivating part of Brazil.

Sandy Guy is an Australian-based free-lance writer who lives Ballarat, about one-hour west of Melbourne. Sandy developed a passion for travel in 1975 when, aged 18, she drove an old car from Melbourne to far north Queensland. She has been travelling ever since.

A journalist for more than 20 years, Sandy has a B.A. in Professional Writing from Deakin University in Melbourne, has worked as a sessional lecturer at the University of Ballarat, and has contributed to more than 50 publications in Australia and overseas.

A mother of four, one of her most memorable journeys was the months she spent backpacking through Italy, Spain and France—on a shoestring budget—with her older children when they were aged 11 and 14.

# BIRDWATCHING IN THE PANTANAL

## By Fiona Leslie, Chester, England

The Pantanal (meaning swamp in Portuguese) stretches from the Matto Grosso in the west of Brazil across to Bolivia and drains into Paraguay's Río Paraná. The area is home to some of the most diverse habitats for birds, from rivers, plains, flooded meadows and tropical forests to humid palm groves. Traveling down the Trans-Pantanal highway from Cuiabá, birds and wildlife abound in the water-filled roadside ditches—from kingfishers and parakeets to capybara and caiman. It's a voyage by boat, horseback, or on foot to see these natural wonders.

An afternoon silent-paddle up the Rio Claro is the perfect way to hear the clacking dawn call of the Chaco Chachalaca, which is soon joined by various noisy Monk Parakeets and Blue-fronted Parrots. Then the softer rising call of the Undulated Tinamou or the Barred and Great Antshrikes competes with the Ringed and Amazon Kingfishers which clatter up and down the banks and the gentle warble of the Thrush-like Wren. A striking Rufescent Tiger-Heron can be spotted in a tree or a Striated Heron patiently poised on a shaded log whilst an Olivaceous Cormorant flies downstream. As the orange sun rises up from the adjacent plains, perhaps a Crested Curassow or a Dusky-legged Guan will be seen clumsily balanced high in a tree or the bright red and yellow flash of a Crested Oropendola dashing in and out of its skillfully woven nests, which dangles from on high like nature's bauble decorations. Where the river slows down and pads form, a disturbed Wattled Jacana flaps awkwardly across the surface, revealing its yellow wing flashes, and nearby in a low bush a Donacobius with its striking black and white tail sits. It is possible to catch a glimpse of the shy, awkward Sun Bittern, then a sudden whoosh from a tall tree to the side and a Black-collared Hawk flaps away. Around the next bend an Osprey swoops down to the surface, its large strong talons extended for a fresh fish meal.

Returning to terra firma, a low-branched tree is bed to ten slumbering Guira cuckoos. Across the plains of roaming cattle, the Great Rheas live beside the Great and Smooth-Billed Anis, Bay-winged Cowbirds and Cattle Egrets. Pairs of Southern Lapwings peck grass with Buff-necked Ibis here from the Tierra del Fuego. In a rut pool darts a Solitary Sandpiper and a Limpkin, and in a nearby pond White-faced Ducks paddle. Here fly Savannah and Roadside Hawks, as well as Snail Kites. The water-filling meadows are dotted with the huge white forms of Jabiru Storks, their large stick nests shared with squawking Mitered Parakeets. In a palm grove, Hyacinth Macaws feast on hard nuts whilst the distinctive water-drop-like call of a Troupial resounds. The persistent hammer of a Blond-crested Woodpecker is one of many of that family here up with the Toucans and Trogons. In a tree near the lodge sings a sweet Saffron Finch and in bushes bob Golden-billed Cardinals with Grayish Saltadors. The list of birding possibilities here is awe-inspiring and endless.

---

PANTANAL TRAVEL TIPS: April is the best time of the year to go, when the waters from the rainy season recede and the birds return to the area in droves. The Pantanal is of course a prime place to view birds, but it is also a great location to spot other wildlife. Among the animals in this area (about half the size of France) are river otters, jaguars, deer, crocodiles, and iguanas, so don't just keep those binocular pointed skyward.

---

Pantanal Wetlands. Photo courtesy of Brasil Tourism Embratur.

# IGUASSU FALLS—A BRAZILIAN PERSPECTIVE

By David Vincent, Lenox, Massachusetts, U.S.A.

At the precipice of the Salto Union gangplank, with a several hundred-foot-high curtain of water, enveloping mists and a thunderous concussion drowning out all other sound, one feels almost a part of the majestic Iguassu Falls. It's not difficult to imagine Spanish explorer Cabeza de Vaca, in the year 1549, awestruck by the very same view.

Long before Europeans ever set foot in this subtropical jungle region at the border of Brazil, Argentina and Paraguay, the indigenous Gauraní revered Iguassu Falls as a sacred location and the inspiration of tribal lore. The name Iguassu is derived from Tupi-Guaraní and means "great or big water." According to legend, a god coveted a beautiful young girl named Naipú. She spurned his affections and instead fled with her mortal lover down the river by canoe. Stung by Naipú's rejection, the god cleaved the land beneath the river, creating the waterfalls and converting Naipú to a tree in the middle of the falls and her lover to a rock at the base, forever unable to touch.

Geologists have a different version of the falls' inception, believing them to be the result of a volcanic eruption and ensuing earthquake that buckled the land along a fault line beneath the Iguazu River. This accident of nature forged the splendor of Iguassu Falls' 275 individual cascades (during the seasonal low) spread along a horseshoe-shaped rim nearly two miles wide. Taller than Niagara Falls and four times as wide, the spectacle of Iguassu in its lush jungle setting is said to have led Eleanor Roosevelt to proclaim, "Poor Niagara." While roughly two-thirds of the falls are located on the Argentinian side of the river, the view from the Brazilian side has a decidedly panoramic advantage. It is also from the Brazilian side that one can best glimpse the amazing Garganta del Diablo (Devil's Throat, located on on the Argentinian side), the tallest of the falls at nearly 100 meters (about 350 feet) high.

Iguassu Falls can transform a neophyte photographer into a professional, though one should take care not to make a sacrificial offering of a high-priced digital camera to the falls. Getting wet is unavoidable but it's also half the fun. The walkways are brilliantly designed to be unobtrusive and yet permit visitors to walk over, under and along the falls at various points. Some of the perches are not for the faint of heart, but witnessing the awesome power of the torrents of water is a transcendent experience. Zodiac rubberized crafts equipped with high-powered outboards can zoom visitors up to the base of the falls for a high-priced and exhilarating shower. For an even heftier fee, scenic helicopter tours are available.

The small town of Foz do Iguaçu is an excellent option for overnight stays and has much to offer in its own right. The town (and neighboring communities) counts roughly 270,000 inhabitants and over a hundred lodging possibilities. The Iguaçuenses (locals) are composed of a fascinating array of diverse ethnic groups, including Africans, Arabs Chinese, Germans, Italians and Ukrainians. Inexpensive ethnic restaurants and churrascerias (Brazilian steakhouses) abound. The Parque das Aves (Bird Park) is an excellent place to photograph uncaged native, tropical birds.

A worthy side trip can also be made to the Itaipu Dam, the world's largest hydroelectric dam that accounts for nearly a quarter of Brazil's total energy consumption. On a practical note, Foz do Iguaçu citizens approved a controversial name change to "Iguassu" in 2005, in hopes of facilitating web searches by foreign tourists.

David Carr Vincent originally hails from Lenox, Massachussetts, but currently resides in Chicago, Illinois, where he teaches social studies at Glenbrook North High School. A graduate of Bates College in Lewiston, Maine, David earned a Master's degree in Latin American and Caribbean Studies at Indiana University.

Carr Vincent has traveled to 13 countries in Latin America and taught English in Montevideo, Uruguay. He is married to his main traveling partner and best friend, Erin. Some of his craziest adventures while traveling include looking for anacondas in a Bolivian swamp—finding them—and going deep into an unmapped silver mine in Potosí, Bolivia.

## FOZ TROPICANA BIRD PARK By Freyja Ellis

Whilst on the Brazilian side of the Foz do Iguaçu Falls, it is well worth spending an hour or two at the fantastic Parque das Aves Foz Tropicana located opposite the entrance to the falls. An independent park, featuring over 900 birds of 150 species from Brazil and further afield, the park acts as a conservation site preserving some of the endangered species in South America.

The park offers the opportunity to view rare birds and learn more about these and other creatures and their habitats. A wide range of toucans, macaws (including the vulnerable Hyacinth Macaw), parrots (including the endangered Purple-bellied Parrot, Red-tailed Amazon Parrot), hoatzins, ibis and flamingos can be viewed close up. Large screens televise live from birds nest allowing visitors the opportunity to see hatchings and young chicks in the nest. In addition, the park includes butterflies and reptiles such as caiman and boa constrictors highlighting the wildlife of the Amazon.

There are numerous walk-through enclosures allowing close contact with the birds and butterflies, including the mischievous Macaw enclosure towards the end of the 1500 metre trail. There is also the opportunity to have your picture taken with a Macaw posing on your arm—a must for any South American photo album.

# CURITIBA

By Kyle Hedlund, Vancouver, British Columbia, Canada

Kyle W. Hedlund is a Canadian writer and teacher currently living in São Paulo, Brazil. He began traveling after graduation from university in 1992, and has worked his way through five continents. He is presently gearing up for a return to Vancouver, Canada, where he dreams of one day establishing a permanent address.

The craziest place Hedlund has ever visited is Osorezan (roughly Mt. Dread) in northern Japan. It's an old volcano crater filled with mist, crows, and the spirits of the dead.

*Rio is an aging starlet with breast implants and dark roots. She still turns heads, but the make-up is applied quite thickly. São Paulo is a tough-looking guy in a bar. He has a blemished face and a scowl, but once you get to know him he smiles and buys you a drink. Salvador is the band: Commotion and the beat of a drum. Curitiba is the pretty girl sitting hopefully in the corner, ignored.*

Curitiba can best be described as nice, with both the positive and negative implications of the word applying. Brazilians know it as their world-class example of urban order and livability. While the rest of the country, and indeed the world, were becoming more and more automobile-oriented, Curitiba managed to get people out of their cars and onto the buses and sidewalks. The result today is a pleasant "little" city of almost 2 million inhabitants.

*Rio is a fancy restaurant with a dirty kitchen. São Paulo is a working-class lunchonete with plastic tables. Salvador is street vendor food, odd flavours and smells both enticing and repellent. Curitiba is the salad bar at a churrascaria.*

A tourist bus plies a route around the city and environs, completing the 25-stop circuit in a little more than two hours (if you miss one bus, wait 30 minutes for the next). A cheap ticket allows for 4 stops and re-boardings, and leftover stubs can be carried over to other days. I bought my ticket on board and was advised that the botanical gardens, Ópera de Arame, Tanguá Park, and the panoramic tower were the most popular points at which to disembark. Short, recorded descriptions of each stop are given in Portuguese, Spanish, and English. One piece of advice: Once you board, it will take more than 2 hours to make it back to your starting point. Plan accordingly.

*Rio is Catholic, encased in ornament and ritual. São Paulo is evangelical Christian, expectant and convinced. Salvador is, predictably, Candomblé; spirited and sensual. Curitiba is a cult, with free kool-aid for anyone.*

My impression of Curitibans is that they are trying hard to convince the rest of the country that their city is "better" than São Paulo or Rio. Without these two mega-cities in relative proximity, it would be hard for some residents to define themselves. While looking enviously at their more cosmopolitan neighbours, they want to be acknowledged as being in more fortunate circumstances. They would undoubtedly hate for too many outsiders to actually move next door, but they want everyone to share their conviction that theirs is a better quality of life.

*Rio plays bridge and sips Martinis on a patio. São Paulo deals poker with whisky in a smoky room. Salvador does dominoes and beer on rickety outdoor tables. Curitiba offers board games and wine coolers.*

I spent a couple of evenings looking for Curitiba's night life. What I saw were patches of life surrounded by quietness, both in time and space. Perhaps due to the early January holiday season, most shops were closed before dark. It seems to be a place where you find your favourite bar and become a regular. The individual establishments are spirited, but the shadows beyond the welcome signs are empty. Walking back to my homestay, just east of the center, between nine and 11 p.m. was eerily quiet.

*Rio is a beach-front condominium. São Paulo is an urban high-rise. Salvador is a row of restored colonial buildings. Curitiba is a single-family home with a garden.*

So Curitiba is a "nice" place. People live here, meaning there is enough commerce and leisure to entertain an interested traveler. There are far worse places to be "stuck" on business. If travel were a checklist then Curitiba would not warrant a box, but to see and experience everything that makes Brazil Brazilian, Curitiba is a must.

## QUILOMBOS

By Dr. Crit Minster

In colonial Brazil, African slaves frequently escaped their harsh conditions and made their way into the dense jungle, where they set up camps and communities: they banded together for mutual defense and to remain free. The largest Quilombo was Palmares, outside of the city of Recife. It was thought to have as many as 30,000 inhabitants, mostly escaped slaves, at one time. It was attacked and defeated by the Portuguese in 1694. Some quilombos were never defeated: in 1988, the descendents of the escaped slaves were granted legal title to the lands they had occupied for generations.

# SÃO PAULO

### By Stephen Keeling, Southampton, England

São Paulo is truly staggering. One of the world's largest cities and the biggest in South America, it's a vast, sprawling metropolis—approximately 19 million people live in the greater São Paulo area—and it is the financial capital of Brazil. Often skipped by tourists in favour of Rio, São Paulo is far more than just a frenetic business centre: the sheer size of the place can be overwhelming, but it's one of the most cosmopolitan cities on the continent, host to an incredibly varied range of restaurants, bars and cultural attractions that surpass its more famous rival to the east.

The city evolved from a mission established on the banks of the Rio Tietê in 1554, but it was coffee that laid the foundation of modern São Paulo. From the 1870s, a boom in coffee cultivation in lands nearby meant the economy mushroomed, the profits rapidly ploughed into manufacturing.

The need for cheap labour increased immigration, and today, São Paulo's diverse ethnic make-up is perhaps one of its most endearing qualities. Unknown to most visitors, it's the largest Japanese city outside Japan, with over one million of its citizens claiming Japanese ancestry—the district of Liberdade is known as Japantown and is the best place to absorb East Asian culture with a Latin twist. São Paulo also contains sizeable Arab, Chinese, Eastern European, Italian, Korean and Portuguese communities, making it one of the best places to eat in South America, from cavernous churrascarias to Chinese noodle bars. The Jardins District contains the most fashionable restaurants and numerous bars—São Paulo's dynamic nightlife is equally as colourful with Rua 13 de Maio and Vila Madalena hip places to grab a drink.

The Butantã Institute is perhaps the city's most famous tourist attraction, a leading center for the study of poisonous snakes with thousands of deadly serpents on display, but it's also worth checking out the city's absorbing museums. Avenue Paulista, the financial heart of the city, is where you'll find the *Museu de Arte de São Paulo* (MASP), a huge art gallery containing an exquisite collection of Brazilian and European art, complemented by the equally impressive *Museu de Arte Sacra*, located on Avenue Tirandentes and loaded with superb pieces from Brazil's colonial era.

But the best way to get to grips with the soul of São Paulo is through its two most vigorous passions: capoeira and soccer. São Paulo has a vibrant capoeira scene, the Brazilian martial art performed in numerous bars and at events organised by ABADÁ Capoeira São Paulo. For sports fans, a pilgrimage to the Estádio Cícero Pompeu de Toledo in the suburb of Morumbi is a must, preferably on a match day when the raucous atmosphere in the stadium equals the skills on the pitch. São Paulo won the Libertadores Cup and FIFA World Club Championship in 2005, both for the third time, cementing its position as Brazil's most successful soccer team—an awesome achievement.

Ignore your first impressions: São Paulo needs time to be appreciated, but it's one of the most absorbing and energetic cities on the continent, a multi-cultural powerhouse with plenty to do and see.

## MONUMENT TO THE BANDIERANTES

### By Kip Fry

People speeding along the expansive Avenida Brigadeiro Antônio Luís in São Paulo often see the monument to the Bandeirantes, but to them it's only a blur. Only those who stop and get out of their cars will really be able to study the Monumento Bandeiras, the sculpture of the Brazilian pioneers. These people have to admit something: they can feel movement in the sculpture. It moves with the same strain the Bandeirantes themselves had to muster to haul such massive objects across the forbidding landscape.

Several centuries ago, the Bandeirantes clawed their way into the heart of Brazil searching for gold and Indian slaves. The granite monument, possibly 100 feet long, depicts the pioneers as they trudged their way into uncharted territory. They are encumbered with an enormous and obviously weighty boat behind them. Every muscle and tendon shows in these statues, emphasizing the effort that was demanded to achieve such a Herculean task.

Two men on horses lead the way: they are the only ones who have it so easy. Following is a long row of men doing the hard work. Ropes harnessed around their necks, they seem to move as one in a synchronized dance. Behind them is a bare-breasted woman suckling a newborn baby. Even through the hard stone, her gentile features can be seen. She is a native with shoulder-length hair and a necklace of teeth hanging around her neck. Her cheekbones are high. Next to her stands another Indian woman and a man with straight hair and a beard, obviously European.

At the rear of the sculpture is the boat. Here the men push, their legs extended with exertion, calves and thighs bulging. They are exhausted, but that doesn't keep them all from pressing—all but one. A Bandeirante has collapsed and is being carried by his compatriots. Another behind him strains and throws his head back as if calling to God for mercy.

There is a definite irony in the look of the piece. Although the sculpture has a 17th-century theme, it is 20th century in style. The Bandeirantes in Victor Brecheret's sculpture pound through hard, thankless and uncompromising work, done largely in anonymity, while the sculpture's author is famous for their depiction.

People on the Avenida may see the sculpture from a distance. But they should look at it at arm's length, as well. Only then can they see the detail and the stories these faces tell.

# ILHA GRANDE

### By Steven Cassidy, London, England

Ilha Grande is one of the most stunningly beautiful islands you can visit in Brazil. It is touted as 100 percent stress-free, with bountiful beaches, steamy rainforest, rolling mountains and colonial architecture.

The island was cut off from the outside world for a long time and has only recently been accessible to tourists. This means the island is pristine: the signs of mass tourism have not encroached on Ilha Grande, making it an adventure for the independent traveler.

It also has an eerie reputation … visitors have only been allowed since 1994, as before that it was a penal island. Rumour has it that political prisoners were held on Ilha Grande, and mysterious ruins from this period dot the jungle. Even further back, it was Brazil's quarantine station, a leper colony, and before that a pirate nest used by the infamous Jorge Grego.

The only hidden treasures today are wide beaches, excellent diving, abundant hummingbirds and monkeys, and the chance to kick back and enjoy the feeling of all stress dropping away.

The best place to stay is the beautiful town of Abraão. The charming, colourful houses, palm trees, a simple church, and pretty pousadas can be overwhelming. Many of the isolated islanders are descendants of original warders and prisoners. Life goes on in the street—kids chase each other, dogs bark, women stand at gates and men shuffle and watch the world go by … All this isolation has hidden some stunning attractions from the world.

Hiking trails dot the jungle-covered mountains and the beaches are so hidden that fishing boats are the only way to get to them. One of the best sandy spots is Praia Lopes Mendes, which requires half an hour on a fishing boat, followed by ten minutes trekking across the narrow neck of the island on a small trail.

Jungle closes in and the trail passes huge groves of natural bamboo. Ants cover the trail and colourful mushrooms grow on the boles of trees. After ten minutes of walking along the trail, you'll descend and eventually spill out onto Lopes Mendes beach—wow!!

I dare you not to stop and stare. Your eyes gaze out at two miles of uninhabited beach. The curve of snow-white sand stretches in a wide arc and is book-ended by jungle peaks. Palm trees sway above, wild monkeys gambol, and the roaring surf rings in your ears as it crashes against boulders at the far end of the beach.

I consider myself fortunate to have seen it when I did—in another ten years it may have been discovered by the tourist hordes and the time warp of Ilha Grande will have gone forever.

---

ILHA GRANDE TRAVEL TIPS: The island has 16 trails, one of which (number four), takes you to a beach which is good for surfing and where you can pay a small fee to camp. Enjoy the natural beauty of the beach without many, or any, people around.

---

*"Look at me and tell me if I don't have Brazil in every curve of my body."*
*-Carmen Miranda, Brazilian Singer and Actress (1909-1955)*

## CAIPIRINHA

By Michelle Hopey

Ingredients: 2 tsp. granulated sugar; 1 lime (8 wedges); 2 1/2 oz. Cachaça; Ice Cubes; an 8 ounce highball glass or old fashioned style cocktail glass.

Mixing instructions: Loosen the juices of the lime by rolling the lime around, then cut the lime in half and muddle sugar into the lime with a pestle or spoon. Afterwards, cut the lime into small wedges and place them in a glass. Fill the glass with ice and pour in the Cachaça.

Originally from Brazil, this sharp, refreshing drink is popular up and down both sides of the South American continent. In Brazil it's the second most ordered drink and is the number one mixed drink. (The number one all-around drink sold is, of course, cerveja or to non-Portuguese speakers, beer.) Perhaps it is the Capirinha's birthplace coupled with its exotic name, pronounced Cap-er-e-nah, that lends it self to the powerful image of posh, wild Latinos sunbathing along a Brazilian beach or clubbing it in the late night. But whatever the reason for its watering hole fame, tasting the real deal in Latin America is essential, especially since Cachaça, the Brazilian liquor made from distilled sugar cane, is a hard find elsewhere. In fact, in many foreign cities you'll find knock-offs, substituting vodka for Cachaça and in some places it has become a new drink altogether called the caiprivodkas. And while still tasty, these are just not the same as the traditional, sweet-tasting, alcohol-buzzing, Brazilian-created, Caipirinha. Enjoy.

# RIO DE JANEIRO

By Kerry L. Smith, Pembroke, Massachusetts, U.S.A.

Soaring twenty stories above the rippling shoreline of the Atlantic Ocean, the tops of the lush green trees of the Amazon jungle resemble clusters of broccoli. Inaudible are the sounds of roaming monkeys, birds and the rippling conversations between flowing waterfalls and the rocky nooks they caress. From the perch of a hang glider, only the forest's beauty is at hand.

Flying through the air in a tandem flight is possibly the best way to view the breathtaking beauty of Rio de Janeiro's tropical landscape—far up, up and away from the hubbub of Carnival parades or the roar of Jeep engines scaling dusty, rocky trails to the tops of various peaks throughout the mighty Amazon.

An estimated 1.7 million tourists come to Rio every year for the festival each February, when temperatures on the white sand beaches can reach 105 degrees. A majority of out-of-towners sign up for jungle tours to get a closer look at ancient ruins and marvel at the exotic landscape and animal life. However, adventurous travelers in-the-know sneak away from the well-hiked path to take a dip in hidden waterfalls: the icy water will cleanse their souls of bad energy. Occasionally, lit candles can be seen flickering in small pools of water throughout the jungle—their presence is evidence of the Candomblé religion, also known as voodoo.

Romantic photographs can be taken at the site of a Chinese pagoda peeking out from the jungle. From there, an unforgettable view of Rio and the three beaches of Ipanema, Leme and Copacabana are spread out below. One can see the towering statue of Christ the Redeemer, a gift from France that stands 100-feet tall atop Corcovado Mountain (the statue is currently in the running to be listed among the New Wonders of the World). People young and old from all over the world come to climb a lengthy stairwell that wraps around the mountain to bask in the glory of this enormous statue.

After the jungle tour, many take a stroll through the botanical garden nearby; the Jardim Botânico is a sanctuary for over 8,000 species of plants and rare trees, as well as a scattering of ponds and greenhouses filled with colorful flowers. A budget-priced double occupancy hotel room in downtown Ipanema (the beach is just a 10 minute walk or a 5 minute drive away) can cost as low as $70 for five days. Food in Rio is tasty and cheap. One can survive on a diet of delicious black beans and rice, coconut juice (which is served straight up; street vendors cut a hole in the fruit with a machete and place a straw inside) and cups of an energy drink known as Acie (made from a combination of a native purple Amazonian fruit, crushed ice and oats).

Past numerous tiny shops selling brightly painted trinkets—musical instruments, Carnival costumes, Brazilian bikinis and home decorations—is the very popular "four corners," the location of the bar where the song "The Girl From Ipanema" was written. Here, patrons pull up a stool, order a cold Caipirinha, and shake their bon-bons to the sounds of Samba music flowing in through the open windows.

Kerry Smith is a freelance writer living in New York City. She graduated with a Bachelor of Arts from Fitchburg State College in Fitchburg, Massachusetts, U.S.A. and mainly works as a music journalist (she has written for *Rolling Stone*, MTV.com, Vh1.com and the Associated Press). Smith is currently working on a non-fiction novel and writing an encyclopedia about Indie Rock music. When she is not working, she enjoys yoga, salsa dancing and painting.

Her dream excursion is to one day walk along the Great Wall of China.

Hang gliding over Rio. Photo courtesy of Kerry L. Smith.

# THE COLONIAL HEART OF RIO

## By Steven Cassidy, London, England

Behind its packed beaches and modern skyscrapers is the colonial soul of Rio de Janerio. When the Portuguese came they brought a whiff of old Europe with their palaces, forts and tiled houses. Unfortunately, not much remains of this 450-year-old part of town, for Rio was a victim of short-sighted city planning when it expanded in the forties and fifties. Much history has been sacrificed on the altar of progress, and huge skyscrapers now line the Rio Branco. If you know where to look, though, there are some real gems—cobbled streets, dazzling cathedrals and colonial architecture.

The old colonial maps would probably still recognize the area north of Praça XV. The Rua Primeiro cuts through the western edge of the area, home to a tourist market. Here you can buy Brazilian knick-knacks such as shawls, trinkets and plastic reproductions of Rio's famous statue, Christo Redentor. The Rua San José has kept its colonial authenticity; paved with enormous granite cobbles, it houses a colourful flower market. The Largo di Carioca has a book market featuring over twenty stalls, each with perhaps a thousand paperbacks.

Along Rua Chile is a giant wigwam made of glass. This is the modernist Catedral Metropolitana. It looks something like a giant Mayan pyramid reaching into the air from its 625-square-foot base. This is Rio's hat-tip to the modern architecture of Oscar Niemeyer, evident in São Paulo and Brasilia.

At the end of Rio Branco is a truly magnificent boulevard, the Avenida Vargas. At the eastern end, marooned amongst all the swirling traffic is the Igreja de Nossa Candelaria. This church is an expression of baroque sentiment and one of the few remains of that period left in Rio. Stepping inside inspires that sense of awe in a way that only great cathedrals can. The colossal nave reminds visitors of a miniature St. Peter's or St. Paul's, complete with frescoed dome and marble columns.

A trip up in the bondinho (mountain tram) is not to be missed. For the people of Santa Teresa, it is the only way down from their barrio high up on the mountain. You must have some agility and courage to climb aboard a rickety, fragile-looking tram. Once there are enough people aboard, it starts with a jolt. It is reminiscent of a ferris wheel ride as it wheezes uphill. You reach the Arcos da Lapa with a jolt. The aqueduct soars 100 feet (30 meters) off the ground and has only enough room for one tram to cross at a time. The view is astonishing—you can see straight across Rio to the docks.

## SURVIVING THE SAMBADROME

By Sandra Scott

There are some events that everyone should attend at least once in their lifetime: the Carnaval parades at the Sambadrome in Rio de Janeiro should definitely be included in that list. Rio throws the biggest and best Carnaval party in all the land, and the parades at the Sambadrome are the climax of this vibrant festival. The best Samba schools march on Sunday and Monday of Carnaval week. Each of the seven schools which march each night will perform for 90 minutes, a show which includes several elaborate floats and three to four thousand performers in tight formation.

Although exciting and fun, the Sambadrome can also be overwhelming with the large, reveling crowds. Here are some tips for surviving the Sambadrome:

Tickets should be purchased well in advance. Many companies offer 4- and 5-star hotel packages. Sometimes the tickets will be delivered to your hotel. Be warned: budget deals do not occur during Carnaval. Without a corporate or inside connection, most spectators end up with bleacher seating. Be aware of your area number: odd-numbered and even-numbered seats are accessed from entirely different areas.

The non-stop parade starts at 9 p.m. and ends about 12 hours later. To get a good viewing spot in areas without assigned seating, try to arrive three hours ahead of time. Wear comfortable footwear as most people stand the entire time. Tickets include an electronically coded neck tag and entry card. People without these tickets are not admitted. Although there is excellent organization and security, the Sambadrome holds 90,000 people, so all valuables should be left in the hotel safe.

Remember to take a couple bottles of water, some snacks, and a plastic raincoat. The best viewing in the bleacher seating area is on the aisle toward the area where the parade starts. Don't leave your spot unprotected. An empty spot doesn't stay empty long. Vendors with food, beverages, and t-shirts roam the stands. This is not a good time or place to drink alcohol if you really want to watch the parades. The dancing and music are non-stop and intense. Those who focus on drinking do not last long.

It will be daylight when you leave the Sambadrome. It may take 30 minutes or longer to get transportation, so ask a security person which way to go for either the buses or taxis.

# LAPA: THE PEOPLE'S THEATRE

By Suzy Khimm, New York City, U.S.A.

Strapping on my harlequin mask and grabbing a golden scepter, I headed straight into the streets of downtown Rio de Janeiro. Marching, dancing, and waving banners all the way across Lapa, the entire Tá Na Rua street theatre troupe (plus two enthusiastic gringos) dispersed itself throughout the public plaza.

Formed under the premise of "Carnivalizing Theatre and Theatricalizing Carnival," Tá Na Rua could not stand idly by while politicians proposed banning the use of masks during Rio's world-famous celebration. The troupe quickly decided to revert to its weapon of choice: spontaneous public spectacle and rhythmic celebration. The historic heart of Rio's Bohemian spirit, the Lapa neighborhood has undergone an artistic and cultural renaissance that is inciting revolutionary social change, Brazilian-style.

Since the 1950s, Lapa has united intellectuals, artists, politicians, and Cariocas (citizens of Rio) of all stripes under the iconic Arcos da Lapa, whose 42 arches served as an aqueduct during Brazil's colonial period. Much of its colonial architecture recently repainted and renovated, Lapa continues to stay faithful to its Bohemian roots: every weekend, swelling crowds transform its twisting streets and plazas into a vortex of bodies, movement, and music.

While Rio's music scene and lavish Carnival have seduced foreigners for decades, the artists of Lapa are intent on using these infectious traditions to go a step further—to combat local injustice and global inequality. The result: a modern-day social revolution rooted in centuries of Brazilian culture. And there's room for any willing soul to join in.

Leading the charge of Lapa's artist-revolutionaries are the Grupo Tá Na Rua and the Center for the Theatre of the Oppressed (CTO), both of which invite foreigners and locals alike to join their "people's theatre" through workshops, performances, and participatory gatherings.

Formed in 1980 during the Brazilian military dictatorship, Tá Na Rua ("It's in the Street") has brought its politically-driven street spectacles to audiences throughout Latin America and Europe. The group invites both actors and "non-actors" who are passionate about personal, artistic, and social transformation to come and train with them.

Housed directly next door to the Casa Tá Na Rua, the CTO has devised a form of community-based theatre that literally turns its audience members into actors—a technique that has been brought to shantytowns, mental hospitals, prisons, and disadvantaged populations across the globe; the CTO offers short-term workshops and internships year-round.

I had intended to come to Lapa for a morning's workshop; by mid-afternoon, I was a masked king, dancing on a staircase while a devil chased a defiant clown. In the words of Tá Na Rua director Amir Haddad, "To be an artist is a possibility that every human being has, independent of office, career, or artistic background. It's the possibility of full development, complete expression, and the right to happiness." There is no better place to experience the Brazilian spirit of "art for all" than in Rio's Lapa: witness your own transformation from spectator to participant in this historic hotbed of Brazilian popular culture.

Suzy Khimm is a journalist who has contributed to the *Los Angeles Times*, *Christian Science Monitor*, and AlterNet, among other publications. Having reported extensively from Brazil, she is currently based in Phnom Penh, Cambodia, where she is a staff writer for the *Cambodia Daily*. She is a graduate of Yale University.

Her upcoming travel destination is Angkor.

Rio. Photo by Jessica Bennett.

# RIO FAVELAS

### By Gary Walsh, Melbourne, Australia

There are three boys at the top of the hill, each carrying a walkie-talkie and a handful of firecrackers. They are messengers, watchmen for the drug cartel that runs this favela, or shantytown, overlooking some of the richest real estate in Rio de Janeiro.

Gary Walsh has been a travel writer for almost 20 years, based in Melbourne, Australia. He is a former Travel Editor of the prestigious *Age* newspaper and a three-time winner of the Australian Travel Writer of the Year. Now a freelance writer, he has travelled widely on all the continents. Gary has written guidebooks for Lonely Planet and Fodor's and contributes to a range of publications around the globe. He is married with two children.

The craziest location Walsh visited was lively and lawless Peshawar in Pakistan on the Afghanistan border. He was invited to a Pathan tribal wedding that involved feasting and the firing of automatic weapons (for the men), and feasting and dancing (for the women). The sexes were separated at all the ceremonies, and the bride and groom had never met, despite being cousins.

Walsh is soon headed to the Philippines to do a story on Cebu.

The young messengers, barely in their teens, are there to signal the arrival of drug shipments or warn of the approach of police. Until recently, the lookouts flew kites: white for a cocaine delivery, green for marijuana, red for a police raid, but that system became too obvious.

I am in Rocinha, the largest of Rio's favelas, a place where the vast majority of the city's population fears to tread. But I am safer here than I would ever be on the streets of tourist Rio, according to my guide, Sidharta. "You can leave your cameras on your seat. Nothing will ever be stolen from you in the favelas," says Sidharta. The drug barons don't want any excuse for the police to act within Rocinha.

More than a fifth of Rio's population lives in the favelas and although shunned by mainstream society, shantytown residents are not isolated from it. They are the security guards, bellboys, room maids, gardeners and kitchen hands of its homes and hotels.

There's a welcoming group of souvenir stalls as you enter Rocinha on Estrada de Gavea, the main road built in the 1930s as a formula one track. Red brick houses are piled one on top of the other on the steep slopes, five and six storeys high. On the eastern side of the hill they overlook ritzy Gavea and Corcovado, where the statue of Christ the Redeemer stands with its arms embracing Rio. Over the hill the houses have million-dollar views of Pepino beach and the fashionable residential towers of São Conrado.

Rocinha has much about it that is reassuringly normal—three newspapers, two radio stations, three bus lines, a cable TV channel, streets lined with such outlets as a surf shop, pharmacies, bars, cafes, video shops and banks—but there is also an air of threat spelled out in the burnt cars and the graffiti-ridden alleyways. The least busy place I saw was the police station, where a single officer sat slumped in the doorway watching TV. In Rocinha, nobody goes to the police: the community deals with its own problems.

And there are many problems for the community to deal with. There is a chasm between those who can afford to live on the three main roads and those who live in the choked alleyways. The alley dwellers have no street address, so they cannot get bank accounts and find it difficult to get jobs. One section of Rocinha, the Dirty Clothes district, is composed of hundreds of houses built of cardboard that share a single water tap.

But Sidharta was right about one thing. I left Rocinha unscathed, camera and wallet intact, and the following night I was mugged on Avenida Atlântico, beachside Copacabana's main street.

## TOP FOOTBALL STADIUMS

### By Ben Winston and Leigh Gower

They say that South America is the home of real football, but until you step into the cauldron of noise, hub of excitement, and sea of colour there, you cannot understand how right "they" are. Visiting the Bombonero, the "Chocolate Box" of Buenos Aires, home to Boca Juniors, is an experience like no other. From watching the deafening crowd jump up and down, to experiencing the adrenaline of a Boca goal—make sure any trip coincides with a home game there. The surrounding area of La Boca is yellow and blue, every street corner emblazoned in the team's colours. During a game, look out for the only box with yellow seats situated on the half way line. You'll see a little man, hanging over the side, leading the singing and waving like a mad man. Take your binoculars to get a good look at the greatest footballer of all time, Diego Maradona.

Also in Argentina, El Monumental stadium in the Nuñez district of Buenos Aires is noted for holding both the opening and closing matches of the 1978 World Cup. Being the biggest stadium in the country, it is also a concert venue and has seen the likes of The Rolling Stones, Madonna, U2, Michael Jackson, Rod Stewart and the Red Hot Chilli Peppers.

However, Uruguay's Estadio Centenario in Montevideo holds a special place in South American football history for it hosted the first FIFA World Cup and has earned the identity of the "temple of football" since; a landmark to the country's national identity and to the continent's most universal religion.

Other famous South American football grounds include the Estadio Nacional in Chile, the Estadio Hernando Siles in Bolivia and the Estadio Defensores del Chaco in Paraguay.

# MARACANÃ STADIUM

By Wilson Lievano, Bogotá, Colombia

In Brazil, soccer is king and Maracanã stadium is its palace. Every Sunday for more than 50 years, Brazilian fans have known glory and tragedy in one of the biggest stadiums in the world. Built in the center of Rio de Janeiro, the stadium is the home of three of the most popular local teams (Flamengo, Fluminense and Botafogo) and a mandatory stop for all soccer fans.

The stadium hosts an average of 76 games a year, so there is a good possibility that visitors will be able to catch a game and experience the energy of a Brazilian soccer game. The music inside the stadium and the passion of the fans make it a spectacle unlike any other found in the sports world.

The Maracanã (its official name is Estádio Jornalista Mário Filho, but people call it Maracanã because it is located in the neighbourhood of the same name) is accessible by subway. Tickets to the games start at $10, but visitors are encouraged to buy $30 seats to enjoy a good seat and avoid congestion.

Soccer fans can admire the almost circular framework of the stadium, a rarity among soccer fields. Originally designed to hold 200,000 fans, this legendary field was renovated in the nineties and its capacity fell to 103.000, still enough to intimidate visitor teams when the stadium is at full capacity.

Just like the Sambadrome, the Maracanã was built to host the biggest party of its type. In 1950 the stadium was inaugurated just one week before the kickoff of the World Cup. It was to be the first tournament since World War II, and the Brazilians organized everything, hoping to become champions in their own land. Their national team was outstanding that year and they reached the final without trouble.

On the other side of the field they encountered the Uruguayans, a scrappy team that had reached the final with a combination of heart and luck. The first half was scoreless, but just four minutes into the second half, Brazil scored and the party began, the newspapers started to sell hundreds of copies with a big headline that said Brasil Campeão (Champion Brazil). The Uruguayan captain took the ball out of his own goal, put it under his arm and slowly walked to the center of the field, waiting for the roaring cheers of approximately 220,000 fans in the stadium to subside. From that point on, Brazil played their best soccer, but Uruguay scored.

Even with a tie, Brazil was still the champion, thanks to a better goal average. Suddenly, just before the end of the game, the impossible happened. Uruguayan forward Alcides Ghiggia defeated the Brazilian goalkeeper with a shot that instantly transformed the party in the stands into a funeral. Even though Brazil tried again and again, they couldn't score, and the final score was 2-1. The cup went to the Uruguayans, who, for several minutes after the game ended, were the only voices heard in the stadium. After the game, cases of heart attacks and suicides were reported all over Brazil.

The incident, known ever since as the Maracanazo, gave the stadium a legendary status only a month after its inauguration. That reputation has only grown, as some of the best players in history have played in the stadium. Visitors can see where Pelé, arguably the best player in the history of soccer, scored his 1,000th goal, or where he scored his "Gol de Placa", a goal so beautiful that the spectators in the stadium (from both teams) collected money to give him a commemoratory plaque. For a soccer fan, there are few places than are as rich in legends and history as the Maracanã, so if you are in Rio, don't forget to visit the king at its palace and pay your respects.

Wilson Lievano is a Colombian journalist, working for the Spanish version of the *Wall Street Journal*, American edition. He studied social communication at the Externado University in Colombia and received his Master's Degree in Journalism at Boston University.

Egypt is a dream destination because of his fascination with history.

Maracanã Stadium. Photo by Freyja Ellis.

# BRASÍLIA

By Darren Fitzgerald, Los Angeles, California, U.S.A.

Brasília may be the often-forgotten capital of Brazil, but it's also one of Latin America's largest design and construction projects to date.

Growing up in Los Angeles, Darren Fitzgerald saw the world through Hollywood movie sets and edited documentaries. He struggled through most writing classes and had more interest in "Dukes of Hazzard" reruns than reading the classics. He obtained an undergraduate degree in economics from UCLA and an MBA from USC. After two years working in post-soviet Bulgaria through a political revolution and economic collapse, he says he finally developed a semblance of culture and discovered putting his observations about other cultures in a journal was cathartic. Fitzgerald wrote for the Sofia *Kapital* newspaper, but currently owns a fitness performance center with a good friend in San Francisco. His passions revolve around guitar, travel, and writing. His strangest cultural experience was in La Ciudad Perdida hike in northern Colombia. A local farmer took Fitzgerald to his canopied hut where he showed him how cocaine is made.

In 1960, ambition rooted in politics and economic power gave birth to the first capital city built from scratch. You won't find cathedrals adorned with gold, rows of colorful homes outlined by cobblestone streets, airy plazas and fountains. Brasília looks more like an Orwellian dream, a utopia for those with a penchant for conformity.

As far back as 1823, Brazilians dreamed of building an interior capital to profit from the resources of its inland territories. In 1883, an Italian priest, Dom Bosco, dreamed that a new civilization would emerge in the central high plains of Brazil. In 1955, president Juscelino Kubitschek decreed that the new capital be carved out in the state of Goiás. The city was modeled from the "plano piloto" to look like an airplane, with the government buildings in the fuselage, the executive power in the cockpit, and housing in the wings. Kubitschek wanted Brasília to be a symbol of economic power and technological advancement. With a workforce of hundreds of thousands of peasants from the northeast under the lead of the famous architect, Oscar Niemeyer, it was erected in three years.

Brasília is where 1950s sci-fi meets the cold war; where McCarthyism seems rampant; where progress and technology reign over creative independence and self-expression. Stroll up the fuselage, which is a wide and long expanse of crab grass, lined on either side by a uniform row of rectangular, low-rise government offices. Each is emblazoned with large gold letters signifying the building's purpose—Ministério da Energia, Ministério da Comunicação, Ministério da Defensa Ejercita. Imagine a synchronized parade of navy blue suits with 1950s hats and thick black-rimmed glasses filing into their offices at exactly eight o´clock every morning. The offices echo with the beeps and shuffling of mainframe computers. An abacus sits on every flat metal desk. Styrofoam is all the rage, and at any moment a nuclear fallout drill could ensue.

The architecture is a mix of shapeless colored metal towers, concave cement dishes, exaggerated arches reaching into space, and bizarre sculptures. At the foot of the fuselage is the infamous Catedral Metropolitana, a circle of arches curving out at the top, giving the cathedral the appearance of a giant paper crown. Along the side of the cathedral is an enormous white oval rock, which will make you want to call Roswell, New Mexico, on the phone and ask them if they're missing a flying saucer.

The outskirts of the capital are filled with highly spiritual religious groups who believe the fields surrounding the city are ideal landing pads for extraterrestrials. After a day in this 1950s "Tomorrowland" you'll believe the aliens have come and gone and left us Brasília.

*"I will never tire of repeating my commitment to ensuring that every Brazilian can have breakfast, lunch and supper every day."*
*-Luiz Inacio "Lula" da Silva, Brazilian President (1945-)*

## KILO BARS By Freyja Ellis

One of the great features of Brazil is that you can pay for your food by weight. Nicknamed "kilo bars," or "*por quilo*" in Portuguese, due to the per-kilo display price, these are self-service restaurants featuring a wide choice of traditional hot and cold foods and salads served buffet style. You simply make your selections, take your plate to the counter where it is weighed and are charged the per-kilo price. You hold on to your bill and add any further trips or purchases, then settle it at the end.

Several Chinese and Italian style restaurants in shopping malls also follow this concept and for the sweeter tooth you can also find ice-cream kilo bars, complete with a selection of flavours, sauces and toppings, although these often require you to pay as you go.

An alternative to por quilos are set-price restaurants. Similar in concept to the por quilos are rodizios, where you pay first, then take as many trips to the buffet as you wish, or churrascarias which also include barbequed meat on large skewers which are continually brought to and sliced at your table until you have had your fill.

A great idea for large or small groups, meat eaters and vegetarians, and large or small appetites, kilo bars are a reasonably priced and excellent choice when you want a quick and decent meal.

# SALVADOR DA BAHIA

*By Dr. Crit Minster, Rochester, New York, U.S.A.*

The rich culture of Salvador is heavily indebted to its legacy as the port of arrival for many African slaves. The Portuguese dominated the African slave trade beginning in 1452, when Pope Nicholas V issued a papal bull permitting the enslavement of any and all non-Christians. Thousands of Africans were captured by the Kingdom of Congo, sold to the Portuguese, and shipped to their colony of Brazil, where they were unloaded and sold in the city center of Salvador: the district earned the charming name of "Pelourinho," or "whipping post."

Slavery thankfully abolished, a dynamic Afro-Brazilian culture evolved from its ashes and now dominates the city—about 80% of the population is of Afro-Brazilian descent. Traditions fusing African and Portuguese are at home in Salvador. The transplanted slaves brought their religion with them: it is called Candomblé, and it survived in spite of centuries of repression by the Roman Catholic Church and the government of Brazil. An amalgamation of cultural influences, Candomblé incorporates both African and Christian traditions. It is a polytheistic faith, and the different deities, about 50 in all, each have their own unique histories and personalities. Some of these Orishas, or God-spirits, are associated with Catholic saints. For those interested in religion, it is possible to observe certain Candomblé services in Salvador.

Salvador is also known for new traditions, such as the famous capoeira dance, native to Salvador. This cross between a dance and a martial art consists of a series of spins and kicks, although the participants never touch one another. If you've never seen it, it looks sort of like a Kung Fu movie set to music. According to tradition, capoeira started as a way for slaves to practice hand-to-hand combat disguised as dance.

Visitors to Salvador are often surprised and delighted by how much there is to see and do in the city. A number of musical/dance groups have sprung up: a good one to check out is Olodum, which was founded in 1979 and has performed around the world (you may remember them from Michael Jackson's 1995 music video "They Don't Care About Us") The city also sponsors a lively art scene: there are numerous theaters and art galleries. The old town, still called Pelourinho, is home to the best cafes, hotels, restaurants, and nightlife. There are a number of fascinating colonial churches and museums, and Pelourinho is a UNESCO World Heritage Site. If that's not enough, stop by during Carnaval: according to locals (and some visitors) it's more fun than the one in Rio de Janeiro.

The city was for centuries the most important port in Brazil, and the historic forts and fortifications are worth a look. One such landmark is the massive Lacerda Elevator, which was built in the nineteenth century to carry goods from the port to the city above. Beyond the port is the Bay of All Saints, upon which Salvador sits. This maritime graveyard is home to more than 100 shipwrecks and is a scuba diver's paradise.

The unfortunate legacy of slavery forced dislocated Africans to cling to values which could not be taken away: their Gods, their culture and their souls. These precious possessions took root in a green corner of the New World; today their culture blooms in Salvador.

---

TRAVELER'S TIP: Wanna Samba with locals at the most popular place in town? Head over to Beco de Gal located at Avenida Vasco da Gama, 2893, next to Transporte Ondina. Any taxi driver will know where to drop you for a night of gyrating and hip-shaking. Wednesday is *the* night to go, and things pick up around midnight, lasting til the wee hours of the morning. This spot is jam-packed, but with good reason—for over 17 years owner Gal has been offering hot music and a chill atmosphere for Samba shakers to strut their stuff.

---

# THE WAR OF THE TRIPLE ALLIANCE (1864-1870)

By Dr. Crit Minster

In 1864, Paraguay, which had been a reclusive, insular state in the 50 years or so since independence from Spain, used a border skirmish between Brazil and Uruguay as an excuse to declare war on Brazil: their true objective was to gain a port on the Atlantic Ocean. A few weeks later, they declared war on Argentina as well, because the Argentines refused to let them pass through their territory. Uruguay, under Brazilian influence, joined the war as an ally of Brazil and Argentina.

At first, Paraguay looked as if it would win the war. During its years of isolation, Paraguay had militarized, and had a military force larger than that of its three opponents combined. Brazilian naval superiority, however, eventually proved decisive and the balance of the war eventually shifted. The three allies prevailed.

Paraguay was left devastated by the war. Most historians agree that probably as much as half of Paraguay's pre-war population of around 550,000 perished in the war, including as much as 90% of the men. The country was utterly crushed: the only thing that prevented Brazil from incorporating Paraguay into their territory was the fact that Argentina would not allow it.

Repercussions from the bloodiest war in South America since the conquest of the Inca lasted for decades. The Brazilians did not leave Paraguay until 1876. Certain border disputes were not fully settled until 1878. Paraguay owed a war debt to Brazil and Argentina until 1943, and certain cultural artifacts taken during the war were not returned to Paraguay until 1975.

# DIVING IN SALVADOR

## By Dr. Crit Minster, Rochester, New York, U.S.A.

May 10, 1624. The Dutch, jealous of the New World empires of Spain, England and Portugal, decide to establish themselves on the coast of Portuguese Brazil. Dutch privateers attack and capture the city of Salvador. In the ensuing battle, more than 90 Dutch and Portuguese ships sink, most of them off the Banco da Panela near the entrance to the Bay of All Saints. Over the ages, dozens of ships would join them on the bottom of the harbor:

- 1800: The British ship Queen sinks in 13 meters of water near Salvador harbor.
- 1875: British steamship Maraldi gets stuck entering the harbor and is lost in four to 12 meters of water.
- 1876: The Germania hits a reef and sinks near the lighthouse.
- 1903: The Bretagne hits the wreckage of the Germania and also sinks!
- 1980: Greek freighter Cavo Artemidi hits a sand bar and sinks.

These are only a few: there are many, many more ships in the nautical graveyard of the Bay of All Saints.

For centuries, Salvador da Bahia was Brazil's most important city. Today it's a diver's paradise: you can dive every day for two weeks and won't see the same wreck twice. A number of decent dive shops have sprung up, and the city itself is friendly and inviting. The waters in the bay are normally quite warm, and divers most likely will not need a wetsuit.

Salvador was the capital of the nation until 1763, when the capital was moved to Rio de Janeiro, which later was moved to Brasília in 1960. Salvador features a large natural harbor and was a major New World shipping center. Thousands of ships came and went … and some came and never left.

A true wreck diver won't want to miss the Cavo Artemidi. According to local legend, the ship was sunk as part of an insurance scam…but whatever the reason, the Cavo Artemidi is one of the most spectacular wreck dives in Brazil. The massive freighter—it is approximately 160 meters (525 feet) long, larger than a football field—is mostly intact and sitting in water between 30 and 100 feet deep. There are gaping holes in the hull that even novice divers can swim through without any risk of being stuck. Many species of dazzling fish make the wreck their home, including several species of angelfish. It is the largest shipwreck in Brazilian waters and is in a good state of preservation.

Located at the mouth of the bay, the Banco de Panela is home to the remains of more than 90 ships sunk during the Dutch invasion. The area is considered an archaeological site and it is forbidden to remove anything from the site. After 400 years, there's nothing recognizable as a ship anymore, but you'll see anchors, wood scraps, and a cannon or two if you're lucky.

The Dutch pirates eventually lost Salvador: it was re-taken by the Portuguese within a year. Like good pirates, they left behind buried treasure: their treasure is for the eyes, and it's buried under warm blue water, fine white sand and dazzling reef fish that flash silver and gold before darting off into the watery dim.

## TOP SCUBA MECCAS

Divers the world over agree: Latin America has some of the best SCUBA diving in the world. Strap on a tank and hop in—the water's great! Join our readers at their favorite places!

1. The Galápagos Islands, Ecuador (p. 264).
"Most diverse wildlife under the sea." Christina, Seattle, U.S.A.
"A lifetime experience!" Peter Daly, England.

2. Utila, Honduras
Utila, The Aquarium, "Best dive spot off the Island of Utila, Bay Islands, Honduras." Sal, London, U.K.

3. Blue Hole, Belize (p. 170).

4. Salvador, Brazil (see above). "Lots of great shipwrecks." Dr. Crit Minster, Rochester, New York, U.S.A.

5. Cozumel, Mexico. "Home to some of the best resorts in the world." Jennifer Flynn, Ohio, U.S.A.

6. Ocotal peninsula, Costa Rica. "Giant manta rays!" Samantha Davies, Worcester, England.

7. Bonaire (p. 93). "Everyone agrees: one of the best in the world." Gideon Wells, U.S.A.

8. Roatán, Honduras (p. 177). "Great resorts and history." Dr. Crit Minster, Rochester, New York, U.S.A.

# BARRA

## By Steven Cassidy, London, England

Two sinewy lads spin, dodge around each other in mock combat. Percussion instruments chime together creating a two-beat rhythm. The dancers kick, spin, leap and gyrate. Locals encircle the performers as they watch this traditional Afro-Brazilian martial art, called Capoeira. Developed initially by African slaves in Brazil, Capoeira became a way for Brazilians to settle differences without resorting to violence. This semi-balletic art form is a traditional expression of Bahian culture and exemplifies the core of the city of Salvador, known for Afro-Brazilian culture and its energetic, violent and exotic history.

For a free show, you can catch a glimpse of youths practicing Capoeira on the sea wall of Barra. It's the signature of this small beachside suburb closest to Salvador. A picturesque beach town, Barra sits right on All Saint's Bay, the natural harbor for which Salvador became famous during the Portuguese colonial era.

Barra beaches have the prerequisite white sand but also feature plenty of surf and small tide pools to explore, and with the reflection of the sun, the sea looks a shimmering emerald green. The beaches start about 500 feet (150 meters) away to the north at the Porto do Barra and then turns to the east where they run forever along the coast of Brazil. Barra's beaches are friendly, laid-back relaxation zones frequented by locals, while tourists tend to go farther down the coast.

But the attraction that draws all the tour buses is the Farol da Barra, the iconic lighthouse of the city of Salvador da Bahia. The lighthouse represents the birth of Brazil and is where the country started. The lighthouse stands on the site of a colonial fort built in 1534 whose cannons were aimed at the bay and were primed to blast the Dutch, English and Spanish pirates and freebooters who frequently attacked the port.

The lighthouse area itself has commanding views of the bay with stone octagonal walls soaring forty feet into the air, each one topped by a turret. Before you enter the lighthouse, have a wander around its walled circumference to look at the wave-crashed inlets and the views along the bay.

The lighthouse features what is arguably the best museum in Salvador. It has exhibits concerning the history of Salvador and its inclusion on the trade routes from Africa and India. It is also full of interesting information: you can see how deep the water was in the bay from readings taken in the sixteenth century! Brittle old maps show the sweeping beaches, the island of Itaparica and the rocky escarpment upon which Pelourinho (the city center) was constructed. There were plenty of shipwrecks in these waters, and models of galleons, ship lenses and figureheads dot the museum. The massive courtyard has been turned into an open-air restaurant.

Climb the ancient battlements for a great view of restored cannons, the lighthouse tower, and the bay itself. With a little bit of imagination, you can picture a Dutch pirate fleet sailing into the bay, cannons blazing, black flags flying. Visualize it for a moment, then go back down the steps to rejoin your friends for an ice-cold Brazilian beer on one of Barra's fine beaches.

---

BARRA TRAVELER'S TIPS:

Of course there is no way to learn the fine art of Capoeira in a few days or weeks, but if you are up to the challenge of learning a move or two, and perhaps making yourself look like a fool, look no further. Check out these masters in Salvador who can show you the ropes:

If you are looking for a bit more combat in your Capoeira, look no further than intense, ten-day training with Mestre Bamba, located at Rua das Laranjeiras, 01, Pelourinho, Salvador.

Find Mestre Beto Mansinho at the Arte Bahia in Pelourinho, on Mondays, Wednesdays, and Fridays, from 3 p.m. to 5 p.m. The address is Rua Frei Vicente, 32.

You'll find that music plays an integral role in these lessons with Mestre Nô—you will play instruments as well as twirl and kick. Ask around where to find his house, located in the Boca do Rio neighborhood, where he teaches.

---

# SWIMMING WAITERS

## By Freyja Ellis

The coastal city of Maceió contains a range of beach bars and restaurants in addition to a good local craft market. One of the unique experiences offered here is the chance to spend time on a Jangada, a traditional boat, and head two km (1.2 miles) out to a shallow reef. The best, and only time to visit is during low tide when the reef is more accessible. Jangadas can be hired direct from the beach for a pre-negotiated rate and will remain on the reef for as long as required.

Snorkelling equipment can be hired from the boats or you can just spend time swimming on the reef and the sand bank. However, the main attraction is the swimming waiters. One of the Jangadas is set up as a bar where beer is available and Piña Coladas are mixed and served in pineapples. Another is a kitchen where local seafood is caught and cooked before waiters serve food direct to the Jangadas, by swimming with a tray held high above their heads. Delicious and plentiful, the food is worth the trip out to the reef, as is the opportunity to have your food delivered by a swimming waiter.

# FERNANDO DE NORONHA

## By Sandy Guy, Ballarat, Australia

Walk the streets of any Brazilian town in the evening and you'll hear the sound of Brazilian soap operas echoing from televisions in houses, cafés and bars. Latin America has produced more than 100 soaps a year for the past 40 years, and the superstars of these dramas are adored by millions of fans.

To escape their legions of devotees, many TV idols flee to the seclusion of Fernando de Noronha, a cluster of 21 lovely islands and rocky islets 545 kilometres off the coast of Recife in Brazil's tropical north.

Ilha de Fernando de Noronha, the only inhabited island in the group, is home to Pousada Maravilha, an exclusive hideaway overlooking the ocean. Here, suntanned celebrities wearing minuscule swatches of lycra, known as "dental floss" bikinis, bask by a sparkling infinity pool sipping Brazil's favourite drink, the Caipirinha—a cool brew of cachaça (sugar-cane brandy), lemon and sugar.

Celebrities and travellers alike love the relative isolation of the islands, 70 per cent of which were declared a national marine park in 1988. To protect its delicate ecosystems—Fernando de Noronha is blessed with multitudes of birds and is home to one of the world's largest resident populations of spinner dolphins—the Brazilian Government limits tourists to 420 per week. They join the roughly 2,500 locals at this 15-kilometre (nine mile) long slice of paradise which is devoid of traffic, harried commuters or mobile phones.

Foliage-covered islets surround Baía do Sancho, acclaimed as South America's most beautiful beach. To reach this heavenly strip of white sands one must descend a precarious-looking metal ladder down a steep cliff face. But the difficult access is well worth the effort: with colourful fish darting through the turquoise, temperate waters and flocks of seabirds gliding overhead, Baía do Sancho is simply magical.

Diving is sensational around the islands, and local operators compete fiercely to show visitors this underwater aquarium rich with colourful reefs. You don't need to be a qualified diver to take to the waters: escorted by guides for a "baptism" dive, novices can descend into the transparent sea,

> *Here, suntanned celebrities wearing minuscule swatches of lycra, known as "dental floss" bikinis, bask by a sparkling infinity pool sipping Brazil's favourite drink, the Caipirinha...*

which have visibility of up to 30 metres (98 feet), to check out the teeming marine life.

There are ample accommodation choices for less well-heeled visitors to the islands, ranging from room and board in modest private homes to some reasonably-priced pousadas (Bed and Breakfasts). One reasonable option is Pousada do Francês, which has pleasant rooms with air conditioning and typical Brazilian breakfasts of fresh fruit and crusty rolls.

Vila dos Remédios, the island's largest village, is perched on a hill above crumbling Remédios Fort (officially Nossa Senhora dos Remédios Fort), the oldest of ten forts around the islands built by the Portuguese in the late 1700s. The stately former governor's residence, baroque church, and several cafés surround the village's steep cobblestone plaza.

Ilha de Fernando de Noronha has two distinct sides: the leeward sea, facing Brazil, is sheltered from prevailing winds and its beaches are generally calm, while waves pound the shores of the Africa-facing windward coast. Praia do Leão on the windward sea is surrounded by an open, almost treeless landscape. Its sweeping beach, buffeted by wind, is a breeding ground for green and hawksbill turtles, whose hatcheries are spread across surrounding sand dunes.

The biggest task you face each day at Fernando de Noronha is deciding which of its 23 glorious beaches to visit. Hundreds of dolphins pirouette from the waters of Baía dos Golfinhos in the early mornings, when the yellow-pink of a tropical dawn begins to light up the sky.

Later, snorkel and swim amid the unspoilt splendour of beaches like Conceição Beach, and laze under shady trees while the sun blazes down from clear skies. Smiling staff of beach kiosks called barracas, nestle around the island's beaches, keeping you supplied with icy Caipirinhas, slice the top off chilled coconuts, or whip up a fresh juice made with exotic fruits from the Amazon region.

Balmy evenings, when the sky is dotted with bright stars, are perfect for al fresco dining at one of Ilha de Fernando de Noronha's ten restaurants. Wonderful seafood platters and stews can be found at Ekologicus and Nascimento restaurants in Vila dos Remédios, or try feijoada, Brazil's national dish—a potpourri of beans, meats and charcuterie served with kale and farofa (manioc flour)—at restaurants across the island. The coffee, naturally, is excellent—this is Brazil, after all.

Due to its isolation, Fernando de Noronha is more expensive than mainland Brazil. Although there is no limit imposed on the length of time you may stay on the island, visitors pay an environmental preservation tax of around $15 per person per day which increases to around $1200 per month. Given the limited numbers of visitors permitted on the islands, it's wise to book well in advance. Varig Airlines flies daily from Recife to Fernando de Noronha.

*Beach, Fernando de Noronha. Photo by Sandy Guy.*

# COAST TO COAST

### By Fiona Leslie, Chester, England

Boarding the first ferry at the historical Brazilian port of Belém, on the south bank of the river mouth—an unimaginable 320 kilometres (200 miles) wide—you quickly, and literally, "bag" your space, slinging up your hammock, making the knots secure, and storing your bags underneath.

All that is left is to master the jaguar-like lolling in your hammock until casting off on this trans-continental river journey. The river, known in Brazil as the Rio Solimões, will do the rest. The passing stage show rolls like a green conveyor belt of lush exotic trees, plants and flowers, between which flitter parakeets, toucans and macaws. The pendulum-drop cacique nests hang like nature's woven jewels.

Occasionally, evidence of human life is signaled by dugout canoes drawn up at small clearings. Muddy paths lead to a few small wooden plank-built, stilt homes beside plots of banana and yucca plants. Children run amok, laughing and screeching as they jump into the muddy waters and play football. Churches stand out, meticulously maintained in white and sky-blue paint work, almost in defiance of the encroaching fetid fauna.

After a day or two you soon become accustomed to the rhythms of river and boat life. The early morning alarm call of clacking kingfishers is closely followed by the shrill whistle for breakfast. Bread rolls and coffee are accompanied by the gently-rising sun behind, and passing local fishermen in their dugouts tending to their nets. The after-dinner entertainment is watching the magnificent burning sunsets or searching the boat's wake for friendly river dolphins who follow behind.

Larger crafts go by where passengers hold parasols aloft against the beating sun. Long narrow thatched-roofed boats, piled high with bunches of green bananas, chug between village quays. The occasional huge barge lumbers past on its mission to Manaus.

Arriving at the great Amazon city of Manaus is a shock after the tranquil pace of fluvial travel. Amongst this modern commercial centre is the opulent Opera House. Crown of the late nineteenth-century rubber boom, it is decorated with the most magnificent French materials and fashions of the day. Across the harbour one can see a distinct line where the dark waters of the great Rio Negro meet the brown Amazon.

Then it's all aboard again for the next 1100 kilometres (670 miles) to the border at Tabatinga, where Brazil meets Colombia and Peru. After crossing to the Peruvian frontier town of Santa Rosa, you take the next boat for Iquitos. This old Portuguese-influenced city is a doorway to the true tropical rainforest and its abundant fauna and flora. The last sail takes the right fork up the Río Marañon until you arrive at the small bustling port of Yurimaguas.

From here it is but 24 hours overland to the ocean. A combination of moto taxi and Jeeps drive over the beautiful, mystical tropical cloud forest mountains to Tarapota and a bus journey takes you to the coastal desert plain city of Chiclayo. Finally, a mere half hour ride takes you to the historic coastal resort of Pimentel, and, dipping your toes into the cool Pacific waters, the journey is complete.

Boy in hammock on Amazon ferry from Belém to Manaus. Photo by Freyja Ellis.

## MEETING OF WATERS

### By Freyja Ellis

One of the great attractions just outside Manaus is the naturally occurring meeting of the rivers. For six kilometres (four miles) the Rio Solimões and the Rio Negro run parallel until they eventually merge, forming the Amazon. What is unique about this particular meeting and what provides the greatest impact is the obvious visual distinction of the two rivers; the black Rio Negro coming from the flooded rainforest and the brown Rio Solimões with mud sediment from the Andes.

The reason for the separation of the rivers lies within the temperature and velocity of each. The Rio Negro runs at two kilometres (1.2 miles) per hour and has a temperature of 22°C (71°F), whilst the Amazonas runs faster at four to six kilometres per hour (two to four miles per hour) with a slightly warmer temperature of 28° (82°F), and thus the rivers cannot merge

Boats can be organised from Manaus or can be included as part of a tour to the Amazon jungle. On the boat trips, not only is there the opportunity to see the meeting of the rivers close up, but also to feel the difference by reaching out of the boat and dipping your hand into the water.

# ILHA DE SILVES

By Patricia Damm, Pensacola, Florida, U.S.A.

Four adventuresome Americans with reservations at the Pousada dos Guanavenas wanted to drive the 350 kilometers (217 miles) in a pickup truck through the rainforest to a boat launch near the jungle lodge. As it was not the rainy season, the trip would take about five hours.

Patricia Damm is retired and lives with her husband in Pensacola, Florida, where she is a member of the West Florida Literary Federation. She attended Florida Southern College and the University of Marburg/Lahn in Germany. She continues to study languages and do volunteer work with many cultures, both in the States and in Latin American countries. She writes both for publication and personal enjoyment.

Her most bizarre cultural experience traveling was walking hand in hand with children of lepers through an isolated leper colony on the Amazon.

Damm's next trip is to Marburg/Lahn, Germany for the 800th birthday celebration of St. Elizabeth, for whom the town's cathedral was built in the year 1200.

Could the Americans take along a few containers of food scraps for the birds in the aviary at the jungle lodge, asked the Manaus travel agency? Mostly fruit, the cargo (which was beginning to ferment) would travel better in the bed of a pickup than with a boatload of people or in a small plane. The jungle road trip on a clay track up and down densely forested, steeply rolling hills provided splendid photo opportunities.

The boat owner at the launch site looked hesitantly at the containers of "bird food" and was told the hotel had requested it. With a reluctant shrug, he loaded duffels and garbage into his wooden flat-bottomed canoe and ferried the travelers a short distance across Canacari Lake to Ilha de Silves.

For visitors to the remote island town of Silves and its hotel, the Pousada dos Guanavenas, the reward is a magnificent view—a picturesque, thatch-covered roundhouse, built from local materials, surrounded by lush tropical foliage and brilliant bougainvillea. On Canacari Lake north of the Amazon River, the island and hotel are accessible only by boat or small plane. Hotel guests take a pleasant two-hour boat ride from Manaus, eastward down the Amazon River, before arriving to the town of Silves and being transferred to the hotel.

Comfortable rooms line the outside perimeter of two floors. Hewn log verandas and screened porches are strung with inviting hammocks. Buffets of delicious local cuisine are served in the dining room or beside the pool at the top of a bluff overlooking the lake. Macaws, parrots and other exotic birds provide additional beauty as well as song in the aviary adjacent to the hotel.

The town of Silves is a short walk from the hotel, down a clay road. Ambling tourists aren't hassled as in big cities and can watch furniture makers carefully carving wood and fitting pieces together. Depending on the time of day, you may spot giggling children returning to school after a mid-day lunch break. Small shops offer cold sodas and local souvenirs. The heat bothers no one but the tourists. On arrival, bird stuffs in hand, the cheerful bellhops greet the entourage, quickly hefting duffels, totes and garbage onto their shoulders and climbing a sheer and lofty wooden stairway. The Americans follow at a slower pace. Hotel staff meet them with refreshments and broad smiles, informing them the birds were already being fed their catered dinner.

In every aspect the hotel, service and ambience were excellent, and you can't beat its jungle location. Posada dos Guanavenas and the town of Silves provide a most untainted, relaxing experience. And getting there is part of the adventure.

*"Brazil is bigger than Europe, wilder than Africa and weirder than Baffin Land."*
-Lawrence Durrell, British Novelist (1912-1990)

## TOP LIST: RAINFOREST ADVENTURES

Quick! Picture Latin America. Did a steamy tropical jungle come to mind? If it did, you're probably a rainforest traveler at heart. Tropical jungles cover much of Latin America, and are home to caimans, monkeys, birds, river dolphins and thousands more fascinating species. Our readers step out of the jungle long enough to tell you their favorites.

1. Manu National Park, Peru.
"Exotic, fun. Small groups of five, plus guides." Mark Mellander, California, U.S.A.

2. EcoPark Lodge, Brazil (p. 75).
"All of the Amazon is impressive!" Sandra Scott, New York, U.S.A.

3. Brauilo Carrillo National Park, Costa Rica. "True dense primary rainforest—no habitation." Beatrice Oliveri, Eastlake, Ohio, U.S.A.

4. Cuyabeno, Ecuador
"Cuyabeno is one of the marvellous places to meet the rainforest ecosystem and its wildlife in the purest state (Hot Spots Camp)." Esthela Luje, Ecuador.

# TROPICAL HOTEL AND RESORT, MANAUS

By Sandra Scott, Lowville, New York, U.S.A.

From the jaguars to the Segways to the folkloric shows, the Tropical Hotel is an excellent option for the visitor to Manaus. Tropical Hotel Manaus is located in the heart of the Amazon jungle on the banks of the Rio Negro, less than 12 miles (19 kilometers) from downtown. Guests enter to find a four-story atria, lobby bar and the ubiquitous H. Stern gem store.

The long wide hallways with marble floors and white walls accented with Brazilian woods and lantern lights give the feel of an elegant pousada. The property offers 594 rooms ranging from comfortable and quaint accommodations to two-storied luxury suites with a private pool.

Guests will find a number of activities around the hotel to check out during their stay, including a zoo with a rescued jaguar, two swimming pools (one with artificial waves!), five tennis courts, a volleyball court, a sauna and a beauty parlor. It is only a short walk to the public beach. Nature lovers will most likely see more wildlife at the Tropical than they will at a nature lodge.

There is also a shopping arcade with 22 stores, two restaurants, several bars and a coffee shop, a nightclub and convention facilities with seating capacity for up to 1,500 people.

The tourist office can arrange tours to the local zoo and other museums to learn about Amazonia: various tours to the Amazon forest and the historical city of Manaus depart daily from the hotel. There is a boat dock and a seaplane dock.

It is the perfect stop for a day or two before exploring the jungle—or for recuperating after a sweaty jungle safari. For those who want the "jungle with the condo," this is the perfect place. Bring the kids: they have special activities for children. Most guests will find it hard to leave. Nearby is the newest addition to the Tropical family, Tropical Business, a towering building with a panoramic view of the Rio Negro.

www.vivatravelguides.com/104200

# AMAZON ECOPARK LODGE

By Sandra Scott, Lowville, New York, U.S.A.

Less than one hour by boat from the modern city of Manaus, Amazon Ecopark Jungle Lodge is an excellent option for those who want a true jungle experience, without being housed on a boat or in an overcrowded hotel. Located on the River Tarumá, a tributary of the Negro River, the Lodge is the only one authorized by the Brazilian Government Environmental Agency, IBAMA, to maintain wild animals.

The Monkey Jungle immediately adjacent to the Ecopark, houses spider monkeys, squirrel monkeys, woolly monkeys and capuchin monkeys—many of them orphans rescued from forest fires and floods.

Amazon Ecopark Jungle Lodge offers 60 rustic rooms in 20 bungalows. Rooms are air-conditioned, but windows are also screened for those who prefer fresh air. There is plenty of hot water for showers. There is also a natural black water bathing pool, a private beach, a massage room, a game room, and six miles of jungle trails where you can see the flora and fauna up close.

Guests receive the personal attention of a forest guide provided by the Lodge. Activities include nature hikes, a boat excursion to the meeting of the waters, canoe trips, alligator spotting and piranha fishing. Seamless transfers are included in the price, as are all tours and meals.

Chief of Baraçana Village. Photo by Sandra Scott.

# THE GUIANAS

**Not really in Africa**

The Guianas are three very small countries located in the northeastern part of South America. They consist of Guyana, formerly known as British Guiana, Suriname, formerly known as Dutch Guyana, and French Guiana.

Guyana went back and forth between the Dutch and the British many times during the colonial period. It was ruled by the British from 1815 to 1966. Most of the inhabitants are of South Asian or African descent. It is perhaps best known, unfortunately, for the 1978 mass suicide of the followers of the cult of Jim Jones, an American, in the jungle town of Georgetown. Today, it is a small, English-speaking republic struggling with a fledgling democracy. In terms of tourism, this small country does boast an outstanding 300 waterfalls, including the single-drop Kaieteur, over 700 feet deep. Its rainforest is home to 800 plus species of birds.

Like Guyana, Suriname was held at different times by the Dutch and English, who both considered it valuable because of sugar production. After the Second Anglo-Dutch War, Suriname was "traded" to the Dutch for Manhattan. It remained a Dutch colony until 1975. Suriname offers some attractions for tourists, such as jungle tours, fishing and birdwatching.

French Guiana is the only one of the three to still be ruled by a foreign power, in this case the French. It had historically been used by the French as a penal colony, including the notorious Devil's Island, an interesting tourist stop, but the French stopped sending prisoners there in 1951. The colony produces gold and timber, but remains highly dependent on France.

# DEVIL'S ISLAND

By John and Sandra Nowlan, Halifax, Nova Scotia, Canada

From our cruise ship balcony in the steady rain and mist, the three small, lush islands, covered with tropical vegetation, look to be among the most pleasant and relaxing places on earth. Looks can be deceiving.

We are, in fact, 15 kilometers off the coast of French Guiana anchored next to Les Iles du Salut (Salvation Islands), collectively better known as "Devil's Island."

In its day, the infamous French penal colony was the most dreaded of all prisons. It's best remembered today as the site of the Steve McQueen/Dustin Hoffman escape movie, *Papillon*. To the inmates, it was known as "The Green Hell". After attempts at colonization failed around 1850, Emperor Napoleon III decided to exile France's most notorious criminals to this steamy South American outpost located just five degrees above the equator. For 100 years, until its closure in the 1940s, about 80,000 French prisoners were shipped across the Atlantic to rot in remote obscurity at this brutal penal colony. Of the 30,000 or so who managed to escape the torturous experience with life and limbs intact, most were still condemned, forced to spend the rest of their lives on mainland French Guiana coping with heat, humidity and rampant diseases like dysentery, malaria and yellow fever.

Visitors dock at the 70-acre Ile Royale, the central and largest of the three islands. It was here that administrative headquarters were maintained, as well as the military hospital, chapel, numerous solitary confinement cells, death row and the ever-crucial guillotine.

Some attempts are now being made to preserve and maintain the major buildings, but much of the prison area itself has been overtaken by a new group of ruffians: decay, rust, vines and palms. A portion of the complex has been turned into a resort hotel and tourism has become a major source of income, a fact which would no doubt shock the former inmates who wanted nothing more than to get away and never look back.

From the wharf, an old cobblestone path leads to the fine colonial mansion of the prison governor and a small museum. A few steps farther on, in the centre of the island, lay the main ruins. Looking into the dark crevices and crumbling walls, it takes little imagination to visualize the subhuman conditions endured by the inmates. In dilapidated buildings, small, dank solitary confinement cells evoke a shudder from visitors; rusting chains and bars along the perimeter serve as flagrant and haunting reminders that many inmates were shackled to the walls at night.

According to some stories from those days, prisoners often had to work naked under the broiling sun while fending off ravenous mosquitoes and sadistic guards. It's little wonder that many tried to escape. Those few who did make it to the mainland then had to cope with dehydration, malnutrition, sunburn, dysentery, storms and the knives and tempers of fellow escapees.

Devil's Island has now become synonymous with French injustice and colonial oppression in a part of the world that was largely ignored and forgotten. As our ship pulls anchor and heads away from this small archipelago, one can't help but wonder at the irony that these notorious islands, once the source of unspeakable pain and suffering, are now a safe haven for cruise ships, resort pleasures, and a growing army of tourists.

John and Sandra Nowlan are semi-retired, freelance travel writers.

John was an announcer, producer and executive producer with public radio and television in Canada for more than 30 years. In addition to taking four or five trips a year, he still consults on several broadcast projects, is a partner in an animation company and continues to do voice-over work and acting. He has a Certificate in Journalism (King's College), a BSc. (Acadia University) and an MBA (Saint Mary's University).

Sandra was a fisheries scientist and teacher for many years. She's an avid gardener and gourmet chef and has just completed her first cookbook. She holds a BSc. from Acadia University, a BEd. from Dalhousie University and a Master of Science from Cornell University.

Next on the Nowlans' travel list is the fjords of Chile and the Antarctic.

---

## DON'T DRINK THE KOOL-AID   By Dr. Crit Minster

In the 1970's, the People's Temple, a cult from California, followed their charismatic leader Jim Jones into the dense jungles of Guyana. There, they founded Jonestown, which they believed would eventually become an earthly paradise of justice and equality. The promised paradise never materialized, as cult members—even children—were forced to work in the hot tropical sun to provide food for the settlement. As complaints increased, so did punishment: cult members were forced into small wooden shacks or forced to undergo extensive brainwashing sessions.

Back in the United States, family members of cult members were very worried. Their concerns led Leo Ryan, a California Congressman, to lead an 18 member delegation including journalists and family members to Jonestown in November, 1978. When Ryan and his team were finally allowed to visit the settlement, they found deplorable conditions and some cult members asked to be allowed to return to the USA. Ryan agreed to take them home.

What happened next is not exactly clear. On November 18, as Ryan and his team were getting ready to leave with some of the cult members, a small squad of cult leaders attacked them at the airport. Ryan and four others were killed and many more injured. The airplane did take off, and the rest escaped. Back at the settlement, Jones knew his time was up. He ordered all the cult members to assemble, and gave them Flavor-aid (A Kool-aid knockoff) laced with cyanide. Over 900 cult members died. Jones and the other cult leaders later shot one another and themselves.

Although a handful of cult members survived, without Jones the People's Temple soon disbanded. The Guyanese government used the facility as a refugee camp for a while, but it was later abandoned and fell into ruin. Today, the ageless Guyanese jungle has once again swallowed the ruins of Jonestown, and there are no traces of Jim Jones and his attempt to create a Utopia in the sweltering rain forest of Guyana.

# VENEZUELA

### Home of the Liberator, Bolívar

In 1499, when Amerigo Vespucci, an Italian explorer, was mapping the northeastern coast of South America, he saw some little houses on stilts and named the region Venezuela, which means "little Venice" or "second-rate Venice" (depending on who you ask). Either way, Venezuela will probably not remind you much of the fabled Italian city. There are more caimans than canals, more street dogs than street mimes, more parks than palaces.

That's not to say that South America's fifth-largest country has nothing to offer. Venezuela does not have great ruined cities, but what it lacks in ruins, it more than makes up for in natural beauty. Venezuela's most famous natural landmark is, of course, the magnificent Angel Falls, the highest and one of most spectacular in the world. But the great natural beauty of Venezuela doesn't end there: check out the famous tepuis, or lost "islands" of the Venezuelan jungle.

This section will take you not only to Angel Falls and the tepuis, but also to many of the less famous—but equally fascinating—parts of Venezuela. You'll visit the Médanos de Coro desert, the Great Plains that cover one-third of the nation and the beautiful Roques Islands. Along the way, we'll learn about the Afro-Venezuelan community, controversial president Hugo Chavez and the great city of Caracas. You'll likely agree with our writers that "little Venice" has as much—or more—to offer as the one in Italy!

# MOUNT RORAIMA

By Martín Li, London, England

Mount Roraima is one of the most majestic of the ancient and mysterious *tepui* (tabletop) mountains that dot Venezuela's Gran Sabana. These massive, flat-topped mountains rise almost vertically from the remote savannah, forming surreal "islands in time". Roraima's summit is guarded by walls so immense and steep it was long believed to be unscalable, and possibly the last refuge of lost species. Tales of dinosaurs and the dramatic reports of the first ascent inspired Sir Arthur Conan Doyle's classic adventure novel *The Lost World*.

Nothing on the climb prepares you for the eerie landscape on the summit plateau, where fantasy meets reality. As far as you can see, a labyrinth of massive dark rocks, gorges and fissures, extends across a desolate plateau, with many rocks balanced crazily and seemingly impossibly on top of each other. One wrong turn in the rocky labyrinth and you could be lost for hours, if not worse.

Some rock formations resemble giant animals—guardians of this prehistoric domain frozen in time. Exploring further, you reach surprisingly lush valleys, plains of sparkling quartz crystals and enchanting natural pools, some sunken in caverns beneath the ground.

Despite the setting and the legends, there are no dinosaurs on Roraima's summit. The only endemic beast is a tiny black toad with a distinctive yellow marking on its back. Having evolved unthreatened in its habitat, it is blind, unable to swim and can only move at a very sluggish pace. Over half of the bizarre vegetation on Roraima's summit is unique to tepuis or Roraima alone, including orchids and carnivorous plants.

The ascent of Roraima involves a tough but enjoyable trek. From the Pemón village of Peraitepui, you walk for two days across the Gran Sabana, towards the massive bulks of Roraima and the neighbouring tepui of Kukenán. You ford two rivers, and might need ropes if the water is high. You follow a narrow path through lush cloud forest, waterfalls and strange rock formations, hauling yourself up with the help of roots and branches, and scrambling over large rocks. Occasionally where the vegetation thins out, you glimpse magnificent views of Roraima's face and the huge expanse of the Gran Sabana far below.

A keen skier, horse rider and trekker, Martin Li has a passion for exploring the adventure and culture of the world's great mountain regions, especially the Andes, Himalayas and Scottish Highlands. Li's first book *Adventure Guide to Scotland*, was published in 2005. He is currently finishing his second book, describing his 2005 expedition by mule across the Inca heartland of Bolivia and Peru.

Li's previous adventures have included riding a horse across the Namib Desert, trekking to the base of Bhutan's most sacred summit, close encounters with black bears in Alaska and rafting the thundering rapids of Panama's Río Chiriquí.

**MOUNT RORAIMA TRAVEL TIP:**
You can climb Mount Roraima at any time, but the best time to go is the December to April dry season. Be prepared for variable weather at any time of year, and beware that rain will swell the rivers and might make the crossings difficult. For the ultimate *tepui* experience, take a helicopter flight.

## TOMÁS' SAPO FALLS

By Katie Hale

Imagine living behind a waterfall—maybe ideal conditions for moss, but not for a human. Tomás Bernal, a Peruvian hermit, chose to dig out a cave for a home behind Sapo Falls in Venezuela, living among mist and the sound of crashing water for 10 years. The year after arriving at the falls, Bernal opened a touring company, guiding visitors behind the falls on a path he constructed.

Located a mere 10-minute boat trip from the small village of Canaima, tourists visit the falls daily to view the spectacular sight. When the sunlight hits the rushing water just right, a rainbow is reflected and the vista is breathtaking.

Bernal is now deceased, but his son continues to run the company, Bernal Tours. This place was not just a tourist destination for Tomás, but a place where spirit and nature coincided and when you walk behind the falls, the power of the water is not the only presence felt.

# ANGEL FALLS

## By Martin Li, London, England

Hidden deep in the Venezuelan rainforest, the beautiful Angel Falls are one of the most evocative and romantic sights in South America. The tallest waterfall on earth, water plunges almost a kilometre (over 3,212 feet) from the lip of Auyantepui ("Devil's Mountain", one of the flat-topped mountains that dot the Gran Sabana) before it hits the forest floor into Cañón del Diablo (Devil's Canyon). During the rainy season, the falls can split into two or more columns of water, each with its own distinct plume.

The falls are so isolated they weren't discovered by the outside world until 1937, when American bush pilot Jimmy Angel crash-landed his plane nearby while searching for gold. Angel's plane became stuck in marsh on the summit of Auyantepui where it remained for 33 years and Angel's party had to walk for 11 days to make their way back to civilisation (they never found any gold).

Many visitors opt to take a scenic flight over Angel Falls, which is fine, although a flyover on its own is unlikely to do the falls justice—you need to be physically at the falls to appreciate them fully. One of the best ways to visit the falls is to take a two-day journey by Indian dugout canoe from Canaima up the Carrao and Churún rivers. You camp beside the river, cook over open fires and sleep in hammocks cocooned in mosquito nets. For the very adventurous, you can take a strenuous expedition through deep rainforest to the base of the falls. Travelling on foot and in canoes, the expedition will take around 10 days and the going will be very arduous, but you are unlikely ever to forget the experience of being one of the few to arrive this way at the foot of Angel Falls.

### ANGEL FALLS TRAVEL TIPS:

Costs will depend on which of the several ways you choose to see the falls. A flyover is cheapest, followed by a river journey, with the expedition trek option being the most expensive (you will probably need to join an organized tour unless you are an experienced jungle explorer). Also, the falls are located within Parque Nacional Canaima, which has an entrance fee for all visitors.

To reach Angel Falls by river, you should travel between June and September (ideally in July or August), when the rivers are at their highest, but be warned the falls are frequently covered by clouds. In other months, it may be necessary to get out of your canoes at times to allow them to be hauled over rapids and other shallow sections of river and the falls are only thin ribbons.

Angel Falls. Photo by Freyja Ellis.

*"I have no doubt I was someone very interesting in a past life."*
*-Patricia Velasquez, Venezuelan Actress (1971-)*

# CANAIMA

### By Kieron Devlin, Manchester, England

Water and earth explode to life on the Río Coroni, which carves its way through Parque Nacional Canaima towards the jungle settlement of Canaima, Venezuela. As I splashed into a fresh water pool formed from a cave waterfall upstream, water crashed down from a high plateau above, pummeling my ears.

Red and gold shimmers of light bounced off the water and danced across my skin. Feeling astonishingly awake and wonderfully alive, I clambered back onto dry land, using tree roots to scale the wet rocks. With a firm grasp of the person in front of me—a great way to make friends quickly if traveling alone—I dogged my way up the trail, lagging behind my guide who seemed as sure-footed without shoes as I was clumsy in them.

In 1983, charmed by the immense beauty of this park, the unflappable young Peruvian, Tomás Bernal, turned his back on civilization and ventured into the Venezuelan jungle to carve out his own existence. With the same spirit and force of the Río Coroni, Bernal spent the next 10 years exploring his new home, living off of the land, and sleeping in a simple hammock beneath an open air cave overlooking the runoff of two waterfalls. The pathway that Tomás constructed behind Sapito Falls has become well-trafficked by tour groups out of Canaima. It is now the main one-day trek from Canaima Waku Lodge. Even the briefest of excursions to this remarkable area inspire a Bernal-like urge to cut ties with civilization and set up shop in the jungle.

Canaima National Park is about as far away from the hustle and bustle of Caracas as you can imagine. Roads don't even go to the Gran Sabana, the remote plain of imperious plateaus called Tepuys. At almost two billion years old, these scattered rock formations resembling giant table mountains add wonder to the ancient landscape. No wonder they are revered as sacred by the local Pemón Indians. Traditionally the Tepuys were "guardians of the savannah" where soul-stealing spirits lived at the top; as such they had never climbed them until recently encouraged by tourism to do so. It's almost the last remaining zone where dinosaurs might have once laid eggs or gone foraging for food.

The only way to get to Canaima is by a tiny 12-seater plane that flies over the dull reddish-brown Orinoco, one of the longest rivers in South America at 2,410 kilometres (1,498 miles). The plane veered 45 degrees to the left and right, causing my stomach to jump as I gasped at the magnificent waterfall below, falling over a mile downwards deep into the jungle. This is El Salto Ángel, the Angel Falls—that's Parecupa-vena to the local tribes—and it is 17 times the height of Niagara Falls.

The plane lands in Canaima on a tiny field. The Waku Lodge is made up of basic wooden chalets, but the setting is glorious with small huts on the lagoon's beach side although the humming of its generator tends to kill the sound of the macaws and other exotic birds. Steam clouds caused by the falls are emitted from the luscious mineral-rich earth, as shocking colors fall onto a pinkish sand. Even the soil seems to be alive and breathing, so it is not surprising that the entire region has been designated a national park. I don't think there can be many places in the world that boast as magical a landscape as Canaima.

A traveler, writer, teacher and alternative therapist, Kieron Devlin has published travel writing, short fiction both in print and online, poetry, essays and reviews. He is currently working on a novel. Though he originated from Manchester in the U.K., he has spent most of his working career abroad. He's just resettled in London. He has a Master's in Creative Writing from the New School, New York.

Devlin's favourite place is at home, and he wouldn't leave for a trip without a juicy novel to read. His dream destination is Utopia, in sharp contrast to his experience in Riyadh on the first night of Gulf War in 1991, when he was sitting in a sealed bathroom with a gas mask. Next he could be headed to destinations as varied as Hawaii, Blackpool or Prague.

Canaima Falls. Photo by Freyja Ellis.

# RIO ORINOCO

## By Peter Anderson, Christcurch, New Zealand

Leaving behind the sparkling waters of the Caribbean, the flat savannah stretching to the Andes comes into view across the 2,500-metre high mountain range that separates Caracas from the sea. The turbo-prop aeroplane flying from Caracas to Puerto Ayacucho, in the Amazonas State of Venezuela, flies low allowing a closer look at the beautiful views. Fifty minutes into the flight, the Rio Orinoco comes into view. The flight follows the Orinoco to Puerto Ayacucho airport, where friendly local tour guides greet visitors.

Amazonas is the southernmost state of Venezuela, occupying about 20% of the country. However, it is home to only 1% of the population, composed mainly of the different Indian communities.

The Orinoquia Lodge, 20 kilometres south on the banks of Rio Orinoco, is an ideal place to stay as it is situated on the banks of the Orinoco and is built in traditional native style. The units are circular with a double bed on a mezzanine floor under a high, conical thatched roof. They have no windows, are open to the elements, but remain shady on days when the noonday sun blisters down on the rainforest and keep you dry when warm tropical downpours soak the region. Each unit has a bathroom, ceiling fan and mosquito net to keep nighttime visits from local bugs to a minimum. The local chef cooks superb meals and the freshly caught Orinoco catfish, fried with bananas, topped with a white cheese sauce and served with salad is a local specialty not to be missed. For an interesting culinary experience, try catara sauce. Its ingredients include the heads of leaf-cutter ants, peppers and yucca juice.

The four main native Indigenous groups in Amazonas State are the Piaroa, Yanomamo, Guahibo and Yekuana.

The Piaroa (pronounced Pee-ah-row-ah) are the main ethnic group in this area. Their mode of transportation is via the bongo, a form of dugout canoe by which they navigate the tributaries of the Amazon and Orinoco. They collect the lightweight balsa wood, native to the rainforest, for use in their hand-carved sculptures. All sculptures are hand-decorated with natural dyes from plants gathered in the rainforest. Birds, animals and figures from their mythology play an integral part in their art.

When one thinks of the Amazon, thick tropical jungle and unexplored territory come to mind. You'll experience the isolation of the mighty Amazon when you're alone with your boatman on a canoe in the middle of the river, a kilometre from either river bank. Apart from the occasional Piaroa Indian passing in his bongo, the only sign of habitation is the laundry drying on the large granite rocks on the banks of the river.

Fifteen kilometres downstream from Orinoquia Lodge is the beginning of the Atura rapids. On the Colombian side of the Orinoco, a short trek across the granite and tussocks of the savannah a new world opens, with circling vultures, insect-eating flowers, miniature frogs and a spectacular view of the Atura rapids. These and the Maipures rapids further upstream are the reason that a 63-kilometre road was built from Puerto Ayacucho to Sampriago in the south.

The peace and tranquillity of the Piara Creek, a small tributary of the Orinoco, is wondrous and the mangrove trees block the scorching midday sun as the canoe drifts past the occasional Piaroa in his bongo jiggling his fishing line in the water. Kingfishers and butterflies add dashes of colour to the deep green backdrop of the trees. The small, colourful *colibrí* (humming birds), smaller than some of the butterflies, dart from flower to flower searching for nectar that will keep them in a constant state of overdrive. The frantic beating of their wings produces a characteristic hum, which tells the savvy traveller to look for a splash of ruby red or emerald green in the trees above.

Turtle Rock, so named because of its shape, is sacred to the locals, and it is forbidden to walk on or climb it. To the south, are the outlines of the majestic tepuis (Table Mountains). The most illustrious is Cerro Autana: the Piaroa believe it is the birthplace of the universe.

Puerto Ayacucho, with a modest population of 70,000, is nevertheless the largest town in the region. The local museum, Museo Etnológico de Amazonas, is very interesting as it shows the lives and handicrafts of the local Indians. A stroll around the native market is a must: every morning the locals sell carved brightly coloured birds and clothing amongst other items—you can even get catara sauce!

It is not easy to reach the remote corners of the Amazon: but the jungle's unique sights, smells, and sounds, make the trek well worth it.

---

**ORINOCO FACTOIDS:**
In Daniel Dafoe's famous *Robinson Crusoe*, the title character is stranded on an island near the mouth of the river in 1659. Actually, the original title of the novel, which is considered by some the first novel in English, is *The Life and Strange Surprising Adventures of Robinson Crusoe, of York, Mariner: Who Lived Eight and Twenty Years, All Alone in an Un-inhabited Island on the Coast of America, Near the Mouth of the Great River of Oroonoque; Having Been Cast on Shore by Shipwreck, Wherein All the Men Perished but Himself. With an Account how he was at last as Strangely Deliver'd by Pyrates. Written by Himself.* The book is set near the real Rio Orinoco.

The Orinoco River. Photo by Freyja Ellis.

# LOS LLANOS

By John Polga-Hecimovich, Burnsville, Minnesota, U.S.A.

Stretching from the Andes in the west to the Río Orinoco in the east, the flat as a griddle savanna of Central Venezuela is known simply as "Los Llanos," or "the plains." In total, it covers 300,000 square kilometers of Venezuela, or about one third of the country. With few cities, the Llanos' main draw for travelers is its wildlife, although the region is also the spiritual capital of the country and home to the unique and fast-paced joropo music.

It is difficult to visit the Llanos independently, because the wildlife is concentrated around *hatos*, large cattle ranches. Tours based out of Mérida take visitors to special hatos that have developed eco-tourist infrastructure. These trips, generally four to five day jeep and boat safaris, cost around $30-$40 a day. Travelers typically start out from their campsite in the morning to look for animals, return to the hato for lunch and a siesta to escape the midday heat, and then undertake an afternoon trip in search of more wildlife. The days are long, so evenings are spent relaxing around the hato's campfire before retiring to hammocks for the night.

There are two seasons in Los Llanos: dry and wet, in which the land is either flooded or bone-dry. Animals are easier to see in the dry season (December to April) as they flock to the scarce waterholes. At this time, these waterholes resemble fourth-grade biology posters that show an entire ecosystem's collection of plants and animals crowded into a space the size of a living room: caimans and iguanas sunbathe along the shoreline, dozens of herons, egrets, and other birds wade in the shallows, snapping up small fish, and capybara skirt the waters. Just below the surface, the water teems with piranha and bottle-nosed dolphins.

Unlike the more famous Amazon, the Llanos have few trees, and this open landscape offers the ideal opportunity to catch a glimpse of animals that would otherwise be difficult to spot. Consequently, dozens of fish, birds and mammals can be seen any time of the day. Camouflaged animals, like turtles and the enormous anaconda, are actively sought by the Llanos-bred guides, and often detected for a quick show-and-tell and photo session.

But the region offers more than just animals. The town of Guanare is where the Virgen de Coromoto, the country's patron saint, supposedly appeared over 350 years ago to an Indian chief, and pilgrimages are made every year to its shrine. The people and the region's culture are other draws. One Llanero contribution to national culture has been *joropo*. Many Llaneros (inhabitants of the Llanos) play joropo instruments, and it is probable that this music will break out spontaneously on any given night on the hatos. Known locally as *música llanera*, joropo has its roots in Iberian Spanish music, although the composition of its instruments is uniquely Venezuelan: the *arpa llanera* (a sort of harp), the *cuatro* (a small four-stringed guitar) and *maracas*. The rhythm is fast and many of the themes deal with life in the Llanos and the character of its inhabitants.

Los Llaneros themselves tend to be friendly and they love to sit around and shoot the breeze with visitors. A look at the land and their life shows why they are renowned for their fierce independence and resilience.

The Llanos is a perfect destination for anyone looking for adventure, wildlife, a different culture, or merely a change of scenery. Interaction with its animals, whether swimming with freshwater dolphins or fishing for piranhas, is guaranteed, and its friendly people and distinctive music and culture are sure to impress any traveler willing to get a little dirty and take a big step off the beaten path.

---

LOS LLANOS TRAVEL TIP:
The Llanos are difficult to see independently; a tour is recommended. High-end tours can be booked in Caracas. No-frills tours can be purchased from the Andean city of Mérida. Tours usually last four to five days and are all-inclusive, minus alcohol.

---

## THE WORLD'S HIGHEST CABLE CAR

By Leigh Gower

Soaring high above Mérida in the world's highest cable car, the panorama of the scattered city below fades into a seemingly endless terrain of camouflage-coloured mountains, as you climb to an altitude of 4,765 m (15,633 feet).

Under Dictator Marcos Perez Jimenez, construction of this cable car was initiated in 1957 and built with French and Swiss components. It was opened to the public in 1960. The cable car consists of four sections which run for a total length of 12.5 km (7.8 miles), making it both the longest and highest aerial cable system in the world.

The 90-minute trip will take you right up to Pico Espejo (Mirror Peak), a stark slate rock searing through puffs of cloud. Pico Espejo is made out of a stone called Mica Moscovita and is extremely bright when the sun shines on it, producing a mirror-like effect.

If you are fortunate enough to take the ride on a cloudless day, you will be able to see over to Pico Bolivar; facing you between Pico Bomplandt and Pico Humboldt, it is the highest point in Venezuela at 5,000 m (16,404 feet). You stand a better chance of a good, clear view if you are an early bird.

Once a month, the first 600 people go up for half price to make tickets more affordable for locals. As such, it is vital that you book in advance, given that there are only four cars able to carry 60 people each at a given time.

VENEZUELA

# MÉRIDA

By Lorraine Caputo, Columbia, Missouri, U.S.A.

The deluge ends as a pale sun dawns over the ageless mountains. Clouds rise up the forest-brocade mountainsides, into the grey, velvet sky. Fresh snow frocks the higher peaks. Fog hangs in the ragged valleys. This is the northern end of the Andes, near Mérida, in western Venezuela. On the world's longest cable car line, people are already beginning the journey threading upwards to Pico Espejo. From there they may walk to quaint villages like Los Nevados or El Morro, or begin to scale glacier-blanketed Pico Bolívar (over 5,000 meters/16,400 feet altitude), or spend several days hiking and camping through the mountains.

A popular destination for Venezuelans and foreigners alike, the city of Mérida is well-developed for tourism. The municipality features over 30 parks, including a zoo and an aquarium. In Plaza Beethoven, a series of chimes announces the time on the hour: surely you can guess who composed the tune. The Universidad de los Andes is located in Mérida: it offers lectures, concerts and other cultural events. At the University is a modern art museum; the city also has an archaeological and a colonial art museum (all closed Monday). Mérida is also a popular place for foreigners to study Spanish.

The mountains immediately overlooking the city are part of Parque Nacional Sierra Nevada. The entrance to a beautiful section of this park, featuring alpine landscapes and lakes, is on the road towards Barinas. There are campsites in this part of the park, or one can make day trips. A number of agencies in Mérida offer tours to Parque Nacional Sierra Nevada, mountain climbing expeditions and excursions into the *Llanos* (plains).

Near Mérida are a number of charming Andean villages with colonial architecture and artisan workshops. From one of these pueblos, Tabay, one can visit the hot springs of La Mucuy.

The higher altitude and cooler climate of Mérida and the surrounding region make for a wonderful relief from the rest of the country. The tapestry that is Venezuela isn't only composed of threads of tropical beaches and jungle. In that southeast corner is deeply woven a brocade of snow-capped mountains, wind-swept highlands and picturesque Andean villages.

---

**MÉRIDA TRAVEL TIP:**
As with many Andean towns and cities, temperatures in Mérida and the surrounding areas can vary significantly. Daytime can vary between 7ºC and 25ºC while night temperatures can drop to 0ºC. Pack for both hot and cold weather.

---

## WORLD RECORD ICE CREAM

By Freyja Ellis

Mérida is famous for two reasons: the world's tallest cable car and Heladería Coromoto, the shop that holds the *Guinness World Book of Records* title for the most ice-cream flavours in the world. With a current count of 831 flavours, the shop boasts classic varieties as well as some of the most unusual creations you could ever come across.

The small shop was established in 1980 by Portuguese immigrant Manual da Silca Oliveria. A board lists all the past and current flavours on one wall, while another features pictures of famous visitors, articles from international press about the shop and the *Guinness World Book* certificates.

The shop typically has about 70 to 80 flavours on offer every week—the selection depends on which local ingredients are available at the time. Some of the more unusual all-time favourites include tuna (with real chucks of fish), asparagus and chilli pepper. For those who enjoy cocktails, Piña Colada, Pimms, Caipirinha and even beer flavours are worth a try, however the less adventurous can stick to classics such as strawberry, vanilla or mint. As for the risk-takers you could always try Miss Venezuela, Canada, Viagra la Esperanza, or Titanic—the ingredients of which are anyone's guess.

Los Nevados. Photo by Kimberly Nelson Spence.

# LOS NEVADOS

By Pete Nelson, Chester, Maryland, U.S.A

The donkey's slender, mud-spattered legs bend and straighten like steel pistons pumping slowly in low gear, his tiny hooves often disappearing completely into the cracks and crevices of the ancient, rocky trail.

We are high in the Andean Parque Nacional Sierra Nevada of southwestern Venezuela, barely an hour into our five-hour descent from the 4,045-meter heights of Loma Redonda to the whitewashed walls and red tile roofs of a hidden hamlet called Los Nevados.

For the moment, three of the four of us ride: my 20-something daughter, Kim, on one of the mules; I on the single horse; and our escort, affable, attractive, Alvaro, about the same age as Kim. Our muletero, Fransicco—sun and wind-hardened—trudges behind us all, leaning on his hand-hewn walking stick with every other step, hissing and whistling to keep his clearly beloved animals from dawdling among the succulent green snacks growing all around us.

Very early in the morning of the day we were happily rocking and rolling high in the Sierra Nevada. We had flown one of Venezuela's regional airlines to the cultural and economic hub of the Andean region, Mérida. At the city airport, with its sloping main runway, we were met and taken for a hearty breakfast on the top level of the Mercado Principal de Mérida, where six independently operated kitchens serve a common dining area.

Loma Redonda ("Roundtop"), the starting point of our trek to Los Nevados, is one station below the uppermost peak, Pico Espejo (Mirror Peak), of Venezuela's famously long cable car. We arrived with palms outstretched for the magic meds that promised to fend off the wooziness and vague nausea caused by the absence of heavy air our bodies were used to.

Soon, Kim, Alvaro, the muletero and I were riding or walking rocky trails known to have been trodden during the early 19th century by Simón Bolívar and his troops struggling for independence from Spain—and probably for generations before them by hardy indigenous residents of the mighty Andes. The initial waves of altitude sickness that Kim and I had suffered briefly had vanished, replaced by exhilaration for this new adventure.

Riding an animal for several hours on level terrain is uncomfortable enough. Clinging to one tip-hoofing on a steep downward angle for any length of time is soon excruciating. When we stopped occasionally for the animals to nibble and drink from one of innumerable streams, Alvaro dug into his bright purple backpack and pulled out bottled water and fresh fruit and lectured lightly on the varied flora around us. Other than that, we talked little, lost in our thoughts of the history of these hills, real and imagined; of the people we saw among the modest white-walled, red-roofed haciendas and the green of their surrounding fields we passed so slowly; of how far we were from the 21st century that most of this region had yet to enter.

"There," said Alvaro suddenly, pointing ahead and sharply down. "Los Nevados." He smiled broadly, as if welcoming us to his own home.

From our vantage point high above the pueblo, it looked like a child's jumble of toy buildings piled together, pink-tinted and rusty-reddish in the low late afternoon sun. One not-too-straight *calle principal*, surely cobbled, divided the town in half. The short spires of a modest church poked up behind the town. At the risk of schmaltzy overstatement, it was truly enchanting.

Cameras back in our bags, we forged ahead and as Los Nevados emerged as reality, the enchantment was replaced by the strongest yearning I have ever had for a cold beer. Most of the flat facades of the buildings, all white, offered little indication of what might lie behind them, but we soon spotted the familiar white bear on the unmistakable blue logo of Venezuela's premier Cerveza Polar beckoning beside an open doorway.

"¿Hay cerveza, bien fría?" To our delight, yes, they had beer and it was very cold.

Our muletero accepted our offer to join us but he didn't linger. The pockets of his tattered trousers bulging with the bolivares we paid him for his efforts over the last several hours, he trudged slowly back up the main street and onto the trail we had just descended, followed faithfully by his seemingly indefatigable animals.

Suddenly fatigue coursed through our respective bodies, competing with the growing craving for solid food. It was only mid-afternoon, however, so after assuring our overnight accommodations in a youth hostel-like *residencial*, we explored the tiny town, then napped briefly before joining the proprietor and her family for a simple, hearty dinner.

The next morning, we were up early, treated to an overwhelming breakfast, then climbed aboard a long-body Land Cruiser—by far the vehicle of choice throughout these Andean realms—and, still tender from the horse and mule-back trek of the day before, bounced and jolted our way along a narrow, rocky route, rife with tight switchbacks, to Mérida.

---

Pete Nelson lived and worked in Chile and in Venezuela early in an international hospitality marketing career that spanned some 25 years, returning to them both on writing assignments in 2001 and 2003, when the camping-adverse traveler earned the nickname "el mochilero gringo sin mochila".

As the son of an international airline executive, Nelson lived and traveled overseas extensively. He now lives in eastern Maryland where his wife, Cathy, oversees some 50 teachers of English for Speakers of Other Languages in the public school system in the same county in which their daughter, Kim, who spent the 1999 academic year in university in Santiago, Chile, now teaches high school Spanish.

His most bizarre cultural experience was getting his Venezuelan driver's license, sitting in a roomful of applicants while the monitor read the questions AND the answers for the written test, followed by the driving test that consisted of simply driving around the block—solo.

# CULT OF THE AFRO-VENEZUELAN SAINTS

By Lorraine Caputo, Columbia, Missouri, U.S.A.

*Ay, my father San Antonio*
*Where are you, I don't see you*
*I've come to sing with him*
*And I'll be leaving with my dreams!*

*What is it you want with San Antonio*
*That you're calling upon him so much?*
*San Antonio is in heaven,*
*Along with the other Saints.*

Two young men—the guardians of the Saint—begin battling in the street. Their *garrotes* (wooden sticks) clack as the procession arrives at the house where they guard a family's statue of Saint Anthony of Padua. The San Antonians dance to the beat of drums, maracas, and a *cuatro* (small four-string guitar). The procession continues, San Antonio guarded by those young warriors, to the next house.

It is June 13th, the feast day of San Antonio. Processions similar to this one are taking place throughout the Venezuelan state of Lara. In the morning, the revelers attend a celebratory mass in the parish church, where they play music, dance and distribute bread (the symbol of this saint). The procession winds through the streets, a riot of throbbing song, clacking sticks and drums—all aided by the sharing of *cocuy*, a sort of home-brewed booze made of agave cactus. As dusk falls, the procession makes its way back to the church.

But the festivity isn't over. In the evening, San Antonios dance the tamunangue. Of African origins, it consists of seven *sones* (rhythms), most of which consist of battles with sticks—some between men, others between men and women.

The Perrendenga, the fourth son, is a humor-

> *The procession winds through the streets, a riot of throbbing song, clacking sticks and drums—all aided by the sharing of cocuy, a sort of homebrewed booze made of agave cactus.*

ous enactment of the affairs of women and men. In the last son—El Seis Corrido—groups of three couples dance an intricate series of 32 movements. Large celebrations of San Antonio happen in Barquisimeto, especially in Barrio La Unión, and Los Crepúsculos, home of Uyama, considered the most traditional tamunangue group. Other villages in Lara state that honor him are Sanare, El Tocuyo, Quíbor, Canapa and El Tintorero.

San Antonio is one of the saints venerated by Afro-Venezuelan communities, with music and dance rooted in their original homelands across the sea. Forced to worship a new god, their slave ancestors merged their traditions into the feast day of San Antonio, as well as those of Saint Benito and Saint John the Baptist. San Benito—according to lore—hid Jesus one night when the Romans were searching for him and protected him with his drumming.

The Venezuelan Chimbanguele ceremonies are accompanied by drums, flutes, maracas and conch shells. San Benito's feast days are December 28 and 29 in communities on the south shore of Lake Maracaibo, including Gibraltar, Bobures, Palmarito and Santa María.

Saint John the Baptist (San Juan) is honored on June 24 in towns such as Patanemo (Carabobo state), and Agua Negra, Farriar and Palmargo (Yaracuy state). He is believed to bless waters and herbs used in healing. It is said that Simón Bolívar was a devotee of San Juan.

The festivals of San Antonio, San Benito and San Juan are only three manifestations of Afro-Venezuelan religious culture. The ceremonies are an unforgettable experience— their rhythms linger in both mind and soul long after the drums are stowed away.

## HUGO RAFAEL CHÁVEZ FRÍAS By Dr. Crit Minster

Visionary emancipator of the poor? Communist Castro clone? Populist troublemaker? Incompetent dictator? Take your pick. Venezuela's 60th and 63rd president—he was replaced for about two days, by two different men, during one turbulent stretch of 2002—is nothing if not controversial.

Chávez counts among his influences two of Latin America's greatest revolutionaries: Simón Bolívar and Fidel Castro. Like Bolívar, he believes in the power of a unified Latin America, and imagines a united region taking its place among the great powers of the world. Like Castro, he believes in social programs for the poor and close state monitoring of business. Also like Castro, he is very unpopular with leaders of the United States, particularly conservatives: American religious broadcaster Pat Robertson called for the U.S. to assassinate him; Chávez in turn has accused the U.S. of plotting his murder. In one famous quote, he referred to President George W. Bush as "the Devil."

He has survived protests, strikes, a coup and a referendum. He has been accused of supplying weapons to Colombian rebels, of supporting terrorism, of contravening political sanctions by visiting Saddam Hussein in Iraq and of being a subversive influence throughout Latin America. Amnesty International has documented many human rights violations in Venezuela under Chávez. As unpopular as he is with the United States, Chávez remains a figure beloved by the poor of Venezuela. Encouraged by the recent boom in oil prices—Venezuela, with vast oil reserves, is making billions—Chávez recently announced plans to establish (jointly with Cuba) a medical school which will provide free tuition to medical students who agree to work in the poorest towns of the region.

It remains to be seen whether some of Chávez' more drastic reforms will take hold, and if he'll ever achieve his dream of a unified South America. Until then, the one thing that Hugo Chávez can be counted on for is more controversy.

# CORO

## By John Polga-Hecimovich, Burnsville, Minnesota, U.S.A.

The Médanos de Coro look as if God had decided that the Sahara already had enough sand and South America needed its share. Luckily, this national park and its spectacular *médanos* (sand dunes) are not only inexpensive, but accessible. Indeed, the desert is just two short kilometers outside of Venezuela's oldest and best-preserved colonial city, Coro, situated at the neck of the Península de Paraguaná, between Caracas and Maracaibo.

Founded by Juan de Ampiés in 1527, Coro was Venezuela's first capital and is one of the oldest cities in South America. It was declared a UNESCO World Heritage site in 1993, which has halted new growth in the colonial center while encouraging its restoration. Walking through the center of town is almost like being transported back in time, as churches and elegant colonial houses rise above narrow streets, tall trees and cobblestones.

The town's churches make for a great visit, from the Iglesia de San Francisco and the Iglesia de San Clemente to the massive whitewashed cathedral, the oldest surviving church in Venezuela (construction began in the 1580s). However, not everything is colonial. The city features two museums dedicated to modern art, the Museo de Arte de Coro and the Museo de Arte Alberto Henríquez, both located in stately mansions in the center of town. West of the center is the Jewish Cemetery, established in the 1830s by a wealthy Jewish merchant, and considered to be the oldest of its kind on the continent. However, perhaps Coro's most impressive spectacle is the Parque Nacional Médanos de Coro.

The médanos are an improbable environment so close to the city. Two kilometers (one and one-quarter miles) outside of town, a tree-lined avenue dead ends at a small monument, some snack bars, and a large sign; a few steps beyond the tamarind juice and potato chips sits a desert landscape replete with fine grain sand, huge dunes, and little vegetation. The dunes extend north to the Península de Paraguaná, with the Golfete de Coro to the west and the Caribbean to the east. Centuries of wind and waves created this curious landscape, building up a sandbar between Paraguaná and the mainland; the region was once the Caribbean Sea itself.

It is possible to rent horses or dune buggies to explore the dunes, but it is just as satisfying to walk for a half hour, lose the backdrop of the city, and become engrossed in the soothing monotony of desert landscape. There are few distractions: an occasional cooling breeze blows sand around as the 30 meter dunes rise and drop around the occasional lonely plant. Of course, the peace and solitude of walking in this surreal desert is heightened by knowing that town—and a glass of water—is just a short ride away.

---

**CORO TRAVEL TIPS:**
Entrance to the Médanos de Coro is free, and the town is one of the least expensive in all Venezuela. The best times to visit the Médanos are in the morning or in the evening, as midday temperature in Coro can reach 40 degrees Celsius (104 degrees Fahrenheit).

---

Médanos de Coro. Photo by John Polga-Hecimovich.

# LOS ROQUES

By Pete Nelson, Chester, Maryland, U.S.A.

Read no further if vast expanses of crystal clear, glassy water, half-inch high turquoise waves and sand as refined as sugar are not your idea of, uh, nirvana. Los Roques, an extraordinary archipelago somewhere off the 2,000-mile-plus Caribbean coastline of Venezuela, is virtually impossible to describe without daydreaming.

Although fishermen have plied this region for generations, and still do (lobster is the prime catch), the islands have otherwise been relatively unharmed by human touch. A large percentage of Venezuela's land surface has been preserved in the form of national parks or natural reserves. Every square centimeter of these 50-plus islands is protected and regulated by federal directive.

The main island or cay, Gran Roque, is home to several hundred fishermen and/or posada-keepers, a handful of liquor-license holders, two trucks for water and trash, and a golf cart. Here you swim, dive, eat, drink, dance and stay overnight. You can sail to another of a handful of other cays during the day to do the same. The allure of this azure locale is the ultimate retreat.

Boats—power and sail of every size and description—are anchored off-shore or pulled up onto the beach. Creature comforts are guaranteed by generator-provided electricity and a desalinization plant—both of which are well concealed. Only the burbling of the power boats and the occasional rumbling of the two trucks overpower the crashing sounds of the half-inch waves. Nay, I wax too idyllic; there is an airport too with an open-air terminal the size of a living room. Single and twin-engine propeller-driven aircraft—including a venerable DC3 that brings a smile to any inveterate traveler—can be noisy, but the trade winds seem to muffle those occasional daytime-only interruptions.

An hour after our arrival, my 20-something daughter, Kim, and I were skimming across the Caribbean's shimmering surface from Gran Roque to Francisquí (Francis Key), which is just large enough to hold a few visitors. In moments, we could see only the tallest masts waving behind us and the mid-19th century windmill-like lighthouse crowning the hill behind the town. Above us, half a dozen pure white petrel-like birds kept pace, circling and swooping as if challenging our boatman to a race. What made us gasp, however, was their bellies and the underside of their wings which had taken on the exact blue-green brilliance of the water below them, as if they had been spray-painted from below. It was a truly stunning sight.

For many years, the island of Margarita, far to the east, captured the imaginations—and the investment of bolivares—of Venezuela's tourism gurus, as well as a few *extranjeros*. Half a century of heady oil-generated revenue and its concomitant corruption, followed by a decade of real world wake-up calls, have left most of Margarita grossly overbuilt and under-used, opening wide its portals to cheap foreign travel from Europe and elsewhere in South America. Meanwhile, the country's coastline east of the capital city of Caracas all the way to the tip of South American mainland reaching northeastward toward Trinidad remains virtually pristine, albeit with a smattering of exceptions. In deference to local inhabitants—farmers and fish folk—much of this coastline is protected to some degree, as well. There are countless bays, coves, and playas coloradas to explore. Close-in islands, some near enough to swim to, add to this region's charm.

But the cays of our inscrutable archipelago are unsurpassed, sprinkled jewel-like in their platinum setting. The government of Venezuela, its current monumental economic and political problems notwithstanding, is clearly committed to smiling back at one of God's proudest creations.

# ISLA DE MARGARITA

By Leigh Gower

It is quite likely that upon waking up on Isla de Margarita, you will smile and think to yourself "it's just another day in paradise." Only 40 km (25 miles) off the coast of the Venezuelan mainland, and laying claim to an astonishing 82 beaches, it is readily equipped with bars, casinos, five-star hotels and a championship golf course to cater to even the most sophisticated of tastes.

One of the most southern Caribbean islands, Margarita also boasts world class wind-surfing at Playa El Yaque, with its shallow, calm waters and steady, strong winds. The scuba diving, jet skiing and sailing will also please water babies, while at Playa El Agua you can partake in bungee jumping and plane rides. For those less actively inclined, long white sandy beaches like those of Paraguito await you, where you will find a young crowd seeking a good surf, set against a palm-drenched shore.

With an excellent foreign exchange rate of the Venezuelan Bolivar to the U.S. Dollar and Euro, the duty-free shopping on the island also attracts many visitors. Try the local drink, Coco Loco, a brown rum held in a coconut, sold at a number of intersections across the island. And make sure not to miss Juan Griego, an old castle which affords you a magnificent view of the sunset.

A vacation haven, Margarita still unfortunately suffers some of the crime-related problems you will find in other parts of South America. But then, even paradise is entitled to a few problems.

# HOME GROWN SAINTS

By Lorraine Caputo, Columbia, Missouri, U.S.A.

Who knows why, but Venezuela—more than any other Latin American nation—has an abundance of *santos caseros* (homemade saints) who, although revered for generations, are not officially recognized by the Vatican. There's the Santo Rostro in the city of Calabozo, La Yaguara in Carabobo, Machera in Mérida, María Francia in Caracas, the Virgin of Turmero in Aragua, and (of course) Simón Bolívar, the liberator of most of northern South America considered to be semi-divine by many.

Thousands make the pilgrimage to the centers of these saints: cemeteries, country churches or homes. Plaques and *milagros* (small metal charms symbolizing the request) adorn the shrines. Two of the most important of these "homemade saints" are María Lionza and Doctor José Gregorio Hernández.

María Lionza is a local saint whose worship is limited to Venezuela. Also known as María de La Onza, her origins are obscure. One legend says she was the green-eyed daughter of Nívar, a pre-colonial native chieftain. In a nearby lagoon lived a monstrous anaconda who demanded yearly sacrifices. One day María was captured by the serpent—but eating her beauty killed him. María became the owner of the waters. She rules all of nature, flora and fauna, caverns and caves, streams and lakes. Her most holy ground is the mountain Santa María de Nirgua.

Many come to this Sacred Mountain, or the Montaña de Sorte, near Chivacoa in the Yaracuy state, to have ceremonies done. These may be for love relationships, healing, protection, blessings or consultations. Long-distance rituals are also done for those who cannot make the pilgrimage.

The supplicants are bathed in earth and herbs, prayers, candlelight and tobacco smoke. The shamans enter trances, channeling the energy of María Lionza. There is whirling, dancing, throbbing drums. Such ceremonies last for several days. The *curanderos* and *curanderas* live in all parts of Venezuela, and accompany pilgrims to the mountain. Some shamans are available at Montaña de Sorte for those who arrive without a spiritual guide.

José Gregorio Hernández is another saintly product of Venezuela, who is venerated not only in his home country, but throughout Latin America, with churches exhibiting small statues of this medical doctor dressed in a somber black suit and black fedora, and people channelling his spirit for those who are ill.

Doctor José Gregorio was born in Isnotú, Trujillo state. A devout Catholic and Franciscan layperson, he dedicated his life to healing the poor. To this day, people pray for the assistance of this "Servant of God," and many claim his spirit has visited them or has prescribed medicines to cure them. He was beatified by the Catholic Church in 1949, but some believe he will never become a full saint because the "brujos" also call upon him for assistance. His gravesite in the Cementerio General del Sur of the Candelaria Church in Caracas is a pilgrimage site, as is his birthplace.

María Lionza, Doctor José Gregorio Hernández—the Holy Face of Calabozo, Negro Felipe, Yaguara, Machera—these are only a few of the dozens of "homemade saints" that have their root roots in the rich Spanish, African and indigenous soil of Venezuela.

---

HOME GROWN SAINTS TRAVEL TIP:
There are two excellent books (in Spanish) about the popular Saints of Venezuela, both by Mariano Diaz: *Milagreros del Camino* (Caracas: Fundación Bigott, 1989); and *María Lionza, Religiosidad Mágica de Venezuela* (Caracas: Grupo Univensa, 1991).

---

*"Judgement comes from experience, and experience comes from bad judgement."*
*-Simón Bolívar, Liberator of South America (1783-1830)*

---

## GREATER COLOMBIA By Dr. Crit Minster

In 1819, as the various wars of independence in South America were still raging, the man known as the "Father of South American Independence," Simón Bolívar, established the nation of "Gran Colombia," or Greater Colombia. This fledgling nation consisted of the present-day nations of Panama, Colombia, Venezuela and Ecuador. It was Bolívar's dream to unite all of South America into a single great nation, and Greater Colombia was the first step. Bolívar was Greater Colombia's first and only president.

Bolívar was a very charismatic statesman and soldier, and under his leadership most of northern South America was liberated from Spanish rule. He was unable to make Greater Colombia work, however, because once the common enemy—the Spanish—was vanquished, petty regional rivalries began to surface almost immediately which tore the young nation apart. Logistics was another problem: the mountains, rivers and dense jungles of northern South America made communication and government very difficult.

Bolívar, disheartened by the failure of Greater Colombia, intended to leave for Europe in 1830, but died of tuberculosis before he could leave. Nobel-Prize winning writer Gabriel García Márquez' novel *The General in his Labyrinth* is a moving portrait of Bolívar's final days.

# ARAYA PENINSULA

### By Lorraine Caputo, Cleveland, Ohio, U.S.A.

Below heavy fortress stones tumbling to the sea, the salina turns rose in the light of late morn. The surrounding hills are ochre, burnt-orange, rime-white and brushed with thorn trees and cacti.

Since before the arrival of the Dutch and Spanish, the parched flats near the town of Araya have been an important source of salt and, to this day, more than 1000 tons of it are extracted daily. A stone fortress, Castillo de Santiago, was built by the Spaniards to protect the salinas. At the time of construction, it was the most expensive project undertaken in the colonies.

Located in the far east of Venezuela, the Araya Peninsula is embraced on one side by the indigo-aquamarine Caribbean Sea and on the other by the deep blue-green Gulf of Cariaco. The Peninsula offers a stunning desert landscape view; the salt flats changing colors throughout the day as the setting sun casts long, deep shadows over the hallucination-like scene.

Manicuares on the Gulf-side of the Peninsula is renowned for its pottery. It was here that Cruz Salmerón Acosta, one of Venezuela's most famous poets, died of leprosy in 1929. His verses capture the haunting beauty of the region and his home is now a museum. This southern shore of the Araya Peninsula is dotted with small fishing villages that are easily visited by public or private boats. One of these hamlets, Merito, is home to a beachside hostel run by the local high school's tourism studies program.

The Mediterranean climate makes for pleasurable days spent walking through hills of glimmering, polychrome stone scaled by herds of goats. Hours can be whiled away painting this land and seascape in watercolor or words, or swimming in salt-dense waters beneath a starlit sky. This is a land Christopher Columbus acclaimed as *hermosa* (beautiful)—and those who explore the little-visited Araya Peninsula will surely agree.

> *"Don't mess with me, girl."*
> -Hugo Chávez, President of Venezuela (1954-) to United States Secretary of State Condoleezza Rice

ARAYA PENINSULA TRAVEL TIPS:

The ferry is more expensive than the "tapaítos."

The ruins of the Castillo are free; the Salmerón Acosta Museum is by donation.

From Cumaná on the mainland, daily auto-passenger ferries leave for Araya town and frequent "tapaítos" (passenger launches) for Manicuares.

There is also a rough road from Cumaná to Araya, but no bus service.

Guajira girl in national dress. Photo by John Polga-Hecimovich.

# PARIA PENINSULA

By Lorraine Caputo, Cleveland, Ohio, U.S.A.

Up in the northeast corner of Venezuela, two peninsulas join together to form a "T." The western arm is the Araya, with a desert landscape. The eastern arm, the Paria, has jungle-draped mountains that tumble into the sea.

Carúpano is the base point for exploring this fascinating region of Venezuela. It was also once the main port for the exportation of cocoa when that crop was king, and where Bolívar emancipated the slaves of Gran Colombia. Today, it is more renowned for being the only place in the country where the traditional pre-Lent Carnival is celebrated, with processions, costumes and music. This attractive colonial town also boasts a regional museum and a landscaped park on the waterfront.

Traveling east along the Caribbean coast, you'll come across many sandy beaches and cozy posadas. Río Caribe is a fishing village with many colonial buildings painted in pastel colors. Further along the coastal road is Puerto Santo, and the Los Cocos, Medina and Puipuy beaches. San Juan de las Galdonas has many inns and fine restaurants. Beyond that, the road becomes a dirt track of little interest to travelers, with few services available.

Another paved road from Carúpano goes inland and crosses the mountains. Around El Pilar are several expensive posadas, spas and eco-tourism resorts with all-inclusive packages. Many have private swimming pools and offer tours to cocoa farms, beaches, mangroves, the national park, hot springs and other areas. The route emerges at Irapa on the Gulf of Paria. Christopher Columbus called this area "The Gardens." This is also allegedly where Papillon landed after escaping Devil's Island.

The road ends at Güiria, a small fishing town with beaches. From here departs the Trinidad-bound ferry. Boats also leave for Macuro, a tranquil village on the very tip of the peninsula, and for Pedernales, a largely indigenous settlement on the River Orinoco delta. The latter two places can only be reached by boat.

Parque Nacional Paria includes most of the coastal range and the northeastern coastline of the peninsula. It consists of dry and wet tropical forests, as well as a swath of cloud forest. Almost 30% of the bird species reported in Venezuela can be found here, including the scissor-tailed hummingbird, native to this region. There are also two and three-toed sloths, the silky anteater and other animals.

An adventure into the little-visited Paria Peninsula in the Sucre state poses a contrast to its sister peninsula. Where else can one find glittering desert on one side of a plateau and rich jungle on the other? While traveling through the Paria, it is also worth stopping off at one of the many homes offering blocks of homegrown, organic chocolate: the icing on the cake, as it were, of this sweet journey into verdant mountains and crystalline seas.

---

**VENEZUELA TRAVEL TIPS:**

Travelers to Venezuela find that there are frequent checkpoints (*alcabalas*) outside of the main cities. The police or National Guard at these points will often stop traffic and check passports and sometimes luggage too. These stops are compulsory. It is essential to carry passports at all times and not complying with this could result in a fine. If driving, it is also necessary to have all the correct papers for the vehicle.

---

# CARACAS CITY TOURS

By Freyja Ellis

Though Caracas is sometimes described as a city of skyscrapers and shanty towns, there are several wonderful sites worth visiting. These can be reached on foot or, for the more cautious, on an organised city tour. An alternative and more cost-effective option for groups of over three is to hire a jeep for the day, allowing you to visit sights in and around Caracas according to your own itinerary and interests.

Some places of interest within the city include Simón Bolívar's birthplace, Casa Natal del Libertador, now converted into a museum featuring military exhibits of the period. Panteón Nacional is the resting place of prominent Venezuelans, while Parque del Este houses a small zoo and replica of Christopher Columbus' ship, the Santa Maria. The Plaza Bolivar is a historic quarter with picturesque buildings, and Parque Nacional El Ávila boasts a cable car from which you can enjoy the views over this city.

Outside the capital it is worth considering locations such as the Germanic mountain village of Colonia Tovar founded in 1843, or Los Roques, an archipelago of small islands in the Caribbean. Venezuela's first national park, Parque Nacional Henri Pittier, is a great place for birdwatching and hiking experiences.

# THE CARIBBEAN

### No Problem!

The magic of the Caribbean is well-known around the world. Steamy tropical nights, beautiful beaches, piña coladas and salsa dancing the night away are all included in the experience. So pack your Panama hat and come with us to the magical islands for a trip you'll never forget!

### Cuba

Mention the word "Cuba" to five different people and you're likely to get five different reactions. Some will think immediately of the 1959 communist revolution or the Cuban Missile Crisis. Some will think of those elements of popular Cuban culture that are well-known around the world, such as meringue music or Cuban food. Still others will imagine the pre-Castro Cuba of the 1950s, a sort of Las Vegas in the Caribbean, with sizzling nightspots frequented by Hollywood stars and famous singers. The one constant over the centuries has been the people of this island nation. Cubans are passionate, fun-loving, cheerful hosts who love to share and show off their island to foreigners.

### The Dominican Republic

Baseball is the national passion of this tiny nation, which shares the island of Hispaniola with Haiti. In the streets, kids play baseball with sticks for bats, rocks for balls, and anything that won't get up and walk away for bases. A tattered rag or an old cardboard box can serve as a glove.

There is more to this small, laid-back country than baseball, however. The Dominican Republic is home to world-class resorts and beaches which draw visitors from all over the planet. What is especially appealing about the Dominican Republic's beaches is their variety; due to its location between the Caribbean Sea and the North Atlantic Ocean, there is a great variety of sand, marine life, water temperature and current.

Come for the baseball and stay for the beaches, or vice versa: whether you're a baseball pilgrim or a sun-worshipper looking for one of the best beaches in the Caribbean the Dominican Republic has something to offer that will captivate your interest.

### Bonaire

If you've heard of Bonaire, chances are you're a diver. This tiny island, part of the Dutch Antilles, is home to only two towns but dozens of dive shops, and the local government has set aside huge sections of the natural reef that surrounds the islands for perpetual protection. Our one piece about Bonaire is about diving, naturally.

### Puerto Rico

This island may legally be part of the United States—technically, it's a "commonwealth"—but culturally, it's part of the Latin Caribbean. If you don't believe me, just go out salsa dancing 'til dawn, and you'll be convinced. Our pieces about Puerto Rico highlight some of the lesser-known attractions of this wonderful island.

# DIVING IN BONAIRE

*By Sharon Chan, Closter, New Jersey, U.S.A.*

Located outside the hurricane belt in the southern Caribbean, a mere 50 miles north of Venezuela, sits the tropical isle and premier SCUBA diving destination, Bonaire.

A divers paradise, for both the experienced and novice, the waters encircling Bonaire are not only warm (reaching above 80 degrees Fahrenheit) they are almost crystal clear with a water visibility of 100 feet plus (30 meters)—but are nearly untouched, in large part due to its status as a National Marine Park.

Once submerged under the calm, green ocean surface, the rainbow of colors before you is simply stunning. Fish flash a dazzling spectrum from black and silver to sharp, bright red, yellow and blue stripes. As you navigate these mystical waters, look for a sea slug called a mollusk. Although large mollusks tend to be brown, smaller slugs transform from pink to fluorescent orange when you shine a light onto them. Shellfish including gigantic red lobsters, pink crabs and tiny peppermint (red and white striped) shrimp are abundant. Reefs and coral provide the perfect backdrop with colors from purple to orange.

Smooth, crystal clear, still waters, along with no rain drops, and the abundance of shore diving makes this an easy, worry-free zone for novices wishing to learn the art of SCUBA. If you learn in cold, silty waters with poor visibility, you tend to hug the shore and not venture into open water. This was my experience learning off the New Jersey Shore, where there was so much silt in the water that I could barely see my hand in front of me, the waters were freezing so close to shore and there were tons of spider crabs which sort of gave me the willies—not a great first experience. These conditions can discourage one from trying again in warmer waters, but I was glad I gave Bonaire a chance.

By no means is Bonaire only for novices. If you are a more experienced diver and are seeking a challenging adventure, there are many companies that host boat and cave dives. There are well over 100 caves documented on Bonaire and visitors can explore many of them by diving or snorkeling.

If diving is not your thing, Bonaire also offers a variety of water sports and land activities. Kayaking around the mangroves, sailing and windsurfing against Bonaire's gentle winds, and snorkeling are all available. Even if you prefer diving, you might want to give the flippers a rest for an afternoon and head to the Washington Slagbaai National Park. A 13,500-acre national park, it covers roughly one fifth of the northern head of the island. Hike, bike, or even drive through the park to check out the donkey sanctuary and see wildlife including birds, lizards, goats, and iguanas. Be on the lookout for flamingos as well—there are plenty in the park. The park road is bumpy and hilly and it's not easy on the knees, so be sure to watch your step.

Sharon Chan currently resides in Hoboken, New Jersey, USA. She attended the University of New Hampshire in Durham, New Hampshire, and now works as a business analyst in retail. When asked her most interesting cultural experience, she says: "I was dining in Tokyo, Japan, for yakitori, and ordered some sort of chicken dish. When the dish arrived, we realized we had just ordered chicken sashimi (aka raw chicken). I will admit that it was tasty." She hopes to dive the Maldives someday.

Scuba Divers. Photo by Dr. Crit Minster.

# CANDELA ART AND MUSIC FESTIVAL, PUERTO RICO

*By Dustin Ross, Colorado, U.S.A.*

Each October for the past four years, DJs, artists and tropical treasure hunters have made their way down to Old San Juan in Puerto Rico to bask in the warmth that is the Candela Art and Music Festival.

Dustin Ross is a Colorado-raised, Brooklyn-based photographer. He attended Tufts University in Boston, MA, Universidad Catolica in Quito, Ecuador, University of Bangalore in Bangalore, India, and Teachers College in New York, NY. He travels extensively engaging in conceptual photo projects. The craziest place that Ross has ever visited is Sikkim, India. His most bizarre cultural experience was eating cow skin. He dreams of traveling the world, "Stopping through every continent and climate zone," but his next trip will be to Tanzania to do a project on hip hop in Africa.

Candela, also the name of the main club/gallery on Calle San Sebastian in the city, continues to play host to underground musicians from around the world, the lucky few that know this spot is the place to be in mid-October.

Past DJ's have included Bobbito, aka "Cucumber Slice," Rich Medina, Karl Injex and Tyler Askew of Rudemovements, Osunlade, Karen P., DJ Cute, Nickodemus of Turntables on the Hudson, Busquelo, Quantic, Rawjak and Matthias Heilbronn. Artists have included Mode2, Doze Green, Lee Quinones, Dustin Ross, Swifty, Mitchy Bwoy, Ease1, Skwerm, HVW8, Swoon, SBTG, Shepard Fairey, Dzine, Chris Mendoza.

The 2005 highlights included a live sneaker customization by Singapore's own SBTG, who killed it by creating a Candela/Rude Adidas superstar. SBTG painted, printed and glued while his cohort Haz from Rawjak and club Zouk in Singapore was cleaning house on the decks downstairs, accompanied by equally impressive DJ sets from Bobbito and the Rudemovements crew.

Another high-point was a rooftop screening of Pablo Aravena's new documentary on urban art titled *Next: A Primer on Urban Painting*. The movie features many of the artists from past Candela Festivals as well as other painters, bombers and smack-talkers from across the globe.

Friday night club-hangers were privy to a live painting by the HVW8 crew, who by now are well known in the streets of Old San Juan. Festival goers were also treated to a vibrant mix of live music from local plena and bomba groups at club Rhumba and an evening of serious salsa riddims in Plaza de San Sebastian, where a live stage was set up.

Each year the DJ, musician and artist lineup changes. So be prepared for surprises in what is a fairly unorganized, but always high-energy and surprising few days of music and art in the sun.

Most guests of the festival stay at the Gallery Inn right in Old San Juan, a converted plantation mansion filled with sculptures, gardens and even live Cockatoos. Otherwise, Pablo has been known to arrange rooms in other guest-houses and hotels.

Of course, the extra bonuses of un viaje to Puerto Rico include fresh snapper by the beach, Medalla beer by the bushel, all the mofongo you can eat, and beaches with crystal clear waters and palm trees into the horizon ...

To stay up on festival details, check http://lacandela.blogspot.com/ or email festival founder and coordinator Pablo Rodriguez at pablorumba@yahoo.com.

## TOP LIST: BEST HOLIDAYS, FESTIVALS AND FUNKY NATIVE SHINDIGS

If a modern musical festival isn't your thing, check out these other holidays, festivals and funky native shindigs suggested by our readers:

1. Carnival, Brazil (see box on p. 64). "The biggest party in the world." Pete Nagle, Minneapolis, Minnesota, U.S.A.

2. Day of the Dead, Mexico (p. 120). "Locals remember the dead by spending the day at the cemetery eating and hanging out." Chester Hawke, Columbus, Ohio, U.S.A.

3. All Saints' day (Nov. 1), Todos Santos Cuchumatán, Guatemala (p. 145). "Everyone gets drunk and rides horses around." Fabio Donacello, Italy

3. All Saints' day, Santiago Sacatepequez, Guatemala. "Everyone goes to the cemetery where they fly these huge, colorful kites. You have to see it to believe it." Patricia Jaden, Houston, Texas, U.S.A.

4. Festivals at Chiquitania, Bolivia (see p. 314).

5. Inti Raymi (June 24). "Many places, but primarily Cusco. Festival of the Sun, banned by the Spanish but brought back in the 1940s." Dr. Crit Minster, Rochester, New York, U.S.A.

# CULEBRA, PUERTO RICO

By Rona Gilbert, Bowling Green, Ohio., U.S.A.

A mere seven miles long and three miles wide, the sleepy island of Culebra is a feast for the eyes, with rolling hills and some of Puerto Rico's best beaches. Just 25 miles east of the mainland, Culebra seems a million miles away from San Juan's hustle and bustle and cruise ship mania, yet few tourists venture to the island. That's unfortunate, because Culebra offers some of the best opportunities to explore Puerto Rico's rich culture and dramatic natural wonders.

Culebra's first inhabitants were a peaceful indigenous tribe known as the *Tanos* who prospered by farming the area's rich hills and valleys. Their way of life changed rapidly and drastically when the U.S. acquired the island in 1898 after the Spanish-American war. Within three years, the U.S. military had established a firing range on the island and began military exercises, relocating the residents to other parts of the island. After 70 years of bombing, the fed-up islanders staged a series of protests and the U.S. military operations were moved to nearby Vieques.

Today, approximately 2,000 islanders live year-round on Culebra, mostly in and around Dewey, the island's only town. The picturesque island bears few scars from its days as a bombing range. Visitors now find Culebra a tranquil and friendly island, offering rare and unique flora, marine animals, wildlife and birds. About 40 percent of the tiny island is dedicated as national reserve parkland, including many of the beaches. Bays, peninsulas and cays surround dramatic cliffs, sandy beaches and mangrove forests, while Mount Resaca, the island's tallest point, dominates the middle from an elevation of 650 feet.

Culebra's main attractions are a dozen picture-perfect beaches that ring the island, most with long stretches of soft white sand, few (if any) crowds and clear, calm, turquoise water. Playa Flamenco, the most popular and most scenic, is the only beach with restrooms, chair and umbrella rental, along with the only development you'll spot on any of Culebra's beaches: Coconuts, a cozy, laid-back beach bar serving yummy mango daiquiris and heaping plates of fresh grilled shrimp. The locals are a great source of information about where to find some of the island's most secluded beaches, many of which are only accessible via a dirt road, path or trail. And with year-round temperatures ranging from 70 to 80 degrees, there's no bad time to explore the beaches.

Travelers to Culebra won't find chain hotels, restaurants or crowds. Accommodations are primarily in inexpensive guest houses and a variety of lively restaurants serve affordable but tasty fresh seafood and other local delights. Daytime activities include diving, snorkeling and other water activities or browsing a handful of boutiques selling locally made artwork and jewelry, colorful sarongs and tropical knick-knacks. While there's no real nightlife, several watering holes offer up a lively bar scene. From San Juan's tourist strip to military exercises on Culebra, America has left its footprint on Puerto Rico. However, the diminutive Culebra offers a glimpse into authentic Puerto Rican culture and its natural riches.

Rona Gilbert is a freelance writer and public relations consultant based in Columbus, Ohio. She has a passion for travel and enjoys using her writing to motivate others to get out and see the world and to experience new and different cultures. Rona is a graduate of Bowling Green State University in Bowling Green, Ohio.

She shared a favorite story with us: "I met a young man in Belize who was operating a snorkel tour. He talked about how he had planned to move to the United States, to escape the poverty of his country. But within two weeks in the U.S. he turned around and came home. He said Americans were 'crazy' because we worked too hard and didn't know how to slow down and enjoy our lives. He opted to leave all of the supposed comforts of the U.S. and return home to his beautiful third-world country to make a living by sailing tourists on his boat. People live very simply—but very happily—in Belize and I was struck by their way of life. Most Belizeans would never want to live anywhere else."

Culebra. Photo by Rona Gilbert.

CARIBBEAN

# VIEQUES, PUERTO RICO

By Erika Cann, New York City, U.S.A.

I've never been a huge fan of public nudity. But something about Vieques' sun-splashed, secluded Navio Beach moves you in a way no deck of cards and after-hours frat party ever could. You're not actually allowed to get naked at any of Vieques' beaches, but if you arrive at the right beach at the right time, it's still possible to claim a solitary afternoon that will make you feel you've arrived at your own little island enclave. And you just might be tempted to strip.

Erika Cann is a humor and travel writer living in New York City. She also teaches dance to small children and walks dogs. And she is always looking for new opportunities to travel. She never, ever, travels without her lucky Grinch t-shirt. Her most bizarre cultural experience? "Probably dating a Dutch prison psychologist who turned out to be the prison cook and who lived in a crack house. Darn that language barrier!"

Anyone with so much as one adventurous pinky knuckle should spend an afternoon four-wheeling to any of the island's unspoiled beaches. Navio beach, pictured here, served as one of the locations used in the 1963 version of *Lord of the Flies*. On the left side of the beach, the surf has carved into the rocky border a complimentary private cavern that you can duck into and feel the sudsy water wash over your body.

Since the U.S. military vacated here in 2003, tourists are now able to access Red Beach, Blue Beach and Green Beach, which comprise, with a few other formerly off-limits beaches, one of the most important wildlife refuges in the Caribbean. All of these beaches are still amazingly undeveloped. Even if you see a lifeguard chair, there will rarely be anyone sitting in it. Many of these beaches are only accessible via dirt "road," with a rented four wheel drive vehicle. But even if you get behind the wheel of a monster truck, go slow on the blighted terrain, or you might find yourself sipping rum runners while stationed on a plastic donut in the evening.

Vieques is a 21-mile-long island just a few miles off the coast of Puerto Rico. The laid-back vibe here is catching on; think eco-traveler rather than party animal. There are two main towns: Esperanza and Isabel Segunda, the latter of which serves as the port and empties out ferries-full of travelers and residents returning from the main island. Esperanza boasts a low-key main drag of restaurants, shops, and hotels. For travelers seeking luxury accommodation, the Inn On The Blue Horizon is a good bet. Budget travelers will have a great time at Banana's. And as long as you've already gone through the trouble of getting to the tiny island, don't forget to visit the bioluminescent Mosquito Bay, one of the few places in the world where you can bathe in a Tinkerbell-like glimmer that follows your every move.

### PUERTO RICO FACTOIDS:

Puerto Rico was a Spanish colony until 1898 when it was ceded to the United States following the Spanish-American War. It has been a commonwealth of the US ever since.

Juan Ponce de León, the first Spanish governor of Puerto Rico, later discovered, explored and attempted to colonize Florida.

Vieques. Photo by Erika Cann.

CARIBBEAN

96    V!VA List    www.vivatravelguides.com/106421

# SANTO DOMINGO AND CABARETE, DOMINICAN REPUBLIC

By Jessica Bennett, Seattle, Washington, U.S.A.

There are no wallflowers in the Dominican Republic. Either you dance ... or somebody drags you out onto the floor to dance. But whether it's a local cafe, a restaurant or an outdoor picnic, Merengue is the soul of the Dominican Republic—and there's no way to escape its syncopated beats. This fast-paced, hip-grinding, salsa-resembling style will follow you from the bustle of Santo Domingo, which meets the Caribbean to the South, to the land-locked villages of the north. And whether they have Latin percussion and brass instruments or a simple cheese-grater and stick to provide a beat, you can bet there's no standing to the side when the Merengue pipes up.

*La Republica Dominicana*, as it's called in Spanish, is an exotic getaway that possesses the luxury of an all-inclusive resort but the culture of a real Latin American traveler's destination. Whether it is the exotic beaches, the hills, waterfalls and vegetation, or the country's favorite sport—baseball—there is something for everyone on this friendly island. Located on the eastern half of Hispanola (the other half is Haiti), the Dominican Republic boasts great natural beauty, such as plunging waterfalls, emerald forests, and inspirational mountains—you may remember the scenery from the blockbuster movie Jurassic Park, which was filmed there.

It is home to a one of the friendliest cultures around, with natives who are welcoming, warm and accommodating. It is the best place to watch a simple stick-ball game, as baseball is (by far) this tiny country's favorite pastime. Major league baseball stars such as Manny Ramirez, Sammy Sosa and David Ortiz are from the Dominican Republic. The Republic has a rich and fascinating history: one good pre-travel read is DR native author Julia Alvarez's *In the Time of the Butterflies*, which is about three sisters living under the dictatorship of Rafael Trujillo, who ruled from 1930 until his assassination in 1961.

If city life suits you, the island's capital, Santo Domingo, is bustling and somewhat polluted, but nevertheless well-worth the visit. It is the oldest city in the New World, founded by Christopher Columbus in 1492. With its plethora of museums and cobblestone roads, including the first street ever built in the Americas—Calle de las Damas—this city has a rich history that's worth exploring. Also check out the Cathedral Basilica Santa Maria la Menor, officially declared the first cathedral in the New World by Pope Paul III in 1542.

If you are more of a beach bum, check out Cabarete, a tiny northern beach town just 20 minutes away from the Puerto Plata International Airport. The town is spread across a semi-circle of golden sand, and many of its hotels, cafes, bars and discos are beachside. Here are a couple recommended activities: bike tours, available at a number of spots, water sports, and of course, stuffing your face with rice, beans and the national beer—Presidente – at the end of each day.

## MERENGUE

By Michelle Hopey

Unlike the cut-loose twists and twirls of salsa dancing, the merengue is a bit more constrained, but no less energizing.

If you're a newbie to the Latin dance scene, you may not know the difference between merengue and salsa dancing. The upbeat, high-energy of both musical genres are quite similar: both tempos exceed 150 beats per minutes and both are partner dances played at salsatecas or salsa clubs. However, salsa is a seven, sometimes, eight-step dance, Merengue has a simple two step move.

Merengue is like marching—stepping from left to right to left, and again over and over through out the entire song. In a way it is similar to a western slow dance as a couple circles around and around together, but unlike the uneventful generic slow dance, merengue has a booty shake.

With every beat of music, you take a step, which makes learning this dance fairly simple: as you march sideways from left to right, each knee bends slightly. But as the knees bend, the same hip must drop as you make complete weight changes from leg to leg. This weight exchange will naturally swing your hips, which is often the most difficult part of the dance. One you do, you've mastered the merengue.

While Salsa dancing is a great full body aerobic workout, its cousin the merengue compliments it nicely-- toning the hips, buttocks and thighs.

A native dance of the Dominican Republic, merengue emerged around the early 20th century. Derived from the European contredance and seeped in African, indigenous and Creole roots, merengue morphed from its folkloric origins to a more modern dance by the 1930s, when it not only became the national symbol of the Dominican Republic, but also one of the most popular Latin dances as well.

Today merengue music and its dance are heard and seen in Salsatecas around the world. Many dancers enjoy both salsa and merengue dancing, so when the band switches it up from salsa to merengue, its like a whole new club. So, if you're dancing the night away at a salsa club and the tempo changes to include a down beat, and the twists and twirls cease, it's probably merengue time, so hit the dance floor and give the Latin two-step a go.

# PLAYA RINCÓN, DOMINICAN REPUBLIC

By Amanda Kass, Columbus, Ohio, U.S.A.

There comes a point, during the trip to secluded Rincón beach, where you wonder if it's going to be worth it. After all, you've left behind several striking beaches around the small town of Samana to ride for forty minutes in a battered jeep that looks like it did movie stunts in a previous life. You turn off the main road onto a muddy trail and you get more nervous. Where are we going? What if this Jeep dies?

Amanda Kass was born and raised in a suburb of Columbus, Ohio, and despite her extensive travels she haven't found the will to leave. She is currently a junior at The Ohio State University (and yes, the *The* is important). She started traveling in her senior year of high-school when a teacher pushed her to apply to a program produced by the National Council on US-Arab Relations.

Ever since then she simply cannot stay in Columbus without going crazy, and she is constantly trying to figure out travel plans that will also get her credit for school. She'll pretty much go anywhere anytime, the crazier the better. And what's the craziest place she's ever been? "Huaquillas or the brothel I stayed at in Boca Chica, although most of my friends think Kuwait was pretty crazy."

But then, you finally arrive. Open beach, white sands, palm trees ... and you have it all to yourself. Rincón means "corner" and it's an appropriate name: you've found a corner of paradise. For five more minutes you steer your abused jeep in and out of the coconut trees before stopping. Without the racket raised by the jeep motor, you suddenly realize that you're surrounded by one of nature's most beautiful sounds: untouched beach. Waves gently lap the shore, birds call out overhead, and you can almost hear the sun warming the white sand.

Playa Rincón is isolated and secluded, closed off by lush green mountains. On a busy day, you may see another fifteen or so visitors, who tend to spread out: you'll basically have the place to yourself. There are some vendors there and you can rent a chair for the day for about 50 pesos ($1.50, more or less) but you may not need to: the sand is soft and comfortable if you've brought a good towel. There are a few small "restaurants"—shacks with food, really—at one end of the beach where you can pick up a greasy meal and a cold beer.

The easiest way to get there is to enlist the services of a "*buscón*" in Samana. A buscón is a "finder," and it's his job to get you whatever you want, be it a hotel, a trip to the beach, a rental car, a good restaurant or just about anything. You don't need to look for a buscón: they'll find you. They're finders, after all. You don't even need to pay them: they'll extort a commission from all the places they take you to later. They can be very annoying, so either assert yourself early and tell them you don't need their services, or pick one and he'll keep the rest from bothering you.

There's not much to do once you've settled in. No jet skis. No parasailing. No white-shirted waiter offering piña coladas. No volleyball net. Sound horrible? Then go to Cancún. Playa Rincón is for those who want to experience a beach in its pure, virgin form, the way the Dominican Republic must have looked to Christopher Columbus when he set foot here in 1492.

## THE MYSTERY REMAINS  By Katie Hale

The remains of Christopher Columbus lie on a catafalque carried by four motionless kings, high above the ground in the gothic Cathedral of Seville in Spain ... or at least some of the infamous man's bones are entombed here in the impressive church.

Where the rest of Columbus' remains are kept is a fervent, over century-old debate. Columbus requested in his will that his remains be taken to what is today the Dominican Republic. When he died on May 20, 1506 he was buried in Valladolid, Spain, but he only stayed there three years before his bones were moved to Seville's Carthusian monastery. In 1536, both the remains of Columbus and his son Diego were sent for final burial in Santo Domingo.

But in 1795, the French took control of Hispaniola and the Spaniards moved the explorer's bones to Havana for safekeeping. In 1898, when the Spaniards were thrown out of Cuba, the remains were taken back to Seville, where they were entombed.

The debate of where Columbus' bones rested began in 1877, when a box containing bones bearing the inscription "illustrious and enlightened male Don Cristóbal Colón" was found in Santo Domingo's cathedral.

In 2006, a group of Granada University researchers, led by forensic geneticist Jose Antonio Lorente, partly solved the mystery. The team carried out DNA analysis of the bones located in Seville's cathedral and concluded they did in fact belong to Columbus.

According to the Dominicans, in 1795 the Spaniards took the wrong body—Columbus' son Diego, who was buried nearby, instead of his father. Examination of the genetic material from the bones located in Santo Domingo would be crucial to settle the debate, but authorities in the Dominican Republic have not allowed the exhumation of the remains buried under the lighthouse thus far. Although Columbus seems to rest not where he intended to, the possibility that he in fact has two resting places in the "old" and "new" worlds seems appropriate for the eminent explorer.

# LOS CALABAZOS, DOMINICAN REPUBLIC

By Amanda Kass, Columbus, Ohio, U.S.A.

You set your 30-pound backpack on the ground and look back up the "stairs"—not really the best word for the rocky, muddy steps inexpertly carved into the hillside alongside a churned up trench used by mules and horses—and wonder if it's worth it. There are nice places to stay in Jarabacoa, after all. You look down: more steps. Where on earth are they taking you? You heft your bag and resume your trek.

At the bottom of the hill, you find yourself in Los Calabazos, a sort of suburb of the larger Jarabacoa, and look around at the wood-and-mud cabins. It's a place that only a true eco-tourist can appreciate: and if you are a true eco-tourist, you'll fall in love with the place, muddy steps and all. The wood and mud cabins house three people—or four if two can share a bed—and a host of odd-looking bugs that will make you wonder if entomologists are aware of them. The only clues that you're still in the 21st century are the electric lights and an icy shower, which actually feels pretty good after a day of hiking or after simply walking up and down the "stairs" back to Jarabacoa.

Los Calabazos is located right on the Río Yaque del Norte, the country's largest river. This means that there are many excellent places to hike (or nap, depending on your definition of a day well-spent) around the trails and boulders that can be found alongside the river. The best part of Los Calabazos is the experience of living with the locals and sharing their daily lives for a time. The little boys play baseball in the streets, in the fields, around the trees and rocks, wherever they can find a small open spot: they dream of being the next Albert Pujols or Pedro Martínez. The little girls dash around, clapping and giggling. The home-cooked meals are a highlight, especially if you like rice and beans (and particularly if you like them for breakfast, lunch AND dinner).

As darkness falls, you join the locals as they make their way from their homes to the local *colmado*, which must be Spanish for "battered mini-mart," and settle in for a friendly night of chatting, watching TV and gossiping. If you're lucky, someone will bring a guitar and treat everyone to a little bit of live music. You look around at the Dominicans who you have gotten to know in the last few days, chatting, singing and laughing in the twilight. You smile as you realize that it was worth the cold shower, the bugs and even the steps.

## DOMINICAN REPUBLIC BASEBALL By Dr. Crit Minster

In September of 1956, The New York Giants sent a new shortstop out onto the baseball diamond. His name was Osvaldo "Ozzie" Virgil, and he was a native of the Dominican Republic, where baseball was already a very popular pastime. He was the first player from the Dominican Republic to play in the big leagues, and he would soon be followed by an amazing parade of talent from this tiny island—half an island, really, it shares Hispaniola with Haiti, which does not produce baseball players—to the fields and stadiums where America's pastime is played on warm summer days. According to legend, baseball was introduced to the island in the 1860s by American sailors who were there to load sugar.

In the Dominican Republic, baseball is played and followed with a fervor perhaps only approached by the love of soccer in Brazil. It is played 12 months out of the year. Rico Carty, a former all-star major league outfielder who was known as a very talented hitter, holds the honorary rank of General in the Dominican army.

The Dominican invasion of major league baseball commenced not long after Ozzie Virgil took the field in New York. In the 1960's and 1970's the Alou brothers—Felipe, Mateo and Jesús—starred for several teams. Mateo batted .342 in 1966 and over .330 on three other occasions. Felipe was an All-Star first baseman: he now coaches his son Moisés in San Francisco. Meanwhile, Juan Marichal was starring as a pitcher for the San Francisco Giants. Pete Rose called him the toughest pitcher he ever faced and in 1983 he was the first Dominican elected to the Baseball Hall of Fame.

Ever since, Dominican players have had a huge effect on baseball. In the first ever World Baseball Classic, played in 2006, the Dominican Republic sent a team that read like an All-Star game roster: Albert Pujols, Vladimir Guerrero, Moisés Alou, Miguel Tejada, Alfonso Soriano, David Ortiz, Bartolo Colón and Francisco Liriano were included, among others. Sammy Sosa, perhaps the most famous Dominican baseballer of recent years, had retired.

Major League Baseball has realized that the Dominican Republic is a very fertile ground for young talent. All of the professional teams have set up scouting camps there, where young players are selected from an early age to receive professional training and support. These camps have often been criticized for failing to provide for the non-baseball education of the young players that sign on. Nevertheless, for many of the Dominican Republic's poorest, baseball is seen as one way to success. Many big leaguers, such as Sammy Sosa, return to the island and use their major league millions to sponsor schools, teams, and more: they're viewed as heroes by the locals. In the streets, kids do not play soccer: it's all baseball, all the time. They dream of growing up and hitting a home run in the bottom of the ninth to win it all for the Giants, or the Yankees, or the Dominican National team.

# PIÑAR DEL RÍO, CUBA

## By David Vincent, Lenox, Massachusetts, U.S.A.

In the westernmost province of Cuba lies a verdant mountainscape called Piñar del Río. Though close to the capital, the "Green Province" seems far away from Havana's hustle and bustle. Tranquility and scenery abound here, as does that most Cuban of products: tobacco. Piñar del Río holds special acclaim for its fertile valleys that yield a richly aromatic tobacco used to produce the renowned "Habanos" or "puros," as the Cubans call their cigars. The area consists of fertile farmland, tropical forest and odd, gumdrop-shaped mountains and hills called "magotes." The landscape is strikingly reminiscent of Halong Bay, Vietnam or the hill country of Southeast Asia. UNESCO also found the region enchanting enough to classify the Viñales Valley a World Cultural and Landscape site in 1999.

Two mountain ranges crisscross the province, and include Pan de Guajaibón, Cuba's highest western peak. Geologists claim that the ancient rocks found here were among the first on the island to crest through the waters of the Caribbean back in the Jurassic period. This is evidenced by a 270 million year old fossil, as well as deeply eroded notches between magotes and an intricate network of caves. The Santo Tomás cavern, one of the largest in the world, tunnels down some 45 kilometers. Other famous caves include Indian Cave and Cueva de los Portales, where Ché Guevara sought refuge during the 1962 Cuban Missile Crisis. In the Sierra del Rosario Mountains, you can hike to the Soroa Lookout Point, and the "Rainbow Waterfall," a 22-meter (over 60 feet) high, spring-fed cascade. Soroa has been declared a National Biosphere Reserve due to its natural riches, including Cuba's largest orchid garden, over 800 types of plants and 73 different types of birds, several of which are endemic to Cuba. Hikers can also soak in the medicinal waters of the Manantiales or San Juan rivers, and visit the ruins of old coffee plantations.

While most visitors come for the sleepy, pastoral countryside, the city of Piñar del Río is also a worthwhile stop. If nothing else, one should stop by the Guach Palace, considered to be the strangest building in Cuba. The palace was built in the ornate style of early 20th century Catalonian modernism, and today houses the Museum of Natural Science.

Even those who are not cigar connoisseurs appreciate a fascinating visit to a cigar factory. Row after row of skilled "rollers" demonstrate their tactile talents, cutting and rolling leaves of aromatic tobacco. Rollers must reach a certain quota without compromising quality. All the while, radio "novelas," or soap operas, play for their entertainment. Another unique and hedonistic stop is a distillery for Guayabita, a tasty local guava liqueur and rum. During a tour, visitors are educated about the distilling process and treated to free samples. Exercise caution here, especially if returning to the road! In fact, why not just spend another night in one of the fine old haciendas, enjoying Cuba's tranquil side.

*"I don't care if I fall as long as someone else picks up my gun and keeps on shooting."*
*-Ernesto "Ché" Guevara, Argentine Revolutionary*
*(1928-1967)*

## CUBAN CIGARS By Katie Hale

Beware: Once you delight in the smooth, rich taste of a Cuban cigar, no other cigar may ever be as satisfying.

On February 7, 1962 President John F. Kennedy imposed a trade embargo on Cuba, making it illegal for U.S. citizens to buy or import products from Fidel Castro's communist regime. Supposedly, Kennedy put in an order for 1,000 H. Upmann cigars the day before signing the embargo.

It is still illegal for Americans to purchase or import Cuban cigars, but the law hasn't stopped the smuggling of the luxury goods into the U.S. for individuals and the black market. The internet has made it incredibly easy for aficionados to purchase cigars anytime, anywhere.

Cigars are complex: the sizes, colors, flavors and shapes all vary. Age, humidity, tobacco type and production method all affect how the cigar will taste and burn. Cohiba, Romeo y Julieta, and Montecristo are popular and sought-after brands of Cubans.

Built in 1845, El Real Fábrica de Tabacos Partagás is an authentic look into the manufacturing of cigars. Tours are offered in several languages and you can watch workers roll cigars by hand.

If you decide to purchase a Cuban cigar anywhere, make sure it reads "Habana" and not "Havana" on the band—the latter is a clear indication of a fake. If you are in Cuba, only purchase cigars at government stores or well-known factories to ensure you are getting the real deal. After selecting a cigar that fits your mood, sit back and enjoy—but please, don't inhale!

# HAVANA, CUBA

## By Grant Doyle, Sydney, Australia

The thing you notice most about central and *Habana Vieja* (old town) is the noise. Not intrusive, nor deafening; just ever changing and mostly uplifting. Walk down any street at any time of day and you'll be embraced by the gentle din of Cuba's decaying but elegant capital.

Household and bar-room music imbues the city with a constant, throbbing pulse. An open doorway might elicit the shrill of adults arguing, a shopkeeper bartering or a TV blasting. Aging, belching cars and trucks—their mufflers long gone—rumble past. Dogs bark. It's energetic this noise, not irritating at all.

The other thing you soon notice about central Havana are the illegal street hawkers; unlicensed young men who volunteer themselves as tourist guides. Aleisai is one such 'entrepreneur'. By day he's a plasterer. Judging by the crumbling building facades you'd think he'd be swamped with work. "I work five and one half days a week," he asserts. The aftermath of Hurricane Wilma has only added to his workload. But it's his "night job" that generates the greatest income while potentially offering tourists a rare insight into the Cuban psyche.

These unofficial guides are persistent but not annoying: they can't afford to be caught because fines and possible imprisonment might follow. There is nothing threatening in their method or manner. They are a part of the local culture. How you handle the encounter can go a long way to defining your time in Havana. I often witnessed western couples wave the likes of Aleisai away with fear and disdain.

"Where you from?" is usually their first, friendly gesture. Politely declining several "advances" at first, my partner and I eventually ventured at a discreet distance (as advised by Aleisai) into a nearby bar, a few blocks off Obispo, one of the main pedestrian thoroughfares linking the spectacular Plaza de Armas and Parque Central. Aleisai met us there.

Aleisai spoke perfect English. The bar made perfect, albeit expensive, Mojitos. The combination made for an ideal, laid-back evening discussing anything from the country's woes to turtle soup. Later, we climbed winding, rickety stairs past sleeping children to a *Paladar*; an official restaurant run by a family operating straight out of their state-owned home. The menu choices weren't cheap but the experience, priceless.

Aleisai makes some money as a plasterer, and more as a guide, but where he really makes his cash is by selling the national product of Cuba: cigars. He escorted us to several "resellers," educating us along the way in what to look for, what to ask, how to taste and what to pay. Even with his cut, the price you pay is about half of that charged by the official Partegás, or cigar houses.

It's free enterprise at its flourishing best in one of the last Communist bastions. And this is the contradiction that is often Cuba. Opulent, ironic and rotting, often in the same instant. But it's a seductive mix you can't turn down.

Grant Doyle is Sydney based and works as a contract web producer and freelance journalist. He has lived in Europe on and off for almost six years. Schooling was in Australia, leading to a journalism degree and culminating in post graduate Information Technology studies at Charles Sturt University.

His favorite cultural experience: "My most engaging cultural experience might have been spending a week in a Tibetan Buddhist monastery recovering from altitude sickness while trekking the Himalayas. Spartan existence yet brimming with spirituality and dignity." Soon, he'll be off to Athens to research a book he's working on.

Havana. Photo by Will Gray.

# COPPELIA ICE CREAM PARK, CUBA

## By Ellery Biddle, Philadelphia, Pennsylvania, U.S.A

Coppelia is indisputably the largest and most popular ice cream place in Cuba, if not the whole of Latin America. It is not simply an oversized shop or creamery; it is an ice cream park. At the center of the lively Vedado section of Havana, it occupies an entire city block and practically spills onto the sidewalk with luscious greenery—palm trees, magnolia trees, oversized ferns.

Coppelia is a social nucleus for *Habaneros*; kids hurry there after school, teenagers go there on dates, twenty-somethings meet there before going out, families go there after dinner. The idea behind Coppelia was to create a center where everyone could afford to come and enjoy a refreshing treat, and the people of Havana responded by making it into a can't-miss destination.

The park has six entrances, but if you go at lunch or dinner time, you will have to wait for at least half an hour to get in. Waiting at Coppelia is like waiting to ride a Ferris wheel. You become familiar with the petty complaints of the child in front of you and the sweet flirtations of the teenage couple behind you. The staff member at each entrance decides how many people to admit at each interval and thus becomes something of a demi-god. If you are extra nice, you might be allowed in sooner.

When you are finally admitted, you will be taken along the circular cement path and led to a cluster of tables surrounded by rose bushes and magnolia trees that make the air cool and sweet. You will feel victorious. Your waitress, who, like the rest of the staff at Coppelia, wears a maroon plaid kilt and polo shirt, will come and take your order. An "ensalada" will get you five scoops of ice cream for five pesos, which (at the time of this writing) amounted to roughly twenty cents in U.S. dollars. There are usually only two or three flavors available each day, and these are written on wipe-off boards at each entrance. Guava, peanut and chocolate are some of the best.

After a while, your ensalada will arrive in an oblong metal dish with a metal spoon and a small glass of water. The perfect reward for a forty-minute wait in the burning sun, it is sweet and creamy and will slide down your throat in the smoothest, most perfect way you can imagine. Enjoy and don't be afraid to order seconds.

www.vivatravelguides.com/104195

# MUSIC AND DANCE OF SANTERÍA AT CASA ELBA, CUBA

## By Ellery Biddle, Philadelphia, Pennsylvania, U.S.A

The *peña* was in a big, old house that was gorgeous in the way that most houses in Havana tend to be: it was falling apart. Some parts of the façade still had the ornate networks of vines and leaves that had been cut into the original stone, while other sections were crumbled and others had vanished altogether. Different layers of brightly colored paint had peeled off various parts of the exterior and freshly hung laundry waved from the second and third floor balconies, a sure sign that someone was living here.

The show was on the roof. The seats and stage were shaded from the sun by pieces of scrap metal that had been patched together with wire and were held up by several metal poles that may once have been street signs. Lots of people were already there, finding seats, talking and laughing. There were people in their twenties, thirties and forties, parents with their kids and many older folks. Most of the seats were simply rusted metal frames of chairs, the seats themselves improvised with a slat of wood or a few layers of cardboard.

An old woman with a white scarf tied around her head and a cigar in hand climbed onto the stage and introduced the performers. Nine Afro-Cuban men came out, dressed all in white linen and carrying *bata* drums, congos and dried gourds with beads strung around them. The place went quiet and they began to play. A small man with a goatee began a soft beat on a congo drum. It grew quickly, becoming louder, sharper, more demanding as more instruments joined and the rhythm of the congo drums diverged from that of the bata.

One man began to sing of Chango, the male god of fertility in the Yoruba tradition (known to some as Santería). Another soon emerged from the group, leaving his drum behind. He began to dance. Short, quick movements, mesmerizing and yet oddly pedestrian as he became Chango personified. People began to stand and clap with the beat. The dancer's face was moving, bright, big eyes shouting to the audience, squinting and then opening wide as his movements grew more expansive. The audience began to stamp and clap and we realized we had to get up and join. We clapped and watched as the musicians kept going, faster, stronger, more powerful, just like Chango, and then after reaching a climax of sound, it all came back down until the dancer stopped moving, bowed his head and then returned to his place, picking up his drum and joining the group in a soft beat.

They kept playing like this, barely pausing as they went from one song to the next, one god to another. When they finally stopped, three old men quickly rose from the audience, went into the house and returned immediately, each carrying a large plastic bag. They handed each person an aluminum can, the top of which had been cut so that the can could function as a cup. Then, they came around again, each carrying a gallon jug, one of apple juice, the other of peso rum. They say that you will go blind if you drink too much peso rum, but my friends and I decided to go with the flow. We drank out of severed Fanta cans on the roof of an old Havana mansion at sunset on a Sunday as the drums began to play again. We drank slowly. Our throats burned. The show continued. It was one of the best I've ever seen.

# CASAS PARTICULARES, CUBA

*By Melanie Furlong, Nova Scotia, Canada*

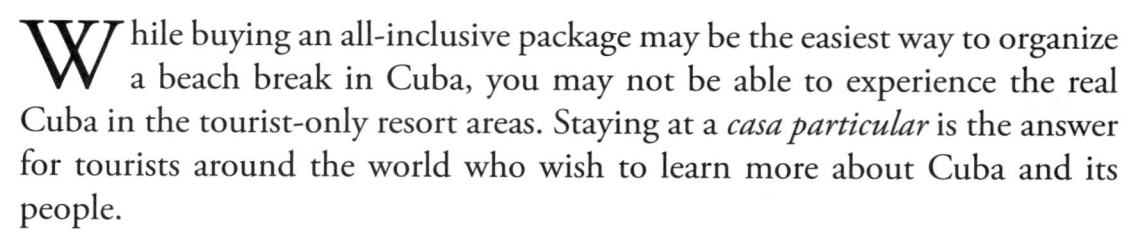

While buying an all-inclusive package may be the easiest way to organize a beach break in Cuba, you may not be able to experience the real Cuba in the tourist-only resort areas. Staying at a *casa particular* is the answer for tourists around the world who wish to learn more about Cuba and its people.

A casa particular is a Cuban bed and breakfast and there are thousands of them around the island. Suzana Sanchez, an elderly Havana widow, has been renting out four bedrooms in her Nuevo Vedado home to tourists since 1995. Clean and bright, the rooms offer air conditioning, ceiling fans, separate bathrooms, double beds, hot water, telephones, security boxes and refrigerators. She also employs two maids and a night guard for the gated parking area at the front of the house.

Paul Lamot, a Belgian citizen who lives near Antwerp with his Cuban wife, began running www.casa-particular.info in 2000 to support exactly this kind of business venture in Cuba. The website is a portal to casa particular sites and provides a list of casas around the country. It connects to 173 casa particular sites in Havana and over 1000 sites in total.

"Casa owners that operate legally are allowed to advertise their place using little fliers that are mostly given to arriving tourists by young people," says Lamot. "Often when you enter a city suddenly motorbikes will appear and they will try to guide you to a casa. That is about the extent that advertising is allowed."

There are no Government statistics about how many tourists stay in casas particulares each year, but Lamot estimates tens of thousands choose to see Cuba this way.

"It is the only viable (and cheap) alternative lodging in Cuba. A casa will cost you half of a cheap hotel and will provide a better room and better meals. Prices for the casas start at 25 pesos.

"Beyond the low prices though," says Lamot, "there is an overwhelming desire with most people to experience Cuba. The 'tourism apartheid' of the government has made the resorts sterile and ghetto-like. People who stay at a hotel in Varadero have not seen Cuba."

Lamot also says that many of the tourists who visit Cuba and stay in anything less than a five-star resort are appalled by the service and food they receive. "Receiving sub-standard services in the hotel creates an image of uneducated and uncaring people. Staying at a casa particular will show you that the Cubans are actually the opposite. The service and care you will receive in a good casa will only create and reinforce the image of the Cubans as an open and helpful people."

The best casas Lamot has seen are in Havana. "I found the most luxurious casas in Havana, but there are some great casas in every town. Santiago can surprise you and Trinidad with its historical buildings has some stunning casas."

In most cases, staying at a casa includes the room and breakfast. Some casas will charge separately for breakfast and any other meals are always to be paid for separately. Lamot says it is advisable to eat at your casa or a *paladar*, a private restaurant, as the quality of the food is much better than it is in state restaurants and the prices are lower.

In a standard casa, eight to 12 pesos convertibles will buy you a good meal.

If you still want to get to the beach, rent a car or hire a car and driver for the duration of your stay. The owner of your casa can help you find a driver and it will be cheaper than renting your own car. Either way, staying at a casa particular will give you more freedom to explore the island and find the Cuba of your imagination.

Melanie Furlong is a freelance writer in Nova Scotia, Canada. She majored in Spanish at Acadia University and married a Cuban in the Czech Republic. She always stays at *Suzana's Casa Particular* in Havana. Soon, she'll be off to England for hiking and horseback riding in Exmoor National Park. She's had enough of roughing it, though: "I think I'm ready for a trip to a five-star spa (anywhere) with daily massages and gourmet food."

## LATIN REVOLUTIONARIES # 4: FIDEL CASTRO

**Cuba (1926--)**

Fidel Castro was born into a wealthy Cuban family in the city of Birán. He began his revolutionary life early: in 1947 he joined the Caribbean Legion, which attempted to overthrow the government of the Dominican Republic. The attempt failed, but Castro escaped on a raft by swimming two miles.

Castro was involved in a short-lived revolt in Cuba in 1953: he was captured, jailed for two years, and then exiled. He met Ernesto "Ché" Guevara in Mexico and the two returned to Cuba in 1956. They carried out a guerilla campaign for two years, defeating government forces in different parts of the country. In 1958, the government mounted a massive offensive against the rebels. When the offensive fizzled, marked by desertions and defeat, the leaders of Cuba began to fear the worst. In December, 1958, President Batista abandoned the country, fleeing to the Dominican Republic and then to Spain.

Castro set himself up as president and within two years had turned Cuba into a communist nation, earning the enmity of the United States. He has ruled the small island nation ever since, defying the U.S. at every opportunity.

# TRINIDAD, CUBA

By Darren Fitzgerald, Los Angeles, California, U.S.A.

On the coastal edge of Cuba's south central valley lies a lively Spanish colonial town where days are spent on the Caribbean and nights in the local salsa club, sipping *Mojitos* under a starry sky. After the buzz of Havana city life, Trinidad welcomes you into a more rural and authentic rhythm of Cuban culture.

The road from Havana winds through the countryside and trails past a lazy creek into Trinidad, ending at narrow cobblestone streets lined with terracotta homes, cigar shops and coffee stands handing out shots of sweet espresso. Families open their doors to travelers, and most stays include breakfast and dinner with family members who offer everything from bicycle rides to opinions on the Cuban revolution.

Mornings start with fresh mangos, pineapples, bananas, fried eggs and a jolt of sugar-saturated Cuban coffee, which energizes you for a 10-mile ride to the sea on a 1940s single-gear Chinese bicycle. The small gravel road to the beach passes through small villages lined with banana trees, and eventually follows the Caribbean coastline to the pristine Playa Ancón. The Soviet-era hotel at the head of the beach is a bit dreary, so keep your eyes on the water, the sand in your toes, a cold Crystal beer in your hand and you'll forget all about it. The day ends with a relaxing ride back with the warm wind and sunset behind you.

*Caballeros* offer horseback rides through Trinidad's lush back country filled with rivers and sugar plantations. Oxen plow the fields while barefoot *campesinos* with leathery skin haul large bags of sugarcane on their shoulders. Children run around taunting the chickens, sheep and goats that dot the hillsides, while old women sway on rocking chairs mending clothes. You cross through several of these plantations until you reach a narrow, rocky trail leading to a waterfall and cave where you snack on banana bread while the horses cool off in the river.

Evenings start with fresh lobster, pulled pork and fried shrimp, served with rice, beans and plantains, topped off by short glasses of 15 year old Havana Club rum. Stroll up to the hillside steps bordering Plaza Mayor and enjoy the balmy night with a frosty Mojito and beefy Cohiba cigar while listening to local musicians. You'll eventually end up at Casa de Música watching live Cuban music under the stars and dancing until dawn with locals and other travelers. The days come and go like a gentle tide on the sand, and for weeks afterwards you can still hear the salsa rhythms, taste the buttery dark rum and smell the warm salty air. It's a slice of Cuba that will never be forgotten.

CUBA FACTOIDS:

José Martí, the hero of Cuba's independence from Spain, was thrown in jail for treason and agitating against the Spanish government in 1869. He was only 16 years old at the time. Although he is revered in Cuba for his poetry and devotion to the cause of Cuban independence, he is best known in other parts of the world as the man who wrote the poem that was put to music in the song "Guantanamera."

On June 6, 1762, The British attacked and captured Havana. A year later, they traded it back to Spain in exchange for Florida.

*"The only force and the only truth in this life is love. Patriotism is nothing more than love, friendship is nothing more than love."*
*-José Martí, Cuban Patriot and Poet (1853-1895)*

## THE BAY OF PIGS By Leigh Gower

On April 17, 1961, Cuban Armed Forces defeated invading American-backed counterrevolutionaries at what has since become known as the infamous Bay of Pigs invasion, in Cuba's Matanzas province. The captured invaders were returned to the United States only after Kennedy's government agreed to pay Cuba approximately $50 million in the form of food and medical supplies.

Visiting the area today you are likely to be surprised. Playa Girón, the site where the actual invasion took place, is a beautiful lagoon of crystal waters and coral reefs right off the shore. To the detriment of the invading force, the U2 spy planes mistook the coral reefs for seaweed. Employing a tour guide here will further help you realize the very obvious strategic disadvantages of the position. Located in the Zapata swamp, the largest in the Caribbean, the Bay of Pigs is an oppressively humid region that would have been quite unwelcoming to soldiers in heavy military gear.

A museum at Playa Girón today commemorates the Cuban victory over an "imperialist" United States. Each year the museum hosts an elaborate celebration on the battle's anniversary, drawing thousands of Cubans who arrive for a day of ceremonies and patriotic revelry. There is also a crocodile farm nearby, but the area is otherwise quiet, best suited to scuba divers or those looking for a tranquil stop. Most of the shoreline is rocky.

The number of tourists has dropped in recent years as a result of hurricane damage and the construction of new resorts on other parts of the island, but the Bay of Pigs is still a significant attraction for those fascinated by an event that helped define the modern era of Cuban-U.S. relations.

# BARACOA, CUBA

By Anna L. Barto, Oaxaca, Mexico

Due to its geographic isolation, Baracoa, Cuba, is just beginning to be discovered by tourists. Those nomads who travel to the remote northeastern corner of the island will be rewarded with an unspoiled colonial village surrounded by secluded beaches and virgin rainforest.

On the horizon looms the most recognizable local landmark, a table-shaped hill called El Yunque, or "the anvil." Baracoa's cobblestone streets are lined with one-story buildings, whose peeling, carnival colored paint jobs and weathered tile roofs add—rather than detract—from their charm. Local people watch you curiously from wide verandas. Some may approach you to sell sweets, but they are not as aggressive as the vendors in Havana.

Baracoa, where cocoa trees grow in abundance, is famous for its white chocolate, sold in round, flat cakes encased in palm bark. Also be sure to taste-test the *cucruchu*, an ambrosia of honey, coconut, nuts and fresh seasonal fruit served in a palm bark cone.

Along the eastern edge of the village runs the Malecón, a miniature of Havana's seaside promenade, which ends in a park dedicated to Christopher Columbus, who arrived here in 1492. His statue, hewn out of a giant tree stump, stares inland with a stern expression. Downtown, in the Cathedral Nuestra Señora de la Asunción, you can see the remains of a wooden cross he supposedly planted at the site.

To the west of town you'll find the tranquil beaches of Playa Maguana and Playa Nibujón. Playa Maguana is the tourist beach, featuring restaurant and bar service, while Playa Nibujón is more rustic and frequented by locals.

Located farther inland, the UNESCO Biosphere Reserve Cuchillas de Toa protects some of the world's last untouched rainforest and its endangered plant and animal species. Among these species is the Cuban land snail, about two inches in diameter with striking spirals of color. It is advisable to hire a guide for trekking or hiking excursions in the reserve. Official government guides can be found at the Office of Natural Parks.

After an active day of hiking and swimming, return to the homey atmosphere of your bed and breakfast, or casa particular, and enjoy a home-cooked meal. Be sure to advise the proprietor in advance. For less than the cost of a McDonald's Happy Meal, your hostess will prepare a feast of traditional Cuban creole food: fried chicken, rice, beans and sweet plantains, or better still, a typical Baracoan meal of fresh seafood, fish stuffed with plantains, garlic-rubbed shrimp or lobster smothered in butter.

Anna Barto is a U.S. expatriate living in Oaxaca, Mexico, where she works as a freelance writer, English teacher, and Coordinator for LanguageCorps Mexico. She writes a regular blog about life in Oaxaca.

She has fond memories of her visit to Cuba: Once, in Havana, she spent the night in the Plaza de la Revolución in order to hear Fidel Castro speak. Soon, she's off to Honduras to visit a friend in the Peace Corps. Her dream vacation? "I'd love to take a culinary tour of Thailand."

## CLASSIC CARS

By Katie Hale

A classic '53 Chevy sits on the side of the road; its deep, emerald green paint job and shiny chrome grill sharp contrasts to the crumbling, colonial off-white facades in the backdrop.

Studebakers, Packards, Fords, Cadillacs, Buicks, Dodges and other vintage cars cruise the streets of Cuba in droves. If you're lucky, you may even catch a glimpse of a Model T Ford. Some have been restored to their original glory, while others ramble along with the help of aging Russian motors.

In a twisted irony, Cuba depends on old American cars for transportation because of the trade embargo imposed over 40 years ago. Until the embargo, Cuba imported more American automobiles than any other country. It is estimated that between 250,000 and 450,000 classic American cars roam this island's streets and highways. To fill the tank of one of these beauties costs a Cuban the equivalent of at least two months salary.

A group of shirtless men hover in the setting sun over the opened hoods of two broken-down cars. They won't be here long. Although there are no junk yards in Cuba, a spare part is always found, the problem is always solved. Losing one of these cars to a mechanical malfunction is simply not an option.

If you can't resist those leather bench seats, tail fins, and chrome details, rent a classic and cruise around Havana's old town or find an open strip of road near the beach. The cost isn't cheap, but can you really put a price on time travel?

# MEXICO

**¡Olé!**

Mexico is a mystery to travelers, it would seem. Many skip it entirely: they go to beaches in the Caribbean, ruins in the Andes, nightlife in Rio, or partake in activities such as scuba diving in Belize, hiking in Ecuador…the list goes on and on. It's almost as if they've forgotten that there is one country that has all of this, and more: Mexico. Even those travelers who do go to Mexico tend to hit the same places: Cancún, Acapulco, Tijuana, Cabo San Lucas. This tendency to ignore the rest of Mexico or only go to the most-visited destinations is doubly puzzling, because Mexico is the closest Latin American country to the United States and reasonable air fares (or even bus fares) are easy to find.

These travelers don't know what they're missing. Mexico is an ancient land, incredibly rich in culture, history, tradition, natural beauty and charming people. Once you get off the tourist trail and leave the Corona-soaked beaches of Cancún and Acapulco behind you, you quickly realize that the best parts of Mexico are the ones that don't offer wave pools, parasailing and the chance to take a picture of a donkey drinking a beer.

In this section, our community will be your guide for a tour through some of the best that this misunderstood land has to offer. Sure, there are pieces about Cancún and Tijuana, and they're great places to visit, but we'll also take you out of the Tequila bars and into a Tequila factory, off the surfboard and onto a horse, riding through a beautiful mountain range, away from the golf courses and into remote jungle ruins. Don't pack a lunch for this trip: we'll stop for some cheese in Oaxaca, try some hot peppers, and even some Mexican jumping beans (okay, you can't eat those, but they are cool).

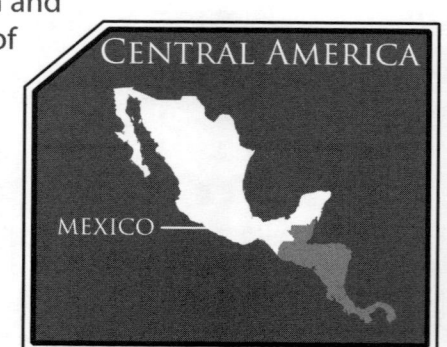

# TIJUANA

## By Dr. Crit Minster, Rochester, New York, U.S.A.

Prohibition was the best thing to ever happen to Tijuana. A small, dusty town best known for a modest cattle ranching industry, the city was considered little more than a place to stay before or after crossing the U.S.—Mexico border. When the United States of America outlawed alcohol in 1919, the conveniently located Tijuana—only 15 miles from San Diego—cashed in. The city built casinos and bars and attracted countless tourists, including many prominent Hollywood movie stars. The city boomed.

The city of Tijuana has never completely shed its image as a place where visitors go to cut loose and have a good time, and the night life is as legendary as ever. La Coahuila, Tijuana's notorious red-light district, continues to hop with after-dark activity. Although the tequila still flows like water, and you're never far from a bar, the city has recently focused on adding activities that don't involve drinking or late-night debauchery.

Jai-Alai, a ball game that involves heavy betting, is a favorite, as are bullfights, dog races, cabarets and water sports on the nearby coast. In an attempt to lure a different class of tourist, the city has also added an amusement park and a number of golf courses. Even as a youthful hellion, the city attracted an international pool of shoppers: the city is a duty-free zone, so prices on many things are lower than they would be elsewhere. The city is also home to several artisan markets, where tourists pick through boxes and contemplate rows of hand-painted ceramics, finely carved wood and bright blankets. Shopaholics will love *Avenida Revolución*, famous for the countless tacky curio shops that line it. Those less inclined to shop-til-you-drop might want to head somewhere else. Bargaining is the norm so polish your negotiation skills before heading into the artisan jungle.

A grueling day of bargaining is sure to leave you famished; it's a good thing that the cuisine of Tijuana is also noteworthy. Order a Caesar salad, if you're a fan: according to local legend, it was invented here (as was the Margarita, so they say). The September 16 festival that marks Mexican Independence is a highlight.

Occasionally derided by visitors for not being "the real Mexico," Tijuana has evolved a new, hybrid identity. With one foot in two worlds, Tijuana's border personality is one of its greatest charms. It is a little known fact that many of Mexico's best and most innovative artists and writers live and work in Tijuana. Their artistic energies are fed by the constant contact with and motion of the border.

Prohibition was repealed in 1933, but Tijuana never looked back. More than just a place to get a cold drink, the city is now selling itself, the mixed-blood offspring of the U.S.A. and Mexico, alive and thriving on the busiest border in the world.

> *"Mexican restaurants slip high-octane beans into virtually almost everything they serve, including breath mints. It is not by mere chance that most of Mexico is located outdoors."*
> -Dave Barry, American Humorist (1947-)

Xochicalco Ruins. Photo by Stephany Slaughter.

# AVENTURAS SOBRE RIELES

## By Lorraine Caputo, Columbia, Missouri, U.S.A.

Not too far from where Pancho Villa led his 1916 attack on Columbus, New Mexico, a new revolution is now brewing in the Chihuahua desert of Northern Mexico. In 1996 all train services—cargo and passenger alike—were halted due to the privatization of this once state-run industry. The *ejidos* (communal lands) and small settlements were left to their own fates. Lacking roads and then rails the locals faced a difficult question: How would they now get their goods to market, see a doctor, or do anything else that required transportation?

A small group of people in Nuevo Casas Grandes therefore decided to maintain 100 kilometers (65 miles) of track. Some of them used to work for the railroad; others are only now learning the trade. With no funding from the government, this is a labor of love—and a conviction of necessity.

Aventuras Sobre Rieles (Adventures on Rails) is the name of this new army of Mexican railroad revolutionaries who now provide regular services to the inhabitants of Ejido Las Heroínas and other settlements along the way to La Madera. They also offer excursions to tourists which help them to cover their maintenance costs. One such special trip is to Mata Ortiz.

Riding the train is a little like stepping back in time, with the train looking rather like a toy compared to its larger kin, the diesel engine. Boarding the old worker transport cars and locomotive, the *trencito* (little train) goes through desert scrublands to this village renowned for its traditional pottery.

Several hours are spent visiting workshops before returning to the city. Another option is an all-day excursion, traveling the entire stretch of open track, to Cumbres. The journey traverses desert populated by roadrunners, lizards, jack rabbits and eagles; poplars, mesquite, cacti and prickly pears; wind and sun-worn adobe hamlets. Then the trencito winds into the Sierra Madre mountains, along a river with pastures, boulders and crags, and through cedar and pine forests. Great blue herons are numerous, as are other types of waterfowl. One then arrives at the Cumbres tunnels of which the oldest is over a kilometer long.

During the Mexican Revolution, a cargo train that was assaulted by guerrilleros derailed and caught fire. It was then hit by a passenger train that could not stop in time, and the tragedy cost over 50 people their lives. Midway down this old tunnel there is an altar to those victims, where offerings are still made in their memory.

On the return to Nuevo Casas Grandes, a stop near Ejido Las Heroínas allows one to picnic on the grassy banks of the river. Mexican families will board, fully equipped with barbecue grills and coolers (for the picnic), so that their grandchildren can experience what it's like to ride a train—and join the Aventuras Sobre Rieles in a new type of revolution happening just south of the U.S. border.

## LATIN AMERICAN MYSTERIES # 3: WHO KILLED LUÍS DONALDO COLOSIO?

Tijuana, Mexico: March 23, 1994.

On the afternoon of March 23, 1994, Luís Donaldo Colosio, a Mexican presidential candidate, was shot in the head in the city of Tijuana during a political rally. He was young, charismatic and the candidate of the ruling PRI political party at a time when that all but guaranteed victory. His assassin, Mario Aburto, was captured at the scene and confessed. It seemed like an open-and-shut case.

Nevertheless, many questions remain.

Aburto has claimed, in phone conversations with his father, that he did not kill Colosio and that he was tortured to make him confess. The video of the murder shows the gunshot but not the face of the killer, who could have been among the security guards surrounding Colosio. The video also shows a shaggy man with a moustache being captured, who bears little resemblance to the clean-cut Aburto. Also, Colosio was shot twice: once in the head, from the left, and once in the abdomen, from the right, two and one half seconds later. All of this contradictory evidence has led many Mexicans to believe in a conspiracy. Even Colosio's parents do not think Aburto did it, or that he acted alone if he did.

Some point the finger at the powerful Tijuana drug cartel, but many Mexicans believe that the assassination was ordered at the highest levels of Mexican government. At the time, Colosio had been selected as the heir apparent to the Mexican presidency by sitting president Carlos Salinas de Gortari. But powers within the party were beginning to suspect that Colosio was more radical than they thought, and that if he were elected, he would betray the wealthy corporate sponsors of the PRI and work for true reform.

This mystery will probably never be completely solved, like the Kennedy assassination, with which it is often compared. Mishandling of evidence and allegations of torture mean that there will always be doubt about Aburto, and if the government or a drug cartel was, in fact, responsible, they've likely destroyed any evidence of their crime.

# BOQUILLAS

By Carol Huang, New York City, U.S.A.

Along the bottom crook of Texas's winding southern border, across from 1,282 square miles (3,320 square kilometers) of protected land in the Chihuahua Desert, is the Mexican town of Boquillas. It is more of a desert outpost than town, with less than 200 people left from its days as a mining settlement in the late 1800s.

Only a handful of shacks remain on a sun-baked bluff overlooking the mud-colored river. If the river is low, you might wade across, but otherwise the only way to get there from the U.S. is by *lancha*, or boat, which you reach by hiking through desert brush and pushing past six-foot riverbank reeds. Usually one or two little boats will be waiting, and for a dollar or two, the men will ferry you across the shallow, sluggish river to Mexico.

The first time I saw Boquillas, my boyfriend and I had spent a day in Big Bend National Park hiking through remote desert canyons, surrounded by the Chisos Mountains and arid land dotted by prickly pears and blue-green agaves the size of wheelbarrows. We unwisely spent a night without mosquito nets on the hard ground as tiny bats swirled overhead, and the next day we hiked to the river where a boatman took us over. As we approached, I saw a couple of deserted shacks without doors on an empty, bone-dry bluff. We hiked up a dirt trail and found a dusty road with a restaurant, bar and a stall that sold soft drinks and bananas. None of the structures had complete walls, and other than a few people hunched in the shade and some panting mongrels, there wasn't much else. Supposedly, the only other Mexican town was an 11-hour drive away. We gulped down two bottles of warm Fanta and left, but I liked the little colony, whose only focus seemed to be the unrushed simplicity of waiting out the heat, surrounded by little more than land and sky.

A few years later I returned. There had been lots of rain and the river was high. Unsolicited, an elderly boatman gallantly carried me to his lancha, presumably so I wouldn't get wet. The rain started to fall as we crossed, and by the time I raced up the trail, pellets of hail had joined the downpour. The town had a new restaurant, so I dashed in to check it out. There were half a dozen locals and three unshaven gringos sipping beers, all staring at the rain and hail beyond the edges of the roof. The unbelievable snippet of conversation I overheard—something about sticking around until the law cooled on the other side—added to the mystique of being temporarily trapped in an old mining town as the grey sky thundered overhead. In seconds it was over, and all of us stepped out to admire the sky as it brightened over the desert.

Carol Huang is a former journalist for Reuters and a graduate of Columbia University's Graduate School of Journalism. She has worked for newspapers in Texas and Nevada and written for various magazines. Stories she's covered include the 9-11 terrorist attacks (*Glamour*, Nov. 2001), the seizure of 800 hostages by Chechen rebels inside a Moscow theater (*Maxim*, March 2003) and the story of Nebiy Mekonnen, a former political prisoner in Ethiopia who translated *Gone With the Wind* from English into Amharic while imprisoned under the Mengistu dictatorship (*American Scholar*, Fall 2006). The craziest place she's ever visited? "For out and out insanity, probably Penny Lane in Nuevo Laredo's La Zona red light district." She hopes to visit the Serengeti some day.

## LA QUINCEAÑERA

By Katie Hale

The transition from childhood to womanhood is an important cultural occasion. In the United States it is sometimes marked by the Sweet Sixteen or debutante's ball; in Jewish culture it's the Bat Mitzvah; but in Mexico, it is *la quinceañera* that is the most significant day in a girl's life.

The celebration of a girl's fifteenth birthday (quinceañera refers to both the celebration and the girl) traditionally begins with a religious ceremony and is followed by a reception with family and friends. At the party, female relatives pass out party favors and family and friends enjoy music, dancing and food. The lavishness of the quinceañera is directly connected to the economic status of the girl's parents.

The quinceañera's court can be composed of all young women (*damas*), all young men (called *escortes*, *chambelánes*, or *galánes*), or a combination of both. The birthday girl usually wears an elaborate and expensive pastel ball gown, only second in ostentation to her future wedding dress. During a ceremony held at the quinceañera's reception, she receives a tiara, bracelet, earrings, cross and Bible or prayer book. The gifts symbolize the quinceañera's faith and never-ending life.

After the quinceañera is crowned, a toast is said in her honor and a huge cake matching her ball gown is cut for all to eat. The fiesta concludes with a *festejada*—a dance to the traditional waltz by the quinceañera and boyfriend or escort. The quiceañera is now no longer a girl, and will be treated as a mature woman by society.

MEXICO

# COPPER CANYON

By Richard Arghiris, London, England

Immense, inspirational and rugged, the Copper Canyons in northern Mexico are as wild as they are lively. Lakes, rivers, springs, waterfalls, rock formations and gorges await exploration in this pristine region, 40,000 square kilometres (25,000 square miles) in area and four times deeper than Arizona's Grand Canyon.

Richard Arghiris is a freelance journalist and writer, born and based in London. His previous work roles are varied. They include being a croupier on Mediterranean cruise-ships, a factory worker in Amsterdam and an auction porter in London. Aside from travel journalism, he devotes a lot of time to fiction writing and is currently working on a novel based loosely on his experiences abroad. His most bizarre cultural experience? "Eating hallucinogenic mushrooms with a shaman in Oaxaca, Mexico."

His passions include hiking, anthropology and the natural world. The Amazon, "the greatest and most savage wilderness on earth," is his dream destination.

Carved out of the Sierra Madre mountains by six rivers, over twenty canyons comprise this astonishing natural wonder. Exceptional evergreen forests pervade the region's heights, while its depths are scorched by a searing, subtropical climate. The 655 kilometres (407 miles) Chihuaha-Pacific railway line traverses the canyons on an east-west axis, providing unparalleled and outstanding views of the land.

At the heart of the region, at an altitude of 2,810 meters (9,200 feet) lies the town of Creel. Surrounded by pine forests, this rugged settlement of log cabins and lumber mills serves as the most convenient jumping off point for canyon excursions. Guides, maps, mountain bikes and four-wheel-drive vehicles are widely available in Creel, served by buses, the Chihauaha-Pacific railway and numerous lodgings.

Close to Creel lies the *Complejo Ecoturistico Arareko*, an indigenous land-owning co-operative or *eidejo* owned by the Tarahumara. There are fifty thousand Tarahumara Indians that populate the region with sparse farms and cabins. They are considered the spiritual and legal custodians of copper canyon country. Their name in their own language is *Raramuri*, meaning "those who run fast." As accomplished long-distance runners, they can cover wild stretches of hundreds of miles barefoot without stopping.

The Tarahumara can be seen in and around Creel in their traditional clothing. The men wear loin-cloths and puffy-sleeved shirts, the women don bright skirts and headscarves.

Simple hikes in the eidejo lead to interesting and unusual rock formations. The Valley of the Frogs contains surreal amphibian-like boulders. The Valley of the Mushrooms holds structures resembling enormous toadstools. The Valley of the Gods, nine kilometres (six miles) away, contains vast phallic shaped rocks worshipped as symbols of fertility and life-force.

Other popular destinations in the eidejo include Lake Arareko and the Cusarare waterfall.

Further flung excursions lead to places like the sweltering town of Batopilas—a rough-looking, brutally arid town, formerly renowned for its mine. The town is most easily reached by a lengthly bus ride, the ultimate in precarious "chicken bus" trips. After rising and falling through several enormous canyons, a drop of 1,800 meters (6,000 feet) to the side, the road makes hundreds of turns and hair-pin switch-backs in a single stretch.

The Chihuahua-Pacific train ride is the perfect conclusion to any copper canyon trip. The westward journey, as far as Los Mochis on the Pacific coast, takes eight hours to complete from Creel. Hour after hour, one incredible edifice rolls on after another. Mountains, canyons, forests, lakes, engulfing stone corridors and monumental pillars. Finally towards dusk, the landscape flattens into desolate, cacti-spotted desert.

---

### COPPER CANYON TRAVEL TIPS:

Creel is accessible via Chihuahua. Buses to Chihuahua run from Mexico City. From there, it's another five hours to Creel. Rapid flights are also available from Mexico City and Los Angeles. Buses run daily to Batopilas and take six hours.

The Copper Canyon railway passes through Creel twice a day in each direction. Heading west to the coast, sit on the left side for the best view. Heading east and inland, sit on the right.

---

Copper Canyon. Photo by Kim Walker.

MEXICO

# BATOPILAS

By Kim Walker, Evansville, Indiana, U.S.A.

At the bottom of a remote canyon in Mexico's Sierra Madre lies the tiny village of Batopilas, a languid place that once thrived thanks to one of the country's richest silver mines. Lavish haciendas and a beautiful cathedral adorned this lush oasis beside its namesake river.

Governor Alexander Shepherd traded American politics for Mexico's silver in 1880 and moved his family, servants and chef to remote Batopilas to manage the mines. The descent into the canyon alone took eight days by mule.

Today the 50 mile (80 kilometer) journey from Creel, a popular stop for tourists traversing the Copper Canyon by rail, takes eight hours by truck. The road, initially paved, winds through pine-forested mountains then abruptly turns to dust. Landslides litter the narrow lane, rutted with potholes, that zigzags down precipitous cliffs. Drivers honk at blind curves and reluctantly inch toward the abyss to create squeezable passing space when faced grille to grille with another truck or wobbling bus on dizzying switchbacks that drop 6,000 feet (1,800 meters). Passengers are free to enjoy the spectacular scenery, as gorges, craggy peaks and meandering rivers give way to a sloping desert studded with citrus trees and organpipe cactus.

Batopilas is considered the treasured jewel of the Copper Canyon. In this mining town where cowboys rumble through the plaza, two general supply stores, a jeweler, a handful of restaurants and a hurache sandal-maker line the town's only street. Tourist accommodations are restored haciendas with flowering courtyards, shuttered windows, Moorish arches and Victorian antiques.

Across the river's swinging bridge, Shepherd's grand mansion is now a roofless ruin overtaken by dense shrubs and purple bougainvillea. In late afternoon, the sun strikes the terracotta structure with brilliant light and draws tourists toward the site. Walking through empty rooms once filled with antiques, and even a grand piano that Tarahumaras hand-carried from the canyon rim, gives one a renewed appreciation for the accessibility of modern life. The seclusion is unbelievable.

Away from town, trails lead up to deserted mines and hills with panoramic vistas, best done with a guide to prevent getting lost or trespassing highly protected agricultural plots. Tourists are free to wander perhaps the most entrancing place of all, the mysterious Lost Cathedral of Saveto. Isolated in a valley 30 minutes from town, a white triple-domed structure nestled in green rolling hills gleams like a fairy-tale castle. Nobody knows who built it, or why.

Jesuit priests had joined silver-chasing Spaniards in Batopilas by 1709, but wouldn't have had reason to build a grand domed cathedral in Saveto, a good day's journey on foot, when the only inhabitants were Tarahumara Indians who resisted organized religion and retreated deeper into the canyons to avoid interactions. Today, local children can't solve the mystery, but will unlock the massive carved door to let tourists poke around the shadowy chambers.

Secrets lie buried in these canyon walls where elusive Tarahumaras still hide. Travelers who take the adventurous journey to Batopilas step back into time, into faded centuries where history, grandeur and intrigue are very much alive.

Kim Walker dabbled in creative writing while completing her B.S. English degree and M.S. in Communication Disorders from SIUC in Carbondale, Illinois. Screen writing soon changed to travel writing after graduate school, when she began working as a speech-language pathologist at a rehab hospital in Evansville, Indiana.

Her love for travel, adventure, writing and photography remained top diversions while working with stroke and head-injured patients and led to the recent creation of Unique Photo Tours. She and her husband lead small groups to various destinations around the globe with an emphasis on cultural experiences, elusive wildlife, historical ruins and special places off the tourist path. On her travels Kim always takes an open mind and respect. In Quito she was treated like royalty and presented with the national delicacy–freshly roasted guinea pig. "A group of smiling locals handed me utensils to cut into the animal, served whole, and nodded approvingly as I savored each bite."

Tarahumara Family. Photo by Kim Walker.

# HIDALGO DEL PARRAL

## By Lorraine Caputo, Columbia, Missouri, U.S.A.

July 20, 1923: Shots ring out from the building on Avenida Juárez in downtown Hidalgo del Parral, in the Mexican state of Chihuahua. A 1921 Ford, driven by the retired revolutionary General Francisco "Pancho" Villa, crashes against a tree. Villa, riddled by at least 15 gunshot wounds, dies almost instantly. Villa is the target, but not the only casualty: retired Colonel Trillo and three others also perish.

The building from which those shots were fired is today a museum (Museo Pancho Villa) chronicling the life, campaigns and death of Chihuahua's most famous adopted son. But Hidalgo del Parral has a history much beyond that of Pancho Villa. Founded in 1631 as a mining center, the city still has over 500 buildings of historical importance, ranging from churches to a hotel once owned by Pancho Villa himself. There is the Casa Griensen, home of the heroine Elisa Griensen. With rifle in hand, she led a group of women and children in resisting the invading United States Army in 1916. The old La Prieta mine—which extracted gold, silver and zinc for almost four centuries—now offers guided tours into its inner chambers.

Every year in July, a several-week long cavalcade through Chihuahua traces the movements of General Villa's legendary *División del Norte* army. The celebration includes art and photographic exhibits, music, dances, theater, round table discussions, lectures and other events reflecting the culture and history of the Mexican Revolution.

The city cemetery holds a great mystery, the locals say. The day after he was gunned down, Pancho Villa was buried here, but several times his grave was defiled. After his head was stolen (some say it is in the possession of Yale University's secret society, Skull and Bones), his family decided to move his body to an undisclosed grave. Years later, an unknown woman died and some say the mayor decided to have her buried in the former Villa site. In 1976 the Mexican government ordered Villa's remains to be moved to the Revolution Monument in Mexico City where they supposedly rest today.

The winds pass through the streets of Hidalgo del Parral, around the spires of colonial churches, through the old mines, bespeaking the centuries of the blood spilled into the sands imprinted by the footprints of the swift Rarámuris. By listening and following its touch, one comes to understand the history of Mexico from the days of Spanish rapine to the Mexican Revolution—and even to this modern day.

---

MEXICO FACTOIDS:

Many westerns have been filmed in the Mexican state of Durango, including John Wayne's *Chisum*.

Dinosaur fossils have been found in Rincón Colorado, Coahuila.

Visitors to the "*Zona del Silencio*"—the zone of silence—near Torreón, Coahuila, claim to have experienced supernatural / extraterrestrial phenomena.

---

## "Respect for the rights of others means peace."
### -Benito Juarez, Mexican President and Statesman (1806-1872)

---

## LATIN REVOLUTIONARIES # 6:  PANCHO VILLA

### Mexico (1878-1923)

The most famous of the Mexican revolutionaries, Pancho Villa—whose real name was José Doroteo Arango Arámbula—was born into a poor sharecropper family in Durango, Mexico. His father died when he was very young. The young José Arango shot and killed the wealthy owner of their land when he was a teenager after the man raped his younger sister. He then fled into the mountains where he joined a group of bandits.

By the time the Mexican Revolution broke out in 1910, Arango had changed his name to Pancho Villa and was the leader of his small force of bandits. Villa believed in the idealism of the revolution and his bandits, already armed veterans, joined the cause. He converted his rag-tag band of highwaymen and thieves into the most powerful military force in northern Mexico. In 1911, his troops defeated the Mexican army at the battle of Juarez. By 1913, however, the country was in total chaos: a former general named Victoriano Huerta, Villa's sworn enemy, had set himself up as president. Villa worked to overthrow Huerta and succeeded in 1914. Villa was rewarded with the post of governor of the state of Chihuahua.

Villa later split with other revolutionary generals and the United States government decided to deny him any more weapons. Villa responded with a series of raids, including one across the border, in which some Americans were killed. The United States retaliated with a punitive expedition of 6,000 men under General John Pershing: Villa escaped. Afterwards, he seemed to tire of the revolutionary life, and retired in 1920. In 1923, he was assassinated in his car: the identity and motive of the killers remains a mystery.

# ÁLAMOS

By Allen Cox, Tacoma, Washington, U.S.A.

According to local legend, the city of Álamos was once so prosperous due to the silver mines that the daughter of a wealthy silver baron, on her wedding day, walked from her home to the church on a path made of silver bars.

In the mountains of the northern state of Sonora, the moguls of Mexico's silver industry left behind a legacy that they called Álamos. In the 18th century, its mines produced more silver than any other Spanish colonial mining project.

Up sprang a graceful *pueblo*, with its central church, its commerce, and its mansions as fine as silver fortunes could buy. Soon, Álamos blossomed into a provincial oasis of high society tucked in the wilds of the Sierra Madre. It became the northernmost jewel in a necklace of "Silver Cities" that spread throughout Mexico's interior.

Despite a few slightly less glamorous distractions in the form of floods, rebellions, and the occasional epidemic, Álamos managed to maintain its general prosperity until the early 20th century, when the Mexican Revolution swept the country like a raging wildfire. The mines closed, the economy declined, and Álamos was all but abandoned.

But not for long—someone soon rediscovered this diamond in the rough. In the latter half of the 20th century, dust flew as ruined colonial mansions were meticulously restored, cobbles in the streets repaired and the infrastructure upgraded.

Today, Álamos is a pueblo of 10,000 people that shines with civic pride. In 2000, it earned the distinction of National Historical Monument (more precisely, 188 individual structures within the pueblo earned that distinction). Álamos was subsequently crowned with the title of *Pueblo Mágico*, one of only a handful in Mexico. Its history, its impressive collection of restored colonial architecture, its rich natural setting in a rare tropical deciduous forest (the home of the famed *brincador*, or Mexican Jumping Bean), and its easygoing people combine in a formula that defines its magic.

Once there, a good place to begin an exploration is *El Museo Costumbrista de Sonora* on the Plaza de Armas in the hub of the historic district. This regional museum provides an excellent orientation and, from there, all the historic structures are within walking distance, making touring the pueblo's colonial heart a simple pleasure.

When I mention Álamos, most people return a blank stare. "Where's that?" they reply, which is precisely what makes the place so appealing. Because getting there requires some special effort (it lacks a commercial airport), Álamos tends to attract visitors who prefer to bush bash off the beaten path.

Allen Cox is a freelance writer from Tacoma, WA. His first loves are: traveling to destinations off the beaten path, primarily in Mexico; hiking in his own backyard—the spectacular Pacific Northwest; and, of course, writing. Besides travel writing, he writes fiction and is currently working on a novel set in Mexico's Yucatan Peninsula. He graduated with a Bachelor of Science degree from City University, has retired from a career in the telecommunications industry, and is a member of Pacific Northwest Writer's Association.

When Allen is not traveling, he volunteers his time tutoring English language skills at a Latino community center in his hometown. When asked about his most bizarre cultural experience, he says: "I suppose standing on the shoulder of a remote highway in southern Mexico, nervously watching my tour guide's van being torn apart by some scary-looking plainclothes drug police in search of contraband could be considered a cultural experience. It was a false alarm; we were squeaky clean."

## MEXICAN JUMPING BEANS

By Dr. Crit Minster

"Mexican Jumping Bean" is sort of a misnomer. They're not really a bean, but a seed pod from a hardy shrub (*sebastiana pavoniana*). Although they're common in Mexico, they can also be found in parts of the American southwest. And they don't really jump, but rather roll and wobble.

All the same, they're a part of pop culture: Mexican kids sell them as "pets" to tourists, and they're a staple of novelty shops all over the southwest. The "jumping" is caused by the larval form of a moth (*carpocaspa saltitans*), which lays its eggs in the seed pods. When the eggs hatch, the moth grub eats the seeds but remains in the seed pod.

Once the seed is gone, the moth larva lives and develops inside the seed pod, and has the odd habit of moving around inside. Not unlike a hamster inside a plastic ball rolling all over the place, the grub causes the seed pod to roll about. Several hundred seed pods under the parent tree, all moving about randomly, looks quite startling!

In late summer, the larvae have matured and are ready to leave the seed pods. They "hatch" from the seed pod and fly off, to begin the cycle again!

# CABO SAN LUCAS

By Kerry L. Smith, Pembroke, Massachusetts, U.S.A.

Cabo San Lucas has been a popular travel destination for newlyweds for years. And for many good reasons: the picturesque beaches, amenity-fueled hotels, ample shopping and food options, and reasonably priced souvenirs—not to mention the view of celebrity bungalows dotting cliffs overlooking the ocean. But there is another side of Cabo, the side for those not swooning, for those in the single life and those in the wedding parties.

Boasting a constant supply of ideal beach weather and friendly locals, Cabo is located approximately 1,000 miles (1,600 kilometers) south of San Diego, California at the southern tip of the Baja Peninsula. English is readily spoken, but the efforts of visitors wishing to practice their Spanish aren't lost. Upon checking into a hotel in Cabo, the first order of business is to strip down to a bathing suit, cozy up to the wet bar and order a frozen Margarita and a basket of chips topped with the freshest guacamole you have ever tasted. Afternoon naps are suggested for those who plan to experience Cabo's vibrant nightlife.

Most hotels offer moderately priced shuttle service into town, where visitors can purchase handmade items for friends and family back home. Silver jewelry is especially cheap in Mexico; but watch out for the exchange rates—which can be confusing—especially after a few daiquiris or shots of tequila.

Sun and sand are great, but nothing makes a trip to Cabo more memorable than a four-wheeling adventure on the Baja peninsula. Group rates are available through different companies. So grab your friends, strap on your helmet and goggles and follow a tour guide along a winding path through the desert to the beach, where you can test out your wheelie or donut-making abilities on an ATV in the hot sand.

After a day on the beach, go for some tasty dinner. Restaurants serve up a delicious array of fresh seafood options and traditional Mexican fare. And while it would behoove visitors to skip the more recognizable and familiar American food chains, a quick visit to musician Sammy Hagar's Cabo Wabo will secure you a delicious bottle of blue agave tequila.

Night owls can opt to take a cruise that begins at sunset from a pier downtown; and while the food on board isn't five-star restaurant quality (the food is buffet style and the drinks may remind some of their college frat party days), the view is stunning— and the live music on board frames the evening perfectly. Party animals should visit the Giggling Marlin, where patrons are greeted by waiters who tempt them into playing musical chairs or doing shots while suspended upside-down.

A trip to "the office," a stretch of beach where a hearty breakfast is served right on the sand and waiters serve lounging patrons piña coladas as they relax on chaise lounges can soothe the roughest hangover. Water activities are easy to find here—rent jet skis at a fair price, or ride on a banana boat or private party boat.

## TOP LIST: BEST PLACES TO SPORT YOUR BIRTHDAY SUIT

Looking for a little risqué fun in Latin America? The climate in this part of the world is perfect for wearing skimpy bikinis—or nothing at all! Here are some of the best places to get "natural," according to our readers.

1. Playa del Amor, Zipolite, Mexico. "Paradise." Jim, U.S.A.

2. Beaches at Manuel Antonio Park, Costa Rica. "Get away from the multitudes and get naked where you have the beach to yourself." Adrian Wetherford, Columbus, Georgia, U.S.A.

3. Sorobon Beach resort, Bonaire. "On a private island!" Ted Lindhall, Miami, Florida, U.S.A.

4. Eden Bay, Dominican Republic. "A great clothing-optional resort." Nick Frost, San Antonio, Texas, U.S.A.

5. Hidden Beach Resort Au Naturel club, Mexico. Kylie Francis, Portland, Maine, U.S.A.

6. Desire Resort and Spa, Puerto Morelos, Mexico. Kylie Francis, Portland, Maine, U.S.A.

# LAS OLAS SURF CAMP

By Jenna Mahoney, New York, U.S.A.

Surfing is really a metaphor for life: You learn how to pick yourself up when you wipe out; the greatest rewards come after you've sweat blood and you realize that balance is essential.

Maybe that's the real reason why Kate Bosworth, Michelle Rodriguez and the rest of the cast of the blockbuster movie *Blue Crush* triggered an entire gender to start surfing. Ever since the movie's release in 2002, girls and women across the globe have been picking up boards and riding waves. Established long before Hollywood launched its surfing spree, Las Olas surf camp offers the ultimate surf-sister experience. You'll learn basic techniques, practice yoga and start speaking like a surfer-dude. Oh, and one more thing: the tagline "We make girls out of women" is totally true.

Las Olas has literally set up camp in a west coast surf town located less than 50 minutes from the bustling Puerto Vallarta. The sleepy spot is home to a number of ex-pats from the Bay area. They've come down for the surf breaks, the cheap beers and the breakfasts at Rollie's restaurant. The beach cove serves as the center of the community. It's got two beach breaks appropriate for all levels. The beginners and some long boarders stick to the sandbar, a gentle and even spot that's easy to paddle out to. Short boarders, locals and more savvy surfers tackle the left. The rocky bottom lends itself to higher crests, longer rides and more opportunities to carve.

Drawn to sand and surf, the "Las Olas girls"—as the locals call them—spend most of the day watching the waves. They hang with the instructors, who run on-land drills and escort them to their appropriate-level waves. Gossip and a crash-course in surfer's lingo are also included. In just a week, you'll master the art of a "pop-up" and learn exactly how to "turtle" (escape a crashing wave without losing your board). Tackling these techniques in a group can assuage fear, doubt and hesitation. Plus, the cheers and encouragement from the rest of the guests keep first-timers and experienced surfers alike motivated. The worry of being the only woman in the water disappears as quickly as a sandbar at high tide, and guests are more likely to stick with and try basic, complicated and carving moves.

Yoga classes compliment the experience. Held every morning on a bluff overlooking the ocean, this practice helps women surfers get limber, focus on balance and stretch sore surfing muscles. Group dinners, beach time and the shared housing help in fostering close "surf-sister" relationships. Las Olas students stay at an expansive villa property overlooking the beach and cove. Each room houses two to four guests and every one of the hotel's little houses is distinct; The size, layout and features vary depending on the natural elements each is built around. For example: One room has an outdoor shower with a tree to provide privacy and some have cold plunge pools on the terraces. It is at these spots that the Las Olas women truly become girls. They sit and chat slumber-party-style swapping stories about love, life and, of course, who caught the sweetest wave.

www.vivatravelguides.com/106683

# PUNTA DE MITA

By Denise Fiske-Chow, San Francisco, California, U.S.A.

Not long ago, Punta de Mita was a place virtually undiscovered by the outside world. Pristine beaches lined the shore, locals spent their Sundays splashing in the crystalline blue-green water and surfers regarded it as the best place to catch a good ride. Then, Mexican President, Salinas de Gotari started to "develop" it, calling it the next Cancún. Now, there are championship golf courses designed by the likes of Jack Nicklaus, mega hotels such as the expensive Four Seasons, and condominiums and timeshares selling like hotcakes. The good news is there is still plenty left for the rest of us to experience.

The peninsula of Punta de Mita lies at the north end of Banderas Bay in the state of Nayarit, Mexico, separating the bay from the open ocean. The translation of Punta de Mita means "point in the middle." Just 22 miles from the famous resort town of Puerto Vallarta, in an area known as Costa Banderas, it offers some of the finest coastline seen in Mexico. The road from highway 200 to Punta de Mita is currently under construction for a much needed widening, probably to accommodate all of the beach-seekers heading to Mita's welcoming shores. You will find luxury hotels, golf courses, and world-class sports fishing for marlin, tuna, mahi-mahi and sailfish. The area is great for surfing, featuring numerous reef and beach breaks. The beach area of El Anclote features a restaurant row, including international delights such as authentic Mexican food, sushi, seafood and European cuisine.

While sitting in one of the beach restaurants, enjoying a cold cerveza and wiggling your toes in the sand, you can look out and see the Marietas Islands. These three small islands sit in a group offshore, and you can hire a local fisherman to motor you out in his *panga*. Here you can gaze into the clear blue water and catch a glimpse of giant manta rays, sea turtles, dolphins and whales, depending on the time of year. The islands are also a good spot for scuba diving, and have been designated a protected area due to the nesting colonies of endangered blue-footed boobies (apparently not only humans flock to Punta de Mita).

The small town of Emiliano Zapata (named for the revolutionary leader) neighbors El Anclote and has a few tiny markets where you can buy basics. There is a small hotel and lots of condo rentals available. The next biggest town is La Cruz de Huanacaxtle, close to the turnoff from highway 200. The main attraction setting this town apart from its other coastal companions is a gas station.

The future will bring more golf courses and a pedestrian walkway along the beach front, with shops, beach access, restaurants, and public rest areas. But as developed as it is, Punta de Mita retains the charm of a place not yet discovered. It offers abundant wildlife such as deer, parrots, peccaries and falcon, and the remote beaches, tropical vegetation and swamps are just waiting to be explored.

# TEQUILA, A WAY OF LIFE

## By Darren Fitzgerald, Los Angeles, California, U.S.A.

The words "Blue Agave" will ring in your ears after a visit to Tequila, the birthplace of that fiery spirit that makes you wiggle your hips. After a tour through a few distilleries and tasting bars you'll see why tequila isn't just a shot with lime and salt, but a way of life.

The town of Tequila lies an hour north of Guadalajara and is home to the world's most famous brands, including Herradura, Sauza and Centenario. The journey into the region takes you through rolling desert hills stretched with fields of blue agave, the cactus plant from which the liquor is brewed.

Tequila is a hot, slow-paced, dusty pueblo centered on a small stone cathedral. The air is thick with the scent of distilled agave roots. The locals wander sluggishly down the main street, which is lined with cantinas selling homemade tequila out of plastic jugs. Start your visit at the museum, where Sauza bottles over 100 years old are aging behind glass cabinets adorned with images of charros and banditos. Stand close enough and you can hear the thunder of horses, crackling pistols and the crash of tequila bottles being tossed to the dirt.

Tequila, which was first introduced to the north as "Mexican Whiskey," has been around for 300 years. Where better to get a taste of this history than at La Rojena, one of the oldest distilleries in the region, and home to the Cuervo brand.

Quite at odds with the drink's 300 year-old legacy, the tour begins with an MTV-esque techno-driven video describing tequila's humble roots. You then go through the production process from soil to bottle. The agave cactus is harvested by hand using flat-nosed shovels to uproot the giant core of the plant, which resembles a mammoth pineapple weighing more than 100 lbs. The cores are lopped in half and thrown into industrial ovens. Baked agave, which tastes like maple brown sugarcane, is shredded and juiced, then fermented and distilled to produce Tequila.

After a few glasses of La Rojena's golden premium añejo, Reserva de la Familia, you'll join the locals in their lazy meandering about town. Saunter into a few of the bars to sample the homemade brews straight from the tap. There's nothing smoother and smokier than an aged tequila created by locals whose hearts ebb and flow blue agave, and you can't leave without a few bottles of your own.

### MEXICO FACTOIDS:

The town of Cocula, just southwest of Guadalajara, is said by locals to be the birthplace of mariachi music.

Local artisans in the town of Tlaquepaque, near Guadalajara, work with such materials as steel, copper, wood, corn husks, leather and papier-mâché. Plus, it's fun to say "Tlaquepaque!"

Agave Fields. Photo by Will Gray.

Agave cores ready for baking. Photo by Darren Fitzgerald.

# EL ROSARIO MONARCH RESERVE

## By Richard Arghiris, London, England

Butterflies fill the sky like clouds of orange ash, pouring over the valley in the thousands. The sun emerges and momentarily illuminates their wings before retreating back into the clouds. The spectacle waxes and wanes, never exhausting itself. Further away, the path curves and descends to the edge of the forest. Beyond it, many millions more butterflies occupy the earth, the air and the vegetation.

Each year, around 100 million Monarch butterflies undertake a migratory journey that spans two thousand miles. Their phenomenal voyage commences in southeast Canada, the monarchs' summer habitat, and reaches as far as their over-wintering homes in the Oyamel forests of the Sierra Madre Oriental in central Mexico. The remarkable El Rosario Monarch Butterfly Reserve, Mexico's only public monarch sanctuary, lies in the state of Michoacán and is accessed from the town of Angangueo.

It is a steep climb from Angangueo into the mountains, up to the sanctuary gates. The view from the approach is hypnotic and the sights in the forest itself are surreal and intoxicating. Butterflies absorb it completely. They coat the fir trees in vast, fiery bunches, weighing down the branches in their numbers.

A deep, flaming orange carpet covers the ground. Occasionally, sunlight breaks through and warms a cluster. Hundreds take flight with dramatic flurry. Rippling upward, they emit the otherworldly purr that is the sound of countless beating butterfly wings.

The entire monarch migration cycle spans four generations. They breed once on the journey

> *The butterflies are symbols of transformation and journey, of life and death, of cyclical progressions and of mystery.*

north, twice during the summer in Canada, then once more on the journey south. Those that arrive in Mexico are the great-grandchildren of those that came the preceding year.

Their arrival in early November also coincides with the world famous Day of the Dead celebration, an important occasion in Mexico when the souls of the deceased are said to return to spend time with their families and loved ones. Coincidentally, perhaps, butterflies occupy a special place in indigenous mythology: they are the souls of dead warriors, migrating to the land of the dead.

Sadly, the Monarch butterflies face several kinds of threat and their migration has been declared an endangered phenomenon. Urban sprawl is devastating their summer residences and their over-wintering habitats face destruction by logging. The Monarch caterpillar's source of food, milkweed, is being steadily eliminated by herbicide from farmers and gardeners. Finally, climate change poses a threat to the Monarchs. The winter of 2002 was particularly harsh and devastated their populations. If such extreme conditions are an indicator of future patterns, the Monarch butterflies will undoubtedly cease their migration to Mexico.

Observing the Monarchs and their ethereal manner, their weightless and entrancing navigation, it is easy to imagine they have transcendental characteristics. More than this, they are undeniable symbols of transformation and journey, of life and death, of cyclical progressions and of mystery. Watching their flight, it is easy to imagine how these remarkable animals may indeed have otherworldly connections, how they could very well be ancient spirits in transit.

---

EL ROSARIO TRAVEL TIP: El Rosario Monarch Butterfly Reserve is open 9:00 a.m. to 6:00 p.m., mid-November to March only. Check with a tourist office for precise opening dates, as these are subject to change.

---

Butterflies at the El Rosario Reserve. Photo by Stephany Slaughter..

# GUANAJUATO, LAND OF FROGS

By Douglas Bower, Overland Park, Kansas, U.S.A.

Doug Bower is a freelance writer, syndicated columnist, and book author from Kansas City, Kansas. He attended the University of Kansas in the mid-70's. He has freelanced for numerous print and online publication including Transitions Abroad, Escape Artist, and International Living. He is a columnist with the California Chronicle and more than 21 additional online magazines. He lives with his wife in Guanajuato, Mexico. His newest book, *The Plain Truth about Living in Mexico*, is out with Brown Walker Press. When he does his travel writing, he prefers a notebook and pen: the old fashioned way. He hopes to explore Mexico in the future, particularly the Yucatan.

When theme parks, beaches, scuba diving, and whale watching have lost their charm after multiple vacations to Mexico, perhaps a visit to The Land of Frogs is in order. The City of Guanajuato, which is called "the Crown Jewel" of Mexico's colonial cities, loosely translates as "the land of frogs" in Tarascan: *Quanax-Huato*. By some accounts, a long-ago inhabitant of the land, whose identity has been lost to time, took one look at the terrain and said, "Nothing but frogs could live here!"

Others say the locals found thousands of frogs in the mountainous terrain. Still other accounts say it was the shape of the mountains that reminded the natives of frogs. Whichever account is true, Guanajuato is a place to get to know.

Guanajuato earned its place in world geography when the Spanish found the surrounding mountains rich in silver deposits. In fact, at one time more than one third of the world's silver riches were mined in Guanajuato.

Though none of the usual summer vacation activities exists in Guanajuato, this city exudes history with every unsteady step you take on its cobblestone streets.

Although small, Guanajuato has outstanding colonial architecture built with the silver revenue from times past. With modern museums, cultural events almost year-round, one of world's oldest universities, and an almost perfect year-round temperate climate, Guanajuato is the perfect alternative to the usual vacation fare.

Many first-time visitors have expressed amazement to find that Guanajuato defies their stereotypical expectation of Mexico. Many who have travelled extensively throughout Europe think Guanajuato resembles a town from Spain or Northern Italy somehow magically transplanted to this side of the planet.

Depending on whom you ask, the City of Guanajuato has a population of between 100,000-120,000 people. It is located in a ravine with the city literally built up the sides of the bowl-like surrounding mountains. If nothing else, a trip to Guanajuato would be worth the time and expense just to marvel at how the Mexicans figured out how to build this city. To call it a marvel is a gross understatement.

Another marvel to behold is Guanajuato's system of underground tunnels. Originally, the Guanajuato River flowed through the centre of town. Numerous devastating floods occurred over the centuries, and engineers decided to divert the river away from the middle of town in the early 1900s. After diverting the river, the riverbed was turned into a maze of underground streets-this time to divert traffic instead of water.

All one need do is visit the Tourism Office to find an English speaking tour guide to take you on an unbelievably rich tour of where Mexico began—at a price that won't break your wallet.

## LATIN AMERICAN MYSTERIES #2: THE CIUDAD JUAREZ MURDERS

Ciudad Juarez, Mexico: 1994-Present

In the past decade, more than 300 mutilated bodies, almost all of them young women and girls, have been discovered in the garbage-strewn deserts outside of the border city of Ciudad Juarez, Mexico. Most of the women were beaten, stabbed or strangled, and about one-third of them show signs of having been sexually assaulted. Many of the women worked in Juarez' infamous sweatshops, the *maquilas*, where they earned less than $60 per week. More than 50 of the bodies have never been identified.

The Ciudad Juarez police department has drawn international attention because of gross incompetence in the case and although there have been many arrests, the body count continues to rise. There have been many allegations of human rights violations: many of the suspects in the murders case have said that they were tortured into confessions. The lack of results has led some to suspect that the police may be somehow involved in the murders. The Mexican federal government has since taken over the investigation, but there has been little real progress. An Argentine forensics team has been brought in to help in the investigation.

There are many theories concerning the killings, including serial killers, gang violence and domestic abuse. Rumors abound about Satanic cults, snuff film producers and international organ traffickers. Most experts believe that if it is the work of serial killers, several may be involved, because the "signatures" are different. Most unnerving of all the theories may be the belief that the killings continue to happen simply because they have not been solved. In other words, killers commit their crime and dump the evidence in the desert because they assume they can get away with it: theirs will be but one more crime on a growing list, with no end or solution in sight.

# LA GRUTA HOTSPRINGS
By Denise Fiske-Chow, San Francisco, California, U.S.A.

Between the little pueblo of Dolores Hidalgo and the town of San Miguel de Allende, in the Mexican state of Guanajuato, is an area renowned for its steamy hot mineral springs. At the 10 kilometer mark along the highway stretching between the towns, you'll find the La Gruta Spa. Walking through the gated entrance is like stepping through the looking-glass; the welcoming façade ushers you from apparent wilderness to a wonderland of self-indulgence. Floral-colored birds accentuate the tropical gardens, making the spas aesthetically, as well as physically, pleasing. Rent a locker for your belongings (the small refundable fee is a recommended investment) and head to the changing room. Don't forget your bathing suit!

Once changed, make your way to one of the three pools into which the waters of a thermal spring have been channelled. Each varies in size and temperature—the depth of the pool determines the water temperature—though the level of enjoyment is invariably the same. Literally translated, La Gruta means "the Grotto," and in San Miguel de Allende this name epitomizes rest and relaxation. The hottest water is in the grotto, entered through a long rock tunnel and lit by a single shaft of sunlight. Once inside, you can take your turn at a shoulder massage from the hot water spout gushing out of the ceiling. Besides relaxing, a popular activity is hopping from one pool to another. The spa also has a restaurant, which is a bit pricey but convenient, as it offers service to the pool areas. A ten minute taxi ride from the spa will drop you off in the stunning colonial town of San Miguel de Allende.

Among the clean-swept streets and exquisite architecture you'll also find good shopping, great restaurants and popular hotels. Shop 'till you drop, and then soak in the healthy waters of La Gruta. It is an experience you won't want to miss.

www.vivatravelguides.com/104038

# MORELIA
By Denise Fiske-Chow, San Francisco, California, U.S.A.

Morelia. Photos by Stephany Slaughter.

Morelia is one of the jewels in the crown of Mexico's colonial history. Its downtown streets are lined by old colonial buildings, looking as Spanish as they did in the 17th and 18th centuries.

The city sits on a 6,400 foot (roughly 2,000 meter) plateau, and is the capital of the state of Michoacán. As big as it is, with a population roughly estimated at 577,000, it is a relaxing place to explore and enjoy. Situated midway between Mexico City and Guadalajara, Morelia is a city waiting to be discovered.

In May, 1541, Viceroy Don Antonio de Mendoza founded a city on the site, calling it Valladolid after his hometown in Spain. When Mexico gained its independence, the name was changed to Morelia, in honor of General Jose Maria Morelos y Pavón, a native son and war hero. Morelia boasts a mild climate, its year round temperature averaging a balmy 73°F. Often, winter temperatures hover around 60°F and summer rarely tops 90°F. Casual dress is the norm, but during the rainy season (summer) don't forget your umbrella.

In 1991, the city was declared a UNESCO World Cultural Heritage site, due in large part to the stunning Spanish-style colonial architecture and distinct artistic flourishes.

City laws now require any new construction in the historical center, be built colonial-style, with arches, baroque façades, and carved pink stone walls. The rose-colored stone shines and the clean streets reflect the pride its citizens have in their city. Morelia, and the surrounding area, is recognized for the beautiful handmade folk art on display all over the city.

The most popular (and highest quality) pieces are the woodcarvings and pottery. Created in many styles, the varying designs and colors indicate which village was home to the artist who created the work. Another sought-after craft product is the fine lacquerware boxes and trays, created with layers of vibrant paint and inlaid gold leaf. The best quality pieces are expensive, but add a colorful flair to any collection.

Morelia's center of activity is the *zócalo*, or main plaza. Shaded by large ancient trees, surrounded by colonnades, and lined by sidewalk cafes, it offers a unique opportunity to sit and mingle with the life of the city. Sunday is family day in the plaza and includes concerts and cultural programs. At night, the Cathedral sitting on the north end of the plaza is lit up and its famous 70 meter high twin towers make an impressive sight. On Saturday and Sunday nights, groups of local university students stroll through the cafes in costume, singing and entertaining the crowds.

Morelia is a city teeming with life, offering the discerning visitor a diverse cultural experience. There is something for everyone, from shopping and meandering through museums to checking out local art and music and indulging in comfortable hotels and great restaurants. To visit Morelia is to marvel at the preservation of the past and pay tribute to the culture of the present.

www.vivatravelguides.com/103934

# PÁTZCUARO: DAY OF THE DEAD

By Darren Fitzgerald, Los Angeles, California, U.S.A.

The indigenous Tarasco Indian tribe who ruled Mexico's central western highlands in the fourteenth century believed death was a continuation of life and the dead could return home every year to visit their loved ones, a celebration called *Día de los Muertos* (Day of the Dead).

Traditionally, the dead were buried with weapons, food, and keepsakes they could offer to the gods in the afterworld. This practice led to the more modern Mexican ritual of decorating gravestones of the deceased with streamers, food, flowers, and other offerings.

Mexico celebrates Día de los Muertos on November 1st and 2nd. The most traditional festivities take place in the town of Pátzcuaro, home of the Purepecha tribe, direct descendants of the Tarasco. Beer-swilling locals and foreigners on a two-day binge detract a bit from its authenticity, but somehow this mix of modern revelry and ancient customs turns out just fine.

Festivities culminate on the island of Janitzio, which lies in the middle of Lago de Pátzcuaro. Thousands of locals armed with coolers of Tecate beer crowd onto the lakeside dock, their breath a clear indication that the festivities started hours earlier. Kids holding carved-out *calabazas* (pumpkins) ask for offerings for the dead. It's like trick or treating in the United States, except they ask for money, not candy, and they do it for two days. Boats lit up in red, white and green (colors of the Mexican flag) take party-goers to the island. The lake is a burst of light as the glowing boats follow a trail of flaming torches somehow stuck into the

> *The dead were buried with weapons, food, and keepsakes they could offer to the gods in the afterworld.*

lake bottom. The light reflecting through the drizzly cool night air looks like a synchronized line of fire-flies in a jungle mist.

Janitzio is a jagged, granite island, which rises out of the water at a steep incline. A labyrinth of narrow stone streets wind up and around to the peak, and every inch is covered with restaurants, food and alcohol carts and souvenir stands masked in orange lights. Halfway up the island sits a small church and cemetery where the crowds tone it down to respect the dead. The church altar is filled with candlelight, flowers, food, and candy skulls, and the traditional orange *cempazuchitl* flowers blanket every headstone. Family members of the dead sit by the graves praying and keeping the candles lit late into the night.

After quietly circling through the cemetery you head to the final destination, a small park at the top of the island dominated by a 200-foot rock statue of José María Morelos, a father of Mexican independence. The park is filled with revelers and Charro bands playing La Banda music while couples wearily bounce along. Just before sunrise, the crowds lumber back down through the narrow labyrinth and pour onto the small dock to catch a boat. It's a quiet ride back, the torchlight fading in the dawn, as the boats deliver the half-awake back to the mainland. If the dead are honored by flowers, candles, and uninhibited drinking and dancing, then Día de los Muertos on Janitzio honors the dead with more gusto than any other celebration in the country.

---

**DAY OF THE DEAD FACTOIDS:**

The Day of the Dead is celebrated on November 1st and 2nd all over Latin America, in parts of the U.S.A. and in the Philippines. It is believed that the souls of children return first, on November first. Adult souls follow on the second.

---

Typical family Day of the Dead display, Ocotapec, Morelos. Photo by Stephany Slaughter.

Day of the Dead display at the Diego Rivera Museum, Mexico City. Photo by Stephany Slaughter.

# URUAPAN

By Denise Fiske-Chow, San Francisco, California, U.S.A.

Uruapan, which in the local Purepeche language roughly translates to "eternal spring," is a city of few tourists and many surprises. From the jewel that is their national park, to the craftspeople that make the beautiful and vibrant cedar lacquer ware, this place is bursting with hidden treasures.

This city of natural and historic wealth, located in the state of Michoacán, serves as a gateway to the Barranca del Cupatitzio-Eduardo Ruiz National Park. Walk just 600 meters from the Central plaza and enter a world of deep forest, picturesque bridges, hidden fountains and winding stone paths. The peace of this place is interrupted only by the roar of water rushing over rocks and cascading into waterfalls.

The park offers a playground, trout farm and, of course, the usual souvenir shops and refreshment stands. At the northwest corner of the park is "Manantial Rodilla del Diablo" (spring of the devil's knee), the birth place of the river *Cupatitzio*. Staring into the crystalline water, you can't help but wonder how far the source goes underground. At the deepest pools along the river, local divers stand at attention, ready and willing to take the 20 to 30 foot plunge for tips from park visitors. The water is clear, cold and invigorating. Don't forget to look up into the high branches of the trees, you may get lucky and see the bright red, pink or orange blooms of wild orchids or bromeliads. An additional 4,500 acres of mountain forest nearby also boasts some of the richest and most delicate flora and fauna in Mexico. To really enjoy the park, spend at least a full day. The hours are 8:00 a.m. to 6:00 p.m. most days.

Another surprising discovery: Uruapan is "The Avocado Capital of the World!" This title is taken very seriously by locals and is manifest in the impressive Avocado Festival. If you are fortunate enough to be in town at this time, be brave and try the avocado ice cream, or even braver and sample the hot avocado punch. There are bullfights, cockfights, and concerts, as well as agricultural, industrial, and handcraft exhibitions. The festival lasts two weeks during November (exact dates vary).

Like the park, the town is ripe with things to discover and explore: the *Mercado de Antojitos Típicos* overflows with typical regional foods, while the *Mercado de Artesanías*, located on the SE end of the park, offers a good selection of high quality handcrafts from all over Mexico. Spend some time exploring the many interesting galleries and museums, or just stroll through the streets. For a break, head to one of the small cafés where you can sit and sip a cappuccino. Or strum your fingers to the beat of jazz, blues, or rock music live in one of the intimate clubs. No matter your tastes or budget, Uruapan offers a range of activities, sites, hotels and restaurants to satisfy you and your wallet. It is a city to relax in, talk to the locals and enjoy the sunshine of eternal spring while appreciating life's little surprises.

Denise Fiske-Chow is currently living in Mexico, where she writes for a bilingual newsletter. She attended California State University at Fresno and has organized and led tours to Costa Rica, Mexico, Hawaii and parts of the U.S.A. She also has traveled to Russia, China, South America and the Caribbean, and hopes to take an African safari someday. Her favorite cultural experience? "Sitting in a grave yard, having a picnic, listening to Mariachi music, while enjoying the carnival atmosphere of Día de los Muertos."

# EL HABANERO

By Katie Hale

Eating a habenero chili pepper is like lighting a firecracker in your mouth; your eyes will water, your throat will close, your nose will run, you'll do anything for liquid to soothe the fire. Although it is believed that the habanero originated in Cuba, it has become such an important food staple in the Yucatán area that most consider it essential to Mexico's cuisine. The peppers thrive in the hot environs of the Yucatán, where over 3,000 tons are grown each year.

A chili pepper's hotness is ranked on the Scoville scale. Most habaneros rate between 100,000 and 350,000 units on the scale—more than 80 times hotter than the jalapeño pepper. Technically, the habanero is not the hottest pepper on earth—the Naga Dorset chili pepper grown in Dorset, England claimed that title in March 2006. However, a product of the habanero—the Red Savina pepper—is still rated as the world's hottest spice by the Guinness Book of World Records.

Recently the habenero saw a surge in popularity in an odd location: Japan. Tohato Inc., a food company, has sold over 25 million bags of the Bokun Habanero (snack rings with sneaking heat) and recently came out with Bokun Babynero, a less spicy version of the popular snack. The boom doubled the production of habanero chilis in Mexico.

Habaneros are not only powerful enough to make you break out in a sweat—scientists found that capsaicin, the compound that makes the peppers hot, causes prostate cancer cells to commit suicide. If you can survive the heat of the habanero pepper, you'll not only enjoy bragging rights, but a chance to boost your health!

# TEPOZTLÁN

By Kena Sosa, San Antonio, Texas, U.S.A.

Snugly fit in the midst of a luscious valley in the Mexican state of Morelos is a pueblo called Tepoztlán, meaning a "town full of copper." As to whether or not there is still abundant copper here, it doesn't matter too much many because the true treasure here is what lies atop Mount Tepozteco.

Kena Sosa is an avid traveler and writer and has lived in both Mexico and Japan, where she lived on a rural potato farm. Originally from San Antonio, Texas, she currently lives in Dallas with her husband whom she met during her stay in Mexico's amazing capital city. She is a teacher as well. She has a Bachelor of Arts degree in English from Our Lady of the Lake University and a Masters of Bilingual Education from Southern Methodist University. Her most bizarre cultural experience? "That would be being chased by screaming crazed schoolgirls in Japan who nearly fainted at shaking my American hand. It was like being the Beatles but without the musical talent."

Like any gem worth discovering, it is not easy to get to. If you take the arduous hike up Mount Tepozteco, along a warm, damp jungle trail, you will be rewarded at the top with a storybook view: an ancient temple built to long-forgotten gods by those who lived in the valley in times long past.

The ancient Aztecs dedicated this mighty temple to Ometotchtli, who was their God of fertility, harvest… and drunkenness! Perhaps Tepoztlán was the first Cancún.

You'll need a break after the hike, and the temple is the perfect place to do so. Visitors sit on the edge and gaze out over the entire valley. From the vantage point of the temple, it is easy to see that the mountains are different from others you may have seen. Instead of being jagged and sharp, the rocks have smooth edges that seem to curve around like the sides of lasagna noodles. Centuries of rain and wind have softened the mountains around Tepoztlán. If you are lucky, you may also spy some fascinating wildlife that inhabits the area including the *pizote*, an odd looking cousin of the raccoon, which has an elongated snout and has a reddish-brown color fur coat.

After taking in the fresh air, the miraculous landscape and the historical aura of the temple that you must work to see, it's time to descend. At the foot of the mountain is the town itself. Like most small towns in Mexico, the streets are lined with tented markets where you can find fresh fruits and local handicrafts. Tepoztlán is also famous for *helados*, or homemade frozen juices. The flavors are usually fruity, and can range from pineapple to more exotic fruits such as the "mamey" and the "guanabana" for under 10 pesos (approximately $1).

A photographer's dream, Tepoztlán is an ideal weekend destination that is easily accessible from the capital and surrounding areas.

---

TEPOZTLÁN FACTOIDS:

During the Spanish conquest of Mexico, Hernán Cortés ordered the destruction of the city when its leaders refused to meet with him.

There have been several alleged UFO sightings in the area, particularly near the ruined Aztec pyramid in the hills above the town.

---

# QUERÉTARO

By Katie Hale

Maximillian I of Mexico stood on the Hill of the Bells in Santiago de Querétaro. Although his death sentence had been ordered, he paid off the firing squad that stood before him to prevent his ominous fate. Six armed guards took Maximillian's bribe and lowered their rifles, but the seventh guard fired one shot into the emperor's head, killing him on June 19, 1867.

Querétaro is an important place to Mexico's history not only as the site of Maximillian's murder, but for the key role it played in the early days of Mexico's independence. Today, Querétaro is one of the wealthiest cities in all of Latin America and is a UNESCO World Heritage Site.

Its clean promenades pass some of the most artfully constructed, colonial buildings in the nation. Among the numerous highlights of the city include the daunting 74-arch aqueduct finished in 1735, La Plaza de la Independencia, the Hill of the Bells where Maximillian fell and the city museum located there, La Iglesia de Santa Clara, Mansión de La Corregidora and the art museum.

Take a leisurely stroll around the Centro Histórico—it is safe and you will not be disappointed with the view of elegant churches, gardens, and colonial architecture dating back to the city's inception over 475 years ago.

# ROAD TRIPPING ALONG THE MICHOACÁN COAST

By Craig Gibson, Ajax, Ontario, Canada

Another day passes as you flip methodically under the broiling sun in piña-colada-saturated Puerto Vallarta. A barrage of time-share pushers and a flock of cruise line victims stampede into your utopia. Don't stress! A new utopia can be found just down the road.

Rent a car, hit the Wal-Mart in Vallarta, buy a cheap tent (or bring your own) and drive south down Highway 200 to the Michoacán Coast, undoubtedly one of the most spectacular and adrenaline-filled drives in Mexico. Escaping the tourist triangle, you embark on an adventure void of trampled paths trodden by the hoards of tourists that crowd the streets of Vallarta. Rewards await you: black sand beaches that burn like a hot coal walk, turtle sanctuaries, secret surf breaks and sunsets that you thought could only exist in artists' renditions.

Beaches like La Ticla entice the surf junkies, while others cradle you in serenity as you soak in natural wave pools and shallow bays while watching the olive sun dip into the martini horizon.

Continue down the highway that chases the setting sun, bask your face in the lights of the heavens and watch in wonder as you pass lush rainforests, uninhabited white sand beaches protected by granite spire guardians and crystal clear waters that will lure seasoned divers.

Worth a sidetrack is Colima, one of the oldest cities in Mexico, founded in 1523 by the Spaniard Gonzalo de Sandoval. Colima rests lazily under a goliath, the Volcán de Fuego, some 30 km (20 miles) to the north. This enormous volcano spews and hisses like a dragon, warning of its volatility. If your timing is right you might be blessed by a display of its power, a spectacularly humbling sight.

At the end of the journey you will find Playa Maruata. Don't blink, or it's gone, and you will continue on a lengthy journey down a stretch of highway (which boasts more *banditos* per capita than the national average) ending in Zihuatanejo, a place made famous to moviegoers by *Shawshank Redemption*. In Maruata, approach one of the local palapas owners and slide them twenty pesos, then set up the tent and stretch out the hammock, crack open an ice-cold Corona, lie back and watch for whale spouts and dolphins jumping on the horizon. You are not on the gringo trail anymore: you have truly found paradise.

In some ancient Mexican civilizations, it was customary to bury the dog with his master because it was believed that the spirit of the dog could carry the spirit of the dead to paradise. Lucky for the dogs from this part of the world, it is a short walk.

Volcan de Fuego, Colima. Photo by Craig Gibson.

Craig Gibson grew up in Ajax, Ontario, Canada. He currently resides in Whistler, BC, Canada. He went to university at Carleton in Ottawa, Ontario. He lives in a ski resort and makes his living in a variety of different ways, writing being one of them. His passions are derived and come to life outdoors. He loves sports, travel and animals. His dream is to write about and photograph the things that he does and loves.

# MISMALOYA

By Katie Hale

A white sand beach backed by a lush tropical jungle—the idyllic place for a passionate affair. It was 1963 and Richard Burton was on set filming *The Night of the Iguana*. Elizabeth Taylor was still married to Eddie Fisher, but she traveled all the way to Mismaloya, 10 km (six miles) south of touristy Puerto Vallarta, to rendezvous with Burton. Their romance attracted a great deal of media attention, forever putting this small piece of coastline on the tourist map.

Mismaloya is now a nice respite from the noisy vacation mecca of Puerto Vallarta, but it still provides all the elements one might need for a romantic getaway: luxury accommodation, delicious food and outdoor sports.

Burton and Taylor married twice, but ultimately divorced both times. Although their marriages did not survive, Mismaloya's turquoise waters and chirping parakeets still hold a romance and charm. It's easy to imagine falling in love on this beautiful beach.

# LA SIERRA HORSE RIDING

By Joanne Stanford, Crawley, Sussex, England

Joanne Stanford is a U.K.-based journalist with six years experience on magazines at IPC and a master's degree in electronic publishing at City University. She now mixes feature writing and in-house sub-editing with running her website, a directory which features more than 70 different riding holidays around the world. Her oddest cultural experience was watching the blowing up of Judas (a fireworks show) during Semana Santa in Mexico. She dreams of someday traveling Africa on horseback.

High above the white stucco mountain town of Valle de Bravo, two and a half hours west of Mexico City, lies Finca Enyhe. The hacienda, with its impressive façade and shady verandas set around a peaceful courtyard, has been lovingly renovated by its owners Lucia and Pepe Schravesande, two of Mexico's most talented horse people.

It is from this setting, with its manicured lawns, thoughtfully decorated bedrooms and glistening pool, that the couple runs their riding holiday: *Calbagatas La Sierra*. The ride itself covers 210 kilometres of some of the most picturesque riding country in the region. Visitors pass through mountainous forests of endemic oak and more than 100 species of pine.

From the Finca at 6,000 feet (1,800 metres) above sea level, the ride gently climbs during the course of the week to 10,000 feet (about 3,000 metres), with an average of six hours a day spent in the saddle and many mountaintop viewpoints affording jaw-dropping panoramas. Each day brings special highlights. On day one it's reaching the tiny village of Los Saucos and being greeted by the school children laughing and giggling, crowding around Pepe for sweets and *satsumas*. Another day, it's filling flour tortillas with hot sausage, cheese and guacamole and retreating to a spot on Lookout Rock, an amazing viewpoint with views of the majestic volcano at Toluca.

Each evening, the horses are stabled at stalls Pepe has built or rented along the way, while the riders are transported back to the five-star luxury of the Finca by minibus or, on one day, a boat across Lake Valle de Bravo. As well as shady forests and mountain lookouts, the ride passes through villages, past hillside smallholdings and through cultivated valleys.

Rather than simply admiring a view of rural life in Mexico-the young girl sitting among a herd of goats, the man ploughing with oxen, the men picking gladioli for the market, children leading donkeys laden with firewood through the forest—this adventure allows the rider to melt into the landscape and become part of the picture.

A charming Mexican couple, Lucia and Pepe are dedicated to taking care of their guests, their staff, the Finca and their precious horses. But much more than this, they are committed to promoting tourism within Mexico in a way that helps to protect their natural environment. A library of books about Mexico's history and the area's flora and fauna can be found at the Finca, and the three-course meals of traditional Mexican fare are always accompanied by thought-provoking and educational conversation.

## LA VIRGEN DE GUADALUPE

by Katie Hale

On the crisp morning of December 9, 1531, Juan Diego was making his way to mass. As he crossed the stark hill, Teyepac, an intense light blinded him, bird-like song filled the air, and a great vision suddenly appeared—a woman who declared herself to be the Virgin Mary, the mother of Jesus Christ.

She told Juan Diego she wished to have a church built on Teyepac and to relay the message to the Bishop. The Bishop did not believe Juan Diego and asked him to produce a miracle. La Virgen appeared to Juan Diego again, and told him to gather roses from barren Teyepac and bring them to the Bishop as proof of his vision. Juan Diego dutifully went to the hill, and although it was winter, found brilliant roses in full bloom. As Juan Diego dropped the blossoms in front of the Bishop, a perfect image of La Virgen de Guadalupe was displayed on his cloak.

The Bishop ordered a church to be built on the site where La Virgen de Guadalupe had appeared. There are debates as to when the original church was actually constructed and the validity of the account. What is known is the original church was replaced in 1709. Juan Diego's mantle is housed in the church, and experts have analyzed the fabric, dating it to the 16th century. Amazingly, La Virgen's image is still clearly imprinted on the over 475-year-old fabric, without any sign of deterioration. In 1745 the Vatican recognized the Miracle of La Virgen de Guadalupe and in 2002, Juan Diego was cannonized by the Pope.

Many churches throughout Mexico have now been dedicated to La Virgen de Guadalupe and on December 12, worshippers gather there for prayer, processions, and fireworks to honor her. She is a symbol that unites both Spanish-Catholics and indigenous groups. Nobel Laureate Octavio Paz once said, "The Mexican people, after more than two centuries of experiments, have faith only in the Virgin of Guadalupe and the National Lottery." Perhaps the Mexican people are better off putting their devotion in La Virgen—she is known to make miracles happen.

# MEXICO CITY AZTEC TOUR

By Kena Sosa, San Antonio, Texas, U.S.A.

Mexico City represents many things to many people. It is colorfully painted by the Spanish language, its record-setting population that continues to grow, and climactic history.

Many assume that Mexico is dominated by the Spanish culture and its Catholic faith, however, travelers with open eyes will find that the Aztecs and their culture did not die after their conquest, but became a sub-layer of the present-day Mexico. The Aztecs lived and built their empire in the middle of a lake at the exact spot they saw an eagle with a snake in its mouth, mandated by prophecy. They were educated and artistic, leading the area in the development of a supreme civilization. Overtaken by the Spanish in 1521, Mexico took on a new character, name and lifestyle. Mexico City is a place of paradoxes amid a beautiful organized chaos.

Chapultepec is the zone where you will find the Museum of Archaeology, where you can get a head start on the indigenous history of Mexico, Central and South America. It is renowned throughout the world and can take a whole day to explore thoroughly.

However, you don't have to go to a museum to experience indigenous Mexico. For a sight that explains the true nature of Mexico and its past, there is the "Plaza de Tres Culturas," or "The Plaza of Three Cultures." A single click of the camera shutter can capture Aztec temple ruins, an incredible Spanish church and modern Mexican office buildings in the same frame. These three cultures are what make Mexico the nation it is today.

Later, explore the *zócalo*, or town square (also the location of the National Palace and Cathedral in downtown) where Aztec dancers frequently put on free shows, complete with drumming, costumes and other demonstrations.

Heading south will lead you to the remains of an ancient pyramid called Cuicuilco. This pyramid is now covered with grass and is missing much of its top layer, but its current state retains the enchantment of the past with the transcendentalist power of the present. Folks flock to Cuicuilco to walk leisurely or pass time, but others use the site to meditate. They hope to harness the energy and purity of the ancestors here and welcome anyone who wishes to join them.

Continuing south to the Dolores Olmeda Museum in the Coyoacán (hungry coyote) area, one can see original Diego Rivera and Frida Kahlo works, as well as the endangered Aztec dog called the *xoloescuintle*.

The xoloescuintle dog is quite rare. It is nearly bald with a tuft of black hair on its forehead and a thick, leathery skin which is very sensitive to the sun. They were the Aztec's constant companion, and on some occasions, a meal. These days they are hard to find, but this museum's garden is home to several of them, as well as some peacocks.

The Aztecs discovered both chocolate and vanilla, however a more unusual food to try would be *pozole*. It is a tomato-based soup made with hominy and meat. It is delicious and succulent and can be found at virtually any restaurant.

Last but not least, a person cannot say they've been to Mexico City without visiting a *tianguis*, or open market. These markets may be difficult to find as they tend to rotate throughout the city. They represent the merchant class of Aztec society who were at the bottom at the caste system of the time. They may not be wearing Aztec garb, but they are continuing a traditional way of life that the blind eye will not see. Peel back the layers of modernization, and find the world that lies beneath.

## THE AZTEC SUN STONE

By Dr. Crit Minster

The Aztec Sun Stone, often called the Aztec calendar, is a massive, 24-ton stone carving currently on display at the Mexican National Museum of Anthropology and History in Mexico City. It is estimated that the sun stone was carved in roughly 1479 A.D. Many tourists don't know the stone was made by Mexican cultures: you can sometimes see an image of the stone for sale on t-shirts in Peru and Ecuador with the title "Inca Calendar!"

The Aztecs believed that they were living in the fifth age of the world: each age had a different sun and each sun represented a different God. In the center of the stone is a grimacing face: it holds a sacrificial knife in its mouth. To the sides, clawed hands hold sacrificed hearts. Many believe the face and hands belong to Tonatiuh, the Aztec Sun God of the fifth age. Around the central figure are four scenes that depict the four previous ages ("suns") of the world. The four ages were jaguar, wind, fiery rain and water. The next ring depicts the 20 days of the Aztec cycle: they have names like deer, rabbit, wind and skull. The Aztec year had 18 months of 20 days each, for a total of 360 days. Five additional days were added every year, and were ominously referred to as "days of sacrifice." The Aztec century lasted 52 years.

The sun stone is one of the most easily recognizable images of Mexico's Aztec history, and no visit to Mexico City would be complete without a trip to the world-class Anthropology Museum to check out the sun stone and countless other priceless artifacts.

Festival in Mexico City. Photo by Stephany Slaughter.

# POLYFORUM CULTURAL SIQUEIROS

By Lorraine Caputo, Columbia, Missouri, U.S.A.

Strolling down Avenida Insurgentes Sur in Mexico City, traffic fumes waft through the forest of modern buildings. Just past the World Trade Center, there's a wall of junkyard materials: worn brakes, rusted rebars and what-not set in ochre concrete. This "sculpture" seems incredibly out of place in this wealthier section of the metropolis.

Hidden behind this sculpture-wall is a twelve-sided building, the Polyforum Cultural Siqueiros. Seen from overhead, it appears to be a giant turtle nesting in the Colonia Nápoles neighborhood. The building is Mexican muralist David Alfaro Siqueiros' masterpiece. Inside and out, there are 8,700 square meters of wall decoration, variously described as mosaics, murals or frescoes. But the technique Siqueiros used is beyond the usual. Expanding on his concept of three-dimensional murals, these works are composed of paint, acrylic and metal on asbestos and concrete. It took six years for Siqueiros and a team of assistants to complete this masterpiece. The Polyforum was inaugurated in December 1971.

On the outside, each of the twelve panels has mosaics fusing ideas of nature and humanity, and is thematically related to the mural in El Foro Universal, the main events room. El Foro Universal is beneath an oval-shaped dome. Here is "The March of Humanity." Covering over 2,400 square meters, it is the world's largest mural.

Seven panels, 24 compositions in all, illustrate the March of Humanity. At one end of the Foro is a man, representing creation, domination and the use of science. At the other end is a woman, representing peace, culture and harmony; the future society. Each holds hands outward, reaching toward one another. On the vault overhead are an eagle, a red star, a white star and astronauts.

The other four panels show the natural world, and the procession of humanity—men, women and children—Pima and Yaqui natives, mestizos and blacks—workers, leaders and demagogues. All show where we have been, and to where we can go, what we can achieve. Parts of the mural are three-dimensional; the lynched black man emerges from the flat space, heaving in his pain.

A sound and light show is offered on Saturdays and Sundays, narrated by Siqueiros himself. The platform where spectators are seated rotates, while each section is highlighted and described with musical accompaniment.

El Foro Universal hosts all types of social, political and cultural events. The Polyforum complex also houses two art galleries with exhibits by international artists, an on-site museum, artisan shop, bookstore, theater, and restaurant-piano bar.

If you're only spending a few days in Mexico City, it's worth going down the Avenida Insurgentes Sur, to the corner of Calle Filadelfia. There, nesting like a turtle, is one of the architectural and artistic surprises of 20th century Mexico City: the Polyforum Cultural Siqueiros.

> *"Every view of the world that becomes extinct, every culture that disappears, diminishes a possibility of life."*
> *-Octavio Paz, Mexican Poet and Essayist (1914-1998)*

## LATIN REVOLUTIONARIES # 9: SUBCOMANDANTE MARCOS

In early 1994, there was a short-lived armed rebellion in the southern Mexican state of Chiapas, in support of the indigenous poor. The Mexican government, fearing that the rebellion could spread, quickly responded with troops, tanks and helicopters. Within a couple of weeks, however, the rebels had hidden their weapons and faded back into the lush Mexican jungle ... and the real revolution began.

The rebel group calls itself the Zapatista Army of National Liberation (EZLN), taking their name from Emiliano Zapata, an idealistic general of the Mexican Revolution who was assassinated in 1919. Under the command of a black-masked figure known only as Subcomandante Marcos, the rebels knew they could never out-gun the mighty Mexican army, and in any event they did not want to: many members of the EZLN do not approve of violence. Instead, after they had captured the world's attention, they turned their efforts to more modern battlefields: the internet and the international press. They have been fighting a war of words ever since, and have gained several important concessions from the Mexican government without the need for violence. The movement is still strongest in southern Mexico and several towns and villages in the region are effectively under EZLN control.

The mysterious Subcomandante Marcos—also known as Delegado Zero—is one of the driving forces behind the movement. Mexican officials believe his real name is Rafael Sebastián Guillén Vicente, although Marcos has publicly denied it and the Guillén family refuses to comment. Marcos communicates with the world through press releases, internet messages and occasional public speeches, where he always wears a black mask. He occasionally leads marches and protests. He is also known to support anti-globalization movements around the world, including a public criticism of the government of Spain in 2002.

# MARKETS OF MEXICO CITY

*By Robyn Leslie, Durban, South Africa*

After a gasp-inducing ride through the back streets of Mexico City with a mad taxi driver named Gonzalo, who was trying to learn English and steer simultaneously, I needed to feel the ground beneath my feet.

Finally standing, I walked through the door and met all 20 million inhabitants of the city at once, most of them cursing the beggars or shouting greetings to their friends five kilometres away. This heaving mass of humanity that extended as far as I could see was my introduction to the street markets of Mexico City.

As a South African, I have seen street sellers. Hell, I considered myself a seasoned marketeer, having visited the Indian spice markets of Grey Street and braved the offal butchery in Warwick Triangle as part of a Saturday morning in Durban. I stalked off towards a small clearing in the crowd, and soon I had disappeared from sight.

The street markets of Mexico City are a whole separate world, full of joy and sadness and humour and pathos. After wandering past a desperate man selling inflatable Valentine's Day roses (in April), I came upon a sideshow designed to entertain the children while parents sold or haggled. I was transfixed by the game they were playing, spinning each child round and whoever fell down last won. I see them in front of my eyes as I write this, small specks of humanity spinning crazily, giggling and screaming with their eyes squeezed shut and fingers grabbing at the air as they lost control.

As I inched my way past tiny ladies carrying large bags of sesame sticks and nameless fried items, I lurched into an old man offering to weigh me for one peso. I was trying to avoid the street sellers who kept pressing crystallised fruit on me, dripping in syrup as bees (an insect everyone was profoundly ignoring) buzzed crazily about their hands.

Covered by a gentle yet firm layer of grime, orange peels and spit become gummed onto your soles. Puddles of water and effluent rise up to suck you down if you are foolish enough to turn your eyes from the concrete upward, gazing at the girls for sale in doorways of gloomy and endless buildings. You can lift your feet up from the ground and be carried forward instead by sweaty forearms, necks and backs of the short, squat women who hustle past, charging through the thronging crowd fueled by the realities of small pockets and large families. Shouting, bargaining and complaining, they leave behind them a trail of grinning men and lost children. No matter, the children are picked up by the next mother in line and are returned somehow after being volubly cursed for their many sins.

The street markets of Mexico City are not for the faint of heart. They extend farther than you believe is possible, and I got lost in them for over three hours. They draw you in and you become part of the lives of those sellers who stare at you like you are not real. After a time in there, you will find your way back to your hostel and go straight to the bar for a drink. It is an experience I would not exchange for any other.

A proud and passionate South African, Robyn Leslie is an environmental and political scientist, focusing on developmental issues such as community development and natural resource management. She studied at the University of Cape Town and is currently wandering around the world, working on any useful and purposeful development project that comes her way! She enjoyed visiting Ecuador, particularly for the Ecuadorian version of Day of the Dead: bread shaped like men, pulverized prunes for juice and family outings to the cemetery. She hopes to visit Madagascar one day.

## TOP LIST: BEST PLACES TO LEARN SPANISH

Looking for a place to learn Spanish, or just to brush up? Our community gives you the inside scoop on the best cities and schools in Latin America:

1. Quito, Ecuador (p. 239).
"The Spanish here is slow and clear! And there is access to many wonderful places to visit." Risa, New York, U.S.A.

2. Oaxaca, Mexico.
"Amigos del Sol is inexpensive. The staff is helpful and friendly and they provide an excellent homestay." Monte Hensley, Albuquerque, U.S.A.

3. Cusco, Peru.
"The teachers are all professionals and Peruvian. They have a wide knowledge of the area, history and the local way of living." Sandra Delgado, Cusco, Peru.

4. Medellín, Colombia.
"One of the best accents and grammar quality is found in the Spanish spoken in Medellín." Colombia South American Explorers Club.

Runners up: Utila, Honduras, (Teri Faught, U.S.A.) Buenos Aires, Argentina, (Aristote Masamba Levi, South Africa) Mexico City, Mexico, (Aristote Masamba Levi, South Africa).

# TAXCO SILVER CITY

By Kena Sosa, San Antonio, Texas, U.S.A.

Two hours to the southwest of Mexico City, not far from Acapulco, sits Taxco, one of the most romantic, charming and important towns in all of Mexico. Resembling a small European village, the streets slope up and down like those of Italy, nesting with white houses donning terracotta-tiled roofs and pink floral accents.

Although its aesthetic charm is enough to attract a visit, many travel through Taxco in search of the mesmerizing abundance of silver found here. One of the largest exporters of silver in the world, this precious metal is the staple on which this town thrives.

Centuries ago, Taxco was the main supplier of silver to Europe, and the quality and artistry of the locals have not declined. Silversmiths here are some of the most talented in the world. This phenomenon is one of the true Mexican arts, a blending of Spanish and indigenous masterpieces. Before the arrival of the Spanish, the locals valued silver as much as cacao, the chocolate plant once considered valuable enough to be used as currency. Locals enjoyed silver's aesthetic quality, but it was not a sought-after luxury because it was so plentiful and common. When the Spanish arrived they assigned a great value to the silver and began extracting it, creating the mining industry which has defined Taxco ever since.

Needless to say, the "silver city," as it is nicknamed, is sprinkled with silversmiths' shops that carry everything from elegantly crafted necklaces and earrings to solid silver sculptures of animals and unique silver art. There is no limit to the styles and qualities of the silver you can find. Jewelers and jewelry-wearers would be hard pressed to pass up the shining trinkets found here.

Towering over the village stands Taxco's towering cathedral, Santa Prisca. Identified easily by its enormous stature with twin bell towers, it was designed and built by town founder Jose de la Borda in the late eighteenth century. The Baroque-styled exterior of the church gives way to a chamber decorated with painted porcelain figures that inspire even the most out-of-practice believer. The decorative stained glass and paintings also make it an unforgettable experience of art and faith.

Don't miss the Museo Virreynal de Taxco to learn more about its history, from its native cultures to the Spanish influence and the current lifestyle of the land.

It is not only silver jewelry and breathtaking churches which make Taxco a heart-fluttering romantic haven. One of the most enjoyable activities is strolling down the quiet brick-paved streets, or lounging while people-watching in the town square, directly in front of the cathedral. For a special date head up to the Taxco Hotel, which has the best view of the city's beautiful landscape.

From this mountain top locale, one's eyes will open their widest to fit in the view of the entire valley—the curvaceous hills, gigantic trees and natural beauty of the untouched areas surrounding Taxco. One need not spend a night at the hotel to visit and breathe air of the most exquisite kind—warm, healthy and clean.

Taxco. Photo by Stephany Slaughter.

*"The Devil is like a strainer that separates the mud from the gold."*
*-Carlos Santana, Mexican Musician (1947-)*

# CATEMACO

### By Lorraine Caputo, Columbia, Missouri, U.S.A.

To the edge of a blue lake in an ancient volcanic crater, jade jungle hills fall. Bird song echoes through the canopies, through the folds of the earth. And through these Tuxtla mountains still roam the spirits of the Olmec ancestors.

This area was the homeland of the mother civilization of all of Mexico, the Olmecs, known for the colossal heads they carved of stone. Catemaco, on the shores of the lake bearing the same name, is the main village of the Tuxtlas region. Along its waterfront promenade are a number of good restaurants offering regional foods (including fresh-water eel) and souvenirs.

Lake Catemaco has a maximum width of 10 kilometers, and can be explored by boat. Tours visit the shrine "El Tegal," where the Virgin Mary allegedly appeared; *Isla de los Macacos* (Monkey Island); *Isla de las Garzas* (Heron Island) and the *Reserva Ecológica Nanciyaga*, (Nanciyaga Ecological Reserve) where "The Medicine Man," starring Sean Connery, was filmed. Playa Hermosa and Playa Azul are beaches near Catemaco town where one can swim in the refreshing waters.

The Reserva Ecológica Nanciyaga has over 250 species of birds, both local and migratory, and crocodiles. Over a hundred species of bromeliads and diverse medicinal plants grow in these forests. This makes the Catemaco region an important center for natural medicine. Every March, on the first Friday, "*brujos*" (shamans) meet for a yearly convention.

Nanciyaga has eco-friendly cabins, campsites and a natural foods restaurant. The spa offers mud and herbal baths and *temazcales* (sweat baths). One can also hike and kayak here.

Near Catemaco is the spectacular 50-foot Eyipantla Waterfall. A 200-step staircase leads to the pool at its base. Another excursion is to *Laguna Encantada*—the Enchanted Lagoon. Oddly, when it rains, the water level goes down; when it is dry, its waters rise.

San Andrés Tuxtla, 13 kilometers from Catemaco, has narrow, winding streets lined with colonial buildings. One can visit the Te Amo cigar factory and learn how cigars are rolled by hand.

Santiago Tuxtla, another colonial town, is a further 15 kilometers on. In the central plaza is the largest Olmec head ever found, weighing in at over 40 tons. The Museo Tuxtleco facing the park offers exhibits on local history and lore, shamanism and an Olmec head.

Indeed, this is the heart of the Olmec homeland. A dirt road goes to one of the most important sites, Tres Zapotes, which is largely unexcavated. Here there is a museum with yet another Olmec head and several stela, including the largest one ever found, and fragments with the oldest Long Count calendar date, equivalent to 31 B.C. Not too far away are three more sites: San Lorenzo Tenochtitlán, Laguna de los Cerros and Cerro de las Mesas.

A journey into Los Tuxtlas is a journey into the mystical origins of Mexico, which survive in its deep mountains and its sapphire waters. This is a place of healing, for the spirit, mind and the body.

## LATIN REVOLUTIONARIES # 3: EMILIANO ZAPATA

### Mexico (1879-1919)

Emiliano Zapata was born in the Mexican region of Morelos to a poor but independent family during the reign of President Porfirio Díaz, who ruled the country with an iron fist. The Díaz regime was known for greatly favoring the rich at the cost of the poor. During his rule, rich landowners took over vast tracts of land and reduced the people to a system of debt peonage. In his home state, Zapata began speaking out against the abuses and was a community leader by the time he was 30.

In 1910, Díaz was removed from office and fled the country. Mexico plunged into a brutal civil war for the next ten years, as former military generals, government officials and popular rebel leaders all raised armies to fight for control. Although he had no formal or military education, Zapata was soon named general of the Ejército Libertador del Sur—the Liberation Army of the South. Wherever the army went, it would "liberate" vast tracts of land from wealthy landowners and redistribute it to the poor. One of the true ideologues of the revolution, Zapata is remembered for one slogan: "Tierra y Libertad!" ("Land and liberty!") and his famous quote "It is better to die on your feet than to live on your knees."

For the next nine years, the Liberation Army of the South remained mobilized, fighting other rebel factions and government forces. Zapata was allied for a while with former Díaz general Venustiano Carranza, but withdrew his support after Carranza seized power. Carranza put a bounty on Zapata, and on April 9, 1919, Zapata was betrayed, ambushed and killed.

Zapata remains an important figure in Mexico: he is seen by many as the true voice of the Mexican Revolution. Several films have been made about him, and in 1994 a popular revolt in Southern Mexico named itself the Zapatista Army of National Liberation: they believed that Zapata's struggle for land and liberty had never come to fruition.

# OAXACA

By Dr. Crit Minster, Rochester, New York, U.S.A.

The people of Oaxaca believe that there is magic in their *Zócalo*, or central plaza. They have fervently believed this since 1529, the year that Alonso García Bravo—the leading Spanish architect of the early colonial era—laid the first stone. Bravo designed the square with the cathedral on one side—erected over the cemetery containing the bones of the Aztec dead—and the municipal government buildings on the other. The belief was that the Zócalo would become a place of balance and harmony between the spiritual and the temporal, and that this spirit would radiate outward through the growing city.

There is still magic in Oaxaca, and the best place to start looking for it is at the Zócalo. It is a haven of tranquility. Tall trees cast their shade upon locals and visitors alike, as they dine on regional specialties at sidewalk cafes. In the evening, lovers walk hand-in-hand through the lengthening shadows. If the mood strikes, they might hire one of several wandering mariachi bands to play them a song. Vendors of everything from fresh basil and nutmeg to Spider-man blow up toys shuffle cautiously along the streets, offering without harassing. Dignified older men and women aimlessly stroll past stately colonial architecture, giving the impression that time stopped in the square four hundred years ago.

The nearby ruins of Monte Albán (about ten kilometers away) draw most visitors to Oaxaca, but it is the spell-binding charm of the city that compels them to return. The city center, with its magnificent cathedrals, colonial homes and architecture, is a UNESCO World Heritage site. The old town's labyrinth of museums, restored homes, markets and quaint cafes and restaurants beckons travelers to stop and explore. From the Zócalo, you can literally wander off in any direction and bump into something remarkable. Head north and you'll find the restored church of Santo Domingo, with its dazzling interior of gold leaf. To the south are the Benito Juárez and November 20 markets, sites of organized chaos, where you can buy delicious Oaxaca cheese, fruits and vegetables as well as souvenirs. To the east is the San Agustín church and the Macedonio Alcalá Theater. To the west you'll find the religious museum and further on, the Monte Albán archaeological complex.

Visitors often leave Oaxaca slightly dazed and more than a little wistful, always promising to return one day. Departing travelers sometimes have trouble discerning what exactly made them fall in love with Oaxaca—was it the food, the history, the architecture, the people? If you find yourself feeling a little melancholy as you're leaving you may want to bear in mind one final legend of Oaxaca magic: according to the locals, if you eat a dish called *chapulines*, you're destined to return to the city one day. The only catch: chapulines are fried grasshoppers. If you find yourself presented with some, take a look around, take a deep breath, and gobble one down: by then, you'll agree that it's worth it.

> *According to the locals, if you eat a dish called chapulines, you're destined to return to the city one day. The only catch: chapulines are fried grasshoppers.*

## TLAYUDAS

By Michelle Hopey

Tlayudas are a fancy name for a simple, delicious, yet outrageously large tortilla creation which is the heart of Oaxaca.

Hand-made and often cooled until crisp, the enormous corn-tortilla is traditionally smeared with black bean paste and lard and then packed with *tasajo* (thinly sliced, dried seasoned beef) or *cecina* (salted pork) special Oaxacan cheese—*quesillo*—and cabbage. Each tlayuda is then cooked open-faced over coals, giving it a smoky, hearty, toasted flavor, and finally folded over into a half moon shape and served. Sometimes meats are garnished on top. Tomatoes or salsa are also common accompaniments.

When done cooking, it looks much like an over-stuffed, extra large quesadilla. Tlayudas are always too large to fit on a plate, considering the ends always hang off.

And don't expect to get a tlayuda in daylight. With many street stalls in town selling the Oaxacan delicacy, tlayudas-stalls are not generally open until 9 p.m. Tlayudas de Dona Martha on Calle Libres is one of the more famous stands and cars line the street until 3 a.m. But Tlayudas de Libres, as it is often called, is in strong contention with Las Reliquias on Avenida Morelos for best tlayudas. Both are authentic, but Las Reliquias is only open from 8 p.m to midnight and is run by a family in their front yard complete with plastic tables and chairs. Dona Martha is a bit more established and sets up grills in the street. In these parts it is said you are either a Tlayudas on libres fan, or Reliquias lover. It's quite Oaxacan to debate this, so as a visitor you might want to do as the locals do, eat at both and then take a stance.

# THE RUINS OF MONTE ALBÁN

By Dr. Crit Minster, Rochester, New York, U.S.A.

The ball game is intense. The players, dressed in padded clothes for protection, dash up and down the court, skillfully moving the ball, using only their shoulders, knees, elbows and hips. Everyone in the city is watching, but the most intent spectators are the priests, who interpret the will of the Gods by the actions of the ball and the players. Finally, the game ends and the winners celebrate: they have brought prosperity to the region they represent. The losers, however, march off sadly—their loss has shown that the Gods are displeased with them and their city-state. The only remedy: the losing team must be sacrificed. The skull of the losing captain will form the core of the hard rubber ball that is used in the next game.

The ball game, called *ollama* or *ulama*, was only one aspect of the culture of the ancient Olmecs, whose civilization was a precursor to later Central Mexican cultures such as the Aztecs and the Maya. No one knows what happened to the Olmecs. This fierce Central Mexican tribe came to the rich valleys near present-day Oaxaca, where they founded a settlement whose name has been lost to history.

Around 500 B.C., some newcomers arrived in the region: the Zapotecs, who defeated or assimilated the descendents of the Olmecs, whose rich culture was then in decline. Together they leveled the top of a mountain and built a mighty city from which they could command three valleys. The Zapotecs named it *Danibaan*, or "Sacred Mountain." They ruled their mountain fortress for centuries

> *The losers march off sadly—their loss has shown that the Gods are displeased with them and their city-state. The only remedy: the losing team must be sacrificed.*

before falling into decline themselves. By the tenth century A.D. the site was almost entirely abandoned.

The Mixtec culture arrived in the fourteenth century, and set up nearby. They considered the ruins sacred, however, and did not occupy many of the larger structures. Instead, they used the area as a burial ground. The Mixtec referred to the ruins site as *Sahandevul*, "at the foot of the sky." The Mixtec lived near the ruins until they were conquered by the Spanish, who named the site Monte Albán after a local nobleman.

One of the highlights of Monte Albán is the *gallery of the dancers*. Among the oldest of the archaeological treasures at Monte Albán, this one includes a series of relief carvings of naked figures in contorted positions. The carvings are definitely of Olmec origin, an intriguing memento left by the first culture to colonize Monte Albán. The exact meaning of the figures is not known, although it may be related to fertility or health.

Over 170 tombs are located at Monte Albán, most of which are attributed to the late-coming Mixtec culture. The most spectacular tomb is tomb seven, which contained more than 500 pieces of gold, silver and jade. Many of the relics from tomb seven are on display at the impressive on-site museum or in nearby Oaxaca.

Today's ball players whine when they don't get a trade they want or when they have to settle for a mere three million dollars per season. They should be happy that no one will be playing with their skulls next season!

*"Perfect order is the forerunner of perfect horror."*
-Carlos Fuentes, Mexican Novelist (1928-)

# QUESILLO—OAXACAN CHEESE

By Michelle Hopey

If you've been anywhere in Latin America, you know, cheese is not the specialty. Usually referred to as queso fresco or queso blanco it is typically served in a block and its consistency is a little like solid cottage cheese, if you can conjure up that image. It's not usually pleasing to the eye, nor is it a renowned palate pleaser.

But there is one Latin cheese, however, that could (and should) rally against any Sharp Wisconsin cheddar or French Brie: Quesillo. Made of cow's milk, the mild, buttery, semi-soft string cheese is a stretched curd cheese which is kneaded, swung into a ball and sold at markets across the Oaxaca region. Quesillo, also called Oaxacan cheese or *Asadero* (Spanish for baked), tastes is like a mozzarella combined with a provolone. While good for easy, on-the-go-pull-apart snacking, it is also a great melting cheese, especially for quesadillas, tlyudas and tostadas. When melted, the Quesillo becomes soft, gooey and stringy, but retains it shape nicely. It's easy to cook with too, just pull apart the cheese and place on whatever it is you are making, no knives needed. If you are a cheese lover, it is quite likely you'll become addicted and eat it everyday while in Oaxaca.

Check with your country on bringing cheese across customs, and if you're lucky, locals suggest freezing it the night before a day of travel. But if you can't bring it home: remember that when in Oaxaca do as Oaxacans do and eat cheese, lots of cheese.

MEXICO

# CHIAPAS

By Nic Havers, Perpignan, Southern France

A visit to Chiapas, in a remote corner of southern Mexico, offers lost Maya cities, isolated waterfalls and indigenous tribes who live as if the Spanish had never arrived in 1519.

The old colonial capital of San Cristóbal de las Casas is a great place to start exploring this Mexican state. The central plaza is lined by colonial mansions, and a short distance north of here is Santo Domingo, a cathedral with a Baroque façade that combines Oaxacan and Guatemalan styles, making it look as if it had been carved from candle-wax. There is a pinkish tinge to the stone.

The most unforgettable experience of this trip is the church of San Juan in nearby Chamula, its village inhabited by Tzotzil-speaking indigenous Maya. These people wear extraordinarily bright costumes and live in houses made from mud mixed with pine needles.

From across the *Zócalo*, San Juan looks like an ordinary white Spanish church. But the hot, sooty interior is crammed with thousands of flickering candles and there are pine needles sprinkled all over the floor. The walls are lined with glass cases containing statues of Saints, some with mirrors attached to their chests, and a man is playing a melancholic tune on a concertina. The burning of incense is choking. All around, people are singing or chanting. Figures on the floor drink from an oily bottle a spirit known as pox, or "white water." They then down Coca Cola, before burping loudly to expel evil spirits. One woman removes a live chicken from the bag beside her, raises it above the candles, and with eyes closed and a look of intense concentration on her face, she chants, and then, shockingly, wrings the chicken's neck.

The Maya hold these healing sessions if they have a problem in their life-if they are ill or their crops fail, for example. The chicken represents freedom because of its wings, and its sacrifice brings back health and good fortune. The dead chicken is kept inside the bag so no one can touch it—it has absorbed evil—and then it is buried in the hills. Whole families come here, sometimes three times a day, to meet with their shaman. They sometimes bring offerings—particularly eggs, because the embryo represents a living thing. Witnessing this ritual is a unique and moving experience-an enduring memory to tell your grandchildren in years to come!

Near the village of Comitán, just outside San Cristóbal, the Hacienda Santa María is worth the bumpy roads to get there. It's a sunny, tranquil spot, with views across a green river valley reminiscent of England with bees buzzing around hives and shady courtyards, and some absorbing 16th-19th century religious paintings in the chapel. The small restaurant serves organic food grown in the gardens. Rooms here come at a budget price, yet have chandeliers and are furnished with antiques.

On a guided tour of Chiapas, you can head down to the Usumacinta River at Escudo Jaguar, bordering Guatemala. Lanchas are narrow, yellow-painted boats with a roof of tin and reeds, which sail you down river to the remote ruins of Yaxchilán where you can explore the *Pequeña Acropolis*.

A climb up 200 steps to Edificio 33 deposits you at a palace with beautiful carvings. There is a headless statue in one room and next door the head is displayed on a plinth. Local Lacandon legend has it that when the head of this statue is replaced upon its shoulders, the end of the world will come. Yaxchilán is an exciting place, exuding an aura of mysticism. It is completely wild, without any tourist trappings and only reachable by boat. Visiting gives you a sense of how the first explorers felt when they stumbled across this city.

www.vivatravelguides.com/104113

# SAN CRISTÓBAL DE LAS CASAS

By Richard Arghiris, London, England

There is a vivid and otherworldly quality to San Cristóbal de Las Casas, a city with a rich colonial legacy, strikingly positioned in the highlands of Chiapas province in southern Mexico. Clean, clear light spills across this city, where colonial mansions rise up between rows of brightly coloured houses. Rich in indigenous culture and history, San Cristóbal de las Casas is an anthropologist's dream.

San Cristóbal's principal authority on Maya culture is the Na Bolom Museum. Na Bolom means "house of the jaguar" in Tzotzil. An essential stop for anyone wanting to learn more about this mysterious culture, the museum attractions include an excellent library and an astonishing photo gallery. Among its acquisitions is a Maya clock, which has no mechanical parts and resembles a hanging mobile. It is purportedly extremely accurate, although few people know how to read it anymore.

Nearby, the *Centro de Desarollo de la Medicina Maya* explores Mayan healing techniques still in use and founded on ancient shamanic practices. Mayan medicine forms an integral part of a complex "cosmo-vision" where extraordinary spiritual realms co-exist with mundane reality. Practically speaking, there are three main branches: herbalism, pulse-reading, and midwifery. The museum contains some excellent exhibits, a medicinal herb garden and a *Temazcal* steam bath. It also has a list of over 900 healers who are all available for consultation.

Nearby San Juan Chamula is particularly renowned for its adherence to ancient traditions. Here the old gods are worshipped as much as the new, and the locally practised brand of Catholicism assumes a vibrant, evocative and thoroughly pagan flavour. Inside Chamula's church, immersed in a fog of incense, shamans engage themselves in strange rituals, sacrificing live chickens before crowds of onlookers. The villages around San Cristóbal are also good places to pick up local handicrafts. Maya textiles are of particularly high quality. Many tours of the area include a trip to a weaver's house, where you are able to buy goods directly and at a discount. This can make your purchases more personal and satisfying and you will also be able to ask specific questions about the pieces you buy. Maya textiles are often laden with symbolic motifs, and their makers are happy to explain their meaning.

Located just 3.5 kilometres outside of San Cristóbal, the Huitepec Ecological Reserve provides an easy excursion into natural surroundings. The reserve is made up of two distinct zones which cover the slope of a dormant volcano. Oak forests dominate the low-lying areas, which as one ascends, slowly transforms into cloud forest. At its heights, the vegetation spills over with lush exuberance—thick green carpets of moss, ferns, bromeliads and spidery extrusions.

Surrounded by green mountains, the mythical dwelling place of ancient spirits, San Cristóbal de las Casas is one of Mexico's most profound and memorable locales. Mystical, indigenous and ethereal San Cristóbal: A visit here is sure to enchant and fascinate.

# PALENQUE

### By Dr. Crit Minster, Rochester, New York, U.S.A.

On the top of a massive stone temple in a lost city near southern Mexico's densest rainforest, there is a small duct that leads from the floor to a chamber deep within the pyramid itself. According to some, the duct was used by Mayan priests to feed the blood of sacrificial victims to the body that lay in the dark chamber, entombed under tons of rock for centuries. The body was that of the mightiest Maya king: *K'inich J'aanab Pakal*, or Pacal the Great. Pacal's descendents revered him as a god, and held elaborate ceremonies on top of his tomb to appease and commune with him. But Pacal did not protect his worshippers: the great city of Palenque would soon vanish under the trees, vines and flowers of the tropical jungle. For centuries this forgotten city would be home only to tribes of monkeys and flocks of parrots and toucans.

Palenque was once known as *Lakam Ha*, capital of the *B'aakal* city-state during the classical Maya era (roughly the fifth century to the ninth century A.D.) During the centuries of B'aakal rule at Palenque, the city became the most important center for culture and commerce in the western Maya area. Without use of the wheel, metal tools, or beasts of burden, they forged a great city from stone: the achievement still boggles the mind today. For almost a century (615-683), Palenque was ruled by Pacal the Great, who built the magnificent *Temple of the Inscriptions* which would later become his tomb.

By the tenth century, the various city-states of the Maya had crumbled beneath wars and natural disasters. Palenque itself was deserted around the ninth century, although local farmers knew of it, referring to it as *Otolum*, or "the land with strong houses." Refusing to succumb to time or the elements, the massive stone city remained standing centuries after abandonment. When the Spanish first visited the city in 1567, they named it Palenque, or "fortress" due to its impressive stone walls and structures.

Unfortunately, these stalwart structures could not withstand the effects of Spanish-led expeditions, which resulted in a great deal of damage to the site—particularly to the palace—over the years. In an attempt to combat further damage, the Mexican government funded two different archaeological and preservation projects at the site from 1949-1952, and again in the 1970's. Although digs have continued, archaeologists estimate that only five percent of the more than 500 structures of Palenque have been uncovered.

Today, Palenque is one of Southern Mexico's most important traveller destinations. Highlights of the site include the imposing Temple of the Inscriptions, which contains Pacal's tomb, and the palace—a maze of high walls and gardens that some believe once served as a royal dwelling. Pacal's great city may have once been forgotten, but neither time nor jungle vines could obscure its undeniable supernatural beauty and mystery.

Palenque. Photo by Will Gray.

*"Solitude is the profoundest fact of the human condition. Man is the only being who knows he is alone."*
-Octavio Paz, Mexican Poet and Essayist (1914-1998)

# PARQUE NACIONAL MONTEBELLO

By Lorraine Caputo, Columbia, Missouri, U.S.A.

Wandering through the grassy ruins of Chinkultik, through ancient plazas with temple mounds, one comes to a small creek meandering through dense leaves. On the other side, high on the face of a cliff, looms a tall temple. El Mirador, the temple clinging to the side of the cliff, seems out of reach to the mere modern mortal.

But it is an easy climb up, and the reward is spectacular vistas over the National Park. Scamper up the hill and you can see the forest canopy stretching to the Guatemalan border, to the Usumacinta River. Thirty kilometers away, as the quetzal flies, the shimmering of the Lagunas de Montebello now and again breaks through the verdant landscape.

These two wonders of Chiapas, Mexico, are located southeast of Comitán, very near the Guatemalan border. Simply head 16 kilometers down the Pan-American highway to Las Trincheras and take the road from there. Thirty kilometers along this camino is the turn-off for the Chinkultik ruins, which is then another two kilometers along a dirt road. Chinkultik is a classic Maya site whose name in Tzeltal means "The Little Sanctuary." Even to this day, peacefulness reigns in this partially excavated and restored site, which consists of 200 mounds in six clusters. The site peaked from 591 to 897 A.D., though evidence shows its final abandonment to have occurred about 1200 A.D. It is one of the few places of the Late Classic Maya period with numerous hieroglyphic inscriptions. A small museum and a "forest" of statues and stela are located near the entrance.

The entire site includes temples, a ball court and Cenote Azul, a sinkhole filled with sapphire-blue water, which provides a refreshing swimming break in the steamy tropics.

Parque Nacional Lagunas de Montebello (also called Lagos de Montebello) is located 65 kilometers from Comitán. Its gorgeous 6,000 hectares are scattered with dozens of lakes and lagoons of every color of the rainbow, from turquoise to red, emerald to black. These colors are caused either by Maya magic or by oxides in the waters—take your pick. The most accessible ones can be reached by private car, or by hopping off the public bus at each one, or—for those who don't mind walking a while—on foot.

The park includes other wonders beyond its lakes, including orchids, quetzals, woodpeckers and various migratory birds. Besides hiking and birdwatching, one can take boat rides on some of the lakes, rent a canoe, or go horseback riding.

Both the National Park and the ruins can be reached by one-day tours from San Cristóbal de Las Casas or Comitán. An even better option is to stay in one of several basic inns on the road to the park, or in the Park itself at one of the lodges or campsites at Tziscao or Laguna Bosque Azul. Then one can enjoy the natural beauty of Lagunas de Montebello National Park and Ruinas Chinkultic over several leisurely days.

## MAKING TAMALES: A CHRISTMAS TRADITION

By Katie Hale

Lil, a family friend who grew up in Mexico and southern California, is almost 80 years old. Even though she has trouble remembering what she did yesterday and her eyesight is failing, she loves to go out dancing with her husband and she loves to cook. She only makes her famous tamales once a year—for Christmas. As Christmas carols start playing in stores and tree lots go up, her family and friends greedily anticipate what awaits. When Lil hands out the hundreds of tamales to the deserving, a clever few stash a batch in the freezer for another day. But usually the tamales just don't last that long ... they are too good to save for *mañana*.

Although eaten any time of the year, tamale-making is an especially important tradition during Christmas time in Mexico. After coming home from midnight mass on Christmas Eve, it is common in Mexico to celebrate with relatives and friends by devouring delicious tamales.

The coming together of loved ones not only to eat the tamales, but more importantly to create them during the holiday season is what makes them an important dish in Latin American cuisine. The food itself is a symbol that represents tradition, family, and togetherness, unlike any other Mexican dish. The days before Christmas Eve, tamaladas, or tamale-making parties, are held where women gather and prepare the tamales. Generations are brought together at these celebrations, and knowledge of cooking and life is passed down between the smearing of dough and the steaming of corn husks.

Ingredients needed to produce this scrumptious food are fresh masa harina (corn dough), corn husks or other wrapper (i.e. banana leaves), a filling (Mexican tamales commonly use pork, but fillers can be anything from lobster to fruit), lard, chicken broth, and sometimes a sauce of chillies or other intense flavors. Making tamales is a time-consuming and difficult process, but no one will ever say the labor is not worth the final product.

Christmas without tamales is simply not Christmas at all. If you are lucky enough to know how to make great tamales, keep your recipe close. If not, you could learn, but the fine art of tamale-making is probably best left to the masters of the kitchen—those like Lil who have been making them for years and who don't need a recipe to make mouths water and stomachs thankful.

# SAN JUAN CHAMULA

### By Darren Fitzgerald, Los Angeles, California, U.S.A.

Pine needles, dead chickens, eggs and soda pop; the staples of worship for the locals of San Juan Chamula, a pastoral village a few miles north of the Mexican colonial town of San Cristóbal. The Chamulans revere San Juan Bautista (St. John the Baptist), and after a few minutes in the central cathedral you might catch yourself wondering, "What does any of this have to do with St. John the Baptist?"

A short ride in a packed VW van brings you to the Chamula valley, which is surrounded by small, forested hills, adobe huts and sheep farmers. Perched atop one of the hills is a burnt-out stone church, which sits in the middle of an old cemetery dotted with different colored crosses—black for people who died old, white for the young and blue for all of the others. The town square is filled with local farmers selling produce and flowers laid out on apple crates and decorative blankets. Women are dressed in typical indigenous attire and the men wear animal hide ponchos and cowboy hats. Facing the square is a large white cathedral with a colorfully painted arched doorway and streamers hanging from the steeple. The real magic of San Juan lies within this church.

The front door is a massive wooden slab studded with pewter rivets. Only a small section of this door is opened, and squeezing past is akin to being birthed into a strange world. You're hit with the pungent fragrance of pine needles as you step into a cauldron of dancing candlelight, wafting incense smoke, and rays of sun illuminating stained-glass windows. The shiny, tormented faces of San Antonio de Monte, Santa Rosa de Lima, La Virgen de Rosario Menor, and El Sagrado Corazón de Jesús gaze at you from the dozens of large wooden cabinets lining the walls of the church.

Your steps on the multicolored tile floor are muted by a soft carpet of pine needles, and families build small altars to San Juan Bautista by clearing away circles on the floor and filling them with candles, eggs, gizzards, dead chickens and bottles of soda pop. They bury their faces in the pine needles, mumble incomprehensibly, smear the gizzards and eggs on the floor, and burp to excess. They believe burping expels evil spirits, so they consume copious amounts of Coca Cola. The barren sections of floor where families have paid their respects are marked by dozens of fading candles drowning in their own pools of wax. Custodians scurry about with scrapers and goat-hide bags, cleaning up the sticky offerings to make way for the next family.

As you head outside and up to that old stone church and cemetery on the hill, you'll see indigenous women roaming over the grassy knolls with their children and flocks of sheep. You might hear some 50s rock-n-roll blaring from one of the adobe huts. It's just one more thing to add to a truly bizarre, but enlightening day, full of diverse and authentic experiences.

---

SAN JUAN CHAMULA TRAVEL TIP: You may need a special pass to enter the church. For a nominal fee, you can pick one up at the local tourist office. Be respectful when you enter: take off your hat, and don't take photos unless you ask permission first.

---

*"The most valuable possession you can own is an open heart.
The most powerful weapon you can be is an instrument of peace."*
-Carlos Santana, Mexican Musician (1947-)

---

## ZAPATISTA WOMEN

### By Katie Hale

In 1910 Emilio Zapata founded a guerilla movement committed to agrarian reform for Mexico's indigenous communities. Zapata and his Liberation Army of the South fought for equal access to land for all sectors of society during the chaotic years of the Mexican Revolution.

Although a minority, pistol-slinging women dressed as men battled alongside their male counterparts. Their reasons for fighting varied from revenge for murdered family members to simply wanting to engage in war.

The most respected female war hero was La Corolena Maria de la Luz Espinosa Barrera. She was granted a pension after service—a rare honor for women of that time. However, La Corolena had difficulties adapting to life after war and became a street vendor who drank and gambled.

Today, women take an active role in the Zapatista Army of National Liberation (EZLN), which exploded onto the world stage on January 1, 1994. One year earlier, the Zapatista women issued the Women's Revolutionary Law, which includes provisions for rights to education, work, health care and other important social matters. The entire Zapatista movement continues to struggle for autonomy, fighting for peace and justice in Chiapas, Mexico and beyond.

# UXMAL
### By Allen Cox, Tacoma, Washington, U.S.A.

Maya legend tells of a dwarf in the ancient city of Uxmal, who claimed to have magical powers. Uxmal's ruler, confident that the dwarf was a fraud, made a foolish wager that if the dwarf could construct a pyramid overnight he could take over rule of the city. By the next morning, the ambitious dwarf had created the great Pyramid of the Magician, and became ruler of Uxmal.

The Pyramid of the Magician, with its distinctive rounded corners and unique and controversial elliptical base (drawing the accuracy of its reconstruction into question) possesses an organic quality, as though it naturally sprang from the earth. There is no other structure with its shape or design in all of Mesoamerica. Also known as *Adivino*, its near-vertical stairway, the steepest on any Mesoamerican structure, rises sharply, 37 meters above the ground. At the summit, the waiting mouth of a serpent is open and ready to swallow any who dare enter the temple.

The stonework at Uxmal is grand in scale and exceptionally ornate in design. Its architects and stonemasons, working in what today is known as the *Puuc* style (named for the region in which Uxmal is located), achieved a height of artistry unrivaled anywhere else in Mesoamerica. John Lloyd Stevens, the American explorer who visited the ruins in the 1840s, likened its scale and grandeur to Egypt's Thebes, but lamented that Uxmal sadly languished in obscurity.

Besides Adivino, two other structures at Uxmal are considered among the most significant in Maya architecture: the Governor's Palace and the Nunnery Quadrangle. The Governor's Palace, renowned for its symmetry and ornamentation, is a massive rectangular structure that covers five acres. The Nunnery Quadrangle, jaw-dropping in the intricacy and complexity of its stonework, consists of four buildings surrounding a vast plaza in the shadow of the Pyramid of the Magician.

It remains a mystery why the ancient Maya would have selected such a location for this grand and important city, which was at its height from the seventh to tenth centuries. The Maya typically settled near cenotes, natural sinkholes that pepper most of the Yucatán terrain and that, even today, serve them well, given the absence of surface rivers. Oddly, Uxmal has no nearby cenotes. Its architects solved their water problem by constructing large underground cisterns to catch rain water. Their worst enemy was drought.

Uxmal is a pleasant one-hour drive into the Puuc hills from Yucatán's capital city of Mérida, and a visit to the ruins makes an easy half-day excursion from the city. The entrance to the ruins has an excellent visitor center with a good restaurant, gift shop and bookstore A pleasant aspect of Uxmal is that it draws fewer visitors than the more famous site of Chichén Itzá, but certainly not because it is less remarkable; the difference simply lies in Uxmal's unwieldy distance from the mega-resorts of Cancún and Playa del Carmen.

## ANTONIO LÓPEZ DE SANTA ANNA
### By Dr. Crit Minster

In 1810, Mexico declared independence from Spain and 16 year old Antonio López de Santa Anna enlisted—on the Spanish side. After several years of fighting the independence movement, he switched sides, allying himself with the charismatic Agustín de Iturbide. He rose to the rank of general and was later instrumental in overthrowing Iturbide, who had declared himself emperor: Santa Anna preferred Mexico be a republic.

In 1824, at the age of 30, Santa Anna was made governor of the Yucatán. In 1829, Spain made one last-gasp effort to retake Mexico. Santa Anna defeated the larger Spanish force at Tampico, for which he came to be considered a hero and a military genius. Santa Anna himself made the most of it, referring to himself ever after as "the victor of Tampico." In 1833, Santa Anna was elected president for the first time. When several states rose up in rebellion, he would personally lead armies out to crush them  In 1835, he brutally put down a serious rebellion in Zacatecas before heading to Texas.

Texas, once a Mexican state, had been allowing American settlers for several years. These settlers eventually tired of Mexican rule and the state declared itself an independent republic in 1836. Santa Anna moved his army north and fought several battles with the rebels, culminating with the famous battle of the Alamo in San Antonio in February and March of 1836. Although the battle was a victory for Santa Anna—the fort was overrun and all of the roughly (no one knows for sure) 200 defenders were killed—more than 1,000 Mexican soldiers perished attacking the heavily fortified Alamo. In April, Santa Anna and his army were attacked by surprise by Texas rebels fighting under Sam Houston. It was a total rout: the Texans killed roughly 650 Mexican soldiers and captured another 600, including Santa Anna himself. Nine Texans were killed, and 18 were wounded. Santa Anna, to secure his release, signed a treaty recognizing Texan independence.

Back in Mexico, Santa Anna retired to his country ranch. But when the French invaded in 1838 to get compensation for unpaid loans, he returned to lead the counter-attack. The Mexicans eventually agreed to French demands, but Santa Anna was a hero again.  His leg was amputated after a cannon shot crushed his ankle. He ordered his leg be buried with full military honors. Within a year, he was president again.

 By 1845, his government had fallen apart and he was forced to escape and head into exile in Cuba. His exile didn't last long, however: in 1846 the U.S.—Mexican War broke out and he was welcomed back to lead the defense. The Mexicans lost the war, partly due to Santa Anna's military incompetence. Once again, Santa Anna went into exile.

By 1853 he was back for one last turn at the presidency.  His conservative allies eventually abandoned him, however, and in 1855 he was overthrown and exiled again, and tried in absentia for treason due to the flagrant corruption of his administration. He lived in several countries for the next two decades before being allowed back to Mexico in 1874, where he died two years later. All in all, he was president eleven times.

# MÉRIDA

*By Allen Cox, Tacoma, Washington, U.S.A.*

The Maya city of *Tihó* once stood where Mérida stands today. In the early 16th century, Spanish invaders laid a relentless 14-year siege to Tihó. The Maya fiercely defended their city, but it finally fell; defeated survivors were forced to build their conquerors a new city out of the rubble of the old. In 1542, the colonial city of Mérida was born of Maya stones, sweat and blood.

Evidence of the conquest is still visible throughout Mérida's historic center. Stones inscribed with Maya motifs are imbedded on the south façade of La Iglesia de Jesús on Parque Hidalgo, giving silent testimony that they once graced the temples of other gods. After more then 400 years, the most telling artifact still stands above the door of the conquest-era Casa de Montejo facing the Plaza Mayor: relief sculptures depicting Spaniards in full battle armor trampling Maya heads under their boots. The Maya figures in the sculptures appear to be crying out in pain: some believe the Maya artisans who created them willfully fashioned the wailing figures in an eternal scream so their voices would never fall silent.

Today's Mérida, the official and cultural capital of the Yucatan, is a vibrant, urban center where traditional Maya and contemporary Mexican cultures overlap. Even though its population has exploded to almost one million, the city retains a friendly atmosphere that welcomes visitors and invites exploration.

The vast municipal market, a few blocks from the Plaza Mayor, is a maze of stalls and shops that beckon visitors to spend the day browsing. After dark, people head outdoors, and the Plaza Mayor, Paseo de Montejo, Parque Hidalgo and Parque Santa Lucia are the spots to be seen. On many evenings, the latter offers free concerts, dance performances, or public readings by nationally renowned poets. In the city's graceful historic center, streets are lined with colonial-era mansions that have been carefully restored to house stylish boutique hotels, restaurants serving Yucatecan and international cuisines, shops, galleries, museums and private residences.

The city experienced a post-colonial building boom in the 19th century, a time when wealthy hacienda owners built European-style mansions along the Paseo de Montejo, making Mérida the "Paris of the Tropics." One of the most opulent of these mansions, a grand Italianate structure, now houses the *Museo de Antropología e Historia*, a must-see, displaying artifacts and exhibits on pre-conquest Maya civilization.

Not only is Mérida itself a fascinating and lively city to visit, but some of the most important archaeological sites in the world lie only a few hours away. Among them are Chichén Itzá, Uxmal, Kabah and Edzna. No visit to Mérida would be complete without a day or overnight trip into the surrounding countryside to explore the ruins. The nearby pueblos of Maní, Ticul and Izamal give visitors a first hand view of small town Yucatán life and the more traditional lifestyles of the Maya who live there.

## LUCHA LIBRE By Katie Hale

A huge arena is crowded with everyone from grandmothers to children holding cotton candy. Small horns held by fans sound and the excitement is palpable. The lights dim and out come two masked, shirtless men full of energy and anger, ready to take each other to the mat.

Lucha libre was born in the early 1930s when Mexican businessman Don Salvador Lutteroth Gonzalez witnessed a wrestling match in Liberty Hall, Texas and decided to bring American wrestlers south of the border, successfully introducing a new sport to Mexico. Lucha libre, or free wrestling, is much like WWE SmackDown!, but with more tradition, history and pomp. The sport itself is also more complex, consisting of more rapid moves and flying leaps.

A luchador (wrestler) can win by pinning his opponent to the mat for the count of three, knocking him out of the ring for a count of 20, making him submit, or by disqualification. However, one on one (*mano a mano*) matches are rare, and crowds usually are told which pair (*pareja*), trio, or foursome (*atómicos*) to root for as each side is identified as the good guys (*téchnicos*) or bad guys (*rudos*). When teams fight against one another, the winner is decided by two out of three falls. To make viewing and fighting more dramatic, sometimes matches have wagers attached. Luchadores can bet their masks; the loser is unmasked and must reveal his true identity. The longer a luchador goes without unmasking, the higher his reputation and standing. If masks aren't bet, hair is, and the loser must shave his head for all to see.

Lucha libre is now one of the hottest spectator sports in Mexico, and is gaining popularity around the world in places like Japan and the United States. The sport has even inspired those with political messages to get involved, dressing up as crusaders like Super Ecologist and Super Barrio and advocating their causes with a rapt audience at hand. One of the most important components to lucha libre are the masks. The luchadores wear masks representing animals, Gods, heroes and other characters. Often in public the luchador will be seen with his mask on—it not only is part of his guise during work hours, but becomes part of his identity.

The most famous wrestler, Santo, who fought for decades and starred in over 50 Mexican films in his prime, was buried in his mask, proving the inseparable bond between the real luchador and the superhero persona displayed in the ring.

Pushing lucha libre into the mainstream was the 2006 Jack Black film, *Nacho Libre*, a spoof based on a real luchador. However, for more of an authentic insight into this wild sport, check out *Lucha Libre: Life Behind the Mask*, a documentary following three generations of Mexican wrestlers living in Los Angeles and their struggles with duty and ambition inside and outside of the ring.

# ISLA MUJERES

By Allen Cox, Tacoma, Washington, U.S.A.

On the 30-minute ferry crossing from the Yucatan Peninsula's Puerto Juarez to tiny *Isla Mujeres*, I am struck by the brilliance of the colors sailing past. Where I come from, these are the colors of expensive modern art and glossy magazines.

The unblemished white sand floor of the Bay of Mujeres reflects a cobalt sky to produce a neon canvas of turquoise. Ahead, a pastel *pueblo* hugs a sugary beach. Silhouetted against a cloudless sky, nearly motionless frigate birds face the wind, suspended like kites, their wings outstretched and their long tail feathers streaming behind them. A pelican fashions his body into a missile and plunges into the bay, emerging a moment later with a good-sized catch flopping into his pouch. I suddenly want fish for dinner.

Isla Mujeres, or simply "Isla" to her fans, is a sliver of limestone, 5 miles long and a half-mile wide. This little island rests easily in the Caribbean, looking back toward the high-rises of Cancún, a world away. Isla Mujeres has been home to a variety of cultures: ancient Maya, modern Mexican and Caribbean.

In October, 2005, Isla suffered from one of the worst hurricanes in its recorded history: Hurricane Wilma. During that hellish three-day battering, nearly anything not made of brick was wrenched apart by the unforgiving winds and tossed carelessly out to sea. Besides fishing, tourism is Isla's livelihood, and the local economy was crushed. The islanders, in a massive clean-up effort, wasted no time in restoring services, bulldozing mountains of beach sand from the streets and repairing damaged buildings. Today they once again stand ready to welcome visitors with open arms.

Those making the pilgrimage to Isla do so to worship the sun and the sea. But for centuries, the island's Maya pilgrims venerated *Ix Chel*, Maya goddess of the moon and fertility. In 1517, Francisco Hernández de Córdoba, the commander of the first Spanish expedition to set foot on the island, discovered several small figurines of the goddess and named the island Isla Mujeres, or Island of Women. For three centuries following Cordoba's visit, the island languished, an uninhabited outpost visited only by pirates and an occasional fisherman. When piracy dried up in the mid-19th century, local fishermen deemed it safe to fish Isla's waters, and soon the *pueblo* sprang up.

In the 1950s and 60s, word got out of a fabled tropical island with pristine beaches and swaying palms, where dining like royalty on lobster and sea tortoise cost a mere pittance. Tourists seeking freedom from the herd found their way to Isla. Some stayed. Isla's Playa Norte, the classic tropical beach of picture postcards, became a mecca of laid-back, topless abandon.

Since those days, the island's population has topped 13,000 and lobster can no longer be had for a pittance. But compared to the mega-resorts of nearby Cancún and Playa del Carmen, the scale remains small and the pace relaxed. It is still the quintessential small town, tropical island paradise in an unrivaled natural setting.

> *"I think of music as a menu. I can't eat the same thing every day."*
> -Carlos Santana, Mexican Musician (1947-)

## DEEP SEA FISHING

By Katie Hale

Isla Mujeres is a place frozen in the past—a place where many people catch their dinner for the night in the brilliant turquoise waters offshore and let their fishing nets dry under the warm Caribbean sun.

This fishing village is a great place for the novice to try their hand at reeling something in—not only does Isla Mujeres offer great opportunities for trawling, it offers cheaper charters than nearby Cancún. International fishing tournaments are held on the small island each year, drawing thousands of experts and amateurs alike.

Although the fishing is great around the Yucatán, the best fishing in Mexico can be found in the Sea of Cortés. The narrow sea between the Baja Peninsula and the Mexican mainland is home to more than 900 species of fish and marine mammals. This sapphire jewel is one of the best places in the world for deep sea fishing and the serious angler should not miss the opportunity to drop a line in the rough waters.

Here marlin, sailfish, grouper, tuna, roosterfish, dorado, snapper and grouper grow to record sizes. If you don't have your own yacht, hire a charter deep sea fishing boat for the day. Prices usually include crew, insurance, fishing tackle and the preparation and/or storage of your catch.

And whether you wrangle that marlin or don't get one single bite, you will not come away empty handed. The beauty of the seascape, the salty smell of the ocean, the cool breeze, and the feeling like you are alone in the world will make your day of fishing—or simply watching—all worth it.

# CANCÚN

### By Dr. Crit Minster, Rochester, New York, U.S.A.

Party, party, party! There is no escaping Cancún's international image as one of the good-time capitals of the planet. College students on Spring Break flock to this gorgeous, sunny city on the Yucatán Caribbean, where they can get more tequila and beer for their buck and the clubs and discos go all night.

Cancún will always be known as a world-class destination for drinking and partying. The largest and most boisterous clubs are on Kukulcán Boulevard: check out The Hard Rock Café, Coco Bongo, Daddy'O and La Boom for no holds bars dancing, drinking, wet t-shirt contests, theme parties and more.

Lately, however, Cancún has made the effort to distance itself from its Spring Break image. To bolster its new family-friendly image, it has added water parks, museums, shows (the clothes-on kind) and more. Parque Nizuc is a water park for families, featuring slides, wave pools and even sharks. Kids and parents can swim with a porpoise at Dolphin Discovery. If you're a shopper, head to the downtown and *Avenida Tulúm*, where handicrafts from all over Mexico are for sale in a variety of shops. If hand-painted masks and ceramics aren't your thing, check out the slick super-malls in the hotel zone.

Of course, Cancún is famous for beaches. The geography of the city—it's built on a sandy peninsula—means that there are miles of gorgeous white sand beaches. The beaches in the northern area of town are better for swimming: the water is rougher on the eastern side. If Cancún's beaches—and all the parasailing, jet skis and other water sports that come with them—aren't enough for you, head to Cozumel, an island paradise right off the coast. It's known for beaches and SCUBA diving.

Once you've had your fill of sun and surf, you'll find that one of the best things about Cancún is how close it is to other attractions in the Yucatán. If you want to see some Mayan ruins, Chichén Itzá, Cobá and Tulum are all within easy day-trip range (and there are no shortages of taxi drivers, tour operators, and other assorted "helpers" who'd be happy to take you there). If you want to see ruins without leaving the city, check out the ruins and reconstructed village of El Rey, right in town.

There are several theme parks within easy reach of Cancún. Xcaret is a Mayan version of Disneyland. Located in Playa del Carmen, it features a guided underwater walk, pools, snorkeling, live shows and the chance to swim with dolphins. In Cancún, Aqua World features snorkeling, SCUBA Diving, jet skis and even a submarine ride.

Cancún doesn't keep statistics on how many visitors come for the tequila and stay for the dolphins, but the fact remains: Cancún is no longer just your father's party town.

## TOP LIST: BEST PARTY TOWNS

Seen all the museums? Gone to all the places your guide book says you're supposed to go? Ready for a little nightlife? Well, put your party shoes on and check out one of these Latin American hot spots!

1. Cancún, Mexico (see above). "During Spring break, Margaritas and Corona flow like rivers in the bars and discos. Each college or university that comes down is more insane than the last." Gideon Wells, U.S.A.

2. Buenos Aires, Argentina (p. 30). "No dinner until 10 or 11 and then up all night!!!" Michelle, Boston, Massachusetts, U.S.A.

3. Antigua, Guatemala (p. 152). "The bars offer specials, so you can drink vile, cheap rum and cokes all night and still have enough money left over for some aspirins in the morning before you start all over again." James DiFiccio, East Rochester, New York, U.S.A.

4. Montañita, Ecuador (p. 263). "There's not a day that goes by that I don't wish I was there." Rich Chiovarelli, New York, U.S.A.

Runners up: Rio de Janeiro, Brazil. Santiago, Chile. Baños, Ecuador, Cartagena, Colombia.

Beach at Cancún. Photo by Stephany Slaughter.

# BAHIA DE SOLIMÁN

By Jenna Mahoney, New York, U.S.A.

Somewhere between Tulum and Playa del Carmen, there's a quiet cove that's perfect for chillin.' Bahía de Solimán is a calm inlet set off from the main highway, which links Cancún with Tulum. The bay has a restaurant, an outhouse and some clearings for visitors' personal hammocks. Best of all, the spot is so remote you won't be hassled by trinket peddlers.

To get to Bahía de Solimán, take a left if you're traveling south. There's a large cracked sign that advertises homemade food and the name "Oscar" (located just south of Xel-Há). An immediate right and a left onto a dirt road eventually leads to the cove's dusty parking lot. There, you'll be greeted by resident hens, ducks and dogs. A few local guys may also give you a smile and a quick "hola."

The large clearing is surrounded by palm trees and strangler figs. It's between these trees that you can set up your hammock and stay the night. As with everything in Mexico, the fee changes, so settle on the price before you hang it. Straight ahead from the parking area sits the coral inlet's beach. The sandy area is actually quite limited in relation to the expansive cove, as it stretches only a few hundred meters across.

To the left sits the area's small restaurant, officially named Oscar and Lalo's. It's a three-walled structure that's open to the ocean, which allows breezes, patrons and animals to pass through with ease. A bar and kitchen are stationed in the back. Plastic tables, chairs and a lone restaurant manager occupy the space. There's also a loud TV that hangs high above the dining room. Planted in the coral-infused sand are some weathered plastic tables. Centerpieces made of coconut sit atop them, serving as anchors for the menus and napkins. What's on the menu and what's actually available may be completely different, so just ask the restaurant manager for some guac, a cerveza and some fresh seafood. Dig your chair into the sand and watch the gentle waves move about the rocky shoreline.

If you see a few kayaks resting on the beach in front of the dining room, ask the manager how much for a rental. Note: You'll need to specifically request a life jacket. They're hidden somewhere in the kitchen or behind the bar. Then, explore the cove afloat (no worries about your belongings—the manager will safely watch them).

Jagged coral abounds at the bottom of the cove, so hop into your kayak as soon as possible. That way, you'll avoid cutting your feet and disturbing the marine life. Once out in the middle of the cove, you can lash your kayak to your friend's and jump out. Just below the surface, you'll find colorful schools of fish, sea vegetation and maybe a lone sea turtle swimming around the inlet's enormous coral reef.

Once back on land, order up another beer, some salsa and tortillas and continue to relax. Not a bad way to spend a day.

Tulum. Photo by Stephany Slaughter.

# COBÁ

## By Allen Cox, Tacoma, Washington, U.S.A.

The ancient city of Cobá, in the Mexican state of Quintana Roo, is a mysterious place, not only for the ghosts some locals claim haunt the ruins, but because 95 percent of the city remains unexcavated, buried under dense tropical jungle. First occupied about 1,900 years ago, Cobá became a sprawling urban center, covering an area of 210 square kilometers. At its peak, it was one of the most heavily populated of all Mayan cities; the population is estimated to have reached 50,000.

Cobá was an important commercial, political, and ceremonial hub, "hub" being the operative word. Wide causeways paved with crushed limestone cut through the jungle, radiating from the city in a complex network like spokes on a wheel. The ancients called these raised roads *sacbé*, meaning "white road," and today visitors exploring the ruins follow in their ancient footsteps. The longest known sacbé travels from Cobá in a straight, unbroken line to the ancient city of Yaxuna, 100 kilometers to the west.

The Mexican government has designated the ruins an archeological-ecological park. Well-trained, knowledgeable guides greet visitors just inside the entrance, offering optional tours of the first structure group. They provide a brief but excellent crash course on ancient Maya society, imparting a wealth of information about Maya religious beliefs, government, social stratification, and how the civilization made use of the natural environment in daily life. They'll also tell you about how the Maya exhausted the natural resources in their lands, which some believe led to their decline. After the tour, the guides turn visitors loose to explore the extensive ruins on their own.

On the jungle paths, visitors are likely to spot a variety of tropical butterflies and birds (including toucans), as well as spider monkeys. We were also spotted by several mosquitoes, who pestered us but didn't ruin the experience.

The most impressive structure at the site is the massive Nohoch Mul pyramid. At 42 meters (the height of a 12 story building), it was the tallest ancient building in the Yucatán peninsula for millennia, before skyscrapers were built in Cancún and Mérida. One side of Nohoch Mul has been excavated, but the other side remains covered by jungle just as archaeologists found it. From the summit, high above the canopy, visitors catch their breath after the steep climb and take in the endless blanket of green spreading out in all directions, broken only by what at first glance appear to be hills, but are actually unexcavated pyramids still covered by jungle.

The tiny present-day town of Cobá huddles just outside the entrance to the ruins. While the ancient civilization at Cobá declined a millennium ago, the Maya clearly never left. It is easy to imagine that those in the modern pueblo descended directly from the ancients who once occupied the mighty city in their back yard.

Doll for sale in market place. Photo by Stephany Slaughter.

# CABAÑAS COPAL

By Liz Kirchner, Carthage, Missouri, U.S.A.

In a world full of resorts dedicated to fine wine and dining, a stay at Cabañas Copal, the palm-thatched Caribbean inn and spa in Tulum, Mexico, is like luxurious camping. Breezy, moonlit, shaggy-chic, five minutes from the grandeur of the Tulum ruins, Cabañas Copal wraps the adventure, romance, and mystery of the Maya Yucatan in candle light and mosquito netting and presents it amidst kayaks, toucans and a magnificent sea.

Liz Kirchner edits scientific literature and leads a deceptively mild-mannered life in the suburbs of Washington, D.C. She graduated from the University of Maryland with degrees in Agronomy and Botany and spent several years in Korea and China collecting data describing Asian home gardens and wild food gathering. That meant roaming the countryside buttonholing surprised Chinese peasants as they hoed peppers and washed their water buffaloes, or popping out from behind mossy oaks to interview Korean mushroom gatherers. No stranger to library stacks or the value of an English-to-Zapotec dictionary, she currently writes travel narrative and essays usually involving food, history, and hiking in places that are startlingly lovely, peculiar, or both.

Designed like a terraced garden, the 47 cabañas are bunched in little groves that have sea views, or are snuggled into the forest; and although they're called "eco-rustic" (all cabañas are without electricity), the spacious beds, tiled showers, adequate hot water, and gobs of mosquito netting in most of the "Hobbit-y" huts is simple, but nothing near primitive. For the minimalist, though, there are two sand-floored abodes without baths serviced instead by the tidy bathrooms down the path, and the communal showers are a pleasant sluice under the coconut palms.

So well laid out is Cabañas Copal that the winding paths make the little nooks seem at once secluded and well attended. Palmetto glades hide pillowed hammocks for two, and, Look! There among the hibiscuses! Lo and behold, you come upon—just in time—two beach chairs perfectly placed for reading your latest beach read, clinking a Corona, gazing at the sapphire-blue sea, or, bare legs entwined, at each other.

The path from reception and greenery-walled restaurant wends past the spa, which offers a body loving pamper-fest of yoga, wraps of mud, aloe, or chocolate, an assortment of therapeutic massages—some at seaside—aroma and crystal therapy and traditional Mexican *temezcal* steam baths. Each service is performed by skilled masseuses and Maya shamans dedicated to their craft.

It is a spa, after all, and the Cabañas Copal balances the yin of lounging under your sun hat all day with the action-packed yang of biking to the ruins or into town, snorkeling the cove, or kayaking the mangrove lagoons of the Sian Ka´an Bioreserve just down the road. The reserve is crammed with wildlife such as nimble spider monkeys and 350 species of migratory and native birds with tours led by knowledgeable, passionate guides.

Cabañas Copal is one of three "sister" resorts strung along the beach. The restaurant, spa, rental, and transportation services of all three are available to spa guests. Each sister has her own well-honed, vertically integrated personality. There is the vivacious Azulik: "adult," says the brochure, and you can't see inside their gates; then there is Zahra, dowdy but serviceable, with a nice little cove and electricity until 11 pm. By comparison, Cabañas Copal is the coltish sister: as tangy a surprise as a fresh-off-the-tree mango.

Undoubtedly, even Paradise has logistical glitches. Although the paths are dreamily candle lined at night, it's easier to avoid garroting yourself with a hammock or mashing an anole if you've remembered to bring a flashlight; and, in the morning as the sun comes thundering up, it may take a while for shower water to arrive, but, hey, relax, you're only a few slow-motion, hair-swinging lopes from the Caribbean Ocean. The water'll come. Everything's fine at Cabañas Copal.

Left: Cabañas Copal. Photo by EcoTulum Resorts. Above: Beach at Tulum. Photo by Stephany Slaughter.

# SIAN KA'AN BIOSPHERE RESERVE

By Nic Havers, Perpignan, Southern France

If Cancún is a place for the hedonist with its loud, late-night bars, American fast food, and over-developed coastline, then the Sian Ka'an Biosphere, two hours to the south, is the antidote. It is a place for the nature-lover, the adventurer, the hopeless romantic, and also where you can still catch a glimpse of traditional Mexico.

Here, you can stretch out on isolated silvery beaches, get close to dazzling wildlife, mix with laid-back locals, and at the end of a long day, kick back with a cold cocktail or two.

*Sian Ka'an* means "where the sky is born" in Mayan. It's reached by a five-kilometre dustbowl road south of Tulum. Biospheres were developed in the 1970s by UNESCO to protect natural areas and wildlife, combining scientific research with sustainable development for locals.

Sian Ka'an consists of 1.3 million acres, with 62 miles of coast protected forever in its pristine condition, including the second longest reef in the world, beaches, a lagoon, savannah and rare wildlife. There are no large hotels, no swimming pools or malls. A visit to Sian Ka'an is all about the pleasures of nature, simplicity and absolute relaxation.

Boca Paila Camps is a small-scale eco-lodge run by the Centro Ecológico de Sian Ka'an, a group involved in research and education programs. They offer two tours: either by kayak along the coast or by boat around the mangroves. The money generated by the tours goes to fund the group's programs.

Rooms consist of a tent-cabin, raised on stilts and reached by sandy lanes winding through the palm forest. The rooms are generously sized and isolated: you retire by way of a jungle path that is washed with moonlight and dotted with flickering candles exhaling incense. The rooms were just made for lovers—a giant bed of billowing sheets and the only sound is the ocean. There is no electricity; instead, there are just two lanterns for light and you won't find many creature comforts. But that's part of the experience.

The eco-lodge's restaurant serves *Xikilpaac*, a traditional Mayan recipe. It's a thick, brown paste, consisting of pumpkin seeds, boiled-down tomatoes, oil and coriander, served in an old-stone pot, eaten with tortillas. Its flavours are intense and wholesome. Time in Sian Ka'an can be spent wildlife spotting, kayaking, fishing, mountain-biking, diving at the nearby Chinchorro Reef, beachcombing or swimming, or remaining horizontal at Copal's spa.

The highly knowledgeable David Reynoso is the resident naturalist guide. He runs several tours, one of which takes you out into the mangroves to spot baby crocodiles, learn about the flora and fauna and visit an unexcavated Mayan temple. David will explain that the Maya traded honey, green and blue jade, ceramics, quetzal feathers, tobacco, onyx, sea snails and shells (for dyes), shark teeth, sharp black obsidian, red cinnabar dust, turtle carapaces, and the most prized object, jaguar pelts.

The channels cut into the mangroves were Mayan trade routes 800 years ago, linking the three-pyramid city of Muyil with the sea. Today, it's peaceful and lined with bromeliads, orchids and red mangrove.

The boat stops at an island that has a 1,000 year old Mayan temple. A carving of a crocodile is prominent. The Maya feared crocodiles. The Maya believed that when they died, they entered the Underworld, where there were different gods. One of these gods is the God L, who appears seated on a jaguar-skin throne, wearing a Moan bird hat and smoking a large cigar.

Nowadays, the crocodiles have fled to the main lagoon, so you are encouraged to throw your life-jacket into the water and float on currents along the channels. This is really fun to do and allows you to observe the giant mangrove roots and brown pelicans dive-bombing for fish. The jaguar, puma, margay and jaguarundi, as well as tapir and 300 species of birds are present in the savannah. The beaches are visited by loggerhead and leatherback turtles, and rare but placid West Indian manatees may be seen offshore.

As a travel journalist, I have visited many destinations around the world. Of all the destinations visited, the Sian Ka'an Biosphere Reserve comes closest to being a genuine, modern-day, earthly paradise, offering an unforgettable holiday.

---

**SIAN KA'AN TRAVEL TIPS:**

The essence of this area is "back to nature." One week spent here will show you the real Mexico. Eco-tourism is prospering here with some wonderful places to stay. The Boca Paila Eco-Lodge is basic but a great way to live in the jungle with low-impact on the surroundings. If you want a bit more comfort, but ultimate relaxation, try Copal. A week exploring Sian Ka'an will not suit people who enjoy nightlife or shopping, but nothing is stopping you combining one week in Cancun followed by one week in Sian Ka'an. Indeed, a two-centre holiday is encouraged in order to truly appreciate both sides of this part of Mexico. The area is inexpensive and very do-able for the average traveler. English is widely spoken and the area is refreshingly free of tourist tackiness.

---

Nic Havers is an award-winning travel writer and editor of *Escapism Travel Magazine*, and lives in Montpellier, Southern France. He enjoys all types of travel but particularly adventure trips and desert islands. One of his favorite places is Marseille, France: "It's a rough diamond sort of place—the ultimate paradox: a beautiful and ugly city, noisy, often dirty, yet beautifully located beside the calanques and the Mediterranean, the bouillabaisse (fish soup) tastes heavenly but looks awful. Many people avoid Marseille, but for me it's Europe's greatest city, it's vibrant, intense and thoroughly un-French—go now." His most bizarre cultural experience? "Visiting the church at San Juan Chamula in Chiapas, Mexico—Mayan women sacrificing chickens in a bizarre ritual, then drinking Coca-Cola to make them 'burp,' thus releasing evil spirits." He hopes to return to the Yucatan Peninsula soon.

# GUATEMALA

**The Land of Eternal Spring**

"The Land of Eternal Spring" is an apt name for this tiny Latin American country: because of its unique combination of latitude and altitude, most of the days are sunny and pleasant without ever getting too hot or too cold. Guatemala has everything a visitor could want: pleasant weather, Mayan ruins, colorful and cheap markets, good traditional food, a battered but serviceable infrastructure, colonial history, friendly people…the list goes on and on.

Like its neighbors, Honduras, Nicaragua, and El Salvador, Guatemala has had to overcome a legacy of a violent civil war. In Guatemala, factions on both sides employed "scorched earth" tactics: to this day, mass graves are being unearthed in some areas of the highlands where the fighting was at its worst. The 1990s brought about a peace treaty between the government and the rebels, but the effects of decades-long hostility presented serious challenges to the stability of Guatemala's infrastructure. Many former rebels, now without a "job," turned to crime, and attacks on buses and cars along rural highways skyrocketed.

Today however, Guatemala is changing its international image as a backwards "Banana Republic." Crime is down and it's safe enough to visit if you take some basic precautions, such as not traveling on night buses. Tourism facilities have improved, but the country is still off the "gringo trail." Thus, in our lifetime, there has never been a better time to visit the Land of Eternal Spring.

History buffs will not want to miss the ruins of the ancient Maya city of Tikal, with its magnificent temples and courtyards set in pristine jungle. If you're a shopper, head to the famous market of Chichicastenango, known as the best in the region. Antigua is a charming colonial city, full of cafes and home to a rowdy nightlife. A visit to Todos Santos Cuchumatán is a step back in time, to when Guatemalan men and women wore bright clothing and spoke an exotic dialect. Come in early November if you can.

Those travelers can get past Guatemala's historical reputation for instability and violence will be amply rewarded with enchanting towns, cheerful people, majestic ruins and stunning natural scenes and wonders. Give the Land of Eternal Spring a chance: you'll be glad you did.

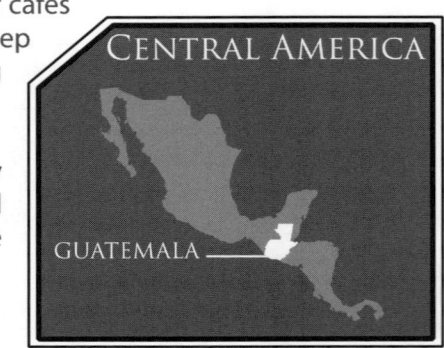

# TODOS SANTOS

### By Dr. Crit Minster, Rochester, New York, U.S.A.

The Spanish conquest swept across two continents and countless islands, leaving death, destruction and disease in its wake. By the time it was over, everything from Texas to Chile was under Spanish rule: some native populations resisted longer than others, but they all were defeated eventually.

Located up high in the windswept, rocky *Cuchumatanes* mountain range, in a remote corner of northwestern Guatemala, the tiny village of Todos Santos was one of the ones that held out the longest. Even today, the townspeople believe that the Spanish were able to conquer them for only one reason: the Spanish had horses. Locals are still passionate about the subject, and every November first, they ride horses all day to prove that the Spanish no longer have that equestrian advantage—and that they never would have defeated them in the first place without it.

Despite the rise of tourism in the region, present day Todos Santos remains an extremely closed indigenous community, devoted to ancient traditions. The men and women still wear their traditional, brightly colored clothing and speak *Mam*, the local language that has not changed since before the arrival of the Spanish. They do not trust outsiders, but have learned to tolerate tourists. The people survive on subsistence farming, tourism and textiles: the men knit finely-made shoulder bags and the women make *huipiles* (a sort of colorful blouse). There are only about 30,000 members of the community living in town and the surrounding areas.

Every year, thousands of visitors descend upon the village in order to see the famous festival, which begins in late October and culminates on the first and second of November. A big part of the festival is devoted to riding horses. Despite being called a "race," this portion of the festival really stretches the traditional sense of the word—there is no competition and no winner—just men riding back and forth on the same stretch of road all day. Most of them are drunk and have been for days. It's part of the ritual. Many fall from their horses and fatalities have been known to occur. The races have religious significance, and if someone dies during the race it is considered an offering to the Mayan spirit world, and the community will have good luck in the coming year. The members of the community save money all year in order to spend it on food and alcohol during the festival.

> *The races have religious significance, and if someone dies during the race it is considered an offering to the Maya spirit world, and the community will have good luck in the coming year.*

Another fascinating part of the festival is the "Dance of the Conquistadores" in which local men dress up as Spanish conquistadores, complete with hand-carved wooden masks depicting blond haired, blue eyed men. They dance in the central square in an elaborate, intricate ceremony, depicting the conquest. The Devil even makes an appearance, in a bright red suit and painted mask. The outfits are elaborate and colorful.

But you don't have to wait for November first to visit Todos Santos: it's fascinating on any day of the year, and if you're interested in traditional native culture, you may want to check it out quickly before the modern world makes it to this remote corner of Guatemala. As with the Spanish arrival centuries ago, the town is currently riding out a tumult of cultural currents. In terms of traditional culture the community is sort of going forward and backward at the same time: although more and more people are abandoning traditions—many are eschewing traditional garb in favor of western clothes—there is a new era of religious tolerance in Guatemala, and long-repressed local religions are making a comeback.

Long ago, the people of Todos Santos exhibited bravery in the face of cultural adversity. They steadfastly preserved local traditions and managed to master the very object once used to by the Spanish to defeat them: the horse. Today, this noble beast has become a symbol of their independence and freedom, high in the rocky Guatemalan mountains. The festival itself—with its flamboyant costumes and equestrian flair—places the town firmly in the saddle of tradition, riding into the future steadily grasping the reigns of cultural change.

Worship in a shrine in Guatemala. Photo by Caroline Bennett.

# NEBAJ AND THE IXIL TRIANGLE

### By Lorraine Caputo, Columbia, Missouri, U.S.A.

The mournful voice of a reed horn, the beating of a drum echo down narrow streets, through misty morning mountains. A feast day is dawning deep in the Cuchumatanes Mountains of Guatemala, in a remote mountain village of the Ixil Triangle.

The Ixil are a small ethnic group descended from the mighty Maya Empire and their area is delineated by three villages: Nebaj, Chajul and Cotzal. Each has its weekly market, where a kaleidoscope of colors collides with the sushes and clicks of the local language, and the intriguing aromas wafting through the air.

Nebaj, the principal town, celebrates its feast days August 12 to 15; Cotzal, June 21 to 24, with conquistador dances; and Chajul, the second Friday in Lent, with a procession of the Christ of Golgotha. According to legend, this statue was discovered in a nearby cave. The Christ was brought to Chajul, but one day it disappeared from the church. Again it was found in the cave. Upon its return, two men were posted to guard the Christ—and they themselves were turned to stone. Over the years, their uniforms have changed according to the political climate: Roman centurions, camouflaged soldiers, or the traditional white pants and bright red coats of Ixil men.

Ixil women wear intricate *huipiles* (embroidered blouses) and woven ribbon head wraps with pompoms. These and other items may be bought directly from the weavers or from cooperatives.

In homes and co-ops, one can study weaving, Ixil language, Spanish and regional cooking. Several women also offer traditional dinners and temazcales (sweat baths) in their homes. A number of community development collectives welcome visitors.

Nebaj, Chajul and Cotzal all have churches dating from the 16th century. All have memorials to victims of Guatemala's 36-year civil war, which hit this region very hard.

The surrounding countryside teems with opportunities for all kinds of hikes: to waterfalls and through the mountains, to traditional villages and those "model villages" set up by the military during the war. One such village, Acul, is known for its cheese. Independent guides offer tours to these sites, and can also arrange ceremonies by *curanderos* (shamans).

To get to the Ixil Triangle, take the bus from Sacapulas. As it climbs and climbs into the Cuchumatanes Mountains, it stops just short of paradise: on a clear day, you can see the Pacific Ocean. Before you know it you're in Nebaj, gateway to the Ixil Triangle: up the green mountains from the Pacific and over the ridge from heaven.

## GETTING FÍJASED IN GUATEMALA

### By Dr. Crit Minster

Guatemala, which has roots in no less than 25 different cultures, has a unique, diverse vocabulary. Guatemalan Spanish is special: many native words have been adopted or changed, and they are commonly used alongside Spanish words in regular conversation. In addition, some Spanish words have meanings peculiar to Guatemala. Here are a few examples:

Fíjase: Literally, "pay close attention." Really, it means "I have some bad news." If you have an excursion planned, and the guide says "Fíjase que ..." then you can be sure the trip is not going to happen. Veteran tourists call this "Getting fíjased," as in "I was supposed to go riding but I got fíjased."

Chucho: a street dog. A *perro* is any dog that is not covered with fleas or belongs to a recognizable race, such as a German Shepherd. All of the mangy mutts you see slinking around the streets are *chuchos*. Chuchos are well trained: if one bothers you, simply pretend to pick up a rock and it'll run away.

"Saber!" Pronounced "saah-ber!" Literally, "to know." Really, it means "I have no idea whatsoever." Usually accompanied by a shrugging of the shoulders or waving hands in the air.

Canchi: White person. Somewhat interchangeable with "gringo."

Chapín: A Guatemalan person. Guatemalans disagree on the origin of the word *chapín*, but all consider it a non-offensive nickname for Guatemalans.

# QUETZALTENANGO

### By Brooke Weberling, Melbourne, Florida, U.S.A.

"Rápido! Rápido! Vamonos!" the man shouts as he hauls a boy up onto the bus. A tiny, weathered woman in brilliantly woven garments squeezes down the aisle, her face barely visible above the seats. The man sitting next to me nods off, his scuffed baseball cap nudging my chin. My American sense of personal space gone, I give in and lean back on the stranger.

The bus weaves through the urban maze of Guatemala City, pausing without warning at unmarked stops to pick up frantically waving would-be passengers. Understanding bits and pieces of the chatter around me, I remember the reason for this trip: I love the Spanish language. I could have enrolled in a class at home in Chicago. I could have opted for the European flair of Barcelona or Madrid. Instead I chose Guatemala, and finally, I had arrived.

The driver makes the sign of the cross and mouths a silent prayer as the bus climbs the mountains to Quetzaltenango, or Xela (shay-lah), as the locals call it. The second largest city in Guatemala, Xela is home to several reasonably priced Spanish schools. A week's worth of lessons—five hours a day, five days a week and housing with a family that provides three meals daily—costs an almost-embarrassing $130. Most people in Xela don't speak English, which makes it easier to practice Spanish. And it hasn't been completely overrun by tourists yet, unlike its magical colonial neighbor, Antigua.

The classes are structured like private tutoring lessons. My teacher, Christian, is an earnest 23-year-old engineering student who teaches Spanish to earn money for college. We start taking daily walks around the city, talking about everything from movies to politics. My Spanish continues to improve through classes and conversations with my adopted family.

My school, like many others in Xela, organizes volunteer projects. One involves helping children from a nearby village find shoes from a slew of new and used gems sent over by a U.S. church. Everyone clamors for the Nikes, the Spiderman sandals and the patent leather slip-ons. For some of the kids, this will be their only pair of shoes.

Through school and my own exploration, I learn about and fall in love with Xela. The heart of the city is Parque Centro América, the main plaza that's always alive with families and Marimba music. Surrounding the plaza are ancient churches and the *Casa de la Cultura*, a fascinatingly funky museum filled with military uniforms, taxidermy and other local artifacts. My favorite piece is the *Diablito del Mar* – the "little devil of the sea"—a clearly man-made construction of someone's imagination. It seems to be constructed of leaves or seashells taped together to look like an underwater monster. It resides in a glass case beside skeletons and other presumably real antiquities.

After more than three weeks in Xela, I sadly bid goodbye to Christian and my family and set off to explore the rest of gorgeous Guatemala. Throughout the trip, I'm glad I set off down the road less traveled and began my journey in Xela. And though I still don't claim to be fluent in Spanish, I will always love the language.

Brooke Weberling grew up in Florida and has lived in Chicago, Ohio, Massachusetts and Pennsylvania. She has worked in writing and communications for various organizations. She holds a bachelor's degree in public relations and international affairs from Florida State University, and a master's degree in journalism from Ohio University. Brooke would never leave for her travels without a camera. This comes in very handy when witnessing unusual Mayan rituals in Guatemala. Her ideal trip would be an around the world excursion with stops in Chile, Ireland, Norway, India, Thailand, Morocco, Egypt and Australia, among others, however her next trip will probably be to Peru to visit her cousin who just moved there.

## LANGUAGE LESSON

### By Katie Hale

Spanish may be the official language of Guatemala, but it may not always seem that way—it is often the second language of the Indian and mestizo populations that form this country's ethnic majority.

There are 23 Mayan ethno-linguistic groups in Guatemala. The Q'eqchis are the second largest of these groups, with over 474,000 members reported in the 2002 national census.

Some of the indigenous languages include Chuj, Mam, Popti, Itza, and Sakapulteko. An important non-Mayan language is Garífuna, spoken by the Garífuna people who reside on the eastern coast of the country.

The Peace Accords of 1996 mandated the translation of some official documents and voting materials into several indigenous languages and ordered that interpreters must be provided for non-Spanish speakers in legal cases. The Accords also mandated that bilingual education would be taught in both Spanish and indigenous languages.

However, it is often only the indigenous communities that must adapt to Spanish-speaking culture. Very few Spanish-speaking Guatemalans ever learn to speak in one of the nation's other native tongues.

# LAKE ATITLÁN

### By Terence Baker, Dartford, England

Lago de Atitlán is reputed to be the most beautiful lake in the world, and it's tough to argue. A stunning backdrop of mountains and extinct and dormant volcanoes complete the already-inspiring scenery at the lake's shores.

Terence Baker was born in Dartford, England, but has lived in New York City since 1993. A writer for Meetings & Conventions, a monthly meetings-industry magazine, he travels whenever he gets the chance, most recently to Chile's Atacama Desert, Assisi in Italy and Zhaoqing in China. He has a Masters degree in English Literature and Creative Writing from Rutgers, the State University of New Jersey, and in his spare time he runs marathons (best time; 2:44:56), writes fiction (no luck yet in being published) and takes photos. Attending the World Penny Farthing (Big-wheel) Bicycle Championships in Evandale, Tasmania, remains a fond memory, as does waking up on Kodiak Island, Alaska, to see sea otters and Harlequin ducks playing on the waves below. He is planning—with his Italian girlfriend Francesca—to visit Mali so as to reach Djenne and Timbuktoo.

The picturesque town of Santiago Atitlán sits on the far side of Lake Atitlán, and it is a good thing that it does. On the other side of the lake, the embarkation spot for memorable boat trips, is the tourist town of Panajachel. Once you've seen Panajachel, hop on the lake ferry and head for Santiago.

Nearing Santiago Atitlán, a maze of floating reeds comes into view, out of which emerge small fishing boats; on rocky outcrops, women wash clothes. The settlements around the lake—there are 12 of them—are all named after the Apostles (Santiago is named for St. James), and halfway across, one sees the *Cerro de Oro* (the "Mountain of Gold") and Tolimán volcano. Most afternoons a strong wind called the Xocomil, "wind that carries away sin," blows across the more than 1,000 foot-deep lake. From the harbor, it is a relatively steep walk uphill to the main part of the town. On the way, shops selling crafts and masks line the route. Small children play football in the dusty street.

I came here to meet someone, for this place is the home of local saint *Maximón*. Ask anyone directions to his home. He changes homes often, but always resides in the house of a member of the local religious fraternity. It is considered a serious lapse of etiquette to visit him but not leave anything, even if it is just a dollar for a photograph. Members of a priestly caste surround him.

Maximón also is known as San Simón or Alvarado, after Pedro de Alvarado, a ruthless conquistador who led the first Spanish expedition into the Guatemala region. His shrine is littered with cups of *aguadiente* (a local booze), cigars, crumpled money and other presents.

It is thought that he is a later representation of an older Mayan god. When the Catholic Church grew in strength, the local people combined the attributes of the older god into San Simón — indeed the name Maximón is a combination of Simón and max (pronounced mawsh), the Mayan word for tobacco. There are shrines to him in several Guatemalan towns apart from Santiago Atitlán, most notably, in Nahualá, San Jorge la Laguna and Zunil.

Beginning on the Sunday following the full moon of the spring equinox (a holy time to the Maya), Maximón is paraded around the town amid great spectacle and noise. On Monday he is then taken to two specific rocks—as he is once every month—down by the lake to be washed. The water used to wash him is bottled and sold: it is considered a sort of cure-all. I must have been there during one of his washdays, for seven or eight men picked him up and started to walk along the road.

## LA CASA DEL MUNDO AND CAFÉ

### By Katie Hale

Set on the gorgeous shores of Lake Atitlán sits the hidden hotel La Casa del Mundo. The decks provide idyllic views of the lake and three volcanoes. Open since 1998 and run by a Guatemalan-American couple, the hotel is a perfect haven for relaxing and enjoying outdoor activities.

Each room is uniquely decorated with local handicrafts, fresh flowers from the on-site gardens, and comfortable beds. Guests can partake in a range of activities including hot tubbing, kayaking, hiking, volcano treks, Spanish lessons, boat tours and trips to local villages.

A family-style dinner is served every night and the staff will accommodate any diet (vegan, allergy, etc.). The full meal is reasonably priced and the delicious food will leave you more than satisfied.

After taking afternoon dips in the swimming holes, sunning on the balcony and getting to know the hospitable staff, you won't want to leave the secluded Casa del Mundo. Sharing knowledge of this secluded spot will be up to you—just be sure to only tell those you trust with your deepest secrets, for this hotel gets its charm partly from its location off the beaten path.

# POSADA DE SANTIAGO, LAKE ATITLÁN

By Dennis O'Connor, Cincinnati, Ohio, U.S.A.

Just before dawn, dozens of angular wooden skiffs embark from the southwestern shoreline at the edge of a village called Santiago de Atitlán. The diminutive armada of boats skillfully manned by Tzutujil Mayans, who have plied the clear waters of this beautiful Guatemalan lake for centuries, now disperse to capture their share of *mojarra*, or lake perch.

Gradually, sun rays illuminate the clouds parting at the peak of Volcán San Pedro, one of three towering volcanoes that form a majestic backdrop for the beginning of another day - part of an endless cycle of life here in the Guatemalan highlands, about 150 kilometers (93 miles) west of the capital city. As their men work the bountiful waters, Mayan women wash clothes along the shore, their colorful huipils—beautiful hand-woven skirts—rolled up just above their knees safely away from the lake's surface. Soon, daylight allows a glimpse of the lake's expanse, its white-capped water stretching roughly 11 kilometers (seven miles) wide and six kilometers or four miles long.

The perfect vantage point to witness this timeless scene unfold is from the wood-fired hot tub at the Posada de Santiago. This one-of-a-kind hotel occupying a couple hillside acres at the lake offers guests spectacular accommodations in private cottages or suites, and exquisite dining inside the spacious restaurant and bar. The food is legendary; every morsel is made from scratch. Coffee is locally grown and wood-roasted daily. The bar is amply stocked for every taste. There also is a lakeside pool adjacent to the hot tub, thatch-roofed "casitas" popping up along the property with hammocks, benches and chairs for the ultimate relaxation. There is even a small library with an eclectic collection of regional interest that merits browsing. And of course, there is the view: the lake, the volcano, the birds, and the indigenous population who move about their lives as though the Spanish conquest of a half-millennium before never arrived.

Proprietors, David and Suzie Glanville, California transplants who have lived and worked here for the better part of the past two decades, are commensurate hosts, offering vast knowledge about the lake and its surroundings, the history of the local people and their many villages that dot the hillsides around the volcanic caldera that created Lake Atitlán millions of years ago. They know every possible pursuit available for visitors—whether it is taking an escorted hike up San Pedro, waterskiing, horseback riding or participating in a walking tour around the village of Santiago de Atitlán, a 10-minute stroll away. David's sage advice to all is "get a drink from the bar and find a hammock."

Located across the lake from the tourist bustle of the village of Panajachel—Atitlán's largest community—Santiago de Atitlán is the epicenter of a way of life found nowhere else, where villagers practice a blend of their ancient religion and Catholicism, grow maize on their hillside *milpas* and sell crafts and goods to the small crowd of tourists who arrive by boat from Panajachel each day for visits. Guests can get a flavor of *Tzutujil* spirituality by visiting the 400-year-old Catholic church at the center of the village, then stopping in at a local home where the Mayans worship *Maximón*—a smoking, drinking effigy who holds court flanked by village elders, moved periodically from house to house so no one family is allowed to accumulate too much juice from the local deity. One can take a photo or two of Maximón for about 10 Quetzales, a bit more than a dollar.

Unlike the day visitors, long after the tourist boats have gone, guests at the Posada de Santiago can witness the ending of the daily cycle: The sun sets and the villagers trek home from their labors. Now the sounds and sights of the night envelope the landscape and over the lake, a soft warm breeze gently carries with it Atitlán's ancient scents.

Dennis O'Connor lives in Cincinnati, Ohio, from which he covers religion, the arts, business—and occasionally—sports, throughout Ohio, Kentucky, Indiana and West Virginia as a full time writer/photographer for a variety of publications and web sites. A journalism graduate from Indiana University in Bloomington, O'Connor has covered the Dalai Lama's dedication of a Buddhist temple in the Midwest USA, met and photographed wildcat coal miners in southeastern Kentucky, and interviewed former presidential candidate George McGovern while on a visit in San Salvador, El Salvador. His sojourns outside the USA have primarily been to Western and Central Europe as well as Central America, although he has traveled to the Middle East. O'Connor treks annually to Central America to meet friends working there and to mine for stories.

The craziest place that Dennis has visited is the middle of Lake Atitlán, Guatemala, made somewhat crazier by the boat running out of gas. His dream trip would be a three-month trek to all the major Mayan sites in Guatemala, Honduras, Mexico and Belize. However, his next trip is to Bavaria, Germany to cover Pope Benedict's visit to his homeland.

Lake Atitlán. Photo by Neruda Marsh-MacNeil.

# PANAJACHEL

### By Dr. Crit Minster, Rochester, New York, U.S.A.

The hand-lettered sign was poorly copied and pasted to a light post. It read simply "Free Quetzal." I understood the words but not the message. "Free," well, that's an easy one, and a quetzal is a beautiful bird, the national bird of Guatemala. The Guatemalan national currency is also called the quetzal. Was someone offering up a pet quetzal? Was there free money to be had somewhere?

Upon further investigation, I learned that "Quetzal" was a young woman from North America who had moved to Guatemala, changed her name to Quetzal and burned her passport, declaring that she was a "citizen of the universe." Quetzal was busted—for overstaying her visa, for drugs, or just for being weird, I don't really know. It seems the authorities in the Guatemalan town of Panajachel weren't taking "Quetzal, citizen of the universe" very seriously, possibly because "the universe" does not issue passports. They locked her up until they could figure out who she was, or at least who she used to be. Her friends, still on the outside, had made the posters and put them up all over town.

One would think the Panajachel police would be used to that sort of thing by now. "Pana," as it's known to locals, is the biggest hippie town south of California. It is located on the banks of Lake Atitlan in central Guatemala, a postcard-perfect lake surrounded by three majestic volcanoes: Atitlan, San Pedro and Tolimán. It's not a very large town, and if you were to remove the hotels, restaurants, cafes, bars and curio shops, you'd be left with some churches, a few dusty streets and the municipal building, where for all I know Quetzal is still waiting for someone to let her out.

Panajachel is all about de-stressing and chilling out. It's a tourist town without a lot of the typical problems that tourist towns have: it's never drunk and rowdy, the crime level is relatively low for Guatemala and even the street kids selling gum, candy and hand-made bracelets are fairly laid back and not as irritating as they are in other places. Many of the full-time residents are Americans and Europeans who moved to Panajachel years or decades ago, seeking a simpler life in a place where it's always warm and sunny and you're never more than a few steps from a marvelous view of the lake and mountains.

Panajachel is a good home base for exploring the region. Up the hill is the town of Sololá, where the residents still wear traditional, brightly colored clothing. The lake itself is an attraction: there is a small beach, but the water is pretty cold and few people swim in it (locals think visitors who do are crazy). There are several picturesque towns around the lake, and tours will take you there by boat. You can shop in Panajachel or in any of the other lake towns: if you're an art lover, take a look at some of the paintings. Some tours offer horseback riding or mountain biking. The market town of Chichicastenango is within day-trip range. There are several Spanish schools in the area as well.

When the sun sets over Lake Atitlan, the three volcanoes change colors, from a rich forest green to blues and purples, and the tourists and some of the residents in town all go down to the waterfront to watch. Perhaps Quetzal is even there, free at last, enjoying the sunset.

---

**PANAJACHEL TRAVEL TIP:**
Panajachel is the only city in Guatemala where they add the tip onto your restaurant bill: look closely at any bill you pay so you don't double-tip. Because of this, service is Panajachel is often bad or slow.

---

Panajachel. Photo by Neruda Marsh-MacNeil.

# IXIMCHÉ

### By Martin Crossland, Miami, Florida, U.S.A.

It was my good fortune to be invited to a Maya ceremony by my friend and tour guide, Vicente Cuscun. His daughter, Nidia Indira, had just graduated from nursing school in Guatemala, and her parents, of Cakchiquel Maya descendent, wanted also to celebrate her graduation in the old ways.

The ceremony was held at the altar in the ancient Cakchiquel capital of Iximché, a few kilometres from Tecpán on the Pan-american Highway. We met at 9:00 am, the ceremony starting right on time. Officiating was the local Maya priest, Cristobal Cojti. Family and friends of Vicente attended the event.

After preparing a fire near the altar and placing coloured candles to the north, south, east and west, pine needles were scattered around it and we were each handed thin coloured candles to help keep the fire burning strongly. To one side was a marimba pura, which is the traditional marimba of just three players without the drums and suits and ties.

Nidia Indira was attired in the traditional huipil and corte of Tecpán, looking a little embarrassed, but also obviously proud of her heritage. Nearby, her school friends were dressed in the latest fashions. Her parents, Vicente and Julia, watched as the priest asked her to kneel on the pine needles in front of the fire. He then proceeded to beseech blessings on Nidia from Maya and Christian deities in Cakchiquel and Spanish.

In the background, the marimba played softly. We were then asked to all kneel around the fire and hold hands to complete the circle. At times we were required to kiss the mother earth, which we all did with varying fervour. The priest explained the conjunction of the deities and the forces of nature. The importance the Maya people have always placed on nature was obvious in his sermon.

After the ceremony, Vicente explained the history of Iximché, which we toured. We also discussed the place of the Maya in today's society, a very complex question and one not easily addressed without sounding somewhat revolutionary. I was shocked to learn that Maya ceremonies were actually illegal prior to the peace accords in 1996. A ceremony such as we were attending would have had to be done in secret 10 years ago. The priest also spoke of the Spanish invasion in such a way as to imply that the Maya still lived in an occupied country. This is an opinion that he probably would not have been able to express freely a few years ago without getting into deep trouble and even today such a viewpoint creates controversy.

It seems that the ancient ways will be sustained, even as the indigenous people enter the computer age. Nidia and her parents are a good example of how these people can accept and acclimatise to our modern westernised world, yet still keep their customs and traditions.

After the ceremony, we were treated to a delicious typical lunch of estofado, skillfully prepared by Nidia's grandmother, and animated by a livelier concert of marimba music. We were surprised to see that Cristobal Cojti was also a gifted marimba player. At 2:00 pm, after several toasts with powerful local cox, the guests bid farewell to the Cuscun family.

Martin Crossland spent six years in the British Merchant Navy and earned a degree in Navigation and Seamanship. Finding that he preferred dry land to the cruel sea, in 1964 he travelled to Peru, where he lived for 12 years (six in Trujillo, six in Lima). In Lima he worked in tourism, and has been working in this profession ever since. He married in Peru, and then lived for ten years in Brazil (Rio de Janeiro). In the 80's, the drop in the value of the US dollar made the United States an attractive destination for Europeans and South Americans, so they moved to Miami in 1982. Since then, Martin has spent a six-year stint in Guatemala, and the rest of the time living in South Florida. "I guess all I can say is that I am a qualified gypsy. Even my name keeps me moving. Where will we end up? Goodness knows, but at this moment, Florianópolis looks awfully tempting." The craziest place that Martin has visited is Maracaná Stadium during a Flamengo-Fluminense football game. His most bizarre experience was a Maya ceremony in a cave underneath the archaeological site of K'umarkaaj in Guatemala.

Mayan Girls. Photo by Scott Eaton.

### GUATEMALA FACTOIDS:

The Quiché Indians are the largest indigenous ethnic group in Guatemala, making up roughly 10% of the population.

In 1996, a major peace accord was signed by the government and rebel groups, ending more than 35 years of civil war.

Guatemala is roughly the size of Tennessee.

Guatemala City has a large Korean community.

The ruined Mayan city of Tikal, in Petén province, Guatemala, once was home to between 100,000 and 200,000 people.

# ANTIGUA

By Dr. Crit Minster, Rochester, New York, U.S.A.

Guatemala, 1541. The two Mayan kingdoms, the K'iche and the Kakchikel, have been defeated by Spanish forces fighting under Pedro de Alvarado, a veteran of the conquest of Mexico and one of Cortés' top lieutenants. The Spanish construction of a capital city in Guatemala is well under way, and Ciudad Vieja is shaping up nicely on the gentle slopes of a majestic mountain.

With a thunderous roar, the supposed mountain upon which they've been building blows its top. A watery mudslide buries Ciudad Vieja, killing thousands and giving the volcano its name: "*Agua,*" or "water." The surviving inhabitants started over a few miles away, laying the foundations for a new city they named Santiago de los Caballeros de Guatemala. This name was a bit too cumbersome, and before long the city was commonly called Antigua Guatemala, or, more simply, Antigua.

Antigua has worked hard to retain its colonial identity and heritage. It was declared a world heritage site by UNESCO in 1979, and local ordinances make it impossible for stores or restaurants to use garish signs or obstruct anyone's view of the marvelous colonial architecture. Even the McDonald's is low-key and almost invisible without its trademark bright colors.

One of the best ways to see Antigua is simply to wander around. It is a very small town, and it is difficult to get lost. Because of its history—a mixture of Spanish colonial accented by frequent earthquakes—there are a number of very interesting colonial-era ruins within the city. One such site is the Santa Clara ruins, where the visitor can wander through tranquil gardens and marvel at

> *With a thunderous roar, the supposed mountain upon which they've been building blows its top. A watery mudslide buries Ciudad Vieja, killing thousands and giving the volcano its name: "Agua," or "water."*

the toppled masonry of what was once a convent. There are many more, and usually the entrance fee is quite low.

Antigua is a must-see for any visitor to Guatemala. It is popular with travelers and ex-pats for good reason: it is a pleasant, beautiful, relatively safe city bursting at the seams with things to see and do. There are good restaurants and bars, lively nightlife, and many activities. The *mercado central* has excellent Guatemalan handicrafts as well as a picturesque local section full of fruits and vegetables. Numerous bookstores and cafes make it easy to pass a pleasant afternoon lounging, while three of the surrounding volcanoes—Agua, Fuego and Pacaya—are conducive to more active days hiking and trekking.

Antigua is also famous for Spanish schools. There are literally dozens of schools, which vary greatly in quality, price and accommodation. If you're interested, a number of these schools have web sites, but that isn't even really necessary: almost all accept walk-ins, and the city is plastered with advertisements. Several even hire local children to pass out fliers to passengers on arriving buses.

Majestically towering over the narrow streets, Agua Volcano still keeps an impassive watch over the city. Agua has been dormant since that fateful day in 1541, but its two siblings, Pacaya and Fuego, occasionally roar at each other across the green valley. Antigua disdains them all: the city has made its sacrifices to the Volcano Lords already. These geological beasts can spit smoke and sputter all they want; colonial charm and quiet side streets still dominate the character of Antigua.

## TOP LIST: COLONIAL PLAZAS TO STROLL IN

In Latin America, strolling through a picturesque main square is a way of life. Most cities are built around a beautiful main square and locals love to slowly walk around it in small groups. If you'd like to join them for a stroll, here's where to go:

1. Plaza Grande, Quito, Ecuador. Jo Edwards, England.

2. Main Square in Sucre, Bolivia. Teresa Colomer, Spain.

3. Main square in Antigua, Guatemala. Teresa Colomer, Spain.

4. Plaza de Armas in Arequipa, Peru. Teresa Colomer, Spain.

5. Plaza de Armas in Trujillo. Teresa Colomer, Spain.

6. Colonia, Uruguay. "Wander around in the early morning and have dinner al fresco in the late evening." Sandra Scott, Mexico, New York, U.S.A.

7. Tarija, Bolivia, "Bolivia has the best traditional plazas." Richard Engan, Minnesota, U.S.A.

Runners up: Plaza de Santa Domingo "One of the most beautiful in the country. It isn't well-known or appreciated." Guadalupe, Ecuador. Main square in Cuenca, Ecuador. "Great views of the church, shady trees and a neat fountain." Main square in Oaxaca, Mexico. "Comes to life at night with wandering mariachi bands."

# VOLCÁN PACAYA

## By Kerrie Hall, Sydney, Australia

It was a small poster on the stone wall at Anna's Café in Antigua Guatemala that tickled our collective sense of adventure. It simply read: "Climb a live volcano tour. Meet here at midday."

So here we are, a bunch of strangers, attempting to reach the top of a live volcano with two boyish guides and a pregnant mongrel dog. In the last rays of light we tramp to a barren plateau. The land is suddenly eerie and alien. Our laboured breathing punctuates the utter silence.

Pacaya stands at an imposing 2,552 metres (8,372 feet) above sea level. In recent history, this complex volcano has reigned terror on local residents with the threat of major eruptions. Since 1965, Pacaya Volcano has erupted almost continuously and is known to launch plumes of ash 6 kilometers (more than three miles) into the atmosphere.

As our vision lingers on the crater, thoughts of female sacrifice come naturally to mind. The ancient Mayas believed the flames and magma gushing from a volcano came from a place as mysterious as the heavens above. The Mayas, Aztecs, and Incas tossed virgins into the fiery mouth of the monster to appease angry gods.

Skirting the edge of a knoll, the earth drops into a deep canyon far below. We trudge onward to the sheer incline and the pot of gold. Beginning the ascent, I refuse to believe that I could possibly reach the top. Two lunges forward, one long slide back. We sink, ankle deep, shoes filled with rusty red granules.

As darkness falls, the Great Volcán Pacaya Show begins. I feel deep rumblings from the earth as I crawl the last few metres to the top. Several dramatic explosions spew a galaxy of glowing red magma as big as trucks from the lips of the crater. The errant fireballs race each other down the mountainside and then disappear into nothingness.

Engulfed in a stream of moist air, bursts of sulphur gas stinging our nose and eyes, we cheer and applaud this ancient wonder. We are on top of the world. Trillions of stars drip from the heavens. A neon-red river of boiling lava slithers down the mountainside like an exotic snake in a deep trance.

I once read somewhere that a group of crazy volcano academics took the temperature of lava from this very same crater. It was 1,970 degrees Fahrenheit. "You could only insert the temperature probe when the wind was blowing away from your body; otherwise you started to cook," they reported.

The immense power and mystery of life on this planet is a revelation to me here. I am perched on a pipeline to the beginnings of the planet and the gateway to Hades. I feel as significant as an ant. Suddenly, a series of ear splitting double explosions fills the silent darkness, followed by a brilliantly lit hailstorm from hell.

On cue, a translucent curtain of tangerine smoke and cloud closes the show. We clap and cheer in a standing ovation. High on the wonder of what we have witnessed, we ecstatically pick our way by torchlight back to the edge of the scree slope.

"OK, let's go skiing," yells Miguel the boy guide. On the soles of boots we slide and lurch downward to the base of the peak, squealing like children drunk on life.

Kerrie Hall is originally from Sydney, Australia. After years of global wanderlust she followed the sun to Queensland's northern tropics, graduating from James Cook University, Cairns, with a Bachelor of Journalism. As a pioneer of the degree course, she organized a foreign news field trip to Bangkok—an epicenter for world news. Two years later she moved permanently to Thailand and was a magazine editor on Phuket when the 2004 tsunami hit the island. Still based on Phuket, Kerrie now works as a freelance writer and editor for international airline in-flight magazines and dabbles in other media projects.

Kerrie doesn't go anywhere without her Aussie papaya ointment—a natural lip gloss and skin cure-all. When visiting Kashmir, India, she was caught in a mortar attack while backpacking in 1997. Her most bizarre experience was attending a week-long Buddhist funeral of a friend who died on Phuket in the tsunami. The local *wat* was full of news crews and the ceremonies went on for days, On the final night, the temple erupted into a huge festive party—as the Thais believe in sending off the soul with much sanook.

View from Pacaya. Photo by Caroline Bennett.

GUATEMALA

# BIKE TRIP IN ANTIGUA

By Martin Crossland, Miami, Florida, U.S.A.

My friend Beat Brunschwiler at Maya Bike Tours in Antigua suggested I join a bike tour. He assured me that it was not a very strenuous trip. Despite having not ridden a bike for any distance of great significance in living memory, I accepted his challenge. With helmet, gloves and a comfortable mountain bike, off I went with a bevy of healthy young ladies from North America and Europe.

Riding a bike on Antigua's cobblestone streets is not exactly easy on the posterior; nevertheless we were soon off the cobbles and onto local dirt roads, riding through villages so small I never knew of their existence. Each one sported beautiful little churches in varying states of decay (resulting from the devastating earthquakes of 1773).

When the road started climbing, I was forced to get off and walk, much to my chagrin: the guide was doing wheelies up this steep stretch!

We finally arrived at the spectacular convent of San Luis del Obisbo, with stunning views over Antigua and the Panchoy Valley. I asked the guide if we were continuing our climb, and he pointed up a steep earth street. I girded my loins and started walking my bike up the hill. Imagine my delight when moments later he caught up with me and told me that the "youngsters" had decided we had gone far enough "up," and now they wanted to go "down."

We now descended at breakneck speed through more villages to the town of Ciudad Vieja, and from there took the excellent highway to the fascinating Valhalla macadamia nut farm. This was a welcome spot to rest and soak up some facts about this remarkable project aimed at introducing the versatile Macadamia nut tree to Guatemala and its farmers. Onwards through San Miguel de las Dueñas to the weaving town of San Antonio Aguas Calientes. Another short uphill walk, and then all downhill and level through coffee plantations back to Antigua.

For someone as out of condition as I, I felt very good having completed the circuit. Was it worth taking the trip? Most definitely yes! This was a wonderful jaunt through a countryside that you can hardly conceive while whizzing by in a car. Too difficult? Not really! If I can do it, anyone can!

---

**GUATEMALA FACTOIDS:**
Carlos Marcello, a notorious New Orleans mobster, was born in Tunisia to Sicilian parents in 1910. To avoid possible deportation to Tunisia, Marcello obtained a false Guatemalan birth certificate. Although it was well known that he was not Guatemalan, The Kennedy administration deported him to Guatemala in 1961. He returned to New Orleans illegally not long after and continued to rule his crime syndicate.

---

## BANANA REPUBLIC OF GUATEMALA

By Katie Hale

The United Fruit Company, today known as Chiquita, has a long and tumultuous history in Central America. Guatemala, controlled by the company, became known as a "Banana Republic," the term coined by famous writer O. Henry in reference to a dictatorship reliant on agriculture. Other countries fell to United Fruit's mighty fist, but none had a more complex relationship with the company than Guatemala.

In 1901 Manuel Estrada Cabrera, then Guatemalan dictator, allowed the United Fruit Company to enter Guatemala for the first time by granting them exclusive rights to transport mail between the country and the United States. Minor Keith, a young Brooklynite and co-owner of the company, saw the country as an investor's paradise and formed the Guatemalan Railroad Company, a subsidiary of United Fruit. He built a railroad between Guatemala City and Puerto Barrios and purchased cheap lots in Puerto Barrios on the pier. The produce was put on to ships sailing to New York and New Orleans, where Americans were eating bananas by the millions each year. In Puerto Barrios institutionalized racism was regularly practiced and non-whites had to yield right-of-way to whites.

Guatemala produced about 25 percent of the company's total output. United Fruit owned virtually all modes of transportation and communication. Its industry was fruit, but its business was monopolization.

Problems still exist today on the banana plantations of Guatemala. Safety and health standards of working conditions are regularly called into question. The fruit of the United Fruit Company may have been sweet, but its legacy has left a bitter taste in the mouths of many living in Guatemala and Latin America.

# RAFTING THE COYOLATE

By Martin Crossland, Miami, Florida, U.S.A.

We leave the Guatemala office at 6:30 a.m. sharp, and soon are off on the motorway to the coast. On the coastal highway, the countryside is emerald green, hilly and forested to the right, and a flat expanse of sugar cane plantations to the left. The sight of the volcanoes that surround Antigua is stupendous. From sea level, they look so much higher.

In Santa Lucía Cotzumalguapa, a small coastal town just north of the Pacific Highway, we sign papers to absolve the outfitter of any responsibility should we never be heard of again. Now is the time to chicken out. None of us do.

We continue down a rutted track ending at the riverbank, which is crowded with locals. This is the big event of the week. The outfitters come regularly with loads of rafters who disappear down the river and are never seen again. Next week, the same people are back with another load. Our guide, Tammy, hands out presents to the children, perhaps to keep them quiet so they won't tell the police about these strange goings on.

The three rafts are inflated; we are assigned our places and issued life jackets and helmets. A quick instruction follows, during which we are informed that most people don't know left from right, and back from forward. We scoff to think anyone could be so dumb. The boatmen will shout orders at us, such as "left forward" and "right backwards," and we must paddle like mad in the direction indicated just like galley slaves, or get forty lashes. Looks like we are going to have lots of laughs!

We start off down the river ignominiously. People fall out of the rafts. The right side paddles forward when they should be paddling backwards, and vice versa. We wonder how we are ever going to finish the trip.

Amazingly we soon shape up, and learn all over again which is right and which is left. Several tributaries fill the river and it starts getting fun, though it isn't exactly Discovery Channel, where half the time the rafts seem to be under water.

The river runs at the bottom of a shallow canyon, with the walls totally covered with vegetation. Birds and butterflies flit around us, and colourful flowering trees cling precariously to the banks of the valley. The sides are formed of smooth black volcanic granite, embedded with large pebbles and boulders. One can only imagine the cataclysm that caused this extraordinary feature. We drift down river, frequently going through mild rapids. At one point we stop and walk to a waterfall that pours from the rim of the valley. It's wonderfully refreshing!

We stop at a small beach for a picnic lunch. While the crew sets up portable tables on the shore, and starts about making sandwiches and salad, we all get to socializing and swimming. By now, city slickers in our group, not used to more physical activity than it takes to sign a cheque or click a mouse, are beginning to feel the burn.

Off again after a well deserved rest, we soon hear a rumble, and round the next bend come to the most exciting rapids of all. The river foams and rushes like a jet from a fire hose between huge boulders. Unfortunately, there is a great tree trunk traversing the most awesome part. Had we continued through this rapid, we would probably all have been decapitated. So we haul the rafts out of the water and carry them around the obstruction.

Next, we spy a waterfall descending straight into the river. We take turns paddling our rafts beneath this impressive shower. Fortunately, we are using helmets, as the water cascades on you as hard as hailstones tumbling from the sky. As the river nears the coast, the canyon walls get less precipitous, and we can start seeing signs of civilisation. We can see sugar cane growing at the edges of the valley, and we pass under an unused railway bridge.

Finally we come to the end of the ride. It is 4 p.m. We have been in the river for 6 hours. Our arms seem to weigh 20 tons each.

As we are changing, we see a man cycle up to the far side. He stops at the edge, calmly takes off his clothes and wraps them in a bundle. He puts them on top of his bike, which he holds above his head, and proceeds to cross. On getting to our side, he dresses, wishes us all "Buenas tardes," and continues blithely on his way.

We don't need entertaining on the way back, as most of us are asleep as we climb back from the tropics to the temperate mountain climate of Guatemala City.

# PUFF PUFF: A RIDE ON GUATEMALA CHOO-CHOO

By Martin Crossland

The humorously named Guatemala Choo-Choo is an epic steam-powered voyage through the countryside. To get to the station, you first have to travel through the city. The high-sounding Avenida del Ferrocarril ("Railway Avenue") is nothing more than a seedy thoroughfare through underprivileged neighbourhoods desperately awaiting the garbage collector. It even passes the red light district, making the day of the scantily clad ladies waving at all the passengers on the train. Frantic vendors hustle to get their carts out of the way before being shattered by the onerous locomotive as we pass through the middle of a market. We cross the impressive Belize Bridge: a high-wire act over the Río de las Vacas, 230 feet (70 meters) below. No protective railings here, so don't lean out too far! If you do have the bad luck to fall overboard, you will conveniently land in the city cemetery way below.

We leave the city and start hootin' and tootin' through little suburban villages. Here one appreciates the population explosion: there are children everywhere you look. The train is an attraction for them and their parents. They run beside the train, laughing and playing, like they do in old-time movies. In a while, we enter a countryside of steep ravines, trestle bridges, and (to the joy of the youngsters aboard) even a short tunnel.

After a two-hour journey, we arrive at Agua Caliente, a beautiful green oasis surrounding a series of thermal hot springs. You can bathe in the naturally heated swimming pool, perspire in a huge steam room or rent a private bathhouse.

# CANCUÉN

By Albert García, Fullerton, California, U.S.A.

It must have been a horrific scene. 1,200 years ago, near the edge of the Pasión River in modern-day Guatemala, more than 30 men, women, and children were executed by lance, spear, and ax. Their remains were tossed into a sacred cistern at the front of an enormous palace. Accompanying them to their final resting place were the precious jades, seashells, and jaguar fang necklaces that symbolized their prestige as the ruling class and nobles of the once-powerful Maya city Cancuén, the "Palace of Serpents."

Albert Garcia, 36, is a lifetime California resident and a graduate student of anthropology at California State University, Fullerton. A self-employed screen-printer, many of his travels have been the result of playing in a punk rock & roll band which took him across the United States several times and twice to Europe. He has also ventured through Guatemala, Honduras, Bolivia, and Peru conducting cultural and archeological research.

Albert wouldn't leave home without music: cassettes, CDs, or an MP3 player, depending on the decade. "Drives and hotels can be dreary and noisy with too much time to kill in both. Music alleviates the noise while easing the hours away." He had a strange experience in western Guatemala dodging skyrockets that were flying off a man dressed as the devil in a small village named Santa Maria Cahabón. The event is called "*Quema del Diablo*," or "burn the devil," and it takes place at the beginning of December as part of a nine day period of religious observances. He was hit once in the hand.

Some dignity and respect was reserved for the very last king and queen of a ruling dynasty dating as far back as the second or third century B.C.: their bodies were buried in full royal regalia 80 meters away in a shallow grave.

To the Maya—for whom life, death, and the supernatural world were closely integrated—the end must have seemed imminent.

Hastily built and unfinished walls around the city suggest there had been something to fear. After the executions, the city seems to have been abandoned, and the fate of its inhabitants is still unknown. Like Tikal, Copán and Palenque, the Maya city of Cancuén simply faded into time and the ageless jungle.

Recent excavations, led by Vanderbilt University anthropologist Dr. Arthur Demarest, highlight an extraordinary new chapter in Guatemalan historical and cultural investigations. Restoration and preservation is aided by the Q'eqchí Maya who reside in neighboring villages. Income raised through tourism will assist the local economy and support the stewardship of the site. The goal of the Cancuén Archeological Project is to establish the three-story, 170 room palace as a center that will attract ecotourists, archaeologists, students, and researchers. The story of the lives, politics and trade and eventually decline of the ancient Maya, is slowly unraveling through the artifacts currently being examined in an on-site archaeology lab.

Unlike larger and more developed Maya cities such as Tikal or Copán, the adventurous and difficult trek to remote Cancuén attracts few visitors. The nearest hotels and restaurants can be found in the town of Chisec in the north-central Guatemalan region of Alta Verapaz. From there it's a two hour trip along narrow highways (often crowded with pedestrians and livestock) and potholed back roads, followed by a scenic boat ride down the Pasión River. Plans are in the works for overnight camping and food service at the site.

Local guides share their perspectives and the latest scientific theories while escorting you through the emerald jungle. Visitors stroll through the ruins of the palace, past a ball court, around half buried temples and to the cistern where the details of the massacre recently emerged.

Crossing the less traveled paths through the colorful Guatemalan countryside is just about worth the trip itself. While there is a chance you might see howler monkeys, rare birds, and woolly anteaters, you will definitely see mosquitoes—thousands of them! Bring a lot of repellent.

Also, bring a lot of film. The excavations are expected to continue for the next decade, which means any visit to Cancuén will be at merely one stage of its reemergence.

## LATIN REVOLUTIONARIES # 7: GASPAR ILÓM

### Guatemala (1940-2005)

Gaspar Ilóm was born Rodrigo Asturias, son of Miguel Angel Asturias, the Guatemalan writer, activist and Nobel Prize winner for literature. Rodrigo adopted the name Gaspar Ilóm from a fictional character in his father's novel Men of Maize. He became involved in the revolution in 1971 when he founded the ORPA, or Armed People's Association. In 1982, the repressive Guatemalan government under Efraín Rios Montt began taking brutal steps to quash the rebellion, which had continued on and off since the 1950s. The move backfired, as it caused the revolution to gain strength.

ORPA was one of four rebel groups that united to establish the National Guatemalan National Unity (URNG), and Ilóm was named its head. He generally directed his forces from exile in Mexico. Ilóm was the head of the URNG from the early 1980s until 1996, when a peace treaty was finally signed. The URNG became converted into a legitimate political party and Ilóm ran for president, but was defeated. He died of a heart attack in 2005. His former adversary, retired general Otto Pérez Molina, upon learning of his death described him as "a brave man, with grand ideas, who did a great deal to bring about the end of the war."

# B'OMB'IL PEK AND JUL IQ'

## By Albert Garcia, Fullerton, California, U.S.A.

In the Maya world, caves are understood to be passageways between the world of the living and the underworld of the dead.

Since ancient times this underworld has been believed to be the realm of gods and ancestors. Named Xibalbá (the place of fright), it is also the home of the "earth monster." Royalty, nobles, and pilgrims would travel great distances to certain caves in order to make offerings and collect the pure waters that seep through the limestone walls and flow from the inner earth. For many in Mesoamerica it is where the very origins of humankind began.

During the Spanish colonial period, when customs and religions of the New World became outlawed and persecuted, rituals had to be performed inside the deep mazes of caverns and caves.

When they found the idols hidden deep within the caverns, enraged European priests would destroy them and punish the worshippers. Despite their greatest efforts, however, these priests could never completely stamp out the traditions of the Maya.

The hidden caves even served the guerilla forces during Guatemala's recent 36 year-long civil war, providing a natural armory for caches of weapons. In the department of Alta Verapaz, just west of the small town of Chisec, the caves B'omb'il Pek (Painted Stone) and Jul Iq' (Wind Hole) are open to adventurous travelers curious about these gateways to the underworld. Both are reached by a short hike across farmlands and over rocky, forested hills. Opened in 2002 through a collaboration of indigenous Q'eqchi' Maya and international archaeologists, the caves continue to serve as centers for traditional ceremonial rites, but now the local economy also benefits from tourism to the sites.

The journey to the underworld, however, is a bit tricky. Ducking under colorful stalactites while stepping lightly around delicate formations on a slick, uneven floor, the visitor must cautiously navigate the treacherous cavern floor. There are no paved routes or lighting, and informative guides, hard-hats and flashlights are necessary and provided with the entrance fee.

Inside B'omb'il Pek, two small holes must be passed through in order to view the rock art on the inner wall. Not for the claustrophobic or broad-shouldered, it requires some maneuvering to squeeze through. Inside the second opening, a stone ledge is all that keeps you from plunging 50 feet into oblivion. An adjacent wall bears images of monkeys and jaguars, painted by the ancient Maya brave enough to enter the earth monster millennia before modern conveniences such as flashlights and hiking shoes.

Deep in the chasm, the guide recommends turning off all lights. The hollow sound of wind passes through; the earth seems to be breathing ... it's easy to imagine a supernatural world residing in such an ominous place.

To see what lies inside the mouth of the earth monster is to experience the Maya world view firsthand—to see the natural landscape that influenced the religion, art, and architecture of one of the world's longest lasting empires. People in this area sometimes say their Mayan ancestors never truly disappeared. Rather, they went underground to where the water flows, and the sounds of their marimbas and celebrations can be heard throughout the night.

CAVES TRAVEL TIPS:

Travel to nearby Chisec requires a days' drive from Guatemala City.

Allow three hours to see both caves.

"New York" in Jul Iq'. Photo by Albert Garcia.

# PROYECTO ECOLÓGICO QUETZAL

### By Denis Burke, Dublin, Ireland

There is always the possibility when doing a community stay that participants will see little more than the adverse effects of tourism on isolated indigenous groups. Not so with Cobán's *Proyecto Ecológico Quetzal*. The inhabitants of Chicacnab (one of two villages the Proyecto works with) have a natural mastery of the art of hospitality. The tiny rainforest village is a genuine treat for those seeking to explore the road less traveled in Guatemala.

Denis Burke has spent most of his life in the country of his birth, Ireland. Since finishing university in Maynooth, just outside Dublin, he has spent his time travelling and living in far flung corners of the world. He now works and studies in Ireland. He wouldn't leave home without a cozy jumper; warmth for the cold nights, a comfort on the hungover mornings and a pillow for the long bus journeys. "Multi functional doesn't get more comfortable." In India he found that the monkeys watching his every move made for a different kind of journey. He longs to undertake an epic campaign taking in all of the Caribbean and South America. His next stop is India again. "I'm going back to write a book. Anyone want to publish me?"

The Proyecto was set up in the late eighties to encourage local farmers to preserve primary rainforest on their lands. The principle is simple: don't cut down the rainforest: make money showing it to nature-hungry tourists. And it works! The traveler arrives in the nearest major town of Cobán, makes some inquiries at the Proyecto's office and within a few days heads off on a very special journey.

We found ourselves taking buses further and further away from life as we knew it, meeting charming characters along the way. Before we boarded the pickup truck that would bring us to the foot of the trail, a young mother insisted we take some pears so we would not be hungry on our hike. The pickup was crowded with farmers and traders. Our guide was easily the youngest on board, not being more than fourteen. He was endearingly shy and made sure we were as comfortable as could be as we bounced down the muddy road to the foot of the mountains.

Once the walking began in earnest the landscape began to change to resemble what might have happened if Peter Jackson had directed *Jurassic Park*. As we approached the village we began to meet some of the inhabitants who spoke *Q'eqchi* to our guide and greeted us in polite Spanish.

While the whole package is marketed as a sort of hike into the wilderness, it is in fact much more of a cross-cultural exchange. Visitors share the family space; usually rustic wooden cabins with bare mud floors and a gorgeous open fire. It is unlikely that the tourist will encounter any wild jaguar but chances are high that he or she will spend ample time with sturdy men and women who work like Trojans and enthusiastic kids who make you feel, genuinely, like part of the family for a few days. Without the slightest reservation we were invited to church and our host's father's home where we met many people who shook our hands, smiled warmly and went on their way as if we were just other people living in the area. We were not made to feel at any time as if we were out of place or, worse, just another pair of foreigners.

If you are en route from Tikal to Antigua or Panajachel this little project is well worth the stop. Guatemala overall was an exceptional experience for us but it was this mini adventure to Chicacnab that made it entirely unforgettable.

## A NATURAL OBSESSION

### By Katie Hale

> Gary squinted up at the sky for a moment and then said, "Martin, we should try propagating these. I brought a species back from Guatemala last week and it was bright orange inside, and it was just beautiful. We'll even name it for you ...We'll make a fortune." Martin tilted his head like a sparrow. "Ah-ha," he said. "Bless its bright orange heart."
> - Susan Orlean, The Orchid Thief

In Susan Orlean's popular book, The Orchid Thief, the delicate flower is more valuable than a prized piece of art or cherished jewel. Orlean encounters those who live for hunting and collecting the rarest species, smuggling them and cultivating them for profit.

Orchids are abundant in Guatemala, and the national flower is the monja blanca, or white nun. The flower is now on the verge of extinction—once it was named the national flower, every orchid collector and Guatemalan wanted a specimen and the flower soon became threatened. The characters in The Orchid Thief would have no qualms about poaching the flower, but you may prefer to go the legal route to get a plant of your own: they are available by mail order from the United States or Europe.

To see the orchids in their natural splendor, visit an orchid farm: Vivero Verapaz, just outside of Cobán, is amazing sight with over 30,000 examples of 600 different species of these rare and beautiful flowers.

# QUIRIGUÁ

## By Dr. Crit Minster, Rochester, New York, U.S.A.

*A new sun rises over the steaming Guatemalan jungle.*

*In the low, green forest, a mighty king stands tall, placidly surveying his realm. He faces north, and the dazzling morning sun throws his face into dramatic relief. He is dressed as befits a mighty king, with an ornate headdress, high boots and elaborate robes. He stands in the same place he stood yesterday, and a thousand yesterdays before that, for a thousand years of yesterdays under the oppressive Guatemalan sun.*

*Around him, his mighty city is in ruins, the grand temples swallowed by the lush jungle generations ago, back when his vigil was still new. The buildings turned to dust as he watched, mute and powerless to stop it. His people are gone, victims of an unknown disaster that took them away from him, away from his severe, stony gaze. Enveloped by thick jungle and shrouded in silence, he patiently waits for the day when people rather than trees are his subjects, and his glorious empire rises again.*

The Maya empire wasn't really an empire at all, but a collection of city-states that were unified by language and commerce. The Maya were great builders, warriors and astronomers, and their culture peaked around 600-800 A.D. before mysteriously disappearing. Historians have a number of theories for their decline, including rampant warfare among the city-states, natural disasters and disease. Whatever the reason, by the time the Spanish arrived in the sixteenth century, the descendants of the Maya were scattered into smaller pockets of civilization spread out over southern Mexico, Belize, Guatemala and northern Honduras.

Quiriguá was a medium-sized Maya city: during its peak (around 500 to 750 A.D.) it may have been home to as many as 50,000 inhabitants. Although it is not a large site, it is noteworthy because of the finely carved stone of the buildings and *stelae*, or tall standing stones. Among these intricately carved stone structures, one of the most impressive is Stela E. The largest of the Mayan stelae, Stela E stands thirty-five feet (11 meters) tall and weighs an estimated 130,000 pounds (almost 60,000 kilograms). Depicted on this massive stone is Cauac Sky, the greatest ruler of the city of Quiriguá during the Maya classic period. Archeologists estimate the stela was finished around 771 A.D. The stone's massive size and foreboding appearance gives the impression that, while the city of Quiriguá disappeared long ago, Cauac Sky continues to rule the jungle. This intriguing remnant from the past is one of twenty or so at the Quiriguá archaeological site.

Besides Stela E and the other magnificent carved standing stones, the area is one of the few places featuring "full-figured glyphs" which is a certain intricate form of Mayan writing into stone. Many of the buildings and temples of the site are still unexcavated. The site also features "zoomorphs", which are great stones carved into animal shapes.

*The impassive king still stands where he has always stood, not minding the ruin around him. He was built to last out of sixty tons of ageless rock, six times taller than he stood in life. He has persevered even as everything around him was reclaimed by the eternal jungle, and to look at his emotionless face, he knows he'll stand tall for generations more, stoically watching the world evolve around him.*

Maya Girl. Photo by Caroline Bennett.

### QUIRIGUÁ TRAVEL TIPS:

Getting there and around: Quiriguá is about 220 kilometers from Guatemala City, and relatively easy to visit as it is not far from the highway that links the city to the coast.

There is a small town nearby but facilities are limited:

Quiriguá is better done as a day trip.

It is a UNESCO World Heritage site.

# MARISCOS

### By Lorraine Caputo, Columbia, Missouri, U.S.A.

Cicadas hum in the heat of mid-afternoon. Sunlight gilds the waters placidly lapping against the shore. This water is warm and so clear I can see the fish swimming about my ankles. Soon sunset will paint the skies above these jungle hills in peach and magenta. Dusk will fall, geckos will chuckle. And the night, ebony, velvety, pierced with infinite stars arrives.

This is the tranquility of Mariscos, on the southern shore of Lake Izabal in eastern Guatemala. When I want to escape, to find a bit of peace, I come here. Days are spent strolling down the country lane to Playas Cocales and Dorada, or up into the hills, past the settlements of rubber tappers and their families. I remember the first time I watched the latex oozing down the groove carved into the tree. The liquid, pooled into a cup, was cool to my touch.

Since the ferries from El Estor stopped crossing the lake, this village has been largely forgotten—except for the few who still remember its pleasures and Guatemalans who take their vacations here. It is both figuratively and literally off the beaten path. To reach this little-known haven, one gets off at the Trincheras Junction on the Atlantic Highway and catches a mini-bus. The last 15 kilometers wind through heavy forest, descending towards the lake sitting on the north horizon. It's not hard to find one's way around here—there's only one road into town. As if to accent the town's remoteness, the paved road abruptly drops into the dusty, dirt street that is Mariscos' main drag. The ferry is gone but the dock is still there. The benches, once used by those awaiting the ferry to El Estor, now make for front-row seats for a dazzling lake sunset.

From Mariscos, one can hire boats to explore settlements along the shores, or to travel to El Estor, the Río Dulce and other points of tourist interest. You can also skip over to a few eco-tourism lodges, if you wish such comforts. Finca Paraíso has a cave and thermal springs, and Denny's Beach is worth a visit. In Mariscos itself, there's sailing, swimming, fishing, diving and other water sports.

Not too far away are the great ruins of Quiriguá, situated amongst banana plantations. Home to the most-intricately carved *stelae*, or standing carved stones, of Mayan artistry, these ruins tower over the landscape, chronicling Quiriguá's ancient, bloody history, such as the glory of the capture and execution of rival Copán's ruler, 18 Rabbit.

Ah, but the greatest secret of all: since the ferry has stopped running, the waters are much cleaner and quieter—so much so that even the manatees love it. Twice a year, in October and again in January-February, they swim up from the Biotopo Chocón-Machacas del Manatí and hang out by the old dock.

Someday I shall return to that plain, little village of Mariscos. Again I shall swim with the fish and resident manatees. Until then I can only reminisce fondly about the evening breeze brushing against palm trees, carrying the scent of almond blossoms. Be assured, that night chorus of cricket, frog and gecko continues in this paradise off the main road of most travelers.

---

*"It is not possible to conceive a democratic Guatemala, free and independent, without the indigenous identity shaping its character into all aspects of national existence."*
-Rigoberta Menchú, Guatemalan Activist (1959-)

Chicken buses. Photo by Will Gray.

# CHICKEN BUSES
## By Neruda Marsh-MacNeil, Cambridge, Massachusetts, U.S.A.

Former U.S. school buses—sometimes still bright yellow and with the district name stenciled in black on the side—get to retire to Guatemala, where they are reincarnated as local transportation. Gringos call them "chicken buses," because you may well find yourself sharing a seat with tonight's dinner! Riding on one can be exciting, exhausting, exhilarating and a real Guatemalan experience.

Traveling various routes across the country, these colorful buses pick-up any roadside straggler. You can be assured no one will be left behind.

When planning a trip to Guatemala, travelers often debate journeying on a chicken buses or modern tourist buses. While perhaps more reliable and comfortable, tourist shuttle buses tend to be more pricey. Chicken buses are cheap, and sometimes safer because you are traveling with locals (and are therefore less likely to have the whole bus stopped and robbed by highwaymen).

But for many, the decision hinges on how much one wants to immerse themselves in Guatemalan life. If you want to see local cultures through the window of a fast-moving bus, go for the tourist transportation: but if you want to be surrounded by local culture on all sides, chickens and all, the Chicken Bus is the way to go.

Everyone finds his own seat at the departure location, putting smaller sacks on the rung bins overhead in the bus and larger items and baskets on the top of the bus. As the bus makes its way through its route, more and more people squeeze on. No one is ever left on the roadside. As a third person slides into the bench-like seat, reminiscent of grammar schools in the United States, you still feel quite comfortable.

As a fourth person slides in with a child or friend on her lap and an enormous sack of carrots in the aisle, you begin to realize what you're really in for. Consider it part of an incredible adventure that will sharpen your perspective on the culture you're visiting. Anyone rubbing shoulders or having full body contact in New York City would find themselves in a very different situation than in Guatemala.

Amazingly, the driver's assistant (known as the *ayudante*, or helper) makes his way through the increasingly crowded bus to collect fares, and all the while merengue, ranchera, salsa, reggae and of course marimba is played at the highest decibel possible. With all of this activity inside the bus, the fact that you're flying around windy roads with gorges thousands of feet just below the bus window goes unnoticed. All the better for some folks, but most will enjoy a window seat if it's possible to get one, to be able to see the small villages and rolling countryside passing by. Don't forget to strike-up a conversation, as people on these buses are good for chatting, especially for information about things to do that guides won't offer.

As one can imagine, it's important to know when your stop is coming up, so that you can start to make your way up to the front or the back of the bus. It is equally important to get the attention of the *ayudante* to retrieve any belongings on the top of the bus, (although somehow the assistant remembers everyone and all of their belongings most of the time). Several guidebooks give some idea of where chicken buses pick up and drop off, but it's not always easy to know which is your stop, or where in the destination city/town the buses will end up. Most people will want to help you—they'll stand at the side of the road with you to get you going in the right direction. Guatemalans are friendly and eager to offer help.

Sure, everyone but the most tight-fisted of backpackers can afford the few extra *quetzales* to take the deluxe bus, leaving the chickens and pigs behind on the chicken bus. But they're missing out. A chicken bus trip, with 90 people, 20 chickens, four goats, two pigs and a dog (not to mention the thirty sacks of potatoes) on a bus built for fifty school kids, listening to *ranchera* music (sort of like Mexican Country music) as the bus zooms around mountain passes is one of the truest and most authentic cultural experiences Guatemala has to offer. So grab a chicken and hop on the bus—you'll be glad you did!

Neruda Marsh-MacNeil originally hails from Cambridge, MA, but now resides in Somerville. She works as a Facilities Project Manager. She wouldn't leave home without her camera, which comes in useful for taking photos of places that she has found to be crazy, such as Valparaíso, Chile. Her dream destination is Scotland and Greece, "… I have to have one?" Her next trip will be to Europe, to visit France.

# CANDELARIA CAVES
## By Katie Hale

Candelaria Caves, located 10 kilometers (six miles) west of Raxrujá, are some of the most extensive and spectacular passageways in all of Latin America. Daniel Dreux "discovered" the caves in 1974 while on a Guatemalan-French expedition, and the best way to access them is through his private property.

Dreux later built an eco-lodge where visitors can now stay. Make sure to venture out your own, however; although Dreux dominates tourism in the area, you are allowed to explore the tunnels on your own, which are considered to be the entrance to the Mayan underworld, Xibalba. Just be sure to pack a headlamp, good walking shoes and a pair of binoculars before you check out limestone stalagmites and bats.

# EL MIRADOR

## By Richard Arghiris, London, England

Far below, the forest is unbroken in every direction. Ancient, ruined cities are silhouetted on the horizon. To the north lies the border with Mexico, to the south stretches Guatemala. To the east, an immense temple breaks through the foliage. Meanwhile, the sunset in the west soaks up the tree-tops with dream-like hues of orange, red and pink.

El Mirador, a largely unrestored and ruined Mayan city in the Petén forest of Guatemala, features some of the pre-Hispanic world's largest ancient structures. More than 2,000 years old, El Mirador contains architectural feats like El Tigre, a magnificent pyramid with a 16,000 square metre base. The pyramid and its enormous scale proves just how advanced early Mayan civilisation was. While archaeologists strive to uncover El Mirador's hidden secrets, their task is not easy. Over 60 kilometers of nearly impenetrable jungle separates the site from the nearest human habitation.

An expedition to El Mirador, undertaken with the support of an experienced guide, can be arranged from the town of Flores—the most convenient jumping off point for excursions in the Petén. The journey lasts a minimum of five days and is accomplished with the aid of mules. It involves two nights camping in the forest and one night at the archaeological site. The hiking is arduous, through thick, dry and sometimes tick-infested forest. En-route sights include workers' encampments, Mayan burial grounds and lesser known ruins like El Tinto.

The walk itself is quite enjoyable. A good guide will inform you about the Petén's flora. "*Pimento*," for example, is a wild herb, typically brewed as a tea. Its effect is strangely hypnotic and the perfect conclusion to a long day's hike, ensuring your aches subside into a pleasant drowsiness. Other locally utilised flora includes a prolific tree used as a blood coagulant and a sweet-smelling tree resin—*copal*, a Mayan ceremonial incense. You will also see fauna in the forest including howler monkeys, toucans, spider monkeys, untold insects and tarantulas. Rarer beasts include jaguars, snakes and pumas.

The view from El Tigre's summit is the highlight of a trip to El Mirador. Where the stars appear wondrously close, one imagines how the Maya had designed their pyramids for astronomical observation. Along with mathematics and time-keeping, astronomy was their forte. But in the Mayan world, science was indistinguishable from religion. As much as astronomical observatories, the pyramids were temples. Upon El Tigre, the city stretched below, priests would perform devotional rites of blood-letting and sacrifice.

Like so many other Mayan cities, El Mirador has been reclaimed by the jungle. Its most ancient structures are now hillocks, mounds and plateaux, overgrown with vegetation. There is a certain poetic symmetry in this. For the Maya, aside from accomplished scientists, were great philosophers of nature. The sun, rain and wind were worshipped as gods and it seems that their fate—both the prodigious rise and mysterious fall of the Maya—is somehow intertwined with the earth and its forces. The pyramids have fulfilled their destinies. They now resemble the mountains they were intended to symbolise.

## BARTOLOMÉ DE LAS CASAS & THE VERAPAZ EXPERIMENT By Dr. Crit Minster

In north-central Guatemala, there are two departments—sort of like a state or county—named Alta and Baja Verapaz, or Upper and Lower Verapaz. The word Verapaz is a contraction of two Spanish words that means "true peace" and there is an interesting story behind it.

In 1537, the great Defender of the Indies, the Dominican friar Bartolomé de Las Casas, was horrified at the brutality of the Spanish conquest. At the time, the most common justification for the conquest was the somewhat illogical notion that in order to "save" the natives—that is, to bring them to Christianity—it was first necessary to pacify or subdue them with military force. Massacres, mass burnings, and enslavement of entire populations was, according to this logic, in the best interests of the natives (at least in the long run). Las Casas didn't buy it. He was determined to show that evangelization of the New World could take place peacefully. He proposed an experiment: if the Spanish crown would grant him a region, he would bring the natives into the fold peacefully. The crown agreed to the experiment (much to the consternation of the conquistadores) and gave Las Casas a region of north-central Guatemala that had been notoriously difficult to subdue: the local K'ekchi people were warlike, defiant, and killed any Spaniards who attempted to enter their territory.

Las Casas hand-picked a team of brave and patient friars and together they slowly began to make peaceful contact with the K'ekchi people. They translated Bible verses into k'ekchi and sent gifts to the local rulers, one of whom agreed to let them come in. Within a few years, the region had been Christianized and Las Casas' experiment was a success.

The story ends badly, however. Once the region was pacified, Spanish fortune hunters, slavers and conquistadores swarmed in, looking for treasure and slaves. The K'ekchi rose in bloody revolt, which was brutally quashed. By the late 1540's, the Verapaz project was in tatters, a victim of European greed.

The region still has the name, however, and local residents are proud of their unique place in colonial history. Today, one of the towns of Alta Verapaz is named Fray Bartolomé de Las Casas in honor of the brave friar who tried to put an end to the senseless violence of the conquest.

# TIKAL

### By Dr. Crit Minster, Rochester, New York, U.S.A.

Tikal, the mightiest of the Maya cities, had languished in decadence for a century and a half. No new great temples had been built, no new history carved into the ageless gray stone. The wars had continued, battles and skirmishes with competing Mayan city-states such as Quiriguá to the south, but there had been no grand victories, nothing that would attract the attention and favor of the Gods. The ruler of Tikal, *Hasaw Chan K'awil* ("Double Moon") commissioned a mighty temple: a pyramid that would reach the sky. Thousands of workers were brought in from the countryside: stonecutters, artisans, laborers. They built a magnificent temple out of stone—it eventually became Hasaw Chan K'awil's tomb: he was laid to eternal rest alongside his wife, Twelve Macaw.

Temple I at Tikal was built around 700 A.D, kicking off a period of construction known as the Late Classic period, when Tikal reached its cultural, social and military apex. Once home to 100,000 Maya, Tikal was one of the most important cities in the Maya empire.

Tikal was "rediscovered" in 1848, when it was visited by the first of several archaeological expeditions (the locals had always been aware of the ruins, so it was never truly "lost"). One of the largest and most important of the ancient Maya sites, the area of the city is estimated to be roughly 60 square kilometers (23 square miles) and may contain over 4,000 structures, the oldest of which date back to around 800 B.C. The most interesting features of the ruins are the central plazas, which have been unearthed and, in some places, restored. The tallest temple is Temple IV, which stands at an impressive 72 meters (230 feet) and towers above the surrounding rainforest (you may have seen it in the first *Star Wars* movie, where it was featured as the exterior of the rebel base).

Tikal is also known for its impressive *stelae*, or intricately carved standing stones. There are over 200 of them at the site, the oldest of which has been tentatively dated to 292 B.C. There is a museum which features ceramics, jade and wood carvings and other artifacts discovered at the site.

An advantage for the traveler is the natural surroundings. The archaeological site at Tikal is only part of a large national park which is home to spider and howler monkeys, parrots, toucans, macaws, and other varied and spectacular wildlife. In fact, it is the only place on earth declared by UNESCO to be both a world culture and nature heritage site.

The stern Gods of the Maya did look with favor on Hasaw Chan K'awil and his new temple: they blessed the city with 200 years of prosperity, a time which saw great accomplishments and the construction of magnificent pyramids. But what the Gods give, they can take away. Around 900 A.D., the stones of Tikal fell eerily silent. The city vanished into the immortal rainforest and the inhabitants scattered like leaves in the wind. The unexplained fall of the Maya is one of the great mysteries of our age. Perhaps it was disease, or strife, or angry Gods. The ageless jungle will never tell.

## TOP LIST: BEST RUINS

Latin America is full of ruins ... but which ones are the most fascinating? Here's what our readers had to say:

1. Machu Picchu, Peru (p. 285).
"The best ancient ruins of the Incas, beautiful landscape as well." Sandra Delgado, Peru.
"What is there to say? Beyond words." Mark Mellander, California, U.S.A.

2. Palenque, Mexico (p. 133).
"Absolutely gorgeous, fascinating." Cynthia Winn, California, U.S.A.
"Incredible jungle surrounded by pyramids," Mark Mellander, California, U.S.A.

3. Chichén Itzá, Mexico.
Teresa Colomer, Spain.

4. Uxmal, Mexico (p. 136).
"Incredible." Mark Mellander, California, U.S.A.

5. Tikal, Guatemala (p. 163).
"Otherworldly." Dirk O'Sullivan, Belfast, Ireland.

6. Tulum, Mexico.
"Almost 20 years ago, it was an incredible setting, jungle, pyramids, Caribbean. I've heard development has ruined it though." Mark Mellander, California, U.S.A.

Runners up: Cusco, Peru, "Beautiful colonial and Inca city, beautiful nature, colonial houses and rich churches, interesting cultural and nightlife." Sandra Delgado, Peru. El Morro, San Juan, Puerto Rico. "This is the fort that surrounds the island of San Juan, Puerto Rico. It was built by the Spanish to ward of enemy attacks. It's beautiful." Susana, Puerto Rico. Kuelap, Chachapoyas, Peru. "Very few visitors, fantastic architecture, less developed than Machu Picchu." Cynthia Winn, California, U.S.A.

# BELIZE

**More than just a tax shelter.**

If it weren't for its famous barrier reef and its status as a tax shelter, Belize might still be an esoteric footnote in Central America, tucked away in the region's lush, green northeastern corner. But SCUBA divers can sniff out a good dive spot like a hungry dog can find a hidden pork chop: it's an instinct, and divers found Belize in the 1980s.

The divers were followed by the deep-sea fishermen, who were followed by the beach bums, who were followed by the birdwatchers and the cavers. Today, if you're not a SCUBA-certified, sea fishing birdwatcher when you go to Belize, you may well be when you leave. Belize isn't simply a place to do all these things: it's a place to do them in style.

Belize is the Central American country that isn't: it may share a border with Guatemala and Mexico, but it doesn't share much else: its citizens speak English, not Spanish, and are mostly descended from African slaves brought in by the British in the 1700s to work in the timber industry. The people of Belize give their land a distinctive Caribbean atmosphere.

For such a tiny country, Belize is packed with things to see and to. Belize's islands (or "cayes") are the best place to visit if you want to SCUBA dive, the birdwatching is first-rate, and in the Crooked Tree Wildlife Sanctuary and there are Mayan ruins scattered throughout, the most notable of which are Altún Ha and Caracol. But you don't have to be a snorkeling, deep-sea fishing birdwatcher to appreciate Belize: there's something here for everyone.

# CARACOL

By Matthew Kadey, Toronto, Canada

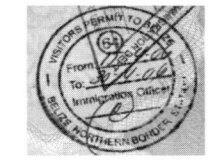

Mexico may have the major Mayan sites of Palenque and Chichén Itzá, Guatemala may be home to the mighty Tikal, and Copán, with its magnificent hieroglyphic stairway may hide out in the thick jungles of northern Honduras, but it is tiny Belize that has the highest concentration of Mayan ruins in the world.

With over 600 sites identified, there's no shortage of opportunities for the traveller to ramble among these timeless archaeological sites. Deep within the lush green jungles of Chiquibul Forest Reserve, lays Belize's most impressive ancient Mayan city—Caracol. The ruins are not nearly as well excavated as other well-known Central American Mayan sites, which is a good thing: Caracol has not lost its rugged charm. Chichén Itzá is for new-age mystics, Tikal is where they make ads for Nike and Tulum is for day-tripping college spring breakers out of Cancún; Caracol has been set aside for true lovers of ancient Mayan culture.

Located on the western edge of the Maya mountains in southern Belize, amid a tangle of thick forest, Caracol remained hidden from modern eyes until 1938 when a logger named Rosa Mai stumbled upon this marvellous wonder. That same year, A.H. Anderson (an archaeological commissioner) visited the site and promptly named it "Caracol" which means "snail" in Spanish, due to the large number of snail shells found at the site. Recent research suggests that the true name of the ancient Maya city was "Oxwitza."

Caracol was a major Mayan city with five plazas, thirty-two large stone structures, five courtyard groups and two causeways. Excavations are currently being conducted by archaeologists from the University of Central Florida, led by Arlen and Diane Chase. One of the perks that comes with a visit to Caracol is the ability to stand over the shoulders of archaeologists as they dig away. So much work is being conducted here that new monuments and carvings are discovered weekly. Currently the ruins cover a total of 30 square miles and once fully excavated they may outsize the mighty Tikal to the west in Guatemala.

Caracol was settled around 300 BC, and occupied well into the Late Classic period of the Mayan empire. At its peak of political power, this mighty city covered an astonishing 100 square kilometers, and supported a population of more than 100,000. Recent evidence indicates that Caracol may have even defeated Tikal in the mid-sixth century.

It's hard to believe Caracol remained hidden for over 1,000 years, considering the towering structure of Caana. The largest pyramid of Caracol Caana, or "Sky Palace," stands around 140 feet high, and is in fact the tallest man-made structure in the whole country. From the top of the pyramid, visitors get the most spectacular view of Caracol and its surrounding jungle and mountain ridges. Birdwatching is top notch as you can expect to see toucans and flocks of brilliant green parrots flying overhead.

Matthew Kadey is a Toronto based freelance writer, photographer and registered dietitian. He has traveled extensively on his bicycle to various global destinations including New Zealand, Belize, Ethiopia, Ireland and Hawaii. He has enjoyed a traditional coffee ceremony in rural Ethiopia and hung out with naked hippies in the Kalalau Valley in Kauai, Hawaii. His travel plans will soon take him to Jordan and Syria, and he hopes to someday visit Bhutan. He never goes anywhere without his camera.

Ruins of Caracol. Photo by Matthew Kadey.

# ACTUN TUNICHIL MUKNAL

By Matthew Kadey, Toronto, Canada

The tiny Central American-Caribbean nation of Belize is a caver's delight: miles and miles of underground tunnels and caverns to explore. Actun Tunichil Muknal, one of Belize's most spectacular caves, was featured in the 1993 National Geographic Explorer film *Journey through the Underworld*: its name means "Cave of the Crystal Sepulchre."

To get to the cave entrance, visitors are first required to hike for forty-five minutes through beautiful but dense jungle: there are three tricky river crossings thrown in for good measure. Access to the cave is gained by a short, refreshing swim through a small blue pool, after which hard hats and lights are needed to negotiate the cave system. It is also possible to repel into this underground labyrinth. Actun Tunichil Muknal is a registered archaeological site and only specially trained guides are allowed to lead groups into the cave—there are no do-it-yourself possibilities here. Besides, entering this dark maze on your own would be suicidal.

Actun Tunichil Muknal was re-discovered in 1986 by archaeologist Thomas Miller. What he found was astonishingly well-preserved Mayan pottery and the skeletal remains of several humans, who appear to have been sacrificed. To date, a total of fourteen individual skeletons have been identified. The most remarkable aspect of this cave tour is that most of these Mayan artefacts are still in place for visitors to enjoy. In fact, visitors are allowed to get so close to these pieces that guides have to be very strict about where people can walk. Although some parts of the cave have been looted, the entrance to the main chamber is not obvious and was left untouched throughout the centuries. Fear of spirits also keeps some would-be looters at bay.

After wading through knee- or even chest-deep water, negotiating small crevices and carefully scrambling up ladders, the tour culminates in the dramatic site of the preserved skeleton of a 20-year-old Mayan woman, "The Crystal Maiden," lying below a rock wall. Archaeologists and historians believe that the girl was sacrificed to the gods.

*"Well, I learned a lot ... I went down to Latin America to find out from them and (learn) their views. You'd be surprised. They're all individual countries."*
-Ronald Reagan, former US President (1911-2004)

## LATIN AMERICAN MYSTERIES #10 : WHAT HAPPENED TO THE MAYA?

Mexico, Guatemala, Belize and Honduras: 800-950 A.D.

The Maya were a civilization of warriors, astronomers, priests and kings, and they ruled northern Central America and southern Mexico 1,000 years before the arrival of the Europeans. But their civilization collapsed and by the time the Spanish arrived in the 1500s, the descendents of this mighty empire were divided into relatively weak city-states that were easy to divide and conquer. The great Mayan cities—Tikal, Palenque, Caracol, Copán—were all lost in the ageless jungle, buried under tons of earth and vegetation.

The Maya carved their history into the solid rock of their cities, creating whole texts in stone, glyphs that have weathered the centuries. Starting about 200 A.D., the stones tell of great kings, mighty cities, wars and alliances. The stones fall silent, however, as one by one the great Mayan cities were abandoned, their inhabitants vanishing into the jungle mists. The last recorded date at the city of Copán is 805 A.D. In 850, Quirigua fell silent. Tikal followed in 869, and Caracol in 889.

Historians have several theories to explain the mysterious demise of this once-mighty culture. Many believe the Maya were the victims of their own success: they say the population outgrew its capacity to produce food, and massive starvation and famines brought about the decline of the empire. Others believe that a severe drought overwhelmed their irrigation systems. A more recent theory that is increasing in popularity is that of civil war. Once believed to be a very peaceful society, evidence is mounting that the Maya actually warred amongst themselves quite often.

The answer may yet be in the timeless rock of the Mayan cities. The Mayan glyphs were unintelligible for ages, but recently, historians and linguists have made significant headway into deciphering them. Perhaps eventually the stones will be able to tell us what happened to those who made them.

# CAHAL PECH

By Melynda Coble, Livingston, Montana, U.S.A.

Sprawled across the top of a hill near San Ignacio, in the Cayo District, is the crumbling Mayan ceremonial center of *Cahal Pech*, which translates to "Place of the Ticks." Its name reflects its history: it was named in the 1950s when archaeological digs were just beginning in the region and the area was a pasture.

From San Ignacio it is a 15 to 20 minute walk uphill to the ruins. The visitors' center plays an entertaining and educational video about the excavation of Cahal Pech and the lifestyle of the ancient Maya. Also in the visitors' center are Mayan artifacts and models of what the center looked like in its heyday.

Immediately outside the visitors' center, Cahal Pech stretches across the landscape with well-manicured lawns, plants in shades of pinks, yellows and every type of green imaginable. Geckos dart up and down large leaved bromeliads and birds chirp and sing in the trees. Pyramid temples, ball courts, palaces, and carved *stelae* (monuments) show evidence of some of the earliest Mayan settlements in Belize.

Most likely, these sprawling structures and their inhabitants arrived 3,000 to 3,200 years ago, with continued occupation running through the Classic period. Around 1,200 years ago, the center was depopulated—earlier than other centers in Belize—but nobody knows why. Excavation of the site began in the 1950s, but there are still large mounds yet to be uncovered. Observing these sections in passing, it's interesting to try and imagine what still lies buried under the ever-growing jungle.

Unfortunately, in the 1970s and 80s the site suffered from chronic plundering, and while some looters were caught and prosecuted, many were not. In 1988, archaeological work resumed at the site, ending the pilfering.

Walking around the quiet grounds, it's easy to imagine rituals and ceremonies taking place here. The average Mayan probably lived nearby in a thatch-roofed hut in the jungle, traveling to Cahal Pech for community occasions.

There are several caves upriver where archaeologists have found evidence of important rituals including the remains of corn, cacao and *anato* seeds. Skeletal remains of infants and adults indicate human sacrifices, probably to the gods of rain and agriculture. Mosses cover some of the stone, making for a slippery walk in sections, and ferns sprout from old walls.

Compared to nearby Tikal, few people visit these ruins, so visitors often have the place to themselves, free to duck through short archways and peer into sleeping centers in relative solitude. Fortunately, ticks are not a problem for the tourist at Cahal Pech and quiet time to explore and reflect on the past is guaranteed.

Melynda Coble is a freelance writer and naturalist guide based in Livingston, Montana, U.S.A. She's used her B.S. in Natural Resource Interpretation from Humboldt State University and M.S. in Environmental Studies from the University of Oregon to explore her world and make (somewhat of) a living doing it. An experienced traveler, she nevertheless feels that her language skills need some work: "Once, I ended up in a nightclub in Spain when I thought we were going to church—I've got to work on my Spanish …" When not traveling, Coble can be found skiing, hiking, backpacking or turning over rocks in the Yellowstone River with her very cute dog, Rigby.

> **FACTOID:**
>
> Bromeliads—family Bromeliaceae—are a large family of flowering plants, including many epiphytes, which are plants that live "in the air" on top of other plants or structures. The most famous member of the Bromeliaceae family is probably the pineapple.

Cahal Pech. Photo by Melynda Coble.

# XUNANTUNICH

By Melynda Coble,
Livingston, Montana, U.S.A.

Elaborate ornaments decorate the sun god's large ears. Pondering eternity, he sits next to the symbol of the moon on El Castillo's frieze. Adorning the west and east sides of the 130-foot tall pyramid, the astrologically themed friezes draw the visitor closer and closer to the highlight of Xunantunich.

Xunantunich was the first Mayan site in Belize to be opened to the public. Relatively small in comparison to other Maya sites, it nevertheless contains one of the highest Mayan structures in Belize—El Castillo. From atop this limestone behemoth, breathtaking views span in every direction: the Belize River Valley, and the Cayo District. Guatemala unfolds on the horizon and the rest of Xunantunich spreads out below.

The site's name means either "Maiden of the Rock" or "Stone Woman," depending on who interprets the Yucatec dialect. Either name stems from an image of a woman depicted on one of the friezes.

In the late 1800s, the infamous Thomas Gann began "excavating" Xunantunich. In reality, he was digging up artefacts which are, sadly, all now lost along with his recorded history. Successive excavations were just as dodgy, with important Mayan artefacts disappearing and dynamite being used to not-so-delicately blast open the structures. In the 1990s a concerted and detailed—and vastly more careful—excavation began.

Archaeologists uncovered eight stelae (monuments) and two altars. Stelae are normally carved, but most of the ones found at Xunantunich are smooth and plain. It may be that they were once covered with painted or incised plaster that has since worn away.

Three main sections comprise the site: the ceremonial center and elite residences, the middle class residences, and the ball court complex where the Maya played a rather vicious game: losers were put to death. More than 25 palaces and temples surround Xunantunich's six major plazas.

And, of course, there is El Castillo looming over the southern end of the complex. The partially excavated pyramid was at one point filled in and built on top of in typical Maya fashion. The friezes have been restored and covered in plaster, both to protect the original work and to clearly display it for the visitor. In addition to the carvings of gods and astrological symbols is a beheaded man, which archaeologists are at a loss to explain. Perhaps his team didn't fare so well on the notorious Mayan ball courts.

www.vivatravelguides.com/104284

# MASEWAL FOREST GARDEN

By Melynda Coble,
Livingston, Montana, U.S.A.

In the days of the Maya, the jungle forests of Belize and Guatemala were more densely populated than they are today. But somehow, this ancient race was able to sustain itself in a way that present populations can not.

To facilitate sustainable development in these verdant, vine-choked lands, an education project began, based around El Pilar—a major Mayan city in the Central Mayan Lowlands. On this section of land straddling Belize and Guatemala, academics and locals toiled side by side to create the Mayan Forest Gardens. A cousin of the precedent-setting Forest Garden Program (developed by Earth Voice and Counterpart International), this project facilitates sustainable development of agricultural and forest lands in traditional Mayan communities.

One such forest garden is owned by Don Berto Cocom in Bullet Tree Falls, Belize. Endearingly referred to as "The Old Man" by locals, Don Berto once cleared his land of native vegetation and planted palm trees in its place. He soon found himself begging his neighbors for the native plants that he depended on, both for food and medicine.

Then, 35 years ago, Don Berto replanted half his land with native plants. Like the ancient forest gardens of the Maya, his network of vegetation is designed around an open canopy that allows light to filter through to the plants and trees below.

Today, Don Berto's Masewal Forest Garden and Medicine Trail is open to the public. The Old Man himself leads visitors along a trail that winds through thick secondary forests and open vistas, stopping at almost every plant to explain its ancient and current medicinal uses. The loop trail passes through an old Mayan quarry and several unexcavated Mayan mounds. Don Berto has found many arrowheads on his property which he has collected and displayed under the thatched roof of his chair-making workshop.

As it is with forests in Central America, there are many, many mosquitoes. Fortunately, the leaves of a particular tree can be squished up and rubbed on a bite to relieve the itching. Perhaps as a joke to himself, Don Berto keeps the identity of this tree a secret until the end of the hour long walk.

A testament to progress in the name of sustainable development, Don Berto finds more use for his forest garden than he did for the palm tree plantation. To spread the word and sow these precious seeds of knowledge elsewhere, he teaches local school children, so that they too can remember the ways of their ancestors.

With people like Don Berto and projects like the Mayan Forest Gardens, maybe one day the area will sustainably support a large population as it did during ancient Mayan times.

# LEARNING TO DIVE IN SAN PEDRO, AMBERGRIS CAYE

By Josey Miller, Chicago, Illinois, U.S.A.

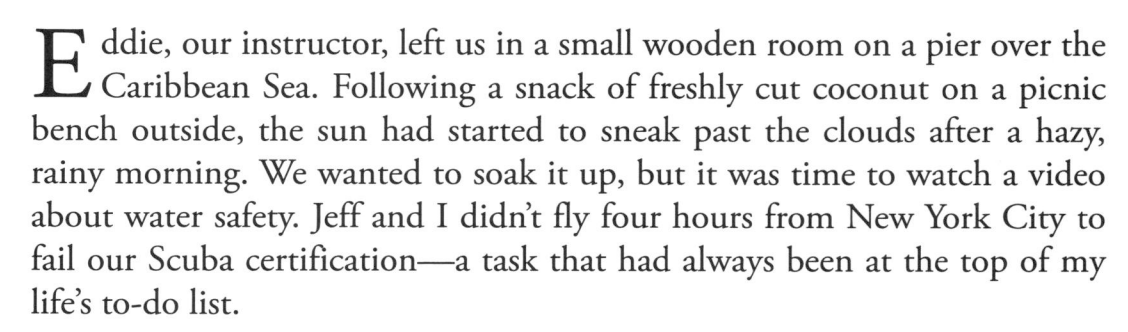

Eddie, our instructor, left us in a small wooden room on a pier over the Caribbean Sea. Following a snack of freshly cut coconut on a picnic bench outside, the sun had started to sneak past the clouds after a hazy, rainy morning. We wanted to soak it up, but it was time to watch a video about water safety. Jeff and I didn't fly four hours from New York City to fail our Scuba certification—a task that had always been at the top of my life's to-do list.

The reefs in Belize are listed as some of the most impressive in the world, and if we were going to do it, we might as well do it right. So we booked a one-bedroom kitchenette at The Palms, and I played (more than) twenty questions with Ana at the front desk before we left; I'd simply never encountered an oceanfront view for under $140 and in my experience things that sound too good to be true usually are. But she was patient, courteous and remarkably enthusiastic—and all of her answers were right on target. My most important question: is there a blender in the room? After all, we'd heard the nightlife in San Pedro on Ambergris Caye left a lot to be desired; the tourists who go there are for the most part hard-core divers who turn in early to wake up with the sun. Jeff and I, on the other hand, were novice divers who refused to forget that this was our vacation, after all.

The puddle jumper from mainland Belize to San Pedro provided beautiful views, not to mention a touch of nausea. But it was only 15 minutes long, and we were able to walk right over to our hotel from the airport; San Pedro is that small. Our Scuba certification course began the following morning bright and early. Over a period of just three and a half days, the course included classroom instruction, confined water practice sessions, and open water sessions —all for just $350.

After learning the necessary buddy signals and basics, such as how to react in emergency situations, we explored the Turneffe Atoll and Hol Chan Marine Reserve. At Hol Chan we actually fed and petted sharks (I wouldn't believe me either, but there are pictures to prove it), and on our way back to shore, dolphins cavorted alongside our boat. Every day after we finished our lessons, Eddie sent us over to Cholo's—the local watering hole where he's a regular for the simple and perfectly understandable reason that, "They serve their beer the coldest." We enjoyed a few bottles of Belikin, the local brew—both there and at Fido's, our preferred lunch spot for rice, beans and "stew chicken" in an atmosphere Jimmy Buffett would write songs about.

After a few hours in the ocean, we were happily drained and ready to be lazy and absorb the unforgettable experience that was Ambergris Caye. Cold beer and hot sand aside, our very favorite "You Better Belize It," memories came from about 60 feet below sea level.

Josey Miller hails from Chicago, Illinois, and currently lives with her fiancé, Jeff, and her cat, Brady, in the West Village of New York City. A graduate of the University of Illinois at Urbana-Champaign, with a major in broadcast journalism, Miller now spearheads the Love & Sex channel of iVillage.com. She is also a singer-songwriter who performs at various venues around Greenwich Village.

Miller is a self-proclaimed "travel nerd" who composes overly meticulous itineraries before every trip and maintains a spreadsheet of dream destinations, including the Galapagos Islands, Moscow, Shanghai, Egypt, Cuba—and practically everywhere in between. She always packs band-aids when she travels. "Not only am I accident-prone, but I like to do a ton of walking when I travel. Plus, they can be used in place of adhesive tape, which comes in handy—and saves space when packing. Multi-purpose!"

## SAN PEDRO: ISLA BONITA By Leigh Gower

"Tropical the island breeze, all of nature wild and free, this is where I long to be, La Isla Bonita." So sang Madonna about San Pedro, principal city of Ambergis Caye, the 25-mile-long island that runs parallel to Belize's own barrier reef. Although she reportedly never visited the island herself, the famed singer certainly captured its essence with her fluid voice and tropical, lazy melody.

The relaxed pace of the island is infectious; golf carts are a primary form of transport here (although the entire length of the island can be walked in 15 minutes) and a popular island phrase is "no shoes, no shirt, no problem."

Ambergris is a limestone coral island that held a thriving Mayan coastal trade centre over a millennia ago. Today its tourist population is abundant and each year the island plays host to San Pedro's International Costa Maya Festival, the only festival of its kind in Central America. With music, food, dancing, parades and a beauty queen contest, the August extravaganza has become a lively occasion, attracting hundreds of excited punters annually.

Recently, however, the island has begun facing problems regarding the preservation of its reef, and the U.N. has been asked to step in and help protect it. According to scientists, the polyp organism that helps build coral reefs— which, in turn, protect beach front properties from hurricanes—are being threatened by global warming. This also bleaches the reefs, which detracts from their natural beauty and the scuba diving, its primary tourist attraction. Preserving this natural sanctuary will prove vital to San Pedro's tourist industry and to the livelihood of the locals.

# SWALLOW CAYE WILDLIFE SANCTUARY

By Melynda Coble, Livingston, Montana, U.S.A.

As Chocolate poles his boat through the water around Swallow Caye, a doughy manatee nose suddenly pokes through the water next to the boat. These are the creatures that sailors once mistook for mermaids? They're cute, but hardly sexy.

Lionel "Chocolate" Heredia has been guiding manatee tours since 1968, but his enthusiasm for these animals hasn't diminished in the least. Belize is the last stronghold of the Antillean manatee in the Caribbean, thanks in part to Chocolate.

The Swallow Caye Wildlife Sanctuary was established in July of 2002 after many years of tireless work by Chocolate and the Friends of Swallow Caye. They are, in fact, cited on Belize's Endangered Species Act. But, the sanctuary alone can't always protect these cuddly (albeit wet) creatures. Chocolate has had to put up his own signs in the water that read "Go Slow" and "Protect my home" under hand-painted cutouts of the inoffensive beasts.

A manatee tour with Chocolate is a must-do for anyone staying in Caye Caulker. He is mentioned in every guidebook and extolled by everyone who has visited the island. But despite all the hype, the tour is worth it.

From Caye Caulker, Chocolate heads the boat towards Goff's Caye 37 miles to the south. At Swallow Caye he turns off the engine and pulls out the pole. (Poles are used to maneuver the boats as engines can maim the manatees.) He and his co-captain slowly pole the little motor boat around the coves and mangrove islands in search of manatees. Some of the "islands" are actually floating pods of red mangroves which can filter the saltwater for nutrients. The manatees swim through the roots of the mangroves to access a lagoon in the middle of the island.

While looking for manatees, dolphins are often spotted, as are cormorants, white ibises and sea gulls. But it is the manatees that Chocolate wants to appear. And suddenly they do, their pudgy faces popping up and bobbing for air on the water's surface.

After floating around the manatee habitat for an hour or two, Chocolate heads the boat to Sergeants Caye for snorkeling, but it's obvious that the best part of the day is over for both Chocolate and the manatees.

---

**MERMAID FACTOID:**

The myth of the mermaid is a common one. Cultures as diverse as the Greeks, Irish and Chinese have versions of the mermaid legends. In some legends, mermaids are said to have magical powers, such as the ability to foresee the future, or the ability to lure men to their doom in the depths of the sea. Many historians believe that the tales told by early Europeans sailing in American waters of mermaids were, in fact, the result of half-glimpsed manatees.

---

## DIVING THE BLUE HOLE

By Degan Beley

If you are in Belize and you are a SCUBA diver—or even if you are somewhere on the Caribbean coast of Central America and have ever had a hankering to know what is down there below the water, then the world-famous Blue Hole should not be missed.

At 480 feet deep and 1,000 feet wide it is the world's largest underwater sinkhole and a diver's dream. A network of caves and crevices appointed with a variety of stalactites and stalagmites unfolds beneath the sapphire waters, home to resident sharks and groupers. The exact depth of the sinkhole was unknown until the early 1970s when Jacques Cousteau brought his research vessel, Calypso, and a one-man submarine to explore the cave system. Due to its unique geological history and location it was declared a UNESCO World Heritage Site and Natural Monument in 1997.

Now, during the high season, dozens of dive boats pass through the reef daily to get to the Blue Hole. It doesn't get crowded, however: the Blue Hole is 1,000 feet across so there is plenty of room for everyone. Recreational divers are only allowed to go to 130 feet and if you're daring enough (and experienced enough) to go to the bottom, it's recommended that you only stay eight minutes or so. You have to be SCUBA certified, but you can get certified by one of the fine dive shops in Ambergris Caye (or surrounds), and head out to the Blue Hole directly afterwards. All you need is a little courage, and some good buoyancy control, and the highly skilled dive masters will make sure you don't stray too far.

You can choose a full day trip that combines two dives at Lighthouse Reef, as well as a side trip and lunch on Half Moon Caye, where there is a red-footed booby colony. From the water the Caye looks like paradise, but the park rangers have clearly made some kind of deal with the mosquitoes, so be prepared to dodge the little buggers as you scamper from the shore through the forest, leaping over colourful crabs, to get to the booby nesting colony.

# TOBACCO CAYE

By Rona Gilbert, Bowling Green, Ohio, U.S.A.

Forty minutes by boat, but seemingly a world away from mainland Belize, a string of small cayes stretches across the tranquil blue depths of the Caribbean. Located about 20 kilometers east of Dangriga, tiny Tobacco Caye is a Robinson Crusoe paradise with a relaxed island vibe where the pace of life slows to a leisurely crawl and visitors drift off to sleep each night to the soothing sounds of waves crashing over the nearby reef.

Just a stone's throw from the longest barrier reef in the Americas, Tobacco Caye is a world-class diving and snorkeling spot. Trips to the nearby atolls (Belize has three of only four coral atolls in the Caribbean) are easily arranged, or you can explore the underwater world by simply swimming out from shore for a peek at colorful coral, tropical fish, giant manta rays, barracudas and even manatees. A tiny lagoon, formed in part by the ravaging wind and rain of Hurricane Mitch (1998), lies on the southern edge of the island offering calm water and is the perfect setting for swimming and snorkeling.

Getting to Tobacco Caye is part of the adventure and while boats leave daily from Dangriga, there are no regularly scheduled departures. (If the boats near the bridge appear unattended, simply pop into the friendly River Café and inquire about the next departure. A little patience is required as the boat skippers usually wait until they have a minimum of four passengers before heading out. If you have to wait, you're best to just relax, grab a cold Belikin beer ("The Beer of Belize") and a snack while you wait. Visitors can also inquire about boat transfers when making hotel reservations, as many hotel owners offer transportation to their guests for a fee.

The deserted isle experience begins with the enjoyable boat ride gliding over the clear bluish green waters; be prepared to leave civilization behind, except perhaps for the occasional lone fisherman. The isolated feeling really settles in as the boat slows to approach the five-acre island, ringed with sandy beaches, palm trees and a smattering of wooden waterfront cabañas.

Originally a trading post for passing ships to pick up tobacco and other supplies, the tiny island is today a popular spot for local fisherman who stop here for a cold drink and to recharge their cell phone batteries. Drop by Mark's Bar and you'll probably find them milling about before pushing off to sea once again. The official gathering spot on the island, everyone eventually makes their way to Mark's to enjoy inexpensive drinks, Caribbean music and to mingle with the international mix of guests.

Simple and rustic, Tobacco Caye's comfortable family-run accommodations add to the island's charm and enhance the exotic island experience. All rooms are near the water, many offer postcard-perfect views and some come with hammocks swaying lazily above the reef.

There are no shops or tourist services (except Mark's) so most hotels include delicious home-cooked meals in the price.

Tobacco Caye is not suited for those seeking a luxury resort experience, but is the perfect place if you want to slip away from civilization, and slide into the natural rhythms of island-time.

---

TOBACCO CAYE TRAVEL TIP:

While less expensive accommodation can be found elsewhere in Belize, Tobacco Caye is inexpensive compared to most of the Caribbean, especially given the beauty of the island and the access to the reef.

---

## BELIZE'S BABOON SANCTUARY

By Leigh Gower

Counting approximately 12,980 acres, the Community Baboon Sanctuary 48 kilometres west of Belize City is the place to go to see one of the few remaining black howler monkey populations in Central America. Home to nearly 2,000 Black Howler monkeys and 200 bird species, among other animals, the sanctuary is a completely volunteer, grassroots conservation program that is entirely dependant upon the work of local farmers and private landowners for survival. Set up along 33 kilometres of the Belize River, the area straddles farmland and forest, through which trails have been carved so that visitors may enjoy the scenery at its best.

The Baboon Sanctuary has four goals: conservation, education, research, and tourism and relies on funding from the World Wildlife Fund. As a result of this, the reserve has been able to assemble a small natural history museum and a visitor center. Black Howlers, known in English as baboons and in Spanish as saraguates, are renowned for their deep, raspy hollering which can sometimes be heard from over a mile away, and help to mark their territory. If you visit on a Sunday you might find yourself navigating the reserve paths alone—this is not advised.

# PLACENCIA

By Martha Simmons, Stockton, Alabama, U.S.A.

Placencia—the long, narrow finger of sand pointing languidly to the southern tip of Belize—offers visitors a thoroughly laid-back experience that can be tailored to almost any age group or style of tourism.

A native of the Gulf Coast of Alabama, U.S.A, Martha Simmons began her writing and photography career in the 1970s for daily newspapers, and has freelanced for national and international newspapers and magazines. Martha is a graduate of the University of South Alabama in Mobile. She now serves as Community Projects Director for the Mobile County District Attorney's Office.

Her most bizarre travel experience? "Definitely, drinking beer with a pig and a Saint Bernard dog at a dirt-floor bar in Evansville, Indiana." She and her husband Doug would like to return to Placencia soon and hope to spend their retirement in Belize.

Placencia glides, rather than bustles, even in the high season. Unlike San Pedro, which has a decidedly Latin lilt and is energetically chock-a-block with people and made-for-tourists businesses, Placencia's people and food are largely Creole or Garífuna, the town has a genuine heartbeat of its own, and the pace is placid.

Visitors may opt for active days spent touring inland Maya ruins and villages, or diving and snorkeling on the coast off nearby cayes (pronounced "keys"), or fishing for tarpon or snook. More relaxing pastimes include sunbathing on the region's gorgeous sandy beaches, taking a boat tour of the Monkey River (where you can expect to see a good deal of wildlife), or grilling fresh lobster for an island picnic. For shopaholics, Placencia offers a few souvenir shops as well as the chance to buy handmade crafts directly from the descendents of ancient Maya, who sell baskets and carvings, necklaces and needlework along the sidewalks and beaches, pulling their goods from backpacks and displaying them on the sand.

Luxury may be had in the moderate- to high-priced resorts on the outskirts of town where one might lounge in lavishly appointed thatched-roof cabanas and see the occasional movie star, or take in breathtaking flora nurtured in a resort's lush tropical garden.

But for the budget-minded—and for tourists wishing to experience the "real" Belize and meet native Belizeans—Placencia Village is the place to hang out. Generous portions of alcohol as well as food and cheap prices make this community a great place for living it up without breaking the bank. The tap water is drinkable. Internet is available. Families, Baby Boomers, hikers, adventure travelers, rich and poor alike mix and mingle peaceably while soaking up the area's sights and sounds.

Bars, restaurants, tour agencies, hotels, cottages, and private residences (as well as the primary school, post office and library) dot both sides of the mile-long sidewalk once listed in the *Guinness Book of World Records* as the "world's narrowest street." Visitors can plunge into village life just by chatting with friendly townspeople, shopping for potent, bargain-priced Belizean rum or homemade snacks at the local grocery, getting ice at the fishing co-op at the docks, watching a game at the *fútbol* (soccer) field, or dancing in the sand with a local at the Sunday afternoon punta rock concert; the sense of community here is strong.

Throughout this charmingly ramshackle fishing village, a distinct Creole cadence dominates the voices and attitudes of the Belizeans who make this town their home. Tourists are welcome, but are well advised to leave impatience and perfectionism back at home. Better to get in step with the locals and slow the pace to match the gentle ebb and flow of the tides along both shores of this salty strip of land. When people in Placencia say, "No problem, mon!" they really mean it.

Hammock time, Placencia. Photo by Martha Simmons.

Parrot eating almond. Photo by Kevin Shank.

# HONDURAS

### Deep Waters

Honduras got its first tourist in 1502. His name—you might have heard of him—was Christopher Columbus, then on his fourth and final voyage to the New World. According to legend, it was Columbus who named the place Honduras, Spanish for "depths."

Back in Columbus' day, Honduras was what we'd call "off the tourist trail." Not anymore. Honduras packs a big punch for such a little country. Historically overlooked by travelers who tend to visit its northern neighbor, Guatemala, Honduras nevertheless has quite a bit to offer.

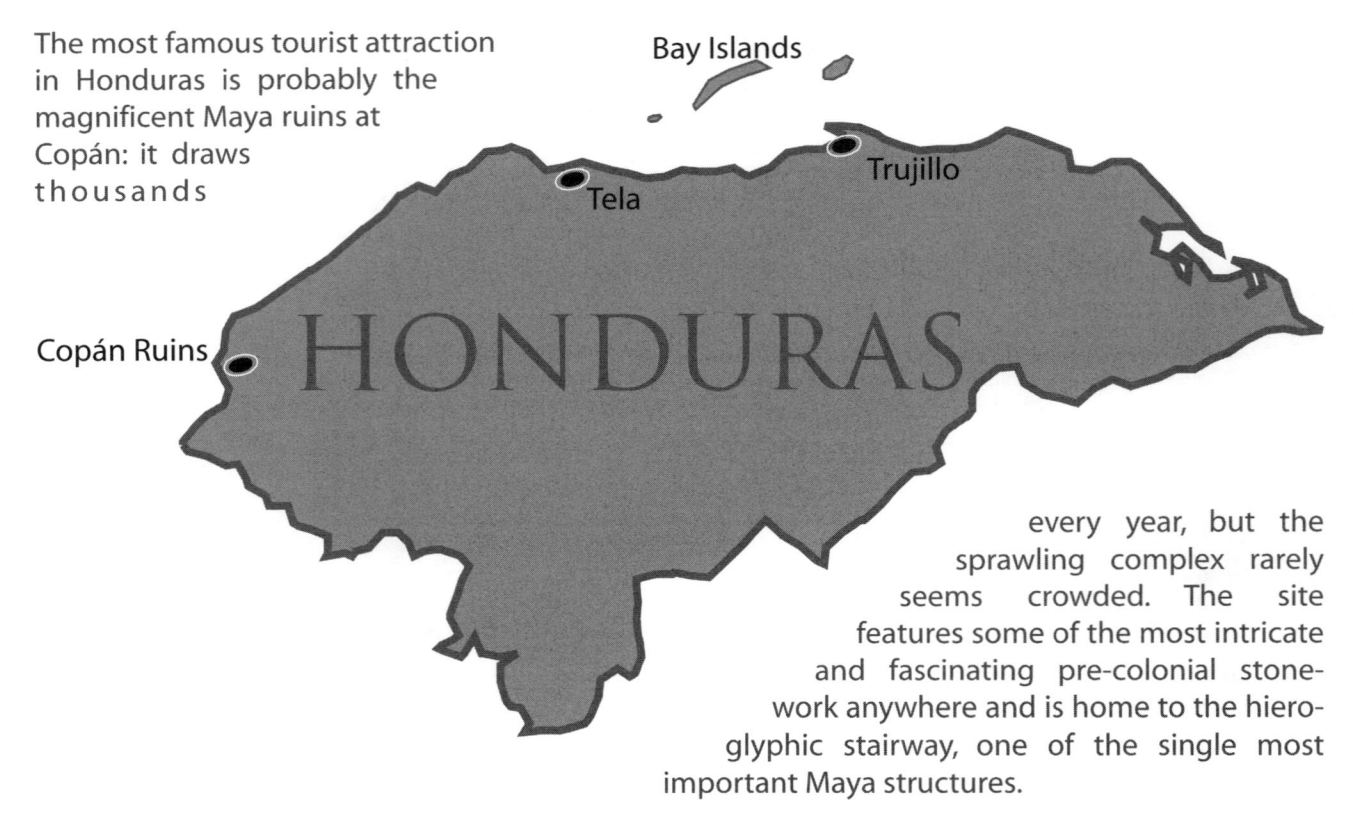

The most famous tourist attraction in Honduras is probably the magnificent Maya ruins at Copán: it draws thousands every year, but the sprawling complex rarely seems crowded. The site features some of the most intricate and fascinating pre-colonial stonework anywhere and is home to the hieroglyphic stairway, one of the single most important Maya structures.

A close second to Copán is the Bay Islands, laid-back havens of swaying trees, cold beer, hammocks…and some of the BEST scuba diving this side of Belize. Join our writers, as they take you to the Bay islands and Copán, as well as the coastal city of Tela and to the most interesting cemetery in all of Honduras.

Columbus is gone, but you can still follow in his footsteps and visit this enchanting land and take a deep breath of the ancient Maya magic that still hangs over it like a wisp of cloud over a sunny beach.

# COPÁN RUINS

## By Dr. Crit Minster, Rochester, New York, U.S.A.

The 15th great warrior-king of the Mayan city-state of Copán, Smoke Shell, had brought his people back from despair. Seventeen years before, in 738 A.D., the neighboring city-state of Quiriguá had defeated his mighty predecessor, 18 Rabbit, in battle. Eighteen Rabbit himself was captured and executed, possibly even sacrificed, by Cuauc Sky, the lord of Quiriguá. During the intervening years, the city of Copán, the mighty southernmost outpost of the Maya lands, had languished in defeat, wondering why the gods had shown them such disfavor.

While kings came and went, the fertile Copán river valley remained occupied for over 3,000 years. The city itself is thought to have begun in the first or second century A.D. and it reached its peak around 400-800 A.D. Along with Tikal, Palenque, Quiriguá and others, this southernmost city was an important stronghold during the Mayan era. Despite initial despair, the reign of Smoke Shell gradually ushered in positive changes for the people of Copán: it was during this time that Smoke Shell and his people threw off the yoke of Quiriguá.

Inspired by his people's newfound prosperity, Smoke Shell decided to complete the grand architectural masterpiece that 18 Rabbit had begun decades before: the Hieroglyphic Stairway, a mighty temple carved out of hundreds of blocks of stones that were destined to withstand time. The hand-carved glyphs—stone symbols—depicted the entire dynasty of the Copán Kings from the dawn of time. Under the rule of Smoke Shell, the stairway grew. New steps were added, and a temple was built on top. The Gods were showing Copán favor once again.

But the favor of the Gods is fickle. Although the lords of Copán ruled for 50 more years, historical records after 805 A.D. fall eerily silent. No one knows why Copán was abandoned, but it didn't take long for the jungle to reclaim the mighty city. Within a generation, the city was lost, swallowed by the dense green rainforest of western Honduras. But like the inhabitants of Copán, the city itself refused to admit defeat: the city's stone structures are remarkably well-preserved.

Since its discovery there has been a great deal of archaeological interest in Copán. The hieroglyphic stairway is the city's centerpiece and one of the most fascinating ruin structures in all of Latin America. The stairway consists of a wide series of ascending steps, elaborately chiseled from massive rocks into skulls, faces and various designs. According to researchers, the stairway is a family tree of sorts, telling the story of the mighty lords of Copán. Tragically, the blocks had fallen out of place in the centuries that the city was lost, and no one knows where to put them any more. The stairway is easy to find: it is covered by a large tarp-like construction to protect it from further destruction at the hands of the elements.

Besides the stairway, the most important single piece of archaeological history found at the Copán site is known as "Altar Q." This relatively small piece depicts all 16 of the major rulers of Copán. Visitors are often drawn to the stelae, or tall, ornately carved standing stones, that can be found in the courtyard. Most of these structures were created during the prosperous reign of 18 Rabbit.

Eighteen Rabbit and Smoke Shell faded into the green jungle and the mists of time, their city deteriorating and falling to rubble, their people scattered. Archaeologists brought them back to life so that they can speak of their Gods and their lives once more.

Copán. Photo by Will Gray.

# TELA

## By Lorraine Caputo, Columbia, Missouri, U.S.A.

Powdery white sand beaches littered with shells. Crystalline blue sea. Verdant landscapes. Walks under the full moon, the warm Caribbean washing across bare feet. The rhythms of punta or reggae of cumbia or salsa pulsating through the night. Of course this is a tropical (near) paradise.

Tela is the most accessible of the attractive towns on the north coast of Honduras, and offers easy access to a number of cultural and natural wonders. The most alluring cultural offering is of the Garífuna ("Black Caribs"). The Garífuna are descendents of the local Arawak-Caribe culture and escaped African slaves. Their music, dance and language reflect this eclectic mix. Originally from St. Vincent Island, the British forcibly relocated them to the Bay Islands off the coast of modern-day Honduras in 1797. Later, they migrated to the mainland coast of Central America, and today can be found from Belize to northern Panama. Some of the most traditional (and most fascinating) Garífuna communities are in Honduras.

In Tela, the Museo Garífuna offers displays on their history, culture and traditions. The restaurant serves traditional cuisine.

To the east of Tela are the Garífuna villages La Ensenada and El Triunfo de la Cruz (the first Spanish settlement in Central America). To the west are Tornabé, San Juan, Río Tinto and Miami. These last two are difficult to get to; Miami is within the Parque Nacional Jeanette Kawas. Jeanette Kawas National Park includes Punta Sal whose many coves were once refuges for pirates. The Park consists of two parts. The peninsula, with white sand beaches, coral reef and jungle, is accessible only by sea (one hour by launch). Here dolphins, monkeys and migratory birds may be seen. Laguna de Micos, the other section, is home to over 350 species of birds. Agencies in Tela offer tours to the park.

Tela used to be the headquarters for the United Fruit Company (now Chiquita). Its imprint can still be seen on the city. New Tela was the residential area for the executives of the company, complete with private beach, fountains and a swimming pool. Today it is an up-scale hotel. Lancetilla Botanical Gardens was established by United Fruit in 1925. It is the second largest tropical research garden in the world and features not only local and regional species, but also those from Asia and other parts of the world.

Sometimes the train still chugs in from near Puerto Cortés and San Pedro Sula. If it is running, it is more direct and quicker than the bus. But no matter how one arrives to Tela, there is good music, incredible beaches, interesting history, fresh seafood, national parks—and a warm Garífuna welcome. This is about as close to a tropical paradise as it gets.

Sunset in Roatán. Photo by Kevin Shank.

# ROATÁN

By Dr. Crit Minster, Rochester, New York, U.S.A.

Outnumbered, outgunned and surrounded, Captain Henry Morgan naturally did what any gentleman pirate would do. He offered his opponent a chance to surrender.

Marcaibo, Venezuela, 1669.

Captain Morgan and his men had ruthlessly sacked the city and spent several weeks celebrating and drinking, but it was time to leave. Upon departure, Morgan discovered that the only exit from the harbor to the Caribbean was guarded by three Spanish war galleons and a heavily armed fort.

The Spanish Admiral, Don Alonso del Campo, scoffed at Morgan's offer of a chance to surrender and prepared for battle. Morgan sacrificed one of his ships by loading it with tar and gunpowder and turning it into the pirate equivalent of a car bomb, sending it into the Spanish blockade. The ship exploded, sinking two of the Spanish galleons and damaging the third: Morgan was able to capture it. As for the fort, he tricked them by faking a land assault, and when the defenders had turned their cannons landward, he simply sailed right past them and into the open sea.

Captain Morgan, the notorious pirate and privateer, had many bases in the Caribbean and off the Spanish Main. One of them was located on a small, sandy island off the coast of present-day Honduras: Roatán.

Today, Roatán is a tranquil island paradise and one of the premier scuba diving sites in the world. An easy flight from mainland Honduras, the island draws thousands of visitors every year to visit its sunny white sand beaches, dive resorts and laid-back small towns. Tourism is king on Roatán and the islanders are very friendly and helpful. One of the more affordable resort destinations in the Caribbean, Roatán has lodgings and services for all budget levels.

Scuba diving is probably what draws most visitors to Roatán. There are two good wrecks: El Aguila and the Prince Albert, both of which feature a lot of sea life and interesting formations. As an added bonus, not far from the Prince Albert is a submerged DC-3 airplane (don't worry, it was brought out on a barge and sunk there for divers to enjoy: it didn't crash). The most famous dive site is probably "Mary's Place," where some volcanic activity long ago caused the reef to crack and split, creating a maze of channels and tunnels, all of which are teeming with marine life. Or you can opt for the *cara a cara* (face to face) dive where specialist dive masters feed sharks for the enjoyment of visitors (don't tell your insurance carrier about this one!).

Roatán also offers a number of other water and beach sports and activities, such as deep-sea fishing, kayaking, sailing and lounging around on the beach. There is also a butterfly garden, an iguana farm, horseback riding and tours of nearby mangroves and rainforests.

Captain Morgan is long gone, but not forgotten. Locals still believe that he left a large hoard of pirate treasure hidden somewhere on the island. So if you go, look around for pieces of eight—but don't be disappointed if the treasure you bring home is fond memories and good photos.

## REEF MADNESS

By John Edwards

Called a "diver's paradise," Roatán is one of the cheapest places in the world to get certified as a scuba diver. Non-divers can explore reefs within swimming distance of the shore and enjoy pristine beaches undisturbed by anything but machete-wielding children selling coconuts, a handful of backpackers and laid-back Peace Corps volunteers on vacation.

Roatán's diving resorts cater to both beginners and pros. All the diving shops provide basic certification for as little as $150 for the four or five-day course. A "resort dive," usually $50, gets you a four-hour course culminating in a 30-foot (10 meter) dive. Certification, snorkeling and scuba rentals are available at a host of scuba shops in West End.

Anthony's Key Resort is considered by many to be the number-one dive resort in the world. It offers seven-night packages, including bungalow-style accommodation on its private key, meals and unlimited dives. Most independent divers stay in the budget paradise of West End, its main road lined with bungalows and guest houses.

Most West-Enders breakfast at Rudy's Coffee Stop, lunch at the Plantation (between West End and West Bay Beach), then dine at The Bite on the Beach. Local bands can be heard most nights playing reggae and country music. Nightlife ends early, allowing everyone another day of reef madness in paradise.

# THE GRAVE OF WILLIAM WALKER

## By Dr. Crit Minster, Rochester, New York, U.S.A.

William Walker was handed over by British forces to the Honduran army to be shot. The Hondurans wanted him dead because they feared he would take over their country. The British wanted him dead because they too were afraid he was going to take over their country: British Honduras (now modern-day Belize). He had a history of doing just that, you see.

If you take a look at a list of the former presidents of Nicaragua, you'll notice something interesting. In between the names of Patricio Rivas (1855-1856) and Tomás Martínez (1857-1867) is a distinctly un-Spanish sounding name: William Walker (1856-1857).

William Walker was born in 1824 in Nashville, Tennessee. A brilliant young man, he had a medical degree from the University of Pennsylvania by the age of nineteen. He also practiced law and spent some time in newspaper publishing. He did all this, of course, until he learned where his true gift lay: toppling governments.

While Walker was developing a knack for anarchy, the United States was expanding. After Texas successfully broke away from Mexico in 1836, Walker conceived the idea of leading other parts of Latin America into rebellion. The new government would be headed up by some of Walker's American cronies. This process—making war on a sovereign nation as a private venture—is called filibustering. Walker led his first filibustering expedition in 1853, at the age of 29. With 45 men, he captured La Paz, capital of Baja California. They managed to hold the city for three months, before Mexican forces drove them out. Back in the United States, he was tried in California on charges of starting an illegal war: the jury acquitted him in eight minutes.

His next venture was more successful. In 1855, he led 57 men to Nicaragua, which was in the midst of a nasty civil war. Together with forces from the rebel faction, Walker and his men defeated the Nicaraguan national army and within a month assumed control of the country. In 1856, he named himself president, and put out the call to mercenaries around the world: he intended to conquer the rest of Central America. In the United States, the Franklin Pierce administration recognized his government.

Despite a rather illustrious career in filibustering, things began to fall apart for Walker in 1857. Many of his men deserted or were wiped out by a cholera epidemic. Forces of other Central American nations, aided by agents working for the American tycoon Cornelius Vanderbilt (he disapproved of Walker's policies regarding trade across Nicaragua), forced Walker to withdraw, and he returned to New Orleans in May.

He was not about to leave the world stage without one final appearance, however. In 1860, he went to Honduras, where he was captured by the British. He was handed over to the Honduran authorities, and he was executed by firing squad on September 12. He was 36.

In the Honduran coastal town of Trujillo, the old cemetery is an overgrown maze of crumbling stones and weeds wilting in the tropical heat. The grave of William Walker can be found here, fenced off from the rest of the cemetery, as if the rulers of Central America fear that he might rise up from the dead and incite rebellion once again. If you're in the neighborhood, pay him a visit: love him or hate him, you have to admit that the ultimate Yankee imperialist had *cojones*.

## TOP MIND-BLOWING BURIAL GROUNDS, CEMETERIES, AND CATACOMBS

Some of the most interesting people in Latin America are no longer with us ... but that shouldn't keep you from a visit! Here are some of our reader-approved places to visit the dearly departed:

1. Chauchilla Cemetary, Nasca, Peru (p. 282). "This cemetery holds the mummified remains of ancient Nascans, dating back between 200 B.C. to 500 A.D. New mummified remains are being dug up in the desert all the time and it's not unusual to find a foot, skull or small bundle containing a mummified child at the surface, which wasn't there the day before." Carol Ann, Scotland.

2. The mummies, Guanajuato, Mexico. Monte Hensley, Abluquerque, NM.

3. Las Lajas Sanctuary, Las Lajas, Colombia. Angela Hamilton, Maxwell, CA, U.S.A.

Runners up:

Santa Clara, Cuba. "Ché Guevara is buried there, in a sort of shrine. There is a museum there." Des, U.K.

Recoleta (where Evita's tomb is). "Also home to José Hernández, famous writer, and many Argentine presidents." Jenny Jones, Ireland.

Monte Albán, Mexico. "The ruins were used by later cultures as a burial site. Tomb 7 is one of the most archaeologically important finds ever." Dr. Crit Minster, U.S.A.

Royal Tombs of Sipán, Peru. "The Lord of Sipán, as he is now known, is considered by some experts to be one of the greatest archaeological discoveries in the Americas." Laura Watilo Blake.

Sillustani, Peru. "The Colla entombed whole families with their riches in these aboveground structures known as chullpas which were usually made from mortar and small stones." Albert García.

Tomb of Pacal the Great, Palenque, Mexico. "Some believe that priests fed him sacrificial blood long after he died." Dr. Crit Minster, U.S.A.

Caracas, Venezuela. Simón Bolívar is entombed here in an elaborate monument. Emily Wiggins, Bristol, England.

San Vicente Cemetery, Bolivia. "Butch Cassidy and the Sundance Kid were buried here ... if you think Cassidy really died here." Gideon Wells, U.S.A.

Iguana. Photo by Kevin Shank.

# EL SALVADOR

**Off the Tourist Trail**

Since the peace negotiations of 1992 El Salvador has been slowly recovering from the violence and instability that made its reputation for decades. Its tourism ministry has gone to pains to highlight the increasingly stable infrastructure of its cities, as well as the pristine attributes of its natural attractions. Despite it being the smallest country in Latin America, much of its Mayan heritage remains unexplored by archeologists. What has been discovered and of interest includes the Joya de Cerén archeological site 1400 years ago buried under volcanic ash and now a UNESCO World Heritage Site. Another legacy of pre-Colombian civilization survives in the San Andrés region, home of the Mayan acropolis.

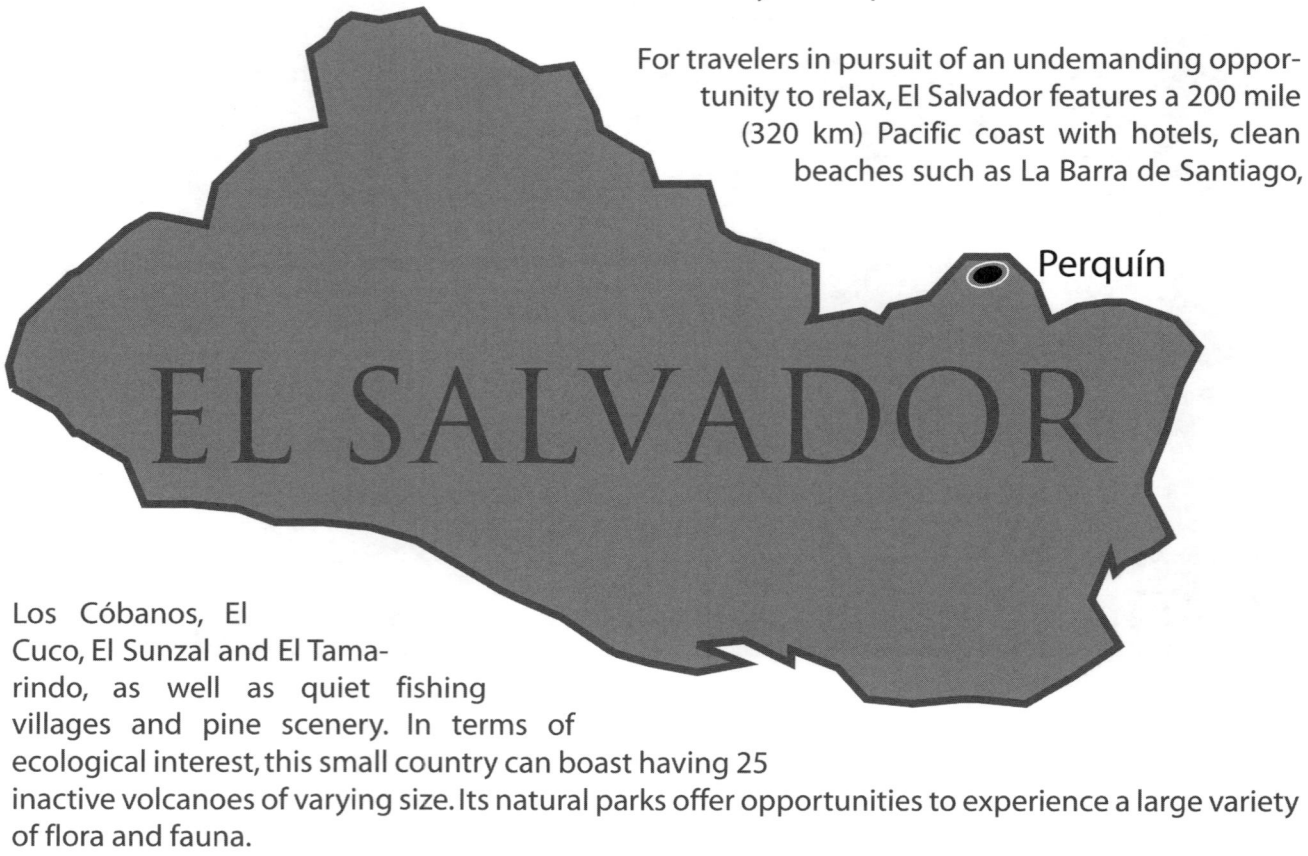

For travelers in pursuit of an undemanding opportunity to relax, El Salvador features a 200 mile (320 km) Pacific coast with hotels, clean beaches such as La Barra de Santiago, Los Cóbanos, El Cuco, El Sunzal and El Tamarindo, as well as quiet fishing villages and pine scenery. In terms of ecological interest, this small country can boast having 25 inactive volcanoes of varying size. Its natural parks offer opportunities to experience a large variety of flora and fauna.

Nonetheless, for many who visit El Salvador, its greatest and most inspiring charm are her people. During the trying times after independence from Spain, El Salvador was a leader in the movement to unify Central America into a larger, more powerful republic. After Hurricane Mitch devastated the country in 1998, the Salvadorans worked together to rebuild. If you visit today, you will find cheerful people who are proud of their country, warts and all, and they're eager to show off El Salvador's admittedly limited tourist attractions. Since the end of the war in 1992, El Salvador has been working hard to develop a tourism industry, and the country is considered much safer than it once was (although "safe" is certainly a relative term).

# PERQUÍN

### By Will Gray, Kettering, England

Some of El Salvador's most turbulent history was played out in the beautiful hills around Perquín, and there are plenty of poignant reminders of the terrible atrocities of the Revolution, none more revealing than the country's most significant museum, situated right in the heart of the former war zone.

Between 1980 and 1992, leaders of the FMLN, the Farabundo Martí National Liberation Front, based themselves in the mountains around Perquín while battling the El Salvadorian military. The military, which forcefully tried to quell the FMLN rebellion, also instigated a ruthless massacre in the nearby town of El Mozote.

Now, former guerrilla fighters lead wide-eyed visitors around the remarkable exhibits, offering fascinating tales of the part they played in the revolution as they point to pictures of their comrades in arms in the surrounding hills.

The museum is filled with interesting photos from the conflict, along with posters and propaganda from various countries, particularly Germany, which openly opposed then U.S. president Ronald Reagan's financial support of the El Salvadorian government. Also on display are many different types of artillery, including a surface-to-air missile and launcher, several kinds of curious homemade bombs, including mines with electric triggers and simple ball bombs, and a range of different guns, all of which were used by the FMLN and some of which were taken in battle from the Guardia Nacional. There is graphically detailed information on the tragedy of the 1981 El Mozote massacre (the most horrific of the many that took place during the conflict) in which 900 men, women and children were brutally slain. There is now a monument to the tragedy in El Mozote, which can also be reached, with a little effort, from the town of Perquín.

On the museum grounds, you can also see the remains of a downed helicopter, blown up by a FMLN bomb that was hidden in a stolen radio. The explosion killed all the occupants, including Lt. Col. Domingo Monterrosa, the head of the Atlacatl Batallion who instigated the El Mozote massacre. This site was also one of the broadcasting locations for Radio Venceremos, "We Shall Prevail Radio." and the makeshift studio, complete with egg cup soundproofing painted with revolutionary declarations, is still in its original condition, just a few meters away from a giant bomb crater which shows how close it came to being destroyed.

Behind the museum sits the small hill of Cerro Perquín, once the site of hideouts and fighting, but now a peaceful park with forested paths, stunning views, and plenty of scars from the past just waiting to be discovered.

On the way up towards the summit clearing are some of the camping places of the guerrilla leaders, gashes in the ground where trenches were dug as hiding places, a clearing where a heliport once stood, a bomb crater and a cave entrance through which tunnels led to hideouts and escape points.

Atop the hill there is a fantastic viewpoint with a 360 degree vista of the wide mountain landscape. Peaceful now, it is an impressive sight with picturesque scenery, making it hard to imagine the atrocious attacks that occurred here just a brief time ago.

*"El Salvador is a democracy so it's not surprising that there are many voices to be heard here. Yet in my conversations with Salvadorians ... I have heard a single voice."*
-Dan Quayle, former US Vice-President (1947-)

## EL SALVADOR FACTS AND FIGURES:

A civil war raged in El Salvador from 1980 to 1992: an estimated 75,000 were killed. One of the victims of the civil war was Archbishop Oscar Romero, a noted advocate for the poor. His story is dramatized in two American-made films: *Romero* (1989) and *Salvador* (1986).

El Salvador is prone to many natural disasters, including volcanoes, earthquakes and hurricanes. In 1998, Hurricane Mitch destroyed or damaged 20% of the country's homes, and killed over 200 people.

El Salvador is the smallest country in Central America and the only one that does not have a coast on the Caribbean.

Approximately 80% of the population of El Salvador is literate: this is up from 26% in 1930.

In 1969, the "soccer war" broke out between El Salvador and Honduras. It lasted five days. Although there were many factors contributing to hostilities, it was a series of three World Cup qualifying matches between the two teams that resulted in riots that provided the "spark." The disputes between the two nations were not decisively worked out until 1992.

From 1865 to 1912, the flag of El Salvador looked a lot like the United States flag: horizontal stripes, with a box in the top left full of neatly ordered stars. The main differences were that the stripes were blue and white instead of red and white, and the "box" was not blue, but red.

El Salvador wrote and enacted new constitutions in 1824, 1841, 1864, 1871, 1872, 1880, 1883, 1885, 1886, 1939, 1944, 1945, 1946, 1950, 1962 and 1983, a grand total of 16 (so far).

# NICARAGUA

**¿Kiubo Mae? ¿What's Up?**

There is just a touch of the surreal, the bizarre, and the magical about Nicaragua. It was ruled for a time by an American filibuster who wanted to turn it into one of the United States (see "the grave of William Walker" in the Honduras section). Lake Nicaragua is home to the world's only species of fresh-water shark. The Mosquito Coast, named after an indigenous tribe, was fought over by England, Nicaragua, the United States, and Spain for centuries until 1894, when Nicaragua claimed autonomy and with little resistance due to its limited strategic value.

In the 20th century Nicaragua's history was dominated by the dictatorial Somoza dynasty, bringing much hardship to its citizens. The socialist Sandinista rebels toppled the Somozas in 1979, and in the years that followed a civil war broke out between the Sandinistas and the Contras, supported by the Reagan administration. However, a popular election did what arms and bullets could not, and in 1990 the Sandinistas lost political control of the country to the more moderate Violetta Chamarro, beginning a new period of increased stability.

These days, Nicaragua is trying to put its past behind it. The nation has been peaceful for years, and tourism is on the rise. It is a beautiful country of beaches, lakes, volcanoes and beautiful parks. Although many have not discovered Nicaragua's charms, our writers have: join them as they take you to the mural workshops of Estelí, the enchanting small towns on Lake Nicaragua and to the mysterious, historical Ometepe Island. Nicaragua still has a touch of the surreal to it: come and see the magic for yourself.

# ESTELÍ

By Lorraine Caputo, Columbia, Missouri, U.S.A.

A jungle, dense with vegetation and animals, wraps around the public library. In a playground, youth defend their nations. On the next corner, ancient to modern-day Nicaraguans confront an eagle clawing Planet Earth. In the hospital the popular history of this country is proudly on display. A few blocks away is the Little Prince.

These are the images of only a few of the over 150 murals that decorate Estelí in northern Nicaragua. For that reason, it was declared "The City of Murals" in 2003.

During the Sandinista Revolution (1979-1990), mural workshops flourished throughout this country. Today, only in Estelí do they survive, preserving the originals and painting new images. Two *talleres*, or workshops, are still active: one at the Casa de Cultura and the other at Funarte, working with hundreds of children and women.

Modern-day Estelí was founded at the end of the 16th century. During the Insurrection (1978-1979), this was an important center of fighting. Then-dictator Anastasio Somoza Debayle heavily bombed the city (in one case, a dud bomb has become a monument). El Carmen Cemetery, west of the city, is exclusively full of those civilians killed during the April 1979 uprising. The Estelí region witnessed extensive damage by the U.S.-backed Contras during the 1980s. The municipal graveyard is full of the tombs of these victims.

To learn about this history, visit the Galería de

> *The Estelí region witnessed extensive damage by the U.S.-backed Contras during the 1980s. The municipal graveyard is full of the tombs of these victims.*

Héroes y Mártires, run by the mothers of these individuals, and El Café del Poeta, operated by María de los Ángeles Rugama, sister of the poet Leonel Rugama.

Estelí is home to many cooperatives and organizations. Some—including Funarte, the Casa de Mujer and Miraflor—welcome volunteers. This is also a center for the study of not only Spanish, but also medicinal herbs. Good cigars are rolled here, and the factories may be toured.

The patron saint days are June 24 to 26, the feast of John the Baptist. During the nights' wee hours, horsemen kick a head through the deserted streets. Another important festival is La Purísima, celebrated with nine days of processions, culminating December 7th.

In the hills surrounding Estelí are a number of attractions. To the south, Estanzuela waterfall cascades into a refreshing pool. To the north are several artisan villages, such as San Juan de Limay, where the locals carve marble, and Ducuale Grande, where pottery is skillfully crafted. To the northeast is the organic coffee cooperative and cloud forest reserve Miraflor, whose main offices are in Estelí.

All these wonders of nature, as well as the history and dreams of Nicaragua, come to life in the discussions of the people of Estelí, and in the dozens of murals that decorate this northern Nicaraguan city.

---

**ESTELÍ TRAVEL TIP:**
The language schools in Estelí are less expensive than in Guatemala, and some offer opportunities for volunteering as well as tours and discussions about the history of the country.

---

## NICARAGUA FACTOIDS:

Before the construction of the Panama Canal, early plans called for a canal to be constructed across Nicaragua.

Nicaragua is the largest country in Central America.

Nicaragua is named after an Indian chief, Nicarao, who ruled the region at the end of the 15th century.

The United States maintained troops in Nicaragua from 1912 to 1933.

After Haiti, Nicaragua is the poorest nation in the western hemisphere.

In 1998, Hurricane Mitch killed 9,000 people and did $10 billion in damage in Nicaragua.

In 2002, former Nicaraguan president Arnoldo Alemán was sentenced to 20 years in prison for fraud and corruption.

Freshwater Lake Nicaragua is home to species of sharks and tuna which have adapted to fresh water.

# SELVA NEGRA

## By Sandra Scott, Lowville, New York, U.S.A.

Cradled in the mountains of central Nicaragua is the sustainable coffee plantation, Selva Negra, and here "sustainable" is the key word. At more than 3,000 feet (914 meters), everything needed to run this little kingdom—from the food on the tables in the lakeside restaurant to the electricity in the quaint, half-timbered cabins—is produced at Selva Negra.

The Hotel Selva Negra has been in operation for 20 years. Eddy and Mausi Kühl, fourth generation descendants of the original German settlers who established the coffee industry in Nicaragua, oversee both the hotel and farm. A little taste of Germany can be witnessed at Selva Negra as each year the hotel celebrates its Germanic heritage with Oktoberfest, complete with draft beer, clowns, and of course, German music and food. The owners have also introduced the traditional Easter egg hunt on Easter Sunday.

The plantation produces a high grade of Arabica coffee produced in an "ecologically correct" manner. By employing ecologically sound processing methods the streams have remained crystal clear and the forest intact.

The Kühls have created a prosperous coffee industry while preserving the natural integrity of the highland forests. Protecting the environment is a main concern. They employ forest rangers to protect the flora and fauna of the area. Selva Negra has a school for the children of its workers; a water powered generator for making electricity and a dairy farm. They are able to provide everything for their family, tourists, and the 600 people who live and work on their land.

Located in the highlands of central Nicaragua, the hills of Selva Negra are draped in green year-round. Fourteen trails, six of which are designed for horses, make this beautiful and pristine cloud forest easy to explore. It is possible to spend hours wandering the trails, marveling at the twisted strangler fig, pausing to locate a singing bird, or stopping to admire the beauty of a blood red flower against the deep green forest foliage. Some of the higher trails offer an impressive view of the rich green valley below.

Howler monkeys, deer, sloth, quail and guatusas all make this remarkable forest their home. Toucans, hummingbirds, and gold finches make the area a bird lover's paradise—the luckiest birdwatchers may even add a quetzal to their list. The forest is also home to an astonishing variety of flora. A visiting botanist identified more than 85 orchids. Selva Negra, in the heart of Nicaragua, is a place where the wonders of nature are just waiting to be enjoyed and appreciated. It is a place that will stay in your memory long after you have said "Auf Wiedersehen."

Horse riding. Photo by Sandra Scott.

### SELVA NEGRA SUSTAINABILITY:

Selva Negra prides itself on its sustainability, which is achieved in a number of ways, including the following:

The animals provide meat including products such as bacon, sausages and ham, milk and cream.

The chickens provide eggs, and there are also quails, turkeys and geese.

The animal manure is used for the home-made fertilizer for growing vegetables to server in the restaurant. The fertilizers include a number of ingredients, such as rice husk, mulch, lake algae, coffee pulp and garbage.

Flowers are grown which are used for displays in the hotel and are also sold locally.

Pest control is also carried out organically.

# JINOTEGA

*By Suzanne Wopperer, Buffalo, New York, U.S.A.*

A battering 1980s civil war fought mostly in the northern forested mountains of Jinotega, Nicaragua virtually eliminated the destination from most travelers' go-to list. This is good news for folks who want to take a romp off the beaten path. Despite a highly successful post-war peace, an excellent urban infrastructure, world-class coffee, and a diverse, handsome and flirtatious population, people just don't visit Jinotega.

If you can maneuver your way through the hot, chaotic and notoriously corrupt capital city of Managua, Jinotega ("HEE-no-TAY-gah") is just a two hour drive into the cool, carefree mountains. Well, the international airport is situated on the northern outskirts, so in effect you could land, head north, and do just what most Jinotegans prefer to do—pretend Managua doesn't exist.

Largely abandoned by the central government, Jinotegans nevertheless do alright. Estimated to produce 40% of the country's domestic products, some 30% of Nicaragua's exports and 25% of its electricity, Jinotega nevertheless specializes in two fine products: cheese and coffee.

Watching the sun set over the mountains, eating a buttery Manchego or smoked Gouda produced by Lácteos Santa Marta and washed down with the pure-filtered mountain spring water Naturalí while watching the sun set spectacularly over the mountains, will make you feel like you've traveled and gone to heaven. A superb front row seat can be found on the third floor of the mountain tavern La Perrera, or The Doghouse, at kilometer 158.5 on the road from Matagalpa.

After the curtains close, help yourself to the buffet and pull up a chair for a film on La Perrera's Cena y Cine (Dinner and a Movie) night. You'll find it all very appetizing, from the over-sized burger to spit-roasted chicken. Try a churrasco—variety plate of grilled meats—fresh salads and cuajada (soft white cheese) on a toasted tortilla. Chef Maximo is an ace at the bar too—he stirs the martinis just right and picks mint fresh from the surrounding gardens for Cuban Mojitos.

On cold, windy nights, the Doghouse's Dame Amanda can be found bundled in her trademark sweater with its Cruella deVille Dalmatian collar. A "media," or 375 ml bottle of the national rum, Flor de Caña, plus good eats will run you around 200 cordobas (about $12) for two people. Stay the night in the cozy inn over the bar and you'll pay some 150 cordobas ($9) extra. For a luxury treat and a hot shower, spend about $40 to stay at the elegant Hotel Café in town just three km (two miles) away, where dinner for two with wine is under $30.

For a nominal fee, but sometimes nothing at all, the nearby nature reserves in wild woodlands welcome hikers and wildlife watchers. If you have to see to believe horses can dance to *ranchera* or *cumbia* music, be sure to schedule your adventure around one of the two annual hipicos, or horse parades. Then grab a beer and go inspect the cattle on show, or attend the rodeo, or go dancing.

In the early '90s, former Contras and Sandinistas were visionary and gifted themselves a national reconciliation initiative, exquisitely unique in its class. Post-war Nicaragua is just that—they've left the war behind and are ripe for economic progress, helped of course by your gringo dollars. Get a move on it—and then take it at your preferred pace in Jinotega. When you return home and your littering co-workers ask you about Jinotega, make sure to tell them there is nothing to do, the people are homely, and bands of marauding bandidos roam the streets.

Born in Buffalo, N.Y., U.S.A., to a family of nine, Suzanne Wopperer joined the U.S. Marines at 17 and worked in communications, language and military intelligence. After serving in the military, she studied international relations and political economy at American University in Washington, D.C. She has worked at the U.S. Institute of Peace in communications and conflict resolution issues and in 2000 she bought land in a Jinotegan mountain forest, where she moved to create the ecotourist romp, La Biósfera. Profit from Naturalí Mountain Spring Water bottled there supports social works, furthering small industry investment, and improving economic conditions in the northern region.

Wopperer is next headed to Cuba, but dreams about riding camel back to Petra, skiing in Switzerland, and dining in Paris.

---

## LATIN REVOLUTIONARIES # 10: DANIEL ORTEGA

Nicaragua
(1945--)

Daniel Ortega was active in opposition to Nicaraguan politics from an early age, and by the age of 22 he was active in the FSLN, the Nicaraguan rebel group also known as the Sandinistas. He was a leader in the movement, in charge of urban warfare. He was arrested in 1967 and remained in prison until 1974, when he was released as part of a prisoner exchange between the FSLN and the government. Once released, he visited Cuba, which had long been a supporter of the Sandinista movement.

He rejoined the revolution and the FSLN overthrew the government of Ansatasio Somoza in 1979. Ortega at first shared power in the new government with four other men, but eventually his faction won out and he was the de facto ruler before long. He was officially elected to the presidency in 1984. He was defeated in 1990 and has lost twice since, primarily due to a number of serious scandals, including charges of blatant corruption from his first administration and allegations of sexual abuse from his stepdaughter. In November 2006, Ortega won the presidential election, embarking upon a new phase in his political career.

# NICARAGUAN DANCE

By Katrina Huntley, Leeds, England

Nicaragua's rich mix of cultures is evident when you come face to face with the locals. Fair hair, blue eyes, Afro curls and pale freckles mix beautifully with indigenous deep brown eyes, maroon skin and thick black hair.

Katrina Huntley is a freelance journalist and creative writer based in the North of England. On the side, she also teaches dance and practises holistic therapies. Huntley studied media and management at Leeds University.

She would never leave home without a really good send off. A sucker for a good party, Huntley has to have one before departing. Presents optional.

The Nicaraguans have seen many foreigners come for a piece of their country in the past centuries. This fact is reflected in the fine Nicaraguan mix of folk dances, celebrations that brim with flavor and influence from all over the world. Each region of the country has its own historic dance with a unique story. This is the result of fertile land and a central position between the Caribbean and Pacific Ocean that made the country a prime target for early Spanish conquests and European settlers. Europeans went to the northern provinces to set up coffee plantations while Africans were brought to the Atlantic coast by the English to work as slaves.

All of these groups brought customs and traditions from their lands, and working closely with the indigenous people, practices were taken up and adapted by locals who developed their own versions of traditional dances such as the Mazkura, the Polka and the Waltz. Jeymi is a dance teacher with the charitable organization CESESMA, based in Matagalpa in the North of Nicaragua. At times she must walk for up to two hours after a long bus journey to reach remote schools for morning class. She gets paid a small wage, but her enthusiasm shines as she gives children in rural communities the opportunity to experience and learn about this rich aspect of their culture.

The children pad their feet in time with the traditional glockenspiel music and once they have the basic steps, Jeymi hands out the long skirts and frilled blouses. The girls aim for a snug fit, the boys looking like farmers in their straw hats and loose trousers. By the end of the class, the girls are floating across the floor, tilting their bodies and shuffling their feet while holding out their big skirts and the boys come weaving in and out without a bump, each using the simple scuffing step and twirl as they tip their hats to their partners.

This is the Nicaraguan Polka, specific to the Northern region, a dance that has its roots in Poland. Every folk dance is complemented by bright and intricate costumes that express strong hints of their origin and local influence. The Dance of the Cutter Ants celebrates Saint Diego and tells the story of a remote village set to lose all their crops due to the threat of destructive ants. The saga goes that the whole village put their faith in the saint and set out armed with wooden branches to bash and batter the ants until nearly all were dead. The dance is a slow, deliberate set of movements that can be seen in the town's yearly procession.

After a turbulent history in which much of the indigenous population was wiped out and few details of their historic rituals remained, Nicaragua was left to adopt a wide variety of styles and influences. It is these characteristics that make the country so distinct, not only in its dance, but in its open acceptance of outside cultures.

It is easy to overlook a country's dance and theatre culture in favor of historic buildings, museums, and famous art galleries. Yet, take the time to explore some of the active arts in a foreign place and you receive some of the most rewarding and entertaining lessons available, along with the opportunity to see locals perform traditional practices and customs in their home land.

Nicaraguan dance. Photo by Caroline Michael.

# LITTLE CORN ISLAND

By Andy Christie, New Zealand.

Like some crazy geographical two-for-one offer, Nicaragua's Little Corn Island feels as if a Caribbean island has drifted over to spend time in Central America. Mainland Nicaragua's lake breezes are swapped for sea breezes, the shadows of volcanoes are exchanged for the shade of coconut palms and even the city plazas morph into golden sand beaches.

After a quick bounce across the open sea from Big Corn Island, arrival on Little Corn Island means either jumping directly into the tide or using a plastic beer crate to a step ashore. Island tempo is easy to fall into. Simply slip out of as many clothes as you feel comfortable with—retaining the minimum required for modesty—and wander.

Little Corn's facilities are concentrated along an area called the "front side." Here, the island's only sealed path connects everything like a social thread. Houses sit resplendent in bright colors, hotels and restaurants waylay the travelers, shops complete with tin shack snack bars, and a health center seems the perfect antidote to the wildlife at The Happy Hut disco.

But the building that attracts the most attention is the dive shop. Daily trips out to the reef are run for divers and snorkelers. Little Corn's healthy reef includes caves, caverns and overhangs. Virtually every reef fish classified as Tropical Caribbean is present in the waters and un-chummed shark encounters are frequent. The sharks are friendly, as are Dive Little Corn's instructors.

Casa Iguana is the best known of the island's accommodations. Set on the breezy far side, the Casa's *casitas* (little cabins) are private and well set up. The Casa Iguana also boasts the island's only internet café run by satellite phone link. However, space is limited and with its popularity the eco-lodge fills up fast, so be sure to make reservations ahead of time.

Ask any traveler and undoubtedly Doña Elsa's, just along the beach from Casa Iguana, will be mentioned as the best place to get lobster on the island. It is prepared slowly, allowing patrons ample time to lounge in the hammocks on the beach front, dozing, drinking, or both.

Although walking after lunch at Elsa's is best kept to a minimum, further north are more secluded beaches. On one of these stunning beaches you'll find Derrick's—described as the place to come and live out Gilligan's Island fantasies. Cabins are constructed of coconut fronds and reeds.

The setting is pure, pristine beach frontage, lined with coconut palms, and there is a coral reef within snorkeling distance. Nightly bonfires add to the feeling of roughing it.

Daytime brings the grocery boat. Fancy a beer? Wave the boat down and order one. Hungry? Try a short walk across the island and follow your nose to the tempting smells of freshly baked coconut bread. The home-baked, all natural ingredient loaf stays fresh for several days.

Your only concern on Little Corn could be the return sea journey to the airport on Big Corn. In rough weather it is possible to miss your flight home again, and again, and again.

Born and raised in numerous cities and several countries, Andy Christie is a traveler by nature, a writer by inclination and somebody who works for the man by necessity.

Before hitting the road, he wouldn't leave home without his sense of wondering what is around the next corner.

"Is being arrested a cultural experience? I've been 'detained' by the secret police for spying in Zaire, and further 'detained' for illegally crossing a war zone in Mozambique."

# BEST PLACES TO STAND IN AWE

Latin America has no shortage of breathtaking sights. Ruins, mountains, waterfalls, deserts and wildlife make this part of the world a bad place to forget your camera! Pack an extra roll or two of film, or an extra memory chip, for these unforgettable places:

1. Machu Picchu, Peru (p. 285)
"Breathtaking, beautiful and mysterious." Danielle Feely, London, U.K.

2. Iguazú Falls, Argentina/Brazil (p. 28 and p. 59).
Peter Anderson, Malaysia.
David Vincent, Chicago, U.S.A.

3. The Galápagos Islands, Ecuador (p. 264).
Almost anywhere in the Galápagos Islands. Paula, U.K. Bartholomew Island, Galápagos. "Climbing to the summit of this spectacular volcanic island at sunset, with Pinnacle Rock thrown into shadow on one side, whilst the spatter and tuff cones, lava flows and lava tubes on the other change to gold." Carol Ann, Scotland.

4. Salar de Uyuni, Bolivia (p. 320). Ann Daly, Australia. "Four days of intense scenery. One hour into this tour, and I was already amazed with the changing landscape. After 15 months of travel, I still rate it as the best tour where I said 'this is incredible' the most times. I did 'that pose' where you open your arms and run towards the landscape because you can't think of anything better to do about 10 times. If this pose doesn't represent the best places to stand in awe, I don't know what does." Jennifer Kotulak, Canada.

5. Atacama Desert, Chile (p. 325).
Atacama Desert, Chile. "So quiet, amazing scenery." Peter Anderson, Malaysia.

6. Perito Moreno Glacier, Argentina (p. 6).
David Vincent, U.S.A. "Blue sky, blue water, blue ice. Huge chunks of ice (about the size on my house) falling into the water creating huge waves and noises akin to a full blown storm ... it's an experience." Jennifer Kotulak.

# GRANADA

By Degan Beley, Vancouver, British Columbia, Canada

Standing in the main plaza at the centre of town, it's easy to imagine that Granada, Nicaragua was once the jewel in Spain's New World crown. Everything from the immense stone Cathedral to the gorgeous colonial homes to the very name of this Central American city have been influenced with Spanish (and indirectly, Moorish) touches.

Degan Beley is a writer and computer technician living in Vancouver, B.C. While she initially went to university for English Literature in Victoria, she later took up an education and career in technology and is now trying finding her way back to her first love of writing and journalism. She takes ongoing classes at the University of British Columbia to that end.

Beley regularly takes time out from her job to travel and write, and she is always in search of an adventure. She wouldn't leave home without a notebook, pen and a camera. The craziest place she has ever visited is small town America. She dreams of visiting Antarctica, but is next going on a driving trip from Vancouver to Ushuaia.

Founded in 1524, Granada dominates the strip of land between enormous Lake Nicaragua and the Pacific Ocean, and is the oldest colonial city in the Americas. Most of the buildings are not that old, however. A fire in 1856 destroyed most of the city, and earthquakes, volcanoes and a thirteen year civil war did the rest. Parts of the Cathedral are original, as well a handful of family homes and the gorgeous blue and white San Francisco Convent (Iglesia y Convento San Francisco).

While not nearly the size of the main Cathedral, the San Francisco Convent is one of the most striking sites in Granada. The traditional bright colored façade favored by the colonists opens onto an enormous welcoming area, from which there is a near perfect view of the city; tiled rooftops give way to swaying palm trees and finally to the distant volcanoes. Situated on top of the hill, it is said that in less stable times it was used as a fortress; having the distinct advantage of being able to see foes coming from either direction.

Inside, the church is filled with treasures: a rose garden carefully tended in the hot Nicaraguan sun, a detailed mural depicting the history of the region since pre-Columbian times, and finally a museum that houses jewelry, clay pots used by people of the area, dioramas showing cooking practices and popular pole dances (similar to the May Pole) and finally the courtyard filled with several pre-Columbian stone statues that were rescued from the bottom of the lake. These are powerful totems, representing the half-world between man and beast—creatures that are half man and half jaguarundi, or half snake, or even completely unidentifiable, seem to leap out of the stone high above the onlookers heads. Just outside you can hear the city continuing on its languid pace, old men rocking listlessly on verandas around the plaza while children play hopscotch.

Not all the charm of Granada is in its history, however. There is a burgeoning artist community that is gaining international attention. Granada's proximity to both the lake and the ocean (not to mention jungles and volcanoes!) has been drawing outdoor enthusiasts and tourism. And beyond all of that, it is the people of Nicaragua that really showcase Granada's charm.

> "Somoza may be a son of a bitch, but he's our son of a bitch."
> -Franklin D. Roosevelt, former US President (1882-1945) in reference to Anstasio Somoza García, Dictator of Nicaragua

## GUANABANA

By Mariana Cotlear

Creamy, sweet, and just a little tangy, the guanabana is the perfect dessert fruit. Its pearly flesh is riddled with large black seeds, and it has a spiky green inedible skin that yields to the touch when ripe, much like an avocado. Native to the Caribbean, Central, and South America, guanabana's light vanilla-pineapple flavor and rich texture make it very popular in the regions where it grows. The fruit becomes very delicate when it ripens, which makes it slightly difficult to harvest and store—it is often directly processed into a pulp, which is later used for blended juices, mousse and yogurts.

# MARKETS OF MASAYA

By Daniel McGlynn, Raliegh, North Carolina, U.S.A.

Visitors to the heart of Masaya are often surprised by what appears to be a medieval castle in the heart of a bustling city neighborhood. Nevertheless, they're delighted to find that the rough, towering rocks of an old Spanish fort now house the Nicaraguan National Artisan Market. Once inside the fort, self-contained booths offer shoppers colorful locally made pottery, musical instruments—maybe even a whole Marimba band—and all the usual souvenirs.

The laid-back atmosphere is conducive to meandering through the market and browsing its wares. Negotiating is a must, and a slight amount of back and forth is expected at any sale.

On Thursday nights, a fee of a couple dollars is charged to enter El Mercado Viejo because it also serves as a venue for cultural events, often featuring folkloric dancing. Brightly dressed performers and well-choreographed dances provide a glimpse into the history and pride of Nicaragua. During September, when the city of Masaya hosts it Fiesta Patronal, the market features live music and hip-jiving Latin dancing.

The smells, sounds, and movement of Masaya's main city market contrast the tranquility and open space of El Mercado Viejo. Housed on the outskirts of town and next to the bus terminal, the city market has an abundance of artisan crafts as well as everyday merchandise. Navigating through the maze of booths and stalls is an adventure in itself. The sing-song call of vendors announcing deals-of-a-lifetime accompany the smell of fritanga (street-food) lingering in the warm, dusty air.

Both markets are intriguing and worth the trip. Prices are pretty comparable at both places, but if time permits, try and head to both for a real opportunity to compare prices and products.

Masaya prides itself on its sense of cultural heritage, so it is worth asking around about ongoing events. The city is easily accessible from both Granada and Managua. There are also many side trips to the nearby Laguna de Apoyo, the Volcano Masaya National Park and the artisan towns of San Juan de Oriente and Catarina.

Daniel McGlynn's travelling started early by exploring the Western United States. While studying the Environment at the University of Colorado, he began wandering internationally. He continued this trend and has fallen in love with Latin American places and their people. He is an educator, writer, paddler and builder.

His dream trip is to explore the Alaskan Coast in a sea kayak.

Ometepe. Photo by Will Gray.

# ISLA DE OMETEPE

By Lorraine Caputo, Columbia, Missouri, U.S.A.

Centuries ago, in the dim past of Central America, a group of wandering Mexica followed a vision south. They believed that they would find their homeland at a place where twin volcanoes rose from an azure sea. Their search was long and their trek arduous, but they reached their destination and founded a city on an island in the middle of a cool lake.

They called their new home Ometepl, and the "sea," Cocibolca. As one travels on the highway running along the western shore of Lake Nicaragua, those majestic twin peaks can still be seen emerging from the slate-blue waters. The island of Ometepe is composed of two volcanoes: Concepción (1,610 meters/5,282 feet), a perfect cone, which often has a spume of smoke wafting from its mouth, and Maderas (1,394 meters/4,573 feet). Being on Isla de Ometepe is like being on Bob Dylan's Black Diamond Bay.

One can't help but wonder if and when Volcán Concepción might blow its immaculate top, and how the island could be evacuated successfully. Indeed, Ometepe had to be vacated in 2000 because of Concepción's increased activity. Today it is safe to visit the island and enjoy its natural wonders. Isla de Ometepe teems with birds and wildlife, even in Moyogalpa, the largest town. At dusk here, green waves of *loros* (small parrots) paint the sky. Hikes along the slopes and to the craters of the two volcanoes provide ample opportunities for birdwatching and for close encounters with monkeys. The southern part of the isle, around Maderas Volcano, has been declared a nature preserve. Since its last eruption 800 years ago, an emerald-green lagoon has filled its crater.

The two main towns on Ometepe, Moyogalpa and Altagracia, are at the foot of Concepción. There are a number of smaller villages, plantations and beaches that one can also visit. At Balgüe is Finca Magdalena, an organic coffee cooperative.

At the narrow waist of the island, between the two volcanoes, is Santo Domingo Beach. Swimming here and all along the eastern side of the island is best, as the water is cleaner. There is no need to fear an attack by fresh-water sharks—it is believed that members of the Somoza family (dictators of Nicaragua for decades) fished the sharks out long ago. Some local fishermen, though, say that in the remotest reaches of the lake, they still net one on rare occasions. At dusk, howler monkeys serenade strollers along the road.

Beyond the natural wonders of the island, the indigenous peoples left behind a number of pictographs around the island. Evidence dating back thousands of years has been found of migrations by the Olmecs, Toltecs, Nahuas, Aztecs and Mayas from the North, and Chibchas, Tiwanakus and others from the South.

The Mexica found their home on a volcanic island on a blue lake: it is worthwhile to follow in their footsteps to this remote paradise.

*"We grew up in a situation where we didn't know what freedom or justice were, and therefore we didn't know what democracy was."*
-Daniel Ortega, former President of Nicaragua (1945-)

## TOP LIST: INTRIGUING ISLANDS & CAPTIVATING CAYES

Some of the best places in Latin America are islands. From the rocky coast of Chile to the sun-drenched beaches of Baja California, our readers have nominated their favorite islands.

1. The Galápagos Islands (p. 264).
 "Most interesting islands in the world!" Christina, Seattle, U.S.A.

 "The islands are very different, each with its own indegenous flora and fauna." Carol Ann, Scotland.

2. San Andres, Colombia.
San Andres & Providencia Islands, Colombia, Angela Hamilton. Maxwell, CA, U.S.A.

3. Floating Islands, Lake Titicaca (p. 296).
"The Mediterranean of South America." Michelle, Boston, U.S.A.

4. Little Corn Island, Nicaragua (p. 187).
"Rough and ready but heaven on earth." Karen, Australia.

5. Utila, Honduras. Rachel Clark, U.S.A.

Runners up:

Roatan, Honduras. Rachel Clark, U.S.A.

Ambergris Caye, Belize. "One of the best dive spots in the world." Dr. Crit Minster, U.S.A.

Cozumel, Mexico. "Great dive spot with lively nightlife." Gideon Wells, U.S.A.

Chiloé, Chile.

# PUERTO DIAZ

### By Daniel McGlynn, Raleigh, North Carolina, U.S.A.

Before arriving in the little fishing village on the Eastern shores of Lake Nicaragua, panoramic views of Volcán Mombacho and Ometepe Island frame the open pasture and fresh-water marsh. Along the road, people are out and about doing any number of daily tasks: collecting firewood, preparing for a cross-community trip, or searching for the rogue cow on horseback. Wide-eyed children stare unabashedly at foreigners before cheerfully returning a friendly wave.

The town itself exists like an island: a few dozen humble homes occupy a rock outcropping that separates them both geographically and culturally from the rest of the region. Most of the Chontales region, and much of the east side of the lake, is based on a cattle economy, while Puerto Díaz and other small fishing towns dotting the shores earn a living on the water.

Making the trek to this side of the lake is a grand opportunity to meander off the beaten trail. Leaving the highway in Juigalpa and bouncing the 20 kilometers down the dirt road towards the port town is like entering a separate plane of existence.

Puerto Díaz is proud of its fish and the two main restaurants happily offer heaping portions of greasy, fried lake fish served with icy drinks. While there is little in the way of tourist infrastructure (according to some, that's the best part of Puerto Díaz) a boat trip along the shores and into some of the nearby creeks can be arranged, and is a great opportunity to explore the unexplored. Visitors should acknowledge that anyone giving you a ride on the water is most likely giving up their work time, and should be compensated accordingly.

If time does not allow for exploration by boat, there are a number of paths and trails that crisscross away from town, up gentle hills and into hidden mango groves. The inhabitants are extremely knowledgeable about the local natural history, and if prompted politely, are more than willing to impart their wisdom. Whether you decide to trail-tromp or spend some time chatting with the locals, Puerto Díaz is rife with adventure for the intrepid traveler.

www.vivatravelguides.com/104356

# GALLO PINTO

### By Daniel McGlynn, Raleigh, North Carolina, U.S.A.

Nicaragua is a country that overwhelms the senses. The intense sun, abundant animals and pervasive music collide with the sound of occasional rain drumming on zinc roofs, the sight of vibrant colors, and the smell of wood fires cooking huge cauldrons of beans. The result is a sensory experience that will leave your head spinning. It is the richness of these sights and sounds that infuse the Nicaraguan food with its powerful tastes and flavors. From gritty corn drinks (*Pinol*) and sweeter corn drinks (*Atol*), to tart juices like that from the skin of a pineapple, *cascara de piña*, or the puckering flavor of the Nancite fruit, Nicaragua's gastronomic venue is as diverse as the country itself.

Chief among Nicaraguan cuisine is Gallo Pinto. The rust-red-tinged dish of beans and rice can be found in all regions of the country and is a flavor unique to Nicaragua. Granted, other nations have traditional dishes of beans and rice, but nothing can compare to some home-cooked Gallo Pinto.

The dish is prepared by frying white rice and red beans separately and then frying them together. The result is a super-fried, red medley that derives its name as a result of sharing the same color as the comb of a rooster. Gallo Pinto is consumed in the *campo* as well as in the city, and is generally eaten for breakfast, lunch and dinner. It can be accompanied with cheese, chili, meat, or bread, but is so tasty as to be enjoyed alone. The Pinto is tastiest when it is fresh off the fryer, but refried versions add a bit of crunchiness. Great pride is taken in the making of the Pinto, so if a plate is exceptionally tasty, or the texture just right, then a compliment to the cook is in order.

Many visitors to Nicaragua develop a taste for Gallo Pinto, but trying to replicate it without the wood fire, the massive amounts of oil, or the rich flavor of a fryer seasoned by generations of use and the country itself is nearly impossible.

# COSTA RICA

**¡Pura Vida!**

Timekeeping is not a phrase that Costa Ricans are very familiar with. "Tico time" regularly means that your bus could arrive within minutes, a few hours, or only the following day—frustrating for anyone insistent on a schedule. But it is precisely this blithe lifestyle and carefree attitude that have earned Costa Rica its slogan "pura vida," or "pure life," and free from the pressures of time, one cannot help but be enchanted by this Central American "Eden."

Costa Rica, the "Rich Coast," is perhaps the most inviting of the Latin American countries for a first time traveler to this region. Following a civil war in the 40s, the country abolished its army in 1949 and has since enjoyed life as a peaceful haven between its often precarious neighbors, Panama and Nicaragua. "We are proud to say that we have more teachers than civil guards" is a famous Costa Rican saying.

Relative safety aside (an influx of Nicaraguan refugees during the 1980s raised the crime level), Costa Rica fulfils every cliché one might associate with a tropical haven, a wildlife paradise and a nature-lover's dream. Chosen by director Ridley Scott to represent the pristine New World in the movie "1492," it is no surprise that it is the home of eco-tourism. Explore both Caribbean and Pacific beaches, see endangered green turtles in Tortuguero, or watch leatherback turtles laying eggs on the Pacific Coast at Playa Grande. Visit a plethora of active volcanoes (Arenal rumbling every 15 minutes) or take a hike through one of the country's many national parks, such as Parque Nacional Corcovado. With approximately 9,000 plant species and 900 bird species, this small country contains 5% of the world's biodiversity, so rest assured you will have plenty to photograph.

And after all this, luxuriating in just a bit of the laziness that the warm climate here makes hard to resist seems only fair. Perhaps this "pura vida" stuff has something in it after all.

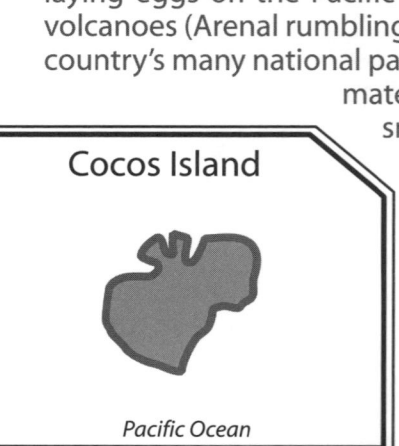

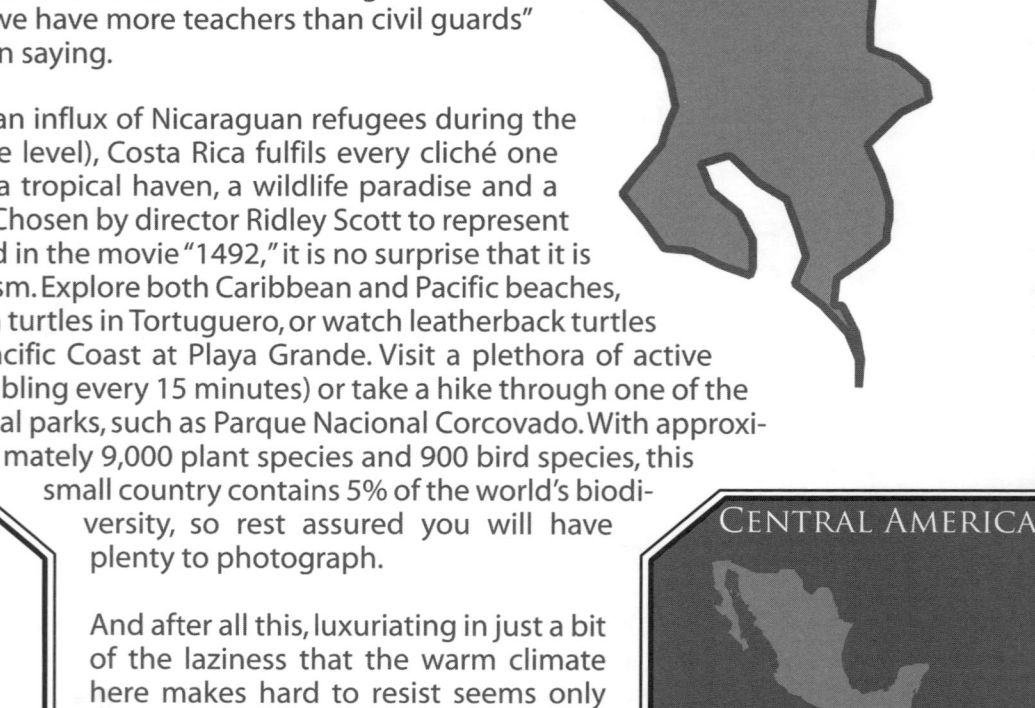

↑ Cocos Islands (532 km)

**Cocos Island**

*Pacific Ocean*

**CENTRAL AMERICA**

COSTA RICA

# RINCÓN DE LA VIEJA

By Hannah Fairlie Agran, Des Moines, Iowa, U.S.A.

Rincón de la Vieja National Park is like a platter of mixed hors d'oeuvres. A little bit of everything, all served in convenient, bite-sized portions, perfect for picking and choosing according to personal taste.

Trails range from easy to strenuous, and they pass through varied landscapes. Some go uphill, others go down. A few lead to picture-perfect waterfalls, one loops around several steamy hot springs, and the showcase hike heads straight up to the volcano's summit.

And because the park is a bit difficult to access—there are no public buses from nearby Liberia—it is less touristy than many of Costa Rica's better known destinations.

Rincón de la Vieja is actually one of two volcanoes in the park. It is classified as active but hasn't erupted since 1998. Santa María, the other, smaller cone, is dormant. Climbing Rincón de la Vieja is a rigorous, day-long undertaking. The trail emerges from layers of forest onto a dramatically bleak volcanic moonscape. Vapor rises from the turquoise crater-lake and floats up into the clouds.

Other hikes are less strenuous, but just as climactic. The path to the park's largest waterfall, La Cangreja, passes alternately through cool, wooded areas and open, sundried plains. Copper-infused water tumbles some 200 feet into a blue-green pool surrounded by eminently lounge-able rocks. Many visitors eat their lunches, swim, or soak their feet before hiking back out.

Near the ranger station, a short, kid-friendly trail leads past scalding ash pits and belching volcanic vents. The air is heavy and sulfuric and iguanas sometimes lounge on the hot stones.

The park is popular with birders, and observant hikers can spot a huge variety of wildlife. White-throated magpie jays, with their jaunty black feathered headdresses, alight on low branches, and lucky hikers might see playful monkeys swinging happily above them. An even luckier hiker might sight toucans, armadillos, hummingbirds and tapirs as well. Even in the park's picnic area, curious coatis snuffle along the ground, their long ringed tails comically upright behind them. Don't feed them, of course, but keep en eye on your peanut butter and jelly!

After graduating from Brandeis University in 2004, Hannah Fairlie Agran freelanced for *Cincinnati Magazine* and taught English for a year on the Boruca Indigenous Reserve in southern Costa Rica. She now lives in Iowa where she is the Assistant Travel Editor at *Midwest Living* in Des Moines.

A teenager in Costa Rica once asked Fairlie Agran, "Snow must be really cold, right?" She was stumped. How do you explain freezing temperatures to someone who has never seen the thermometer dip below sultry, she thought? Suddenly inspired, she compared it to sitting inside the refrigerator and watched as the girl's eyes widened in disbelief. The encounter reminded Fairlie Agran of how little most people have seen of the world they inhabit—and how fortunate she is to have seen all that she has.

Rincón de la Vieja. Photo by Hannah Fairlie Agran.

# VOLCÁN ARENAL

## By Wes Weston, Sarasota, Florida, U.S.A.

There are few places in the world where you can get up close to an active volcano. During the day, eruptions occur so frequently that there's a massive trail of smoke cascading across the sky. At night sparks fly as red lava gushes down the side of the mountain in an uncontrollable fury. The spectacle is absolutely breathtaking, making you wonder if it's actually safe to be so near to all the fireworks.

The Arenal volcano is undoubtedly one very impressive sight to behold. The volcano stands over 1,600 meters (5,249 ft) in all its glory in a perfect conical shape. Arenal was actually thought to be dormant for several hundred years until a massive explosion in 1968 threw rocks and ash for miles, killed 84 people, and devastated the surrounding villages. Since then, it has been very much awake and is considered one of the ten most active volcanoes in the world.

Centrally located in the northern region of Costa Rica, nestled between Lake Arenal to the east and the town of La Fortuna to the west, Arenal is one of the most sought-after tourist destinations in the country. The town of La Fortuna is small but has many shops, hotels, and restaurants to accommodate visitors. It's incredible just to walk down the main street in town with the volcano dominating the backdrop, which is the scene on many postcards.

The activities around Arenal are plentiful, ranging from horseback riding to canopy tours to visiting a magnificent waterfall. There's even a rope swing on the road heading south out of town. It's a great place to take a plunge into a refreshingly cool swimming hole. If you want to get a closer view of the volcano, Parque Nacional Volcán Arenal has several trails leading to expansive vistas for capturing photos of the towering inferno. However, the most extraordinary luxury that Arenal has to offer are the thermal hot springs where you can relax in steaming pools while watching lava explode from the volcano's mouth. There are several different hot springs to choose from, all providing a range of amenities.

A trip to the Arenal volcano is a must for anyone wishing to marvel over the explosive power of nature. It may not be off the beaten path, which means there's a reason why so many people just have to see it.

## TOP LIST: BAD-ASS VOLCANOES IN LATIN AMERICA

1. Nevado del Ruiz, Colombia. It is so high (17,453 feet/5,321 meters) that it is constantly covered at the top with snow and ice. On November 13, 1985, Nevado de Ruiz erupted, melting the snow and ice and sending massive mudslides into the nearby town of Armero, killing an estimated 25,000 people: it was one of the worst volcano disasters in history.

2. Agua, Guatemala. Although it has been inactive for almost five hundred years, it went out with a bang, destroying Cuidad Vieja, the original capital of Guatemala, in its final eruption in 1541.

3. Cotopaxi, Ecuador (p. 248). The highest active volcano (19,388 feet/5,911 meters) in the world, it has twice destroyed the nearby town of Latacunga. The 1877 eruption melted the snow and ice on top; mudslides traveled for miles. The bad news is that Cotopaxi is due: it last erupted in 1903.

4. Popocatepetl, Mexico. The highest active volcano in the northern hemisphere (17,802 feet/5,426 meters), it has erupted 8 times since 1920. In April 1996, five climbers were killed when a section of the crater rim suddenly exploded.

5. Pacaya, Guatemala (p.153). Had been dormant since 1860, but erupted in 1961 and has been constantly erupting ever since. On a clear night you can see the bright red lava as far away as Guatemala City. Popular with tourists, but go with an armed guard because there are many thieves on the trails.

6. Poás, Costa Rica. Has erupted 39 times since 1928. Often throws huge clouds of steam into the air when the water in the crater lake comes into contact with lava.

7. Galeras, Colombia. Scientists estimate that Galeras has been active for more than one million years. Its last major eruption was in 1886, but nine hikers and scientists were killed in 1993 when a medium-sized eruption took off part of the top.

8. Colima, Mexico. Mexico's most active volcano, Colima forces massive evacuations every few years, most recently in June 2005, when it sent a cloud of ash three kilometers (almost two miles) into the air.

9. Reventador, Ecuador. Has erupted at least 30 times since the arrival of the Spanish to the region. Its 2002 eruption sent a massive plume of ash into the air, which blanketed Quito, miles away. Its name means "Exploder."

10. Irazú, Costa Rica. Although it last erupted in 1965, covering the capital city of San José with ash, it is still very active. It is a popular tourist attraction.

# TABACÓN SPA

By Erika Cann, New York City, New York, U.S.A.

The first indication that life was about to slow down was on the drive from the airport, where we passed Costa Rican workers hand-painting the white perforations that divide the road into lanes that are either coming or going, depending on how you see things. Moving closer to our destination, the Tabacón Hot Springs Resort and Spa, Volcán Arenal loomed ahead like a friendly monster. Even from afar, I sensed the paradoxical effect of this volcano, inspiring tranquility as well as apprehension.

At Tabacón, you will leave your everyday troubles behind, partly because of the peaceful setting, and partly due to the active Arenal volcano, which appears to always be on the verge of blowing into the stratosphere: it has a way of keeping your troubles in check. In truth, pyroclastic flows in 1975 and 1993 almost wiped out the hotel and all its guests, this guest included. The hotel is periodically evacuated: including only a few days after my most recent visit.

Active volcanoes aside, Tabacón is a playground for grownups. Volcanic activity has carved a forest of thermal pools into the earth. Arenal provides an underground molten heating system for these springs, which vary in temperature according to their proximity to the volcano. It's no wonder the Guatuso Indians believed the God of Fire lived inside the rumbling mountain. Spend your evening steeping in the pools, but keep your eyes on Arenal, who frequently drizzles a steady orange neon bolt from his mouth, piercing the backlit stars.

Inside the hotel, rooms are stylish, with furniture and art handcrafted by local artists. Some of them boast luxurious deck side hot tubs. Visit the Iskandria spa to enjoy a banana mint facial, the coffee sugar body scrub, or my favorite, the volcanic body wrap, after which you will be led naked to a nearby spring to rinse off the volcanic mud. Exotic flowers and butterflies abound in Tabacón's gardens, and the quaint town of La Fortuna is a five-minute ride away. Arenal, the dutiful sentry, keeps a constant watch, a looming photo opportunity.

The hotel provides booking for various day trips; we chose an intermediate-level whitewater rafting trip, which turned out to be a wonderful refresher course. Our teenage guides made sure I didn't fall out of the raft, and treated us to a carved watermelon at the river's edge. The tour operator can also book you for waterfall rappelling and other hair-raising adventures.

For three days, I enjoyed a perfect, unobstructed view of the volcano. In this short time, I grew to regard Arenal as a natural compass, happily replacing my subway map and my Blackberry. "Should I get the camera?" I mumbled every few hours from the pools, the massage table, between bites of various meals. On our last day, I gathered my photo equipment, and went outside only to be greeted by an amorphous, smoky mound where Arenal had stood majestically for the last few days. Until we meet again, Arenal, for now our time together is only in my memory.

COSTA RICA TRAVEL TIPS:
- Bring a good amount of cash with you, as ATM machines can be picky about accepting cards.
- Try to speak Spanish, even if you don't know much. English is widely spoken and it can be tempting to stick with a language you are familiar with, but you are in a different country after all.
- Pack clothing that dries quickly. Costa Rica is very humid and you will likely be active and outdoors much of your time.
- Malaria isn't really a big problem in the country, but other problematic diseases carried by mosquitoes are, so wear DEET when in bug-infested areas.
- If you rent a car, here are two local rules of the road: stick your left hand out the window and wave slightly if you want to merge left (have your passenger do the same if you want to merge to the right), and flick your lights if you want oncoming traffic to slow down so you can turn left.

# SAN JOAQUÍN DE FLORES HEREDIA

By Leigh Gower

San Joaquín de Flores in Heredia is an excellent destination for Spanish students who want to escape the hustle and bustle of San José. A quiet community set amid green fields, it is the perfect place from which to take day trips to the Café Britt coffee plantation or the Alajuela Butterfly Farm.

The small town of only 10,000 residents is also home to one of the oldest churches in Costa Rica, founded in 1797. The church takes it place of pride in the centre of town. Another church, the centennial church, has been declared an architectural and historical heritage site and was built with stones brought to the town one at a time in carts. One resident has claimed that because cement was not widely known about in the mid-nineteenth century when it was constructed, the builders used a mixture of egg whites, sand and lime to put the stones together.

San Joaquín remains a peaceful town with stunning views of the nearby mountain range. It is a place where you can really hear yourself think, but also close enough to the big city for you to be able to catch a movie, do some architectural sightseeing and eat out aplenty. For travelers seeking authenticity in a real *pueblo tico*, San Joaquín is an absolute must.

# TORTUGUERO

By Cyril Brass, Vermilion, Alberta, Canada

A true natural wilderness deep in the tropical jungles of Costa Rica, Tortuguero National Park is considered one of the most biologically diverse regions in the country. It is a hidden treasure of fascinating views, incredible wildlife and exotic flowers for any outdoor enthusiast, birdwatcher or nature lover.

Cyril Brass combines his passions for travel, photography and writing into a lifestyle full of adventures and memorable experiences. He currently works as a professional photographer specializing in the areas of sports, special events, nature, travel and commercial photography. His work has been featured in wildlife publications such as *Creaturesall Magazine*. In the past he has led guided adventure tours and completed photo assignment work in Costa Rica.

His most bizarre cultural experience was had while on an African safari through Kenya and Tanzania, when he danced with the beautifully decorated Maasai warriors.

This coastal lowland region was declared a National Park in 1970 by the Costa Rican government, primarily to protect the green sea turtle population from extinction. In Spanish, *Tortuguero* means "Region of the Turtles." The Tortuguero beach, stretching some 22 kilometers (14 miles), is the most important nesting site of the green sea turtle in the Western Hemisphere.

From July to mid-October, this endangered reptile visits this beach to lay eggs. During the turtle-nesting season, guided night walks are available for visitors to experience this amazing natural wonder. The leatherback and hawksbill species come to nest here as well, but they are far less common.

The National Park was also created to protect a unique series of natural inland waterways with a high concentration of flora and fauna species. This intricate network of man-made canals and fresh water rivers creates a sort of inter-connected water highway. Traversing swamp forests and meandering through secluded lagoons, this easy flowing waterway system is the only means of getting around in the area.

Cerro Tortuguero is the highest point in the park, reaching 150 meters (500 feet) above sea level. A short but adventurous climb to the top is rewarded with stunning panoramic views of the canals, forests and coastline. This forest-covered hill resembles the shape of a turtle and some consider it a possible navigational marker for the green sea turtles.

Located within the park boundaries is the village of Tortuguero, a gathering place for travelers interested in visiting the turtle museum, hiking in a tropical rainforest, strolling along the beach, or shopping for souvenirs. The friendly residents possess a mix of African and Spanish cultures found only on the Caribbean side of Costa Rica.

Touring the canals by boat is the best way to experience the lush vegetation and abundant wildlife. You can spot iguanas basking in the trees, sloths climbing in the forest canopy, herons searching for fish or caimans resting along a sunny riverbank.

Flat-bottom motorized boats carry nature enthusiasts deep into the wild jungle through the forest-lined canals searching for snakes, monkeys, lizards, river turtles and macaws. The local naturalist guides have seemingly telescopic eyes, enabling them to spot the local inhabitants, well-camouflaged to the untrained eye. Smaller waterways branch off the main canal, allowing tour boats to explore this fascinating region more closely.

Relax and enjoy the natural beauty all around as the boat drifts silently through the tranquil backwaters. The tropical plants, dense vegetation and interesting wildlife showcase an impressive spectacle in the northeastern region of Costa Rica. For a truly extraordinary experience in a natural wildlife sanctuary, travel to Tortuguero National Park.

### TORTUGUERO TRAVEL TIPS:
There are no roads to Tortuguero. The only way to access the park is by boat or small plane. Daily flights travel from San José and Limón to Tortuguero. Consider a tour, as the area is not easy to navigate, even for independent travelers. The village of Tortuguero does offer both accommodation and restaurant options, making it an easy base while exploring all of the natural beauty and wildlife the surroundings offer.

Basilisk lizard. Photo by Cyril Brass.

# MONTEVERDE

## By Michelle Hopey, New Hampshire, U.S.A.

Perhaps it's the rugged dirt road, or maybe it's because it's perched up high in the cloud forest, with difficult access. It's likely that it has something to do with the amount of biological diversity that thrives here, or it might just be that the colorful, friendly and warmly inviting locals are what make Monteverde a tropical utopia. All those reasons give Monteverde, Costa Rica a magnetic pull, continually drawing in a flow of visitors with its intense, mysterious tropical charm.

Straddling the continental divide at 1440 meters (or 4662 feet), Monteverde, meaning "green mountain," is often a day trip for folks visiting Santa Elena, but staying in Monteverde is perhaps the best way to see and experience the true essence of the town, which was founded in 1951 by a group of Quakers from North America. It is reported that this group was jailed for dodging the Korean War draft, and after their release they sought out a place to live which would cultivate peace and harmony: they found Monteverde. Back then, their goal was to buy land in Monteverde and clear some forest for daily farming. Soon after, it was realized that the forest cover was essential to protecting the locality and so 541-hectares were set aside for preservation.

In 1972, after studying birds in the cloud forest, George Powell, along with Monteverde resident Wilford Guidon, came together to create a reserve by adding 328 more hectares to the 541 already owned by the Quakers, and the famous Monteverde Cloud Forest Preserve was founded. With the preserve soon came a science observatory which soon hosted researchers from around the world studying the high biological diversity of plants and animals. Today, the Preserve covers 10,500 hectares, with 90 percent of it virgin forest, contains over 2,500 plant species—including 420 different kinds of orchids—100 species of mammals, 400 bird species, 120 reptilian and amphibian species and thousands of insects. With such a global presence in science community, residents found a way to incorporate the biological treasures and fame with its goal of a healthy self-governed community devoted to sustainable living practices.

As the visitors came so did the concept of eco-tourism, which Monteverde nearly conceptualized. A few eco-tourism snobs today will say Monteverde is a has been, considering the village saw a heyday in the early 1990s, when its popularity boosted it into the spotlight, only making it more popular. Other visitors will say it's a nice town, but that there is nothing too exceptional to do, considering that the more exciting stuff happens down the road at Volcan Arenal, and others will say its too filled with travelers who want to go, just to say they've been. But the real Monteverde isn't a place to discover, it's a place to experience and the real experience of Monteverde is seeped in the town itself and the people who live there.

Since the village of Monteverde focuses on building and sustaining a strong community within itself and visitors, residents are extremely friendly, hospitable, honest and well-educated. Call it the Quaker influence, but locals want to share their town with you, and learn about yours, treating you as if you are long-lost family. To get a real glimpse of Monteverde, stay with a local family in their home and participate in community events as they do. A homestay always gives you insight to the culture you are visiting. Volunteer, even for a day, at the town's school, or with one of the social organizations around town. Make sure to check out or even take a course at the Monteverde Institute (MVI), a community organization founded in 1986 by residents and visitors as a member-governed, Costa Rican non-profit educational association. The MVI is focused on the geographical, social and cultural reality of Monteverde communities. Its purpose is to incorporate community service at all levels.

To explore the cloud forest, you'll need a trained guide, preferably one from a research station or a local that is a member of the Monteverde Guides Association, an organization that trains guides without any economic interests. Without an expert, you are likely to only see insects and hummingbirds, but a guide will be able to take you further into the cloud forest, off the well-worn trails to see howler monkeys and sloths. They'll be able to school you in the large varieties of hummingbirds and medicinal plants as well.

Whatever reason compels you to visit Monteverde, remember that to understand Monteverde is to understand the people of this unique town. Monteverdians love their town so much, that visitors should feel lucky that they even let tourists in, but then again if they didn't, they wouldn't be the friendly, easy-going folks they naturally are. So, in a way, you can't really be upset that residents have yet to approve paved roads, connecting it to the Panamerican Highway. It's still a bumpy, dusty and scary two-hour ride up to the mountains. While no roads means no economic development, Monteverdians don't seem too concerned, and why should they? For centuries people have naturally felt the town's radiating charm and come looking for the peace they are likely to find.

## MONTEVERDE ZIPLINING

### By Leigh Gower

High above the treetops, one can't help but feel like Tarzan swinging through the rainforest. Of course, you are rather better equipped with harnesses and clips than Tarzan ever was, as you partake in the Monteverde Cloud Forest Sky Trek, and rather than passing through the trees, Sky Trek takes you right over the forest canopy. Nevertheless, an adrenaline rush will certainly overwhelm you as you jump off platforms and speed down cable lines, the longest of which is 427 meters long (1,400 feet) and 127 meters high (417 feet).

If having your feet on the ground proves a more appealing option, however, the Sky Walk tour includes 2.5 kilometers (1.6 miles) of trails and six suspended bridges, the longest of which is 300 m (984 feet), across deep canyons. Nature enthusiasts will be thrilled to encounter vast collections of plants, trees and wildlife—but make sure to bring binoculars and rain gear with you, as this is a cloud forest. There are also two observatory towers for a 360-degree panoramic view of the Guanacaste, San Carlos, the Puntarenas lowlands and the Gulf of Nicoya.

Be warned, high winds and elevation mean you could end the journey soaking wet, but for an exhilarating view of the rainforest from new heights, Sky Trek will not disappoint.

# LOS ALTOS AND CHOCOLATE

## By Sandra Scott, Lowville, New York, U.S.A.

There is a secret place between heaven and earth, but like all secrets it is best when shared. On the Altos de Pinella in Guanacaste, Costa Rica, is Los Altos de Eros, where guests can relax in chocolate heaven. It is the epitome of chocolate decadence.

The day begins with the call of the howler monkey and ends watching the stars reflecting in the shimmering pool. The strains of Andrea Bocelli make it so magical you will think you can fly.

But between the howler monkey and Bocelli is a spa day that is a chocolate dream. It starts with a walk down the teak steps at the end of the swimming pool to the lush and tropical Spa de Eros. The Spa has been meticulously carved from the side of a hill. The views of the ocean and the tropical forest are breathtaking and calming, inducing feelings of tranquility. Truly a place between heaven and earth. Actually, it is heaven on earth.

The water falls over the natural stone from the hilltop pool, splashing into a small pool where hibiscus flowers float. The scents of jasmine and sandalwood fill the air. Soft music melds with the sounds of nature.

The day of chocolate decadence starts with Spa de Eros' aromatic signature massage—so soothing, so relaxing, so rejuvenating. Naturally, only pure and natural ingredients are used. What follows is beyond the wildest imagination of the chocolate lover. Nothing surpasses the luxury of soaking in the Balinese tub with the spa's specially prepared "Chocolate Decadence," soothing waters with chocolate, essential oils, flowers, and the scenery to take you to a place of supreme tranquility.

Just when you think it can't be any better—it does. While soaking in the Jacuzzi, gazing in wonder at the view, the gourmet lunch arrives. And, what a lunch it is! An array of fresh fruit, mahi mahi, and salad is accompanied by a chocolate fruity smoothie and wine. Then it gets better—the dessert arrives—Chocolate Terrine, an elegant combination of four great flavors—chocolate, chocolate, raspberry and chocolate!

After lunch, the hedonistic chocolate spa day continues with the ultimate in facials, the "Chocolate Dream" facial that cleans, tones, and moisturizes the skin. What a dreamy, relaxing, rejuvenating chocolate day!

Los Altos de Eros is a treat for all one's senses. The staff of this luxurious property focuses on personal attention. It is a special place where the location, the service, and ambiance are unsurpassed. And, for the chocolate lover, it is Chocolate Heaven.

Los Altos Spa. Photo by Sandra Scott.

### LOS ALTOS DE EROS TRAVEL TIP:

Feeling like you need to burn off some of those chocolate calories? The resort provides a day-long yoga immersion program, private and semi-private yoga classes, and the popular sunset yoga session. Not only are the classes taught by experienced professionals, the setting among lush greenery and oceanic vistas is one that will leave you feeling truly relaxed and rejuvenated. And if you've had enough of the chocolate (doubtful, but always a possibility), the resort also offers a yoga cuisine complete with fruits, vegetables, salads, smoothies, fish, and high-protein, gourmet dishes.

# LEATHERBACK TURTLES AT PLAYA GRANDE

By Degan Beley, Vancouver, British Columbia, Canada

Deep in the inky depths of the world's oceans, one hardy species has remained unchanged for nearly 120 million years: the great leatherback turtle, so named because in place of the traditional turtle shell they have five bony plates held together with fat and skin.

Once a year, the females crawl up onto the beach to lay their eggs on beaches distributed among the shores of South America, Panama, the Antilles and Costa Rica, including Playa Grande (and adjacent Tamarindo) in Costa Rica. As the females lay the eggs, the males circle tirelessly 100 metres offshore until it's time to move on.

The tiny community of Playa Grande consists of a hotel, a turtle museum and a pizza parlor, while larger Tamarindo to the south has an airstrip and considerably more amenities. Both are surf Meccas, but after moonrise the only people on the beach are there for the turtles. The beaches are part of the Las Baulas National Marine Park (which extends far into the sea), created to provide a protected area for the nesting turtles. Park rangers patrol the beaches, protecting the turtles and their nests from poachers and any potentially threatening obstacles.

The Earthwatch Group is also established in the area to aid in ongoing research about the turtles and to help in conservation efforts. Through education, the Playa Grande community has turned from poaching to conservation and is eager to pass that message on to visitors.

> *Through education, the Playa Grande community has turned from poaching to conservation and is eager to pass that message on to visitors.*

A good first stop is the turtle museum, where you can learn of the many dangers and horrors facing the leatherback. Also of interest is Hotel Las Tortugas, where guests are invited to eat their dinner by very dim candlelight, as a consideration to the turtles that are easily distracted by bright lights.

The nesting season is from October to February with the turtles being particularly active during high tides. However —early risers beware—the turtles only come ashore at night and the tours don't get underway until well after 10 p.m. Tourists are not allowed on the beach by themselves; they must go with a ranger and attend an information session beforehand. Here guides give a brief lesson, in a schoolhouse crawling with cicadas, of what can be expected on the excursion. They also outline the rules: no touching the turtles, no walking in front of the turtles, no talking, no flashlights, no cameras with flashes, no wandering away from the group.

Even with all the restrictions (or perhaps because of them), it is a truly powerful and reverential experience. The leatherback turtles are in danger from discarded plastic bags that they mistake for jellyfish, one of their favorite foods, as well as fishing nets, motorboats and environmental destruction due to condo developments. The Earthwatch Group predicts that if these destructive, careless behaviors continue, the leatherback turtles could become extinct in our lifetime.

## TOP LIST: WILDEST WILDLIFE EXPERIENCES

Some of the most fascinating inhabitants of Latin America don't walk on two legs: instead, they fly, swim, waddle or run on all fours. Many people come to Latin America simply to see these marvelous animals. Our community faves:

1. Spotting Golden Tamarin, Mexico. "Beautiful and amazing." Sandra Scott, New York, U.S.A.

2. Torres del Paine, Chile (p. 341). "Wild guanacos and ñandus are all over the place." Strawberry Reynolds, Virginia, U.S.A.

3. Jaguar sightings, Suriname. Sam Crothers, Pennsylvania, U.S.A.

4. Pampas, Bolivia. Ann Daly, Australia.

5. Galápagos Islands, Ecuador (p. 264). "Swimming with hammerhead sharks is amazing." John Anderson, Chicago, U.S.A.

6. Cuyabeno Reserve, Ecuador. "Howler monkeys keep you up all night." Sarah Duniway, England.

7. Manu Reserve, Peru. Ann Daly, Australia.

8. Isla Magdalena, Chile. "Amazing colony of Magellanic penguins." Francis Saunders, Vancouver, British Columbia, Canada.

9. Iguana park, Guayaquil, Ecuador. "Dozens of huge iguanas in a park right in the middle of Ecuador's largest city!" James Dificcio, East Rochester, New York, U.S.A.

COSTA RICA

# MAL PAÍS

By Jenna Mahoney, New York City, New York, U.S.A.

The quest for simple paradise ends at a tiny fishing village on the edge of the world. Its name is Mal País. Yes, if you translate the name of the town you get "bad land," but that refers to the rocky coastline. And it's thanks to the village's moniker that this spot has been kept so secret and sacred.

Mal País is located on the southeastern tip of Costa Rica's Nicoya Peninsula. Starting from the Pacific coast, the tiny pueblo stretches only over about six kilometers east to west. Mal País sits between the Cabo Blanco National Park and a quiet surfer Mecca called Santa Teresa. The people of Mal País embody the friendliness of the Pura Vida (Pure Life) anthem. And it's the perfect destination to experience nature in her purest form: expect to see horses galloping down the beach, monkeys hiding in the trees and a myriad of maritime species living amongst the shore's rocky enclaves.

A stay at the Swiss-owned Hotel Surf The Place is the perfect complement to the area's easy going vibe. The property features a modern villa, five breezy bungalows, a small pool and quiet main house surrounded by tropical gardens. Each of the estate's structures are scattered over a sloping hill. The intimate houses exude a feeling of cozy privacy. Guests can hear the gentle crash of the waves against the rocky shore located only about 150 meters away. Each cottage also has a hot-water bathroom and safe as well as an overhead fan and views of the Pacific Ocean.

If you're with a group, stay at the property's villa. It's a modern air-conditioned house set apart from the rest of the property. The Place also offers three smaller guest rooms located in the main house. This structure houses a quiet bar complete with relaxed cushioned seating and a few tables. In the morning, the open-air space transforms into a leisurely breakfast area. The tables are rarely over-crowded and guests linger as long as they like over eggs, *gallo pinto* (rice and beans with a kick) and rich Costa Rican coffee.

And when you're done, there's a number of activities on offer in Mal País—no need to rush, though. The folks at The Place can arrange horseback outings, kayak rentals, hiking excursions, yoga classes and massage services. Then there's also lounging by the property's small pool and walking along the rocky shore. Remember you've found the end of the earth: A little piece of paradise, so you can do as little or as much as you like.

www.vivatravelguides.com/103938

# SURFING IN MAL PAÍS

By Cat Hartwell, New York City, New York, U.S.A.

Mal País may not be a town for everyone. However, the long journey is well worth the trek for the die-hard surfers who are promised miles and miles of perfect breaks and beaches that aren't overcrowded like the more frequented shores of Jacó and Tamarindo.

It takes an hour and a half ferry ride from the nearest mainland port of Puntarenas and an additional two-hour drive through rocky, mountainous terrain just to arrive at the secluded little village.

Upon first glance, Mal País is by no means "pretty"... particularly in the dry season when the dust from the dirt roads covers everything it touches, and local sanitation workers have to spray molasses on the streets at night so that businesses aren't affected by the dirt.

But once you get off the roads and onto the beaches, the sights are breathtaking and the weather perfect. It is true that every person in town spills out daily to watch the sunset, many taking it in while catching the last waves of the day.

Experienced surfers can find everything they need at the local Cordoruy surf shop, run by a couple of ex-pat Americans who have been living in the area for more than a decade. The shop, located right on Playa Carmen, has a wide selection of clothing to buy, boards to rent, and even quality surf lessons for all levels right in their front yard. Cordoruy is a great place to stop in even without buying anything—as a popular local haunt, there is always someone who can offer advice on tides, and where the best beaches can be found.

One surprisingly doesn't have to travel any farther than Playa Carmen or the many beaches of Santa Teresa to catch some of the areas most choice waves, especially good for beginners. Heading further up north to Manzanillo and Playa Hermosa offers bigger breaks and even less crowded beaches. A little further up the road, Mal País Surf Camp offers lodging, surf lessons, movie nights, and even one of the town's most reputable party scenes.

With its extremely hard to reach location, Mal País is truly off the beaten path. Those determined enough to get here can spend weeks discovering the many secrets this dusty little surf haven holds.

# SANTA TERESA'S SODA

## By Jenna Mahoney, New York City, New York, U.S.A.

After a day of getting your butt kicked by Santa Teresa's epic waves, you'll need to refuel. And there's no better place than the Soda at Mama's house. Talk to the Ticos and they'll agree: Mama makes the best fish sandwiches around. And she's also got the only vegetarian yucca burgers in the land.

In Costa Rica, Sodas are actually roadside cafes. Most are an extension of private homes that just happen to serve food to visitors. It's rare that you'll find a printed menu, set price list, or an outdoor sign to indicate its existence. Such is the case at Mama's. The Soda at Mama's is located opposite the ocean. Her house sits on the only street that runs through the entire town. It's built into a small hill just a few hundred meters from Santa Teresa's popular surf spots—El Carmen and Playa Hermosa. Six or so plastic tables sit on a concrete porch that extends from a small home—that's the indication that you've made it to Mama's.

Take a seat and greet Mama. Then ask her what she has that day. (Note: It's rare that Mama actually leaves her kitchen, so you've got to politely yell through her open kitchen door). Her answers generally range from fresh-from-the-sea ceviche, melt-in-your-mouth fresh fish sandwiches, hand-cut spiced yucca patties or simple spaghetti. As with everything in Costa Rica, Mama's specialties are served with pinto, a spicy fry-up of beans, rice and lard. Yes, even the pasta.

Order a few *cervezas* and observe Tico life while you wait for your delicious dinner. Often Mama will have a daughter or neighbor helping her in the kitchen and serving as a waitress. You can listen to them tick away in Spanish and all the while you'll hear Mama dicing, slicing, and frying your food. In the next room, there's always a television blaring. Since it also opens onto the Soda's "dining room," you'll catch dad, some brothers and passing primos moving in and out of the house. Everyone says "hola" and they've all got a smile.

As with everything in Costa Rica, things may move slowly at Mama's, but since you feel as if you're part of the family, you won't mind the wait. That, and the food's not only the best, it's also made with some serious homemade lovin.'

## SURFING TRAVEL TIPS:

Costa Rica is one of the best places to surf, due to its warm water, accessible breaks and abundance of surf camps. Here are some tips if you decide to catch a wave or two on either (or both) of the coasts:
- Best breaks occur on the northern Pacific coast from December to April; central and southern Pacific coasts from May-November and on the Caribbean Coast from November-March.
- Leave your wetsuit at home—water temperatures rarely drop below 25 degrees Celsius.
- Black sand beaches like Playa Hermosa are *really* hot in the middle of the day and reefs on the Caribbean side can be shallow and sharp, so take care!
- Wanna try surfing for the first time, or are just need some more tips from a pro? Try these surf camps that promise to have you balancing on a board in no time: Witch's Rock Surf Camp, Pura Vida Adventures (camp for women only) and School of the World.

## JACÓ

### By Katie Hale

Surfboards sit propped next to doorways and tourists walk barefoot in the streets, sand stuck between their toes from a long day on the beach. Jacó is a popular resort for Costa Ricans and foreign visitors alike—especially ones who favor great waves. Nearby Playa Hermosa offers some of the most consistent breaks in Costa Rica. Located two hours from San José, Jacó is an easy escape to find both lazy days in the sun and a party atmosphere simultaneously.

If the early morning waves aren't calling to you, head 15 kilometers (nine miles) north to Carara National Park to view the beautiful scarlet macaws. Their red, blue and yellow plumage is brilliant and these social birds will sometimes talk to passersby.

In town, rent a moped and cruise around the small streets and the main drag that runs parallel to the coast. The passing view of palm trees and gray sand lapped by blue-green water is gorgeous, but don't let it distract from driving too much!

Back in Jacó, the sun slowly falls into the Pacific Ocean, illuminating the sky with hues of mandarin, fuchsia, and lavender. The tranquil scene is misleading though—Jacó is the one of the biggest party towns in Costa Rica and when night falls, the fiesta begins complete with dancing, drinks and gambling.

# MANUEL ANTONIO NATIONAL PARK

## By Cyril Brass, Vermilion, Alberta, Canada

Abundant wildlife, diverse ecosystems and stunning beaches are some of the things that make Manuel Antonio National Park one of the top wilderness areas in Costa Rica.

Unique in its land coverage, the Park spreads over a small portion of tropical rainforest and includes a significant offshore area out into the Pacific Ocean, encompassing small, uninhabited islands. Although the fame of the park has grown in recent years, and it is now a well-known tourist destination, it is still a must-see for the visitor to Costa Rica.

There are four beaches within the park area, each of which is outstanding. The two white sand beaches, Playa Espadilla Sur and Playa Manuel Antonio, are bordered by lush, living rainforest. Gentle waves brush up on the fine grain coral-white sand and the warm turquoise water allows visitors a chance to take a refreshing swim after a few hours of hiking the park trails.

The seven kilometers (4.3 miles) of marked trails will take intrepid nature enthusiasts deep into the humid tropical forest. The well-groomed trails meander through dense jungle growth to secluded coves, observation lookouts and a captivating waterfall. Take time for a picnic lunch at a one of the coves while soaking up the natural beauty of forest and sea, then take in the panoramic vistas along the pacific coastline before crossing a shallow creek whose origin is a picturesque waterfall sheltered by rich vegetation.

One of the easier walking trails is the Perezoso trail, named after the sloth, which can be sometimes seen in the area, as it favors secondary forest growth.

Another trail winds its way up through the forest-covered cliff of Punta Catedral (Cathedral Point). Once an island, it is now connected to the mainland by thousands of years of sediment and sand buildup. It is a worthwhile hike up the narrow path as it encircles the point, providing incredible views of the bird sanctuary islands and majestic open seas.

The diverse ecosystems provide excellent habitats and refuge for a wide variety of flora and fauna. Abundant wildlife can be spotted on the forest-lined trails, high on the tree canopy and on the pristine beaches. If you're lucky, you'll spot a coatimundi digging in the underbrush debris for bugs and insects, see a sluggish three-toed sloth climbing high overhead in the thick foliage, see colorful crabs scurrying on the damp forest floor or enjoy the white face capuchin monkeys playing in the trees above the trails. Other known species within the park are caiman (a sort of alligator), armadillo, agouti, deer and squirrel monkey. Manuel Antonio National Park is one of the few remaining habitats for the adorable endangered squirrel (titi) monkey.

Just as the wildlife is protected, so is the tropical vegetation of primary and secondary forests, mangrove swamps and lagoons. The endangered black locust, the poisonous Manzanillo tree, mayflower, balsa and palms provide a deep green background to the unspoiled beaches.

## LA MANSIÓN INN By Sandra Scott

Bats are not my favorite mammals, and normally anything associated with the furry, night-flying animal sets me shrieking. But when I checked into La Mansión Inn near Manuel Antonio, on the Pacific Coast of Costa Rica, and received a coupon for a free drink in the Bat Cave Bar, I just had to check it out. The fact that La Mansión is an upscale inn with a stunning view of Manuel Antonio Beach and the Pacific Ocean helped alleviate my fears—well, some of them.

The owner, Harry Bodaan, has clasped hands with notables from all walks of life. The entryway includes photos of Bodaan with personalities that run the gamut from Elizabeth Taylor to George Bush to Mikhail Gorbachev. They are just some of the people he met during his days as president of the Press Clubs in Washington, D.C., and Moscow. Celebrities have stayed at La Mansión and frequented the infamous Bat Cave and I was determined not to be left out of this select group.

La Mansión's location on the hillside allowed Bodaan to create the Bat Cave Bar without displacing the bats. The low-lit bar, hewn out of solid rock, is the only one of its kind in all of Costa Rica. Although the Bat Cave entrance is through a wooden door that looks like it was designed for Snow White's dwarfs, nothing here is Disneyesque. One wall is the natural rock formation complete with a small waterfall.

After the first sip of Bat Cave Juice—a yummy, fear-reducing combination of Liquor Perfecto Amor, chocolate liquor, cream, and sugar—I began to loosen up. The soothing sound of the waterfalls was also a help. With my angst and phobia under control, I wanted to see the bats. I finally worked up the nerve to look at the ceiling. No bats.

What? "Where are the bats?" I demanded, my nerve fortified by a Bat Cave cocktail. Diego, the somewhat frenetic but entertaining bartender, pointed: "There, behind the glass." Sure enough, there they were, hanging around their bat cave. It was comforting to realize I was hanging out in one Bat Cave and the bats had their own separate bat cave. It called for another round of Bat Cave cocktails.

Bats are not the only creatures sharing the La Mansión property. Beside Bodaan's three pampered pups, each morning I'd sit on the balcony of my room waiting for a troop of squirrel monkeys to scamper by on their morning forage for food.

For more information, check www.lamansioninn.com/cavebar. The accommodation is expensive, but a value considering it is rather upscale, and best suited for those looking for an intimate getaway with excellent service in a natural setting.

# HORSEBACK RIDING: A FAMILY AFFAIR

By Cat Hartwell, New York City, New York, U.S.A.

One of the best parts of staying in Costa Rica's southern Pacific coastal region is the bounty of eco-tourism activities a traveler can find. Hiking, kayaking, mountain biking, sports fishing—the list goes on and on.

But for the adventurous soul, there may be no better way to see the countryside than via horseback (and it certainly makes getting to the top of a mountain a lot easier). Although there are many tour guides offering scenic outings on horseback, perhaps the best of these outfitters is Don Lulo's Adventure Trip to Nauyaca Falls, one of the main natural attractions of Costa Rica's southern Pacific coastal region. Most of the tours offered by Don Lulo are appropriate for riders of any level and experience and include a full day of riding, swimming, meals and two guides to ensure a safe trip.

Don Lulo's Horseback Ride to Nauyaca Falls is a family-owned and operated enterprise from start to finish. The family home acts as the start of the journey, where riders pick up their horses, buy souvenirs, and chat with the man and lady of the house. Don Lulo's two sons then lead small groups up a mountainside and across two rivers, stopping halfway up the mountain for a homemade Tico-style breakfast at Don Julio's house—another family establishment.

Following breakfast, the tour continues to the top of the mountain, wrapping up at two gorgeous waterfalls that drop 150 ft. and 65 ft. respectively into a refreshing and crisp pool. Upon arrival to the falls, tourists can swim, sunbathe, and the more daring can dive from the falls. Lucky riders may persuade one of the tour guides to put on a very exciting show and dive from a rock that is at least thirty feet up.

After drying off, travelers get back on their horses and make the hour and a half descent back down the mountain, again stopping at Don Julio's house, this time for a delicious lunch (both meals are included in the tour fee). Don Julio's house also features a makeshift zoo, with toucans, iguanas, and other exotic creatures that people can photograph and interact with. At the bottom of the mountain, riders return their horses to the family home and have one last chance to buy souvenirs before making their way back to their hotels with memories, photos, and very sore bottoms to remind them of the day's adventure.

Cat Hartwell is a 27-year-old musician-by-night, hustler-by-day just trying to make it in NYC. She graduated from Boston University in 2001 with a degree that she sometimes uses in film & television, and moved to the big city to find herself in a touring pop band and editor of an urban lifestyle magazine within a year.

Now, in her second music group (a southern dance-punk band called Holy Hail), she finds herself paying the bills with jobs in fashion and television and skipping town to see the world whenever she can.

Hartwell's craziest experience was a three-day rampage through Istanbul. "It's amazing how much you can get done when you only have 72 hours." When she went to the Middle East in 2000 with a friend, she had bright red hair with blonde highlights, and all the kids were going up to her saying "Spice Girl! Spice Girl! You look like Spice Girl!!"

Her ambition is to hit all seven continents, but her next trip will be to Barcelona.

## HOTEL MONO AZUL

By Leigh Gower

Looking for a place to stay in Manuel Antonio? Look no further than the Hotel Mono Azul (in English, "Blue Monkey Hotel"). Located a mile up the hill going towards the park, this reasonably priced accommodation offers comfortable, rustic rooms surrounded by immense greenery and a tasty selection of food (the fruit smoothies are not to be missed).

The hotel is also home to the non-profit organization, Kids Saving the Rainforest, and ten percent of the hotel's profits go towards educating local children about rainforest conservation. Attached to the hotel, the gift shop exhibits original pieces of artwork and indigenous crafts made by local children; a percentage of these profits also go to the foundation.

Mono Azul offers a number of excellent tours. Particularly recommended is Rafa's Mangrove tour, which can be booked from the hotel. While other tour guides recommended by larger hotels bring along food to attract monkeys, Rafa insists that this severely detracts from the animals' natural habitat. But have no fear—you will see plenty of monkeys on Rafa's tour because his "children" know him very well and regularly come jumping onto his boat to visit and say hello. Hold onto your camera and sunglasses!

Rafa's knowledge of the wildlife in these waters is nothing short of amazing and he will point out snakes, deadly crabs, birds and other animals which the untrained eye might miss. Be careful though, he enjoys putting deadly crabs in his mouth for your viewing pleasure, which he happily admits could kill him with one pinch. That would make for an interesting journey back to the shore.

COSTA RICA

# PEACE OF MIND

### By Cat Hartwell, New York City, New York, U.S.A.

Two kilometers away from the main drag of Playa Dominical exists a little getaway known only to the very plugged-in and well-informed traveler. Local Dominical residents also hold this little secret close to hearts, because they know that it is here, at this special little place, that they can congregate daily and tap into a little bit of paradise and a lot of relaxation.

Coconut Grove is a small resort offering cozy beachfront cottages run by two Americans that have permanently retired to their favorite town in Costa Rica. Over the years, they have built the resort by themselves piece by piece. In addition to the cottages, Coconut Grove has an oceanfront swimming pool and a gazebo fully stocked with barbecue equipment and hammocks to lounge around on. The owners, Richard and Diane, love the Grove so much that they have built their own home right in front of the property, and it functions as both the reception area and the hub of all activity. The couple is known to throw a pretty hip party from time to time, and friends from far and near gather to enjoy their beautiful, idyllic estate.

Coconut Grove offers more than just lodging and a place to congregate. A couple years ago, Diane envisioned a place where both locals and guests at the Grove could practice yoga in the mornings and enjoy other physical activities all day long. Soon after, the open-air yoga studio at Coconut Grove was built. Offering sunrise yoga and Pilates classes throughout the week, the studio is the perfect place to enjoy the pure natural splendor that the Grove has to offer. Built by Richard and a couple of local men, the coconut wood and thatched roof perfectly fits the aesthetics of the resort. The classes are taught outside where yogis and yoginis can peacefully watch the waves crash a hundred yards away. Sometimes, an iguana wanders by or a flock of butterflies flitters past.

Yoga classes are taught every Monday, Tuesday and Friday by Jennifer Smith, a yogi who has been teaching for seventeen years, while Pilates is taught on Wednesdays and Thursdays. Popular with both locals and guests, the classes are intermediate to advanced, and because they are held on "Tico time" they can last anywhere from an hour and fifteen minutes to over two hours, depending on the teacher's state of mind. After classes, locals tend to gather and catch up over coffee and snacks, while guests meander over to the pool or beach for some more relaxing. Whether staying at Coconut Grove or elsewhere in Dominical, an early morning class here is the perfect way to start a day in this South Pacific town.

Baskets. Photo by JenFu Cheng.

*"The more freedom we enjoy, the greater the responsibility we bear, toward others as well as ourselves."*
-Oscar Arias Sánchez, Costa Rican President (1940-)

# VOLUNTEERING ADVENTURE IN COSTA RICA

By Richard Christiano, Lexington, Massachusetts, U.S.A.

As a young man—before I began working full-time and raising a family—I was fortunate enough to travel often, and after a 25-year hiatus, I decided to rekindle my passion for travel. Being older and, hopefully, a little wiser this time, I knew I wanted to experience more of a country and its culture than is normally experienced during a typical sightseeing vacation. Once I began investigating opportunities, my research led me to a New York company called "Cross Cultural Solutions" which sponsors volunteer opportunities in various parts of the globe. To give it a try, I signed up for a one week "insight abroad" program and chose Costa Rica as the destination.

My preference and expectation was to work with kids who have disabilities. My teenage son is autistic, and like any parent would, I had developed skills in this area. I was somewhat surprised to learn, two days before my departure, that I was to work at an HIV clinic in Cartago, Costa Rica, building an organic garden. It was rather far afield from what I had indicated on the very thorough questionnaire they had me submit, but I thought that if that's where they needed me, that's where I'd go.

Like many, I'm familiar with the facts of HIV, but haven't had a lot of direct contact with people in the advanced stages of AIDS. After working in the garden and swinging a pick ax for several hours a day, I spent time with the residents. We talked about life, politics and their own situations. It was up to the patients whether they wanted to mingle with the volunteers and it usually depended upon on how much energy they could muster. Everyone in the clinic was quite weak and was there to recuperate.

I was struck by one gentleman in particular who I conversed with daily. His name was Fernando and he was a very distinguished-looking older man of what I guessed to be about 65 years old. Fernando spoke of the years he spent as an owner of a restaurant/bar on Costa Rica's Caribbean coast. Although most of our discussions needed a translator, the conversation flowed. He told me of a cross-country bicycle race he competed in as a young man, and won, and he spoke fondly of his departed wife. On the last day of my assignment I found out he was actually 81 years old. I think his innate, gentle nature and aristocratic bearing served him well. Unlike others, he never mentioned how he contracted the disease.

Surprisingly, several of the residents weren't reluctant to talk about their situation. One man had lived a sexually irresponsible life and spoke with surprising humor of his misperception that the disease would never strike him. Another woman, a housewife, was unfortunately infected by her philandering husband.

The star of the clinic was Carolina, a little girl barely over one year old that stayed with her mother, a patient at the clinic. For whatever medical reason, they could not determine if Carolina was infected or not until she was 18 months old—and an unspoken hope existed in all that she would be spared the consequences of this terrible illness. They still didn't have the results when I left.

In addition to the satisfaction we received from building an organic garden and providing the residents with fresh, healthy vegetables, I made some friends and I think I made a small, positive difference in their lives. On my last day at the clinic, everyone gathered to present me with a memento for my efforts; a small wooden building façade to represent the clinic. A long speech in Spanish accompanied the gift and a card, signed by everyone. I was quite touched at their overwhelming appreciation which was not just for my hard work but for my understanding.

A volunteer vacation is not for everyone, but if you're not afraid of hard work and want to see a country from the inside out, it's an incredible adventure. I'm sure much of the enjoyment I experienced had to do with the Costa Rican people I met and their wonderful outlook on life. The quality of the program was also a major factor. One week is a good way to evaluate if this is the type of adventure you want, and so for my next visit I'll almost certainly spend more time. I was able to do a little sightseeing in the three days before my assignment began, but I wish I had scheduled an additional three or four days to see more of the country.

If your idea of travel to another country includes getting off the beaten path and experiencing what life is really like away from the hotels and beaches, a volunteer vacation might be a something for you to consider.

Richard Christiano is once again traveling the world after a 25-year hiatus. He has worked at Harvard University for the past 20 years and is a graduate from the University of Massachusetts with a master's degree in Education from Cambridge College. In addition to his full time job as Director of Facilities for Harvard Business School Publishing, he also teaches in a continuing education program at Boston University and is an adjunct professor at Wentworth Institute. His very athletic, 17- year-old autistic son is his constant companion and future traveling partner.

Christiano dreams of exploring Ethiopia and currently has a trip planned to climb Mt. Rainier in Washington State (his second attempt).

# OROSÍ

### By Hannah Fairlie Agran, Des Moines, Iowa, U.S.A.

The views from the road into Orosí are as stunning as the town is charming. Buses and cars slowly wind along the edge of a lush valley anchored by a snaking river and carpeted with verdant coffee fields. The steep hillsides, dotted with colorful houses and patches of forest, cradle the town center, where most of the valley's 10,000 residents live.

Coffee is a large component of the local economy, but the town has grown to comfortably accommodate a small tourist population. Orosí's location—a half hour from Cártago's magnificent *Basílica Nuestra Señora de Los Angeles*, an hour from Irazú Volcano, and less than two hours from San José—and its low-key atmosphere make it an ideal base for exploring the region and experiencing small-town Costa Rica firsthand.

Orosí's two main streets run parallel through the town, flanking the all-important soccer field in the city center. Most businesses, including the supermarket, bank, butcher, and bakery, line one side of the main street, while Orosí's famous Iglesia San José Orosí sits along the other. Built in 1743, the squat white structure is the oldest continuously operating church in Costa Rica. The church courtyard is attractively landscaped, and a religious museum filled with dusty relics is open most days. Orosí has developed a solid infrastructure for tourists.

Accommodation ranges from budget to upscale, but nothing is shockingly expensive. Visitors can sample traditional food, enjoy homemade pizza on the main drag, nurse lattes at a comfortable coffeehouse, or have a beer at a local bar. For an even more authentic experience, many travelers enroll for a week or two at Montaña Linda, a foreign-run Spanish school with strong community ties. Students can opt for a full immersion and live with families in town, or they can stay at the nearby hostel, which offers maps and walks into the surrounding countryside.

Although it is fun to hike into the hills, strolling around town is a pleasant alternative. Residents are used to visitors and greet passers-by with a musical "Buenas!" as they go about their errands. Pickup trucks laden with seasonal produce trundle through town, and men and children zip by on bicycles. Stray dogs roam the streets, patrolling their imaginary territory. A soccer ball is nearly always in play on the central plaza. It is typical Costa Rican life—unaffected, friendly, and utterly *tranquilo*.

---

**OROSÍ TRAVEL TIPS:**

Visit *El Museo de Arte Religioso* to view religious artifacts and artwork housed in the former monastery. The church is open every morning and the museum is open seven days a week. Also worth stopping at is the *Mirador de Orosí* located on the road to Paraíso. This vantage point offers breathtaking views of the valley below.

---

*"Your hands are not clean to fight communism when you don't fight dictatorships."*
*-José Figueres Ferrer (1906-1990), former Costa Rican President, to U.S. interviewers*

---

## MONTEVERDE DAIRY FACTORY  By Leigh Gower

The story of the Monteverde Cheese Factory is one of quality dairy produce and—perhaps surprisingly—international history. In order to escape the draft of the Korean War, with which their religious beliefs heavily conflicted, a group of seven Quaker families from the U.S. moved to Costa Rica. In 1953 they founded the dairy factory in order to make a living, and today it is a thriving producer of excellent cheese.

The factory produces approximately 17 different kinds of cheese. The Monteverde's Gouda was the first pasteurized cheese made in Costa Rica. During the factory tour you will watch the cheese-making process and learn how they make milk and ice-cream. The factory adheres to a list of stringent ethics under the eco-friendly attitude that the Quakers insisted upon years ago. If the dairy's tempting smells are not enough to entice you, the samples offered at the tour's end will surely convince you to get in line and purchase a tub of ice-cream, assortment of cheese or other dairy treats.

Some interesting facts and figures: The factory earns an astonishing approximately 10 million dollars a year and employs over 1,100 of Monteverde's 11,000 people. They buy milk from 250 farms in the area, produce around 1,550 kg. (3,417 lbs.) of cheese a day and are a primary supplier of cheese throughout Costa Rica. The cheese factory's employees union also owns the only gas station in Monteverde, without which the nearest gas pump would be 35 kilometres (22 miles) away!

# CHIRRIPÓ

By Hannah Fairlie Agran, Des Moines, Iowa, U.S.A.

As an inexperienced hiker, I didn't think I would survive the two-day trek up Chirripó, Costa Rica's highest peak. I puffed and panted behind my friends, focusing my eyes on the myriad of toggles and straps on their packs and cursing myself for agreeing to come along.

We hiked the first 14 kilometers (8.6 miles) by day, marveling at the mystical foliage, swirling fog, and grand vistas. The second morning, we left the rangers' base camp at three a.m., hoping to reach the top before dawn. I followed the intrepid, bobbing head lamps above me, pausing periodically to catch my breath and look back at the tumbled landscape of scrubby trees and jutting peaks spread below. As the black sky melted into rosy oranges and pinks, I clambered up the final rocks and huddled with my friends, 12,529 feet (3,818 meters) above sea level, watching the sun rise over bands of soft clouds.

Chirripó crowns the Talamanca range, southern Costa Rica's geological backbone. The indigenous tribe that named the peak was surely inspired by the crystal lakes nestled below it—Chirripó means "Land of the Eternal Waters." However, modern-day hikers will be just as impressed by the stunning range of ecosystems that blanket the mountainside. In some areas, towering bamboo stands flank the trail, and in others, branches heavy with moss hang overhead. Jewel-like blue ants crisscross the path, and beady-eyed lizards dart among the damp leaves.

Higher up, the forest opens onto an eerie landscape scarred by fires, where charred trunks twist about like hands reaching out from graves. It is re-

> *Higher up, the forest opens onto an eerie landscape scarred by fires, where charred trunks twist about like hands reaching out from graves.*

assuring to find the base camp hostel, Los Crestones, tucked in a pretty valley, several kilometers below the satisfyingly windswept summit.

Because Chirripó is such a popular destination, the steep trail is well maintained, though slippery and muddy during the rainy season. You must register ahead of time, in San Isidro or at the ranger station in the village of San Gerardo de Rivas because you can not hike Chirripó if you don't, plus beds are limited at the camp. Most people cover 14 kilometers (8.6 miles) on the first day, as we did, leaving before eight a.m. and arriving at the hostel mid-afternoon. The facility is spare, but clean, and the young staff is friendly. The cheerful communal kitchen is well stocked, and there are blankets, sleeping bags, and gas stoves available to rent. Temperatures approach freezing and electricity is unreliable, so warm clothes and flashlights are essential (only one person in our group braved the cold water showers).

On day two, many groups rise early for the final five km (three mile) stretch to the summit. Sunrise at the top is worth the dark climb. Some people spend two nights at the hostel, resting their muscles and exploring the lakes, but others head back to San Gerardo after reaching the peak, as I did. San Gerardo offers several food and lodging options, all catering to the Chirripó crowd.

On our last night, warm and clean, we clinked glasses over steaming banana pancakes and regaled new arrivals with the tales of our climb.

---

**CHIRRIPÓ TRAVEL TIPS:**
When climbing Chirripó there are a few essentials you should not go without. Here's a short list to make your adventure a bit more comfortable: plastic bags (it rains—sometimes a lot—and you don't want everything getting soaked), sunscreen, extra food and headlamp.

---

## LA FINCA DE MARIPOSAS

By Leigh Gower

One of the most popular excursions close to San José, La Finca de Mariposas—the Butterfly Farm—in Alajuela, north of Costa Rica's capital city, will surely add a flutter of color to your travels. Opened in 1983, the Butterfly Farm was the first commercial farm of its kind in Latin America and today exports thousands upon thousands of butterflies to Europe each year. Since butterflies only live for on average between three weeks and a month, frequent shipments are required to replenish European exhibits.

At the farm, in the subtropical climate of the La Guacima suburb in Alajuela, visitors take part in a two-hour tour during which the life cycle and natural history of these beautiful insects is explained. Photographic opportunities abound, particularly in sunny conditions when the butterflies tend to be most active. In fact, the spectacular colors of the butterflies are their means of protection from predators.

Today the farm is home to over 500 butterflies from some 40 species, 50 tropical plants and a scenic waterfall. Since each type of butterfly will feed on only one specific plant, the 50 different tropical plants are needed just to maintain the plethora of butterfly species. If you are keen to observe the economics of the farm, make sure to visit on an export day when you can watch thousands of pupae being packed for shipment.

# RÍO PACUARE RAFTING

## By Cyril Brass, Vermilion, Alberta, Canada

"Paddle hard!"
"Hold on!"
"Take a break!"

Ah, the commands shouted by your friendly, experienced river guides while aboard a wild rafting expedition on Costa Rica's Río Pacuare.

Nestled deep in the Costa Rican tropical rainforest, the Río Pacuare is a whitewater enthusiast's dream, paddling down one of the world's most rugged rivers, maneuvering through the turbulent waters, deep in the heart of densely forested gorges, cascading waterfalls, narrow passages and pounding rapids.

Far removed from civilization, the Río Pacuare descends from the Talamanca Mountain Range, pouring onto the lowland plains near the town of Siquirres, then curving its way eastward toward the Caribbean. High annual rainfall generates great volume of runoff, creating consistent opportunities for whitewater rafting trips year round. However, the best time to battle the rapids is during the rainy season—May to November.

Profiling the more wild side of the country's eco-adventures, the Río Pacuare has been named an official Wild and Scenic River by the Costa Rican government, the first waterway in Central America to hold that honor. This renowned river plunges through an unexplored jungle of primary and secondary rainforest. The protected region is still inhabited by the indigenous Cabécar Indians. In a wilderness of dense vegetation, the thick undergrowth also provides an isolated sanctuary for jaguars, monkeys, sloths and many other animals and birds.

The Pacuare has some of the world's most challenging whitewater. With the majority of the rapids recorded as Class III and IV (whitewater with irregular, long, difficult rapids), paddlers enjoy stretches of white knuckle rapids interspersed with relaxing floats that allow them to catch their breath and soak up the beauty around them. Free-spirited adventurers are rewarded with a thrilling action-packed ride of twists and turns, foaming water, huge waves and breathtaking scenery.

Each rafting excursion begins early in the morning, as rafters are collected at their hotels in San José. Enjoy a scenic drive along the foothills of the Irazú and Turrialba volcanoes on the way to the river "put in." Professional bilingual tour operators and guides will take care of you through the entire adventure. Safety and paddling instructions will be explained before hitting the water. Protective safety gear is always worn while on the river. A safety kayak accompanies the rafts during the voyage down the raging river.

Rafting the Río Pacuare is an excellent choice for an adventurous ride filled with stunning natural beauty and breathtaking rapids. Whether you're an expert or beginner, nature lover or thrill seeker, rafting the Río Pacuare will be an action-packed, unforgettable experience.

---

FACTOID:
Ever wonder what Class III rapids really entail? All of that rafting jargon sometimes can be confusing, and if you don't know what you're getting yourself into, you can be headed for serious trouble. Here are the definitions of the classes to clear things up.
Class I (easy): Fast moving water, with small waves. Very few obstructions that can be easily dodged with little training.
Class II (novice): Straightforward rapids, where occasional maneuvering may be required.
Class III (intermediate): Rapids with moderate, irregular waves. Scouting is recommended for the inexperienced.
Class IV (advanced): Intense, but usually predictable rapids. Scouting is usually necessary the first time down because of likely dangerous hazards.
Class V (expert): Extremely long, obstructed, and violent rapids. Proper equipment, training and rescue skills are needed for navigation.
Class VI (extreme and exploratory): These runs have almost never been attempted. These rapids are only for experts and have severe consequences.

Rafting. Photo by Cyril Brass.

# FROM GROUND TO GRANDE: COSTA RICAN COFFEE

By Katie Hale, Corvallis, Oregon, U.S.A:

Any die-hard coffee drinker will tell you that first cup of Joe in the morning is essential to start the day off on the right foot. For the true coffee connoisseur, no watered-down cup of grab-and-go java from the corner store will do.

Finding that perfect blend is no easy task. That's why many consumers compromise, leaving it up to mega-corporations like Starbucks to deliver their daily caffeine buzz. These middlemen offer freshly brewed espresso intended to lure the coffee junkie in, and they keep them coming back with trendy, exotically titled coffee blends, warm scones, and Norah Jones melodies that play seductively in the background.

You won't find Starbucks in Costa Rica ... at least not yet. Central and South America produce more coffee than any other area of the world, but it is Costa Rica in particular that has set the standard for coffee production.

Coffee was introduced to Costa Rica in 1808 from Cuba. In 1821 the government started giving out free coffee plants and ensured that families who produced coffee would live a tax-free life. Juan Mora Fernández was elected the country's first head of state in 1824. He encouraged the cultivation of coffee with land grants for growers. These land owners saw rapid wealth, creating a new class of Costa Rican elite. The rest of the 19th century saw a dramatic rise in coffee exports and overnight, Costa Rica changed from a fledging third world country, to a more successful and dominant nation due to its coffee cash crop. In 1843, the first coffee export to Britain was shipped. Soon after, the U.K. heavily invested in the trade, becoming its main buyer until World War II.

Costa Rica is an ideal place to cultivate coffee because of its land and climate. Its volcanic-rich soil, high altitude, afternoon sun, plentiful rain, and cool evenings together create perfect conditions for yielding beans that are rich and intense in flavor. The most famous coffees types by region are Tarrazú, Tres Rios, Herediá, and Alajuela. The Tres Rios region near the Pacific Coast produces coffees that are mild, sweet, and bright. The Tarrazú region, which is located in the mountains of Costa Rica, produces a complex, heavier coffee. A "classic" Costa Rican coffee is clean, balanced, and strong.

Unlike many coffees, Costa Rican coffees are generally identified either by the estate or farm (*finca*) on which they were grown, or by cooperative or processing facility (*beneficio*) where they were processed. This information, which is often available to the importer, is seldom passed on to the consumer, except in the case of well-known estates like Bella Vista or La Minita. Hacienda La Minita cultivates the most sought after coffee in all of Costa Rica, thanks to clever marketing and product quality.

Coffee harvesting in Costa Rica is mainly dependent on the cheap labor of Nicaraguan immigrants, who make around $12 a day picking coffee cherries. After the cherries are picked, they are transported to the *beneficios*, where they undergo washing, drying, removal of the skin, and sorting.

There is nothing like the aroma of fresh coffee—whether it be from fields of growing coffee plants or brewing espresso. When you return home from Costa Rica, and find yourself standing in line for five minutes for that *macchiato*, it will definitely seem worth the wait, since you now know it that it takes six years for a coffee shrub to bear fruit. But even if your ordered blend is harvested from Costa Rican mountain-sides, there is no doubt; you will miss the authentic flavor only available back in the paradise nation itself.

Katie Hale is a fourth generation San Diegan, and grew up in both California and Oregon. She recently graduated from the University of Oregon with a B.A. in Journalism. Her first trip abroad at age 17 to Ghana, West Africa, left her with a bad case of wanderlust she hasn't since been able to shake. She has traveled extensively throughout Europe solo and hopes to next visit Southeast Asia.

Hale's most bizarre cultural experience was living in a neighborhood in a city with two million people, where no one had seen a white person before. Getting spit on, making kids curious enough to touch you, and being whistled at daily can only make a person stronger.

She is a recent addition to the V!VA Travel Guides team, and currently resides in Quito where she is attempting to sharpen her Spanish and salsa skills.

## GUARO By Leigh Gower

Even with my limited comprehension of Spanish, I understood that Guaro was not a drink for the faint of heart. Made from distilled sugarcane, *aguardiente de caña*, as it is generically known, is a potent, if unrefined beverage that will quite literally numb parts of your body after a measly couple of shots. The local brand is bottled by Cacique, which means "Indian Chief," and it is thought that the drink was invented by the Guaro Indians although this remains unconfirmed. The red- and black-labeled bottles boast the image of "Cuatro Plumas," the four-feathered Indian chief. The drink's popularity is probably a result of its affordable price. Where Guaro is being consumed, you may hear the locals chanting a celebratory song to the draft, such as the Moonshine anthem, translated here:

"From the sugarcane comes the Guaro.
Caramba! The cane is a good fruit!
If you crush the cane you can suck the Guaro from it's waters.
El Guaro, you are the one who said you would never forget me.
Come—let's get drunk until the sunrise starts the new day!
It's popularity is a result of it's low price."

COSTA RICA

# PLAYA ZANCUDO

### By Hannah Fairlie Agran, Des Moines, Iowa, U.S.A.

Step onto Playa Zancudo, look up or down the beach, and for kilometers in either direction, you will see ... nothing. Just a serene expanse of sand, sky, and water punctuated by swaying palm trees and bleached driftwood. Perhaps you'll spot a handful of guys playing soccer or a couple lying out on a blanket, but it's most likely you'll have a wide swath of the six-kilometer beach to yourself.

In touristy Costa Rica, this sort of seclusion is hard to come by without making a determined effort to leave behind the hotels and restaurants of the more popular destinations. But at Zancudo, you can eat and sleep well and enjoy a practically private coastal oasis. The biggest factor in Zancudo's low-key atmosphere is its geographical isolation. It is perched on a slender spit that juts out from the mainland opposite the Osa Peninsula. Visitors arrive from Golfito, and most forgo the long, bumpy bus ride in favor of a scenic boat-taxi trip along the shore of the Golfo Dulce.

The water taxis are just beat up old speedboats, and the drivers don't bother with pointing out landmarks or wildlife. Nothing fancy—just cold water splashing into the hull and salt spray clinging to your hair as the little boat skips over the waves under a blazing tropical sun. You'll arrive in Zancudo wetter, rosier, and, in all likelihood, mellower, than when you left.

Many of Zancudo's full-time residents are ex-pats. Some run hotels, cabinas or restaurants, and others live in the large homes that dot the shoreline. Unlike in some beach towns, however, where foreigners feel like an intrusion, here they blend in among the sand and sun. The buildings are nearly all hidden among the trees, and they are strung out along a single sandy road. There is no nightlife to speak of, other than laughter and conversation over drinks or desserts.

The inexpensive hotels cater to weekend visitors, while pricier places offer week- and even month-long options. The restaurants are outstanding, serving delicious meals in comfortable, friendly settings. The outsiders who have moved here do not want it to change, but they don't mind sharing it with others who want to escape the blaring party scene at Costa Rica's better-known beaches.

Even the ocean matches the mood here. Though there is excellent surfing at nearby Pavones, about 15 kilometers south, most of Zancudo's waves are too small. The warm water is lovely for wading, kayaking, or cooling off after a frisbee toss, and it is ideal for night swimming. Many evenings, the sea sparkles with phosphorescence. As you move, a glittery track lights up behind your feet, hands, and hair. On starry nights, the magical effect is magnified, as the shimmering water mirrors the twinkling sky. Standing in the luminous waves, staring up into the silent night, it is easy to see why so many visitors, having come once, never want to leave.

---

ZANCUDO TRAVEL TIPS: For a place to meet people that radiates relaxation, head for the Cabinas Sol y Mar. Join in a volleyball or horseshoes game or pick up one of the boogie boards lying around and hop in the lulling waves. If you aren't feeling energetic, grab a good read at the book exchange, order a drink at the bar, sit back and soak up the afternoon rays.

---

## HOMESTAY AT FLAMINGO BEACH

By Leigh Gower

The small concrete hut with its corrugated roof greeted me as I peered out of the bus window and over the two thin pieces of barbed wire—barely redeemable as a fence—at my home for the coming month. I had arrived in Potrero, on the northern coast of Costa Rica's Guanacaste region, and for all purposes of intent, the absolute middle of nowhere.

Potrero is a tiny coastal town and, like so many Costa Rican communities, it is centered around a soccer pitch which, when not being used for play, becomes the roaming ground of aimless village chickens and dogs. With few distractions on offer in the town itself, apart from the tranquil beach some mere footsteps away, I contentedly prepared myself to be devoted to my Spanish lessons.

The nearby Spanish school, CPI, in Playa Flamingo offered an excellent standard of study set in a clean modern complex complete with a swimming pool for use between classes. Flamingo is a relatively upmarket town where lots of yachts dock and which also hosts a stunning beach where you can go boogie boarding—but beware of the tide; it gets extremely strong without much warning!

As my Spanish improved I took part in after-school activities including outrigging and snorkeling to a deserted beach nearby, a trip to the Arenal volcano and La Fortuna waterfall and even a weekend trip to Granada, Nicaragua.

After a month of lessons, my Spanish had come on in leaps and bounds and my stomach had finally grown accustomed to being served *gallo pinto*, a traditional dish of rice and refried black beans, for breakfast. My tan wasn't looking too bad either.

# OSA PENINSULA

By Thomas Plunkett, Aurora, Ohio, U.S.A..

Hidden at the edge of lush tropical secondary rainforest, on a secluded stretch of sand on the Golfo Dulce, sits the Iguana Lodge. A beautifully handcrafted jungle eco-lodge, the Iguana is an exotic, magical place set smack-dab in the middle of one of the most biologically diverse environments on earth.

The owners, ex-pats from Denver, Colorado, live 30 feet up in the air in a 2,500 square foot tree house built into in a massive native hardwood tree. The entire property is remarkable—a small grouping of immaculately clean bungalows amidst the rainforest are intertwined with manicured connecting paths leading to the beach, bar, restaurant, main lodge, Japanese hot bath or off into any direction for exploring the ripe green flora and fauna. The close contact with nature is truly amazing.

After waking in the early morning to the eerie shrieks of howler monkeys, my wife and I sat for coffee on our veranda while troops of white-faced capuchin monkeys cavorted around our bungalow, dropping slowly down to our railing barely five feet away to eat bananas we tossed to them. After breakfast, we moseyed down to the private secluded beach, just 200 feet from our room, and watched as sea turtles hatched in the sand and struggled to crawl the 30 yards into the ocean. It was utterly fascinating to observe this event. My wife and I did pick up a few stragglers and hand-delivered them into the water before watching them swim away.

Iguana Lodge is a bird watcher's paradise. In a single, easy paced walk through the jungle you can spot hundreds of colorful native birds as well as three-toed sloths, leafcutter ants, boa constrictors, you name it. This area is teeming with wildlife. The water is just as full of life: if you're lucky, you may get to snorkel alongside a monster whale shark, as they are known to swim just off the beach.

We hired an English-speaking guide from the lodge, Juan Carlos, who took us alone into the Golfo Dulce in a 23-foot powerboat in search of wild spinner dolphins. After an hour or so of searching in the open ocean, we found a huge pod with at least 120 frolicking dolphins. Quickly, we scrambled over the side and Juan Carlos threw us a tow line. We were equipped with swim masks and as he slowly towed us through the water, to our amazement, hundreds of wild spinners at least ten feet long swam right up next to us. They were so close, I could nearly touch them. They seemed as curious about us as we were about them. After 45 minutes, the pod left the area. We found a quiet spot to snorkel and then had lunch on the boat. Total cost for this day-long unbelievable experience—$45 per person!

If you want to enjoy a very affordable adventurous vacation that has exotic animals, beautiful scenery, perfect weather, is safe, has clean water, hot showers, nice rooms and friendly staff—this is it!

Thomas Plunkett was in the air force when he was first exposed to the wonders of travel and has been hooked ever since. He is now a fire department captain.

One of the craziest places he's traveled to is Goose Bay, Labrador, in the Arctic Circle when it was 122 degrees below zero. His work schedule allows him plenty of time to travel, which he takes full advantage of.

Tree frog. Photo by Mauricio Fonseca.

# PARQUE NACIONAL CORCOVADO

### By Wes Weston, Sarasota, Florida, U.S.A.

Her words didn't offer much reassurance. "Avoid crossing too far up the river because you may encounter crocodiles, and don't cross too close to the mouth of the river because sharks like to feed there," was the last thing the ranger told me at the La Leona station where we entered Parque Nacional Corcovado.

I neglected to pass on this sage advice to my father and his friend, who had flown in to join me roughly 24 hours before on this trek through Costa Rica's most exquisite tropical preserve. It would be much more fun to tell them once we entered the river crossing. Timing is everything.

Our destination, the La Sirena ranger station, was about 15 km (nine miles) into the heart of Corcovado. As we made our way in and out of the living corridors of the tropical forest and along secluded coastal beaches, a revelation hit me like a shot of guaro. We had been walking more than three hours and hadn't seen another living soul other than some scarlet macaws, several monkeys, and a group of coatamundis (that I suspected was following us).

I had lived in Costa Rica for a year, traveled from one end to the next, and would never have imagined there's a place in this country where you can go more than one hundred paces without running into another gringo. Had I indeed found paradise? Parque Nacional Corcovado certainly sits apart from the rest.

It's the largest of 13 national parks and resides on the Osa Peninsula in the southwest region of Costa Rica. To get to Corcovado, it's just a short 10-hour bus ride from San José to Puerto Jiménez, then a 1.5-hour taxi ride to Carate, before you can hike one kilometer to the park entrance at La Leona. You have to want it, and that's what makes Corcovado so difficult for those travelers without a great deal of time. But once you get there, the park's majestic beauty is so invigorating that you'll never want to leave.

With its pristine vistas and uncharted territories, Corcovado´s tranquility is only surpassed by its abundant bio-diversity. The park is home to roughly 140 different mammal species, 400 bird species, and 500 species of trees. As they say in Spanish, *"increíble!"* Four ranger stations are connected along a network of timeless trails providing sanctuary to nature lovers, hikers, and tourists alike.

After four days exploring the wonders of Parque Nacional Corcovado, my comrades and I were forced to leave this plush utopia due to an inescapable force of nature known as "work." Nevertheless, I had found what I was looking for this entire time: a place without ongoing construction work that prohibits a highly anticipated mid-day siesta or loud discos blasting reggaeton until sunrise. I found a place that seemed to be surrounded by as much life as there were stars in the night sky. I had found paradise. And that ... is Pura Vida.

## TOP LIST: GLORIOUS NATIONAL PARKS

Think enjoying nature in Latin America is sipping a piña colada on a golden beach? Think again! Mother Nature has many faces in this part of the world, and some of the most beautiful spots have been preserved as national parks. These are some of our readers' favorites:

1. Torres del Paine National Park, Chile (p. 341).
"Dramatic landscapes with glaciers, lakes and snow-capped mountains make it one of the best National Parks in the world." Teresa Colomer, Madrid, Spain.

"The most amazing mountain scenery and hiking, even for near beginners like me." Chris Hurling, U.K.

2. Corcovado National Park, Costa Rica (see above).
"The most beautiful place of the world I have seen so far! An incredible abundance of wildlife—we have seen nearly everything living there ... tapirs, parrots, puma, monkeys (three different species), crocodiles, a shark ... just amazing. Together with an astonishingly beautiful hike with river crossings and marvelous beaches and forest parts ... " Annika Guse, Germany.

3. Manuel Antonio National Park, Costa Rica (p. 202).
"A small park along the Pacific Ocean with abundant wildlife and white sand beaches." Cyril Brass, Canada.

4. Tayrona National Park, Colombia (p. 225).
"Huge national park in the northwestern tip of Colombia. The Lost City is within the park. The park offers stunning beaches, snow-capped mountains, rainforests." Colombian South American Explorers Club.

"Chill out where jungle meets white sand beaches with coconut palms." Chris Hurling, U.K.

4. Cotopaxi National Park, Ecuador (p. 248).
"The splendour of the Cotopaxi Volcano makes it to be one of the most important of the world." Teresa Colomer, Madrid, Spain.

5. Glaciers National Park, Argentina.
"It houses several of the best glaciers of the world." Teresa Colomer, Madrid, Spain.

6. Tortuguero National Park, Costa Rica (p. 196).
"Located in a remote part of northeastern Costa Rica, this park is true natural jungle with a network of freshwater canals to explore the natural beauty. This park is also the nesting site for the endangered green sea turtle." Cyril Brass, Canada.

7. Villa La Angostura, Argentina.
"All in one. Nature, lakes, mountains, incredible flower explosion, snow, and all the sports you can imagin." Villa La Angostura Neuquen Patagonia, Argentina. "Don't lose the opportunity of visiting paradise on earth!" Eduardo Arce, Argentina.

# COCOS ISLAND DIVING

By JenFu Cheng, Roseland, New Jersey, U.S.A.

Not everyone looks for the opportunity to be in close proximity with sharks. But if you are one of those rare souls, there are few places in the world more impressive than Cocos Island.

It is certainly no easy feat to reach this unique location. Sitting 550 kilometers (340 miles) off the Pacific Coast of Costa Rica, Cocos Island National Park is a 36-hour boat trip from the mainland. But those with enough patience, determination, and motion-sickness medication will be treated to an unforgettable experience.

Getting to Cocos Island isn't the only challenge. The water is warm (25-28° Celsius) but unpredictable; thermoclines cause the temperatures to plunge significantly in places. The dives are generally deep (25-30 meters) with potentially strong currents. These factors and variables make Cocos Island a poor place for beginners to hone their skills: don't go if you're not totally confident in your gear and abilities.

Over 300 species of fish have been identified in the waters of Cocos Island, but it is the large pelagic migratory species (chief among which are sharks) that provide for the jaw-dropping experiences. The rocky, underwater pinnacles and small satellite islands provide perfect sites for cleaning stations where hammerhead sharks and other pelagics gather to remove parasites. The Alcyone and Dirty Rock sites are particularly amazing. In the open water, enormous schools of fish gather in "bait balls." These spiraling orchestrations of thousands of fish dance against a deep blue backdrop, that is, until a group of predators decimates it in a matter of minutes!

Cages? What cages!?! Diving with the sharks in Cocos Island is a rather "exposed" situation. While whitetip sharks rest comfortably on the ocean floor during the day, at night they roam the rocks *en masse*, hunting in "packs." One almost pities their prey, cowering in small rock recesses. What a way for them to spend each night! For the most part, the whitetip sharks pay no attention to the divers, so one can have a "front row seat" to this incredible action.

With huge schools of hammerheads, countless whitetips, occasional silvertips, and many other species, Cocos will definitely not fail to thrill.

JenFu Cheng M.D. travels the world with the goal of capturing in photographs the essence of his passions. He learned the technical aspects of photography through a voracious appetite for books and magazines on the subject. However, being an avid climber, hiker and SCUBA diver, his inspiration has come from a close connection with his subject matter. Cheng sees photography as a means of exploring new facets of each sport as well as communicating to others his love of the outdoor world.

His next trip will involve heading down to Grand Cayman to help teach a group of paraplegic teenagers how to SCUBA dive.

Diving. Photo by JenFu Cheng.

COCOS ISLAND FACTOIDS: It is the largest uninhabited island in the world. Michael Crichton wrote *Jurassic Park* with this place in mind. Pirates made Cocos a stopping off point and a home base, especially during the 1800s. It is estimated that if the treasure recounted in the lore and legends from long ago is still hidden in Cocos, it is worth around $1 billion.

COSTA RICA

# PANAMA

**The Land Divided; The World United**

With the Caribbean Sea to the north, the Pacific Ocean to the south, the land that connects Central and South America provides its own unique charms among her Latin neighbors. It features the largest rain forest in North America, making it home to wildlife (including 900 species of birds) not found elsewhere in Central America.

The country whose name refers to "many fish and butterflies" is also home to one of the most modern capital cities in Central America, Panama City, a major mercantile and banking center whose economy is currently experiencing unprecedented growth.

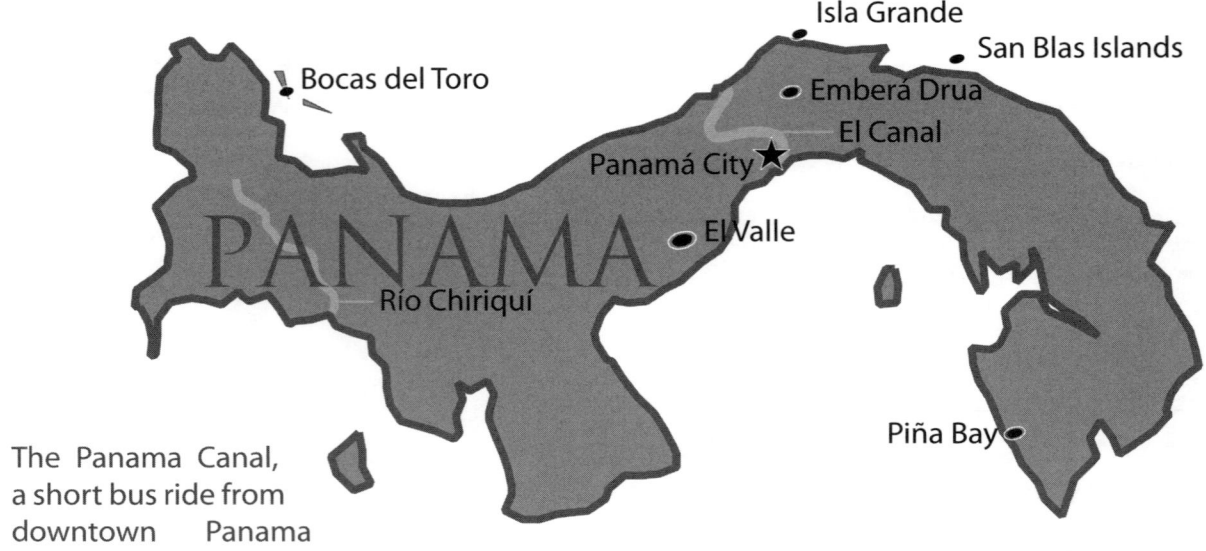

The Panama Canal, a short bus ride from downtown Panama City, is an engineering marvel and an integral part of Panama's economy and history.

In the realm of culture and sports, Panama lays claim to being the home country of such internationally recognized musicians as Rubén Blades, Billy Cobham, and Miguel Bosé and an extraordinary roster of boxing (Roberto Duran), baseball (Rod Carew) and fútbol (Rommel Fernández) champions, among scores of athletes excelling in many other sports.

The Caribbean coast features some dazzling getaways like the Bocas del Toro Archipelago. Home to six large islands and dozens of little ones, this archipelago is one of the fastest growing areas in Central America. Also worth a visit are the fascinating San Blas Islands, numbering over 365 (one for each day!), and with a high concentration of indigenous populations.

Bordered by Costa Rica and Colombia, Panama's long rainy season is from April to January; the climate is always tropical: steamy with late afternoon showers and temperatures averaging 27ºC – 30ºC (80ºF – 85ºF) year-round. A practical paradise, offering abundant wildlife, natural beauty, and some of the best adventure tourism in Central America, this isthmus should not be overlooked.

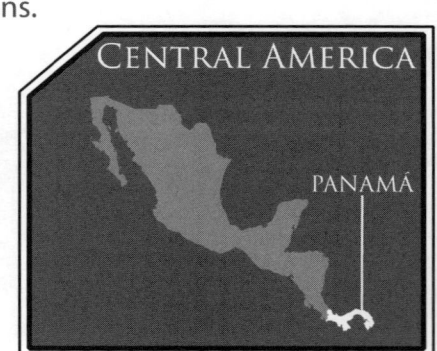

# BOCAS DEL TORO

## By Wes Weston, Sarasota, Florida, U.S.A.

Cruising through the narrow canals on the Río Changuinola, your motor boat passes by simple wooden canoes powered by a man with a single oar. The river banks are completely overgrown with a lush tropical forest, home to brightly colored birds that squawk and chatter as you pass. The bank is lined with decrepit houses on wooden stilts where barely clothed children play in the muddy water: you wonder if you've somehow gone back in time to a simpler era when kids did not need Game Boys to be happy. As the backdrop opens up into Bahía de Almirante, misty islands materialize not far off in the distance. You've reached the amazing archipelago of Bocas del Toro.

Located in the northeastern corner of Panama, Bocas del Toro (loosely translated as "the Bull's Mouths") features a wide variety of activities for all tourist types. You can surf some of the most explosive waves on the Caribbean, snorkel over magnificent coral reefs, explore a picturesque tropical reserve, or lounge on pristine white beaches.

Perhaps one of the most spectacular features of Bocas del Toro is not just the journey to reach this paradise, but how you get around while there. Boats are the main source of transportation: visitors have to use water taxis to go island hopping and arrive at some of the area's more exclusive beaches. The two most popular destinations within Bocas del Toro are Isla Colón and Isla Bastimentos. Isla Colón is by far the most developed of the islands, offering a wide selection of accommodation and restaurants. The small town of Bocas exudes a vibrant Caribbean feel and is the perfect location from which to explore the surrounding islands.

Popular beaches such as Big Creek and Playa Paunch produce waves that will thrill surfers of all levels. Isla Bastimentos is the next island over and a mere 10 minutes ride by water taxi. The island has no roads but does have a network of concrete pathways. Exploring Bastimentos on foot is a unique way to get a feel for the island's character as you walk up and down small hills and in between wooden houses and locally owned family businesses. Parque Nacional Marino Isla Bastimentos, on the eastern side of the island, is a nature reserve which protects various mangroves, coral reefs and several endangered species: it is a spectacular spot for nature lovers. Bocas del Toro is one of the greatest treasures in Panama, with its plush natural beauty and distinctive cultural vibes. The only way to truly appreciate its flavorful environment is to see it for yourself.

BOCAS DEL TORO TRAVEL TIPS: The best way to arrive at Bocas del Toro is by water taxi. This can be done from either the towns of Changuinola or Almirante. Lodging in Bocas ranges in price but there are plenty of places for budget travelers. This is a popular tourist destination so it never hurts to make reservations in advance.

Bocas del Toro. Photo by Cia Bernales.

# RIO CHIRIQUÍ RAFTING

### By Melynda Coble, Livingston, Montana, U.S.A.

Running the Chiriquí Viejo means bouncing and bobbing through umpteen rapids. It might mean flying through the air, getting sucked under the boat and spat out the other side. It definitely means having the time of your life.

The Río Chiriquí Viejo flows through Panama's southwestern province—Chiriquí—near the border with Costa Rica. The landscape is as beautiful as it is diverse, and sits along the flanks of Volcán Barú, Panama's highest point.

The Chiriquí rapids are fun and big; it is some of the most exciting whitewater to run, but the scenery is the most impressive part of the day. Cormorants, kingfishers, vultures and other birds glide over the river, landing on rocks to fish, or soar into the jungle on the other side.

Between the countless class II-IV rapids, river runners can stare in awe at the waterfalls pouring into the river or try to spot elusive spider monkeys chattering in the trees and iguanas sunning themselves on fallen logs. It's the jungle that people think of when traveling to Central America, but without the effort of hiking through thick vegetation or being eaten by tiny bugs. This trip is the easy, but exciting, way to discover the tropical rainforest.

The raft guide points out the "Tourist Tree"—red with peeling bark—and a "Panama Tree" which Panamanian Indians used to make canoes out of to cross the Panama Canal before bridges and modern boats took their place.

Hopping out of the boat, passengers can float through a short, flat section of river with sheer canyon walls closing in on either side. Water weeps through the walls, growing vines, ferns, large impatiens and intricate colorful bromeliads. The sky cuts through the narrow opening above, illuminating the tiny canyon and river.

At the lunch spot, rocks can be cracked open to reveal fossils; reminders of how old this place is and how much has changed since those molluscs lived here. Dynamic as the river, but always in the present, this trip is about being excited and content in the now.

---

**PANAMA FACTOIDS:**
The first European to visit present-day Panama was Christopher Columbus, in 1502.
Because Panama is crooked, if you go from the Atlantic to the Pacific via the canal, you will actually travel south-east.

---

## TOP LIST: WHITEWATER RAFTING

Abundant rainfall, lush green forests, top-notch guides and equipment, multi-day jungle trips ... Latin America is a river rafter's dream. So strap on a life jacket, pack a lunch, and hit the river! Here's what our contributors had to say about rafting.

1. Toachi River, Ecuador. "Descends through the cloud forest—gorgeous vistas and wildlife." Dr. Crit Minster, Rochester, New York, U.S.A.

2. Chiriqui Viejo River, Panama. Melynda Coble, Livingston, Montana, U.S.A.

3. Pacuare River, Costa Rica (p. 208). "Good for everyone from beginners to pros." Chester Rice, Des Moines, Iowa, U.S.A.

4. General River, Costa Rica. "Class III-IV rapids in a beautiful tropical setting—it'll take your breath away." Erin Keyes, Vancouver, British Columbia, Canada.

5. Acequia River, Venezuela. "An unforgettable adventure." Kyle Preston, Nevada, U.S.A.

6. Apurimac River, Peru. "Widely considered one of the best in the world ... a must-do for big water fans who are anywhere near Peru." Jimmy Haynes, Quito, Ecuador.

7. Amacuzac River, Morelos, Mexico. "It passes through a canyon ... our guides were top-notch." Lou Coyne, Ithaca, New York, U.S.A.

# EL VALLE

By Alpana Varma Chariatte, New Delhi, India

As you arrive in the town of El Valle, a large sculpture of a sleeping Indian sits on the hilltop overlooking the city. As legend has it, the native Indian was in love with one of the Conquistadors, but under her fathers ruling, was forbidden to marry him. In grief, she killed herself and found her composure in recline.

Indeed El Valle or literally, "the Valley," is a town of history and legend and of flowers and fruits.

Located on an extinct volcano about 120 kilometres (74 miles) from Panama City, El Valle is a quiet weekend resort, offering a surprising number of activities for adventure. The town has a year-round spring-like climate thanks to its verdant hills and 600 meter altitude. The weather is a big draw for anyone weary of the scorching heat in other parts of this tropical country. But don't be fooled: the afternoon sun can be scorching. Visitors are frequently greeted by the *Bajareque*, a brief, light rain shower, which can scatter the sun's rays, but be careful the sun is still there and is as bright as ever (i.e. bring sunscreen!).

Situated in volcanic territory, hot springs are common here. One can take a mud bath in the volcanic earth and then soak in open-air thermal baths, all under the cool shade of trees.

To balance relaxation with adventure, check out the tropical rainforest around the *El Macho* waterfall. A brief tour on foot is an exhilarating experience as one treads over rickety wooden bridges through dense foliage, watching for rare birds such as the gorgeous toucan. For those who are more daring, there is the canopy adventure attraction in which you can "imitate Tarzan" and fly above the jungle floor by way of cables and pulleys.

There is also an orchid nursery which houses the rare white orchid that is the national flower of Panama. The ubiquitous mango tree is a temptation in the month of March with delicious green mangoes dangling tantalizingly from its branches.

The tropical forest also contains remnants of past civilizations—the rock carvings called petroglyphs which have yet to be deciphered. A little church in the city center and the adjoining museum elaborate on these mysterious carvings, and also give a glimpse of the town's cultural heritage. In the center, a walk along the quiet streets affords a glimpse of enormous, exquisite villas that sweat wealth and luxury. Some have private mini golf courses and swimming pools alongside sprawling gardens and duck ponds.

An El Valle activity that cultivates both relaxation and adventure is the Sunday market. You can buy local handicrafts along with exotic fruits and vegetables. Wooden trays painted in brilliant colors are the traditional crafts of this region. Appliqué embroidery made by the natives of the San Blas islands is also readily available here. No matter what your objective is, whether adventure or relaxation, you are sure to find it in El Valle.

Alpana Varma Chariatte has lived in Zurich, Switzerland, since the year 2000. Currently, she's doing a doctorate in Social Anthropology at the University of Zurich. Before that, she lived in New Delhi, India, where she was a business correspondent at the leading national daily, *The Times of India*. She did her MA in Political Science at the University of Delhi.

Varma Chariatte and her husband are avid travelers who mostly prefer destinations of cultural importance. One such place was Las Vegas, where she was surprised by the city's art scene: "It was fascinating to see so much artistic creativity amid abundant kitsch and display of opulence in Las Vegas." They both hope to visit China, particularly Beijing and Shanghai, sometime in the future. For now, she'll have to settle for a vacation in Northern Italy "just to get some respite from our hectic daily routine."

---

**PANAMA FACTOIDS:**
Panama seceded from Colombia in 1903 with the help of the United States, who wanted to complete the canal project abandoned by the French in 1887. Panama has no army. It does have a police force, and small maritime and air forces. More than 900 species of bird have been identified in Panama.

---

# VOLCÁN BARÚ

By Katie Hale

Shrouded in clouds, sleeps Volcán Barú—the only volcano in Panama at 3,475 meters (11,410 feet) high. Once an active beast, the volcano is now extinct, looming over Panama's central highlands like a quiet guardian.

You can reach the summit by foot or 4x4, but hiking is probably the better option, as vehicles have difficulty navigating the rough terrain. The all day climb is approximately 14 kilometers (nine miles) one way and winds through orange fields and misty forests where quetzals hide out.

Drier weather from January through April promises optimal conditions to visit Barú. Bring gear to camp overnight and you will be rewarded with a sunrise over the Pacific and Atlantic Oceans—the summit is the only place in the world where both bodies of water can be viewed simultaneously.

# PANAMA CITY

## By Alpana Varma Chariatte, New Delhi, India

When the English pirate Henry Morgan plundered and razed Panama Viejo in 1671, the first European settlement in the Pacific was lost, only to be rebuilt two years later a few miles away. His onslaught from the rear, the side of the Río Chagres, took the inhabitants by surprise as they had braced themselves only for a possible attack from the ocean ahead of them.

Founded on August 15, 1519, Panama City served as the base where all the gold originating in Peru was gathered and then directed to Portobelo on the Atlantic side, to be shipped to Spain.

As you walk among the ruins that are left today, you find signs of daring, perseverance, adventure and organization by a people who undertook a long, arduous journey in pursuit of wealth and grandeur in unknown lands.

The importance of the church in colonial times is very evident. In addition to the Cathedral, there are six convents with their churches and the San Juan de Dios Hospital. You can take a guided tour of old city with a member of the tourist police, an innovative Panamanian institution, whereby a policeman not only looks after the security of tourists but also gives a detailed historical account of a site. A major restoration effort is currently under way to bring back the city's colonial splendor: part of it is being funded by the government of Spain.

The city had no walls for protection and the Cathedral, the layout of which is shaped like a cross, also performed a defensive function. Next to the Cathedral is the Treasury, where the gold was kept, adjoined by a monastery, the bishop's quarters and the slave market. The street through which the slaves would escape to the forest on the mountain still exists today. A largely Afro-Panamanian town still exists on the mountain today: they are the descendents of these escaped slaves.

The rebuilt city, called Casco Antiguo, or the old quarter of Panama City, is surrounded by battlements and a wall. Unfortunately, this area was plagued by frequent fires and little remains of what was originally there. Its development received a big boost when, in the wake of the gold rush to California, the trans-Panama railway was constructed in 1846.

A number of ornate buildings in French, Spanish and Italian style can be seen here, housing the national theater, the Cathedral, the church of St. Francis of Assisi and the History Museum. Many historical buildings were reduced to slums, when in the early 20th century, the well-to-do citizens left for greener pastures in newer neighborhoods where they could move into American-style garden villas. Now there is an attempt to restore this colonial architecture with UNESCO help.

The construction of the Panama Canal generated a boom at the end of the 19th century. The fascinating account of not only the Panama Canal, but also the arrival of the Spaniards in the continent, is provided in the Interoceanic Canal Museum. Unfortunately, the information is only in Spanish. It is housed in what was originally the Grand Hotel and later became the office of the French company in charge of digging the canal.

This ever-changing city is now once again in the midst of a construction boom, this time consisting of high-rise condominiums and office buildings. Being a major banking centre and located close to the free-trade zone of Colón, the city's importance as a business centre is constantly growing. More importantly, Panama is trying to attract retirees (mainly from the U.S., but also from South America, as well as Europe), with ample incentives to settle in its inexpensive cities. Some of this urbanization is quite haphazard in the Paitilla and Punta Pacífica neighborhoods. A new upscale neighborhood in Costa del Este aims to be the new Miami, with a well planned layout, ultra-modern luxurious apartments in skyscrapers, business centers, malls, not to mention the breathtaking ocean views.

Panama City. Photo by Alpana Varma Chariatte.

# THE PANAMA CANAL

### By Lorraine Caputo, Columbia, Missouri, U.S.A.

Kuna women are rolling up their *molas* for the night, and lovers are strolling the old sea wall atop the *Bóvedas* in the Casco Viejo sector of Panama City. A mango-colored sunset reflects off the bay, casting a deep shadow onto a ship just finishing its journey through the Panama Canal.

This is where the Canal ends for some and begins for others, whether traversing it or in learning its history. Below these Bóvedas is the Plaza Francia, where 12 plaques tell the story of the heroic but ill-fated French attempt to build this Canal (1878-1889). The statues staring into the approaching dusk include one of Ferdinand de Lesseps, builder of the Suez Canal and chief engineer of the *Compagnie Universelle du Canal Interocéanique*. His attempt to build a lockless canal through this isthmus was misguided: countless problems of geography and disease forced the French company into bankruptcy.

Further up the street is a bust of Spanish King Carlos V. In 1579, he commissioned a feasibility study of digging a ditch from the Atlantic Ocean to the Pacific. But the world would have to wait another three centuries until technology caught up with the dream. On one side of the Cathedral Plaza is the *Museo del Canal Interoceánico*, a must-visit for those who wish to understand the Canal. Well-designed exhibits go beyond just historical and technical explanations; they also teach the social and economic impacts of five centuries of trans-isthmus travel. The U.S. had long thought about building a canal across the narrow waist of Central America. The Panamanian route, then part of the territory of Colombia, was already under contract to France. The Americans' original plan, through Nicaragua, was vetoed by Congress. When the French company went bankrupt, Colombia rejected the U.S.'s offer to acquire the contract. In 1903, the U.S. (with three naval warships) encouraged Panama to gain its independence from Colombia, and immediately signed a treaty with the new government acquiring the sovereign rights to the canal and to the territory extending five miles from either side of it. After an initial campaign to eradicate yellow fever and malaria, the Canal was completed, using a three-lock design. It opened in 1914.

The U.S. Canal Zone was contentious for Panamanians, who wished to see the economic benefits of this passage through their country. In 1977, the Torrijos-Carter Treaty was signed, promising to turn sovereignty of the Canal over to Panama on December 31, 1999. Miraflores, the set of locks closet to the Pacific end of the Canal, is situated just across the road from former U.S. Army Base Fort Clayton. Nearby, a statue honors high school students killed in the 1964 "flag riots." Panama still commemorates the "Day of the Martyrs" on January 9. At the observation deck, visitors can listen to bilingual commentaries about the history of the Canal and passing ships. The new Visitors Center also has exhibits, a gift shop, theater, snack bars and a restaurant. Buses leave for the Miraflores Locks from the Plaza de Mayo. There are a number of other attractions along the Canal:

- The Old French Cemetery, where over 20,000 persons are buried.
- Barro Colorado, a wildlife-abundant island in Gatún Lake, location of a Smithsonian Institute biological research center.
- Parque Nacional Soberanía, a rainforest with walking trails.
- Colón, the Atlantic terminus of the Canal, with the second-largest duty-free zone in the world.

The Isthmus can be crossed by public bus or train. Boat tours through the Canal itself are also offered. To watch the passage of the ships through the Panama Canal is a marvel, making the "great ditch" worthy to be called "The Eighth Wonder of the World."

## MANUEL NORIEGA

### By Katie Hale

Espionage. Exile. A decapitated head sent via the U.S. mail. Although it sounds like the makings of a great movie plot, the real life of Manuel Noriega could not have been more interesting if it *were* fiction.

The man that would manipulate the U.S. government, overthrow regimes, and dupe many into believing he was president of Panama was born in Panama City around 1938. He received his education and training at the Military School of Chorrillos in Lima, Peru and the infamous School of the Americas, then located in Panama.

A career soldier, Noriega was promoted to Lieutenant of the Panamanian National Guard in 1968. The years that followed were tumultuous ones for Panama's military rule, and Noriega was accused of being involved in several coups. Involved or not, he rose higher and higher in the ranks until 1984 when he took the reins of the country. The first presidential election since 1972 was held and the winning opponent ended up decapitated and tortured among allegations of fraud.

Although a CIA agent for the United Status for over 30 years, Noriega was working as a double agent—using his inside access to U.S. top secret information, selling classified U.S. information to Cuba, facilitating the sale of restricted U.S. technology to Soviet bloc countries, and selling arms to Cuban-backed guerrillas in Latin America.

However, it was not the knowledge that Noriega was trafficking large amounts of drugs into the U.S. that upset the government up north—it had been aware of his illegal actions since 1972. Instead, it was disturbed by his growing independence and intimacy with enemy nations.

In 1989, U.S. forces invaded Panama, captured Noriega, and brought him to Miami for trial. He was convicted in 1992 of drug trafficking, racketeering, money laundering, and was sentenced to 40 years in prison. No longer a man of espionage and drug dealing, Noriega found God behind bars, and awaits his scheduled release date—September 9, 2007.

# ISLA GRANDE

## By Alpana Varma Chariatte, New Delhi, India

*If there is paradise on earth, it is here, it is here.* These oft-quoted lines, written in another language, for another place, come repeatedly to mind when one merely looks around when on Isla Grande. The name is a misnomer, as it is actually a rather small island in the Caribbean, off the mainland town of Portobelo, which is located an hour and a half from Panama City.

Much of Isla Grande is protected and open only to limited tourism. Hopefully, the restrictions will protect this gorgeous, emerald paradise forever. Covered by virgin tropical rainforest, there are two walking trails, one leading to a lighthouse and the other leading to the other side of the island where you will find a postcard-perfect beach, known as La Punta. The beach is surrounded by coral reefs, which give the water a greenish hue. A little further down the beach, the waters are ideal for snorkeling and scuba diving. With the water perpetually at 28 to 30 degrees, no matter what the weather may be like, a dip in the water is always heavenly.

The lighthouse affords a panoramic view of the vast horizon, an infinite space dotted with green, hilly islands where palm trees sway gently next to crystal blue waters.

If you want to go to the beach but don't feel like a sweaty hike through the tropical rainforest to get there, you can take a boat. Not only is the boat a cool, refreshing alternative to a steamy hike, but you'll have the added bonus of getting a good look at the mangroves. The way the roots and branches are entangled to create a solid mass on the shallow ocean floor is fascinating.

Our boat driver took us to another island where he lives in a charming village. Most of the houses are painted in brilliant colors and the walls are decorated with sea shells. The people are mostly dark-skinned descendents who have made the island their home since the colonial era. They make a living from fishing, trading coconuts and tourism. They are disarmingly friendly and happy to receive visitors.

Our boat driver told us about another island, which was once used by the people as a cremation ground. A few years ago, it was bought by a Spaniard, who burned all the vegetation down to exorcise the place and has since planted palm trees all over the grounds. It stands out as an unusual sight, as it has no natural vegetation, only a massive white mansion.

One could spend an eternity here, put all worries behind oneself and savor the bounty that nature has provided to this place.

For accommodation, the Banana Village Beach Resort is perhaps the best option; the only one offering international standard comfort and food. There are 18 little cottages, with three rooms each, which except during Carnival time (last week of February), are never really full, giving the place an air of quiet exclusivity.

---

**PANAMA FACTOIDS:**

Unlike some of its Central American neighbors, Panama is rarely affected by hurricanes: it is too far to the south.

The first ship to sail through the Panama Canal was the *S.S. Ancon*, a U.S. cargo ship, on August 15, 1914.

---

## THE PANAMANIAN-CHINESE By Katie Hale

The heat felt like walking into a sauna. Murky water was chest high. Mosquitoes hovered in swarms, secretly carrying malaria. Through all if this, the men had to continue to work, laying tracks and pounding steel.

During the 1850s, over 1,000 Chinese came to Panama to help construct the transatlantic railroad. The men were looking for fortune, and instead found a nightmare. With them they brought the comforts of home: tea, rice and opium. These familiarities would not be enough to soothe them during the arduous working days and the long, lonely nights. Within months, over 400 Chinese railroad workers committed suicide. They hanged themselves, wrapping their long, black ponytails around their necks, and then to tree branches, or fell on their sharp machetes. Opium was the only thing keeping them alive in a state of fog, numbing the harsh realities of daily life in the Panamanian jungle.

After the completion of the railroad, Chinese were continually enticed through the "coolie trade" to come as contract laborers, as slavery was slowly outlawed. Today, many large cities in Latin America today have Chinatowns due to these migrations.

In 1903, after Panamanian independence, a law was passed forbidding Chinese immigration. In the 1940s, the Chinese ran the grocery trade in Panama, which created anti-Chinese sentiment and resentment. Presently, Chinese immigrants are forbidden to own businesses, but Chinese-Panamanian citizens are allowed to do so. Currently around 200,000 Chinese live in Panama, accounting for 6.5% of the population—more than any other Latin American country. There are over 20 Chinese-Panamanian community organizations. The past of the Chinese-Panamanian is a tortured one, but the legacy of their strength can be felt every time a train rumbles by on the tracks of the world's first transcontinental railroad.

# EMBERA DRUA VILLAGE

By Kim Walker, Evansville, Indiana, U.S.A.

There are not many places left in the world where outsiders can sneak a peek at another culture seemingly lost in time, a place where inhabitants live off the land, dress in native attire, practice ancient pre-Columbian traditions and use medicinal herbs still undiscovered by western civilization. Panama's Embera villages, deep in the rainforest, are such a place.

According to stories passed down through the generations, the Emberas migrated from South America's Amazon to Colombia's Choco region in the 16th century, then crossed into Panama's rugged Darien Gap to escape the Spanish conquistadors. Semi-nomadic, they moved through the Darien's impenetrable jungle in tiny communities, erecting stilted, thatched huts along riverbanks ten feet off the ground to protect themselves from jaguars, flooding and rival Kuna and Waounan tribes. They thrived in the living forest, fishing in the rivers and hunting rodent-like pintado, monkeys and wild boars with blowpipes, poison darts and 12-foot spears.

In the last century, the Emberas were forced to move yet again. Hunting yields in the Darien dwindled when Latinos moved in and Pan-American Highway construction crews decimated their food supply. In the 1970s, political turmoil, Colombian guerillas and drug traffickers finally forced most of the 15,000 Emberas westward, toward the central part of the country where they settled along the Chagres River, not far from the Panama Canal.

Native communities living within what is now the 129,000 hectare Chagres National Park have had to adjust to restrictions established in 1996. No longer permitted to hunt, log or domesticate animals, Emberas now must depend almost solely on fishing. To create economic solutions for their growing needs without compromising their culture, some villages are turning to tourism. Most visitors to Drua village come for the day, but a few tour operators from Panama City offer overnight stays. Trips begin with a hour's drive north to Lake Alajuela, where visitors transfer into a motorized, teetering canoe for the one-hour journey.

The sounds of nature are all around, from the calls of a toucan to the rush of a waterfall. A young Embera boy perched at the bow with pole-in-hand and a turquoise loincloth flapping against his dark skin, expertly navigates the rapids as stoic blue herons standing in the sand impassively watch. Thatched roofs of stilted huts, clustered together in groups of 15 to 20 families, become visible peeking through a lush jungle dense with banana palms. Coasting to shore, tourists are welcomed with music emanating from deer-skinned drums and bamboo flutes. Bare-breasted Embera women with long silky hair and bold-patterned skirts lead visitors to the communal hut where the Noko chief speaks through an interpreter. Women demonstrate their timeless weaving techniques before serving lunch—fried tilapia and plantains wrapped in giant leaves. Barefooted villagers perform languid native dances before day-trippers leave. Giggling children find amusement playing in the sand or surprising guests with pet monkeys. Afternoons are spent hiking with the medicine man, swimming in the river, or relaxing in hammocks until darkness falls.

In the flickering candlelight, the medicine man tells stories of lost love and black magic before visitors drift off on floors of open-sided thatched huts 10 feet off the ground. Tranquility blankets this gentle village, centuries removed from the bustle of modern city life.

*"Regarding the Panama Canal Treaty negotiations, they will find us standing up or dead, but never on our knees, never!"*
*-Omar Torrijos, Panamanian Revolutionary (1929-1981)*

## TABORCILLO

By Leigh Gower

A mirage of palm fringed, white sandy beaches, it is no wonder that John Wayne fell in love with Taborcillo Island and bought it as his own private retreat. With extensive plant and animal wildlife, and exotic fruits to tantalize the hungriest of palates, the island is just a 30-minute flight from Panama City or 40-minute boat ride, and has remained, perhaps surprisingly, almost free from human harm.

Taborcillo is situated approximately three kilometers off the Pacific coast, across the way from Punta Chame, and on the outskirts of the Las Perlas Archipelago. Today the island is owned by Ralph Hübner, publisher of the *Who is Who* guide in Europe, and a resort and theme park have been constructed on the island in honour of the man himself—John Wayne City. The island's old mango trees were planted by the "Duke" himself.

Although much of the island is now controlled by a development company which has divided it into residential plots, visitors are ensured a good feel of the great actor's presence amid its streets designed, in tribute, in the style of an old western village. You can even "lock" someone up in the jail cell on Main Street. The island remains very private as it can only accommodate between 53 and 58 people at any one time. A truly tropical west-meets-south-sea island haven.

# KUNAS OF SAN BLAS

By Martín Li, London, England

Behind you is thick, misty forest. In front of you, the sea. Moored beside a rickety wooden pier is your "taxi"— a precarious looking dugout canoe. Your destination lies a mile offshore: the mysterious Kuna island of Achutupu. Achutupu isn't large, but is densely packed with thatched dwellings and dotted with squat palms. Smoke rises gently from a few huts. Bright flags flutter from others. Wooden canoes are anchored by small docks and inlets; others poke out from open shelters. Beyond the island energetic waves crash over a reef.

Only 49 of the 365 San Blas islands are inhabited. The majority of these are similarly packed with dwellings constructed around the frames of sturdy tree trunks, with thatched roofs, earth floors and walls of cane or bamboo. The Kunas, a native indigenous group, are accomplished mariners who have long paddled and sailed across the ocean in small dugout canoes. One of their few concessions to modern influence is the outboard motors they use for longer journeys.

Few ancient tribes have preserved their traditions as staunchly as the Kunas. Leading a coastal existence that has changed little in centuries, they survive from fishing and trading coconuts, and live virtually autonomously from the Panamanian state. The Kunas are fiercely territorial and the government consults them on all proposals, including road building, which could affect their territory.

Walking around Achutupu is surreal. All the women wear traditional dress: distinctive mola blouses constructed around patterned silk squares; rings through the nose and ear piercings; headscarves; and forearms and lower legs strapped with bright strings of beads, worn for life from a young age. Despite obvious overcrowding, islanders reserve space for a basketball court, which, along with the nearby stores, forms the hub of local life. The community governs its affairs in the large Gathering House. The Chicha House is the other important public building and is where islanders celebrate locals girls coming-of-age. Women maintain a revered status in Kuna society and reaching puberty is commemorated by a series of ancient rituals and feasts. The culmination of these is the "Long Chicha," a drinking festival that lasts three to four days.

The Kunas are not only independent but also seem very contented. Groups of villagers chat in good humour and the sound of laughter often rings out across the island. Children greet visitors with happy cries of "Hola!" Such is the nature of these happy coastal dwellers.

San Blas Islands. Photo by Terence Baker.

# TROPIC STAR LODGE

By Paul Imbessi, Ocean City, New Jersey, U.S.A.

If you're going to Pinas Bay, Panama, you're probably going to one place: Tropic Star Lodge. And you're going for one reason: some of the best deep sea fishing in the world.

Located 150 miles from Panama City, on the Pacific, in the southeast portion of Panama, sits Pinas Bay. Situated in the Darien jungle, set into a mountainside, near the northern tip of Colombia, is Tropic Star Lodge.

But there are no roads for the 100 miles or so between Panama City and Pinas Bay, which makes travel more like an adventure straight out of a Hemingway novel. After a charter plane lands in lush jungle with vegetation crawling over mountain and cliff as far as the eye can see, you snake through a remote village until you hop on a canoe that motors its way to the famed fishing resort.

Tropic Star Lodge was originally built in 1961 by Texas oil tycoon Ray Smith. He opened the up the lodge to the public in 1965, under the name Club de Pesca. The club was sold to Edwin Kennedy after Smith's death in 1968. Kennedy gave it the name Tropic Star Lodge. In 1976, Conway D. Kittredge of Florida bought the resort and to this day the lodge is operated by Kittredge family.

Two hundred and fifty International Game Fishing Association records reside at Tropic Star Lodge and big game fishing has made the lodge famous around the world: Black and blue marlins are the big catches, along with sailfishes, tuna and dorado.

The weather is what you would expect from the jungles of Central America: hot, humid and sunny. There are two main seasons to watch out for: dry and rainy. The dry season lasts from January to April, and the rainy season lasts from May to December. Depending upon what you want to catch, certain times of the year are better than others.

All species of billfish can be caught year-round, while black marlin season primarily runs from December through April. Pacific sailfish are abundant from April to July, and striped marlin season is mid-March through May.

Boats are provided to all of the guests at Tropic Star, complete with captains and mates. Each boat is about 35-feet long, and all are old sport fishermen boats, Bertrams, which run well and are sure to get you in and out of the bay safely.

Back on shore, guests sleep in fully equipped air-conditioned cabins, swim in the fresh water pool, sip Margaritas and swap stories of the day and feast on a gourmet dinner overlooking the bay.

After working as a business and health reporter for *IndUS* Business Journal, a bi-weekly newspaper that covers the South Asian business and health community, Imbessi recently switched to web-journalism and is currently a content producer for Philly Media in Philadelphia.

Originally from Ocean City, New Jersey, he doesn't like to stick out when he travels: "I guess the one thing about traveling that I hate is when I look like a tourist. I know a lot of other people say that, but I grew up as a local in a tourist town, which means I really don't like people who litter and get mad at you when you give them complicated directions. I like to assimilate into a community as quickly as possible and love to get lost in cities. Trips with thin itineraries are the way to go!"

# PLAYA BONITA RESORT

By Sandra Scott

What a wonderful concept—turning military installations into five-star resorts! The InterContinental Playa Bonita Resort and Spa is a brand-new luxury destination resort on the Pacific Coast of Panama. Only 30 minutes from Panama City, the resort, which opened in March 2006, is located on property that was once home to a U.S. military base.

Nestled on a sweeping private beach and surrounded by lush tropical vegetation, the resort's architecture is inspired by a fusion of Mediterranean, Colonial and Panamanian styles. Punta Bruja Nature Reserve, which hosts all types of exotic birds and wildlife, is adjacent to the hotel.

Playa Bonita Resort and Spa offers guests a convenient location, with a wide array of outdoor activities like snorkeling, deep-sea fishing, and historical tours. And because it is located in a duty-free zone, it is also a great place to shop.

Or, skip the shopping and just walk the beach, nap in one of the hammocks, or play in the water. Enjoy lunch around the pool or feast on fresh seafood in the dining room.

The resort's Bonita del Mar Spa is a holistic spa offering a wide variety of treatments including soothing therapies, seaweed wraps and facials. The spa includes 12 treatment cabins, jacuzzi, steam room and sauna. For guests who want to enjoy the natural surroundings, outdoor massages are also available.

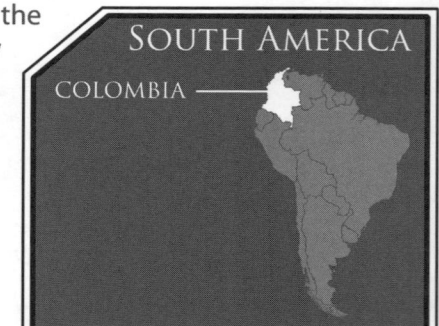

# COLOMBIA

¡Acarachas!

Colombia is a study of contrasts. It is a nation of beautiful mountains, lush valleys, and photogenic landscapes…that just happen to be perfect for growing coca, which is made into one of the most destructive and addictive substances known to man. It is home to some of the friendliest, happiest people in South America, who welcome visitors to their home…and ruthless, cold-blooded, remorseless murderers and kidnappers who target tourists and foreign businessmen. It produced Gabriel García Márquez, Nobel Prize winner for Literature, one of the world's most celebrated writers, who produced the epic masterpiece of magical realism, 100 Years of Solitude…and Pablo Escobar, the nefarious drug lord, a teenage car thief whose blood-soaked rise to become the seventh-richest man in the world is the stuff of dark legend.

There are some signs, however, that the positive side of Colombia is finally beginning to beat out its dark side. The armed struggle between leftist rebels and the government has cooled lately, and Colombians are beginning to hope for some sort of settlement. Tourism is on the rise, as international travelers are beginning to rediscover the magic of this great land.

In this section, join our writers as they take you on a tour of this land of contradictions. Visit lovely, historical Cartagena, where Spanish governor Don Blas de Lezo and 3,000 men held off a British fleet and force of over 28,000 led by Admiral Edward Vernon in 1741. You'll stroll on the beach at Playa Blanca, visit a famous cathedral carved into salt deep in a mine, and see the lost city of Ciudad Perdida, one of the oldest ruins ever discovered.

It's unfair to judge the whole nation by a few bad apples. Let our writers show you the Colombia that isn't in the world news, the Colombia beloved by its citizens, the beautiful nation that will once again take its place as a tourist paradise when it puts its tragic present behind it. See you in Cartagena!

# PLAYA BLANCA

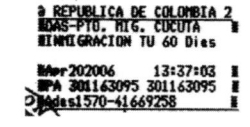

By Darren Fitzgerald, Los Angeles, California, U.S.A.

After weeks of hard trekking and a few late nights in the old colonial city of Cartagena, I was looking to put my tired body in the sand and gaze off into the blue horizon. With the mid-day sun still stinging our eyes, a couple of traveling companions and I arranged transport to Playa Blanca, which lies on the edge of a jungle, an hour's boat ride from Cartagena. Making our way in a *lancha*, which was a small, questionably seaworthy, minimally appointed boat, we passed the time in the company of our drivers—a motley crew of local *Costeños* whose boating skills were as undeveloped as the paradise we were approaching.

As the boat crested in on a slow rolling wave, we took in the Spartan amenities—a gentle blue tide and a narrow, long strip of white sand backed by thatched roof huts and lazy, bowing palm trees. Locals offering fresh shrimp, necklaces and massages meandered up and down the beach, while distorted funky salsa music flowed from the huts. We made our way to the Wittenberg cabañas just up the beach, a popular haunt with the gringos and where accommodations were no more than a hammock swinging from a large front porch. I strung up my hammock, grabbed my book and sarong, put my feet in the sand, and drifted into the first of what would be many tranquil days. Playa Blanca was the cool-breeze therapy I needed to recharge my traveling spirit, and somewhere between dips in the Caribbean and napping in my hammock I began to wonder if I'd ever leave this little strip of paradise.

I started my days at dawn, rolling out of my hammock to swim in the water and watch the sunrise. Then I strolled into one of the huts for scrambled eggs and Caribbean corn fritters, washed down with mango juice and strong coffee. The most taxing decision of the day was whether to lie down by the shore or higher up on the beach under the shade of a coconut palm.

By early afternoon I wandered into another hut for a plate of fresh grilled snapper and tomatoes and onions with plantains, then off for more strolling, swaying, and napping. Sunsets were spent with my companions at yet another hut with bottles of local beer and more grilled fish. The evenings ended by playing a few hands of cards and strumming guitars to the light of low burning gas lanterns until sleep crept in, preparing us for the next day of bliss.

---

EMERALDS FACTOID:

Colombia is an excellent place to buy emeralds. The emeralds mined here are thought to be particularly special because of their coloring—they are a shining green. There are at least 150 emerald deposits in Colombia—the most important mine is at Coscuez. Brazil is also an important emerald source. Emeralds can be bought in Colombia significantly cheaper than in other places, but be careful that you are buying the genuine article.

---

*"Wisdom is that which comes to us when we no longer need it."*
-Gabriel García Márquez, Colombian Writer (1928-)

---

# TAYRONA NATIONAL PARK

By Freyja Ellis

Parque Tayrona, located at the juncture of the Caribbean Coast and and the foothills of the Sierra Nevada, is the most popular national park in Colombia. Just 35 km (22 miles) east of Santa Marta, the park contains 1200 square km (463 square miles) of unspoiled white beaches and lush mountain landscapes.

A 45-minute walk through the jungle path leads to the section of the coast where most of the accommodations are located. Visitors have the choice of staying in eco-friendly log cabins, sleeping in hammocks or pitching tents on the beach. Arrecife is extremely popular with younger people, while El Cabo is quieter with a greater choice of cabins.

Clearly one of the great attractions is the picturesque coconut-tree-lined beach, broken up by rocky boulders. The relaxing atmosphere and friendly people add to the charm, and many visitors stay longer than anticipated. For those interested in nature, the park offers many birdwatching, scuba diving, snorkelling and wildlife viewing opportunities. Lucky visitors might catch a glimpse of sea turtles nesting on the beach. The more energetic can undertake a trek to El Puebilto, an indigenous hill settlement of the Tayrona Indians (the park is named after them), or simply explore the depths of the beach forests.

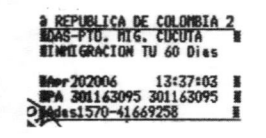

# CARTAGENA

### By Wilson Lievano, Bogotá, Colombia

Cartagena has always attracted visitors. In its early years, most of the visitors were unwelcome. The frequent attacks by pirates forced the Spanish, who used the city as a key port for shipping Inca gold to Spain, to fortify the city. In 1741, during the war between England and Spain, British Admiral Edward Vernon assembled a fleet of 180 ships and over 28,000 men with the intention to take the city. Don Blas de Lezo was in charge of the city defenses, but with only 3,000 men under his command, his efforts seemed doomed to failure.

De Lezo, a man who had lost an eye, an arm and a leg fighting for the Spanish crown in Europe, was a master of siege tactics. He retreated to the inner walls and forced the British to advance. Vernon's assault resulted in the death of 800 of his men, and the capture of 1,000 more. Meanwhile, the malaria, cholera and dysentery decimated the remaining British forces. After 36 days of siege and the loss of half of his men, Vernon retreated and de Lezo was acclaimed as the savior of Cartagena.

Nowadays, this city of 750,000 inhabitants on the northwest coast of Colombia welcomes visitors from all over the world. The walled city, once filled with taverns and soldier quarters, is now one of the most exclusive spots in the city. Most of the architecture is from the Spanish colonial period, dating to approximately 100 years after the Vernon siege, with colorful fronts and balconies adorned with flowers. In the Santo Domingo Plaza, visitors can enjoy a meal in one of the many restaurants and admire "La Gorda Gertrudiz," one of the sculptures donated to the city by Colombian artist Fernando Botero. Motorized traffic is not allowed inside the walls of the city, but a ride in a horse carriage or a walk on its cobblestone streets make exploring the city a romantic journey.

The Castillo de San Felipe de Barajas, where de Lezo directed the resistance, has been restored. Visitors can walk through the dark and narrow passages of the castle (not recommended for people suffering from claustrophobia or a heart condition) and learn about its history and architecture.

Cartagena was also, by decree of King Felipe II, the South American outpost of the Inquisition Holy Office Court. It is now a museum, where you can see authentic instruments of holy torture. And you thought no one expected the Spanish Inquisition.

The modern city expanded outside the wall. The neighborhoods of El Laguito and Bocagrande house many hotels, restaurants and nightclubs that feature local rhythms from the popular Champeta, Vallenato and Reggeaton to the traditional Salsa and Merengue intertwined with electronic and dance music.

Visitors looking for sun and beach can go to Islas del Rosario, a group of islands 15 to 20 minutes in boat from Cartagena. Pristine beaches and coral reefs are the main attraction, but visitors can also enjoy the aquarium and the seafood restaurants around the island.

Unfortunately, the only place you can't visit in Cartagena is the tomb of Blas de Lezo, the defender of the city who died a few months after defeating the British and was buried in an unknown location. However, his legacy is honored with a statue in front of the walls he defended.

> *"I never re-read my books. It scares me."*
> *-Gabriel García Márquez, Colombian Writer (1928-)*

---

**CARTAGENA TRAVEL TIP:**
Water taxis can be taken from Muelle de los Pegasos, which is the dock area. Here you can find lots of companies offering trips to Rosario Island. Perhaps the cheapest way of doing this is on a tour arranged through a budget hotel. The more people, the better the deal. Water taxis are used by the locals to get around, but they can also be taken to interesting sites such as Fuerte de San Fernando, where the movie *Romancing the Stone* was filmed.

---

## CHIVA PARTY BUS By Freyja Ellis

A highlight of any trip to Cartagena is a night spent on the Chiva Bus, a traditional, brightly painted, open-air wooden bus. At the last pick-up stop a *papayera* band boards the bus, the free bar opens and the party starts. The band plays whilst the "director," complete with microphone, encourages singing, dancing and consumption of the free-flowing alcohol.

Taking a city tour through the picturesque streets of Cartagena, the director explains the pirate history of this colonial walled city. Stopping at historic Las Bovedas, passengers can disembark and dance to the sounds of the local bands, enjoy traditional foods, take advantage of the bar and even have their picture taken with a baby sloth.

After about an hour, the horn sounds and passengers board their respective buses for the last stop of the tour: a local disco where free admission and a welcome cocktail are included in the Chiva Bus price. Passengers can choose to stay and continue the party until the early hours of the morning or re-board the bus at 11:30 p.m.

# SANTA MARTA

### By Lorraine Caputo, Columbia, Missouri, U.S.A.

Jumbled boulders beneath an opalescent sunset. Jade-green waves. Screeching parrots. Banana ships entering the harbor while local fishermen prepare to go to out to sea. Strolling along the seafront park. Taking a nighttime dip in the sapphire Caribbean.

Could this tranquility actually belong to the second most important Atlantic coast port of Colombia? Santa Marta hides her treasures well to the casual visitor who has come for the larger gems of her region: Ciudad Perdida and Tayrona National Park.

Santa Marta was the first Spanish city founded in South America, at the foot of the Sierra Nevada Mountains where they cascade to the sea. On a clear day, their snowy peaks edge the horizon. This is a port that was repeatedly sacked by pirates and the place where Simón Bolívar died. He lived his last days at Quinta de San Pedro Alejandrino, now a museum to the Liberator.

Santa Marta is a frequent host of music, theater and other festivals. Centro Cultural San Juan Nepomuceno and the Alianza Francesa offer movies, art exhibitions and lectures almost nightly. The free Museo de Oro, with a good archaeological collection and impressive vault of Tayrona gold, is a recommended visit before going to the Lost City; English-language guides are available.

To the south of the city are two pueblos of interest. Aracataca is the hometown of Gabriel García Márquez, author of the famous novel *One Hundred Years of Solitude* and winner of the 1982 Nobel Prize for literature. His childhood home is now a museum. It is worth spending several hours—or even several days—in this real-life Macondo. García Márquez' stories seem to leap to life here. Near the old train station is a statue of Remedios (a character from *One Hundred Years of Solitude*) and her yellow butterflies.

Ciénaga is a lagoon full of bird, animal and plant life. On its east shore is the town of Ciénaga, surrounded by banana plantations. The railroad station plaza is where the 1928 massacre of banana workers occurred, mentioned by García Márquez in his classic work.

Near Santa Marta are the beaches of Rodadero, offering all services for the higher budget tourist and excursions to an off-shore aquarium, and Tanganga, popular with backpackers and SCUBA divers.

The greatest pearl of this coast is Parque Nacional Tayrona. White sand beaches and emerald jungles filigree its crystalline waters. A paradise, many spend days here, lost to the outside world, snorkeling, swimming and swaying in a hammock. A pleasant walk through the jungle leads one to Pueblito Chairama, a Tayrona site.

Then there is the most splendid jewel: Ciudad Perdida. Not discovered until 1975, visitors can enjoy a six-day hiking tour to the most important of the Tayrona culture ruins.

Blinded by the shimmering wonders near Santa Marta, many overlook her simpler pleasures. Days spent waiting for trips to Ciudad Perdida and Tayrona National Park can be spent pleasurably basking in the tropical breezes, taking cooling mid-day siestas, wandering down narrow streets lined with colonial buildings, sitting beneath the shade of Parque Bolívar or cafés and enjoying the culture this small-town city offers.

Tayrona National Park. Photo by Freyja Ellis.

## GABRIEL GARCÍA MÁRQUEZ

By Dr. Crit Minster

Colombia's best-known writer, Gabriel García Márquez was born in Aracataca, Colombia in 1928. His early career as a reporter is reflected in many of his later works, notably *Chronicle of a Death Foretold*, which blends journalistic and novelistic styles.

The middle of the 20th century was witness to a major literary phenomenon in Latin America commonly referred to as the "boom." Of all of the boom writers, García Márquez is arguably the most high-profile, and his works are considered major pieces of literature. He has also gained fame outside of Latin America, with translations of his works selling millions of copies worldwide.

His best-known novel is probably *One Hundred Years of Solitude*, which tells the story of the fictional Colombian town of Macondo. The novel introduced much of the world to the Latin American literary movement referred to as "Magical Realism." He was awarded the Nobel Prize for Literature in 1982.

# LA CIUDAD PERDIDA RUINS

## By Darren Fitzgerald, Los Angeles, California, U.S.A.

We were in the middle of the Colombian jungle, being drenched by the typical afternoon downpour, when our guide Rodrigo told us our camp had hot showers and a Starbucks. That Colombian sarcasm provided a much needed laugh near the end of our first grueling day into what was to be a six day, 36-mile trek to and from *La Ciudad Perdida*, the Lost City, the oldest pre-Colombian city ever discovered.

Built a millennium ago by the Tayrona Indians, and later inhabited by the Kogi tribe, La Ciudad was abandoned for centuries. Not until after grave robbers discovered it in 1975 did archaeologists begin their excavation. The beauty and historical significance of this find can only be appreciated through the adventure to reach it and the encounter with the Kogi Indians.

We hired two guides and a mule out of Santa Marta, the north coast Colombian town whose sweltering heat and humidity provided a taste of what awaited us in the jungle. On that first day out, right around the time I was feverishly shaking the fire ants out from between my toes, I questioned my sanity for signing on for this journey. However, the jungle's beauty soon surpassed its challenges. We cooled off in deep river pools and devoured fresh mangos from the trees lining the trail. As the sun set over the misty jungle, we shared our days' adventures, swaying in hammocks while listening to the jungle critters chatter in their nocturnal playground. Our dawn wake up call was a symphony of birds and reflections of the sun through the rising jungle steam.

The finale to reach La Ciudad was a canopied staircase of 1600 cracked, slippery, moss-ridden stones ascending from the river. I felt like I was climbing an ice sculpture, which led up to the city's old stone ruins and a vista of a 200-foot bridal veil waterfall cascading from the hillside. What was most astonishing were the Kogi Indians living in the bamboo huts dotting the hillsides. They are considered one of the only indigenous tribes to have survived the Spanish colonization intact; they did this by hiding in the northern Colombian jungle. They exist as they have for the last millennium, draped in white cotton garments and beaded necklaces, roaming the jungle barefoot collecting wood and fruit, and hunting wild boar. My temporary coexistence with this tribe prompted a solid gut check that evolution is best measured spiritually.

I returned to the trailhead on my last day dirty and worn, but content and emotionally satiated. My first cold beer sent me back in my chair, satisfied for pushing myself to experience an ancient culture and the fertility of a jungle that has sustained a bloodline for a 1,000 years.

Entrance to the Lost City. Photo by Dominic DeGrazier.

### LA CIUDAD PERDIDA TRAVEL TIPS:

Guides are arranged through tour companies out of Santa Marta. Treks leave a few times a week so be prepared to stay in Santa Marta for a couple of nights.

On the trek, the weather is hot and humid, so cool and loose-fitting clothes are required. Water proofed hiking boots are a necessity, but climbing sandals are also very helpful for the river crossings along the route, as the currents can be fairly strong. Other handy items include a sarong to use as a towel and as a light covering in the evenings. Mosquito repellent and sun tan lotion are vital. A water purification system or tablets are a good idea too.

It is highly recommended to check the most recent travel advice before embarking on this trip—kidnappings of travelers have been known to occur in the vicinity.

# PARQUE NACIONAL DEL CAFÉ

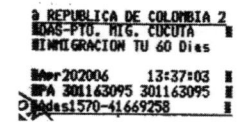

By Wilson Lievano, Bogotá, Colombia

If Juan Valdez, the image of Colombian coffee through the world, had a farm, it would probably be on the grounds of the Parque Nacional del Café, the theme park for all things coffee related.

Located in the town of Montenegro, Quindío, 160 miles north of Bogotá, in the heart of the coffee growing region of Colombia, the park is a blend of mechanical attractions, eco-tourism, and family entertainment. All pay homage to the production of the smoothest, tastiest coffee in the world.

The park sits in a small valley. To get there, visitors can take a cable car which gives a broad view of the park and its surroundings or a path that allows them to see and touch all the varieties of coffee plants that are grown in Colombia, along with several other varieties from around the world. The path forks, one way leading to the auditorium where twice a day a dance troupe performs the typical dances of the region. The other arm leads to several stations where park officials explain step-by-step how the coffee goes from the Colombian highlands to your favorite mug.

Both paths converge on a big colonial-style square filled with statues and stores. During the Christmas season, the square has a large tree and live re-enactments of the Nativity. From the square, visitors can walk to the mechanical attractions area that has everything from carousels for the kids to roller coasters and go-karts for the grown-ups. A little further down the road is the lake of the legends, a place that offers boat rides and several tales of the myths and legends of the original inhabitants of the region.

There are buses that take visitors to the park, but for convenience visitors are encouraged to rent a car and drive there. No visit to the park is complete without taking some time to sit in one of the many coffee houses scattered all over the park to enjoy a *tinto* (the name that locals give to a cup of regular coffee). These shops also offer a wide variety of candy, made from coffee (of course).

The Parque Nacional del Café is a tribute to one of the products that make Colombians proud. Families, nature enthusiasts and wide-eyed java-heads will enjoy themselves here. While you are in the park keep an eye open for Juan Valdez and his trusted mule Conchita: they will gladly invite you for a cup of coffee.

*"The basic dream of many Colombians is to have a secure nation without exclusions, with equity, and without hatred."*
-Álvaro Uribe Vélez, President of Colombia (1952-)

## COLOMBIA'S TURN TO TOURISM

By Ricardo Segreda

Is Colombia too dangerous to visit? The South American nation's notorious infamy for kidnapping, drug trafficking, guerrilla warfare, para-military groups, corruption and general chaos has for decades made Colombia a pariah for world travelers, almost on a par with its civil war torn neighbors in Central America during the 1980s. The U.S. State Department warns that "travel to Colombia can expose visitors to considerable risk." It is such that Americans working for the U.S. in Colombia are not allowed to use buses, and can only travel between major cities via air.

However, the State Department also acknowledges "violence in recent years has decreased markedly in most urban areas," which only gives a vague hint of what by word-of-mouth and the internet has become one of the biggest travel phenomena of the millennium's first decade. Whether attributed to President Alvaro Uribe's law-and-order crackdown on guerrilla violence or the resurgent growth in Colombia's economy, Colombia has experienced a growth in tourism unparalleled in its history. Forty-five new hotels were constructed last year to accommodate the high volume of foreign tourists visiting one of the most geographically and culturally exciting countries in all of Latin America.

The standard rules still apply: stick to large cities, well-patrolled beaches, and the most familiar and protected tourist attractions. Taxis are advised for transportation at night (and only from known cab companies). And while in large cities, avoid any situation that could put you at risk for kidnapping or robbery.

With that in mind, a growing number of travelers are booking trips to enjoy such landmarks as the port city of Cartagena, one of the oldest (1533) colonial cities in the West, as well as Bogotá and Medellin, with their clubs and culture. Paradoxically, one factor contributing to Colombia's tourism renewal is that its still mostly negative reputation has mitigated an overcrowded tourist environment. So go enjoy Colombia, use common sense, and don't tell your friends.

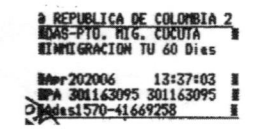

# MEDELLÍN

By Carol Huang, New York City, New York, U.S.A.

Flying to Medellín without my passport didn't seem wise, but we were already at the Bogotá airport and debated whether we should go back to my friend's apartment to get it.

"The hitch is, if I make it on board, they might not let me back on," I reasoned.

"Then you'll be stuck in Medellín forever," Hugh replied.

I doubted this, so I decided to wing it. Not the best idea, but, really, was it any crazier than going to a city once called the murder capital of Latin America anyway?

It's been more than ten years since police gunned down Medellín's most famous drug lord, Pablo Escobar, and though crime has fallen precipitously, the city is still struggling to emerge from the hands of paramilitary groups who control vast stretches of the country.

But Hugh said the city was gorgeous, and as our plane angled down to the Aburrá Valley less than an hour later, I believed him. Below us sprawled lush, green, undulating land that was richer and greener than any countryside I'd seen in more than a decade of traveling. Another 40 minutes by taxi along a curving road that cut between broad-leafed palms on a sloping mountainside and we were in Medellín—Colombia's third-largest city and the capital of Antioquia, a northwestern state bordered by the Caribbean Sea and cut through the middle by the Andes.

Nestled at 5,000 feet (1,500 meters), the City of Eternal Spring was stunning: domed cathedrals, cobblestone streets and neighborhood gardens bursting with geraniums, carnations, chrysanthemums and roses. The city offered surprises at every turn—from its squeaky clean metro (Colombia's only subway system) which whizzed past old colonial buildings, to El Tesoro, a luxury mall with trendy retail stores such as Diesel and Sketchers. We rode a cable car 1,300 feet (400 meters) up to the mountaintop neighborhood of Santo Domingo, peering down at rooftops where laundry flapped in the breeze, and drank lattes in the renovated downtown district where corpulent, larger-than-life bronzes of artist Fernando Botero reclined in an outdoor sculpture garden beneath the sunshine.

The best surprise came that night, when we found our way to Parque los Periodistas, an underground club district where recordings of Moby, Shakira and salsa blasted from the open doorways of one tiny, cement-shack bar after another. Latin punk rockers, goth teens with metal piercings and hipsters in plaid pants crowded the streets, along with stunning young women swinging waist-length hair. Drummers and guitarists on the sidewalks vied to be heard, competing with fire-eaters for our attention, while junkies nodded obliviously on the curb. We plunged into the mayhem, entering a nameless club blasting Led Zeppelin. Squeezing past a mass of writhing bodies to reach the bar, we ordered shots of *arguardiente*, a fiery, clear brew like Tequila, and started dancing. I realized then that I did not care if I made it back to Bogotá or not.

## LATIN AMERICAN MYSTERIES #6: WHO KILLED JORGE ELIÉCER GAITÁN?

Bogotá, Colombia: April 9, 1948

In 1948, Jorge Eliécer Gaitán was a young, up-and-coming Colombian politician. He had served as mayor of Bogotá, Minister of Education and Minister of Labor. From a humble background, he was very popular with Colombian poor and working classes, who he constantly fought to defend: he had supported strikes and workers movements in the foreign-controlled fruit industry, even going up against the powerful American United Fruit Company in 1928.

By the late 1940s, Gaitán was a figure beloved by the poor and despised by the wealthy: even some members of his own Liberal Party thought he was too extreme. He advocated land reform and other concessions to Colombia's poor. In 1947, Gaitán rose to a position of leadership in the Liberal Party, and many believed that he would be the country's next president in the 1950 elections.

On April 9, 1948, Gaitán was shot and killed by Juan Roa Sierra, who was subsequently lynched by a furious mob: his motives were never known. Some believe that he acted alone: Roa was known to be unstable and had asked Gaitán for a job on several occasions without being granted one.

However, many Colombians believe there was a larger, more sinister conspiracy. The CIA was known to protect the interests of American big business in Latin America, and in 1954 it would intervene in Guatemala on behalf of the same United Fruit Company that Gaitán had defied in 1928.

Gaitán was murdered during the ninth Pan-American Conference, organized by the United States to oppose the spread of communism in the Americas. A protest of the conference was taking place, organized by the Latin American Youth Congress. One of the organizers of this counter-protest was young firebrand Fidel Castro, still ten years away from his successful takeover of Cuba. Castro had an appointment to see Gaitán later in the day he was killed. Some believe that the Bogotá police ordered the killing to keep the popular Gaitán from speaking in support of the protest.

Whatever the reason, Gaitán's death led to a massive three-day riot known as the "Bogotazo," in which thousands died. This, in turn, kicked off the period of Colombian history known as "La Violencia" in which as many as 300,000 people were killed over the course of the next decade as citizens loyal to the rival Conservative and Liberal parties fought in the streets.

# VILLA DE LEYVA

## By Terence Baker, Dartford, England

Villa de Leyva (also spelled Leiva) is a magical, colonial town 100 miles northeast of Colombia's capital, Bogotá, and a stage fit for any novel by this country's favorite son, Gabriel García Márquez. Dominating the walking town—full name: Villa de Nuestra Señora de Santa Maria de Leyva—is one of Colombia's largest cobble-stoned squares, in the center of which is a small Mudéjar-style fountain. Around the square are whitewashed, two-story houses, small shops fronted by covered walkways boasting slender columns and plaques chronicling former citizens. In the middle of one of the sides is a humble church, where you can sit outside and watch children running to school. This is the perfect place to watch people emerge from sleep, a coffee in one's hand and the strains of Colombian rocker Carlos Vives coming from a tinny jukebox. The sparseness of the architecture makes the plaza seem immense.

On the weekends, things get busy here, with Bogatá's elite city slickers fleeing to second homes; during the week this town, founded in 1572, reverts to being a sleepy haven. Foreign tourists are few. Politicians are reputed to now own the villas scattered in the surrounding hilly countryside that once belonged to narcotraffickers. A knock at the correct door will result in cheap milk direct from the cow sniffing at you, and an amble around town is an experience unlikely to be forgotten. Small plazas open into narrow walkways, which reveal restaurants and the occasional priest emerging from the darkness of a monastery. A cemetery, seemingly taken out of New Orleans, adds to the town's unique ambiance.

Three hundred yards from the square, the tarmac runs out, trails leading to both grand ranches with horse stables and to poor housing with livestock, ruddy-faced children and stoic parents. Hang around outside some of the churches on a late Sunday morning, and after hearing the voices of unseen nuns chanting mass, you can rent horses to visit the nearby archeological site of Los Infiernitos (The Little Hells) that displays long lines of phallic dolmen-shape statues. The ride across the stony scrubland and along narrow roads also is enjoyable.

The places to stay here are equally memorable. Choose between the Hostería Los Frayles, which has a sister property in Bogotá, or the more expensive, equally colonial Casa de los Fundadores. Cheaper accommodations can be had in private homes. A small bus terminal links Leyva to Bogotá, and this is the way to travel here, if only so someone else can do the talking if an army patrol is encountered. It is relatively safe in this area of Colombia, but common sense definitely should prevail. Do a little research, don't be afraid to ask questions and then enjoy one of South America's hidden jewels.

---

VILLA DE LEYVA TRAVEL TIPS:

A site worth a visit outside of Villa de Leyva is El Fósil, located six kilometers east of the town. It can be reached by taking a taxi, cycling or walking along the road to Chiquinquirá. Here you can find an almost complete fossil of a *kronosaurus*, a sort of prehistoric crocodile.

---

# FERNANDO BOTERO

### By Dr. Crit Minster

The most famous living Latin American artist, Fernando Botero (1932-), is best known for his paintings of very fat subjects. His art is abstract, in that the colors, figures and people depicted are not meant to be a representational likeness of the subject. The obesity of the subjects is designed to mock the bourgeois middle class. In one portrait, a corpulent family of four poses by an apple tree and even the pet monkey is grossly overweight.

Born in Medellín, Botero had limited exposure to art at an early age, as most commonly accessible art in Colombia at that time was of religious images such as Madonnas and crucifixes. He originally trained as a matador, and bullfights and bullrings figure prominently in his early works. In his teens, he went to Spain and Italy, where he studied art and art history. He spent a few years in Mexico, where the murals of Diego Rivera and others greatly influenced his work. He moved to the United States in 1960 and has lived in New York and Paris ever since. In spite of his long absence, his paintings continue to display a distinctive Colombian flavor.

Botero is very highly regarded in international art circles, and is becoming well-known outside of Colombia and New York. In the last few years, his work has become increasingly political. In 2005, he released a series of paintings and sketches concerning the U.S. torture abuse scandal at the Iraqi prison of Abu Ghraib. He has also tackled issues from his native Colombia, such as a rebel gas cylinder attack that killed 120 people in a church in May 2002.

"I grew up with the idea that art is beauty. All my life I've been trying to produce art that's beautiful to discover all the elements that go to make up visual perfection. When you come from my background you can't be spoilt by beauty, because you've never really seen it."

—Fernando Botero

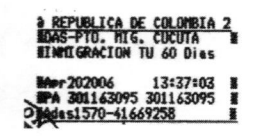

# ZIPAQUIRÁ

## By Wilson Lievano, Bogotá, Colombia

The dark passages beneath the mountain had been traditionally associated in the Christian culture with hell and the devil, but a group of miners transformed their workplace into a place of worship which became a symbol of their devotion.

For more than 500 years, the salt mountains that surround the town of Zipaquirá, Colombia have been exploited, first by the Muiscas, the native culture of the region, and then by the Spaniards and their descendants. After Christianity was introduced into the region, the miners started to hang religious images in the walls of the mine for protection. The fervor of the workers inspired the government to build a shrine in the mines. The project was completed in 1954 and soon began to attract visitors.

The salt cathedral is a must-see for Catholics that visit Bogotá, (Zipaquirá is just 15.5 miles from Bogotá and is accessible by car or train), but the architecture and the fine carving of statues and religious symbols appeal to all kinds of visitors.

The current cathedral is not the original one. As time passed, the water that seeped in from outside (rain is frequent in the region) started to damage the cathedral and pose a threat to visitors. In 1990, the government closed the shrine and started to build a new one 197 feet (about 60 meters) below the old cathedral. The project was completed in 1995 and now covers 2.1 acres of underground tunnels and chambers.

The cathedral is composed of three sections: first there is the Stations of the Cross, where small shrines carved in salt guide visitors through the scenes of the passion and death of Christ. The tradition says that depending on the gravity of your sins and your willingness to repent, you can take one of three stairs to the next level. The more sins, the longer the stairway. Cold tunnels illuminated by blue and white lights lead to the second section, the dome. A ramp takes the visitors deep into the mountain where they can see in the distance a 52-foot cross carved into the wall of the central chamber of the cathedral. Mass is held there every Sunday and on special occasions.

At the bottom is the central chamber, which is supported by four columns that represent the four evangelists and a round marble sculpture of the creation of man, inspired by Michelangelo's Sistine chapel fresco painting. The chamber is also decorated with several angel sculptures meant to be a reproduction of the Pietà, as well as a Nativity scene carved in stone. Further down, there is a concert hall and a path that leads to the surface and a small park dominated by a statue honoring the salt miners that worked in the mine over the centuries.

Entrance to the cathedral is $5 USD for adults and $2.50 USD for kids under 12. There are no religious requirements for admittance. Persons with heart conditions, fear of darkness or enclosed spaces are not encouraged to take the tour. But for the rest, the experience of descending into the darkness might bring them closer to God.

Zipaquirá. Photo by Freyja Ellis.

# EL MUSEO DEL ORO, BOGOTÁ

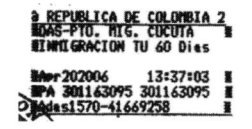

## By Wilson Lievano, Bogotá, Colombia

Legend tells that when the Muiscas, the native culture of what is today Bogotá, Colombia, had to crown a new *cacique*, or chief, they congregated at the nearby Guatavita lagoon. Their candidate was then covered in gold dust, and he and the tribe's shamans would sail to the center of the lagoon in a raft loaded with offerings of gold, emeralds and other precious objects. As the shamans offered the precious objects to the god of the lagoon, the would-be cacique would jump into the icy waters. If he emerged unharmed, he became their new leader.

This legend, which later came to be known as the myth of El Dorado, lured many greedy Spaniards to Muisca territory with the promise of incredible wealth, but aside from some pieces of gold and jewelry found at Guatavita lagoon, no one has ever found the mythical place. But in 1939, to honor the memory of the Muisca and to preserve the Colombian archeological heritage, the Colombian government created its own Dorado: El Museo del Oro, (the Gold Museum) a permanent collection of more than 35,000 ornaments, tools and art pieces made of gold by all the native pre-Hispanic cultures of Colombia.

One of the most famous pieces of the exhibit is a representation of the legend of El Dorado. It is a raft with figures that represent the cacique and his priests made in solid gold. The level of detail of this piece and its historic significance have made it the image of the museum among Colombians. There are other fascinating pieces, such as the Poporo Quimbaya, a golden urn decorated with perfectly round spheres, an especially hard achievement since these cultures didn't know the metallurgical techniques used in Europe at the time.

The museum, located in downtown Bogotá, has three floors; the first floor houses temporary exhibitions. The second floor displays the main collection: a voyage through the history and customs of the tribes that lived in the center, south and north of Colombia organized according to the type of metallurgical process they used.

Along the way, visitors will also hear the legends, myths and stories that are associated with some of the pieces. Other pieces were made during the Spanish conquest and tell the story of the native resistance and defeat at the hands of the Spanish invaders.

The third floor contains a history of gold and its significance to the pre-Hispanic cultures, along with an exhibit of pieces from cultures originally from the Colombian southwest. By 2007 the museum hopes to open two new exhibits about the cosmology and the technology of pre-Hispanic societies.

The museum has its own stop on the *Transmilenio*, Bogotá's mass transportation system. To visit, get off the Avenida Jimenez line at the station Museo del Oro and walk two blocks to the museum. Entrance to the museum is $2 from Monday to Saturday. Sunday, the entrance is free.

---

BOGOTÁ TRAVEL TIPS:

Because entrance to the museums is free on Sundays, the Gold Museum has a long queue. Expect to wait for two hours or visit on a different day. The Bogota Beer Company is a good place to get draft beer in pint glasses. There are several locations scattered around Bogotá. Head to the Juan Valdez Coffee Shop to get a taste of premium Colombian coffee, or pick up some gifts.

---

Bogotá Gold Museum. Photo by Freyja Ellis.

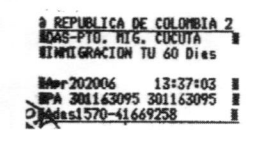

# GAY BOGOTÁ

By Chris Hurling, London, U.K.

Whether you are gay or not, Bogotá is a wonderful city. But it is especially welcoming to gay and lesbians travelers who have little choice in the historically macho Latin society.

Chris Hurling was born on the south coast of England in 1964. Following his chemistry studies at the University of Bristol, he was attracted by the brights lights and buzz of London, but no longer by chemistry, so Chris initially went to work for the famous department store Harrods in London, where he was sponsored for a post graduate diploma in marketing. He now specialises in customer relationship marketing in the financial services sector. Based in London, Hurling spends all his spare cash on travelling, and recently spent nine months in Latin America.

Hurling never leaves for his travels without zip lock bags. He had some bizarre experiences in India, particularly on the sacred Ganges river where holy men were chanting mantras, bodies were being burned on ghats and dead cows were floating on the river next to the candles that he had floated on the river...in sharp contrast to his ideal trip, which would be a gastronomic culinary tour of Puglia or Tuscany in Italy, a trip that he would find to be orgasmic, if a little bourgoise.

Aside from the gay popular scenes of colorful Rio de Janeiro and Buenos Aires, word on the street is that Bogotá, with its friendly *chicos* and *chicas*, cheap and accessible shopping, and unlimited number of cultural activities, is home to the third largest gay culture scene in South America.

So if you are gay, bisexual, or gay-friendly and want to check out what Bogotá has to offer, the best spot in town to make your home is Chapinero, a downtown neighborhood. From here, it is easy to access tourist sights, including La Candelaria and shopping in the Zona Rosa during the day, while in walking distance of the action at bars and clubs at night. Hotel Nación, which is just half a block from the trendy Village Café, has a very friendly atmosphere, but if you are on a less strict budget you should go for one of the upscale hotels in Chapinero or Zona Rosa.

Once settled in, head out for a day of sightseeing and shopping. Scope out the many free, but wonderful museums and galleries Bogotá has to offer. Visit Museo del Oro, Donación de Botero and Museo del Siglo XIX (great coffee in the beautiful courtyard). There are also lots of churches—Santa Marta is worth a look, and sometimes has concerts. La Candelaria is good to walk around, and if you take the cable car to Monserrate, you'll be in for a stunning sunset as the city lights up.

Pack lightly, as it is always fun shopping in Zona Rosa. You will find all the top labels, and for much cheaper than in the US or Europe—Diesel jeans go for half price! Shops and boutiques line the streets, but you should also go into the Centro Commercial Andino and the new Rápido shopping centres.

Once you have shopped until you drop, take a rest and then return to Zona Rosa for dinner. While there is traditional food served in the Colombian chain Crepes and Waffles, you can also opt for some of the tastiest international cuisine in all of Latin America. The Thai restaurant The Wok, is highly recommended and there is also a microbrew pub with good bar food.

For after dinner drinks, hit the trendy The Village Café. A comfortable bar with tasty cocktails, even if it is a bit pricey for Bogotá, it's a good place to start and find out what is happening in town for the week. The super cool El Recreo de Adán in Zona Rosa is also lovely and a very welcoming gay bar. You might also want to try La Oficina as well.

As the night grows late, Lotus, which is next to *Teatrón*, Bogotá's largest gay club, is the best place, especially on a Thursday night. You can dance and talk with gorgeous guys or gals until 7 a.m. while listening to 1980s pop-rock and chart music on the main dance floor, while house music plays in the other room. If you are in town on a Friday night, try The Closet in Calera, which is a drive away in the hills. If you do get lucky, and you are not going back to his or her place, there are special "love hotels" on the same street as Teatrón.

## LATIN AMERICAN MYSTERIES # 8: WHERE IS THE WRECK OF THE SAN JOSÉ?

Off the Spanish Main: June 8, 1708.

In June, 1708, a fleet of Spanish treasure galleons and their warship escorts was making for Cartagena harbor, looking to take on provisions before heading across the Atlantic to Spain. Among them was the massive San José, carrying 64 cannons and somewhere between seven and eleven million pesos—perhaps as much as 350 tons—of gold and silver coins. Although a British war fleet was rumored to be in the area, the Spanish captains felt they could safely make it to Cartagena without incident.

The winds died down and the fleet was unable to make it to Cartagena harbor, however. On the afternoon of June eighth, a small fleet of British warships led by Admiral Sir Charles Wager and the HMS Expedition attacked the Spanish convoy. The battle lasted all day, and the Expedition and the San José exchanged several broadsides. After one such volley, the San José exploded and within 15 minutes it had sunk. Only 14 men survived out of a crew of 700.

The wreck of the San José sits somewhere off the coast of Colombia, near the Baru Islands, about sixteen miles from the harbor at Cartagena. The wreck—and all of the treasure—is lost in some 2,000 feet of water, which is why it has never been found. Today, it remains one of the greatest shipwreck treasures yet to be salvaged.

Gold Museum artifact. Photo by Freyja Ellis.

# ECUADOR

**¡Chévere! ¡Cool!**

It's tough to believe that there is so much to see and do packed into this Andean nation, roughly the size of Nevada. Certainly it's a country with a lot of geographical superlatives: the Galápagos Islands, of course, where Darwin discovered evolution, and still the best place to see it in process; the snow-capped Cotopaxi and Chimborazo, not only the highest active volcanoes in the world and a magnet for climbing enthusiasts the world over, and the rich Amazon basin, where indigenous shamans will offer cleansing rituals for adventurous explorers.

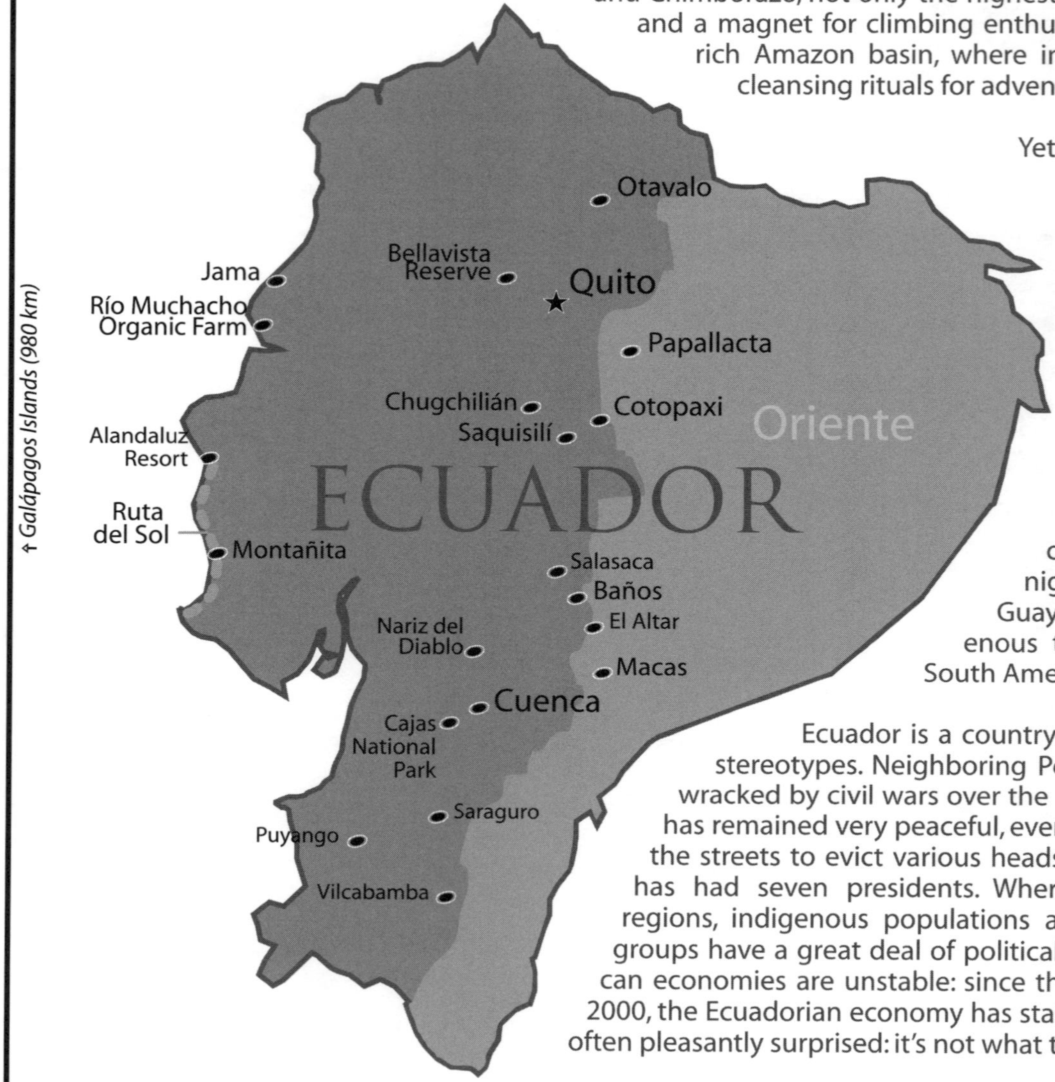

Yet against such spectacular geographical competition, Ecuador's urban and cultural attractions hold their own; the rich colonial architecture of Quito, the first city in South America to be claimed by UNESCO as "Cultural Patrimony of Humanity", as well as in such towns as Cuenca (similarly honored by UNESCO for its historic center), the exciting (if risky) nightlife in the port city of Guayaquil, while the Otavalo indigenous textile market is the best in South America.

Ecuador is a country that defies expectations and stereotypes. Neighboring Peru and Columbia have been wracked by civil wars over the last few decades, but Ecuador has remained very peaceful, even as the citizens have taken to the streets to evict various heads of state: since 1997 Ecuador has had seven presidents. Whereas in other Latin America regions, indigenous populations are marginalized, here native groups have a great deal of political clout. Whereas South American economies are unstable: since they adopted the U.S. dollar in 2000, the Ecuadorian economy has stabilized. Visitors to Ecuador are often pleasantly surprised: it's not what they had imagined.

Those who have visited Ecuador tend to report the same thing: it's the friendly, outgoing people of this small nation that make a trip there so memorable. Come for Galápagos and stay for the rafting, birdwatching, mountain climbing, colonial cities, food, scenery, hiking, shopping and horseback riding, and many cultural activities, and you'll learn what the friendly Ecuadorians already know: this is a great country. ¡Que chévere! as the locals like to say; How cool!

Ecuador has a special place in the hearts of those of us who produced the book you now hold in your hands: get comfortable, turn the page, and you'll soon see why.

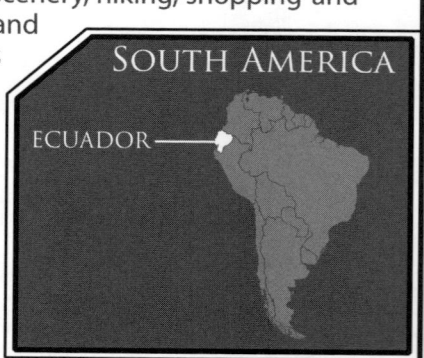

# OTAVALO

## By Dr. Crit Minster, Rochester, New York, U.S.A.

You pick up the sweater with an appraising eye. It might be the right size, it might be a little small, it's tough to tell unless you try it on. "How much?" the hopeful vendor asks in English: you get the impression he could ask you the same question in Spanish, Quichua, German, French, and possibly even Swahili. You lift your gaze from the sweater in your hands to the rest of the items in the stall. The back wall is hung with hand-woven wool tapestries, every color of earth and sky, geometric designs, landscapes, animals and fish. In front of you, finely embroidered white blouses hang from the stall's frame on twisted coat hangers. On the table between you and the vendor, neatly folded and stacked scarves, shawls, sweaters, hats, bags, and ponchos await your attention. To the right is another stall, another hopeful vendor, another pile of sweaters: to the left, the same. The sun is bright overhead, tourists and beggars jostle you on their way past, and you can smell the greasy pork and fish being cooked two blocks away in the food market. The sights and smells, sun and sounds swirl dizzyingly in your mind: looking back at the sweater, you feel a profound sense of surrealism. You ask yourself: "Where am I?"

The Otavalo market is an experience best appreciated with all the senses, if you can keep them from being overloaded. Colors dazzle the eyes, sounds and smells assault you from all sides, and the things you touch often have startling textures, from soft-as-a-cloud alpaca teddy bears to rough woolen tapestries to cold soapstone sculptures.

During the Spanish colonial period, the natives of Otavalo—about two hours north of Quito—became very skilled with textiles, and over the years the Spanish, followed after independence by powerful Ecuadorian families, began setting up factories to produce and sell the sweaters, blankets, rugs and more, produced by the industrious locals. In recent times, the Otavalo natives have organized the market themselves and now keep their profits, making them the wealthiest native ethnic group in Ecuador (if not all of South America).

The market has been a tradition for over 100 years in Otavalo: Saturday is the best day to go, when hundreds of vendors set up stalls over an area encompassing roughly ten blocks, but the vendors have learned that tourists don't only come on Saturday, and you can find vendors and stores on any day of the week. It's not just for textiles: you'll find jewelry, wood carvings, watercolor paintings and more. It is the largest market in Ecuador, and one of the largest in the world. It attracts visitors from around the globe: listen closely and you may hear Japanese, English, German and a dozen other languages.

You decide to buy the sweater and begin negotiating at $14. You thought you wouldn't like the bargain game—what sort of store has no price tags?—But you find that it's sort of fun, this battle of wits with the vendor, a game of give and take, bluffs and tricks. In the end, you're the proud owner of a wool sweater that cost you $10, and you're feeling pretty good about it. You turn and look down the block: more stalls, as far as you can see. Behind you, the same. Time to resume the hunt again … maybe a scarf this time, or a chess set for your nephew, or a shawl for mom …

### OTAVALO TRAVEL TIPS:

On Saturday mornings, Otavalo also holds an animal market. This can be found slightly out of town. It is important to get there early—the animal market is over by 9:30 a.m. It is recommended to stay overnight in the Otavalo vicinity if you have an interest in visiting the animal market.

Photos left to right: Otavalo woman shimmying goods and Otavalo textiles. Photos by Katie Hale.

# HACIENDA PINSAQUI

## By Dr. Crit Minster, Rochester, New York, U.S.A.

December, 1863: Colombia and Ecuador have been at war for two long years. Ecuador has lost two pivotal battles: the battle of Las Gradas in July, 1862 and, more recently, the battle of Guaspud on December 6, 1863 when Colombian forces occupy Ibarra, the "White City" in the north of Ecuador. The people of both nations, tired of years of strife and war, demand that their governments make peace. Ten miles south of Ibarra, representatives from both nations meet in a stately country home. There, they hammer out the details of a peace treaty, naming it after the estate. The Treaty of Pinsaqui is signed on December 30, 1863.

Established during the colonial era as a textile workshop and the country home of prominent Ecuadorian families, Hacienda Pinsaqui is one of Ecuador's most historic and stunning country homes. The signing of the famous treaty is only one episode in Pinsaqui's fascinating history. At its height, the hacienda employed more than 1,000 local artisans, and in the early part of the nineteenth century, the famous leader of the struggle for South American independence, Simón Bolívar, often stayed at the hacienda when traveling between Ecuador and Colombia. In 1867, an earthquake destroyed the hacienda, which was rebuilt shortly thereafter.

This prestigious local landmark has been in the Freile-Larrea family for generations: a member of the family, Modesto Larrea, served as the ambassador of Ecuador to Spain and Chile (look around on the walls: you may spot a framed photo of him with Frida Kahlo). The historic hacienda was converted into a first-class hotel about 10 years ago and feels more like a home. The surrounding estate is a maze of well-kept, beautiful gardens, patios, airy hallways, unique guest rooms (all of which have private bath and either a wood stove or a fireplace) and fountains. Emerald hummingbirds flitter around the flowering trees and plants of the gardens. The rustic chapel still features original colonial art and statues.

Of particular interest is the bar area, which is the only part of the hacienda to survive the 1867 earthquake. It is a charming, cozy room with a large fireplace and decorated with old saddles and equestrian trophies won by Pinsaqui horses over the years. Guests are invited to the bar for a nightly welcome cocktail, occasionally presented by the owner himself. A local Andean music band completes the ambience.

Pinsaqui is located almost exactly between the towns of Otavalo, Cotacachi and San Antonio de Ibarra. This is good news for shoppers: Otavalo hosts the largest native handicraft market in South America, Cotacachi is known for leather goods and San Antonio de Ibarra is famous for woodcarvings. With one foot in the past and one in the present, Pinsaqui is a unique place in the highlands of Ecuador.

---

### ECUADOR FACTOIDS:

Rumiñahui was a famous Inca general who advised fighting back against the Spanish conquistadores. Today, many things in Ecuador are named for him, including a volcano and a bank.

When measured from sea level, Mt. Everest is the highest point in the world. When measured from the center of the earth, however, Ecuador's Chimborazo Volcano is the highest point, 3,219 meters farther from the center of the earth than Everest.

Trout farming is a thriving industry in the highlands of Ecuador, where they are raised in special tanks and ponds.

---

### LATIN REVOLUTIONARIES #1: SIMÓN BOLÍVAR

(1783-1830)

The "George Washington of South America," Simón Bolívar was born into an upper-class family in Caracas. His parents died while he was still young, so he went to Spain to complete his education. He returned to Venezuela in 1807, where he was soon involved in the independence movement. Although Caracas declared independence from Spain in 1810, Napoleonic Spanish forces re-established control of the area in 1812 and Bolívar was forced to flee to Cartagena.

Revolutionary leaders granted him military command in 1813 and he began what is known in Latin America as the "Admirable Campaign." Bolívar's armies swept across northern South America, liberating cities and regions. A series of setbacks, however, forced Bolívar to go to Jamaica, where he lived in exile in 1815 to 1816. He returned to South America in 1816, aided by Haitian forces, and began the battle for independence anew. He liberated Venezuela and Colombia in 1821 and Ecuador in 1822. Peru followed in 1824.

In 1821, Bolívar was named president of the nation of "Gran Colombia," which included much of Venezuela, Panama, Colombia and Ecuador. Bolivia was added later, taking its name from Bolívar. The large nation proved unwieldy and difficult to govern, however, and by 1830 Gran Colombia had dissolved into the smaller nations that make up northern South America today.

# STUDYING SPANISH IN QUITO

By Paula Newton, Seaton, Devon, England

"Hola! ¿Qué tál?" This is not a good start. It's the first day and we're already bewildered, shuffling around, looking at the floor. One brave chica responds, "Estoy bien." The rest of us collectively hang our heads in shame and an aura of embarrassment pervades. Why did we not try harder with our self-learning books and CDs? The hard realisation of how little we know and how tough the next four hours will be is starting to sink in.

An efficient señora hands us each a chunky textbook, full of alien-looking words and exercises. She jabbers something at me—from her actions, I understand that I am to be taught by Mercedes, a woman with a pleasant, warm and friendly face. She beckons me to a room and my immersion Spanish begins.

There's no hanging about. Within seconds of entering the class, the lesson commences, full-steam. Rapidly we construct sentences with the new verbs and tenses that I learn. Here, as in most of the Spanish schools in Quito, no English is spoken. I receive The Look every time I utter an English word. She rolls her r's in a way that seems physiologically implausible. However, slowly, over the next few weeks, I do learn enough to get by and hold a relatively decent conversation. The learning is interactive and tailored to suit the individual. To increase my vocabulary we play Scrabble, exchange recipes, visit museums and explore local markets. It is fun; we laugh at my ghastly mistakes, and I swiftly learn what not to say. The dictionary is used sparingly—unknown meanings are described via comical charade-style actions or explanations rather than directly translated.

Competition is fierce and schools sell themselves on their extras. Internet use is free here. There are complimentary salsa classes, cookery classes, fascinating lessons in culture and Ecuadorian history and a free city tour. A small fee pays for optional weekend excursions to the beautiful surrounding countryside—Otavalo Market, Quilotoa Loop, Papallacta Hot Springs. The atmosphere at the school is welcoming and sociable—students and teachers alike are congenial. This enhances both the learning process and enjoyment. Many students also stay with local families to speed up their Spanish education and discover and integrate themselves into the local way of life.

Ecuador's Spanish learning industry is thriving. With an easy-to-understand accent, inexpensive classes and its position as a kick-off point for many key points on the Gringo Trail in South America, Quito is well-positioned. The city's popularity is reflected in the large number of schools that can be found within a few square miles of each other. Named as a UNESCO World Heritage Site in 1978, Quito's pretty colonial charm and stunning backdrop high up in the Andes add to the attraction of studying here. At 2,800 metres (almost 10,000 feet), whilst close to the equator, the gentle year-round spring-like weather is another draw.

At four hours a day (not including homework), there's no doubt that the program is intense. However, most schools boast a six to eight week path to fluency. For price, surroundings and enjoyment, Quito must be the *numero uno* choice in Latin America.

Paula Newton is V!VA's operations expert. With an MBA and a background in the Interactive Television industry in the U.K., Paula is the organising force behind the team, and the Managing Editor for V!VA List Latin America. In a step outside her day-to-day role, exchanging the business suit for a backpack, she also contributed writing for the Ecuador chapter and editing for all sections throughout the book. With an insatiable thirst for off-the-beaten-track travel, Paula has ventured extensively in Europe and Asia, and most recently in Ecuador. She currently lives in Quito. Paula never leaves for her travels without a good supply of patience, which is, "remarkable because I don't have any when I'm at home!" The craziest place she has ever visited is Hanoi, Vietnam. "I have never seen so many motorbikes in one place, following no obvious traffic rules."

The most bizarre cultural experience she had was watching Indonesian men in a remote coastal community in eastern Lombok paint their toenails with pink nail polish brought to them by the tour guide. This was followed up with a dance including a strange mix of 1970s disco and the very traditional music of the locals.

### LEARNING SPANISH TIPS:

Try to learn three verbs per day.

Watching children's TV shows in Spanish can help with understanding.

Reading the newspaper in Spanish can help to increase vocabulary.

Immersion is a good way to quickly learn Spanish. If learning in a Spanish-speaking country, it is definitely worth spending the extra pennies on a homestay experience.

Find a Spanish-speaking girlfriend/boyfriend!!

The Basilica.
Photo by Suco Viteri.

www.vivatravelguides.com/103388

# QUITO HOMESTAY

*By Katie Tibbetts, Middletown, Connecticut, U.S.A.*

Katie Tibbetts' sense of adventure has taken her around the globe. A native of Connecticut, U.S.A., she received her Bachelor of Arts and Post Graduate Degree in English Literature from the University of Otago, Dunedin, New Zealand.

Upon graduation she moved to Seoul, South Korea, for a year where she taught English and traveled Asia. Her passion for hiking, climbing and the great outdoors has taken her extensively through Australia, Europe and Ecuador.

Majestic snow-capped peaks, bustling markets, and shy but friendly natives. These are the elements of armchair travel, the source of that voyeuristic surge of inspiration felt while thumbing through glossy travel books and magazines.

Post-card perfect landscapes and safe, self-contained cultural encounters. This is the stuff of expensive packaged tours where everything is painstakingly planned, right down to the cute pink umbrella in your cocktail. Check out the local sights and sounds with your friendly guide and at the end of a long day check in to your hotel, complete with cable TV, and those fun little crème-filled mints on an over-fluffed pillow. This is zoo travel: you can see it without having to get uncomfortably close to it. Picture-perfect and neatly packaged, complete with continental breakfast buffets (included of course!), and air conditioned suites (view of spewing volcano extra)—don't pet the natives, please.

Fine for some, but not for me. Give me cold electric showers, rice and potato dinners, and drinking games with drunken uncles. The blood and guts of travel by the seat of your pants, outside the First World comfort zone: a country skinned and served uncooked and underdone. Red, rare, raw, and dripping with the unrefined realities of everyday living in a foreign country: Ecuador, alive and kicking.

Stripped bare of the travel brochure bombast and tour guide diplomacy, the country may appear dishearteningly lackluster, and surprisingly similar to the life back home. No ad-agency adjectives or airbrushed photos: a homestay in Ecuador promises the willing traveler a very different spread.

*Snap.* Breakfast with the family, sipping coffee and discussing the latest political gossip.

*Snap.* Christmas dinner. Tossing back drinks and enjoying the warming tingle of inside jokes and that easy, liquid conversation between brothers and sisters, mothers and fathers.

*Snap.* Crowded on a couch with your Ecuadorian family, sharing a blanket, and watching poorly dubbed American horror films.

And these are just a few highlights. While living with an Ecuadorian family, one can expect unexpected encounters with the mundane mechanisms of everyday life. You will have the rare opportunity to eat, sleep, live, and breathe *Ecuador*. A homestay may not boast five star hotels, gourmet spreads, or *National Geographic* natives. In fact you'll be lucky to get red meat and green vegetables once a week.

There are no class five rapids to write home about. No survival stories of hairy encounters with men in loin cloths. And you may as well forget about top ten lists of "picture-perfect landscapes" and "things to see and do before you die." What a homestay does provide is a wild adventure into the heart and soul of a country, its natural rhythms and the heartbeat of its people. It is a rare opportunity to drop the accoutrements of an outsider and don the apparel of an insider.

Packaged tours, while certainly convenient, do tend to serve the country on a silver platter. Plucked of stray hairs and injected with aesthetically appealing souvenir-shop-markets, majestic mountains, and built-for-tourist towns. The wildest adventure, perhaps, involves traveling into the hearts and minds of those who inhabit the country and discovering the subtle similarities and differences between your life and that of your host country family.

It is about sitting at its kitchen tables, eating its food and drinking with its uncles. Living with a family in Ecuador offers the opportunity to roll up your sleeves, brush up on your Spanish and dive into the strange and bizarre events that inevitably accompany the uncut, unrefined, realities of family life in a foreign country.

## BASILICA DEL VOTO NACIONAL
*By Kathleen Fisher*

The Basilica del Voto Nacional is a favourite with daring travelers, who scale its grey and rough-hewn heights for the best views of Ecuador's capital.

Construction on the Basilica started in 1883 to mark the country's renewed devotion to Jesus Christ, as decreed ten years earlier by president Gabriel García Moreno. Despite over 120 years of history, the church is relatively new compared with others in Quito's colonial district. In fact, it remains technically unfinished, which is hardly surprising, considering almost penniless local church-goers provided the funding.

Nonetheless, this neo-Gothic structure is magnificent, rising 112 metres (367 feet) from the ground to its spire top. The Basilica emits the romantic eeriness of late 16th-century novels, emphasized by a series of bird-like gargoyles, perched and watchful, on its parapets. In defiance of all notions of occupational health and safety, a trembling gangplank and iron ladder deliver hot and dirty climbers to their final destination—the rosebud-encrusted bell tower.

Most clang the Basilica's bells before enjoying the majestic views from the statuesque Virgin of Quito south of the city's Old Town and modern skyscrapers to the far northern suburbs, a 360-degree spectacle unmatched in this city.

# QUITO CLEATS

### By Katie Tibbetts, Middletown, Connecticut, U.S.A.

One sunny day in Ecuador, a milking cow, an old man, and an eight-year-old-girl made the grueling trek across a muddy field. In an unlikely turn of events, I had become the center of what some might call a good start to a bad joke. And despite the notes of laughter dancing about the air, this was no joke. Something very serious was about to occur. Among women. In Ecuador.

Anyone who knows Ecuador (and who fancies bubble baths, has a penchant for gossip, and loves … no hates … no LOVES chocolate) has probably experienced the thick blue vein of machismo that courses through nearly all healthy Y-chromosome inhabitants of this Latino country. Besides bullfights and the ever-so-charming catcalls, there is no better way to assert one's masculinity than by donning short shorts and running around shirtless with a bunch of other sweaty men.

When put this way, it is perhaps a bit strange that *fútbol* would be the national pastime of a country brimming with conservative Catholics and barrel-chested men with swaggers that would shame a Texan. Then again, if the bar-room brawls in England and roughed-up refs in Brazil are any indication, this no sport for someone light in their boots (or cleats). Given the importance of fútbol in a country ruled by machismo and *mujeriegos*, it is not surprising that soccer has yet to capture the interest of young Ecuadorian women.

But despite the whistles, sensual Latino serenades, and skin-tight tanks, a new species has come to inhabit Ecuador's cultural landscape: the female *fútbolista*. Sporting the same apparel as her male counterpart (but the shirts stay on), this cleat-crazed beast is ripping up fields around Ecuador. Bravado with a feminine flair: this is the character of these all-women matches.

Having lived and breathed soccer since the age of seven, I was desperate to lace-up and hit the turf in Ecuador. Mention of this desire, however, was met with snickers, sneers, and sideway glances from both men and women. Clearly, I thought to myself, I had picked the wrong country to pursue this internationally recognized and revered sport. But Latin America has always had its renegades, and ladies lacing up on the fútbol fields outside of Quito are no exception.

Thanks to the pioneering efforts of a few fearless women (and a flurry of phone calls in broken Spanish) I found myself once again sporting cleats and panting my way up and down a fútbol field. I use the term "field" loosely to refer to a converted cow pasture with the makeshift metal goalposts awkwardly sticking up from either end.

Our weekly Sunday matches were brutal, elbows flying and tempers flaring. You might think this was a typical match between two competitive teams—except for the slightly-peeved heifer who refused to share her space and occasionally had to be beaten off the field of play by the old man wielding a large, rather painful looking stick. Maybe she, too, wanted to play. And unlike the matches back home, in these I was just as likely to receive a pass from a robust 45-year-old woman as I was her gangly-and-grinning eight-year-old daughter.

Struck dumb by the sight of my mud-encrusted clothes and socially mind-blowing new activity, my Ecua-brothers stammer out a few sentences in Spanish. "But are they any good?" one asks, incredulously. *Who needs skills when you're a Latina woman with an attitude. Let them be on the receiving end of one of those elbows, I think to myself.* An image of a matador being gored by his bull flashes before me. All I have to do is show them the ball-shaped bruise on my leg, and they give a nod of approval. Of course, I conveniently failed to mention that after the game we gossiped our way back to one of the women's houses for fresh squeezed pineapple juice and finger sandwiches.

---

# THE HAUNTED MUSEUM

By Dr. Crit Minster

On the corner of García Moreno and Sucre streets in the colonial center of Quito sits a majestic building that was once the Central Bank of Ecuador. In the 19th century, the building also served as the national mint, and was home to an enormous coin press that is still on the premises.

The first official minter of Ecuador was one William Jamesson, an Englishman. According to legend, at night some of the mint and bank workers used to slip into the building and make their own counterfeit money using the coin press. Jamesson found out about it, and put a stop to it, but not before a good deal of counterfeit money had gone into circulation. Jamesson dedicated himself to finding all of these counterfeit coins … and some believe that he is still doing so, more than a century after his death.

Today the old Central Bank building is home to the numismatic museum, and houses an impressive array of currency from Ecuador and around the world (it is worth a visit if you're interested in coins, bills and money). During the daytime, the museum is full of tourists and schoolchildren. At night, however, the guards and watchmen say they're not alone in the building. Several claim to have heard the sounds of footsteps and the clinking of coins, and to have felt cold, eerie blasts of air as they make their patrols.

All of these watchmen believe the same thing: that it is none other than the ghost of William Jamesson, roaming the halls and going through the exhibits searching for false coins. So go and visit the coin museum if you dare, but first check the coins in your pocket, and if any of them don't look real, leave them outside!

Numismatic museum: Garcia Moreno and Sucre, old town. Hours: Monday through Sunday, 9:00 to 5:30.
Source: *Ecuadorian Ghost Stories*, by Mario Conde.

# BULLFIGHTING AT THE FESTIVITIES OF QUITO

By Paula Newton, Seaton, Devon, England

The trumpets blare a theatrical fanfare. A small doorway in the ringside opens, and dazed and confused, the massive brown bull catapults into the centre of the ring. Bemused, it suspiciously eyes the spectators, wondering what is going on.

The bull doesn't get long to think—one-by-one, three Toreros in highly ornate costumes appear from the sidelines, waving shocking pink capes, provoking the bull. Irritated, it charges across the ring. The Toreros leap for shelter around the ring's edge. The Matador keenly watches from the edge, assessing its behaviour as the bull attacks the wooden fence with its horns, trying to reach the elusive Toreros.

The crowd goes wild. The Plaza de Toros is packed—Quiteños have been queuing all week for tickets to today's spectacle. The men don cowboy or panama hats, shirts and jeans and pour red wine into their open throats from *botas* (wineskins) and cheer. The ladies are dressed more appropriately for a night on the town rather than an afternoon on the concrete seats of the bullring. Every so often, the crowd breaks into a verse of "El Chullita Quiteño," a rowdy local anthem.

From above, the trumpets proclaim the entry of Picadors on horseback. Their dazzling costumes glitter in the midday sun. The bull, bewildered by this turn of events, and now angry from the taunting, turns its attention from the sheltering Toreros and takes up the new challenge, hurtling towards one of the Picadors. The horse, whilst armoured, takes the full weight to its side. The Picador lances the bull in its back below its horns. The blood flows heavily, bubbling out of the bull and dripping onto the sand. The Picadors exit as a daring and nimble Banderillero runs at the bull and stabs it in its back with banderillas, which dangle precariously from the bull.

The Matador enters the ring and the crowds cheer. This is what they have been waiting for. He holds a small red cloak concealing a razor-sharp sword. Weakened, the enraged bull charges at the cloth, hoping to gore the arrogant Matador with its sharp horns. Gasps of terror take hold as the ferocious bull briefly gets lucky—the Matador is knocked to the ground. Trembling with fear, the crowd watches in horror as the Matador is gouged in the leg. A worried Banderillero offers aid, frantically waving his pink cape and angering the proud Matador who shoos him away and breaks free of the horns. The dance between bull and man continues and the beast tires, blood spewing from the holes in its back. Sensing its fatigue, the Matador conceals his blade beneath the cape. In a climatic finale, he reaches between the bull's horns and, with all his strength, plunges the blade between the beast's shoulder blades and into its heart. The bull drops.

As the corpse is dragged from the arena, from within the assembly, dozens of red roses fly at the victorious Matador, symbolising the throng's enjoyment of the show and appreciation of his technique and daring. He strides around the ring bowing and catching the roses. This pleases the people, who cheer more.

The Festivities of Quito last for 10 days. During this time there are daily bullfights—at a rate of six bulls per day over a 10 day period, a total 60 bulls are killed. However repulsive this may seem to some, few protest. With its roots arguably in Minoan Greece, brought to Latin America by the conquistadores hundreds of years ago and still thriving here today in Ecuador, bullfighting is here to stay.

## CUARENTA

By Paula Newton

Cuarenta is a card game, played in Ecuador, particularly in the Sierra.

The word Cuarenta is Spanish for "forty." Forty is both the score needed to win the game and the number of cards that are used from the deck. The eights, nines and tens are removed from the pack to reduce the number of cards to forty. The game requires either two or four players. If there are four players then players double up into teams, with the players sitting opposite one another. Each player receives five cards which are dealt all at once to that player. Once the first set of five cards have been played, the players are each dealt another set of five cards until all forty cards have been played.

The aim of the game is to be the first to reach a score of 40. The person to the left of the dealer plays first, and play continues in a clockwise direction. Points are scored by "capturing" the cards of the other player/team. Cards can be captured by matching the card of another player that has already been placed on the table, or by playing a card that is the total of some of the cards already played (e.g. playing a five when a two and a three are already on the table), or by playing the next card in a sequence. In any of these scenarios, the winning player takes the cards that have been captured from the table, and each of these counts as one point towards their score.

Other elements of the game include capturing a card through *caida*, which is winning a card by matching the card just played by the last player. *Limpia* occurs when the table is completely cleared by a player who manages to capture all of the cards that have been laid. Both of these moves are awarded two points.

In Quito, the game is especially popular during the period of the Festivities of Quito in late November and early December when many offices finish up early for the day and workers relax together playing Cuarenta and drinking a *cerveza* or two.

# TELEFÉRIQO

### By Paula Newton, Seaton, Devon, England

Having recently opened in July 2005, Quito's "TeléfériQo," or cable car, is a very pleasant option for whiling away a few hours. Morning is the time to go, as there is greater chance of sun, clear blue skies and majestic, sweeping vistas.

Eighteen gondolas, each carrying six people, are available to sweep you at a tranquil pace up the mountainside. You wait with trepidation at the allotted spot from which you will clamber into the gondola. As it swings around the corner, you hop on, excited and a little nervous. It takes eight to 10 minutes to soar up the mountain; cables humming, the gondolas swing precariously in the wind and you gasp as you try to cast from your mind thoughts of snapping cables as seen in the movies. As the journey progresses, the buildings below get smaller and Quito seems like a toy town in the growing distance. The people at the base become specks in the distance.

Arriving at the top, at 4,050 metres (13,300 feet), you are surrounded by amazing views. Follow the pathway to the view place—from here you look down on the dwarfed Panecillo, clouds, the old town and on planes landing at the airport. In the distance, the city limits of Quito are enclosed by glorious snowcapped Cotopaxi, Cayambe and Antisena volcanoes. There is nowhere better to view Quito's spectacular settings than here, up in the clouds.

Expensive boutique shops and an equally pricey restaurant offer you good quality products, souvenirs, chocolates, and even oxygen for those struggling with the altitude. You are a captive audience and will pay over the odds for a cup of coffee and a piece of chocolate cake in the swanky restaurant owned by Juan Pablo Montoya. You sip on your drink and admire the spectacular view to Quito's north and east.

Adventurous souls can also hike to Ruca Pichincha volcano from the top, but the hike is tough going at this altitude. Temperatures at the Ruca can drop below freezing and the weather changes rapidly so it is necessary to be appropriately clothed. The hike takes from two and a half to three and a half hours depending on speed and fitness levels. The ecosystem at this height is known as páramo. It is wild and austere, but supports an incredible diversity of life. The tall páramo grasses swish in the gentle breeze, one of the few sounds other than the tramping of your feet and you might spot an Andean fox or rabbit scurrying about its business, or a condor gliding overhead.

As you glide down the mountain, the garish Vulcano Park amusement park gets closer and closer. You start to hear the squeals of joy and terror coming from the rides. You feel smugly satisfied knowing that the ride you just took was the most rewarding of them all.

---

*"I have painted for half a century as if I were crying in desperation."*
-Oswaldo Guayasamín, Ecuadorian Artist (1919-1999)

---

## THE VIRGIN OF QUITO

### By Dr. Crit Minster

Quito's most recognizable landmark is almost certainly the Virgin, a 45-meter/148-foot-tall white statue of the Virgin Mary that looks out benevolently over the northern half of the city. The statue is always easy to spot, as it is on top of the Panecillo (literally "small bread roll") hill just south of Quito's old colonial area.

Panecillo hill was, for centuries, home to a small Spanish fort. The location was perfect: the hill commands all of old town as well as the valleys to the north and south. Later, it was selected as the site for the massive statue, which is a reproduction of an original, much smaller statue on display in the San Francisco church.

A visit to the Virgin is a must-do for travelers in Quito. The view of the city is great (only the view from the top of the TeléfriQo is better), there is a good restaurant, and sometimes local vendors sell souvenirs. It's included on most formal city tours.

Quito Old Town. Photo by Maximilian Hirschfeld.

# PAPALLACTA

## By Paula Newton, Seaton, Devon, England

High up in the páramo, at 10,800 feet above sea level, the Papallacta thermal springs are the epitome of bliss. At an average temperature of 104 degrees Fahrenheit, the pools are a welcome retreat from the chilly daytime temperature of 57 degrees. Whilst being very peaceful to loll about in, the pools are also purported to have healing properties.

Slide into the steamy waters and worries seem to slip away; it's not hard to believe that these waters can help flush toxins from the body. Framed by rugged, bleak peaks, the vistas are almost as refreshing as the water. Relaxing and unwinding in the springs against a panoramic backdrop of jagged, isolated mountains is quite extraordinary. A kaleidoscope of colors—blues, greens, and grays—melt into one another in the steamy setting. This swirl of colors collides with the sight of soaring peaks and delicate hummingbirds fluttering about to form an image that is captivating and picturesque. Pulling away from the warm embrace of the water is as difficult as the views are beautiful.

The surrounding beauty is breathtaking—and so is the cold air that greets the bathers exiting the pools. Despite the initial chill, the combination of cold air and hot pools is oddly, yet delightfully refreshing.

Drift lazily from pool to pool and experience all the varied temperatures that the springs have to offer. A romantic, night-time dip in the pools under clear skies and twinkling starlight, or an early-bird bathe accompanied by the rising sun are both invigorating. At the break of day, the pools are especially peaceful and the sight of the mountain peaks through the mist rising from the pools in the morning sunlight is truly magical. After an afternoon dip, don woolly clothes and head for the warmth of the restaurant for a tasty, wholesome meal of fresh trout, the regional specialty. For those who tire of bathing in the pools, massages and other luxurious and therapeutic treatments in the spa add a delightful finishing touch to an already indulgent stay.

### PAPALLACTA TRAVEL TIPS:

When visiting Papallacta you should remember to bring warm clothes. It can get cold at this altitude, particularly if you are staying overnight. For a quieter day-trip to the springs, visit on a weekday if possible. Weekends are more crowded, but this can be a good time to practise your Spanish, as you will find many Quito residents have made the trip to the pools, and will be keen to talk to you. If taking the local bus to Papallacta, remember to wear a decent pair of walking shoes because there is a short (20 minute) hike from the bus stop to the springs. Finally, don't forget the sun screen. While cloudy up there, due to the high altitude and proximity to the equator the sun can burn quickly.

# OYACACHI

## By John Polga-Hecimovich

For a more off-the-beaten-track experience than Papallacta, the isolated community of Oyacachi is a fine example of rural development in the Andes, and it boasts hot springs, ruins, artisan work, and amazing hiking for tourists anxious to escape the Gringo Trail. The village lies in the expansive Cayambe-Coca Ecological Reserve, stretching from Volcán Cayambe down the eastern cordillera, and is so far off the beaten path that few outsiders had even ventured there until the first road into town was built in 1985. The road is still relatively rough, although the views more than make up for the bumpy ride: the rolling hills and patchwork fields around Cangahua give way to towering mountains and páramo grasses that finally yield to rushing waterfalls and the Oyacachi's verdant green valley.

The Termas de Oyacachi, a community project that benefits the village, is the reason most travelers make the trip from Quito or Cayambe. They aren't quite as stylish as the waters in the nearby village of Papallacta, but just as warm and with fewer crowds. There are currently five pools, and the hot springs complex has changing rooms, showers, and bathrooms as well as space to cook and camp.

The current 400 or so residents of Oyacachi are said to be descendents of the Caranqui tribe, who sought refuge there after an Inca massacre at Lago Yahuarcocha, near Ibarra. Interestingly, artifacts found near the Oyacachi River about 40 minutes east of town give evidence of a prehistoric migration from the Amazon to the Andes. In more recent history, the town was a way station for people traveling between these two regions. In fact, one of Ecuador's best treks is an old Inca trail that begins in Oyacachi at 3,140 meters (10,300 feet) and descends some 1,000 meters (3,300 feet) through the thick vegetation of the ecological reserve, ending in the Oriente town of El Chaco. The trek should appeal to serious birders, who can see and hear red-crested cotingas, black billed mountain toucans, and the shining sunbeam hummingbird.

# EL ORIENTE AND THE WAORANI

By Kathleen Fisher, Canberra, Australia

Fifty years ago, five young American missionaries flew their small Mission Aviation Fellowship (MAF) plane into Ecuador's eastern jungle, aiming to turn the country's fiercest head-hunting warriors to Christianity. The Waorani people, then known as Auca, responded with barbed spears, butchering the visitors and ransacking their plane.

It would be easy to assume this was the last contact between the MAF and the Waorani. Not so. The event sparked an influx of volunteers wishing to carry on the work of the men now known as the "five martyrs." Today, MAF workers provide vital services, including air ambulances, to one of the least modernized cultures in South America. What's more, travelers can join pilots, as suitable, on their daily flights for a unique glimpse of remote Amazon village life, accessible only by air.

An international organisation, MAF has three bases in Ecuador, including one in Shell, a peaceful town in the Southern Oriente. Two hours from Baños and 20 minutes from Puyo, it's not a tourist destination—in fact, it owes its existence to the oil company of the same name, a military airbase and a cluster of American missionary groups.

My MAF flight starts with an ID check by local military and a weigh-in at the mission's hangar. My fellow travellers include a nurse from Hospital Vozandes (run by another group of Christian missionaries) and a recovered patient returning to his jungle home. Our other "companions" will travel in the hold—two giant, gasping catfish, as long as my arm-span and wrapped in wet cloths. At other times, passengers include mothers with newborns, snake-bite victims, government teams undertaking immunisation and health education programs, and clucking chickens.

From the air, the jungle looks like an emerald labrynth, an eternal green carpet of life and vitality. The tiny Cessna buzzes and rattles, and we chat with our pilot, who clearly knows this journey inside-out. After 30 minutes, we descend onto a slick jungle airstrip and Waorani people rush to meet us—fortunately, without spears and blowguns.

The village is hot and humid, filled with sweet fruity scents and chirping crickets and frogs. The heritage of the people is one of head-shrinking, cannibalism and vicious blood feuds. They are delighted to show us their village—a rambling cluster of thatched huts on stilts. We are invited into a one-roomed home and feast on finger-sized bananas while the woman of the house mends a woven bag. Three shy girls sit under hanging bunches of green bananas, while a couple of boys giggle and sway in a hammock. Then we paddle nearby in a shallow river, watching women with swift reflexes snatch hand-sized fish from the water. A pet monkey rattles overhanging branches and butterflies drift by like scraps of blue and orange paper.

As we buckle up to leave, children press their huge dark eyes against the plane's windows. The grass on the runway whirls and flattens as we take off and they dash after us on broad, splayed feet never touched by shoes — they are as thrilled as we are by the encounter with people from an unfamiliar world

Kathleen Fisher is an Australian writer and photographer, specialising in arts and lifestyle. Although she has been writing for over 10 years and has traveled extensively, writing about her adventures is a relatively new string to her bow. She wouldn't leave home without her camera and a blank notebook to record her experiences. Her favourite places are raw and energetic, with plenty of opportunities to mingle with locals—one time including tasting local "treats" in Cambodia, such as insect larvae, chicken tongues and deep-fried grasshoppers. She has an Honours degree in creative writing and a Graduate Certificate in photography.

She yearns to explore Zimbabwe, her husband's childhood home, but her next trip will be driving 1,200 kilometres across her own country on the Nullabor Plain.

Waorani Girls at home. Photo by Kathleen Fisher.

ORIENTE TRAVEL TIPS:

Roads conditions are not good in the Amazon region. Roads are being developed into the Oriente region, however be aware that conditions on them are not great due to the effects of natural disasters such as flooding.

There is significant development of the oil industry in the Ecuadorian Amazon. This causes deforestation and pollution amongst other problems.

A pair of rubber boots is a very handy accessory in the jungle. These will protect your lower legs from insects and other creatures, and are also useful due to the humid and wet weather conditions. If staying at a lodge, it is most likely that you will be able to hire or borrow boots—most lodges hold stocks of boots in many sizes.

# EATING LEMON ANTS IN THE RAINFOREST

By Dr. Crit Minster, Rochester, New York, U.S.A.

You're hiking through the thick, steamy jungle of Ecuador's rainforest. The hot sun overhead is softened by the dense canopy of trees, vines and other lush, green plant life. Far off, a parrot shrieks, and hairy spiders scamper over the muddy trail in front of your feet. Suddenly, there is a break in the impenetrable wall of green: you've stumbled into an open space, a dry patch of ground dominated by a lone tree. Nothing else grows within about twenty feet of it.

According to local belief, the strange open space in the middle of the dense jungle is the home of a malignant forest spirit. In the local language, it's called a "devil's garden" and they are fairly common in parts of the Ecuadorian and Peruvian rainforests. If you're with a local guide, however, he or she will not avoid the spot: instead, he or she may break a twig off the tree, split it open to reveal dozens of tiny brown ants ... and invite you to eat them!

The ants are, in fact, edible. They are called "lemon ants" because of their vague tangy, lemony taste. Feel free to have a try: it won't hurt you and is likely to become one of your most memorable experiences in the rainforest. But the ants are more than a tasty jungle treat: together with the lone tree in the middle of the clearing they make up one of the most remarkable symbiotic relationships in nature.

The ants (*myrmelachista schumanni*) and tree (*duroia hirsuta*) work together to survive and thrive in the competitive forest. The ants get the benefit of a home, and it's a good deal—some ant colonies are thought to have survived for more than 800 years. The trees gain the advantage of room to grow—the ants are the only known insect species to produce their own herbicide, a toxin that poisons other plants in the area, allowing their home tree to get the sunlight it needs. The ants bite into the leaves of any other plant species that tries to take root in the area, injecting formic acid which slowly kills it.

Don't plan on making a meal of lemon ants; they're very tiny and you'd probably have to eat the whole colony before you felt full. But the next time you find yourself in the devil's garden, stop for a moment and enjoy the rainforest's version of dessert!

Eating lemon ants. Photos by Dr. Crit Minster.

> "I am proud to be a madman. Mad people speak from the heart and see with their souls. The people understand this. That is why they call me 'Crazy Abdala.'"
> -Abdala Bucaram Ortiz, Ex-President of Ecuador (1952-)

# MACAS

### By Lorraine Caputo, Columbia, Missouri, U.S.A.

A gold and fuchsia sunset erupts across the sky above a virgin jungle stretching across the horizon. A rainbow emerges over the eastern Amazonian hills and the gravel-braided Upano River. To the west, the snowy Sangay volcano glows lava-red. As darkness closes in, the song of night flows through the rough-hewn streets of Macas.

Nestled in the eastern part of Ecuador, six hours south of Puyo, the sleepy jungle town of Macas was founded at the end of the 16th century as a missionary outpost. Today, it serves as a center for exploring the natural and cultural riches of the area.

Take an excursion to Sangay National Park, home to three volcanoes, including Sangay itself, which is one of the world's most active volcanoes continuously spewing ash, stones and fumes; Tungurahua, also presently active; and Altar. The park's ecosystems range from tropical rainforest to páramo (barren highland) and glacial. Fauna include majestic condor, mountain tapir, puma and ocelots.

Hiking can be very arduous and a good guide is highly recommended. Hiking to the Sangay Volcano will take about seven days. On the way to the Park, near the villages of Santa Rosa and Guapala, is the Complejo Hombre Jaguar archaeological site. Little is known about these ruins, composed of numerous tolas (burial mounds).

Macas is in the midst of Shuar territory. Once known as the "head-hunting" Jívaro, these indigenous people allow visits to traditional villages only with approved guides, in order to learn about their misunderstood culture.

At the confluence of the Kapawari and Pastaza rivers is the Kapawari Ecological Reserve, working in cooperation with the local community. The Achuar-styled complex is set in an area rich in biodiversity, and is reached by plane and canoe.

Tour agencies may arrange short or long treks into the jungle or Sangay National Park, whitewater rafting on the Río Upano, or other adventures. In the city itself, there is an archaeological museum and a recreational park rich in orchids and with great views of the Upano River valley. A few kilometers north, on the Cupueno River, is La Cascada, which offers great swimming, a water slide and a picnic area.

Macas offers an alternative route into the cultural and natural richness of the Ecuadorian Oriente. Whether to visit a Shuar community, or merely to gaze upon Sangay glowing on the horizon, a visit to this town promises to be unforgettable.

---

**RAINFOREST FACTOIDS:**
It is estimated that tropical rainforest once covered 14% of the earth's surface: currently, it covers about 6%. According to some estimates, as many as 50,000 species a year of plants, animals and insects may be lost due to rainforest deforestation around the world. Although 25% of modern western pharmaceuticals are derived from rainforest ingredients, less than 1% of all rainforest plant and animal species have been thoroughly tested by scientists. One hectare of rainforest may contain more than 1,500 plant species, including 750 species of trees.

---

# RAFTING IN THE ECUADORIAN AMAZON

### By Chris Sacco

Boasting legendary status with whitewater enthusiasts, the Ecuadorian Amazon is home to scores of easily-accessible rafting runs ranging in difficulty from class I to class V.

The best place to begin your rafting or kayaking expedition is in the jungle town of Tena, which was once an important colonial trading post, but is now the commercial center and capital of the Napo Province. There is no shortage of rafting and kayaking tour operators in Tena, and many have offices at the northern end of town on Avenida 15 de Noviembre.

Two rivers, the Río Tena and Río Pano, course directly through the center of town and there are numerous other rivers, streams, and waterfalls waiting in the great green expanse of forest that stretches beyond the city limits, as far as the eye can see.

Early January is the ideal time to plan a trip, as the rivers are at their peak. You might just coincide with the Napo River Festival, organized yearly by the Ecuadorian Rivers Institute to celebrate and raise awareness about the Napo Watershed, which is home to Río Napo, the last remaining free-flowing tributary to the Amazon, as well as numerous other creeks and rivers, including the Ríos Jatunyacu, Misahuallí, and Anzu.

In addition to experiencing some of the world's finest rapids, rafters and kayakers exploring the Napo Basin can expect encounters with lowland Quichua indigenous and possibly Quijos and Chibcha Indians. It's possible to visit many of these communities to observe and sometimes participate in traditional dancing, the preparation of chicha (an alcoholic drink made by masticating maiz, rice or yucca and fermenting the juice), shamanic rituals and blowgun competitions.

Whether you want to brave the endless rapids and nasty holes of a class IV or meander lazily down a class II river while soaking up the wonders of the rainforest, a whitewater trip in the Ecuadorian Amazon will change you forever.

# COTOPAXI

By Chris Sacco, Hamilton, New York, U.S.A.

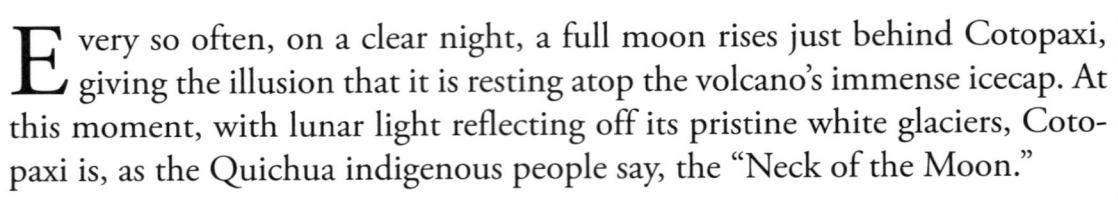

Every so often, on a clear night, a full moon rises just behind Cotopaxi, giving the illusion that it is resting atop the volcano's immense icecap. At this moment, with lunar light reflecting off its pristine white glaciers, Cotopaxi is, as the Quichua indigenous people say, the "Neck of the Moon."

In addition to contributing to *V!VA List* and the *V!VA Travel Guides Ecuador* book, Christopher Sacco has worked extensively on the last three editions of the *Rough Guide to Ecuador*. He has written for numerous magazines and newspapers such as the *Washington Post* and *The Economist* Intelligence Unit. Sacco always leaves for his travels with a good book.

He had some crazy trips visiting the Ecuador-Colombia border area while updating the Rough Guide to Ecuador. He once had a strange experience sleeping in a llama barn in the Uyuni Salt Plains in Bolivia after being trapped between two flash floods. "It's odd asking dirt poor Bolivian peasants to lend you a blanket and spot next to their livestock ..."

Cotopaxi's majestic cone, which at 5,897 meters (19,300 feet) is one of the highest active volcanoes on Earth, juts forth abruptly from the high-altitude grasslands and bucolic fields stretching south from Quito all the way to the Peruvian border. This soaring peak reaches so high that it is clearly visible 60 kilometers away in the nation's capital, despite being ringed by half a dozen other mountains, each exceeding 4,500 meters (14,800 feet) in height.

In addition to being among the most impressive and beautiful peaks in the Andes, Cotopaxi has become a favorite destination for outdoor enthusiasts, in part because even novice climbers can summit its lofty peak. Hovering close to the forbidding 6,000-meter figure, this mountain is perfect for anyone seeking to bag a high-alpine ascent. The route has changed over the years, due to shifting of the glaciers triggered by global warming, but it generally takes you up the right side of the volcano's north face to the huge rock wall called Yanasacha, and then cuts back left, traversing a steep slope to the summit. Ascending along this route takes between five and seven hours, and the descent approximately half that time. Cotopaxi can be climbed year round, but December and January are considered the best months.

While Cotopaxi is the crown jewel of Cotopaxi National Park, the most popular protected area in Ecuador, there is plenty more to do nearby, including two other great ascents, Cerros Rumiñahui and Sincholagua, which are within sight of the volcano. These two mountains are often climbed to acclimatize in the days preceding the main Cotopaxi climb.

If you are lucky enough to have a clear morning, Cotopaxi's summit provides dreamy views of the mountainous Andean landscape spreading out hundreds of kilometers in every direction. Or better yet, if you plan your climb during a full moon, you may just catch a glimpse of the indigenous Cosmo Vision that gave Cotopaxi its name.

---

**CLIMBING COTOPAXI TRAVEL TIPS:**
Proper acclimatization, good fitness and training are essential before attempting to climb Cotopaxi. It is worth spending at least a week or two in Quito, and summiting one or two other peaks first. Be ready for an early start - the climb commences at any time between midnight and 2 a.m.

---

Climbing to the summit of Cotopaxi. Photo by Suco Viteri.

# HACIENDA SAN AGUSTÍN DE CALLO

By Dr. Crit Minster, Rochester, New York, U.S.A.

The sun had been setting a little earlier every night. The inhabitants of the majestic Andes began to worry, as they did every year: what if this year, the sun simply continued to set earlier and earlier until it disappeared altogether? For three days, the priests prayed, fasted and sacrificed guinea pigs and llamas, and on the shortest night of the year, they celebrated the annual festival of Inti Raymi, honoring the Sun God and imploring him to return for another year. The Sun God listened: on the next day, sunset was a little later, indicating another prosperous year for the crops of the Incas.

The festival of Inti Raymi was banned by the Spanish colonial administration in 1572 as pagan and anti-Catholic. It went underground and survived, and Andean natives began celebrating it again in the 1940s. Ironically, Spanish colonial writers had written about the festival, and their descriptions of it helped modern Andeans re-create it. The most important Inti Raymi celebration takes place in Cusco, Peru, but there are other, smaller celebrations including Ecuador's at Hacienda San Agustín de Callo—one of the best places to celebrate.

The site was an Inca fortress, an outpost between the great Inca imperial cities of Quito and Cusco. The Spanish took over the fortress and turned it over to the Augustinian order, who built a convent there. The Incas were peerless stonemasons, and the original walls are still as solid as they were the day they were built. The Augustinians built over the Inca walls, incorporating them into their convent but not covering them up. In 1921, the hacienda passed into the hands of the Galo Plaza family, which boasts two presidents of Ecuador in the past hundred years. The family has owned it ever since and converted it into a luxury hotel.

The Hacienda itself is gorgeous. The owners have artfully worked the original Inca walls into the design and left them bare whenever possible, and on a clear day there is a good view of the majestic Cotopaxi volcano from the patio. It is possible to visit the hacienda without staying there: many people come for lunch.

The local indigenous groups consider the site to be part of their cultural heritage, and often have traditional festivals on the grounds. The festivals should not be missed, as they feature natives in full traditional dress donning bright, colorful attire. The most important festival is Inti Raymi, the festival of the sun. It is held on June 24, the winter solstice in the southern hemisphere.

The chapel at the Hacienda is particularly interesting. It's squared-off, small, and resembles a prison cell more than a church, with its solid stone walls on three sides. Religious statues sit in stony nooks in the wall, and a bench too wide for the space stretches across the narrow room. They seem out of place, as if they were an afterthought, a concession to the fact that the room could never be anything but an Inca structure.

As many distinguished guests over the years have learned, the ancient and modern worlds come together in a memorable fusion at Hacienda San Agustín de Callo.

The Chapel. Photo by Diane Newton.

## TOP LIST: CHARMING COLONIAL HOMES

The colonial period left its mark on Latin America in many ways. One of the enduring legacies has been beautiful old homes and architecture. Most of the votes received were for haciendas in Ecuador. Check out these colonial gems if you get a chance:

1. Hacienda Pinsaquí, Ecuador (p. 238). Teresa Colomer, Spain.

2. San Angel Inn, México D.F. Teresa Colomer, Spain.

3. Hacienda de los Morales, México D.F. Teresa Colomer, Spain.

4. Hacienda San Agustín de Callo, Ecuador (see above). Teresa Colomer, Spain.

5. Hotel Monasterio, Cusco, Peru. Gideon Wells.

6. Hacienda Cusin, Ecuador.

# BLACK SHEEP INN

By Carla Walli, Edmonton, Alberta, Canada

The Black Sheep Inn is more than a place to stay; it is a truly unique experience. Located in the heart of the Ecuadorian Andean highlands and overlooking the Río Toachi Canyon, the Black Sheep Inn and its owners, Michelle and Andres, adhere to an ecologically friendly style of travel. They even offer a 10 percent discount for those arriving by bicycle; "Thank you for not polluting!"

Carla Walli is from Edmonton, Alberta, Canada, and works for the Provincial Government of Alberta as a Resource Consultant. She graduated from the University of Alberta in 2001 with a Bachelor's degree in English and then returned to complete her honors after-degree in Women's Studies and graduated in 2003.

Walli has written various editorial pieces for the Alberta Government's provincial newsletter and has an ongoing review column in the inter-office newsletter. In addition to her current love-affair with Latin America, she has also traveled extensively through Europe, Asia, and the Middle East. In her spare time, She can be found studying Spanish over a latte, or shaking up a Hula storm with her Polynesian dancing troupe.

Serving family-style vegetarian meals, made with ingredients fresh from their very own backyard garden and farm, the Black Sheep Inn encourages guests to get to know one another and share travel advice. The Sunday morning breakfast includes plenty of pancakes and music by the jazz greats. The Inn features a sauna, a zip line, and composting toilets. They also sell Tigua paintings and other crafts made by local artists with proceeds going directly to the artists themselves.

The long and arduous journey by bus to the tiny whitewashed and friendly little village of Chugchilán is worth it when the weary traveler arrives at the door of the Black Sheep Inn. Fantastic photo opportunities abound as you pass through the villages on the ride from Latacunga to Chugchilán. After the steep incline to the front door of the Inn, past a flock of the namesake black sheep, freshly-baked cookies and chocolate brownies await. The delicious fresh cheese board, courtesy of the local European Cheese factory, and the first class Chilean wines are a must after a long day exploring the romantic and mysterious cloud forest.

An oasis of activity for the avid day-hiker, the Black Sheep Inn hands out area maps to all guests, with an endless possibility of hiking trails. The particularly challenging four to six hour hike from the glistening turquoise waters of the Laguna-Quilotoa Crater Lake, down through the Río Toachi Canyon and up to Chugchilán, is not to be missed. Michelle and Andres can arrange guides and horses to traverse the tough trail. Mountain bikes, available for rent from the Inn, are another exciting way to explore the stunning scenery of the highlands.

The stunning beauty, all-inclusive prices (breakfast and dinner included), the easy-to-explore landscape and the friendliness of the local villagers will entice travelers to extend their stay in this haven of tranquility.

This eco-lodge was the winner of the 2005 *Smithsonian Magazine*'s Sustainable Tourism award, was named by *Outside Magazine* in 2003 as one of the top ten eco-lodges in the world, and earned the Best in a Mountain Environment by the First Choice Responsible Tourism Awards. The Inn offers its guests an exciting and educational travel experience, while benefiting the local community and the surrounding environment.

## TOP LIST: MOST ECO-FRIENDLY PLACES

There is a growing eco-tourism movement in Latin America. There are many eco-lodges and environment-friendly places that are well worth a visit for the responsible traveler. Here are just a few voted for by our community:

1. The Rio Muchacho Organic Farm, Ecuador (p. 262).
"An oasis for ecofriendly travelers, great self-sufficiency model, organic agriculture, permaculture, alternative energies ... masses to learn." Ruth Mears, New Zealand.

2. The Black Sheep Inn, Ecuador (see above).
The Black Sheep Inn, Ecuador, "Wonderful owners. bathrooms with beautiful views. A sauna, sheep. What else do you need?" Risa, New York, U.S.A.

3. Mindo and various of its accommodations, Ecuador.
"Nature lovers paradise! Birds and butterflies galore, mellow folk, and loads of adventure on the river and in the woods. It's a gem." Bob Mark, Vermont/Washington state, U.S.A.

4. Monteverde, Costa Rica (p. 197).

Runners up: Santiago de Querétaro, the capital of the State of Querétaro, Mexico, "Many plazas connected by andadores, meandering pedestrian walkways, in the cleanest city I've encountered in Latin America." Sandy Leach, Knoxville, U.S.A. Hosteria Alandaluz, Manabi, Ecuador.

# LA CASA DE MAMA HILDA'S

### By Michelle Hopey, New Hampshire, U.S.A.

Sunken valleys. Patches of green and brown acres of land quilted together. Gargantuan peaks of mountains and hills with vertical slopes of cows, sheep, goats, pigs and llamas.

Perhaps the best place to view the amazing Andean scenery is from the Ecuadorian highlands itself, along the now famous Quilotoa loop. And while the tourist trail that follows this circuit has been well-paved, primarily to view the Laguna Quilotoa- a stunning blue volcanic crater lake—those who stay in the mountain oasis for more than a day and see this land by horseback will be the only ones privy to the real beauties of this place, the landscape and people.

Tucked away, high-up in the mountains, three and a half hours by bus from Latagunca on a rocky dirt road is the rural pueblo of Chugchilán. It is perhaps the best location to hunker down while exploring these mountains. In Chugchilán you get fresh, brisk air, warm piercing equator sunshine, windy, dirt roads and clunking pickup trucks. Unfazed and uninhibited, the raw indigenous culture is nearly unscathed. A low population mixed with friendly smiles and family warmth makes you revel in this place you've found. But perhaps the best part of Chugchilán is taking up staying with Mama Hilda.

Mama Hilda's Hostel is a modern cozy lodge, with super-clean bedrooms and baths to boot. You are treated to breakfast, a delicious, home cooked dinner, and the company of Mama Hilda, a meaty and short, yet warmly loving grandma that dons two signature braids that rest perfectly off her shoulders, and a large amiable smile stretched across her face. Mama Hilda and her family run this show—while Mama cooks the meals, her children, grandchildren and nieces and nephews are cleaning the property, building new bedrooms, farming for produce, herding the cattle, flaming the pigs, and guiding visitors up over the mountain—by foot or by horseback—to the great crater lake.

To experience the best of what Mama has to offer, plan on staying with her and the family for two nights. The buses from Latacunga arrive at Mama Hilda's in the afternoon which is perfect for you to check-in, get comfy in your room and get your bearings down in this ever-so small town.

Late afternoon is perfect for relaxing in one of the hammocks while rich savory smells of dinner waft in the air. Dinner is scrumptious, warm, hearty winter meal, eaten, of course—family style. Inevitably, Mama cooks up a dish using the Andean seed, quinoa which is much like couscous, and she prepares meat, potatoes, rice—typical Andean fare. Mama will wait on you hand and foot; rarely does she take a seat—she works to please and won't let you leave until you are full-bellied and happy. The warm-fuzzy family atmosphere will make you want to trade in some relatives for these ones. Since there is no heat in the rooms, guests typically stay in the dining room where there is a fireplace. Travelers trade tales well into the night while playing cards, reading, drinking (the only thing you'll need cash for outside of the room price) or making plans for the next day's activities—hiking or horseback riding.

Over an early morning breakfast of fresh, hot bread, jam and fruit (sometimes eggs too) is the perfect time to chat with Mama and her kids about horseback riding or hiking to the crater. While the hike is an amazingly steep adventure, and satisfying aerobic work-out, if you've come to experience the Andean high-life and take in all the scenery, you're likely to see much more from the saddle of horse. The horses will take you high-up on the ridges where you marvel at the peaks or peer over the deep green valleys while in the midst of llamas, sheep, pigs and goats. And like Mama herself her children are kind and comforting, so if you've never ridden horseback before, they will settle worries and ease you into a magnificent ride.

If you're lucky, your guide may invite you to have lunch with friends living near the lake, a real chance to see how a local family lives, void of any tourist dollars. A soccer game with the local children, after the meal isn't unlikely either, but watch out: they're the undiscovered national stars just waiting to be signed. Read: they are incredibly dynamic soccer players.

After a likely defeat, you'll be driven back to Mama's hostel where you can wash-up and warm-up to another one of Mama's hot, home-cooked savory meals. It's guaranteed to soothe any aches from the earlier ride. And whether you are headed off for a good nice sleep and leaving the next afternoon, or catching the 3 a.m. bus back, it's rare that you can sneak off without one of Mama's generous big hugs, and like a good, true Mama, she might even pinch your cheeks.

Flowers in the Ecuadorian countryside. . Photo by Dr. Crit Minster

# SAQUISILÍ MARKET

By Dr. Crit Minster, Rochester, New York, U.S.A.

I suppose it's a little like an Ecuadorian Wal-Mart. I mean, you can get everything you need there. Food. Clothes. Household stuff. There's a food court. You can buy music and the latest DVDs—if you don't mind that they've all been pirated and don't really work very well. You can even get your hair cut and your knives sharpened.

The similarities stop there, though. There's no photo lab, not much of a lingerie section, and you won't find any greeting cards. There are no shopping carts, but if you have a llama, feel free to load him up. (Shopping carts don't wander off to nibble grass while you're looking for shampoo, but then again you can't pat a shopping cart on the head). The stuff in the food court definitely isn't what you're used to, unless of course your Wal-Mart stocks pig heads, miniature fish fried in grease, or guinea pig on a stick.

Oh, and you can't use your credit card.

The Saquisilí market is one of the largest remaining indigenous markets in Ecuador. The famous Otavalo market sold out years ago: it's all tourist stuff now. But Saquisilí has stuck to its roots: every Thursday, hundreds if not thousands of indigenous people in the mountains south of Quito pack up their burros (donkeys) and llamas early in the morning and make the long trek to Saquisilí. They bring their excess produce: a few onions, some carrots, potatoes, perhaps even some chickens or a pig. They arrive when it is still dark out and set up shop, hoping to make a little extra money or at least get a fair trade for what they've brought.

As the people pour into town, the square comes to life. In the butcher shop, they slaughter sheep, pigs, goats, cattle and llamas and sell them off bit-by-bit. Even the heads are sold: they make good soup. The food-sellers drizzle in one-by-one and fire up their stoves: they'll begin to fry fish, boil chicken and make rice. Some specialize in juice: pineapple, orange, blackberry and more, including some that you've probably never seen before.

The Saquisilí market is more than a trip to the grocery store for the locals. As it has been for centuries, market day is an important social event. The men and women who come to market wear their Sunday best and spend as much time socializing as they do buying and selling.

Although the market is gradually becoming more touristy, it still maintains that authentic edge that provides visitors with a unique view of native life. More and more visitors, perhaps a little turned off by the commercial Otavalo market, come to Saquisilí for a less touristy taste of traditional highland life. The vendors have been quick to spot this, and you'll find stalls devoted to selling Otavalo textiles, Tigua paintings and Pujili ceramics. Unlike Otavalo, however, these stands have not yet become the focus of the market: they're secondary and the exception to the rule.

Set foot in this spectacular market and you'll be stepping back in time. Bring your camera, bring your llama, and above all bring an open mind: this is one of the last places in the world that won't ask "paper or plastic?"

## REGGAETON By Mariana Cotlear

"Hips. It's all in the hips." Any cursory explanation of Latin dance will start with this mantra. It is a chicken-and-egg question of which came first—the rhythm or the movement—but Latin Americans seem to create music designed to fulfill an intrinsic desire to wiggle and shake. Infectiously danceable, reggaeton is no exception—this wildly popular blend of hip hop, reggae, dance hall, and salsa understands this organic desire to dance and exploits it.

The boom-ch-boom-ch of its ubiquitous Dem Bow beat is as addictive as it is inescapable. Coupled with its shocking, sometimes clever, and often crude lyrics, reggaeton is a natural draw for the youth of Latin America. This is definitely not their parent's salsa; yet, rather than renounce the legacy of merengue, cumbia, bachata, and all else that came before, they borrow from each of these genres to create something that is distinctly their own. And, judging from the grinding and hip-shaking that inevitably accompanies the music, they surely haven't lost their love of dancing.

This musical genre has taken the world by storm in just a few short years. Born in Puerto Rico or Panama—depending on who you ask—its provenance is slightly more complex. The genre takes root in Jamaican reggae. Panamanian artists began translating popular songs and got hooked on the beat that now characterizes most, if not all—reggaeton, known as "Dem Bow," a Jamaican riddim named after the song that first popularized it back in 1991.

The Panamanian sounds migrated to Puerto Rico. The island's not-yet-reggaeton artists took a page from their mainland backyard, New York City, and began to incorporate the lyrical style and content of the island's nascent rap *en español*. In the mid-90s, the name "reggaeton" was finally coined.

Popular songs talk about dancing and having a good time, but like the gangster rap it parallels, reggaeton is also flush with themes of violence and sex. The male-dominated genre features women mainly as sex objects or convenient call-responders who confirm the male protagonist's virility, i.e. " ... papi dame lo que quieres," and everyone's favorite, " ... dame más gasolina."

Far from its underground origins, reggaeton has writhed its way firmly into the mainstream. In Puerto Rico, it was once denigrated as a lewd, low-class music. The government even attempted to ban the aptly named grinding dance that accompanies reggaeton called "perreo" (it roughly translates to "doggy-style"). Nowadays, Puerto Rico is the proud exporter of reggaeton's biggest stars, such as Daddy Yankee and Tego Calderón. One can hear the throb of Dem Bow 24-hours a day in all neighborhoods—look around, and you'll probably catch bystanders shaking their hips.

# SALASACA: DAY OF THE DEAD

By John Polga-Hecimovich, Burnsville, Minnesota, U.S.A.

Día de los Difuntos, or Day of the Dead, is without a doubt one of the most important and highly respected days in the Ecuadorian highlands, taking place on November 2nd. A chance to experience it firsthand in a community such as Salasaca will never be forgotten. Mumbled monologues and the pouring of alcohol onto the ground might, to many Westerners, seem like scenes from an anthropology class, but these rituals are quite the norm for members of the indigenous community of Salasaca. On this day when families celebrate the spirits of their ancestors through elaborate gestures such as the sharing of food, drink, and good conversation with the deceased.

The dry and dusty town of Salasaca, located 14 kilometers from Ambato on the road to Baños, is home to one of the most distinctively indigenous communities of Ecuador. In addition to their characteristic clothing - men wear long black ponchos and women dress in naturally dyed bayetas (a type of female poncho) and black anakus (wrap-around skirts)—the community is known for its tapestry weaving. Many of the tapestries sold in the more popular markets of Quito and in Otavalo are in fact woven on wooden looms in Salasaca and generally, prices of textile goods in the central plaza, where vendors sell what they have woven, tend to be lower. The other principal economic activity of the community is highland agriculture, the main produce being corn and potatoes. Fava beans, barley, wheat, and agave plants and their cuchinilla bugs which are used for dying are also harvested.

Día de los Difuntos is also known as Finados. On this day, villagers celebrate the spirits of the dead by dressing in their finest clothing and sharing food, alcohol, and conversation with them. The Salasaca, as they call themselves, wake up early and walk in groups to the cemetery with supplies of food and drink. Hunched over graves and speaking softly in Quechua, they pass around bowls of chocho (lupine beans), corn, hominy, potatoes, bread, and cuy (guinea pig), eating some with their hands and leaving some on the tombs of their beloved. Drinking also begins early and, as the "spirits" flow, conversations between the living and their dead begin to grow more animated. It is not long before liquor bottles and cartons of boxed wine are piled high next to the flower-covered crosses and simple headstones.

Although it may appear bizarre to western onlookers, to the Salasaca and other highland indigenous groups, this process is one of renewal and reconnection with their roots. Participating in or merely observing this holiday provides a unique insight into the indigenous Andean cosmology.

*"The Indian rebellion carries morning in the protest of their shovels."*
-Jorge Carrera Andrade, Ecuadorian Poet, from "Indian Rebellion" (1902-1978)

## SAUCY, SEDUCTIVE SALSA

By Michelle Hopey

*Salsa.* The mere word conjures up a colorful, spicy, hot image.

Translated as "sauce" in English, salsa is not only a tomato-based dip for tortilla chips, but it is also an up-beat music genre—identified by its percussion base and fast pace—which is celebrated with its own dance throughout Latin America.

Although passionate and sensual, Salsa dancing isn't about bumping and grinding. Said to be created by African slaves brought to the Caribbean by the Spanish, salsa is for cutting loose, casting away worries and allowing the hips to shake to the seven-beat pattern. At the heart of it all, salsa is about enjoying oneself and being oneself.

A partner dance, salsa consists of seven basic steps, with a multitude of variations and styles, giving name to Cuban salsa, cha cha, and mambo. It is danced to music with a recurring eight beat pattern. The male is typically the leader. He steps out with the left foot on the first count, and on two and three, brings the right foot forward. On count five, six and seven, he steps backwards, taps and steps forward again. The woman does the identical motion, just reversed. Together they move back and forth as one. With each step there is a shift of weight from left foot to right. With this, the hips will naturally swing side to side and the more the knees are bent, the weight is shifted and the more the hips will shake.

Visitors to Latin America don't always understand salsa with its close physical space, high tempo beats and liberal movements. Intimated by such, many gringas, and even more gringos, are scared to give this spunky, choreographed dance a try.

With all responsibility on the male, it's no wonder gringos get nervous. He is the leader. Rumor has it that if the male is a good salsa dancer, the woman doesn't have any choice but to be good too and vice versa.

But the one thing any beginner, male or female can do wrong is to be stiff, the purpose of salsa is to kick-back or up, shake the hips, relax and let go.

# BAÑOS

## By Katie Tibbetts, Middletown, Connecticut, U.S.A.

Nuestra Señora del Agua Santa is alive and well, working miracles in the ever-popular town of Baños. Quiet coffee-sipping mornings slip into hectic afternoons as clouds lift from the surrounding hills and foreign and Ecuadorian travelers alike emerge from their hostel havens.

By mid-afternoon, the streets buzz with activity and people of all shapes, sizes, and styles spill onto the café-lined sidewalks. They have shaken the alcohol-induced stupor from the previous night and are eager to embark on the day's adventure.

Such is the essence of Baños, where time drifts liquid-like from day to night and night to day, with the same fluidity as the Río Pastaza below. One part rowdy, two parts relaxed, a pinch of adventure; shaken, not stirred, garnished with a sprig of the sub-tropical and served with a side of local hospitality. This is the cocktail that makes Baños the hip, friendly, slightly cooler cousin of Quito that it is.

For the young and young at heart there is endless opportunity to get the heart pumping. From horseback riding to mountain biking, canyoning and climbing to river rafting: the countryside around Baños is as rife with adventure as it is bountiful in beauty and abundant in waterfalls.

Or stay in town. From the pilgrim's Basilica to the Swiss-owned bistros, from Mexican to *melcochas* (toffees), Baños has tradition-with-a-flair covered. The town is touristy, but not suffocating. The locals are friendly, but not over-the-top. Days filled with street shopping and café-hopping, massages and medicinal baths melt into wild nights of dancing and drinking to the *thump de thump thump* of Reggaeton and disco-tech. Yes, the weekends can be a bit mad, but is that such a bad thing?

Call it dirty, call it a tourist trap, but Baños has a pro for every con. And if your hunger is more for authentic cultural encounters than handmade candies and crafts, then head to one of the local Spanish schools. Or, better yet, sit and chat with a local store owner.

Like the locals, this place has kept things real, developing its own authentic identity in the process. In a place where even the street dogs are friendly, it's hard not to just relax and—don't tell anyone—enjoy being a tourist for a while.

---

### BAÑOS TRAVEL TIPS:

Baños is located in the shadow of the mighty Tungurahua volcano, and has been evacuated in 1999, and more recently in 2006. Check on the latest status of the volcano before traveling to Baños. Provided the town is safe to visit, tours can be taken at night time to view the volcano and its sputtering. A Chiva tour usually includes a hot drink. If it is cloudy it is not worth taking the tour.

Baños candy maker. Photo by Katie Hale.

# LAGUNA DEL ALTAR

### By John Polga-Hecimovich, Burnsville, Minnesota, U.S.A.

Also known by its Quichua name, Capac Urcu, or "almighty mountain," El Altar (5,320 m/17,400 feet) is not the highest volcano in Ecuador, but it is one of the most impressive. The view from the Collanes Plain, down below, is humbling: eight snowcapped peaks rising up and standing vigil over a crater lake that tumbles down the open west face of the volcano.

Flocks of birds circle above, crowning the majestic landscape with open wings. Hundred meter waterfalls spill off the páramo surrounding the giant "C" shaped crater, and a rocky approach leads to the turquoise lake, the Laguna Amarilla. In short, this mighty mountain is a stunning, majestic volcano located in Ecuador's wild backcountry, and a trek to its flanks, its crater, or its crisscrossing ridges is a high-altitude trip almost unheard of outside the Andes and the Himalayas.

The Spanish called the mountain "El Altar" because its many peaks resemble the shape of a colonial church altar. Not surprisingly, the scale of El Altar and the surrounding mountains really do seem to mimic the design of a cathedral. Unlike more popular climbs in Ecuador, such as Cotopaxi or Chimborazo, El Altar is further removed from both the highway and cities. Consequently, a visit is not a one day endeavor, but a three day round-trip trek through unspoiled páramo, boggy lakes and creeks, and remote snow-covered ridges, all of which mean a dearth of tourists. Due to the difficult terrain, the safest way to see El Altar is with a guide, although serious trekkers could probably manage fine without one.

The trek begins in the hamlet of Candelaria, winds upwards through fields and pastures, and then ascends to the páramo and elevations of 3,800 meters and above. After four or five hours of hiking, trekkers arrive to the soggy Collanes Plain, an insane full frontal view of El Altar, and a campsite managed by Candelaria's Hacienda Releche. A number of treks are possible the following day, including ones to the Laguna de Mandur, Laguna Negra, and the Campamento Italiano on the snowy south slopes, the páramo of the northern ridges, and the yellow-tinted crater lake. The latter hike is a half day trip from the campsite, through rocky debris leftover from an October 2000 flood, past high altitude polylepis trees, and onto the smooth ledge of the cave-filled crater. From the crater, occasional cracks and creaks can be heard as chunks of ice break away from the glacier and drop into the lake.

It is possible to hike to the crater and make it back to Candelaria in one long day, but this is not recommended. It is better to witness the spectacle of the sun setting over El Altar from the front of the lake, as light streams in through the corridor of the Collanes Plain, highlighting its serpentine rivers and marshy páramo. The sky turns orange, then red, then purple over the enormous crater, and clouds gather around the rim, in one of the finest natural spectacles in the Andes.

---

LAGUNA DEL ALTAR TRAVEL TIPS:

The best times to visit are from December to March. Bring plenty of food, cooking gas, warm sleeping bags and trekking clothes for the cold, rubber boots for the Collanes Plain, and walking sticks and climbing gear if ascending higher than the crater (i.e. attempting an ascent of one of the peaks). Candles (and matches) as well as flashlights are also indispensable, because the campsite has no electricity.

---

# HUMITAS

By Dr. Crit Minster

If you spend enough time in Ecuador, sooner or later (most likely at breakfast) you'll be presented with a soggy corn husk, stuffed with some unknown substance and served piping hot. Congratulations! You've just been given humitas, one Ecuador's least-known traditional foods.

In Ecuador, humitas are made of cornmeal, onions, and occasionally a bit of cheese. This mixture is wrapped in a corn husk and steamed (in other South American nations, it is acceptable to boil or bake them, but the very notion is heresy in Ecuador), and is best enjoyed right out of the steamer. They're vaguely sweet and Ecuadorians are quite fond of them, selling them from vending carts, in restaurants and at bus stations.

Other countries have their own versions of humitas. In Chile, they add basil, hot peppers, or other flavors and can be baked as well as steamed. In Peru, they tend to prefer them a little sweeter, and often add raisins or cinnamon.

The tamale is the cousin of humitas, and is particularly popular in southern Ecuador. It is made in a similar fashion to the humitas, but generally is sweeter, and may include bits of chicken, pork, raisins and (occasionally) chopped olives. Tamales are usually wrapped in large leaves (such as banana leaves) instead of corn husks.

So when you're looking down at the soggy, steaming corn husk, don't pass it on: dig in and enjoy one of Ecuador's most authentic traditional foods!

# THE DEVIL'S NOSE

## By Chris Sacco, Hamilton, New York, U.S.A.

Thirty kilometers into the ascent of Ecuador's towering western range, a railway snakes up a mountain known as *La Nariz del Diablo* (The Devil's Nose). This nearly vertical wall of rock was the greatest natural obstacle engineers encountered during construction of the country's train system, and the decision to go up it instead of around was one of a string of blunders that nearly smothered the dream of connecting Ecuador's two largest cities, Guayaquil and Quito, by rail.

Today, the Devil's Nose is the highlight of a fantastic rail trip that meanders through the rich tapestry of cultivated fields and rugged highland spread across the southern half of Ecuador's 400-kilometer long Central Valley, aptly christened "The Avenue of the Volcanoes" in 1802 by the German explorer Alexander Von Humboldt.

The journey begins in the picturesque city of Riobamba. Like many cities in the Ecuadorian Andes, Riobamba sits in shadow of a giant volcano, Chimborazo, which at 6,310 meters (approximately 20,702 feet) enjoys the dual distinctions of being Ecuador's highest peak and the furthest point from the center of the earth, thanks to the bulge at the equator. The train travels south from Chimborazo through a few small towns and large expanses of open country before arriving at Alausí, where it begins a hair-raising descent of the Devil's Nose. Most travelers sit on top of the rail cars to take advantage of the spectacular vistas provided by the engineers' ingenious solution of carving a series of tight zigzags into the side of the mountain, which allow the train to climb a gradient of 1-in-18 from 1,800 to 2,600 meters, by going forwards then backwards up the tracks.

A hundred years after it was constructed, the steep grade of the Devil's Nose stretch of track precludes its use as a freight or efficient passenger line, but affords the perfect means for present-day explorers who want to discover the rugged and breathtaking Ecuadorian countryside.

*Climbing onto the train. Photo by Freyja Ellis.*

### DEVIL'S NOSE TRAIN RIDE TRAVEL TIPS:

It is possible to take the train from stations other than Riobamba, such as Cajabamba or Guamote, and even just from Alausí to just experience the Devil's Nose part of the ride. However, the countryside for the earlier part of the journey, ahead of the Devil's Nose section of the ride is extremely beautiful and the local villages interesting and it is recommended to at least take the train from one of the earlier stations, if not all the way from Riobamba itself.

In terms of clothing, layers are in order. The ride starts early in the morning, and it will be cold, so warmer clothing is needed. Later on, as the morning progresses, there can be rain, or the weather can heat up - it can get hot on top of the train, so don't forget sunscreen.

Cushions to sit on cost extra—they don't come included within the price of the train ticket.

The train stops in some of the stations for longer than others, and in some places it is possible to take a bathroom break and stretch your legs. Listen to the conductor to find out when the train will be leaving the station. If all else fails, the train will hoot before it leaves. That is your last warning to jump aboard.

The train does not leave every day, so it is worth checking in advance which days it is running before traveling.

# CUENCA

By Chris Sacco, Hamilton, New York, U.S.A.

While wandering around Cuenca, it's easy to forget you live in the 21st century. The city's cobblestone streets, towering cathedrals, and marble and whitewashed buildings give it a colonial air unequaled in Ecuador and rarely rivaled in Latin America.

Officially known as "Saint Ann of the Four Rivers of Cuenca," it's not surprising that the city sits amidst four rivers. The most visible of the four, the Rio Tomebamba, runs through Cuenca's colonial heart, separating it from several newer residential areas to the south. The historic district's compactness, grid-like layout, and numerous readily identifiable monuments make it easy to navigate. There are quaint B&B's, fine hotels, and inexpensive hostels peppered throughout city center, as well as good cafes, bars, and eateries and nearly all are within walking distance of the main sites.

Cuenca's nearly limitless sightseeing opportunities begin with the two cathedrals on either side of the main plaza, Parque Abdón Calderón. The beautiful rose window and celestial blue domes of the New Cathedral (Catedral de la Inmaculada) dominate the skyline while the bell tower of the Old Cathedral (El Sagrario), built in 1557, radiates a more subtle charm. Not far from the plaza, there are half a dozen other worthwhile sites, including Las Conceptas, a fortress-like complex that occupies an entire block and houses a working monastery and a museum displaying centuries' worth of religious artifacts and artwork, and the Museo del Banco Central, which contains a permanent collection of black and white photographs of 19th and early 20th century Cuenca, as well as displays of art and archeological pieces.

Those searching for signs of indigenous cultures in Cuenca won't find much in plain sight because even though Cuenca's story began long before the arrival of the Spanish—it was originally a Cañari settlement called Guapondeleg believed to have been founded around 500 AD—little evidence of its pre-Colombian past survived the Spanish Conquest. Nevertheless, those interested in indigenous cultures will not be disappointed by the Museo de las Culturas Aborígenes, which displays a private collection of 5,000 archeological pieces representing over 20 pre-Columbian cultures of Ecuador. Also, some Inca walls and stonework may be found along Calle Larga, Avenida Todos los Santos, and along the river, although they don't compare to Ingapirca, Ecuador's most important Inca ruin, which is located about 70 kilometers north of Cuenca on the Pan-American Highway.

In addition to being the cultural Mecca of Ecuador, which recently earned it the honor of being listed as a UNESCO World Heritage Trust site, Cuenca has become a favorite destination among international travelers because it provides easy access to some of Ecuador's best protected areas, El Cajas and Podocarpus National Parks, and it's a painless three-hour drive from Guayaquil and the southern Ecuadorian coast. If you've only time to visit one place in the Ecuadorian Andes, it should be Cuenca.

*La Catedral de la Inmaculada Concepción. Photo by Dr. Crit Minster.*

### CUENCA TRAVEL TIPS:

In addition to cathedrals and churches, Cuenca has a pretty flower market that is well worth a visit. This can be found on Córdova between Torres and Aguirre, just around the corner from the main square and cathedrals.

Another market to stop by is the 10 de Agosto indoor market. Here you will be overwhelmed by a sea of fruit and vegetables and vendors eager to sell. Wander upstairs and try an Ecuadorian speciality—roast pig. There is a special section of the market that you will come across with a number of women selling the roast. It comes usually with a boiled potato and some salad.

Surrounding Cuenca there are a number of little towns and villages that make for an interesting half-day excursion. Perhaps visit Gualaceo and stroll through the market looking at the strange array of fruits and vegetables. Or head to Chordeleg where there are many little shops selling ceramics. Chordeleg is also famous for its jewelry—there are many shops set around the picturesque town square.

# HIKING IN THE CAJAS NATIONAL PARK

## By Paula Newton, Seaton, Devon, England

Hiking up to a wild craggy peak early on a clear, sunny day in Parque Nacional El Cajas it is possible to view an amazing panorama of glistening lakes and untamed páramo grass, often with not another soul in sight.

Approximately 30 kilometers west of Cuenca, spread across 29,000 hectares, the Cajas National Park is simply breathtaking. The glacial park topography is bleak and wild. Littered among the jagged peaks and weathered valleys are more than 250 stunning cerulean lakes. At an altitude between 3,300-4,500 meters, the ecology of the park is firmly within the páramo region, where beautiful orange-flowered chuquiragua plants flourish among a variety of greenery, including the páramo grasses, lupin and quinua trees. In this inhospitable environment, the fauna is remarkably diverse, with hummingbirds, Andean gulls, ducks, woodpeckers and condors, living alongside wildcats, deer and llamas. In contrast to the austere eastern side, the western side, of the park is concentrated with thick cloud forest. The weather can be hostile, dominated by biting winds, rain, fog and even snow on occasion. When set against the equally unforgiving landscape, the harsh climate adds to the sense of immense solitude that the area inspires.

Despite its intimidating appearance, the scenery within the Cajas National park is truly outstanding. Opportunities for hiking in such a beautiful, yet austere and isolated environment are few and far between. Three to six hour hikes are the most common, but it is also possible to spend several days trekking throughout the park. The anticipation of extreme weather whilst already enduring the biting wind inspires an undeniable spirit of adventure. Navigating up the rocky landscape against the gusting winds, makes for a tough-going hike in several spots. In some areas the hillsides are so steep that grasping the lush páramo grasses is the only way to keep from slipping and tumbling downwards at great speed. Sliding down the slopes may not be such a great disaster as soft spongy vegetation grows around the swampy lakes below. While hiking is by far the most popular pursuit in the park, other active options include camping, trout fishing, or praying for miracles to the Virgen de Cajas, who allegedly appeared in the park some years ago.

For those choosing to explore the park on foot, guided walks are highly recommended – getting lost in this remote, brutal wilderness is not advisable. Another advantage to hiring a knowledgeable guide is that they can help in identifying some of the more timid wildlife that exists here. Hunting these shy animals involves stooping in silence, while perfecting the fine art of not-batting-an-eyelid. Crouched behind the isolated outcrops of peculiarly knotted trees that form mini-forests throughout the park, contemplating the awe-inspiring atmosphere while waiting for animals to make an appearance is incredible. Although the park is teeming with wildlife it is sometimes difficult to believe.

Having braved the severe weather that the park can bestow, hikers feel an enormous sense of elation after conquering this strenuous hike. The perfect ending to this challenging trek is to indulge in a hard-earned feast of fresh trout or piping hot chicken stew at one of the quiet, family-run hostelries nearby.

The Cajas National Park. Photo by Will Gray.

# BELLAVISTA

### By Paula Newton, Seaton, Devon, England

All around us, a peaceful humming sound prevails amid a rainbow of colour. Nearly twenty hummingbirds are swooping in on feeding platforms. This is what we came for, and we aren't disappointed. Little finches—which appear enormous in this environment—cannot edge their way in to the feeder and merely fade into the backdrop of the real showstoppers: the flitting colibris. Try as you might, you cannot take it all in, there is too much fluttering and colour.

This is Bellavista Cloudforest Reserve, one of the few times in your life when you might actually want overcast weather. The cloudier the skies are, the more active the hummingbirds. And the grey skies make for a perfect backdrop for the multi-coloured friends whom you have come to admire. That said, the butterflies prefer the sunnier weather. Well, you can't have it all.

Bellavista, an eco-friendly resort, is located approximately 90 minutes northwest of Quito. As you leave behind the smog and dirt of the city, you head out into the cloud forest, where the road snakes around mountains and gorges, the landscape changes and greenery dominates. Forest spreads for miles in every direction further than the eye can see. It looks like jungle, but looks are deceptive. This is not jungle but bosque nublado, or cloud forest, a very specific type of ecosystem, loosely defined as being a forest where there is cloud cover at the vegetation level. On the southern edge of the Choco-Andean biodiversity hotspot, the Bellavista Reserve itself is part of the Mindo area of international importance for birds.

It's not hard to see why. It is thought that there are at least 330 different species of bird in this region. Everywhere you look there are hummingbirds of all shapes and colors. The site is literally buzzing with them. The hotel has leaflets to help you identify them. The Booted Racket-tail is easy. It has little white fluffy booties and is much smaller than the others. But there are countless other species here—the Speckled Hummingbird, the Andean Emerald, the Tawny Bellied Hermit, the Green Violetear and the Collared Inca to name but a few. It is truly a birding paradise, with no effort required.

While you take lunch in the 360º dome restaurant, you can continue to watch the birds all around you—the feeders have been strategically located around the restaurant to maximize opportunities for watching these pretty creatures and the sugared water within them ensures that they keep coming back. As we eat, a Blue Winged Mountain Tanager clunkily lands at one of the feeders, dispersing the hummingbirds momentarily. Also beautiful, it seems huge in comparison to its smaller cousins. On one of the many guided walks that are available, Toucan Barbets can be spied squawking in the trees above. The numerous winding trails and maps allow for fascinating self-guided walks. At night, the harder-to-spot owls perch on posts, seemingly undisturbed by the goings-on, and it is possible to take pre-dawn hike to spot the Cock of the Rock, a most unusual sight.

Birds aside, this environment also fosters an incredible variety of butterfly and orchid species, and this ecosystem is known for its wealth of mosses and ferns, in particular a large diversity of epiphytes, or "air plants" that grow on trees. Taking a trip away from the resort, in Mindo village it is possible to visit a butterfly and orchid farm. The butterflies compete with the hummingbirds for beauty, variety and color. Finally, a few minutes drive from the village takes you to a waterfall, where after a sweaty half-hour hike in these hot and humid conditions you can pause for a dip in the refreshingly cool river at the bottom of the hill.

*Hummingbird at Bellavista. Photo by Freyja Ellis.*

## FIONA LESLIE'S TOP BIRDS:

What are the most sought-after birds by avid birdwatchers coming all the way to South America? Here is one birdwatcher's list:

1. Harpy Eagle
2. Andean Condor
3. Hoatzin
4. Hyacinth macaw
5. Andean Cock-of-the-rock
6. Amazonian umbrella bird
7. King vulture
8. Buff-necked Ibis
9. Sun Bittern
10. Torrent Duck

Honorable mention: Scarlet macaw, Long-tailed potoo, Red-tailed comet (hummingbird), Orange-backed troupial, Oropendulas, Toucans, Long-tailed hermit hummingbird, Frigate bird, Maguari stork, Jabiru stork, Southern screamer, puna flamingos, King penguins, Peruvian pelican, Wandering albatross.

# DRIVING LA RUTA DEL SOL

By Paula Newton, Seaton, Devon, England

Late in the afternoon, we turn a corner on the dusty road and spy our goal—the balmy, azure Pacific Ocean, white apartment buildings sparkling in the sun and the sea reflecting the clear blue sky. I have been promised paradise, and this view secures the dream.

Six hours driving from Quito brought us here, to the province of Esmeraldas, winding along the scenic route through the mystical, mountainous cloud forests of Mindo, then rapidly dropping altitude whilst increasing humidity and traversing through the warmer lowland banana plantations. An aggressive four-day drive, our tour begins in the city of Esmeraldas in the north. Our route will take us through pretty little coastal pueblos and party towns from Atacames through Perdernales, Canoa, Manta, Puerto Cayo, Puerto López, Montañita and finally to the large port city of Guayaquil in the south.

Stopping for the night in Atacames, a lively beach town, we head for the beach to watch the sun set. The beach stretches for miles, eventually framed by craggy cliffs. Beach vendors sell trinkets and wiry men lazily lob a volleyball over a makeshift net. Everything is orange as the sun seems to drop out of the sky; within 15 minutes it disappears over the horizon and complete blackness ensues.

In the open air beach side shack, the ocean breeze cools and soothes burnt skin. Cocktails are ordered. I opt for a tri-color, sickly, red, green and yellow drink, and sip slowly whilst the deejay beats out reggaeton and local men woo the gringas, teaching salsa and promising eternal love.

Morning comes and the trip continues. The sun blazes down on the car. Photographic opportunities abound and frequent stops are made to capture the sweeping landscapes, the mangroves, the local life, and the bright orange and pink flowers against a backdrop of greens, ranches, coastal villages. We share a warm Pilsner mixed with cola and munch on crackers. The radio blares and we sing along, warm and satisfied, salty skin sticking to the leather of the seats. It is difficult to feel anything other than elation in this sunny, sandy haven.

We take a break from the driving in sandy Perdenales. No gringos here. The hot sand burns my feet as I dash into the glistening waves of the warm Pacific that crash down onto the beach. The fishermen are bemused; they pause from their *fútbol* to observe this crazy chica splashing to cool off from the heat of the mid-afternoon sun.

Our home for the second night, Manta, feels like the original Sin City with dark, seedy-looking, and empty streets. Maybe it's the time that we arrive—late—scouring the deserted streets for a decent hotel, that make this city more menacing than it needs to. There is a large U.S. Marine base here. There is no reason to stay for long.

On the road again, the vegetation changes as we reach Machalilla National Park, the foliage is heavier, the roadsides more forested. We turn a corner and from nowhere, a marine iguana skedaddles across the road, narrowly escaping death. Every few miles, a secluded cove, a beautiful little island, an unusual bird appears, as if for our viewing pleasure alone.

Montañita is a surfers heaven. This funky little hippy town in the south serves as our third night's rest and watering hole, and it emanates a relaxed, warm vibe. The youth and travelers in the town are on the beach, gathered around a roaring fire. The beer flows fast and dancing by firelight is atmospheric, reminiscent of the ambience of a grungy music festival back home.

Slightly worse for wear, the drive continues south. Vultures circle overhead—carrion is nearby. A huge flock of pelicans darken the sky, flying north. A family of donkeys ambling along at an idle pace greet us at a beachside stop along the road—mother, father and baby, completely in tune with coastal life—nothing happens quickly here.

After driving almost the entire length of the Ecuadorian coastline, our trip draws to a close. The port town of Guayaquil is nearing, smoking on the horizon. Ecuador's largest city is a sprawling urban maze and a world away from the lazy beach side towns of our recent days. Strolling down the Malecón 2000, we recall snippets from the trip. We climb the Cerro Santa Ana hill; the recently gentrified bars are pumping. Overlooking the city we drink a toast to returning someday soon.

## TOP LIST: TOP LATIN AMERICAN COCKTAILS

Latin America is a great place to enjoy a drink or three! Be sure to check out these local cocktails, some of which are not available at home:

1. Caipirinha, Brazil (p. 62). "Refreshing and smooth, this Brazilian cocktail is sort of like a boozed-up limeade. Be careful: they go down smooth and are stronger than you think!" Gideon Wells, Scottsville, New York, U.S.A.

2. Mojito (p. 287). "Smooth and sophisticated. Great to sip on in a slick bar after a few days hard trekking." Mary Jones, Ireland.

3. Pisco Sour, Peru or Chile (p, 334). "Tasty, good for you!" (Peru). Mark Mellander, California, U.S.A.

4. Margarita. "Delicious frozen or otherwise, and available in a great variety of flavours, from Mexico in the north, right down to the tip of Chile in the south." Matilda Skipp, U.K.

5. Canelazo, Ecuador (p. 348). "Served hot, the Canelazo is made with sugar cane liquor, naranjilla juice and sweet cinnamon water. Best enjoyed outside on a cold night." Dr. Crit Minster, Rochester, New York, U.S.A.

Runner up: Chicha, Bolivia. Made from chewing on corn. Delicious!

# PUNTA PRIETA GUESTHOUSE

*By John Polga-Hecimovich, Burnsville, Minnestoa, U.S.A.*

Miles from the nearest village and filled with the sound of waves crashing into its cliffs, Punta Prieta calms the restless and soothes the burdened. This guest house offers creature comforts, fresh seafood, and all of those intangibles that go with its location: a salty breeze that rejuvenates the spirit, a deserted beach that begs for company, and an atmosphere that makes relaxation no chore.

Punta Prieta is a tourist-free oasis in the middle of a stretch of coast between Pedernales and Canoa that attracts many Ecuadorians and foreigners alike in search of peace and solitude. Perched atop a rocky cliff, it offers eight different and affordable cabins, a central restaurant with stunning views north and south along the coast; other distractions include a movie and DVD collection and a billiards table. Punta Prieta's owner, Alonso Ordoñez, has decorated the grounds with art. He also feeds a slew of iguanas that live outside the main building, and keeps a Galápagos tortoise that is at least 60 years old. In addition to the usual amenities, cabins have refrigerators, kitchen access, and wonderful views. Travelers on a budget can camp on the beach for a minimal fee, and have access to the showers and bathrooms.

Vacationers are also drawn to Punta Prieta's tours of nearby tropical dry forest, a rare ecosystem that can appear dead to the untrained eye. In reality, because half of the year is completely dry, those plant species that have survived have adapted and tend to lose their leaves in the dry season. They include palo santo "trees" (actually bushes), ceiba and balsa trees and the tagua palm whose malleable nuts are carved and sold in highland markets such as Otavalo. Unfortunately, like other tropical forest habitats, this unusual ecological zone is disappearing at an alarming rate. Tours can be made on foot or on horseback, and their duration depends on the visitor's preference. A more relaxing hike from Punta Prieta follows the beach along craggy cliffs to an unusual rock formation. This structure, el Arco, is a natural stone arch formed by water erosion that stretched over ten meters into the air. The arch sits three kilometers north of Punta Prieta, and is accessed by simply following the beach at low tide; a round trip hike takes between two and three hours.

After the daytime beachcombing, exploring, or simply chilling out, the sinking sun promises that the day's catch will soon be cooked up in Punta Prieta's kitchen. The restaurant sits on the edge of the cliff, and salt air wafts in from three sides as the waves continue their rhythmic solo 15 meters below. It isn't hard to understand why many families, couples or backpackers end up spending much more time here than they planned; the reality of work or school couldn't be father away.

## LATIN AMERICAN MYSTERIES # 1: THE GALÁPAGOS AFFAIR

In 1929, Dr. Friedrich Ritter, an eccentric Berlin doctor, arrived on Floreana Island with his mistress/patient Dore Strauch. Dr. Ritter had a medical degree, but believed that the mind could cure diseases: today, we would call him a "holistic" doctor. They left their respective spouses to set up an Eden in the far-off Galápagos Islands, and their affair made them popular in the European press. Soon they started getting curious visitors who came all the way from Europe. Most didn't last long, but in September of 1932, Heinrich and Margret Wittmer arrived with Heinrich's 12 year old son from a previous marriage, Harry. They set up a homestead not far from Ritter and Strauch.

The Wittmers and the Ritters didn't have much in common, and the two groups kept to themselves. Their peace and tranquility was severely disrupted, however, with the November, 1932 arrival of "The Baroness." Looking like the star of a bad S&M movie—she regularly wore black boots and riding pants and kept a whip and a pistol handy—she used the name of Eloise Baroness Wagner de Bosquet and claimed to be Austrian nobility. She set up home in Post Office Bay with her retinue of three men: Germans Rudolf Lorenz and Robert Phillipson and Ecuadorian Felipe Valdivieso. The German men were apparently both love slaves, and the Ecuadorian was there to work.

Not long after her arrival, the three groups of settlers began to have problems. The Wittmers and Dr. Ritter and Ms. Strauch suspected that the Baroness was stealing items and mail from them and lodged complaints. The governor of Galápagos was forced to come to Floreana to check the reports, but he fell under the spell of the Baroness and even invited her to his home. By March of 1934, the situation of all three groups had taken a turn for the worse. The area was suffering from a severe drought, heightening the tension and requiring more work from everyone. Dr. Ritter was becoming abusive towards Dore Strauch, forbidding her from doing non-essential work. According to the Wittmers, Strauch showed no signs of wanting to leave the doctor in spite of his increasing violence and cruelty.

Meanwhile, at the Baroness' camp, Rudolf Lorenz had apparently fallen out of favor, and Phillipson was beating and starving him. He would often show up at the Wittmer home for food, and would stay until the Baroness and Phillipson came for him. One day, the Baroness and Phillipson vanished. According to Margret Wittmer, they told her that they were going to Tahiti on a ship that was waiting for them in the harbor. There is no evidence, however, that there was such a ship, and a search of their home indicated that they had taken almost nothing with them, including items that they would have wanted even on a very short voyage. They also never turned up in Tahiti.

Not long after, Lorenz left the islands on board the ship Dinamita, bound for Guayaquil. The Dinamita also vanished. The bodies of Lorenz and the ship's captain were later found, mummified and desiccated, on Marchena Island, where they died of dehydration and starvation. Marchena is not the way they would have gone to go to Guayaquil.

In December of 1934, Dr. Ritter, a vegetarian, died after eating some chicken that had gone bad. As he died, he cursed Dore Strauch, leading many to believe that she had poisoned him. Although there have been many inquiries, no one has ever gotten to the bottom of the disappearance of the Countess and the deaths of Lorenz and Ritter, and "The Galápagos Affair" remains one of Latin America's most enduring mysteries to this day.

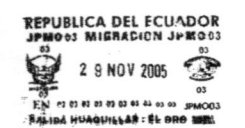

# RÍO MUCHACHO ORGANIC FARM

## By Warren Linde, Springs, South Africa

The Río Muchacho Organic Farm is nestled between semi-arid hills and beside the river from which it takes its name. A 15-minute bus ride from the nearby village of Canoa affords fantastic scenery of the *bosque seco* or "dry forest" region of the Manabí province.

In a blink of an eye, one is transported to a place where life slows down. Also called Río Muchacho, the small community's major source of income is agriculture and cattle grazing. Large herds of cattle can be seen grazing or being milked in the early mornings. Located in one of the driest regions of Ecuador this river offers lovely warm weather for most months of the year, which can be a welcome change from the cool "winters" of the high Andes.

But what makes this place special is not the beauty of the nightly sunsets, the tranquility of the lifestyle, the rolling hills and the stark landscape or even the cool breeze from the banana leaves on a hot day. What makes the Río Muchacho Farm really special is the people who own and run it. After only a three day visit, when the time came to take leave of the owner, Dario, I felt like I was saying farewell to an old friend. Dario has worked for many years in and around the Bahía de Caráquez area of the Manabí coast, promoting the environmental cause. He was instrumental in saving the last mangroves in the area, which can be seen on Isla Corazón.

There is plenty to do and see on the farm, like making chocolate and roasting your own coffee; seeing a troupe of wild monkeys; horseback ridding; shrimp fishing and much more. The quaint little thatched chalets fit right into the surrounding landscape. The trickling river and singing frogs lull one to sleep at night. Meals are eaten together with the staff, the owners and the group of international volunteers who help out on the farm. Everything is home-grown, organic and delicious.

Keep your eyes open for the ever-present hummingbirds which often have their meals (nectar from flowers) right next to you. The Río Muchacho Organic Farm and all of the environmental projects it is involved with stands out in my mind as one of the most interesting and beautiful experiences on my travels around Ecuador. The beauty of this place originates from within the hearts of the people involved.

www.vivatravelguides.com/103714

# ALÁNDALUZ RESORT

## By Penny E. Schwartz, Long Island, New York, U.S.A.

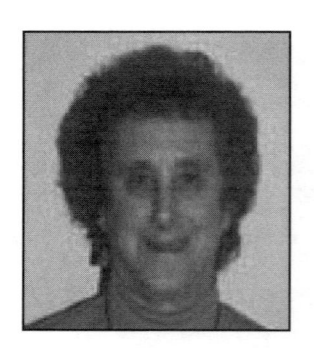

Awakening to the sounds of peaceful crashing surf is just one of the special moments to be savored at Alándaluz Resort. Near Puerto López along Ecuador's El Ruta del Sol, Alándaluz was built some 16 years ago. What began as an ecological project to utilize the local bamboo, ended as a lovely and lush resort where time seems to stand still. About 100 families helped construct the resort using native bamboo and stone, giving the local economy a boost, as well as a way to recycle local materials.

The eco-resort's logo is "A Passionate Embrace for Life," and everywhere at Alándaluz the visitor sees evidence of this philosophy. Beds of organically grown vegetables and small groves of bamboo dot the grounds, along with bromeliads, orchids and indigenous flowers of many hues. Most of the fruits and vegetables served in the indoor-outdoor dining room are grown on the grounds, with a percentage of the crop given to the resort's employees, so that nothing is wasted.

Dinner one night included one of the resort's specialties, a local fish prepared in peanut sauce and tucked into a thick bamboo stalk with a door cut into it for ease of eating. The name of the dish, "El Viudo," comes from the tale of a sad widower who regained his happiness and passion for living when he tasted this preparation. Another dish served in a natural container is "Encocado," which blends coconut milk with seafood and other locally grown ingredients and arrives at the table in a coconut harvested on the resort grounds. Locally grown pumpkins are also utilized for both flavoring and food service. The kitchen has revitalized the use of a number of endemic fruits and vegetables that were once important to local residents but have fallen out of favor.

Public areas are large and inviting, shielded from the sun by leafy overhangs or bamboo trellises. Inviting hammocks hang everywhere, even inside the hotel rooms, encouraging guests to relax and enjoy the gardens and beach front with its pure white sand.

The resort owners believe strongly in replenishing the earth and promoting responsible tourism, but not at the expense of either luxury or pleasure. Accommodations are first-rate, whether in rustic wooden cabins or charming turreted stone cottages that resemble fairytale castles. Fireplaces, windows with inviting views, colorful bedspreads, and rugs add to the charm.

Expeditions in the area include visits to Isla de la Plata, part of Machalilla National Park, where many species similar to those on the Galapagos reside. Also nearby is Cantalapiedra Wildlife Sanctuary. Close to the resort itself is also a magnificent and unusual church built of bamboo in a lacy pattern that lets in light and air while enclosing its parishioners in the embrace of nature, just as Alándaluz Resort folds its guests in the embrace of nature.

---

Penny Schwartz grew up on Long Island, within walking distance of the beach, and graduated from New York University with an English degree. Travel has always been a pivotal part of her life. During college, she met her husband on a student tour of Europe. After spending several years in Chicago, they settled in Redlands, California, where they raised two children and she earned an M.A. in English Literature from the University of Redlands.

Schwartz has been a freelance writer in the areas of arts, theater, restaurants and travel for 25 years and has also taught journalism and English as a Second Language. A lifelong traveler, she has visited close to 70 countries, at last count, and loves learning about and experiencing other cultures and lifestyles.

# MONTAÑITA

By Katie Tibbetts, Middletown, Connecticut, U.S.A.

Sun, sand, surf, and locals as warm as the weather make Montañita a spectacular stop for weary travelers in search of a little R and R. Nestled along the south west coast of Ecuador, this charming ocean-side gem has all the flavor and flair of a hip beach town without being too busy or over-the-top touristy. Dusty dirt roads wander past palm trees and simple adobe buildings with bamboo roofs and brightly colored facades. Inside, bohemian-looking beach-goers lounge about, sipping tropical drinks or flipping through dog-eared paperbacks. The main street leads directly to Montañita's most popular attraction: the beach.

Jutting out of the sand at one end of the beach, the craggy outcropping known as La Punta serves as a natural beacon marking the best surfing spot on the coast. From here the beach stretches as far as the eye can see, bordered by turquoise water and tropical vegetation, making it the perfect playground for surfers and sand bunnies alike. Time seems to slip by as the afternoon sun gives way to spectacular sunsets and beach bonfires at night.

During the day, the main beach is filled with foreigners and Ecuadorians alike, sprawled out on beach towels and accompanied by either sun lotion bottles or beers (mostly beers). Vendors wander up and down the beach front selling a variety of items, from exotic tropical fruits and drinks to jewelry and T-shirts. In addition to excellent waves, Montañita also boasts an array of hotels, restaurants and bars that tempt visitors with mouth-watering menus and refreshing cocktails. Despite its popularity as a hot surfing spot, the town maintains a relaxed almost-island feel, where visitors can enjoy languorous afternoon strolls, the drinks are always cold, and even on the busier weekends there is room to breathe.

At times it feels like the town itself sleeps during the day, saving its energy for the long night of partying ahead. Unlike other trendy beach towns, Montañita maintains a distinct small town charm. The two faces of Montañita—one characterized by colorful, funky restaurants and hostels catering to a host of international travelers, and a slightly less flamboyant but certainly just as captivating section where sun-wizened old men chat in doorways and chickens converse in the street—combine to make for a very unique chilled-out atmosphere. The eclectic beach crowd and a variety of international and national cuisine infuse the laid back atmosphere with a distinct multi-cultural flavor that is sure to rejuvenate even the most jaded of travelers. Indeed, this is a place where you can find a lot to do without really doing much of anything.

In the high season, from December to August, prices tend to rise along with the temperature as people from all over flood into town. Although prices are lower from September to November, the lower temperatures and rarely seen sun make for a slightly less spectacular beach experience. In general, seafood aficionados should stock up on Montañita's marine fare, as it is cheaper (and better) here than inland. In particular, the traditional ceviche dishes are sure to please the palate. Of course, everything tastes better when it's served with fresh salt air, sun, and an ice cold beer.

Despite its popularity, Montañita is still well within the reach of even the most miserly backpackers. Hostels range between $5 and $15 per night, depending on whether you visit during high or low season. Most restaurants serve up a variety of dishes that are sure to satisfy the taste buds and the budget: average main meal $2 to $5. Beers and cocktails are also cheap, but then drinking is one of the Montañita must-dos.

## TOP LIST: BEST BEACHES FOR TANNING AND SCANNING

Time to hit the beach? Latin America is home to some of the best beaches in the world! Here are some of our readers' favorites.

1. Ipanema Beach, Rio, Brazil.
"On sunny days, which pretty much cover the calendar, Ipanema is the place to be and to see ..." Kyle, Vancouver, B.C., Canada.

2. Cartagena, Colombia (p. 226).
"You just have to feel the atmosphere of this amazing place." Rache, Pilot Butte, Canada.

3. Montañita, Ecuador (p. 263).
"Watching the surfers." Paula Newton, England.

4. Canoa Quebrada, Brazil.
"Nice and quiet, with lots of nice restaurants and cheap places to stay!" Rache, Pilot Butte, Canada.

5. Máncora, Peru (p. 271).
"Year-round sun, warm waters, clean white sands and surfing with the dolphin." Freyja Ellis, Scotland.

Runners up: Playa Rincón, Dominican Republic. "A corner of paradise." Amanda Kass. Salinas Beach, Ecuador. Jorge, Ecuador. Santa Fe, Venezuela. "Quiet and a little rustic." Rache, Pilot Butte, Canada. Playa Potrero, Costa Rica. "Off the track, not much people watching, but a fabby place to get away from it all." Rache, Pilot Butte, Canada.

# THE GALÁPAGOS ISLANDS

## By Dr. Crit Minster, Rochester, New York, U.S.A.

Leaving behind the smog, traffic and fast food of Quito, an airplane flies two hours west and eons backward in time. The Galápagos Islands is a land that time forgot, a rugged and unforgiving paradise where the air, land and sea are home to species found nowhere else on earth. It is a zoo without cages: each island is its own harsh laboratory of evolution, adaptation and competition. The marine iguanas understand this: stoic black dragons that seem to have crawled out of the volcanic rock itself, they share the lordship of these islands with the birds, tortoises and sea lions. They were here first, and they will permit you to visit, but they know that you couldn't stay even if you wanted to. You're not tough enough to share their rocky bit of paradise.

Fun and sun? Surf and sand? Forget it. If that's what you're looking for, go to Cozumel. A visit to Galápagos is an expedition, a chance to walk in the footprints of Charles Darwin. It's not about the beach, it's about the birds, fish and animals, and simply put, there is no better place to see them than here.

In a sense, there are no species that are purely native to the islands. The islands were never connected to any continent: every resident reptile, mammal, bird and fish arrived after the islands were born of thunderous volcanic upheavals in the deep crevasses of the Pacific Ocean. Once these animals found themselves on these rock-strewn, desolate islands, survival dictated the long process of adaptation. Ages later, the island species no longer even resemble their cousins on the continent.

The most famous resident of Santa Cruz Island is about 80 years old, has no teeth, and weighs somewhere around 200 pounds. His face has all the wrinkles you'd expect for someone his age: he has a sort of worn, leathery look about him that reflects a life mostly spent outdoors. He's in good health for his age, however, and enjoys his vegetarian diet; he has a penchant for papayas. He is a full-time resident of the Charles Darwin Research Station, where they sincerely wish that he would have more sex. They call him Lonesome George, and he is the last surviving Pinta Island giant tortoise.

But even George and his sad tale have to share the spotlight in this magical place. There are more than a dozen endemic species on Galapagos: animals that can be found nowhere else on earth. Not counting George, there are ten surviving species of giant Galápagos tortoise: four more have gone extinct. The Galápagos penguin is the only one to live north of the equator. The flightless cormorant has lost its wings to evolution: there are few predators to flee. The iguanas are marvels of adaptation—the land iguanas eat spiny cacti with ease, while the marine iguanas can survive a 15 degree drop in body temperature while they eat underwater algae. Even the nondescript little finches have their share of the fame: Darwin used the thirteen different endemic species of finch as an example to prove his theories (one variety can suck blood!). Even some marine species are endemic: the Galápagos shark is a gray reef shark only found in the islands.

For all the rugged vistas and parched, rocky trails, the Galápagos is actually a very fragile ecosystem. In the early days of exploration of the islands, passing whaling ships often took tortoises for food: this resulted in the extinction of four different species. The first settlers released goats into the wild. This did provide food in the short term, but now they're considered an ecological disaster: they destroy the vegetation and ruin the habitat of other native animals: the tortoises and iguanas in particular have been badly affected. Introduced plants such as the sour apple and blackberry have taken over acres of park area, forcing out native plants in the process. Domestic dogs and cats that escape and breed in the wild are considered a serious problem as well. Efforts to control these animals and plants have met with mixed success: for example, goats have been successfully eradicated from some of the islands.

There is hope: concerted efforts of park staff, international organizations and tourism operators have helped greatly in recent years to protect the islands and the animals that live there. And don't let the gloomy human record in the Islands discourage you from a visit: as long as you closely follow the instructions your specially trained naturalist guide gives you, you'll not cause any damage.

There is a reason why the Galápagos Islands are one of the top three visitor destinations in South America on any list you check: they're magnificent. Enjoy the white sand beaches, lounge on a luxurious cruise ship, but bring extra rolls of film or digital memory cards for the real stars of the islands: the flora and fauna of one of the last original places in the world.

Galapagos Sealion. Photo by Michelle Hopey.

# WILD ALBATROSS MATING

By Carol Ann, Rhynie, Scotland

The walking trail is nothing more than a metre-wide swath from where the biggest and most dangerous boulders have been removed. After stumbling along for half an hour trying not to sprain an ankle, it comes as a bit of a surprise to find that this rocky terrain is both the take-off and landing strip of the waved albatross of Española Island, Galápagos.

At up to one metre tall—roughly the size of a large turkey—these spectacular birds create heart-stopping moments as they wobble and lumber to the edge of a basalt cliff, before taking off into the wind to become graceful flying creatures. Their landings are just as spectacular, as their splayed feet bounce like skis across the boulders, wings acting as airbrakes, until they are slow enough to be able to stop. Their legs appear thin and fragile, but unlike human beings, they are clearly masters of this inhospitable terrain. These basalt cliffs, on the most westerly point of picturesque Española Island, are the only nesting sites for the ten to twelve thousand pairs of waved albatross that remain on this planet. Like many humans, these beautiful birds also mate for life and have a very lengthy, noisy and complex courtship ritual. The young adults are very sociable and, before they finally choose a mate, island visitors can often see them in groups practicing their courtship displays. They seem to dance, bowing and parading around each other, heads swaying from side to side in an exaggerated way, as they perform a strange nasal honking. At some unknown signal, necks stretch and heads are thrown back to point directly at the sky, before beaks descend and clack together in a parry of fencing moves.

It may be many years before these young adults finally select a mate, but when they do, the female will lay a single egg between mid-April and July. Both parents will incubate the egg and after it hatches, one will stay with the young chick whilst the other feeds. Bigger chicks are left in nursery groups while their parents spend longer times at sea searching for their favourite food—tasty squid! By November the juvenile birds look as if every day is a "bad hair day." These ugly ducklings don't have long to develop their striking adult plumage—in late December the adult birds will leave the island and fly out to sea. If the juveniles haven't fledged, they will be unable to fly or catch food for themselves and will die. Each day, as sleek feathers develop and straggly down falls off, they exercise growing wing muscles, lifting their heavy bodies further and further off the ground.

Before long, a few stumbling steps between the boulders, become a clumsy, wobbling run, until the albatross manage to take off for the first time. Once in the air, they fly naturally and gracefully circle around a few times before coming into their rocky airstrip for the first of many bumpy, but well-mastered landings.

Now a grandmother in her late fifties, Carol Ann lives in the foothills of the Grampian Mountains in Scotland. After 34 years in the IT industry she has 'retired' to indulge her passions for travel, writing and photography. Her personal experiences over three decades of extensive travel, seeing many sacred places, spectacular landscapes and meeting indigenous peoples, has given her ample source material for writing and has allowed her to explore the links between sacred landscapes, their legends and underlying geology. In spite of an increasing tendency to short-term memory loss, she continues to learn and is currently studying for a Geosciences Degree with the Open University. She is also a published children's author and regularly gives talks and slide shows about her travel experiences. Ann would never leave Horace behind when leaving for a trip, Horace being "a small teddy bear given to me by my eldest son when he was 14."

## WILD TORTOISES ON SANTA CRUZ ISLAND

By Carol Ann

To early pirates and sailors calling at the Galápagos Islands, the giant tortoise was easy prey and a convenient source of fresh meat. Given the added bonus that they could be kept alive without food or water for up to a year in the hold of a ship, it's not surprising that tortoise populations were decimated almost to the point of extinction. High on the list of anyone's Galapagos itinerary is a visit to the Charles Darwin Research Station on Santa Cruz Island. For many visitors (especially those on a quick trip) this is the only place where they will see the iconic giant Galapagos tortoise. As part of a special breeding plan, the research station is home to hundreds of young tortoises from islands where their species is under threat. Here they are reared in safety before being released into the wild at three to five years old. By this age they are too big to be eaten by feral dogs, cats and rats and stand an 85 percent chance of survival.

But seeing tortoises in open pens in a protected environment is not the same as seeing them roaming free in their natural habitat. If you want to see them in the wild, take a trip up into the lush, green highlands of Santa Cruz, to the El Chato Tortoise Reserve, accompanied by a national park guide.

Inside the national park boundary, it's not uncommon to find one of these giants shuffling along a footpath, or moving into the undergrowth with unexpected speed and agility. Nor is it unusual to find a communal mud hole with dozens of tortoises of all shapes and sizes, wallowing and wading in the brown, sticky ooze. Stand quietly for a while and a rhythmic, wheezing sound may emanate from nearby bushes—this is the sound of tortoises mating; the smaller female wedged into the undergrowth, whilst the larger male pushes against her. Another thing you will notice is how healthy these tortoises look. With their bright eyes, scaly faces and jaws full of tender green leaves they are clearly in tortoise heaven, safe from the clutches of passing sailors.

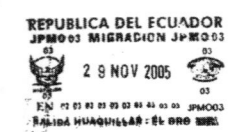

# SNORKELING IN THE GALÁPAGOS

## By Dr. Crit Minster, Rochester, New York, U.S.A.

A black eel with bright green stripes slithers blithely along the sandy bottom, weaving in and out of small rocks and patches of seaweed. Sea lions swim circles around you, playfully darting at your mask or nipping your fins. A marine iguana clings to a mossy green stone, gnawing off bits of algae and seaweed. A reef shark sidles up for a closer look and glowers at you for a moment before turning and disdainfully swimming away, as if you're beneath notice. A school of surgeonfish passes by, chomping on coral and spitting out sand as they go.

Memorable snorkeling in the Galápagos is easy: if you're near any island, chances are you can strap on a mask, jump into the water and you'll see something amazing. The water is generally quite nice, although often cooler than you might expect. If you have an underwater camera, be sure to bring it—there are many species to watch and photograph, including numerous endemic ones, species that you'll only see in the Galápagos.

The Devil's Crown is a circle of craggy rocks that rise out of the sapphire waters off the north coast of Floreana Island. The jagged rocks—far too small to be considered islands in their own right—are home to blue-footed boobies, frigate birds and marine iguanas that seem to make their home on any warm, sunny rock in the islands. The premier snorkel spot in the Galápagos, the Devil's Crown is a favorite haunt of numerous marine species, including a wide variety of fish, sea turtles, sharks, eels and rays. The swift currents can be treacherous for beginning swimmers, but if you're up to it, don't miss the chance to dive in.

Sea Lion Island or "Isla Lobos" is a long, narrow cay off of San Cristóbal Island that protects a small, tranquil bay. As you would expect, there is a large colony of sea lions there, frolicking in the water and lounging on the rocks. Perfect for beginners since the water is shallow, warm, never rough and full of bright things to see. The sea lions often play with swimmers, and there is a good chance you'll see a sea turtle or ray.

A massive rocky island in the unmistakable shape of a sea turtle surges out of the water towards the sky off Española Island. Xarifa, more commonly known as "Turtle Rock," is a good place to see white-tip reef sharks, sea turtles, rays, scorpionfish and other fish. Turtle Rock is good for all skill levels—although the currents can be tricky and the water is sometimes rough but the island always shelters part of the water, making the swimming easy.

Underwater, the Galápagos is every bit as magical as it is on the "enchanted islands" themselves. The majestic sharks, shy eels and dazzling bright colored fish never fail to impress: you can't take them with you, but you'll never forget them.

*"The people of Ecuador today have decided to save the republic, a republic of hope, in whose streets and green fields should flower dignity, hope, equality and happiness."*
-Alfredo Palacio, former President of Ecuador (1939-)

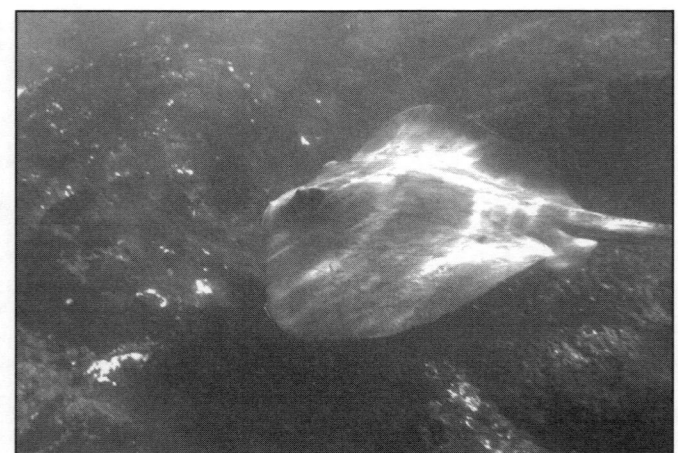

Stingray. Photo by Dr. Crit Minster.

# SARAGURO

By Allison Korn, Washington, D.C., U.S.A.

Arriving in Saraguro is a one-of-a-kind experience; there is literally no place like it in the world. What makes this small city so unique are the inhabitants, the Saraguros. The Saraguros are distinctive in their dress, traditions, and history, and are unlike any other indigenous group in Ecuador.

Originally from the Lake Titicaca region in Peru, the Saraguros were moved to their present location by the Incas as part of the Mitimae system. As a result, the Saraguros have maintained their age-old traditions and have become leaders in the indigenous movement, both in Ecuador and internationally.

Saraguro is famous for its beautiful weaving and jewelry, which can immediately be observed upon arrival. The typical dress of the women includes a black, outer-skirt which covers a more colorful embroidered one, together with a black shawl held closed by an intricately designed metal *tupu*, or pin. Around their waists are brightly woven belts and their colorful, beaded necklaces are often so large that they hang over their shoulders. The dress of the men is most notable for the calf length black pants and ponchos. Both men and women wear white felt hats with flat wide brims and their hair in one long braid.

To really get a feel for Saraguro it is worth it to have a guide take you not only through the city, but to the surrounding towns, which hold just as much Saraguran culture. A great place to start is at Fundacion Kawsay, whose goal is community ecotourism and revitalization of the indigenous culture and ethnicity of Saraguro. With them you can take tours of weavers' workshops, medicinal plant projects, as well as take hikes to sacred waterfalls where traditional ritual cleansings are still performed. The profits of this organization go directly to the different communities visited, so you know exactly where your money is going. And if you have a hankering to pick up some Kichwa, this is the place to do it, as most people in the area, especially in the surrounding towns, speak this native language.

At 64 kilometers North of Loja, there are not very many places to stay the night in Saraguro, although Fundacion Kawsay has the most comfortable hostel just outside of town with beautiful views. There are also the Hotels Samana Wasi, Sara Allpa, and Saraguro, all budget and adequate. The best place to eat is Mama Cuchara, serving typical meals on the main plaza and run by the indigenous federation.

A trip to Saraguro is truly eye-opening and refreshing; there are very few tourists and it is home to beautiful countryside and a fascinating culture.

Allison Korn was born in New York and grew up in Washington, D.C. Her undergraduate studies of Community Health and Human Rights took her through Bolivia, Ohio, Costa Rica, Nicaragua, and Brooklyn and the Bronx. She is currently living in the mountains of Cuenca, Ecuador where she works at a women's shelter and a study abroad program. In her free time she plays the violin and chats with her two sheep, Mayu and Pancho. Her dreams include raising alpacas, growing her own vegetables, and becoming a midwife. Her most bizarre experience was negotiating her way out of a taxi filling up with water that stalled while driving through a river in Bolivia. She dreams of working on an organic permaculture farm in India.

## CHARLES DARWIN (1809-1882) By Dr. Crit Minster

One hundred and fifty years after the publication of his many books and papers, Charles Darwin remains a powerful, contentious, controversial figure. To some, he is the intrepid scientist who was the first to shine a light into the eternal process of change and adaptation by which all creatures on the earth have survived and developed over millennia. To others he was the pawn of the devil who did Satan's work by destroying man's faith in the divine. A man of science, he will forever be remembered for one of his many theories: the theory of evolution.

Born in 1809, young Charles Darwin experimented with many fields of study in his early years. His experiences would serve him well when he signed up for a scientific voyage aboard the HMS Beagle from 1831 to 1836. He visited South America, the Pacific, the Galápagos Islands, Australia and Africa. Darwin collected specimens and wrote letters home, which were edited by his friends and colleagues into scientific papers. Upon his return, he was a celebrity. He spent the next few years cataloguing his specimens, giving talks and living the life of a respected scientist.

Meanwhile, a radical theory had been forming in the back of Darwin's mind. Although his stay in the remote Galápagos Islands had been relatively brief, he recalled how the tortoises, mockingbirds and finches on the islands had been similar but different, each perfectly adapted to their environment. It occurred to Darwin that perhaps they were all descended from one single species of tortoise, finch or mockingbird that had made its way to the islands eons ago. If this notion does not sound very radical to you today, remember that at that time most Europeans were Christians who believed in the biblical account of Creation, which tells of how God made every species on earth exactly as it was—the idea that species could change over time was not only radical; it was heresy. In secret, Darwin started exploring his new theory.

In the late 1850s, Darwin's hand was forced. Alfred Russel Wallace, a talented biologist working in Borneo, was working on a similar theory and intended to publish his findings. Darwin edited his notes and presented his theory jointly with Wallace in 1858. The theory soon turned into a controversy that shook Britain and the western world. The idea deeply offended sectors of British society. Darwin himself, increasingly ill from tropical diseases he caught while on the Beagle, remained mostly aloof from the controversy regarding his theory.

Charles Darwin died on April 19, 1882. The controversy between evolution and creationism rages on today, as parents, churches and school districts debate over what to teach to children.

# THE PETRIFIED FOREST OF PUYANGO

By Dr. Crit Minster, Rochester, New York, U.S.A.

With a thunderous roar that shook the ground for miles, the top of the volcano exploded, sending tons of slushy mud into the nearby valleys and dropping a thick layer of ash over a vast area. The ash settled over the mighty Araucaria trees, hurled to the ground by the blast. Over time, the ash began to harden, and before it could erode away, the area was covered by water, as irresistible geological changes turned what was once a forest into a swampy lake. Under the black waters, the trees, still entombed in the mineral-rich ash, began to change. As the ages passed, silicon, carbon and other minerals from the ash and water seeped into the wood, hardening and preserving it even as the original biological structure of the tree disappeared.

Centuries passed. The land which was once a forest and then a shallow sea was pushed out of the water and became a forest once again. The land began to naturally erode, and the once-flat land became hilly. More centuries passed, and the trees, which had not seen the light of day for millions of years, were slowly exposed, no longer wood now, but stone.

The largest field of exposed petrified wood in the world is found just south of the Ecuadorian city of Loja, not far from the Peruvian border: its name is El Bosque Petrificado de Puyango, or the Puyango Petrified Forest. Massive stone logs 70 million years old cross the trails, fallen giants from a bygone age. Petrified forests are rare: wood usually decomposes once it dies, and Puyango is considered a very significant source of information by scientists, especially as most of the trees are in the Araucarias family, which are rarely fossilized. There are marine fossils in the park as well, a remnant of a time even before the trees, when the area was a shallow sea.

However, there is more to Puyango then petrified wood. In the local language, Puyango means "dry, dead river," and for good reason. The region is considered a dry tropical forest, a rare ecosystem as most forests in the tropics tend to get a good deal of rain. The area is a protected national park, and features a diverse ecosystem with unique wildlife—more than 130 species of birds call the forest home for some, if not all of the year. It is also known for many beautiful species of butterflies.

For some, the best part will be the fact that Puyango is well off the gringo trail: it's very remote, and the nearest city of any size is Loja, about four hours away.

PARK FACTOIDS:

The Park is 2,568 Hectares, or about 6,570 acres. The oldest fossils in the park are marine fossils estimated to be about 500 million years old: the area was once under water. The tree fossils are considered to be about 70 million years old. The nearest town with any sort of tourist facilities is Alamor. From December to May it is the rainy season, and the dry season is from June to November. It's preferable to visit during the dry season.

## MANUELA SAENZ

By Dr. Crit Minster

Born in Quito in 1793 as the illegitimate daughter of a married Spanish nobleman, Manuela Saenz led one of the most fascinating lives in the history of Latin America.

Forced into a convent because of her illegitimate status, she was kicked out at the age of seventeen when it was discovered that she was carrying on an affair with a Spanish military officer. Her father arranged for her to marry James Thorne, a wealthy Englishman who was much older. They moved to Peru, where Manuela lived as an aristocrat and became involved in the planning of the independence movement.

In 1822, she left her husband and moved back to Quito, where she met Simón Bolívar, the hero of South American independence, and they began a torrid affair. Although she lived with Bolívar for a short while, they spent most of their time apart as he traveled a great deal in pursuit of independence. On September 25, 1828, she saved his life by helping him escape an assassination attempt.

Bolívar died two years later of tuberculosis. After his death, anti-Bolívar factions in Peru and Ecuador conspired to exclude her from any position of influence, and she wound up living in Jamaica for some time. She moved to a small town in northern Peru, where she lived by selling tobacco and translating letters that North American whalers wrote to their lovers in various ports of Latin America. She died penniless in 1856.

Today, Ecuadorians (and Quiteños in particular) have embraced Manuela Saenz as one of their own. She is considered a national heroine and is the subject of the first ever Ecuadorian opera. You can visit the Manuela Saenz Museum in Quito: Barrio San Marcos, Centro Histórico.

# VILCABAMBA

By Brenda Flynn, Flemingsburg, Kentucky, U.S.A.

What immediately strikes you about Vilcabamba, a small town near Loja, Ecuador, in the southernmost range of the Andes, is the idyllic temperature. It stays between 65 and 85 degrees Fahrenheit year-round.

The nights are balmy, with playful breezes that tease your hair and make for perfect late afternoon naps in a hammock, strung between two palm trees. The days are never unbearably hot or dry, even when you're astride a Paso Fino pony, riding trails through water-forged gullies and alongside the plunging rock-faced cliffs of the nearby *Parque Nacional Podocarpus*. Vilcabamba is truly an oasis, hidden in a patchwork quilt of banana plantations and sugar cane fields.

Formally founded in 1756, Vilcabamba is structured like most small Ecuadorian towns. It has a central square surrounding a small park and several small tourist or food-related businesses. The streets are paved, fading into limestone paths outside town, where they wind up mountains and through dense forests.

Vilcabamba maintains the mystical aura of being a place of earthly longevity: the Latin American Fountain of Youth. The name Vilcabamba translates from the Quichua as "Sacred Valley." According to local legend recently backed by scientific evidence, inhabitants regularly live to be more than one hundred years old. Is it the water, pure mineral water from ancient glacier snows and deep limestone aquifers? Is it the air, free of chemicals, having thousands of acres of rainforest growth to filter out any harmful pollutants? Or, is it the richness and variety of natural organic foods, grown in the volcanic soils of the small valley? Hard, physical work probably plays into the mix as well.

Just outside of Vilcabamba sits Parque Nacional Podocarpus, a safe haven to well over 500 species of birds and several endangered and threatened species of large mammals, such as the giant armadillo and mountain tapir. It also boasts one of the world's most diverse habitats, from lower-altitude rainforests to cloud forests to sylvan forests and alpine ecosystems. There are two natural-flowing rivers, the Chamba and Yambala, so naturally hiking and trail riding are just two of many outdoor activities available for visitors in the area.

A great place to stay in Vilcabamba is the Madre Tierra. For a reasonable price, you're treated to a cottage suite with hot showers (artistically designed in mosaic tiles), romantic atmosphere, colorful patio hammocks, and two delicious gourmet meals per day. Choose between several spa services, such as hot clay baths, colonics, steam and sauna, facials, full-body massages and reiki, for less than $10 per visit. The mineral clays, dug fresh every morning from a "secret" spot, are renowned internationally for their therapeutic qualities. Licensed masseuses knead every square inch of muscle, relaxing you and making the short walk down the winding stone stairway of the garden spa almost impossible. Combine those with a warm, friendly staff that dine with guests outside on a covered lanai with lit aromatherapy candles, native music and a mystifying sense of calm, and you have enough reason to visit Vilcabamba.

Having worked with a newspaper for 18 years as a news artist and journalist, Brenda Flynn left in 2004 to pursue other creative interests and freelance her writing skills. She recently moved from Florida to Kentucky to open an art gallery and studio in an 1840s-era commercial building in a small town near Lexington. She has some travel advice for readers: "Even if you're really good at throwing darts, if you go to one of those non-touristy pubs in England, and you're female, it's best not to shoot better than the local hero. And, never spit on the sidewalks in Germany, even if you did take a bite of candy and it happens to be licorice, and you hate licorice."

Flynn finds tourist traps irresistible: "I'm a roadside attraction junkie, so if there's a big ball of twine out there, I have to find it."

## BREAKING THE BANK

By Katie Hale and Dr. Crit Minster

In 1999, on the brink of economic collapse due to a failed banking system, falling oil prices, and natural disasters, Ecuador made a tough decision—to give up its national currency, the Sucre, and officially adopt the U.S. dollar in its place. The move was extremely unpopular with the people, and then-president Jamil Mahuad was ousted (in part) because of it. Nevertheless, dollarization went forward. In the summer of 2000, both currencies were accepted at the rate of 25,000 Sucres to one dollar, up from 7,000 Sucres to the dollar less than eighteen months before. By the fall of 2000, all Sucres had been removed from circulation.

Reaction to the move has been mixed. Most Ecuadorians admit that dollarization has helped stabilize the economy, largely by forcing the government to adopt fiscally responsible policies. However, most Ecuadorians also feel that in general, the cost of living has gone up significantly since 2000. There is also the question of national pride: populist candidates often promise a return to a national currency, although some experts warn that the Ecuadorian economy is not yet ready for such a move.

One way that Ecuador has retained some national pride is in the minting of coins. Ecuadorian coins are the same size, denomination and weight as their US counterparts and feature past presidents and national figures. They are used interchangeably with US coins in Ecuador.

Ecuador is not the only nation in Latin America to use the US dollar. Panama adopted the dollar as its official currency in 1903, alongside its own currency, the balboa. El Salvador dollarized in January 2001.

# PERU

**The Land of the Incas**

Think of Peru and you'll probably think of Machu Picchu, the sprawling, magnificent country retreat of the mighty Incas, perched on a lush, emerald mountain deep in the Andean wilderness. While it is true that the lost city of the Inca is high on everyone's list of must-sees—and rightly so—there is much more to Peru than Machu Picchu.

When the Spanish conquistadores arrived in Peru, led by Francisco Pizarro, they were able to exploit a civil war between Inca brothers Huascar and Atahuallpa and subjugate the Inca Empire. Within ten years, the greedy conquistadores were at each other's throats as they fought like dogs over Inca loot: Pizarro himself was hacked down in the street by rivals. The 19th century brought a war of independence from Spain followed by a war with Chile. In recent years, the country was beset with turmoil as the Maoist Shining Path guerillas waged an insurrection in the 1980s and 1990s.

Don't let this history deter you from visiting this marvelous country: it's currently very peaceful and well worth a visit. The Peruvian Amazon, a vast, dense, steamy, wonderful jungle wilderness, is still fairly pristine and remote. On the other side of the country, the Ica Desert is where people go to see dinosaur bones, sandboard, and visit the Nasca Lines. The Pacific Coast is home to several fantastic areas, including the Paracas National Reserve. If you like the sophisticated, big city life, Lima and Cusco are where you want to be.

Nature buffs will find themselves in heaven: there is a lifetime's worth of hikes and treks in Peru's snowcapped mountain ranges, where they can appreciate Peru's unforgiving, eternal beauty as they trek through pine forests, past sapphire lakes, across frigid slopes and along rocky ridges in the footsteps of the Incas themselves.

Sure, come for Machu Picchu, but don't short-change Peru (and yourself) by only visiting Cusco and the ruins. The country should not be judged for the shiniest jewel in its crown alone.

# MÁNCORA AND PUNTA SAL

*By Freyja Ellis, Benbecula, Outer Hebrides, Scotland*

The tiny little beach town of Máncora, Peru, consists of one main road, running north to south. It is home to no more than 8,000 full-time residents, most of whom are fishermen or work in the many hotels and restaurants. Some are beach bums who came to surf and never left.

It's easy to see why: Máncora is sunny year-round, the water is warm, the beer is cold and the surfing is excellent. What more could a surfer ask for? The laid-back friendly and night-time partying character of surfing towns the world over prevails in Máncora. The town is a great stop-off point for travellers from or heading to Ecuador or those just wanting to relax and soak up the atmosphere of the best beaches in Peru. Despite its tiny size, it has everything you need: plenty of ATMs and a bank to exchange money, internet cafés, and pharmacies in addition to the usual hotels, restaurants and hostels, the least expensive of which are clustered at the south end of town. Needless to say, there are souvenir stands and surf shops every few feet.

Surfing with the experts takes on a new meaning in Máncora: the instructors are great, but the real pros are the dolphins, who often splash around and break waves right next to you! If you opt for lessons from someone with hands and feet instead of fins, you can choose between surfing and kite surfing lessons. But that's just the beginning: in addition, the town also offers horse riding, deep sea fishing, diving, windsurfing and water-skiing activities. But who needs all of that? Many decide to simply spread out a towel or sling a hammock and relax on the clean, white sandy beaches.

Whereas Máncora is the most well-known in the area, a number of neighbouring beaches offer lesser tourist facilities but good surfing, diving and fishing. Beaches of note include Las Pocitas Beach (4 km south of Máncora), Vichayito Beach (10 km south), Los Organos Beach (13 km south) and Punta Sal (23 km north).

Punta Sal is worth a special mention as it is considered by many to be the best beach in Peru and offers a tranquil setting of white sandy beach broken up by carob trees and the occasional picturesque rock formation. Small fishing boats come and go, as they have for centuries. A small beach resort town, Punta Sal, has a handful of comfortable hotels, some with restaurants and swimming pools. The Hostal Hua, in addition to rooms and a restaurant, offers camping on the beach. You'll need your own camping gear, and it is important to be mindful of tides when selecting your pitch unless you like waterbeds! There are no shops in Punta Sal, although emergency supplies and basics are available from the restaurants. In fact, you needn't go hungry or thirsty because the bars and restaurants open early and stay open until the last person leaves.

With its clean warm waters—the same ocean currents that come to Galápagos arrive here—Punta Sal is ideal for swimming, snorkelling or diving. Local fishermen offer the opportunity to fish in traditional, paddle driven reed boats or deep-sea fishing. For the less active, the quiet beaches offer opportunities for relaxing in average daily temperatures of 26ºC/73ºF or exploring the coastline and the many crab pools. At night, locals and visitors alike gather on restaurant terraces or around cheerful beach bonfires, watching the majestic sunset as another day in paradise turns into another soft Pacific evening, bringing with it the promise of another sunny day tomorrow, the same yet unforgettable.

Freyja Ellis hails from Scotland, although now lives in London, and holds graduate and postgraduate qualifications in Business Studies and Marketing and is a chartered marketer and member of the Chartered Institute of Marketing. On completion, she undertook a career break and spent seven months traveling extensively through South America covering nine of the 13 countries, including the Galápagos Islands. Prior to this she has spent time traveling through Asia, Australasia and Europe and extensively through Southern and Eastern Africa and has lived for three years in North America.

Her most bizarre cultural experience was in Port Douglas, Australia, when a visit to a local pub revealed a local tradition—cane toad racing. This involves placing the poisonous toads, with a bucket over them, in the middle of a table and then releasing then and betting on which one hops off the table first. She found this event hilarious because, as the toads reach the floor, pub visitors hop up onto tables and chairs to avoid being touched by the toads and their poisonous skin secretions. Ellis would never leave home for travels without her sense of humour.

## CEVICHE By Mariana Cotlear

All along the coast of Peru, legions of hungry natives can be witnessed lunching on a combination of marinated raw fish, lime, onions and *aji amarillo* (a spicy yellow pepper). This wildly popular national dish, known as *ceviche*, comes in many variations, but its premise is always the same. Very fresh raw fish—usually *lenguado* (sole) or *corvina* (sea bass)—is cut into small chunks, scattered with onions and chopped aji, then doused in lime juice, left to sit for a few minutes, and served. Traditional ceviche is accompanied by *choclo* (corn on the cob), *camote* (sweet potato), and *canchita* (toasted corn kernels), with some extra aji amarillo sauce on the side. Alternatively, ceviche can be garnished with anything from *chifles* (fried plantain chips) to popcorn. Variations on traditional ceviche can include anything that comes from the sea; ceviche mixto includes pretty much everything.

A milder variation on ceviche is known as *tiradito*. Here, the fish is cut very thinly, carpaccio-style, and covered with a creamy sauce made from lime and mild aji amarillo. Again, the variations on tiradito are endless, as the dish is constantly being reinvented by adventurous chefs.

A delicacy you might be served along with your ceviche or tiradito is leche de tigre (literally, "tiger's milk"). This "juice"—the extra marinade from the ceviche mixture—is known in the popular lore for its invigorative properties. Alternatively, you might choose to wash down your meal with a Pisco Sour or an ice-cold cerveza. Peruvians fiercely claim ceviche as their national dish, but it has become popular across Latin America—particularly in Mexico, Ecuador, and Chile—as well as among trendy eaters in wealthier countries to the north.

# SURF'S UP! PICO ALTO AND CHICAMA

By Brad Balkus, Newbury, Massachusetts, U.S.A.

Brad Balkus resides in Massachusetts, where he works as a middle school technology education teacher.

He never travels without music and the craziest place he has visited is Samoa. Balkus is currently dreaming about heading to the Maldives to surf.

Like the lost Inca city of Machu Picchu, Peru's surfing scene could be characterized as a forgotten wonder. Surfing in Peru started more than 2,000 years ago when fishermen surfed the incoming waves on reed boats after a long day at sea.

This ancient art is still practiced today in many northern villages where the pace of life has changed little since ancient times. Today, modern surfing is an important part of the coastal culture where many of the best surfers in the world can be found tearing it up on some of the planet's best waves.

Peru's 2,500 km (1,500 miles) of rocky coastline is arguably the holy grail of point breaks. Huge southern hemisphere storms pump swells northward to the coast of Peru year round. There is never a lack of swell, and at times there cen be too much. Peru's big wave breaks like Pico Alto, located near the happening surf town of Punta Hermosa, can hold waves in the 30-foot-plus range. Big wave surf contests at Pico Alto draw professional surfers from all over the world.

If big wave surfing is not your style, Peru's meandering coastline offers many waves for all ability levels. Just a short drive from Pico Alto is all it takes to find breaks that will produce waves that are much smaller than those at the top spots. The Lima area alone offers 20-plus surf breaks from knee high beaches to double OH (over head) hollow points.

The climate in Peru is generally temperate with the best swells arriving between January and June. Water temperatures usually stay between 55ºF-65ºF (12-17ºC). With much of the coastline covered in thick fog and clouds for weeks at a time, a wetsuit and booties are recommended (except in the extreme north) along with some serious nerve to surf large waves in chilly, dense fog.

Perhaps the most intense waves for the die-hard surfer though, are found at Chicama. What turns a routine surf trip into a soul surfer's pilgrimage is the break at Chicama. Not only a muse for Hemmingway's *The Old Man in the Sea*, this tiny fishing village also boasts the world's longest wave. On a good swell, Chicama will break for more than a mile (1.7 km) and provide surfers with rides timed at over three minutes. The distance and currents make paddling back to the takeoff spot nearly impossible, so surfers must walk back along the beach or take one of the waiting taxis back to the starting point. There are a couple of local places to camp and hostels in the area, and fresh fish for dinner can be purchased from the local fisherman. This wave is truly a natural wonder and a must-see for anyone with an adventurous spirit and love for the ocean.

# PEDRO SARMIENTO DE GAMBOA

By Dr. Crit Minster

Pedro Sarmiento de Gamboa (1532-1602) was a Spanish writer, conquistador, astronomer, scientist and adventurer. After an early career as a soldier in the various wars of 16th century Europe, he immigrated to the New World in 1555. After a brief stay in Mexico, he went to Peru. In 1568, he discovered the Solomon Islands, which he promptly took in the name of Spain. The islands were too remote for Spain to govern, however, and no Spanish force of any size ever stayed there long.

In 1569, he began working for Francisco de Toledo, the new Viceroy of Peru. In 1571, Sarmiento de Gamboa produced a book, *History of the Incas*, in which he defends Spanish rule in the New World. In 1578 he was named commander of all naval forces in the Pacific off the coast of Peru: his mission was to capture or kill the notorious pirate Sir Francis Drake. Drake escaped, but Sarmiento saw the need for a permanent Spanish settlement on the Strait of Magellan.

In 1583, Sarmiento de Gamboa founded the city El Rey Don Felipe (named for King Philip II) on the bleak Strait of Magellan. Recalled to Spain, he was captured by the British, who released him with a letter from Queen Elizabeth to King Philip II. On the way, he was captured by French Huguenots and held for four years until 1588. In his absence, the city he had founded failed: all of the settlers deserted or starved. In 1587, Thomas Cavendish, a British pirate, visited the ruined site and renamed it Port Famine.

Sarmiento de Gamboa went into semi-retirement in Spain, editing and writing. In 1602, at the age of 70, he was commissioned admiral of a fleet of Spanish ships headed to the New World. He never made it back to the New World that he loved so much, however: he died on board not long after the fleet left Spain.

# HUACA RAJADA

By Laura Watilo Blake, Cleveland, Ohio, U.S.A.

The swing of a shovel from a grave robber's hand in northern Peru in 1987 began a dramatic series of events that would eventually lead to one of the most important archaeological finds of all time. The looters had literally struck gold—and silver—on an eroded pyramid of adobe near the desert town of Sipán. However, what they left behind would reveal a wealth of knowledge about the Moche civilization, an ancient culture predating the Incas.

The remnants of a royal leader remained undiscovered in his gold- and silver-laden tomb thanks to the quick response of Peruvian archaeologist, Walter Alva, and local authorities. The Lord of Sipán, as he is now known, is considered by some experts to be one of the greatest archaeological discoveries in the Americas.

Even though the artifacts that have been found thus far are now located 50 kilometers (30 miles) away at a huge pyramid-shaped museum, Tumbas Reales de Sipán in Lambayeque, visiting the archaeological zone has a way of bringing context to its history. The residents of Sipán contribute to the maintenance of the Huaca Rajada funerary center and offer guided tours.

When visitors gaze upon the Lord of Sipán's tomb, they actually see his stunt double decked out in the finest costume jewelry. Surrounding him were the bodies of eight servants, concubines and warriors, whose lives were cut short in assisting him on his journey to the spiritual world. One of the interred was missing a foot, perhaps keeping him on this worldly plane to guard the burial site.

If visiting the Huaca Rajada is considered the appetizer, a trip to the Tumbas Reales de Sipán museum is the main course. After all, the majority of its visitors want to see the precious metals from the tombs. The treasures are displayed in the order they were found, as if visitors to the museum themselves were excavating the tombs from the top to the bottom.

The grand finale is The Lord of Sipán's regalia. He wore a three-foot-high semilunar gold crown. His ears were covered by golden orejeras encrusted with turquoise and lapis lazuli. In his nose, a nariguera hung down in front of his mouth. He carried a gold scepter and dagger carved with Moche figures. On his feet were silver sandals that rarely touched the ground because he was carried everywhere he went. Photos alongside the artifacts show the pieces as they were found in the earth, while detailed descriptions in both Spanish and English chronicle how the archaeologists removed and carefully restored the treasures.

The Sipán treasures have finally received the royal treatment they deserve. But as a reminder of the historic information that was dangerously close to being lost to the world, the museum also features recovered artifacts from the ransacked tombs at Huaca Rajada. The Moche artifacts were found in many parts of the world, but with international help—from the U. S. Federal Bureau of Investigation and Sotheby's Auction House among others—the priceless treasures have made the journey back to northern Peru where they belong.

www.vivatravelguides.com/104039

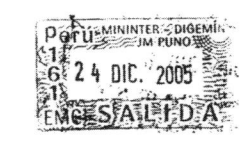

Laura Watilo Blake is a journalism professional with 15 years of experience in writing, editing, design and photography for traditional and online media. Originally from Missouri, Watilo Blake is based now in Cleveland, Ohio, although her husband might argue that she spends more time abroad.

One of her strangest experiences while traveling was had while in China. No matter where she went in the country, she was chased by paparazzi—okay, not exactly. Strangers wanted her to pose for photos with their dad, their sister, their children and themselves. Watilo Blake recounts, "It was as if they had never seen a blonde American woman before." It was an experience that has made her more culturally sensitive, who now realizes how pygmies must feel when the tourists show up with their cameras.

# CHICLAYO

By Stan Kimer, Raleigh, North Carolina, U.S.A.

Although Chiclayo is Peru's fourth largest city and is home to interesting ruins and impressive museums, it receives few tourists. The area was once inhabited by the ancient Moche and Sipán civilizations which adorned their leaders with gold that rivals that found in King Tut's tomb.

One route from Chiclayo can start with a visit to the Sipán and Túcume ruins of the Moche and Lambayeque civilizations, where several great gold artifacts have been uncovered over the past few decades. Near Chiclayo are the three museums of Sicán-Ferreñafe, Bruning Museum, and Tumbas Reales de Sipán; depicting the lives of local cultures that lived 1,000 to 2,000 years ago, and displaying some spectacular, priceless gold pieces. The most modern of the three museums, Tumbas Reales de Sipán, closes the museum tour with a dramatic room of life-size figures that move and rattle instruments to ancient Indian music.

There are several other charming sites close to Chiclayo. One special trip would be heading to the beach of Pimento around noon, where just as in ancient times, fishermen paddle themselves out into the wild ocean waves in small, single-person reed canoes for fish and crabs. Around noon each day, dozens of these fishermen return to the beach in the tiny crafts rocked wildly by the waves. There is a tingling anticipation and excitement along the beach as each fisherman arrives on shore and his family and friends him help pull his heavy boat ashore and then examine the catch for the day. As you participate in this daily ritual, you will magically feel transported back to a simpler time of 1,000 years ago when people subsisted off the sea.

Less than half an hour north of Chiclayo is the small charming colonial town of Lambayeque. It contains a grand, yellow cathedral and across from it is Casa Montjoy, which claims Peru's longest balcony. Travelers around the Chiclayo area can experience all these historical treasures, sights, and sounds without seeing another single tourist!

In lieu of staying at a modern hotel, one can instead stay with a local woman who built two small apartments on the second floor of her home and now offers them to tourists and visitors. Her home is located in an average, middle class neighborhood about half a mile from the center of Chiclayo, making it very easy to walk to downtown with its gorgeous town square and magnificent gold filled cathedral. Locals frequently go to a side chapel in the cathedral and pray reverently before a huge, sparkling, gold religious ornament upon which sits a huge white holy communion wafer.

Stan Kimer is currently Director of Global Sales Operations for IBM's Consulting Services, where he has worked for over 26 years. He received his BS from Georgia Tech and an MBA from the University of Chicago. Kimer's passions outside of work include exotic travel and photography, and so far he has visited over 50 countries on six continents. In addition, he is involved in stamp collecting, coin collecting, Metropolitan Community Churches, the N.C. Council of Churches and his local Georgia Tech Club. Kimer lives with his domestic partner of 15 years, Rich.

His most bizarre cultural experience was getting stranded in a remote town in Haiti after several kids punctured all of his car tires, and then negotiating with the kids' "friends" to repair the tires.

www.vivatravelguides.com/103708

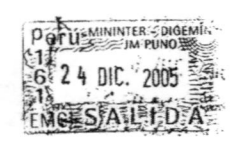

# IQUITOS AND THE JUNGLE

### By Will Gray, Kettering, England

Iquitos is Peru's gateway to the Amazon, where there are opportunities to swim with dolphins, fish for Piranhas and see a host of bird life in one of the many riverside retreats.

The small but bustling town, which sits on the banks of a tributary to the mighty Amazon, is a fascinating place to launch your trip. The pleasant main square contains the Iron House, designed by Gustave Eiffel, and an artisan market, complete with a riverside promenade, which offers a place to take a gentle stroll by day and to drink, party and watch the street entertainers by night.

The easiest and most exciting way to reach the port is on one of the many motorcycle taxis, which zip you through the streets to within inches of all obstacles in their way, before arriving at the place where the Amazon trips embark. There you can board one of the metal boats tied to the jetty, each one of which has space for around eight passengers (pick one with fewer occupants for a more comfortable journey).

Even though the boats whip along as fast as they can, it takes three hours to get to the most remote parts of the jungle, where the greatest opportunity of seeing wildlife exists. The river soon flows into the mighty Amazon, where it widens and changes color from brown to blue. Only once you are back on one of the tributaries, however, does the animal life explode with the arrival of storks, herons, dragonflies and flying fish.

The jungle lodges, which sit on stilts to raise them out of the high-rising river in the wet season, are relatively similar in looks but differ in levels of luxury and comfort. Most will offer the essential mosquito nets and plenty of hammocks on which to kick back and relax as well as jungle guides to show you the vibrant life of the rainforest. A three-day trip offers enough time to get out and explore through jungle walks and river trips.

At the lodge, bird calls wake you from your slumber. After a hearty breakfast, you are led through the jungle where leaf-carrying ants trot across your path, banana spiders cling to webs above your head, furry black caterpillars and big hairy tarantulas hide in sodden tree stumps and, if you are lucky, monkeys swing from the trees. Seeds and maggots are available to test your jungle taste buds, while vines dripping pure water can be chopped to quench your thirst. Piranhas swim in the river waters and are there to be fished with primitive rods, making a tasty lunch. Vultures, cormorants, kingfishers, ospreys and eagles rule the skies until the clouds arrive to scare them away, occasionally bursting into a spectacular rainforest downpour, where the only shelter offered is by the trees on the banks.

The jungle is a thrilling place to explore and offers a tantalizing mixture of pleasure and pain. The pain of heat, humidity and mosquito bites is counteracted by the pleasure of raw wildlife, papaya juice, hammocks and relaxation in the shade, and the ride back to Iquitos arrives all too soon.

www.vivatravelguides.com/103424

# BIRDWATCHING IN IQUITOS

### By Fiona Leslie, Chester, England

Arriving at the remote jungle city of Iquitos, which is only possible by plane or boat, the intense heat and humidity promise that you are entering the gateway to one of the richest areas of biodiversity in the Peruvian Amazon. A tour of the Pacaya-Samiria National Reserve affords the most wonderful opportunities to witness birds and animals in their truly tropical rainforest habitat.

At dawn and dusk, the jungle comes alive with flying colours and a cacophony of calls. Majestic birds, from scintillating scarlet, blue and yellow macaws to the distinctively-billed toucan and Black-collared hawks, soar overhead. Going steadily upstream striking white-faced saki monkeys curiously peer down, and the occasional three-toed sloth slumbers in a tree top. A white-necked Cocoi Heron leads the boat further upstream while a small flock of large-billed terns perch on a log. At the river's edge, some basking turtles look strangely out of place this far inland. Here, spot a Rufescent Heron, and there a brilliant red flash of a Ruby-capped Tanager, or the more common Greater and Lesser Kiskadees parading their cheery yellow stripes. Oropendulas and caciques bob in and out of their woven pendular nests, whilst a pair of silver-beaked tanagers shy away in a low tree. As the river opens, Yellow-hooded Blackbirds busy themselves in a bush and a Scarlet-headed Blackbird flashes past.

A softly-paddled night boat trip up to an ox-bow lake is a tense ride through the unknown darkness around. Caimans skulk around the banks, their eyes shining in the torch light. Careful observation finds the round sturdy profile of a Horned Screamer perched on a low, overhanging branch, whilst a troop of Black Monkeys crash about noisily in the canopy above. A short torchlight trek in the undergrowth reveals Nightjars, enormous frogs in the leaf litter, and a female Pink-toed Tarantula settled onto a fallen nest which, at the size of your palm, is still a mere youngster.

At the lake by the lodge, the early morning visit of a Sun Bittern, flapping awkwardly and revealing its strikingly patterned wings, is a treat, while the Blue-crowned and White-eyed Parakeets begin making their presence known loudly and clearly in the surrounding palm trees. After the initial cacophony of the dawn chorus, the forest sounds die down and it is possible to pick out the chirping of woodpeckers, Olivacious Woodcreepers, thrush-like wrens and a colourful Yellow-rumped Cacique or a White-eared Jacama in a dark corner of the forest. A shrill but delicate cry is a tell-tale sign of Pygmy Marmosets, their tiny pink faces looking strangely aged and timid as they stop to peer at the human interlopers.

The Amazonian forest around Iquitos has an enormous variety of birds and natural wonders on offer and should not be missed on any trip to Peru.

# CARAZ

By Claire Peltier, Paris, France

Between the twin extremes of the arid Cordillera Negra and the high-peaked, icy Cordillera Blanca, the town of Caraz has a sunny, pleasant climate year-round. Sitting at a height of around 2,200 meters (7,200 feet), lower than the nearby and more touristy town of Huaraz, it is an ideal place to acclimate to the altitude and take amazing sightseeing tours.

Roughly 200 years old, the town is built around a Plaza de Armas and, like most villages in Peru, it has a grand colonial church that somehow seems slightly out of proportion to the rest of the tiny village.

At the north end of the village, you can see the Chavín ruins of Tunshucayco (the Chavín culture is one of the oldest of Peru, inhabiting the area from about 1000 B.C. to 300 B.C.) which consist of fascinating excavated walls. Without any signs, guides or tourists around, one enjoys the rare privilege of walking around among the ruins without being disrupted, of discovering secret tunnels and taking different paths that lead to superb views of the colorful valley.

On the way back to the village, slightly off track, a creek runs through a landscape of grass and beautiful trees—it looks like paradise.

Traveling would not be as interesting without the possibility of meeting people, and Caraz is one of the best places to encounter real Peruvian culture. In Caraz, tourists simply blend in, while the local population displays an honest, yet subdued curiosity as to their visitors' origins and reasons for trekking all the way to their village.

Women traveling alone will appreciate not being harassed, as well as the ease with which women and children initiate conversation. They are not intrusive or aggressive, but polite and kind, which makes any visitor feel welcome.

Caraz is ideally located for all sorts of active sports and for exploring the two mountain ranges by its sides, perfect spots to take a closer look at the snow-capped peaks of the two mountain ranges. It is a warm and comfortable base camp for trekking in the Cordillera Blanca and the best place to return to and rest, taking a last glance at these amazing mountains, in a town that has lost track of time.

Claire Peltier grew up in Paris where she studied marketing. After a bit of travel, she started working for an auction house eight years ago in London. For two years she has been living in Paris and New York for her work.

In Africa, she had a difficult run in with an armed guard. While visiting Guinea. she took a picture of a ferry; it was in a remote place lost in the forest. The guard wanted to arrest Peltier becuae it was not permitted to take a picture of a strategic point. It took 30 minutes of discussion for her to be released and the best part was she got to keep her film.

Peltier would love to travel to Antarctica and the Silk Road (end to end).

## TOP LIST: BEST PLACES FOR BIRDWATCHING WITHOUT BINOCULARS

South America is a birdwatcher's paradise. Literally thousands of species flap, flitter, and chirp their way through the jungles, deserts, lakes and rainforests of the region. A few of the more spectacular birds are quetzals, hummingbirds, hoatzins, condors, toucans, tanagers and perhaps the most famous birds of all—the unassuming Darwin's finches of the Galápagos. Bring your checklist, your binoculars and your tape recorder and follow our readers to their favorite spots:

1. The Brazilian Pantanal (p. 57).

2. Mindo, Ecuador. "Easy access from Quito. Fantastic for lovers of hummingbirds." Risa, New York, U.S.A.

3. Galápagos, Ecuador (p. 264). "Spectacular wildlife that can be viewed close-up." Carol Ann, Scotland.

4. Iquitos, Peru (p. 274).

5. Cuyabeno, Ecuador. "We saw over 30 species of birds in about three days. And they were unusual beautiful birds." Risa, New York, U.S.A.

Runners-up: Colca Copper (condor spotting). Iguazú (some rare species are found there). Atacama Desert for flamingos. Monteverde, Costa Rica.

# HUARAZ AND THE CORDILLERA BLANCA

By Will Gray, Kettering, England

An often overlooked area of Peru, the Cordillera Blanca offers a wilderness of high mountain hiking and true adventure for those who want to take it. To get the most out of the four or five-day Santa Cruz hike, which encompasses high altitudes, extreme terrain, and rapidly changing weather, it is best to hire a tour guide with local knowledge.

Heading out of Huaraz, the picturesque road splits the white-topped mountains of the Cordillera Blanca and the blackened hills of the Cordillera Negra. Stop along this ribbon of mountain road and fuel up with the local *chicha* brew before climbing right to the trailhead at Cashapampa. After strapping packs to the donkeys, the trek begins with a long, shallow climb on a path that runs beside a tumbling river. Leaving the misty mountains in the distance, the route continues on into the tall-walled Santa Cruz gorge before camp is set beside the river as the sun begins to sink into the night sky.

The following morning, the trail reaches the end of the gorge at the Ichicocha lake, a reed-filled lagoon home to Andean geese, and the surrounding mountains are revealed. From there it is on to Jatuncocha, a deep blue glacier-fed lake at 4,100 metres (13,400 feet), and then a climb up to the second camp as the valley opens out into a rolling plateau.

The view from camp two, Taullipampa, at 4,250 metres (13,900 feet) is spectacular, with the mountains of Quitaraju, Taullapampa and Alpamayo, once voted the most beautiful peak in the world, forming a row of pyramidal summits on one side; Paria, Piramide and Artesonraju create an icy panorama on the other and the lakes, now long left behind, hiding in the valley below.

The next day begins with a tough climb up to the 4,700 metres (15,400 feet) Punta Union pass, chewing coca leaves to alleviate any altitude sickness as you go. Past a vibrant blue glacier lake, the route reaches the top, and there offers sweeping views of valleys tucked between the rugged mountains on which you stand. From here the trail drops into the Huaripampa valley, eventually winding through meadows which, at certain times of the year, overflow with flowers.

A long walk will eventually find the campsite and an overnight break before continuing on through small settlements like the farming town of Wallipampa, where villagers and cattle live harmoniously, surrounded by the captivating scenery that unfolds beneath Chacraraju mountain. At Vaqueria, the sight of towns in the distance incorrectly suggests the final destination is near.

Before winding to an end, the trail witnesses a change of scenery and follows a white-water river through a forest of moist and mossy trees. One more overnight stop here, then another rocky climb takes you back into the clouds at 4,800 metres (15,700 feet) and through the Portachuelo de Llanganuco, which offers the finale: high views over snowy peaks with Huscarán, Peru's highest peak at 6,768 metres (22,200 feet), towering above the valley below. From here the trail drops down past two lakes, eventually leaving you to meet the lift back to Huaraz.

Cordillera Blanca. Photo by Maximilian Hirschfeld.

Cordillera Blanca. Photo by Natalie Potter.

# LIMA

By Michelle Hopey, New Hampshire, U.S.A.

The guidebooks terrified me. The way most described it, I was about to get mugged, knifed, gunned down or assaulted in some fashion. They said I could never take a taxi, walk alone or a ride a bus, and that my hotel would be scary, unless, of course, I was staying at a luxury hotel. So, as I sat on the plane flying through the Andean night sky, it's no wonder my feet began to dance nervously. As I flipped through one of my travel guides, I began second guessing myself: why on earth had I chosen to travel to Lima of all places? I knew the answer. As a curious writer, I had yielded the internal call to explore Cusco, Machu Picchu and the mysterious Sacred Valley. Since I was flying into Lima as a start-off point, I decided that I should visit this 6.4 million person metropolis—one of South America's major cities and economic hubs. After all, it was founded by Spanish Conquistador Francisco Pizarro, and nicknamed the City of Kings. For three centuries Lima was the greatest city in South America. I figured there had to be something to it.

But as the grand ol' bird smoothly landed at Aeropuerto Internacional Jorge Chavez my heart raced, causing a slight tightening in chest. My thoughts kept circling back to my friend Claudia, who didn't particularly enjoy Lima when she visited either: "If you have to go to Lima, get the heck out of there as fast as you can," she had said. As I said goodbye to what now felt like a nice, safe plane (ironic, because I hate flying), I was surprised and felt instantly eased when I walked into the Lima airport: it was clean, modern and downright nice. I didn't know what I had expected—something depressing, I suppose, and this sure wasn't it.

Neither was most of Lima, as I soon discovered. In fact, Lima as it turns out, is a culturally rich but modern city on the rise. Lima could very well be the next big thing, maybe even the next Buenos Aires. The abundance of cultural nightlife in Lima makes this Latin America city sizzle, its pulse is upbeat and electric. I'm not just talking about hot sweaty bars stuffed with designer youths. In a way, it has a whiff of the Buenos Aires night scene. Art aficionados will love the evening exhibits put on by several of the Miraflores galleries, while musical enthusiasts can get drunk in the sounds of the Orquestra Sinfonica Nacional, one of the best in Latin American. If you like performing arts or music you shouldn't leave Lima without visiting a Pena—a bar that hosts dancers dressed in elaborate costumes who passionately groove to local music. Cultural events, such as poetry slams, independent films and concerts are always offered by the Centro Cultural Ricardo Palma.

While the unemployment rates in the 1980s and 90s contributed to the demise of the city and rise in crime, Lima also suffered from intense pollution, mostly emitted from the large number of cars and industry that has emerged. The smog, combined with a heavy fog, called *garua* which blankets the city from June to December, makes Lima seem dark, gloomy and scary. But under it all, Lima is a colorful city, and in recent years as the government has cracked down on crime and made many tourist areas safer, the city as a whole with its reputable gastronomic scene (including signature fish dishes) musical talents, lively historic and contemporary art scene, terrific performing arts and cosmopolitan shopping venues—has become a great place to explore.

In 2003, under the mayor's orders, the old city got clean. For years, the historic center, El Centre, had been considered an unsafe area not worthy of any attention. But like so many South American cities that hold exquisite architecture and rich history all that was needed was bit of money and a whole lot of loving.

Today, Plaza de Armas located in El Centre as is the square where Lima declared independence from Spain in 1821, shows off its beauty and safe. The renovation of this area has also made it easier and safer to visit some of the Centre's most unique treasures such as the Inglesia de San Francisco which houses catacombs with tunnels that reportedly hold bones from 75,000 people, or the Museo de Arte de Lima, a Peruvian art museum.

Farther away from the center, the Museo de Oro del Peru, Lima's gold museum has with tons of Pre-Inca and Incan artifacts, and the Museo Nacional de Antropologia, Arqueologia, e Historia del Peru has the most well-preserved collection of pre-Colombian artifacts, perhaps anywhere.

If you are still nervous to be in Lima, you may want to find lodging in Miraflores or San Isidro. A very touristy section of town, Miraflores is safe (but remember tourists equal pickpockets) with plenty of Limenos and tourists walking around in the day and even at dusk. As I experienced, Miraflores isn't necessarily a gringo-land. Wealthy residents from the south of Lima, and business people alike frequent this *barrio*, since it has some of most exquisite high-end boutiques and some of the swankiest restaurants around.

Lima may be on the cutting edge, but it's an edge worth exploring. Its raw vibe mixed with its new sense of pride is sure to bring this once Spanish capital back into the spotlight. And although there will always be dark streets not to go down, and phony taxis preying, just use your common sense and remember many South American countries are always evolving—that's why they are developing nations.

## LA U VERSUS ALIANZA: FIERCE FÚTBOL RIVALRY

By Mariana Cotlear

Graffiti-covered brick walls bear the clichéd slogans of political campaigns past and present, while ancient concert posters peel off buildings. These sights are common across the developing world, but there is something about Peru's urban aesthetic that is unique to this country. If you look closely, you'll notice that just about everywhere the letter "U" appears, it is surrounded by a crude circle of spray-paint.

This graffiti symbol is the logo of Universitario de Deportes (affectionately known as "La U"), one of Peru's two top football teams. They, along with Alianza Lima, make up the country's most intense athletic rivalry. Traditionally, the players of La U were known as the "rich kids," white, middle class university students. Alianza, on the other hand, was made up of lower class blacks and mulattos. Their rivalry grew to symbolize the ethnic and economic disparity in Peru.

The teams are no longer split along such clear-cut socioeconomic lines, but the intense rivalry persists between the two teams. Fans of Alianza avoid the letter "U" like the plague. Their fan organization, known as "Comando Sur," for its location in the southern part of the stadium, is spelled "Comando Svr"—insurance that no La U supporter can turn the word into their rival's logo.

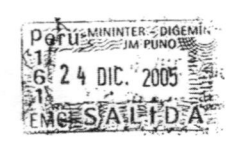

# TRADITIONAL CRAFTS AND SHOPPING

*By Michelle Hopey, New Hampshire, U.S.A.*

Every country has its textile, pottery or art that it's famous for. But Peru is an exception. It has so many quality choices—almost too many. If you're a shopper, you'll enjoy Lima and Cusco and not only for cheap prices. From hand-woven tapestries, beautifully crafted silver jewelry, knitted sweaters, scarves, gloves and clothing boutiques—it is a challenge to choose: traditional folk art or modern contemporary painting? Antique tapestries or newly woven weavings? Ceramics or CDs?

Soft, cozy, finely knit alpaca sweaters are one of the best buys in Peru. While they might be really expensive by Peruvian standards, the cost would still be much higher in Europe or the United States. Alpacas evolved thousands of years ago developing a fine hair with remarkable softness, fineness, length, warmth, and strength. Finding the right alpaca sweater or product is worth a little shopping around. Alpaca products, from sweaters to gloves to hats to ponchos are abundant through-out Peru, and especially in Cusco. There are 22 different natural colors of alpaca and baby alpaca makes the most luxurious and soft products.

While there are many high-end stores where you can get gorgeous sweaters at a hefty price—acrylic fakes are abundant too. Don't get duped. Real alpaca is beautifully made; the texture is super soft and feels like cashmere. If it's too silky though, it's probably been spun with polyester and if the texture is too rough, it's been spun with sheep's wool. These still make fine products, but just aren't what you thought you were paying for. The label also makes a difference. A real alpaca sweater will have the label of the person who made it, or company. Most often, true alpaca items are found in mid-to high-end stores in Cusco and Lima.

Since you are in the land of the Incas, artists have designed some exquisite pre-Colombian art work that you can purchase nearly anywhere from street markets to museums. A range of Inca designs are painted in a variety of colors from bright oranges and reds to earthy browns and stone blues. Relatively cheap and beautiful, they make great wall hangings for framing. They also make good gifts. Most artists and galleries have suitable packaging so that you can take it home with out damaging it.

Intricate tapestries are another great purchase. Indigenous people still use these today to hold their babies, or carry fruits and vegetables. In Lima there is a store on the southwest side of the Plaza De Armas which sells these delightful tapestries in a range of colors. Also in Lima at the Avenida la Paz Market in Miraflores, many tapestries can be found, of rich, deep reds and blues.

The closer you get south towards the silver mines of Bolivia, the more you will begin to see silver stores. Earrings, rings, necklaces, bracelets, jacket pins, hair pins, silverware, serving plates, candle stick holders and frames can all be found in both Lima and Cusco. Many are one-of-a-kind and most are handmade.

Lima tends to be more expensive, but, at the same, there are a slew of exceptional silver stalls especially at the market on Avenida La Paz in Miraflores. Here unique designs can be found, and many are created into Incan symbols, which are filled in with red, blue and green crushed stone to complete the design. Necklaces and decorative pins are mostly done in this motif.

Cusco on the other hand—and even though it is still a tourist town—tends to be cheaper for silver, probably because it is closer to Bolivia. But in Cusco there are many, many shops along Plaza de Armas, which although nice for variety, require more sifting through to make sure what you're buying is true *plata* (silver). Always ask what type of silver it is. Since silver is a soft metal in its purest form when mined, it's too soft to be used for jewelry and other items. So it's mixed with other metals to make it more durable. Only .925 is pure sterling silver, meaning that .075 is an additive, usually copper is added to make a pure 1000 parts silver. So anything around .925 is a good bet. In Cusco you might also want to head up towards Calle San Blas, will find many small, funky independent jewelry boutiques that have some incredibly exciting finds.

Finally, follow the guidelines below for securing and buying some great quality Peruvian products regardless of which town you are in:

First trick of the trade: From September to May is considered low season and many shop owners are likely to cut you a deal. Second tip: As in all of South America it bargaining is accepted and expected. Don't feel bad or feel like you should give more because they are small indigenous shop owners. Indeed, if you don't many locals will actually be offended. Third hint: If you can pay in cash, do. You are likely to get a bigger discount on the items you are purchasing. This includes high-end stores where credit cards are common, and readily accepted. The fees associated with credit-card payments tend to be higher than discounts, so it's worth their while.

## LATIN REVOLUTIONARIES #8: ABIMAEL GUZMÁN

Peru (1934—)

Born in the Peruvian province of Arequipa, Abimael Guzmán developed two interests at an early age: academics and communism. He earned degrees in philosophy and law, and before he was thirty he was working as a professor of philosophy at the San Cristobal of Huamanga University in Ayacucho. While there, he became involved in various communist groups, and even visited China. He became head of a communist group that followed the Chinese model: it was named the Peruvian Communist Party, but was commonly called "the Shining Path" after a phrase written by José Carlos Mariátegui, the group's founder: "Marxism-Leninism will open the shining path to revolution."

By 1980, Guzmán had adopted the *nom de guerre* President Gonzalo and had gone underground. Soon the Shining Path was ready to begin its guerilla war against the Peruvian government. In the 1980's, the group controlled vast stretches of the country and even carried out brazen attacks in Lima. The Shining Path was particularly ruthless, killing thousands in their effort to destabilize the Peruvian government. The resulting civil unrest is thought to have left more than 70,000 dead at the hands of the Peruvian Army as well as the Shining Path.

Guzmán was captured in Lima in 1992 and subjected to a very public trial. Found guilty in three days, he was sentenced to life imprisonment. His public appearance on Peruvian TV in 1993 to announce a peace with the Peruvian government greatly weakened the Shining Path movement. He remains in a Peruvian naval prison.

# ICA DESERT

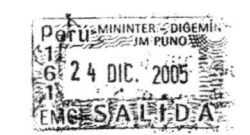

By Dr. Crit Minster, Rochester, New York, U.S.A.

Carcharodon Megalodon ate whales. A member of the shark family, this monster of the sea had a bad attitude and teeth the size of frisbees. One of the largest predators ever, it probably measured as many as 20 meters (65 feet) and weighed as much as 25 tons. With a maw that measured 1.8 meters (6 feet) wide by 2.1 meters (7 feet) this beast of beasts could swallow a buffalo ... whole!

The bones of the mighty Carcharodon Megalodon, as well as many other marine animals, can be found in the parched stretch of land known as the Ica desert. Located near Ica, Peru, this desert was once a shallow ocean basin before a tectonic upheaval pushed it above sea level. Local guides know all of the best places to find fossils in this parched wasteland, and the lucky visitor may even find a Carcharodon Megalodon tooth. Some of its teeth have survived, deeply embedded in whale bones.

The sands of the Ica desert hide more than the bones of dead fish, however. Before the arrival of the Spanish, local cultures used the desert as a sacred burial ground. Unfortunately, grave-robbing is still something of a local industry. Those relics that have survived the rampant scavenging can be viewed in the regional museum in Ica.

The desert surface is also conducive to a number of active adventures, equally as interesting. Among these sand-sports, sandboarding is one of the most popular. As the name implies, it involves sliding down a sandy dune on a sort of surfboard. You can also tear through the desert on dune buggies, mountain bikes or four-wheelers: you can rent them (and guides) in the nearby town of Ica. Most travelers stay at the Huacachina Oasis, a speck of green in the gray desert. There is a small lake there, surrounded by numerous hotels and tour operators.

Beyond its bones, burial grounds, and sandboards, the Ica desert still holds at least one mystery: the Ica stones. According to local legend, a farmer discovered a cave full of more than 15,000 stones with designs etched into them after a heavy rain. He was busted for selling them to tourists, and then sold his collection to Dr. Javier Cabrera, who maintains a private museum of the stones in Ica. The designs show many different scenes, such as medical procedures including heart and brain surgery, as well as humans hunting dinosaurs. Most scientists believe the Ica stones to be a total hoax, but the curious may find the museum to be well be worth a visit. Either they're a legitimate historical find, or they're evidence of how much work people will put into creating and propagating a profitable scam. Questionable authenticity aside, the stones are intriguing and make for an interesting excursion.

Fortunately for swimmers and surfers, the last Carcharodon Megalodon went to shark heaven about 1.2 million years ago (although there are those who say there could still be some lurking in secret corners of the world's deepest seas). If you want to see one, you'll have to go to Ica, and don't forget your sandboard!

---

**ICA DESERT TRAVEL TIPS:**

When heading out in the desert, make sure you hire an experienced guide that not only has a proven track record in the area, but is knowledgeable about paleontology. Make sure you pack along a sun hat, sunscreen, at least a gallon of water per person, per day, extra tires (sharp rocks are prone to puncturing even strong tires), and cotton clothing.

---

## LATIN AMERICAN MYSTERIES # 9: THE ICA STONES: REAL OR HOAX?

Ica, Peru: 1966-Present

In the dusty Peruvian desert town of Ica, Dr. Javier Cabrera runs a museum housing his personal collection of over 10,000 stones carved with intricate, fascinating designs: he insists the stones are genuine evidence of an advanced ancient culture. Some of the stones—which he says are hundreds of years old—show scenes that would be considered impossible, such as men hunting dinosaurs and brain and heart surgery. Unfortunately, he is not backed up in his claim: other than the stones, there is no other evidence—such as ruins or ancient burial grounds—of the alleged people who carved the stones.

It is difficult to get to the bottom of the mystery: it is not possible to date the stones or the designs etched upon them. According to local legend, after a heavy rain a farmer discovered a cave full of more than 15,000 stones with designs etched into them. The man started selling the stones to tourists and to Dr. Cabrera, but was eventually arrested and charged under a Peruvian law which prohibits the selling of ancient cultural artifacts. Under threat of prison, he confessed to carving them, but later retracted his confession, and has been flip-flopping ever since. The original "cave" where the stones were found has never been located. One piece of evidence supporting the theory that the stones are authentic is the sheer volume of them: some estimate that it would take one man over forty years, working every day, to carve all the stones in Dr. Cabrera's collection.

Most scientists believe the Ica stones to be a total hoax, but the curious museum may well be worth a visit. Dr. Cabrera and his family have always maintained that the stones are genuine, and no one expects this mystery to be cleared up any time soon. The Ica stones are evidence either way: either of an ancient culture or of how far people will go to perpetuate a profitable scam.

# SANDBOARDING AROUND ICA

## By Claire den Hoedt, Rotterdam, The Netherlands

A curvaceous, tan valley and high mounds of wavy desert sand stretches out for miles with little else near, while soft sunlight casts shadows against the real, but seemingly unreal dunes. A desert has never been so pretty.

Claire den Hoedt originally hails from Rotterdam in the Netherlands. On her travels she wouldn't leave without her backpack, " ... well, it's practical, isn't it!" The craziest place that she has ever visited is Pisco in Peru, and her most bizarre cultural experience was staying on one of the islands in Lake Titicaca, with a family who were quite poor, but who seemed to live a happy life. She longs to travel to Patagonia, however, her next trip will not be so far flung. She will be traveling to Sardinia, Italy.

Just five kilometers (three miles) outside of Ica, Peru, in a small town called Huacachina are some unique sand dunes. Not only are they an amazing landscape to witness, they beckon to some of the most extreme adventure-seekers out there: sand boarders. These hills taunt sand boarders with their smooth slopes and unruly enormity, calling on them to grab board and hit the sand.

I didn't really know what sand boarding was when I first arrived in Ica, nor did I know that it was possible to board, which is just like snowboarding, on sand. Testing my limits on my South American journey, I declared a "why not" and signed up at one of the several tour operators in Huacachina.

Off we went in a sand buggy into the dunes, racing with high speed as we went up and over, and up and over the hilly dunes. Several times we stopped on top of a dune, with wind whipping us in the face as we grabbed a board and just like snowboarding, positioned our feet in and kicked–off, gliding across the sand as the speed suddenly increased, our hair flapped in the wind and we experienced the thrill of sand boarding.

A few people on my tour had no snowboard experience, and those who were too nervous to try standing up chose to belly board, also a common and fun way to sail down the dunes. I belly boarded once and found it to be exciting and funny as you flew down the hills very fast and had to break by putting your feet in the sand. The only real issue I had with belly boarding is that I laughed while going down, making me eat some soft, grainy sand.

Not only did I learn to sand board, but with dunes as high as 100 meters, (325 feet) I came to understand that sand boarding is a popular sport in this region of Peru, hosting a yearly international sand boarding competition in Cerro Blanco, a enormous dune 14 km (eight miles) north of Nasca.

From Ica, take the bus from Plaza de Armas to Huacachina. Most hotels in Huacachina have sand boards for rent. If you're in Ica, don't miss out on sand boarding. There are few places in the world to do it and it is certainly a thrill.

The Ica Desert. Photo by Maximilian Hirschfeld.

### SANDBOARDING TIPS:

For those who have already tried snowboarding, sandboarding should be fairly straightforward.

For beginners, start with smaller dunes first and get some practise before moving onto bigger and steeper dunes.

Wear a snowboarding helmet to protect your head.

Rocks can damage the board, and it is not recommended to sandboard on areas that are grassy, because this can damage the environment by destroying the grass, and thus damaging the dune.

Take the same route up the dune each time, treading in the footprints of others where the sand is more compacted.

# NASCA LINES

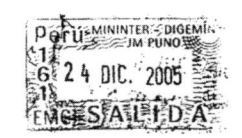

### By Dr. Crit Minster, Rochester, New York, U.S.A.

Four hundred and forty kilometers (275 miles) south of the Peruvian capital of Lima, an inhospitable desert is home to a spider, a monkey, a pelican, three hummingbirds, a whale, a dog … and an astronaut.

Ages ago, a mysterious culture etched more than 300 figures and shapes into the barren desert rock outside of the present-day town of Nasca, Peru. No one knows for certain why they did it. The culture that created them vanished into the dusty desert winds, and for centuries the drawings waited alone in the ageless wasteland. These mysterious designs weren't discovered until the 1920s when they were spotted by pilots of the first commercial flights in the region. Those who ventured into the desert to investigate dubbed them "The Nasca Lines."

From ground level, the intricate designs appear to be nothing more than a confused jumble of shallow ruts in the sand and rock of the parched desert. When viewed from the air or an observation tower, however, the shape of these drawings—known as "geoglyphs" in the scientific community—becomes apparent. Some of them are massive: one of the hummingbirds measures 123 meters (400 feet) in length. Another line is 65 kilometers long. Some of the figures are geometric, such as trapezoids and triangles, and others represent animals. The "astronaut" is a bulb-headed humanoid with round eyes. Some say the figure represents an alien; others say he's a man in a space suit. Interestingly, two of the designs, the whale and the monkey, represent animals that are not found anywhere near the lines. Such figures are considered evidence that the makers of the lines were traders or pilgrims … or space aliens.

Like their origins, the exact age of the lines is still unknown. The Nasca culture did live in the region for several centuries (roughly from the first to the ninth century A.D.), but there is no empirical way to date the lines. The recently discovered city of Cahuachi, located nearby, may yet reveal some answers.

Besides dispelling the cloud of mystery surrounding their age and origins, preserving the Nasca Lines is one of the biggest challenges facing Peru today. The elements in the desert are harsh and the lines are naturally eroding. Human intervention, however, is proving much more destructive: advertisers and political campaigns have carved messages in the rock between the designs, and new copper and gold mines are slowly scraping away the remaining integrity of the lines. At nearby Cahuachi archaeological site, grave robbers threaten to loot the recently discovered tombs. The area has recently been designated a UNESCO World Heritage Site, which should help in preservation efforts.

If these efforts fail, perhaps the aliens will come back and fix their landing pad.

---

NASCA LINES TRAVEL TIPS:
The best way to see the lines is from a small plane. These depart from nearby Nasca, and also from the town of Ica, which is slightly farther away. Costs of a fly-over vary, but are not too expensive. A cheaper but less satisfying option is to take the highway into the desert (by bus or taxi) and visit the three-story observation tower, which affords decent views of three of the lines. Take your motion sickness pills before taking the flight: the small planes swoop, bank, and do everything but turn upside-down in order to give visitors good views of the lines! There are a variety of hotels in Ica and Nasca, including some nice ones at the Huacachina Oasis.

---

## LATIN AMERICAN MYSTERIES # 4: THE NASCA LINES

Nasca desert, Peru: time unknown

Etched into the ageless desert outside of the Peruvian town of Nasca, you will find about 300 drawings and designs carved into the ageless desert floor. There are dozens of recognizable drawings, including hummingbirds, condors, a spider, a monkey and a whale. The drawings are generally attributed to the Nasca culture that lived in the area centuries ago, but even this is not known with certainty. What the drawings mean has been one of the biggest mysteries in Latin America since their discovery in the 1920s.

Despite an abundance of theories, the Nasca Lines remain a mystery today. Maria Reiche, a German mathematician who dedicated her life to studying the drawings, believed that they reflected constellations of stars in the night sky. Although her theory is plausible, subsequent studies indicate no astrological evidence to support it. Erich Von Daniken, a Swiss writer, suggested in his book *Chariots of the Gods* that the Nasca lines were a landing strip for extraterrestrials. Others believe that the lines were intended to serve as walking or running paths: priests or participants would follow the trails during elaborate ceremonies aimed at pacifying the Gods. Still others argue that the lines mark the location of important aquifers and underground rivers.

Unless the extraterrestrials show up and land in their spaceship, the Nasca Lines are likely to remain a mystery for a while, although recent discoveries at nearby archaeological sites may shed some light on this ancient mystery.

# CEMENTERIO DE CHAUCHILLA

## By Albert Garcia, Fullerton, California, U.S.A.

The long, lonely dirt road that steers off the highway from Nasca to Chauchilla heads straight into low hills, crossing a vacant, almost lunar landscape. It is difficult to imagine even an isolated homestead thriving amidst this inhospitable desolation.

At the road's end, footpaths guide you to several open pits, shielded from the sun by raised poles and wood-slat canopies. Inside lie some artifacts of the culture that flourished here from 200 B.C. to 800 A.D., including ceramics, textiles and stone tools alongside mummified remains.

Nearby, the mysterious Nasca lines, scratched across southern Peru by an ancient civilization, have left the world guessing as to their meaning and purpose. There is, however, no mystery regarding how this mysterious ancient culture cared for its dead.

Located about 30 kilometers (19 miles) from the small town of Nasca, the *Cementario de Chauchilla*, or Chauchilla Cemetery, features bones, textiles, hair, and even some skin that were preserved in underground vaults constructed of mud bricks and buried for over 1000 years. The Nasca people wrapped their deceased in finely embroidered cotton cloths before coating them with a resin and placing them into tombs in crouched positions. Grave offerings were stored beside them, possibly in anticipation of their protection in the next realm. The resin and textiles kept out insects and bacteria, slowing the decay process while the hot climate and arid soil created an environment suitable for natural mummification.

Today, centuries later, bleached white skeletons, some still with dreadlocks, crouch upright on the floors of their ancient tombs, favoring visitors with creepy grins. The few sightseers stand by silently, mystified. The mummies stare back, appearing just as amazed at the passage of time that has brought them together with us.

Although the arid desert protected the remains from time and decay, it could not safeguard them from *huaqueros*, or grave robbers. Over the years, poles were stuck into the ground to locate the tombs and mummies were ripped apart in the search for anything thought to be of value. Nothing exemplified this tragedy more than a simple gaze across the ground where, until 1997, in a scene more fitting for forensic anthropologists than tourists, broken pot shards and litter, human rib bones, shoulder blades and skull fragments lay scattered across the grayish-brown desert floor. Today, the burial sites have been reconstructed although many "scars" remain in the sand.

A visit to the Chauchilla cemetery takes about three hours, including travel time from Nasca. The tour can be purchased as part of a package with flights over the Nasca lines, which can save a few dollars. The price includes a side trip to local artisan workshops, where one can observe traditional methods of gold extraction and ceramic firing and, of course, buy souvenirs.

In a morbidly interesting way, Chauchilla presents a view of culture that cannot easily be forgotten.

Mummies, Chauchilla. Photo by Albert Garcia.

*"If you are killed because you are a writer, that's the maximum expression of respect."*
-Mario Vargas Llosa, Peruvian Writer (1936-)

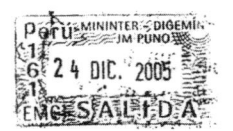

# CORDILLERA VILCABAMBA

## By Martin Li, London, England

Northwest of the timeless Inca city of Machu Picchu lies Vilcabamba—a wild, densely forested region of cold uplands and hot sub-tropical valleys, bordered by the Urubamba and Apurimac rivers. Following the Spanish conquest, most of the surviving Inca royalty fled into the steep, overgrown Vilcabamba mountains, where they held out for several decades and made their final refuge.

The overgrown route through Vilcabamba is dominated by high peaks as it climbs from the cloud forest below Machu Picchu and crosses the spine of the range before descending into another steep canyon. The going is heavy and difficult, and maps of the region are often unreliable. Getting lost in the jungle is a real possibility if traveling without knowledgeable local guides.

After Machu Picchu, the superbly atmospheric yet seldom-visited Choquequirao is one of the best-preserved major Inca ruins, perched on a wooded spur high above the Apurimac. The site isn't mentioned in any chronicles of the Conquest and its precise purpose remains unknown, which adds to its allure. More important historically, Vilcabamba was home to the post-Conquest Inca capitals. The ruins of Manco Inca's capital, Vitcos, occupy an elevated position at Rosaspata.

In a nearby valley stands the magnificent White Rock, a huge outcrop of white granite, 52 ft. (15.8 m) long, 30 ft. (9.1 m) wide and 25 ft. (7.6 m) high, covered in complex carvings, flights of steps, seats and square projections. Each year on June 24th, locals re-enact the vibrant Inti Raymi festival (the most important pre-Hispanic festival, paying homage to the sun). This is a much better alternative to the tourist-packed festival at Cusco.

Deeper in the jungle, Espiritu Pampa hides the ruins of many Inca buildings, temples and palaces, almost completely covered with vines and lush tropical growth, all beneath a towering canopy of trees. This is believed to have been the site of Vilcabamba the Old, the Incas' final stronghold. The poignant last capital of the Incas marks the end of the magnificent, but short-lived, Inca empire. It was here in 1572 that Tupac Amaru, the last Inca emperor, was captured by the Spanish, hauled off to Cusco and executed, thus bringing to an end the Inca dynasty.

### TUPAC AMARU FACTOIDS:

The last indigenous leader of the Inca, Amaru was a representation of resistance against Spanish invasion. He set up a permanent, peaceful settlement for his people in the Vilcabamba province following the conquest of Cusco. In 1572, the Spanish overtook the Vilcabamba empire, captured Amaru, brought him to Cusco, and executed the man who would forever be remembered for determination in the face of opposition.

# EL CAJÓN

### By Mariana Cotlear

As far as beautiful instruments go, the *cajón* is not much to look at. The name means, literally, "box" in Spanish, and that's basically what it is. But don't be fooled by this percussive instrument's simple six-sided shape: when touched by the hands of a well-trained musician, this box produces an impressive array of beautiful sounds.

Thought to have been adapted in Peru by African slaves who used shipping crates as a replacement for their traditional drums, the cajón now plays an important role in Peru's *musica criolla*. The *cajonista* sits atop the cajón and hits, slaps and taps along its surface to produce a beat, which resonates through the box's opening in the back. It is truly amazing to witness the dizzying pace with which an adept cajonista can use his fingertips and palms to create powerful music.

Globalization has brought the cajón into a surprising array of musical genres. Spanish flamenco musician Paco de Lucía popularized its use in modern flamenco. It has also been spotted on tour with prominent American pop acts, including the Dixie Chicks and Destiny's Child.

# THE INCA TRAIL

## By Jussi Ruottinen, Helsinki, Finland

Jussi Ruottinen hails from Helsinki, Finland, but currently resides in California, U.S.A. He is a photographer and is working on his degree in tourism which he will receive from Laurea Polytechnic, Finland. He aims to combine a photography, travelling and writing career in the future. He enjoys traveling around the world and spends most of his spare time aside from traveling doing fine art, stock and freelance photography.

Ruottinen wouldn't leave home without his camera gear. The craziest place he's visited is Iceland, "Because it's very different from any other places in a good way. Their culture and beliefs are very unique and the nature is spectacular and haunting." He yearns to visit northern parts of the world, including northern Europe, America and northern Asia.

Winding through the majestic Andes is the 45 kilometer (30 mile) hike known as the *Camino del Inca*; the Inca Trail. Most hikers stay at the center of Peruvian tourism in Cusco, before heading out to the trail that takes hikers up, down, inside and out of Inca history to arrive at the most breathtaking of all historical ruins: Machu Picchu.

Most hikers begin the Inca Trail at a point a few hours away from Cusco by bus, while the hike itself takes from two to four days to complete depending on where you begin and how quickly you want to move on. Right away, hikers experience the mind-blowing beauty of the Urubamba River and the breathtaking vistas of the noble Andes. The climate shifts along the hike, and there is no telling what will be around the next turn. From highland vegetation to jungle flora, any lover of plants, flowers and trees will surely find themselves in Eden. Fans of birdwatching will also enjoy distinguishing between the hundreds of species found on the trail. Not only do the natural sights captivate visitors along the way, but the smaller Inca ruins like Llaqtapata, Runkuraqay and Sayaqmarka are not to be taken for granted. The only drawback of the Inca Trail is the whiplash one can get from trying to take in everything at once!

More spiritual types will enjoy the Inca Trail as well. Behind the lingering mist that provides occasional glimpses of the surroundings, a waterfall appears next to the trail; rugged snowcapped mountains gaze down upon their guests when their cloud cover is blown and the summit of "Dead Woman's Pass" seems attainable for a minute before disappearing a moment later. Hikers are thrown into the carnival of a constantly-changing environment.

The Inca Trail is certainly not for the faint-hearted. At 4,200 meters (13,800 feet), the summit will quite literally take your breath away. Even young people in decent shape find it hard to catch their breath climbing thousands of steps in the thin Peruvian air. Overestimating one's abilities can be dangerous on this journey, but the reward at the end is definitely worth the risk.

On the morning of the fourth day, hikers reach the Sun Gate, the gateway to every hiker's dream before arriving in Peru: the mysterious ruins of Machu Picchu. Although no one truly knows what Machu Picchu was used for, many historians have taken a guess. One suggestion is that it was a gathering place for the enlightened; Machu Picchu may have been an extremely selective place for learning allowing only one percent of the Andean population knowledge of its existence. A more probable suggestion is that it may have been the last stand for the Andean people against the invading Spanish. Since a high percentage of female skeletons were found during excavation, it has been theorized that the Incas sent their women to Machu Picchu, hoping they would have a better chance of survival.

What is certainly known about Machu Picchu and the Inca Trail is that they were discovered by an American archeologist Hiram Bingham in 1911, though Bingham thought it was the city of Vilcabamba. While excavating Machu Picchu, Bingham noticed an overgrown path from the Sun Gate towards the Sacred Valley. It took researchers several years to complete the journey, but what they uncovered was the Camino del Inca. Nowadays the Inca Trail consists of only about 30 percent of the original path, but is a spectacular and memorable journey nonetheless.

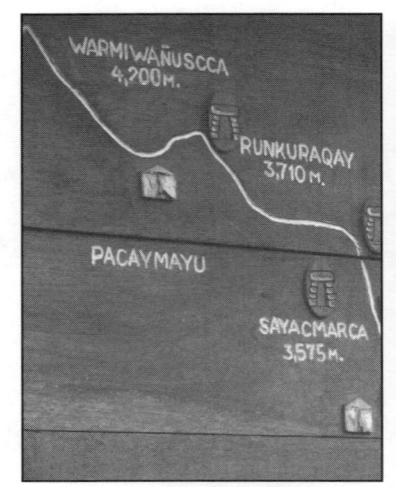

Inca Trail signpost. Photo by Michelle Hopey.

Donkey along Inca Trail. Photo by Jussi Ruottinen.

# MACHU PICCHU

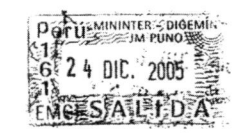

## By Dr. Crit Minster, Rochester, New York, U.S.A.

*Above all, there is the fascination of finding here and there under swaying vines, or perched on top of a beetling crag, the rugged masonry of a bygone race; and of trying to understand the bewildering romance of the ancient builders who, ages ago, sought refuge in a region which appears to have been expressly designed by nature as a sanctuary for the oppressed, a place where they might fearlessly and patiently give expression to their passion for walls of enduring beauty.*

-Hiram Bingham III

July 24, 1911. A light rain falls and the Andean rainforest is lost in a gray haze, the dazzling green of the vegetation blurred amid the thick fog. Two men and a boy climb an ancient trail through the dense trees, heavy vines and twisted roots of an ageless jungle. Off in the distance, a bird calls. One of the men turns and looks: it is obvious from his garb that he is a stranger here. The young boy leads the way, and does not pause: the birds are part of his world.

The path opens up onto a terrace where a few local families have reclaimed farm land from the eternal jungle: beneath their meager crops the stranger can see evidence of an ancient stone wall. His heart, already racing from the climb, begins to beat even faster. He is searching for the lost city of Vilcabamba, a mighty Inca fortress spoken of in the Spanish chronicles but since lost to time and the timeless jungle. He follows the boy even higher, onto a high plateau dotted with small hills.

The boy says something and the stranger waits for the other man to translate: this is the place. The boy walks to one of the hills and brushes away the accumulated dirt and vegetation of centuries to reveal intricate stonework: this is no hill, but a building, reclaimed by the forest many years before. The stranger, Hiram Bingham III, Yale archaeologist, explorer and adventurer, looks around and for the first time sees not natural hills on a plateau but a city, swallowed by the jungle and lost to time. Excitedly, he asks his translator again what the locals call this place.

"Machu Picchu," the man replies. "It means 'Old Mountain.'"

You've seen the photographs.

You've jealously listened to your friends tell you about their trips there.

You've seen the *National Geographic* special.

That's all well and good, but understand one thing: there is no photograph, slide show or story that can capture the sensation you feel when you first cast your gaze upon Machu Picchu. Not even the National Geographic Channel can do it justice.

As dawn breaks on the summer solstice, the mountain peaks that surround Machu Picchu are the first to light up in the pure sunlight of the breaking day. Slowly creeping down into the valleys, the light hits the lost city of the Incas, passing precisely through one of the windows of the Temple of the Sun and illuminating the ceremonial area. Six months later, on the winter solstice, the sunlight will pass directly through a different window. Years ago, Inca stonemasons and holy men designed the space of the windows down to the centimeter.

The Sacred Plaza, which includes the Temple of the Sun, is part of a larger holy area, which many experts believe was the ceremonial and spiritual heart of the city. Uphill from the Sacred Plaza sits an enormous stone structure which has a shape roughly similar to Huayna Picchu, a nearby peak with a rounded top which is easily visible from the ruins on a clear day. The name of the stone is *Intihuatana*, which means "hitching post of the sun." It is believed that the most important ceremonies of all—the ones meant to ensure the continued blessing of the Sun—took place there. Many Inca cities and temples contained such a structure, according to records, but these were destroyed by the Spanish who wished to extirpate Inca idolatry.

The Condor Temple was constructed to resemble, of course, a condor in flight. Many experts believe that the Condor Temple was used as a sort of religious dungeon: prisoners may have been held and tortured there. Funerary Rock, which was supposedly where members of the Inca royal family were mummified, sits uphill from the rest of the complex and is one of the best places for a photo.

Hiram Bingham III came and left, taking thousands of priceless artifacts with him (it's still a sore subject in Peru: ask anyone), but he could not take the timeless soul of the majestic city. Today, many believe that Machu Picchu is a central point of natural energies as old as the earth itself. You may choose to believe them or not: but do not pass judgment until you visit it for yourself and open your mind to the soothing harmony of the Lost City of the Incas.

---

**MACHU PICCHU TRAVEL TIP:**

Don't let the pesky sandflies at this amazing place ruin your experience: don't forget strong insect repellent!

---

Machu Picchu. Photo by Maximilian Hirschfeld.

# AGUAS CALIENTES

By Bonnie L. Jernigan, Duxbury, Massachusetts, U.S.A.

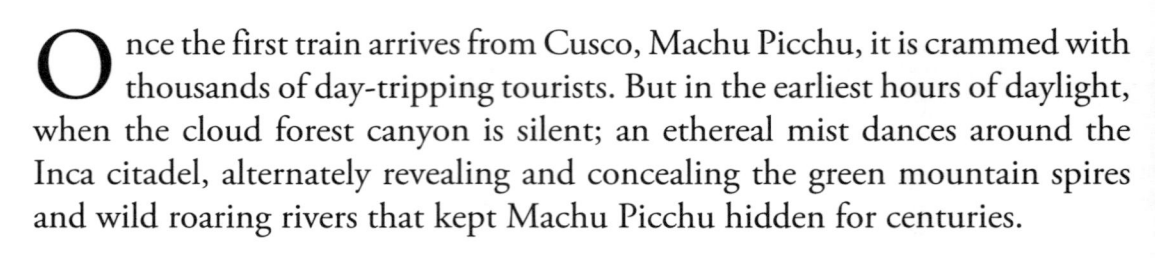

Once the first train arrives from Cusco, Machu Picchu, it is crammed with thousands of day-tripping tourists. But in the earliest hours of daylight, when the cloud forest canyon is silent; an ethereal mist dances around the Inca citadel, alternately revealing and concealing the green mountain spires and wild roaring rivers that kept Machu Picchu hidden for centuries.

Bonnie Jernigan lives south of Boston in a small Massachusetts coastal town. After earning a theater degree from the University of North Carolina at Greensboro, she worked in the Blue Ridge Mountains as a magician's assistant, being cut into three pieces six times a day. Next, she was stage manager for the North Carolina Opera touring program, and between shows began to wander off the beaten track, discovering small town characters and attractions and writing stories about them. Upon moving to Cape Cod 25 years ago, and becoming a mother, she was hired by a local newspaper as a features writer and editor. Her articles have appeared in local, regional and national publications.

Connections made through her family's involvement with student exchange organizations have led Jernigan to travel in South America several times in the past few years, and she can't wait to go back again.

To witness this mystical performance of vapors and haze, and to experience a relatively uncrowded Machu Picchu—without committing to arduous days of an Inca trail trek—arrive the day before. Spend the night sleeping under a luxurious alpaca blanket at Machu Picchu Pueblo Hotel, a boutique hotel in Aguas Calientes, the village at the foot of the mountain that is home to the great lost city of the Inca.

Whitewashed guest cottages with working fireplaces nestle into terraced hills, surrounded by waterfalls and nature trails. The intent, according to the management, is to re-create the ambience of a royal Inca retreat, with spa services and a first-class restaurant, decorated in local antiques and pre-Columbian artifacts.

Rising just before dawn, spend an hour or two climbing a steep footpath, enjoying the scent of orchids and the company of butterflies. If you don't want to hike, hop on the morning's first bus, and ride the zig-zag road to the top. Upon reaching Machu Picchu, you should have plenty of time to explore the ruins and even walk to the Sun Gate before the train whistle sounds in the village below. Let that be your signal to leave before the throngs of tourists arrive on the next bus.

Head back down and have lunch while you listen to the Andean ensemble playing in the Pueblo Café, which overlooks the chocolate-brown waters of the roaring Urubamba River. Then wind your way up the cobbled streets of Aguas Calientes, and find the namesake hot springs. Soak there, surrounded by craggy ledges covered with drooping bromeliads. People speaking in a cacophony of languages, familiar and unfamiliar, create a sort of international soup, and you can be part of it.

The village is colorful and worth experiencing, with shops and hostels catering to tourists and backpackers who flock to Machu Picchu from all over the world, so the hotel offers a welcome haven from the hustle and the hordes.

Indulge in a massage or visit the sauna built of native bamboo and scented with local eucalyptus. Take a walk with a naturalist guide, who will lead you past a working tea plantation, along forest walkways leading to ancient petroglyphs.

With an emphasis on eco-tourism, the property includes a sanctuary which is home to 16 species of wild hummingbirds, as well the world's largest collection of native orchid species in their natural habitats.

There is a tangible connection with the culture that existed here before Machu Picchu became a destination that would attract the world to this remote Andean outpost, where every morning, before the multitude ascends, clouds still waltz around stiletto peaks, in an age-old dance.

## HUAYNA PICCHU CLIMB

By Will Gray

Machu Picchu may be spectacular to explore, but climbing Huayna Picchu, the towering rock that watches over the ancient Inca site, will really blow your mind.

Standing at the base, the top looks very high and far away, and it is. There are steps all the way up, however, and after signing in at the bottom it is a grueling but thrilling climb of between 40 minutes and one-and-a-half hours, depending on your level of fitness and finesse on the steep, stony ascent.

The path leads up and up, offering views below (if you dare look down). You will reach a tight cave through which you must squeeze in order to reach the top. Once you find your footing and look up, you'll be rewarded with a jaw-droppingly awesome view, a 360-degree panorama of forested mountains and the Inca temples of Machu Picchu. Not for the faint-hearted, it is like standing at the top of the Empire State Building, only without the windows, railings, or coin-operated binoculars.

After such a nerve-wracking climb it is good to spend plenty of time on top, relaxing and taking in the view before attempting the head-spinning descent. Plenty of heart-in-mouth moments accompany the return journey down the precarious steps buffeted only by the sheer drop-off below. Once back at the bottom, the café by the site entrance allows you a well deserved rest, and plenty of time to ponder your Huayna Picchu experience.

# WILLKA T'IKA ECO-LODGE

By Michele Gentille, Brooklyn, New York, U.S.A.

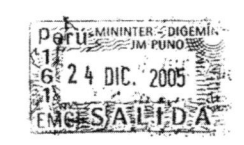

The Sacred Valley in Peru has an unmistakable aura of mysticism about it. It makes sense that some clever person would build an idyllic retreat there, just a short drive from the astounding mountain city of Machu Picchu.

Willka T'ika, which means "sacred flower" in the Quechua language, is an eco-lodge. The property is located at the foot of the Andes and has seven beautiful gardens containing flowers, medicinal plants, organic vegetables, fruit and grains.

Carol Cumes is originally from South Africa and studied yoga, shamanism, flower essences and meditation in the 1970s. She started building the Willka T'ika Garden Guest House in Urubamba village after moving to Peru in 1995. She currently also heads a non-profit organization that raises money for new schools and libraries in nearby, isolated mountain areas. The lodge itself is staffed by locals, all Quechua-speaking neighbors, who grew up within a five-mile radius of it, and who seem to be as equally versed in the culinary arts as in medicinal herbology and local culture.

Rooms are spacious and beautifully decorated with garden views. On top of that, they are connected to solar water panels and have real working bathrooms—not something to be taken for granted when traveling through the South American countryside.

In the cooler months when you crawl under the comforter, a hot water bottle has toasted your sheets with warmth. When the morning sun glitters through the lush greenery at your window, all you hear are the twittering birds outside.

From early in the day you are able to help yourself to strong, blissfully organic coffee. The menu is totally vegetarian. Breakfast includes freshly baked whole wheat bread, scrambled eggs, fresh cheese, and beautiful platters of fresh fruit and avocado. Other meals feature dishes such as sweet potato soup, quinoa patties with romesco sauce, vegetable casserole and fruit cobbler. The majority of organic fruit and vegetables served are supplied by the gardens onsite. There is always hot water for tea in the main gathering room, along with a variety of teabags and a basket of fresh herbs and coca leaves. In Peru, coca leaves are considered a kind of panacea—good for altitude sickness for cleansing the blood, for use in poultices, or just as a tonic.

The grounds feature plenty of spots for quiet meditation, including an area where a 500-year-old Lucma tree thrives, "fertilized" by the large crystals placed at its base. There are also three outdoor solar-heated baths, a yoga studio, massage rooms, a crystal bed and an outdoor fire pit.

During our stay, we were treated to a prosperity ritual performed by two shamans, who also brought handmade goods to sell. They had walked three days to reach us and stayed for three days, until we left.

Willka T'ika caters to groups of five to 30 people, some of who are there for yoga or meditation retreats, and others who are simply touring local sights. You have to arrange a stay ahead of time since it is a guest house, and functions differently than a regular hotel.

Michele Gentille believes true traveling is an important kind of rebirth, and finds it a kind of dissent that promotes growth rather than conflict. She is a freelance writer based in Brooklyn, New York, focusing on food and the people, art and culture, and inevitably travel, as these subjects are so entwined. She graduated from L'Ecole de Cuisine in France in the early 1990s and has been doing something in the culinary arts ever since—writing, cooking, consulting, photographing, or missing it.

Gentille's dream destination is Llhasa, by donkey and foot, but will soon be found in Barcelona, Spain, sipping Priorat, tasting tapas, and practicing yoga.

## GET YOUR MOJO ON

By Michelle Hopey

Probably one of the most refreshing Latin cocktails around, or one of the most refreshing cocktails anywhere for that fact, Mojitos are cool, relaxing and full of spunk, just like Latin America itself. So, whether you're sitting by the beach, pool, cabana or dance floor, order up a Mojito and tap into your inner mojo.

Ingredients:
4 oz. clear white rum
3 oz. clear fresh lemon or lime juice
3 sprigs of fresh mint
2 teaspoons sugar syrup
2 tablespoons of water
Dash of soda water

To prepare:
Heat sugar and water together until melted. Muddle mint sprigs with sugar syrup and lemon juice. Add rum and top with soda water. Garnish with spring of mint leaves and lime slice. Serve with a straw.

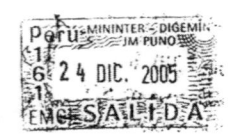

# OLLANTAYTAMBO

## By Martin Li, London, England

Nestled deep in the Sacred Valley, Ollantaytambo (or "Ollanta" as the settlement is often called) is a wonderfully atmospheric cluster of old stone houses set along very narrow cobbled streets and dominated by soaring mountains on all sides. Ollanta is the last surviving Inca settlement, boasting some of the only Inca houses still lived in today. Many houses retain their solid walls with characteristic interior niches and foundations of huge interlocking blocks, supported by massive cornerstones. More incredibly still, water continues to babble along an original Inca water channel lining one of the streets. Residents still draw water from the channel for washing and cleaning, although no longer for drinking.

A statue of the Inca warrior Ollantay dominates the main square, which remains surprisingly tranquil despite the comings and goings of tourists and their noisy buses. Ancient yellow and cream painted buildings cluster around the square. One of these is the tiny church beside which is a small market with several thatched stalls selling a variety of food and snacks. Moto taxis (covered, motorised tricycles—like tuk-tuks) provide local transport between and around Urubamba and Ollanta, although even these struggle to navigate Ollanta's narrow streets.

Perched on top of a steep mountainside above Ollanta are the famous fortified Inca ruins, protected by a flight of deep defensive terraces that contour beautifully up the near-vertical terrain. This was the site of an important battle during the great rebellion of 1537, when Manco Inca tried desperately to liberate Peru from the Spanish Conquistadores. There are some 15 terraces, each rising about three metres high. Gazing up from the bottom, the terraces meld into one huge barrier of daunting stonework.

Staring up at this intimidating masterpiece of Inca engineering, it is easy to imagine the terror the Spanish must have felt as they tried to storm the fortress. Discovering the Conquistadores in the act of a surprise attack, native soldiers hurled a barrage of missiles down on them while archers shot arrows from the terraces, before Manco unleashed his final weapon: diverting the river and flooding the plain, forcing the Spanish horsemen to retreat.

An afternoon visit to the ruins is perhaps best capped off with a tasting of the local drink: chicha. As in the rest of the Sacred Valley, many houses in Ollanta display red (sometimes blue) bags on the end of sticks hoisted over their doorways, indicating that the residents sell the maize beer that was once the royal drink of the Incas. A trip to one of these chicha houses makes for a fascinating encounter with the locals and an evening you're not soon to forget—depending, of course, on how much you drink!

---

**OLLANTAYTAMBO TRAVEL TIP:**

Tourist trains stop at Ollantaytambo on the way to and from Machu Picchu, although they are expensive and can get packed. A cheaper alternative is to travel by local bus. After the hustle and bustle of Cusco, Ollantaytambo provides an excellent and relaxed base from which to explore the Sacred Valley, either before or after a visit to Machu Picchu.

---

Ollantaytambo. Photo by Martin Li.

# CHOQUEQUIRAU

By Julie Koppel, Westlake Village, California, U.S.A.

Although a bit tricky to access, your efforts are well rewarded upon reaching Choquequirau, a remote ridge-top Inca site. Currently, the ruins can only be reached on foot, but this will soon be changing as UNESCO is funding tourist authorities to make this site more accessible to the masses.

It is best to go now before the trek becomes strewn with gringo garbage and straggling walkers, breaking the delicate silence. The trail to Choquequirau can be reached from the town of Cachora. To get to Cachora, you can take a bus from Cusco heading towards Abancay, but make sure to ask the driver to let you out at the turn-off for Cachora. It is about an hour's walk to the beginning of the trail from Cachora; just ask any of the friendly locals who will more than gladly show you the way.

The trail is very well laid out and it is not necessary to have a guide, but it is highly recommended because the trail is steeper and more challenging than those which most Westerners, even experienced trekkers, have come across.

The trail starts out flat for about two hours, before a three-hour descent to the Río Apurímac. It is possible to camp alongside the river, but there is a camp site approximately 30 minutes prior to the river, and this spot is better for its solitude and lack of mosquitoes. Besides, it is not every night that you can fall asleep on an Inca terrace, under a blanket of shooting stars and the Southern Cross.

Once across the bridge over the Río Apurímac, the precipitous ascent begins. Despite there being switchbacks built into the trail, it feels as if you are climbing straight up the side of the mountain, with Choquequirau always looming in the distant clouds.

After about three-hours, you reach the "town" of Santa Rosa. It consists of a small shack (where it is possible to purchase Inca Kola) and a small religious monument, which makes for a great place to seek shade from the burning sun and rest your weary legs. You can also find a lot of bamboo sticks in the area to aid your climb.

Another three hours of ascent brings you to a flat part of trail, where you can find open fields of grass along the cliff's edge. To reach the Inca site, you continue down the rolling trail for about an hour and a half. There is a viewing area about an hour before the site, where you can take in the full vision of the condor-shaped Choquequirau and surrounding agricultural terraces.

It is an enthralling place to sit and enjoy the greatest aspect of the area's beauty, its secrecy and solitude. Alone on the path, this magical place is entirely your own, minus the few Peruvian workers you pass along the way. Without seeing any other gringos, you finally have the opportunity to experience the nature of Peru as it is meant to be experienced: in quiet contemplation.

From here, you can carry on down the path to explore inside the ruins, which are bigger than Machu Picchu.

It is about a four or five hour climb back up the mountain, and again Make sure to take along plenty of water from the tap at the camping site. Once you reach the top of the switchbacks at the end of the ascent there is a much-needed shelter, where you can seek cover from the wind and collapse into a heap of exhaustion and gratitude at having had the privilege of partaking in such a mystical and unforgettable experience.

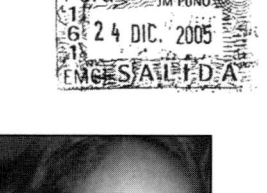

Originally from Westlake Village, California, Julie Koppel graduated from Washington University in St. Louis with a B.A. in Psychology. Following graduation, she spent a year working and traveling throughout Australia, Thailand, and Cambodia, as well as volunteering at a conservation sanctuary in New Zealand. Upon returning to the U.S., she served as a member of AmeriCorps NCCC (National Civilian Community Corps).

She has spent the last year in Peru constructing cleaner-burning stoves in the Sacred Valley, in South Africa interning with an environmental justice group, and in the Benin Republic in West Africa, at a refugee camp for Ogoni (Nigerian) refugees, starting up an educational project. Koppel is currently a frontliner for Greenpeace and working on a master's degree in Socio-cultural Anthropology at American University. Her most bizarre cultural experience abroad was had in West Africa; she was placed on her knees in the dirt and doused in the oil and water of Christ in front of 850 refugees (she's Jewish). That, and trying to explain to people in Mississippi that vegetarians don't eat bacon.

# VOLUNTEER IN PERU By Michelle Hopey

The perfect way to get off the gringo trail, take a rest from the hustle of travel and do something outside yourself while still feeling as if you are experiencing a new culture, is volunteering. Maybe you want to pitch-in at a health organization, cook-up food at an orphanage, teach pre-natal care to indigenous women, plant crops, clean-up a river, or help protect the rights of local Inca Trail porters—there are a thousand ways to volunteer in Peru, and in Latin America as a whole.

But there are many misunderstandings about volunteering in Latin America. Do an internet search for "volunteering in Peru," and you'll come up with many opportunities. Many will say the shortest term possible is one week, if that. Others will say it costs $1500 for 10 days without lodging. If you're looking for short-term volunteer work, you can find it and if you can't spend money to help others, than don't break the bank—you don't have to. One-day or a few hours can make a child laugh or lift an ill-man's spirit. Often, the small local places that need your help aren't advertising on the internet or with agencies, so look for local, on-the-spot volunteer opportunities once you are in the country.

Local Spanish schools are often a gold mine for finding volunteer options. And in tourist heavy cities like Cusco, Arequipa, Lima and Máncora you'll find plenty of small shops offering-up volunteer possibilities. But its good to note that while these are all great ways to find short-term positions, longer term ones typically take time, hence the extra costs, and going through a reputable organization is recommended. A great place to start your search is www.volunteerabroad.com.

# CUSCO

### By Dr. Crit Minster, Rochester, New York, U.S.A.

Illiterate, ill-tempered, cruel and ruthless, Francisco Pizarro was considered one mean SOB even by the other Spanish conquistadores that he led up the misty slopes of the western Andes in 1532. Pizarro and his 180 soldiers were following tales of a city in the mountains, high in the clouds, where there would be gold beyond their wildest dreams. A city that was home to an empire that stretched from Colombia to Chile, from parts of Brazil to the Pacific. They were searching for the fabled city of Cusco.

Pizarro and his men found and captured the city, the great stone capital of the mighty Inca Empire. By then they had already overtaken the city of Cajamarca, where they captured, ransomed and executed Atahuallpa, the last of the Inca emperors, and without a leader, Cusco fell without a great struggle. Although Pizarro did not last very long—he was assassinated by his own men, hacked down in a Lima street in 1541—the city became part of the Kingdom of Spain.

The new lords of the city did what they could to erase all memories of the old Inca Empire. They built cathedrals on top of temples and moved into the homes of the ruling Inca class. But they soon found that they could not destroy the stone walls constructed over the centuries by Inca masons: they were far too strong and well-built. Even gunpowder could not knock them down.

That's good news for the modern visitor to this fascinating city. You can walk down the streets of Cusco and still see mind-boggling Inca stonework, which shows no sign of aging even after more than 500 years of exposure. Some of the stones weigh several tons, and the most amazing part is that they are fitted together without any sort of mortar or concrete. Many of the old churches, colonial homes and convents show a distinct mixture of Inca and Spanish styles: Cusco is the best place in the world to see this combination.

There's more to Cusco than old stone walls. The city is a modern mecca of tourism: if you're going to visit, plan on spending at least a week. The can't-miss site, of course, is nearby Machu Picchu, the lost mountain city of the Incas and one of the most impressive sites in all of South America. There are two ways to get there: by train or on foot, via the Inca Trail. Hiking the Inca Trail can take anywhere from one to four days, depending on where you get off the train from Cusco to Machu Picchu. The hike is grueling – Cusco lies at an altitude of 11,500 feet—but well worth it if you're in good shape. The train can get you to the ruins and back the same day and leave a couple of hours in between for a visit.

The region around Cusco is known as the Sacred Valley, and includes several ruin sites including Sachsaywaman, Pisac and Ollantaytambo. The best way to visit these sites is to buy a special pass that will let you into all of them: any travel agency can sell you the pass. Hikes and ruins not your thing? Cusco has top-notch hotels, restaurants, good nightlife and some great shopping—silver jewelry, intricate paintings, hand-woven rugs and of course, the grape liquor, Pisco. The museums are excellent: some of the best ones are converted old convents and monasteries. You can visit the small towns around Cusco, and even take a hot-air balloon ride.

Pizarro and his men turned to dust centuries ago, and some of them are buried in this city in the clouds. Cusco is still a mythical city, drawing visitors from all over the world. They don't come for gold and silver, however: they come for the wealth that comes from experiencing a magical city deep in the Peruvian Andes.

www.vivatravelguides.com/103419

## STATUE TO STATUE IN CUSCO

### By Will Gray, Kettering, England

A trip between the two towering statues that look down on the city from opposite hills is one of the best ways to take in the many sites that Cusco has to offer.

The walk begins at the Cristo Blanco, which can be reached by taxi and a short walk, or a longer but nevertheless interesting stroll through cobbled streets, up the hill, past the Sacsayhuamán Inca ruins. The ascent to the statue from the road is a tough one up steps and then a steep trekking path, but what a view you get at the end! At this height, even the clumsy and wing-less feel like they're gracefully soaring above the cloud patterns on the city below.

The path back down follows more cobbled streets that seem straight out of Yorkshire, England, before reaching San Blas square, a vibrant haven of Peruvian artesanía. The area is full of art shops, where it is possible to buy popular bright blue, modern art paintings, as well as other souvenir stalls selling everything from t-shirts to embroidered goods. Scouting for art aside, an afternoon can be spent climbing the never-ending streets that zigzag amongst the colonial buildings in this picturesque area of Cusco.

You will pass through several other small and pretty squares en-route to the main square, the Plaza de Armas, where a break for lunch provides a welcome rest from the long stroll. After a look at the cathedral and the churches of Jesus Maria and El Triunfo, around the square, it is off again. The next stop is a craft market that backs onto one of the city's many old Inca walls.

From here it is easy to find the main road where you will find an occasionally working fountain and a towering monument to the ninth Inca, perched between the two lanes of the thoroughfare itself. This is home to many of the stray dogs that roam the city, so you will quite probably attract a new friend to accompany you on the walk up the second hill to your final destination.

The statue of another Inca warrior appears as you head across the road through twisting streets that climb into the hills. You may even encounter some locals at home here. When the streets eventually lead you to your final destination, another fantastic birds-eye view of the city is unveiled. If timed right, this makes the perfect spot to take in the sunset.

# LOCAL EMERGING ARTISTS

By Michelle Hopey, New Hampshire, U.S.A:

As Elvis Presley exploded onto the American rock and roll scene in the 1950s, the Peruvian contemporary music scene started an inferno of its own, only to see it crash and burn in the late 1960s with the banning of what was called, "alienating, Yankee" American rock music. But that was 40 years ago.

Today, contemporary rock music in Peru is on the rise, and while still maintaining a somewhat underground scene, artists like Miki Gonzales and classy Susana Baca have hit a new cord, making a serious mark, perhaps even the upswing that Peru has been seeking all these years. Peru's rock scene is going to explode one of these days, and as history shows, the rise and fall of Peru's economy and development is linked to this rock scene's growth. Despite a small commercial industry, Peru is crawling with top-grade musicians, but you'll only hear them at small concerts, bars or clubs. Not witnessing one of these performances is to not fully experience modern day Peruvian culture.

Traditionally speaking, Peruvian music consists of folkloric sounds. Afro-Peruvian music came from slaves the Spanish brought, with lots of raw, up-beat tunes. Most artists today have found a way to use their Andean or Afro roots to cultivate rock and roll, alternative rock or new age rock styles. It's been a hard road, but they are arriving. This music is a mesh of Latin sizzle, acoustic sounds, grunge, electronic vibes, smooth and deep voices.

As Elvis was making his mark, so were popular Peruvian bands like Los Incas Moderno and many others—it looked like rock and roll was going to sweep Peru and it continued in the 1960s with British beats and American surf songs becoming the rage. But in the late 1960s and early 1970s, thanks to then-General Juan Velasco Alvarado, rock music, Peruvian or otherwise, came to a halt. It is said that Alvarado banned all things to do with the import of American rock music and also banned concerts—including Peruvian shows—in major venues, making what seems to be a serious mark on contemporary Peruvian music.

In the late 1970s and early 1980s, Peruvian rock was pushed further underground with the popularity and airtime of salsa and disco. With no media support, no outside influences and a bad economy there was no commercial rock. The underground scene, however, thrived because frustrated and angry youth found an outlet that resonated: bad boy British punk rock, impacting Peruvian music and giving gusto to its new scene. As the economy built muscle and liberalization began, the underground world began to emerge in the 1990s, albeit, with few promoters and little airtime. Finally, with the initiation of MTV's Latin America division in the early 2000s, Peruvian bands captured the spotlight, giving them the well-deserved air-time they deserved.

Only one Peruvian has truly broken through the commercial surface. Susana Baca is a Peruvian singer of Afro-Peruvian descent and is the queen of the Afro-Peruvian revival. In 2002, Baca became the first Peruvian to win a Latin Grammy (best folk album, *Lamento Negro*). With her deep, poetic voice, Baca's music is a mixture of contemporary and traditional Afro-Peruvian sounds complemented indigenous Peruvian instruments and accented by Cuban and Brazilian influences.

Then there are folks like Miki Gonzales who was on the rise in the late 1980s and 90s, but didn't make it big until 2004 when he threw himself into the spotlight with Café Inkaterra which sold locally at number one for several weeks back in spring 2004, but still lacks serious commercial fame. Musician and producer, Gonzalas, has studied traditional Afro-Peruvian and Andean music since the 1970s. His music has always fused traditional Andean music with jazz, rock and pop. His style is now classified as Peruvian remix, since his most recent work has mixed electronic music with popular and traditional music.

And while there have been success stories, there have also been stardom one day, not the next. In 2002, Líbido, a fun-upbeat dance band, also received recognition, with nominations for a Latin Grammy Award and then won the Best South-West Artist honor at the MTV Latin American Awards in 2002, one of the first times that a Peruvian musician or band has received international attention. But in 2005, with the departure of drummer, Jeffry Fischman the band, began to slip and has spiraled since. Another popular Peruvian rock band, TK has a similar story and in 2006 announced their break-up.

There are thousand of Peruvian musicians to discover and as history shows, soon some of the rising stars will be set into stardom and before they are, you might want to get a glimpse of the best music. So, when in Peru, do just that—and revel in these sweet, unique sounds of contemporary Peruvian music.

## SING IT ... LATIN STYLE By Michelle Hopey

With Latin Music heating up mainstream music, here are a few of the big players and ones to watch:

Name: Los Amigos Invisibles     Country: Venezuela
A Latin dance band that experiments with disco and acid jazz, Los Amigos Invisibles are spicy and fun. Although they had moderate success with a few albums and songs from 1995 to 2003, it wasn't until they released *The Venezuelan Zinga Son, Vol. 1* in 2003 that they began to see commercial success. The album also got them a nomination for a Latin Grammy for Best Alternative Latin Album. Funky and spirited, Los Amigos have a brand of their own, and are ones to watch.

Name: Shakira     Country: Colombia
Perhaps the most famous female Latin singer of all-time, Shakira has turned the billboards upside down on at least four occasions with hits like, "Wherever, Whenever," and "Hips Don't Lie." Not bad for a young rock goddess from Colombia. While she has just got her groove on in the past four years, she keeping improving at the speed of light, so its safe to say that Shakira hasn't even peaked yet—almost unimaginable.

Name: Gustavo Santaolalla     Country: Argentina
As a composer with blockbuster hits like *The Motorcycles Diaries* and *Brokeback Mountain* attached to his name, Gustavo Santaolalla is one to watch ... and listen to. An eclectic rock musician from Argentina, this composer—and president of Surco Records (which holds the Juanes label)—Santaolalla won an Academy Award for *Brokeback*. He's on the cusp of something big, and it's very likely that acceptance speeches are in his future.

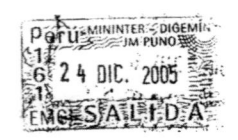

# MADRE DE DIOS RIVER

## By Bonnie L. Jernigan, Duxbury, Massachusetts, U.S.A.

Meandering from the Andes to the Amazon, the Madre de Dios River snakes through the rainforest region known as the biodiversity capital of Peru. The variety of plant life in a single hectare of this wild jungle far exceeds what a coast-to-coast traveler might catalogue in the entire United States; one tree may be home to more insect species than in all of Great Britain.

While nearly half of Peru lies in the Amazon Basin, most guidebooks devote only a few pages to this territory. Without decent roads and with only a few towns of significant size, the area remains remote and relatively undiscovered by tourists. A mere trickle of travelers, no more than 50,000 a year, make it to Madre de Dios, compared to the nearly half a million who flood Machu Picchu. Nonetheless, the region is surprisingly accessible. Every day, flights from Lima and Cusco land at the jungle frontier town of Puerto Maldonado. From there, Reserva Amazónica, a rainforest lodge smack in the middle of a private ecological reserve, is an easy hour away by motorboat.

Inkaterra, the 30-year-old company that pioneered ecotourism in Peru, operates Reserva Amazónica and looks after the surrounding swath of jungle. Some forty huts surround a main pavilion that includes the dining room, as well as an upstairs loft with balconies for birdwatching and stargazing.

The huts are simple structures, built on raised platforms in the indigenous style. Crisp sheets on the beds are comfortable; hammocks on the front porch are heavenly. But be warned: this accommodation isn't for everyone. Aside from generators that power the kitchen for a few hours every night, there is no electricity. Gas lanterns and torches light the way after dark; it's lovely, but hot showers and hair dryers are out of the question.

Nature is all around and can sometimes be too close for comfort. Guests may find themselves sharing their room with a gecko on the ceiling, a frog by the toilet, or even a giant hairy-legged spider on their bath towel. Birdsong and raucous screeches pierce the thick air. But the monkeys and the macaws—along with all the other mammals, birds and reptiles that live in the rainforest—work at not being seen, so visitors to Reserva Amazónica are assigned a guide who knows what to do and where to look, vastly improving the odds of actually spotting wildlife. Speedy lizards startle as they dart across the forest floor. A sudden rustling calls attention to capuchin monkeys overhead. Take a long look, and notice the iridescent blue beetles living in a staggeringly tall kapok tree.

Even a single night's stay provides a sense of the rainforest, but more adventuresome excursions are part of the package for people who wish to stay longer. Drink sweet milk from a coconut at a local farm, and learn first-hand why the jungle is better suited to small subsistence patches than large-scale agri-business. Cruise the river at sunset and search for the black caiman, an endangered Amazonian cousin of the crocodile. Rise before the sun for a trip to Lake Sandoval, an isolated oxbow lake created over time in a place where the winding Madre de Dios gradually etched a straighter course. Part of a protected preserve, Sandoval is home to parrots, pirañas and wild pigs, as well as endangered giant otters regularly seen fishing there. Gliding across the water in a heavy canoe, you might see the red belly of a green kingfisher flying low over the glassy lake.

One of South America's largest canopy bridges is the newest addition to Reserva Amazónica, making it possible to literally walk through the treetops for more than a quarter of a mile. Millions of species, many still undiscovered, spend their entire lives in this realm where, until recently, only scientists ventured. Inkaterra, backed by an alliance that includes National Geographic, believes projects like the canopy walk will attract more tourists. Their dollars may also slow the destruction of the rainforests by protecting them succumbing to large-scale agribusiness.

## TOP LIST: PLACES YOU WON'T SEE TOURISTS

Sometimes, you get sick of being one more gringo on a bus. If you want to get off the tourist track, here's some places to try:

1. Colca Canyon, Peru (p. 273)
"This is on the tourist trail, but very seldom visited." Carol Ann, Scotland.
Casa de Mama Yucca—hotel where there are not many tourists, Colca Canyon, Peru.

2. Cajas National Park, Ecuador (p. 258).
Cajas National Park, near Cuenca, Ecuador. Angela Hamilton, Maxwell, CA, U.S.A.

3. Colombia (p. 224).
"Colombia is still a place where you'll hardly see tourists and that's why the few tourists who decide to visit the country are not only amazed by the country's beauties but gladly surprised that the security situation is much better than in other popular destinations." Colombia Board, South American Explorers Club, Colombia.

4. Atacama Desert, Chile (p. 325).
"Tourists are very few and far between in this magnificent landscape." Carol Ann, Scotland.

Runner up: Manu Biosphere Reserve, Peru. Sam Crothers, PA, U.S.A.

# COLCA CANYON

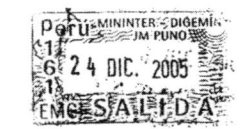

### By Will Gray, Kettering, England

The serene flight of the condor is the main draw of Colca Canyon, a giant scar cutting across the earth's surface. This awesome landscape is one of the few natural homes to these gigantic birds.

Starting off from the picturesque town of Arequipa, one of the jewels of Peru, a two-day journey, usually made in a battered old 4x4 truck, is the best way to see the condors at the right time. The trip itself is as challenging as it is spectacular, and a great way to enjoy the full attractions of the area.

Leaving behind the towering El Misti volcano, you soon hit the dirt roads and speed through plains dotted with grazing vicuñas before stopping for a cup of coca tea at a roadside café in the middle of nowhere. The road then runs over the second highest pass in Peru, rising up to 4,800 metres (15,800 feet) and offers spectacular views, before the nail-biting descent to Chivay.

This small town is the gateway to the canyon, but has a charm all of its own. One of its local attractions is its hot springs, a fantastic open-air venue to kick back and relax, providing you can forget about the pungent sulphur smell, proof that it is naturally fed by heat from the earth's core.

An evening in town can be spent taking in a meal at one of the local restaurants or going to the local folk show, complete with pan pipes, recorders and dancers, before tucking up under the blankets to fend off the cold high-altitude night air in preparation for an early morning departure. The following day starts with a hint of anticipation in the air. The small village of Yanque, with its charming local community, makes a good breakfast stop before continuing on as the valley begins to roll with terraced hills, bumping into bleak altiplano along the way. If you are lucky, the sun rises up to create a misty grey and black silhouette of the spectacular mountain range that unfolds on the road ahead.

Against this marvelous backdrop, you will encounter the most famous place in the Colca Canyon, the Cruz de Condor, where, at around 8 a.m., these giants of the skies take flight, their 3.5 meter wingspan outstretched to make the most of the rising morning air. The inevitable tour buses arrive in droves, of course, but if you are lucky the condors will continue to fly long after the camera-toting crowds have left the canyon's edge. The birds are spectacular, but do not leave before you have taken time to explore the canyon itself, because the views are breathtaking. This area is bursting with natural beauty and it is possible to walk through the towering cacti right to the edge, where you can catch a glimpse of the stomach-churning drop to the floor below before hitting the road and heading back to civilization.

---

COLCA CANYON TRAVEL TIP:

Although this area can be enjoyed any time of the year, it is best to avoid during the rainy season (December to March) when landslides and mud make hiking nearly impossible.

---

Small village, Colca Canyon. Photo by Maximilian Hirschfeld.

# AREQUIPA

By David Vincent, Lennox, Massachusetts, U.S.A.

In a high valley at an altitude of 2,380 meters (7740 feet), shimmering under a deep azure sky, sits Peru's "Second City," Arequipa. Bathed in more than 300 days of sunshine annually, a more hospitable climate would be hard to find. In fact, the Incan forbearers at the site supposedly quipped in their native Quechua, "Ari, quepay," which means, "Yes, stay." More likely, the name came from the Aymara words "ari" (peak) and "kipa" (near the mountain). That mountain would be El Misti (the gentleman), which towers over the city like a sentinel and has become its enduring symbol. The regal volcano stands at 5,822 meters (19,098 ft.) and with its snow-capped, perfect cone, dominates a magnificent view, which also includes the mountain Chachani (6,075 meters, 19,931 ft.) and the volcano Pichu-Pichu (5,669 m, 17,798 ft.). The fertile Arequipa valley has been inhabited for between 7,000 and 8,000 years and was "established" in 1540 as one of the earliest and most important colonial settlements. Arequipa soon became a critical junction in the huge overland shipments of silver from the mines of Potosí, Bolivia. Some of that wealth managed to remain in Arequipa, evidenced today by remnants of colonial splendor.

Glinting in the noon-day sun, "La Ciudad Blanca" (White City) cuts a striking image. Almost all of Arequipa's colonial buildings were constructed of *sillar*, a chalky white volcanic rock, that besides its luster is a stalwart rock in an earthquake-prone area. A rich architectural legacy is apparent in Arequipa, with the fusion of European and indigenous building styles. A visitor will find a wealth of buildings with ornate Baroque facades, stout walls, archways and courtyards.

The central Plaza de Armas is considered one of the most strikingly beautiful in Peru and all of South America. Showcasing an ornamental fountain, dotted with swaying palms and ringed by colonial buildings, it is a delightful space to relax and watch the locals and tourists serenely go about their business. At the north end of the Plaza is the magnificent Basilica Cathedral of Arequipa, which was rebuilt in 1656 after being destroyed by earthquake. A more recent massive earthquake struck on June 23, 2001 and severely damaged the Cathedral; its twin spires (one of which collapsed) have since been restored. Aiding the reconstruction effort was the fact that in December 2000, UNESCO declared the historical center of Arequipa a World Heritage Site. Incidentally, this author arrived in Arequipa just one day after the devastating quake to find a city in mourning but already rebuilding as it had resolutely done so many times before.

One of the true gems of Arequipa is the Monasterio de Santa Catalina, built in 1580. The sprawling monastery with narrow corridors and brightly-hued walls cloistered hundreds of nuns and attendants until 1970, when it was it finally opened to the public (only 20 nuns currently remain). Though "cloistered," throughout most of those centuries the nuns hardly lived an ascetic or austere lifestyle. Many had personal servants, and the nuns hosted musical performances, gave parties and generally lived lavishly. Each family paid a hefty dowry to admit their daughter to the convent. Sor Ana de los Angeles was a nun at Santa Catalina who came to prominence in the 17th century. She was believed to be prescient and performed extraordinary healings both during and after her life. Sor Ana's body was exhumed 10 months after death and had allegedly not decomposed. After her death, many afflicted individuals were healed upon devoting themselves to Sor Ana, or touching an object that had belonged to her. In 1985, Pope John Paul II visited the monastery for the beatification of Sor Ana.

From this author's perspective, the "Second City" of Peru should be one of the first stops. You just may succumb to the beauty and delightful climate of La Ciudad Blanca that has enticed so many others to "Yes, stay."

Arequipa Convent. Photo by Freyja Ellis.

Peruvian girl. Photo by Freyja Ellis.

# HIKING EL MISTI VOLCANO

By Michael Davies, Vancouver, British Columbia, Canada

On February 20, 2005, I was picked up from my hostel in Arequipa, Peru at 5 a.m., along with three other tourists, and taken to the base of the El Misti Volcano. The drive up to the base offered some of the best views of El Misti in all its glory, standing tall in the light of dawn, all 18,000 feet (6,000 meters).

The steady, steep grade of the volcano made the hike up incredibly difficult from the start. The snow line was still low on the slope from the previous winter, and the coming spring had only just begun to warm the air in the valley below. We were to stay at base camp that night, so each of our backpacks was stuffed with food and supplies.

Over ridges and through gullies, we hiked for six straight hours in the driving rain and sleet. The altitude and weather sucked the wind right from my lungs and I was sure that I was about to pass out when we finally reached base camp. The views of Arequipa and the rest of the valley were clouded and the reality of being on the side of a volcano became all too apparent. Only the peaks of neighboring mountains rose from the clouds and shone in the dying late of the afternoon. Isolated and chilled to the bone, we set up camp.

Our guides woke us just after 5:00 a.m.; with tents ill-equipped for the grim weather we faced, and a little tight for our group of tall Canadians, we were soaked to the bone and still exhausted from the previous day's hike. The tents had clearly been designed for smaller people and better weather!

Three and a half hours of hard hiking later, we found ourselves scrambling over and around a patch of enormous boulders. The trail to the summit had been so obscured by snow that our guide had accidentally taken us to an area strewn with large rocks; the hike battered our already-spent bodies. The altitude was getting to me, and the view of the ground in front of my feet was intermittently blurred, making foot placement very difficult. I was succumbing to the perils of altitude sickness. "Only a few more minutes and we'll be there," I said to myself over and over, but the headaches were rocking me from the inside out.

Only 500 meters (1600 feet) or so from the top, I began to feel really nauseous, and no amount of coca leaves could stop the ravages of the altitude from breaking my will to continue. Together, the weather and a poor night's sleep had sapped my usual athleticism and energy and turned me into nothing more than a shivering, green-faced young man on the side of a volcano.

Our guide recognized the urgency of getting me back closer to sea level, and decided our best route down to base camp was by leaping down the fall lines and sliding on our heels on the finely crushed pebbles remaining from avalanches and previous eruptions. The four-hour hike up turned into a 30-minute stroll downhill to base camp. Another two hours of descending by trail through the rain, and we were back at the jeep and on our way back home to Arequipa, watching out the back window the elusive summit of El Misti grow further from our reaches.

Michael Davies is a musician from Canada, who writes the music and lyrics for a band called Sinfoni, and also records and produces bands in studio.

His dream adventure is to go ocean kayaking from the Alaskan border along the western shore of British Columbia, down to Vancouver. Next he is likely traveling to Cuba or Iceland, where he will hopefully be able to put his new Icelandic language skills to use.

Andean flowers. Photo by Suco Viteri.

# LAKE TITICACA HOMESTAY

By Freyja Ellis, Benbecula, Outer Hebrides, Scotland

My first stop after arriving in Puno for the trip to Lake Titicaca, was the Uros Floating Reed Islands. The area consists of 45 artificial Totora Reed islands, anchored by poles in the ground, although only a few are accessible to tourists. On the island, I was treated to a tour and introduction to the Uros who still live a traditional lifestyle of hunting and raising cattle, although signs of the 21st century are evident in solar power panels and TV!

Whilst on the island I was offered the chance of riding on one of the traditional reed boats, something that is not only relaxing, but also a good insight into how the Uros travel.

After an hour, I boarded the boat again and headed a few hours across Lake Titicaca, the highest navigable lake in the world at 3,800 metres (12,467 feet), to Amantani Island. Here, we disembarked and the guide assigned us our families, trying to closely match them to our preferences. I was assigned, with two others, to a family with four children and the lady of the house met us at the pier. The host families live in simple houses and the accommodation offered is basic. My family had no electricity and only an outside toilet with a single room for guests. Conversation can be difficult as Quechua is the primary language, although our guide gave us a basic phrase sheet prior to our arrival. Luckily the children spoke Spanish, so with the help of phrase books and sign language, we managed some basic conversation.

After a quick settling-in period, we were offered lunch which consisted of potato soup, followed by potatoes and boiled eggs. Afterwards the locals and boat passengers enjoyed a game of football before a tour around the island, with our guide explaining the history of the island and islanders. The island itself is barren, but beautiful, with a handful of villages and ruins situated between the two peaks of the island, Pachatata (Father Earth) and Pachamama (Mother Earth). A walk three times around the ruined temple at the top of the island is said to grant wishes.

After watching the sunset, we headed back to our respective families for dinner and the evening's entertainment. We were dressed in traditional dress. Men wore ponchos and hats whilst the women wore petticoats, bulky skirts, white embroidered blouses and black embroidered scarves. A dance was put on in the local school to the music of local bands. The dancing was traditional, but easy to follow. The cold beer and the beautiful, clear night sky rounded out a fun night.

The following day, after a breakfast consisting of coffee and pancakes, we were taken down to the pier, where we said goodbye to our host families and sailed the short distance to neighbouring Taquile Island, where roles are reversed and the men are renowned for their knitting. Whilst still protective of its local customs, the islanders have adapted to tourists and there are several small restaurants and a co-operative store.

The island itself is rugged with many Inca and pre-Inca ruins dotted on the hillside and the paths alongside the terraced hillside are shared by an assortment of cows, sheep and locals. Traditional dress is also worn on Taquile Island, and the men wear embroidered, woven red waistbands (*fajas*) and embroidered wool stocking caps that indicate marital status; red for married men and red and white for those who are single. After a time exploring the island we headed back to the boat and I relaxed on the deck as we sailed back to Puno, arriving late afternoon.

> "Going to Peru is well, if you ever have an opportunity in your life to go there, you should do it because it is absolutely mind-boggling."
> -Dean Stockwell, U.S. Actor, (1936-)

## QUECHUA WORDS By Michelle Hopey

The most widely spoken native American language, it is reported that nearly 10 million people today throughout South America speak some form of Quechua. This ancient language has many different dialects and variations. The list below details common words that are useful today in the Lake Titicaca area and specifically on the Isla Amantani.

| ENGLISH | QUECHUA |
| --- | --- |
| Good morning | Allin punchay |
| Hello | Allillanchu |
| I am fine | Allillanmin |
| My name is... | Nokan sutimin |
| What is your name? | Imata sutiki? |
| I am from... | Nokan kani... |
| Where is the bathroom? | Maypitaj wanu? |
| Can I help you? | Yanaparisayki? |

# SILLUSTANI

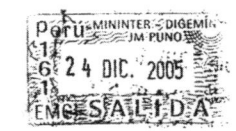

## By Albert Garcia, Fullerton, California, U.S.A.

If life on the stark highlands near Lake Titicaca was as difficult as experts believe, the graves of the ancient people who lived there deserve the commemoration that Sillustani offers.

Called "the people of the south" by the Inca, the Colla are considered part of the Aymara ethnic group. They inhabited the frosty, desolate valleys around the saltwater Laguna Umayo for hundreds of years. A sacred plateau, Sillustani, rises from the shore of the surrounding lake and contains cylindrical tombs that rise like silos across the hilltops. The Colla entombed whole families with their riches in these above-ground structures known as chullpas which were usually made from mortar and small stones. Some were coated with stucco which has slowly dissolved with time. Others, possibly the tombs of noblemen or the wealthy, were built using enormous blocks of stone meticulously carved to create a smooth, rounded outer surface. Incredibly, the perfect shape of the stones allowed them to be stacked over 12 meters (39 feet) high without the use of mortar.

Sillustani is located about 35 km (20 miles) outside of Puno, a popular town on the Peruvian shore of Lake Titicaca. The road there is rough but scenic. Several tour agencies arrange day trips and hotel pickups, and package trips to other local attractions are usually available. Plan to spend about three to four hours with a guided tour.

Many of the chullpas bear the scars of intentional destruction by looters and of natural destruction by time and weather (lightning rods are now in place on the larger tombs). Still, Sillustani has endured as a memorial for hundreds of years to the surviving souls who eke out an existence in this harsh perimeter of the world. At 3,800 meters (12,500 feet) above sea level, with coarse terrain and often freezing winds, Sillustani serves to remind visitors of the endurance and adaptability possible in all of us.

Sillustani. Photo by Albert Garcia.

# LÚCUMA

### By Mariana Cotlear

A visit to Peru is not complete without a taste of the lúcuma fruit. This wildly popular fruit is native to the Andean region, where its inhabitants treasure its distinct flavor and unusual texture. This taste is notoriously hard to describe; it is rich, mild and sweet, but these words hardly do the lúcuma justice.

Covered by a stiff, shiny, dark green outer skin, the lúcuma's interior is a contrasting yellow-orange. This hue has become part of the Peruvian color vocabulary—stick around and you might overhear someone complimenting or criticizing their neighbors' lúcuma-colored facades.

The fruit's dry and starchy pulp is not usually eaten on its own (though it can be) but is most often used in preparations of desserts such as mousses, cakes, shakes and ice cream. In fact, lúcuma is the most popular ice cream flavor along with the ubiquitous chocolate and vanilla (and it goes very well with chocolate fudge).

Peruvian ex-pats across the world can be heard yearning for the taste of this very special fruit, which is rarely accessible outside of Peru and parts of Ecuador and Chile. So, if you happen to be in the area, do yourself a favor and sample all the treats the lúcuma fruit has to offer.

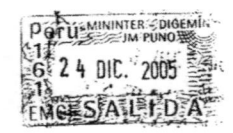

# CARNAVAL IN PUNO

## By Michael Davies, Vancouver, British Colombia, Canada

Twenty-four hours on planes, and 19 hours by bus; I had gone from snowy Calgary, Canada on the first of February to the warm and beautiful sunshine of Puno, Peru by the fourth. This little town is set in the southeast corner of Peru, and was rumored to be the spot for Carnival, so I high-tailed it from Lima, a 16-hour bus trip, to check it out.

Perched in the mountains on the shore of the highest navigable lake in the world, Lake Titicaca, Puno was said to be the birthplace of the original rulers of the Inca Empire. It also had its day as a port facility to Bolivia (which shares the lake with Peru) in the 1800s.

I was awakened by loud drums and horns, people yelling and an atmosphere that buzzed with excitement. Today was the start of "La Virgen de la Candeleria," a festival specific to Puno alone. From my hostel room window, and as far as I could see down the streets in every direction, there were huge groups of people dancing and playing music. They were clad in bright costumes, and all were playing their hearts out. Carnival had begun.

Throughout the day there were parades of people, one group after another, all playing the traditional celebratory music of their home regions. The sun was shining and the weather pitched a perfect summer day. People were drinking and laughing and dancing in the streets and it wasn't even late afternoon yet. All about the city there were street vendors selling large bottles of beer.

The music raged well into the night. All the young people raced about the streets with aerosol cans of white foam, spraying anyone not already covered. A friend and I were drawn into the foaming game, so while we drank our beers from the balconies overlooking the streets, we'd pick out our targets; kids, men, women, dancers! Then we'd race down out of nowhere and cover the helpless victims in white froth!!

It was electric. Regardless of my poor Spanish, people just wanted to share a drink and some good times.

Never mind, this was only the first night of what was a solid week of amazing times. Great music. Great times. Great people. Puno had been rumored to have the biggest Carnival celebrations in Peru, but I would venture to say that these celebrations were some of the biggest this side of Rio.

Puno. Photo by Maximilian Hirschfeld.

### CARNAVAL FACTOIDS:

Carnaval is widely celebrated throughout Latin America. Festivities kick off in the run-up to Lent. Traditionally, the most important days are usually the Saturday through to the Tuesday before Ash Wednesday, when fasting used to begin.

The name Carnaval has been claimed to come from the Italian words "carne" and "vale," meaning "farewell to meat."

In the highlands of Peru, a popular custom is to throw water at people. As a gringo you are likely to be a popular target!

Carnaval is very important in Cajamarca, Peru, where a Carnival queen is elected and there are competitions of friendship and song.

Other important Carnaval celebrations in Latin America are celebrated in Brazil, Bolivia and Colombia. The Bogotá Carnaval is celebrated later in the year, in early August. On the other hand, important Cuban carnavals are celebrated in July.

Señoras. Photo by Maximilian Hirschfeld.

# BOLIVIA

## The Tibet of the Americas

Bolivia is literally in the clouds: long time visitors and residents will tell you that it's as close as you can get to heaven in this mortal life. It is a land of extremes. In just about any category, Bolivia is out on the skinny part of the bell curve: it's the highest, coldest, most traditional and poorest nation in South America (not counting the Guyanas).

Rugged Bolivia isn't for everyone. Being landlocked, there are no beaches, no Club Med, and not too much in the way of five-star, internationally famous resorts. That being said, if you like your native culture authentic (as opposed to canned "authentic" jungle village, highland town or gaucho ranch "trips"), if you like your mountains majestic and snow-capped, and if you like to step off the beaten tourist trail every now and then, Bolivia is for you.

In this section, we'll take you through Bolivia's fascinating history with trips to the old Spanish mines of Potosí, on the trail with Butch Cassidy and the Sundance Kid and to Lake Titicaca, home to indigenous cultures in South America for millennia. Bolivia doesn't skimp on culture, and neither do we: we'll show you the festivals at Chiquitania, the Sun Island festival and the famous Witches' Market of La Paz. Along the way, we'll take some time out for adventure: how about a bike ride on the world's most dangerous road?

Bolivia borders Paraguay to the east, Chile and Argentina to the south, Brazil to the north, Peru to the west, the majestic Andes beneath and Heaven above. Isn't it time you checked it out for yourself? While you're waiting to buy your ticket, turn the page and join us on our trip to South America's answer to Tibet.

# LAKE TITICACA AND THE ISLAND OF THE SUN
## By Martin Li, London, England

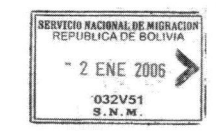

Lying at the northern edge of the Altiplano, or highlands, and straddling the Bolivia-Peru border, Lake Titicaca's intense blue waters are sacred to many cultures. The lake was the cradle of Andean civilization and remains known as the mystical birthplace of the Inca Empire. When viewed through the crystal clear light of the Altiplano, beneath the snow-crowned peaks of the Cordillera Real, it's easy to understand how the lake's crystalline waters became associated with mystical events.

The lake's original name was Khota Mamma ("Mother Lake"), and was only renamed Titicaca after the Spanish conquest. The lake has two sections. The smaller southern section, known as Wiñay Marka ("Eternal City"), is comparatively shallow, which led to the legend of a city lying beneath the lake. The discovery of remains of a settlement and an ancient temple on the lake bed in 2000 bolstered this theory. Whether or not the legend is true, one need not look far to find a bizarre city resting peacefully on the surface of the lake.

Originally constructed by the Uros in an attempt to escape the brutality of Spanish forced labor, the "floating islands" known as Islas Uros are composed of matted tortora reeds and are home to a truly unique local culture. Carrying on the traditions of their ancestors, the Uros fish, hunt birds and ply the lake's waters in traditional reed boats made of lashed-together bundles of totora.

In the south of Lake Titicaca are two islands of unique importance to Andean history: the Island of the Sun and the Island of the Moon. The Incas revered these islands and built religious shrines and facilities on both, converting them into a great pilgrimage destination and shrine complex.

The beautiful and tranquil Island of the Sun is prominent in Andean mythology and littered with Inca ruins. Few places can match the island for capturing the overwhelming solitude that so characterises Lake Titicaca, surrounded by glorious vistas rimmed by snow-capped peaks.

The island is a delicate patchwork of steep fields and terraces of different hues of green, yellow and brown, criss-crossed by stone terraces and zigzagging walls tumbling down to sand beaches and the lake's intense blueness. Inca emperors would visit the island each year and stay at the palace of Pilko Kaina in the south, close to the island's largest community of Yumani.

Today, most visitors to the island still climb the Inca Steps to Yumani, beside which spring water cascades down the Inca Fountain. Yumani perches on the island ridge and enjoys superb views across the Island of the Moon to the Cordillera Real beyond.

The ruins of the Chincana labyrinth (thought to be an Inca monastery) hug the island's northern tip. The nearby Sacred Rock marked the conclusion of the most important Inca pilgrimage. According to the creation legend, the first Incas, Manco Capac and Mama Ocllo, rose from the lake near here to begin their ministry to bring civilisation to the world.

Even knowing nothing about its history and mythology, visiting the Island of the Sun is an intensely serene experience. With the Inca legends added in, the experience verges on the spiritual.

---

**TORTORA OF TITICACA:**
The abundant reed plant, known as *tortora* in Spanish or *t'utura* in Aymara, is invaluable for the people of the Lake Titicaca region. Once cut, it is dried in the sun, and then used for a variety of purposes because of its strong, yet foam-like quality. It is not only used to make boats for transportation, but also to construct roofs and houses. It is sometimes fed to animals, and is even edible for humans, resembling celery in taste.

---

Reed boat, Lake Titicaca. Photo by Martin Li.

# OFFERINGS TO PACHAMAMA

### By Carol Ann, Rhynie, Scotland

At the southern end of Sun Island on Lake Titicaca is a sacred place, used by the local Andean Indians and their Kallawaya for rituals and offerings to Pachamama, the Earth Mother. The Kallawaya is a fortune teller or native doctor of the Andean Altiplano and this one is a small man, dressed inconspicuously in a white shirt and dark trousers. With thin sandals on his feet, he walks purposefully south along an unseen trail through eucalyptus trees, past a stone monument until he reaches his destination, a small, round stone enclosure. On his back, a grey sheet encases a medley of strange shaped objects which are clearly heavy, because he's bent over forwards to balance the weight.

Once inside the stone hut, the grey sheet is emptied of its contents. First he takes out a pile of wooden logs half a metre long and proceeds to build a square-shaped stack around a pile of shavings and small twigs. We admire the view—this is a beautiful spot with the snow-capped Cordillera Real and the sacred mountain, Nevada Illampú in the east and the southern shore of Lake Titicaca in the west. It's mid afternoon. The sky is clear and very blue, the lake surface is placid and the sun is still very hot.

We turn back to the Kallawaya who is now dressed in a bright red, sleeveless poncho with an intricately patterned woolen hat on his head— he is ready to begin a ceremony which has been handed down through his family over countless generations.

The offering package was bought from the Witches' Market in La Paz and every item has a special significance. The contents can vary depending on the price paid, but this one contains a small llama foetus, coca leaves, sweets, small gold and silver coloured trinkets, images of the sun and the moon and crushed quartz and other crystals. We take turns to present the offering to the north, south, east and west, saying a few words to Pachamama in each direction. We are asking for peace and prosperity for the Lake and the people who live around it, but the words can change, depending on the occasion.

Offerings to Pachamama are made to celebrate marriages and births, to ask for rain and a bountiful harvest, to ask for luck in exams, anything the giver chooses. The package is finally handed to the Kallawaya who murmurs his own incantations before placing it on the wood stack and lighting it. The heat from the fire is fierce and we move away to the edges of the stone enclosure, where we sit and watch as the logs and offering burn down to embers.

The ceremony is complete, the Kallawaya is thanked for his services and we leave the sacred area to its guardian spirits, beckoned on by the need for a cold drink and a seat in the shade.

www.vivatravelguides.com/104130

# THE PEOPLES OF LAKE TITICACA

### By Carol Ann, Rhynie, Scotland

As our small wooden boat comes alongside the island, strong brown arms reach out to help me ashore. Looking up, I see twinkling eyes in a wrinkled, leathery face, a beaming smile that shows crooked, white teeth and short dark hair sticking out from a knitted woolen hat with ear flaps. I step carefully onto the thick mat of reeds, half expecting it to move with my weight, but it's firm and robust—I have arrived on the floating reed islands of Lake Titicaca.

These particular reed islands have been built by the 32 surviving families of the Urus-Iruitos, using techniques that have helped them to survive in this area for over 7,000 years. Despite modern influences, these families still speak Pukina (language of the ancient Tiwanaku) and Quechua (the language of the Incas) and have chosen to continue their ancient traditions and way of life, as part of a Bolivian sustainable tourism project based around Quewaya Island, in the southern part of the Lake.

This first floating island is an agricultural space, with a small greenhouse containing herbs and vegetable seedlings and an outside vegetable patch. Once the reed base has thickened and rotted sufficiently, larger crops such as potatoes and root vegetables will be grown here as well. On nearby Quewaya Island is an even larger greenhouse, where the use of biological fertilizers (the droppings from guinea pigs and quails) allow the Urus to optimize year-round food production and become more self-sufficient. The humble totora reed has many uses, in addition to the constant replenishment of the base beneath our feet.

On a second floating island, dried reeds have been used for building sleeping huts, a "tee-pee" style gathering space, small cooking shacks and traditional reed boats. They are woven into the conical, brimmed hats which the village headman and his family wear to keep off the sun; and new shoots are peeled to reveal a nutritious snack which tastes like sugar cane. As I peek into one of the cooking huts a young, smiling Urus girl shows me earthenware pots containing fires fuelled by burning reeds. These fires heat a pot filled with a delicious stew of freshly caught king fish and potatoes which we are all invited to taste.

Each day the headman and his family are joined by other Urus-Iruitos from nearby Quewaya, all dressed in colourful ponchos, hats and eye-catching, multi-layered skirts. They provide an additional income for the village by selling finely patterned, hand-made bags, scarves, rugs, bowls and trinkets to passing visitors.

As I take in this colourful spectacle, I'm aware I have been welcomed as an honoured guest and I feel privileged to have met these people and shared a glimpse of their unique way of life.

# MADIDI

## By Kelley Coyner, Texas, U.S.A.

The flight to Madidi foreshadows the park's tremendous topographic diversity. The small airplane provides front row seats to some of the world's highest peaks including Illampú (21,276 feet/6,424 meters), Illimani (21,201 feet/6,322 meters), and Huayna Potosi (19,974 feet/6,088 meters). The view is up close and personal: note the roadways wending across the steep landscape, past houses perched on craggy hillsides and nestled in rugged crevasses. Just beyond the highest ridge, the snow covered Apolobamba range plunges into the warm, humid lowlands of the Amazon Basin. Following the landscape, the plane swoops over cliffs, gliding past small farms and densely wooded areas, finally coming to rest on the grassy runway in Rurrenabaque.

Boasting 200 species of mammals, 1,000 species of birds, and 100,000 varieties of insects and arachnids, Madidi is one of the most biologically diverse protected areas on Earth. Birders will be pleased to hear that nearly 1,000 species of birds call Madidi home (in contrast to the mere 800 in all of North America!). An uncounted number of plant species can be found in Madidi; during a recent reconnaissance trek, researchers identified 15 new species of fern flourishing in a single valley of the cloud forest. The physical environs include rainforest and cloud forest, the Amazon's only pristine savannah, not to mention a series of class five rapids and world class fly-fishing along the Tuichi, a major tributary to the Amazon.

If you don't like spiders and snakes, instead check out the birds and monkeys. Formerly a hunting area for the Tacana indigenous community, Chalalán was home to little wildlife ten years ago. Today birders (and non-birders) can view the Amazon screamer, midget kingfisher, birds of paradise, nesting hummingbirds and more. With careful coaching from a guide, the less experienced birdwatchers can learn to spot the flocks of blue and gold macaws and handsome toucans socializing in dense canopy overhead.

If the idea of 1,000 species of birds doesn't excite your senses, keep your eyes peeled for tree frogs bouncing along the branches of walking cypress trees or snakes slithering up one of the at least six varieties of palm trees or across the strangler vines. Besides creatures of avian, arachnid, and amphibian origins, the 25 kilometers of trails that wind through Chalalán harbor a host of other interesting creatures. Palm-sized, brilliant blue moths flitter alongside shimmering butterflies creating an intense kaleidoscope of colors. The lucky may see a puma or red brocket deer: fresh tracks often parallel the trail.

If your daytime trek leaves you hungry for more wildlife, take a night hike through the boggy understory, where you might spy the laser-like red eyes of caimans and the hammock-shaped webs of social spiders (the ultimate arachnid extroverts of the rainforest, the social spiders congregate in groups numbering in the hundreds). You might even catch an anaconda or a tree boa in the beam of your flashlight. Visitors often come face to face with tapirs, peccaries or wild pigs and capybaras, the world's largest rodent.

This bastion of biodiversity is also a great place to spot monkeys swinging from the trees. Bands of hundreds of yellow squirrel monkeys socialize along the rivers and lakes. Brown capuchin monkeys look like the monks for which they are named, while the piercing shrills of red and black howler monkeys crash through the canopy. Keep an eye out for the newly discovered golden titi monkey, a shy family man that travels in small groups through this area.

Return through Rurrenabaque on Sunday and experience market day. Dugouts brimming with bananas and other products tie up on the muddy bank. Locals shop for necessities from fuel to oranges, plastic hair clips to mosquito nets. While you await your plane, check out the emu at the Safari hotel or grab a brew and round of fresh air billiards at the aptly named Mosquito Bar. Regardless of how long you spend exploring this astounding area, you're sure to leave feeling like you've just scratched the surface of what Madidi has to offer.

## CHICHA

By Leigh Gower

Made from a yellow maize commonly known as *chicha de jora*, Bolivia's national alcoholic beverage, *chicha*, dates back to the days of the Inca Empire when women were taught how to brew the drink in special feminine schools called Acllahuasis. These women were usually the Aqllakuna, or "chosen women," of the king.

Made from corn which is traditionally chewed and spat out before being allowed to ferment, the drink manifests as thick, pale and yellow with a slightly bitter after taste, which it has been said is reminiscent of hard apple cider, and is famed for its alcoholic strength. It seems an enzyme in the saliva of the chewer releases the desired starch in the maize.

Not to be confused with hookah smoking of the Middle East, also sometimes referred to as chicha, academics cite the origins of the word chicha being the kuna word chichab, meaning maize. Chicha held ritual significance for the Incas who believed their grain was a gift of the gods, and thus consumed it in large quantities during religious festivals. It is tradition to drop a bit of chicha on the ground before and after drinking it as an offering to pachamama, the Inca earth goddess.

Gringos alike have called chicha the moonshine of the third world for its potent effects. It has usually been considered the alcohol of the poorer classes because it is cheap, but for travelers offers the chance to get thoroughly drunk for pennies. Once a staple of Andean towns, few continue to make the drink today—the best in Bolivia is said to be in the small town of Punata in the Cochabamba region (ask for "dona Berta"). If walking through the Bolivian highlands you come across a home flying the traditional white flag out front, you can be sure there is chicha ready for you to drink inside.

# TREKKING THE CORDILLERA APOLOBAMBA

By Martin Li, London, England

Centuries ago, the Incas built hundreds of kilometres of trails, paths and roads to link the various parts of their mountain empire. Today, with Peru's celebrated "Inca Trail" to Machu Picchu groaning under the weight of thousands of trekkers, savvy adventurers are searching for alternative Inca paths to explore. Bolivia offers several such Inca trails, of which the route through the Cordillera Apolobamba is arguably the most scenic and fascinating, and certainly one of the least trekked.

High, wild and remote, the Apolobamba trek offers breathtaking Andean wilderness, a glimpse into the heart of ancient cultures and guaranteed sightings of wildlife including alpacas, vicuñas and rare, majestic condors. The trail begins in Curva, the home of the Kallawayas, a group of mystical healers and fortune tellers who treated Inca aristocracy, and whose vibrant way of life survives today. Passing sacred sites where Kallawayas still sacrifice llamas, the trail climbs towards Akhamani, the Kallawayas' most sacred summit. Along the way, you can hand-catch trout from a tiny stream for supper.

Trout or no trout, continue up the trail where you'll scramble over dark, steep rocks to a succession of high passes. As is the local custom, place white stones on the summits to ask for good luck and strength. If your requests are answered, you might be lucky enough to see condors soaring magnificently overhead at the passes. A camp high up on a steep path called "Mil Curvas" ("thousand curves") promises a bitterly cold morning, but also the incredible sight of Akhamani bathed in brilliant morning sunshine against the backdrop of a cloudless blue sky and possibly a late-rising moon. From the 5,100 m (16,700 feet) Sunchulli Pass, the snow-covered Apolobamba peaks stretch into the distance to your left. To your right, the Sunchulli glacier towers above the calm turquoise Laguna Verde, beyond which scowls a dark, brooding ridge protected at its base by an impossibly steep screen. Most Apolobamba treks end at the misty stone town of Pelechuco, but those in search of even finer scenery should continue north for one more day.

Those who continue on to summit the Katantika Pass are amply rewarded with some of the most stunning scenery in the Andes: glaciers and crevasses glinting as the sun plunges towards the valley far below, illuminating a tranquil, trout-filled lake bordered by Inca paving, and possibly another condor perched not far above your head.

A stone cross marks the most sacred point of the pass, the landscape beyond mellowing markedly from jagged, icy summits to endless rolling pampas and eventually Peru. You'll probably want to lay a stone at the cross, most likely more in gratitude for this spellbinding vista than to ask for any more good fortune.

> "You must not judge people by their country. In South America, it is always wise to judge people by their altitude."
> -Paul Theroux, American Travel Writer and Novelist,
> from "The Old Patagonian Express" (1941-)

Cordillera Apolobamba. Photo by Martin Li.

# COROICO

By Chris Sacco, Hamilton, New York, U.S.A.

Dozens of black dogs sit stoically at the edge of the road, weathering the gloom of the winter morning, and as we drive by, their long snouts and obsidian-colored eyes swivel in pursuit.

I can't say exactly when the first one appeared; maybe an hour outside of La Paz, but the memory of the ominous canines haunted me until we reached the last narcotics checkpoint at the mouth of the legendary road to Coroico. The dogs' terrible poise was disquieting, but it was their eyes that truly worried me. They seemed to speak, and, as we approach the precipitous descent into the Yungas Valley, their gaze screamed "danger".

For three and a half hours we wound our way down from the barren heights of the Cordillera Real northeast of the capital through the steep, forested slopes of sub-tropical Bolivia. Many consider this stretch of road, locally known as the "Highway of Death," to be the most dangerous in the world. And with good reason: it drops 3,000 meters in less than 70 kilometers and has swallowed hundreds of travelers over the years. Makeshift crosses and piles of stones mark dozens of places where buses and cars have plunged over its sheer cliffs.

If anything merits such a hair-raising trip it's Coroico, a picturesque town that clings to the side of a lush mountain covered with a tapestry of orange and banana groves, coffee and coca plantations. Coroico is popular among Bolivians and foreign travelers seeking a reprieve from the bone-chilling winters of the highlands. The climate is divine and the views from just about everywhere are arguably the best in the country. Moreover, inexpensive yet marvelous accommodations and restaurants pepper the village and surrounding countryside. Perhaps the best part of Coroico is its relaxed pace; nevertheless, there are plenty of opportunities to hike and go horseback riding, and there is excellent rafting just a few hours away on the Rio Coroico, which has over 30 rapids that range in difficulty from Class II to Class IV.

On account of Coroico's unexpected splendor, coupled with a subconscious fear that the journey back to La Paz would be our last, we stayed for two days more than we had planned. When we finally emerged from the Yungas intact, if not a little worse for the wear, the black dogs were still there. They sat as before, unflappable against the wind and rain, watching us drive off towards the city. That night at a pub, a table of Bolivians overheard us recounting the day's hazards and told us that "the dogs embody the souls of travelers who have perished on the road to Coroico." I believed them. I believe them still. For whenever I remember Coroico, it's not its superb climate or hotels that come first to mind, but the knowing eyes of the lonely black dogs.

www.vivatravelguides.com/103430

# MOUNTAIN BIKING THE WORLD'S MOST DANGEROUS ROAD

By Martin Li, London, England

Starting high in the rarefied air of the Bolivian Andes, the steep and bumpy road from La Paz plunges 3,600 metres (12,000 feet) during the spectacular 64 km descent to the lush, sub-tropical Yungas and the sleepy town of Coroico. The narrow—occasionally very narrow—track hugs the sheer valley side as it snakes through dramatic, verdant scenery, surrounded all around by soaring Andean peaks. In places, the road is barely wide enough for one vehicle, let alone two.

Twisting beneath waterfalls and rocky overhangs, an unprotected drop-off to near certain death is a constant travel companion. A fatal accident every fortnight is not uncommon on the Coroico road, and the Inter-American Development Bank has declared it "the world's most dangerous road."

The ride begins at La Cumbre, a desolate, windswept pass at a chilly 4,700 metres (15,400 feet). A few turns of the pedals and you are swept away by gravity over beautifully smooth high-altitude tarmac, soon hurtling downhill at tear-streaming speeds approaching 80 km/hr. At 20 km, the smooth tarmac ends at the head of a yawning valley. The landscape is still lofty and steep, but has mellowed from bleak, high Andes to dense, lush cloud forest. The road is now a stony, unsurfaced single track hewn out of the sheer mountainside, hundreds of metres above the valley floor. You can follow the thin brown strip for tens of kilometres as it descends into the distant haze—with an unprotected outer edge for as far as you can see. This is it: "the world's most dangerous road."

Even with a death grip on your brakes, you'll feel you are going too fast over the loose gravel and might skid frequently. No matter how hard you concentrate on controlling your speed and maintaining a safe distance from the edge, it's impossible to ignore the many poignant reminders of tragedy. You pass crosses, memorials and bunches of flowers at chillingly-frequent intervals.

One of the eeriest features of the road is that you can only hear traffic when it is distant. The dense foliage and blind corners smother the sound of nearby vehicles so much that you can turn a corner and find yourself confronting the massive grille of a lorry or bus that has seemingly materialised out of nowhere. The road here is bone-dry and you lose visibility totally behind dust clouds whenever a vehicle passes.

In just one day, you cross high, windswept Andean passes and snow-covered plains, plunge joyously through dense cloud forest, and by late afternoon are sipping Margaritas in a bar in the tropics. You descend nearly 3,600 thrilling metres, with barely a need to pedal, and defy the spectre of death that has stalked you for most of the journey.

But such an adrenaline-rush comes at a price. Your body will ache. It won't be saddle-soreness and it won't even be your legs or arms. It's your hands that will be throbbing from constantly braking for so much of the descent. Hopefully, though, your tired fingers will just about manage to clutch onto your Margarita glass.

# LA PAZ

## By Martin Li, London, England

La Paz is Bolivia's principal city and at 3,600 meters (11,811 feet), is the world's highest capital. Although Sucre is Bolivia's official capital, La Paz is the actual seat of government and commercial centre. Spanish conquistadores founded the city in 1548 on the site of Choqueyapu, a busy Aymara village located on the strategic trade route between the Bolivian silver mines and the Pacific ports. Bolivia has the highest proportion of indigenous people of any country in South America, a fact not lost on any visitor to La Paz.

Relatively untouched by tourists, La Paz offers visitors a fascinating and genuine glimpse into South American life.

The drive from the airport to the city centre is unforgettable. You bump along poor roads passing slums and street markets until, rounding a corner, the ground suddenly falls away on one side and the great bowl of La Paz unfolds before you in what can only be described as one of the most dramatic skylines anywhere in the world. Modern skyscrapers soar from the pit, where a carpet of squat adobe dwellings claw their way up its steep lip, the diameter of which stretches nearly five km (three miles) from rim to rim. Majestic Illimani's three snow-covered peaks dominate the horizon while all around, the Altiplano and snow-crowned summits of the Cordillera Real stand out against the deep blue sky.

The poorer districts of La Paz lie higher up and the wealthier districts lower down. The shanty adobe houses of El Alto, the satellite district that now contests La Paz for size, sprawl from the edge of the Altiplano high above the city centre. In contrast, the lower Zona Sur region is warmer, wealthier and altogether more comfortable than the city centre, and is favoured by expatriate families and wealthier Bolivians.

Notwithstanding the comforts of Zona Sur, nothing captures the essence of La Paz like the city centre: breathlessly steep cobbled streets lined with vendors; pulsating, seemingly—endless markets; and a huge population of indigenous women clad in bowler hats and brightly coloured traditional costumes, all set against the backdrop of Illimani and the chatter of Aymara.

Aside from the effects of high altitude, La Paz is an easy city to navigate on foot. A single main road lined with skyscrapers runs along the base of the canyon through the heart of the city centre, various points along the way being Ismael Montes, Mariscal Santa Cruz, Villazón and 16 de Julio ("the Prado"). If ever unsure of your location in La Paz, simply head downhill or towards the skyscrapers to return to the city centre.

Though cuisine is not often regarded as one of Bolivia's more noteworthy points, the food can be delicious and invariably inexpensive. One of the highlights of local dining is the *almuerzo* or fixed lunch, which generally consists of a starter or salad, large bowl of soup, main course, dessert and possibly coffee, all for $1-2. *Salteñas*, mid-morning snacks of beef, chicken or vegetarian filling in a pastry ball, are also a delight. Don't miss the delicious meat dishes of *lechón* (roasted pork), *chicharron* (deep-fried pork) and *anticuchos* (night-time beef heart kebabs—sounds disgusting, tastes divine). You can also purchase superb fruit and vegetables at ridiculously low prices in any of La Paz's many food markets.

---

LA PAZ TRAVEL TIP:

For an incredible 360-degree view of the city, visit Parque Mirador Laikakota. To get the best views, walk past the playground to the far end of the park. Don't forget your camera. Located on Avenida El Ejército in Miraflores. Open daily from 8:30 a.m. to 7 p.m.

---

La Paz. Photo by Martin Li.

# WITCHES' MARKET

By Dr. Crit Minster, Rochester, New York, U.S.A.

Time to make out your shopping list. Let's see … a dozen eggs, some milk, you're low on toilet paper, some pork chops … oh, and don't forget the dried llama fetus, because you never know when your home will need protection from someone trying to hex you!

Wandering around the Witches' Market (El Mercado de las Brujas) in La Paz is a cultural experience like no other. The hills of Calle Linares, not far from downtown La Paz, (where the market takes place) become a maze of wizened vendors, smiling toothless behind tables laden with dried animals, potions, clay figures, candles, incense and bunches of pungent herbs. There are rolls of snakeskins, small, grinning figures of Andean men with play money sticking out of their tiny pockets (a prosperity charm) and remedies for everything from stomach ailments to lovesickness. You don't have to be a witch or a warlock to purchase something: the vendors are accustomed to foreigners and are happy to tell you what everything is used for. Today, much of the business done at this traditional market is with tourists.

"The dried frogs bring money," a cheerful crone assures me. "The clay figures are for many different things." There are dried armadillos for home protection, burnt llama fetuses for prosperity, and any number of charms, potions and candles that promise a better sex life. (Let's see … more money, better sex life … sounds like the spam folder on my e-mail account.) The dried llama fetuses (which, by the way, look extremely creepy: you may mistake them for desiccated birds) are traditionally buried under homes when the foundation is set: they bring security and prosperity. Some estimate that upwards of 95% of Bolivian homes have a llama fetus in the foundation.

I ask the woman if she knows who Harry Potter is. She gives me a blank look, and I assume that Harry and his friends must do their shopping elsewhere.

You can even purchase spells. Want a special someone to fall in love with you? No problem. Kids getting bad grades in school? Not for long! Starting a new business venture? You won't need a marketing plan if you have the power of white magic on your side. If you want to simply know the future, you can have your coca leaves read, sort of a South American version of telling the future with tea leaves. The coca leaf reading is still very popular with Bolivians, although relatively few tourists try it.

Tradition is important in Bolivia, and many Bolivians still seek out these traditional mystics and healers. The Witches' Market in La Paz isn't the only one in the country: other cities have them as well, although they're smaller. It's fortunate that such bastions of traditional Bolivian culture remain, although the time may soon come when the Witches' Market only caters to foreign tourists. I suggest you hop on your broom and get there before it loses its unique charm!

## TOP LIST: TRADITIONAL MARKETS WITH FLAIR

Native markets remain one of Latin America's biggest tourist attractions: people come from all over to find art, gifts, and that special one-of-a-kind item for a friend back home. These are some of our readers' favorites:

1. Otavalo, Ecuador (p. 237).
"Incredible mix of locals and tourists and quality products." Larry Clark, San Diego, U.S.A.

2. Witches Market, La Paz, Bolivia (see above).
"You'll find things here you'll never see anywhere else in the world - llama foetuses, condor feathers, etc." Carol Ann, Scotland.

3. San Telmo Market, BA, Argentina (p. 31).
"Such fun energy with art, antiques and street tango shows." Patty Buckworth, U.S.A.

4. Mercado Libertad, Guadalajara, Mexico.
"Largest open air market in Mexico—stupendous." Mark Mellander, California, U.S.A.

5. El Pochote Organic Weekend Market, Oaxaca.
"Fresh, organic breakfast, fresh juices and other organic products in the small, but beautiful outdoor El Pochote marketplace." Rachel Tussel, Michigan, U.S.A.

Runners-up:

21 Noviembre Markets, Oaxaca, Mexico. Michelle, Boston, U.S.A.

Chichicastenango, Guatemala. "Colors, sounds, and odors assault you from all sides." Dr. Crit Minster, U.S.A.

Mercado Aldolfo Lisboa, Manuas, Brazil.

# OFF THE BEATEN TRACK IN AND AROUND LA PAZ

By Kelley Coyner, Texas, U.S.A.

Most known for its extreme altitude, ladies with bowler hats, the coca museum, and witches market, La Paz also has many lesser known treasures to share. Depending on what tickles your fancy, there are dance and dinner fests (known as *peñas*), treks on ancient Incan roads, museums squeezed behind colonial side streets, textile exhibits and secret shopping finds, as well as a terrific children's museum whose views of the city alone are worth the trip.

Located on former fair grounds, Kusillo is not just for kids. Associated with the Kipus Foundation's interactive children's health and culture programs, this place has plenty to keep parents and progeny alike busy. For a striking view of the city, hop on the outdoor elevator (known as the funicular) or head to the playground on the upper level. If sweeping views and heights aren't your style, try something with a little artistic flair: kids can try their hand at local crafts and everyone can spend some time checking out the crafts from La Paz and around the country.

Calle Jaén, located very close to La Paz's major plaza and cathedral, harbors great views of the city's remaining Spanish colonial buildings, as well four museums. The Precious Metals museum, which exhibits Inca and Tiwanaka work, is a sure win, as is the Museo de Instrumentos Musicales de Bolivia. The latter displays an array of charangas, horns, drums and other music-making devices from the past and present. Get in touch with your musical side, as you bang and pluck your way around exhibits of play-it-yourself drums, harps, and pianos. A great chance to fill the colonial courtyard with your own version of musical genius.

Like the city itself, the clothing donned in La Paz is a refreshing blend of traditional and modern. You can learn more about Inca, Aymaran and other textiles at the Museo Nacional de Etnografía y Folklore or the Textiles museum. COMART on Illampu features a range of wearable works downstairs and a display from the recently revived weaving district of Tarabuco upstairs. Millma, which exports to exclusive boutiques in the U.S., features beautiful contemporary alpaca sweaters and other garments at significantly lower prices than you will find back home.

If you're in the mood to get the old heart pumping, go for a trek on the area's Inca Roads; day treks of all kinds abound around La Paz. Be sure to exercise some caution, though, as routes change every wet season. The two main Inca Roads—the Choro and Takesi—have yet to change, however. You can day hike or hire a guide and walk the entire road in a couple of days.

If you're a little green from the altitude, but want to get out for some air, try Pongo, located just 15 minutes past La Cumbre, or Summit, on the world's most dangerous highway. You can take a turn fishing for trout, or buy some at one of the stands (we recommend number 17 and 23). Or you can head to the Valle de La Luna for a lookout over really funky sand and rock formations.

www.vivatravelguides.com/104031

# MUELA DEL DIABLO

By Kelley Coyner, Texas, U.S.A.

According to Bolivian *abuelas* (grandmothers), *Muela del Diablo* (the Devil's molar) can be a dangerous place. The hole at the base of the mountain is supposedly enchanted and draws in dogs and young men who are swallowed by its darkness and never seen again. In this part of the Andes, myths and legends of mountain devils abound. The devil figures prominently in the local carnival dance, and special amulets are made for rituals performed to protect miners who enter the mountain.

To the unsuspecting observer, Muela del Diablo appears like nothing more harmful than a broken tooth jutting out from the mountains that surround the bowl-shaped valley that is home to the capital city of La Paz. For many years, the Devil's Tooth was the venue for trekkers seeking to acclimatize to the altitude before taking on a multi-day trek. Despite its rather ominous history, it remains a beautiful half day walk that provides a spectacular view of the city of La Paz as well as the scenic gorges that surround it. During the fall, winter, and spring (roughly April to November), the walk also boasts spectacular views of the Cordillera Real, including Illumani and Murato. 40 bolivianos and a predisposition for taxis chugging along nearly vertical mountain roads will get you to the Pedregal cemetery and from there to the Muela del Diablo trailhead (if your driver isn't careful, your visit to the cemetery may be permanent!).

Follow the trail up to a small plateau, where you can gaze at the scenery and stop for a picnic. The hardier can continue on, and scramble up the rocky outcropping. Take care as there is lot of scree, or loose rock, which can be particularly challenging on windy days. The summit is reachable, but only with climbing gear, strong legs and a hankering for heights. While in the area, avoid walking across fields, even small ones, as this is seen as a sign of disrespect (and because you may trample potato plants).

If you happen to be at the Muela on All Saints Day, which is celebrated on November 2, head to the cemetery at San Pedregal, where you can experience some of the most vibrant and colorful celebrations in the area. For hours on end, the air is filled with the music of bands playing in the smaller graveyard, close to the start of the trail. As you enjoy the music, notice the lavishly decorated graves, which are adorned not only with crowns of flowers, but also special breads and other food stuffs to feed the spirits of the dead. Tents selling food and drink for the living, along with carnival rides, ring the perimeter.

As for the dangers of the cave, you'll have to decide for yourself.

# TIWANAKU

### By Albert Garcia, Fullerton, California, U.S.A.

Surrounded by sweeping views of the dusty Altiplano, the ruins of Tiwanaku (also known as Tiahuanaco) are one of Bolivia's most visited cultural treasures. Stone walls and temples stand in majestic contrast to the desolation of the northern highlands. Solemn faces carved into giant monoliths stare silently across the plains, concealing the advanced knowledge of an ancient culture that cheated the elements and thrived in this cold, windswept valley.

Tiwanaku was constructed 13,000 feet (4,000 meters) above sea level near the southern shore of Lake Titicaca. Spanning almost 3,000 years, its cultural influence reached from Bolivia into the modern-day nations of Peru, Chile and Argentina. During its peak (between A.D. 500 and 950) some historians believe between 10,000 to 60,000 people lived near the city center. Their perfected method of food production, raised field agriculture, is still in use by many indigenous Aymara today. The drive to the site crosses plains extending from the western side of the snow covered Andes through an endless landscape of fields, farmlands, and traditional villages. A museum at the site begins the tour with collections of artifacts from years of excavations, including elongated skulls and musical instruments.

Sometimes referred to as the "American Stonehenge", Tiwanaku is recognized as one of 754 World Heritage Sites. The walls and temples are built with precisely cut stone blocks, one of which weighs over 130 tons. Archaeologists are still trying to understand how, exactly, many of the stones were transported from quarries up to 100 km away. During the summer solstice, locals celebrate with folkloric dances and music while thousands gather to watch the sun's rays pass through the massive Puerta del Sol (Gateway of the Sun). The giant gateway bears an image found on pottery and textiles in many regions outside of the city. Referred to as the 'Staff God', it is likened to Viracocha, the creator god of Inka religion, though a lack of written records has prevented scholars from determining definitively that this figure represented Viracocha for the early Tiwanaku people. Tiwanaku serves as a unifying symbol in Bolivia, a nation with almost 200 revolutions and military coups in the past 200 years. In January of 2006, the newly elected president, Evo Morales, an Aymara Indian, celebrated his victory at the site in a traditional ceremony complete with native dress and music.

Excavations are often conducted at and around the site to understand its remaining unknowns. What is known, however, is the widespread influence of Tiwanaku on Andean culture. According to archaeologist Javier Escalante, this influence "transcended the borders of its capital, covering diverse and distant areas" of South America. To see Tiwanaku, in other words, is to see where Andean culture began.

## SAN PEDRO PRISON

By Katie Hale

Luxuriously decorated apartments sit overlooking La Paz and snowcapped mountains; children run in the courtyard; the Coca-Cola-sponsored soccer team plays a lively game; diners enjoy a leisurely lunch in neighborhood restaurants; grocery stores sell fresh goods; men read the newspaper as their shoes are shined. The scene could be that of an upper-class, gated community. In a way, that's exactly what it is. However, the people behind these gates cannot come and go as they please.

Looks can be deceiving—these men and women aren't here for a little R and R—they were caught committing serious crimes like murder or smuggling millions of dollars worth of cocaine. They are now living behind the gates of San Pedro Prison in La Paz, serving hard time.

The gates cannot keep out the problems of the outside world. Like any city, San Pedro Prison has a dark side. There are drug lords, daily acts of violence, and many inmates are addicted to smoking cocaine base, which is readily available from laboratories inside the prison walls.

The prisoners without money live day to day like they would on the streets and are confined to small cells. Here in San Pedro, money can buy a sense of freedom. Prisoners must purchase their own cells, and the more money spent, the more lavish and comfortable the living quarters. One prisoner didn't like the four-star wing of the prison, so he constructed a new building and designated the penthouse for himself.

There are 200 children of inmates living in San Pedro. Under Bolivian legislation, it is legal for children under six to live with their incarcerated parents. Often wives of imprisoned husbands live here to cut down on expenses. Although living conditions are not ideal, the family can stay together as one unit.

San Pedro is open for illegal tours and entrance is around $7. Once inside you will be escorted by a guide and be given someone to act as your "protection." The prison does not allow cameras, but past visitors inform that this rule is not strictly enforced and you may want to document the amazing view from the inside—of course at your own risk.

For an fascinating account of the prison, read *Marching Powder: A True Story of Friendship, Cocaine, and South America's Strangest Jail* by Thomas McFadden and Rusty Young.

# TIWANAKU OFF THE BEATEN TRACK

By Kelley Coyner, Texas, U.S.A.

A number of small towns nearby Lake Titicaca offer wonderful spots for traveling off the beaten track. The following are some of the best locales.

Most people rightfully come to Tiwanaku for the ruins and museums. The new museum explains the traditions of this ceremonial capital which has been at the epicenter of Andean culture for 1,000 years, and the influence of this ancient culture is obvious around town. Walk to the church built by colonial-era tin magnates. After a visit to the museums and ruins, the statues should seem familiar. Much of the stone used to build these came from the Tiwanaku structures. After a long day of touring, you may just want to catch some sleep. Take a break from napping at the overlook outside of Tiwanaku. On a clear day, it may be one of the best views of the Corderillo Real. If you yearn to taste llama, a staple of the Tiwanaku diet, stop at the Tiwanaka Inn.

Located 15 minutes by car from Tiwanaku, the historic port of Guaqui offers views of Lake Titicaca and the Corderillo Real of the Andes. The port was a key hub for transportation in the 1900s and now holds restored steam locomotives of the era. After a flood inundated area in the mid-1980s, both the water port and the rail operation closed. Today you can poke around the original warehouses on the rail sidings and take a peak at the locomotives. If you are lucky enough to find someone with the keys to the secured warehouse and you can take a look at an English-made, small steam locomotive from 1914 (La Hualaycha) and a medium-sized locomotive also of English descent, No. 6 (La Illimani). In 2007, the Bolivian-based Quipus Foundation hopes to open the first in a series of museums on site and thereafter you will be able to hop aboard one of these old trains for a ride around the area.

Less than a kilometer away from the port, the town of Guaqui hosts a recently restored colonial church. Built in 1624, the walls exhibit exquisitely painted mantles and the altar is covered in silverwork typical of the era. Be sure to tuck your head into the small chapel dedicated to El General Tata Santiago, a local hero who has been sanctified by the Catholic Church here. He's the soldier riding a white stallion at the rear of the chapel. If you happen to visit in late July you may see the Morenada, a traditional dance of parish festivals and the Carnival.

On the way to Tiwanaku, the road passes alongside Laja—once the original site of La Paz. Finding the cold, arid winds of the Altiplano too much to bear, the Spanish relocated to below the *seja* or edge of the Altiplano. The colonial church still stands off the road in the little town—just follow its towers to get there. The toll booth marks the exits for Laja as well as a snack stop. Aymayran ladies in blue aprons sell fresh, flat bread for a Boliviano a bag, or about 15 cents. The bread is best when it is still warm.

Students keen on the early civilizations of South America should venture to Chiripa, a small village located on the Taraco peninsula, at the southern arm of Lake Titicaca. Between the church and the soccer field is an ongoing excavation of a subterranean temple, believed to have belonged to one of the earliest cultures on the lake. The gate is usually padlocked, but ask around for the mayor who can let you in and provide you with a brief overview of the site. The site is not physically astounding, but its historical significance will send a chill down your spine.

---

MORENADA FACTOIDS: The Morenada was the first African dance in Bolivia. Dancers wear costumes representing the wealth of mine owners that can weigh over 100 lbs. The dance itself represents the forced march of the African slaves that were brought to Bolivia by the Spanish and Portuguese to work in silver and gold mines. Many of the slaves died from a result of being overworked or altitude sickness.

---

## LATIN REVOLUTIONARIES #2: ERNESTO "CHÉ" GUEVARA

(1928-1967)

Born to wealthy parents in Argentina, Ché Guevara earned a medical degree in Buenos Aires in 1953. He abandoned his medical career, however, and traveled around Latin America in the early 1950s, eventually winding up in Guatemala in 1954. Guevara fought with the socialist government against a CIA-led coup, but the efforts were in vain and he was forced to flee the country.

In Mexico, he met Fidel Castro, the firebrand Cuban revolutionary and went with him to Cuba in 1956. Eventually Guevara, Castro and others were able to topple the Cuban government in late 1958. With Castro taking over as leader, Guevara ascended to Minister of Industries and other important positions. Guevara also took on the task of spreading the communist revolution: using Cuban resources, he supported failed insurgencies in Panama and the Dominican Republic in 1959.

In 1965, Guevara disappeared: eventually he was found to have gone to the Congo to support communist revolutionary forces seeking to replace the Congolese government. The revolution failed, in part due to US-aided intelligence gathering by the Congolese. Guevara returned to Cuba, but soon disappeared again. He had gone to Bolivia to help local communists overthrow the government there. Once again, his efforts were in vain: this time, he was captured and executed by Bolivian forces in October, 1967.

# TREKKING CONDORIRI TO HUAYNA POTOSÍ

## By Kelley Coyner, Texas, U.S.A.

Starting about an hour outside of La Paz, the Condoriri to Huayna Potosí trek packs a remote, world class trek into three days and two nights. This short interval has it all: views of the Cordillera Real llama herdsman and their flocks, glaciers, 18,000 foot passes, sand pits, fantastic fauna and flora, mining ruins, crystalline waters and a close up look at Huayna Potosí from multiple lookouts.

The drop-off point is a two and half hour walk from the Mt. Condoriri base camp. The relatively short walk is somewhat dull compared to the landscape yet to come. Drop your bags, set up your tent, and take a hike to the edge of the receding Condoriri glacier, named for its condor-like appearance.

Poking around the vicinity is interesting in its own right. Base camp is next to an enclosure for llamas and pack animals. A small settlement nearby supports the base camp: the herdsmen, guides and cooks live there.

The *cholitas*, local women sporting traditional skirts, petticoats and hats, will be glad to take you vizcacha hunting with their traditional sling shots, though you're best to turn down any invitations: they're an endangered species, despite being an important part of the local diet. Technically a rodent, the vizcacha looks like a cross between a rabbit and squirrel. The cracks and crevices in the rocky outcroppings surrounding the camp provide a communal burrowing area, rather like a vizcacha condo complex. At dusk, dozens of the critters scurry in and out. The unfortunate ones become dinner.

After an overnight at camp, you're ready to hike. The next day's trek traverses rolling ridges and valleys and a series of lakes. The first lakes and ponds are shallow, silty, and greenish-white in color, and fed by glacier melt. Around these ponds are spongy bogs with tiny flowering plants. The lakes that you will pass later in the day are fed by an elaborate, rock-hewn irrigation system. Some of these lakes are now trout farms. Toward the end of the day, the trail passes through an old mining community. The region's hills and valleys are riddled with abandoned mines, which in their day constituted the economic mainstay of the area.

The second night's sleep-over spot is only partially sheltered from the howling winds. The gusts, along with the temperature drop, discourage most from leaving their tents after bedtime. The condensation from the breath of two trekkers was enough to cover the inside of the tent and the sleeping bags with a crusty frost by dawn. Dawn is wake up time both because it so hard to sleep at 15,000 feet and because there is a hard hike ahead.

The last day's trek provides close–ups of the dramatic recession of the glaciers in this area. The schlep over the highest point at a little more than 18,000 feet is across a scree slope that was completely covered by a glacier just twenty years ago. After passing to the other side, there is a relatively easy 90-minute ramble on dusty roads and well beaten paths through rolling hills and pristine lakes. The trek ends at the base of Huayna Potosí. There are magnificent views of the mountain from the trail and your efforts are rewarded at the *refugio* café with a terrific view of the glaciers.

## QUINOA

### By Michelle Hopey

The United Nations has already declared it a superfood, NASA is considering feeding its spaceflight crews with it, and supermarkets across the U.S. Canada and Europe are on the look-out for this new phenomenal food called Quinoa. Not bad for a tiny 1/8 of an inch seed hailing from the Andean highlands of South America.

Despite its recent move towards popularity though, Quinoa, (pronounced KEEN Wah) is nothing new. In fact, Peruvians have been eating the cereal crop since as far back as 3,000 B.C. In Quechua, the dominant language of the Peruvian Incas, Quinoa is known as *chisiya mama* or "mother grain." However, not to out the Incas or anything, but Quinoa is actually not a grain, but rather it is a seed that is grows from the Chenopodium or Goosefoot plant. Many often assume Quinoa's status as a grain because it is small and well, grainy. Plus its nutritious content—a unique amino acid composition combined with high calcium and phosphorus and a low sodium content, makes it seem like a grain. Plus, it's gluten-free and easy to digest.

Light and fluffy when cooked, Quinoa is similar to couscous or rice. It can be used in a variety of dishes, historically in Peru and Bolivia it is commonly used in soups and as portage. The glory of Quinoa though, is that it can been creatively added, substituted for, or simply used in nearly every dish from soups pasta, salads, cereals and can be fortified in breads, pastries and cookies. Although it has a mild nut flavor when baked, raw Quinoa can taste quite bitter and can be crunchy and hard since it protected by a coating called saponin. Saponin can be toxic to the body, so before cooking the first step is to remove the saponins by soaking the seeds in water for a few hours and then running water over it. Most boxed quinoa, however, has been pre-rinsed before packaging.

After rinsing the seeds, its time to cook the Quinoa, which is very similar to cooking rice:

Measure one cup of dry Quinoa, rinse in a strainer, and put the grains into a two-quart saucepan. Add two cups of water and a dash of salt. Cover and bring to a boil over high heat. Turn heat down to low and let sit for 15 to 20 minutes. As the seed cooks, the germ unfolds itself and forms a tiny white spiral circle. Quinoa, like rice can double its size during the cooking process. But when it's done, fluff it with a fork and add it to whatever you please, because not only will it be nutritious, but it might just become your next comfort food.

# AMBORÓ NATIONAL PARK

By Kelley Coyner, Texas, U.S.A.

Bolivian travel literature is filled with stories of travelers lost in the jungle. Some miraculously make it through, like Yossi Ghinsberg, who made it back to civilization after nine days lost along the Tuichi river in Madidi. Some were never to be seen again, such as the plucky British surveyer Col. Fawcett who apparently became lost shortly after embarking on his last quest to find the lost city of Atlantis (maybe he found it and decided to stay). Even the briefest excursion to Amboró National Park vividly demonstrates how easy it is to get lost in the wilds of Bolivia; it also explains why the intrepid and adventurous are drawn here.

Located in the eastern lowlands of Bolivia, Amboró comprises three distinct ecosystems: the Amazon River basin, the foothills of the Andes Mountains, and the Chaco desert. The small villages of Buena Vista to the north and Samaipata to the south and west are the staging areas for a variety of treks, from short one-dayers to a seventeen-day trek that traverses the entire park. Day trips cut through fern forests, heading towards condor nesting sites and secluded waterfalls. A two-day trek might include dozens of river crossings, captivating vistas of volcanic lakes, tunnel gorges, ridge walks, and field crossings—all this as the trail winds past small farms located in the managed resource portion of the park.

Fabled among birders as an avian paradise, the Amboró National Park contains more species of birds than all of North America. Even the unseasoned birder may spot condors, parrots, boa birds, and parakeets. Veteran birders will undoubtedly add to their life lists as they make their way through even a small corner of the park.

The park is also home to numerous insects, mammals including big cats such as pumas and jaguars, the world's largest rodent, the capybara, the tapir, and reportedly more types of butterflies than any place on earth. In the area surrounding the campsite sponsored by a local community, no fewer than a dozen varieties of butterflies dip and dive around summer flowers. The elusive Blue Morpho darts among flowers in open fields and along dim forest paths.

Little wonder that even a short visit to the park may result in sensory overload. The Spanish, after all, despised it, calling it *Infierno Verde* or "Green Hell." Of course, they wanted to pass through it on horseback and were quickly mired and lost going up and down gorges, hills, and canyons that lurk beneath the thick tropical and subtropical forest. In the end, the same hellish green may be what saves the park, both dissuading new settlements and attracting voyagers who relish such natural sanctuaries.

### AMBORÓ PARK FACTOIDS:
Although no one is allowed to live within park boundaries, over 18,000 people live within the buffer zones of the park and currently threaten the ecological well-being of the area. Unregulated oil exploration, hunting, fishing, tourism, logging, and slash and burn agriculture put the park in danger of major degradation. Many tourists are taking part in eco-tours when they visit to cut down on human infringement of the natural environment as much as possible.

## EVO MORALES' JUMPER

By Leigh Gower

His behavior breaks the norm on many accounts. He is single, shared a flat with other MAS officers before election, and following the election, cut his salary by 57%. But nothing marks Evo Morales' leadership more distinctly than the red, white and blue striped alpaca sweater he regularly sports to meetings with world dignitaries.

An Aymara Indian, Mr. Morales is believed to be the first indigenous president in Bolivian history, and, as such, has refused to adopt the formal suited look employed by the majority of world leaders. He greeted French President Jacques Chirac in short-sleeves and stood open-necked next to Venezuela's Hugo Chavez. Most impressively however, he donned "the sweater" on four continents following his December 2005 election.

The Bolivian president's sweater has even received international attention: a Mexican radio station wrote a song about "the sweater;" which goes in part:

*The president-elect of Bolivia/Has a sweater, nothing more/It's striped, cozy/The truth is, it's not so pretty/Ohhhh, yeah/Buy him another sweater already.*

Morales' casual cool has certainly been received well by his electorate. Reuters reported that Bolivians were pleased Morales had remained true to his roots with the sweater, or *chompa*, symbolic of his remaining a man of the people. Remarkably, it has also become a fashion item. Knitwear company Punto Blanco claims it will sell copies of the sweater as "a symbol of the president."

# LA GRAN CHIQUITANIA

By Geoff Groesbeck, Hamilton, Massachusetts, U.S.A.

La Gran Chiquitania—"The Great Chiquitania"—may well be South America's last undiscovered paradise, a vast land of quiet, pristine natural beauty, blessed with a unique culture and fascinating history. Slumbering in the remote eastern plains of Bolivia's Santa Cruz province, it is a refuge and a delight for the traveller who has been everywhere and done everything, but who still seeks that elusive final frontier.

There's no one in your rear view mirror in the Chiquitania. You may go the rest of your life without meeting anyone who's made this trip...but many who'll wish they had. And your timing is perfect: 2006 marked the opening of the Lanzamiento Mundial de las Misiones Jesuitícas Chiquitos, when the Jesuit mission settlements open to the world in all their glory.

A region with a unique culture, history, people, and environment, the Chiquitania is an unforgettable experience from start to finish. It's also everything your parents would want it to be: safe, peaceful, and it won't cost you an arm and a leg. It's ridiculously cheap—you'd be hard pressed to spend $500 USD in a week in the Chiquitania for everything, including lodging and transportation.

The product of a remarkable fusion of two civilizations, European and native American, its fascinating legacy remains intact to this day. Its world-famous Jesuit mission churches, each a breathtakingly beautiful architectural wonder and spiritual monument built in the midst of an idyllic wilderness, were established by intrepid Jesuit missionaries between 1691 and 1760. Six were designated World Heritage Sites by UNESCO in 1990, and seven survive intact, their original glory lovingly restored in every detail.

Others come for the Renaissance and Baroque musical and theatre extravaganzas (celebrated in world-famous festivals held every other year throughout the region's major towns); an astounding heritage of sacred art and architecture; abandoned colonial ruins slumbering in pristine settings and a wealth of centuries-old customs and folklore handed down from one generation to the next that still play a dominant role in daily life.

Some come for the colourful folklore and traditions maintained here and nowhere else. Still others come for the beautiful hand-wrought art that has fascinated collectors and scholars for centuries. Yet there is more than cultural attractions. Nature rules here, and the options are limitless, from luxurious cabañas and the slow pace of life in towns like San Javier and Concepción, to charming frontier settlements like Santa Ana and San Matías; from the honeymoon villages of Santiago de Chiquitos and Roboré to empty, eerie landscapes and petrified forests of the pathless Serranía Santiago and Serranía Sunsas.

You can visit historical wonders from prehistoric drawings in long-forgotten caves and rock faces in the remote outposts of Quimome and Motacusito to primeval forests larger than entire countries; from the northern edges of the trackless Gran Chaco to the watery wonderland of the Pantanal; from the amazing "Tree of Life" carvings and the energy-radiating El Torre in Chochís to secluded balnearios and wide-open plazas; and of course, the astounding flora and fauna of no less than five of Bolivia's ecological crown jewels: Noel Kempff Mercado; Otuquis; San Matías; Santa Cruz la Vieja; and the Ríos Blanco y Negro National Wildlife Reserve.

San Xavier. Photo by Geoff Groesbeck.

---

Geoff Groesbeck spent his formative years alternating between Portugal's ridiculously sunny Algarve coast and Massachusetts' somewhat sunny North Shore. Briefly dallying in Japanese at Harvard, but coming to his senses after his first exam, he walked a fine line between jaunts in global finance and financing global jaunts, before deciding upon the latter as an infinitely preferable vocation.

Until recently an academic at the Massachusetts Institute of Technology, Groesbeck now works closely with several non-profit organisations in and around Santa Cruz, Bolivia, and has written extensively on Bolivia and Paraguay.

His particular field of expertise is the Jesuit missions of Bolivia's remote Chiquitania, for which his writings and website have won international acclaim.

His most bizarre cultural experience was when he wandered into a Bolivian café on an intensely hot day, only to be greeted by a chorus line of young girls dressed as Father Christmas (in red fur-trimmed mini-skirts), urging him to try the house speciality: Indian curry.

# FESTIVALES DE MISIONES DE CHIQUITOS

By Geoff Groesbeck, Hamilton, Massachusetts, U.S.A.

If you had to choose the most unlikely place on earth to take in a Baroque concert, one with musical instruments, scores, and settings completely faithful to its seventeenth-century origins, where would you choose to go? Chances are you couldn't possibly top the remote jungles and plains of eastern Bolivia. Yet this is exactly what you'll find if you are fortunate enough to travel to the mission settlements of the distant Oriente.

There are 15 of these idyllic settlements, each founded by peripatetic Franciscan and Jesuit missionaries in the seventeenth and eighteen centuries and nearly lost in Bolivia's vast, largely unexplored Amazonian basin. Each location offers a stunning display of musical virtuosity every other year in late April, with concerts held in the towns' beautiful colonial-era churches (six of which were named World Heritage Sites by UNESCO in 1990).

These festivals, painstakingly organized by the Santa Cruz-based non-profit group Asociación Pro Arte y Cultura, last for 11 days and are collectively known as "Festivales de Misiones de Chiquitos." They are perhaps Bolivia's finest attraction for the culturally minded traveler. Since their quiet beginnings in 1996, they have consistently attracted world-class performers and are now numbered amongst the most important classical musical festivals anywhere in the world. In the 2004 festival alone, nearly 1,000 performers from 22 countries performed more than 120 concerts in these timeless communities.

The location for these festivals is not as strange as it may seem at first. The Oriente is a traveler's paradise—the finest of many within Bolivia—and the regions where these festivals take place, the Moxos, Guarayos, and Chiquitos mission towns, have some of the richest cultural traditions in all of Latin America. Here and here alone, European tastes merged with local indigenous traditions to create a hybrid culture that for a time bordered on the utopian. To the amazement of the few visitors who make it as far as the Oriente, this polyglot culture has survived in an essentially unchanged form to this day. And there's nowhere better to see, hear, and experience it than at these festivals.

The festivals are a remarkable revival of a centuries-old musical phenomenon: missionaries trained their native "charges" to become phenomenal craftsmen in several fields, but especially so in music. The Chiquitano tribes in particular had an amazing ability to adapt to and incorporate European motifs into their artistic output. Complex European musical instruments and scores were effortlessly assimilated in the depths of the Bolivian forests by the Chiquitano under the tutelage of the missionaries.

This output eventually led to each mission having not just a truly world-class church (courtesy of the missionaries), but also an orchestra staffed entirely by indigenous peoples. Often these tiny settlements also had schools of music and instrument making as well. Imagine this, in a town of about a thousand inhabitants, hundreds of miles from the nearest settlement of any size, and you begin to get a vague idea of what the Jesuits and Franciscans, in partnership with these indigenous peoples, managed to create … and what is still preserved intact to this day in these festivals.

## TOP CAPTIVATING CHURCHES AND CONVENTS

The early Spanish colonists were very religious and constructed many churches, convents, monasteries and other religious structures. The city of Cuenca, Ecuador alone is rumored to have 52 churches—one for every week of the year! Our community have suggested their favorites in Latin America:

1. La Compañia, Quito, Ecuador.
Teresa Colomer, Spain. "Exquisite." Paula Newton, England.

2. Santa Catalina Monastery, Arequipa, Peru.
"A whole city block of the most charming Spanish colonial buildings. A city within stone walls." Mark Mellander, California, U.S.A.

3. Santo Domingo, Oaxaca, Mexico.
"Simply stunning." Mexico, Michelle, Boston, U.S.A.

4. La Compañia, Cusco, Peru.
Teresa Colomer, Spain.

5. Church of St. Thomas, Chichicastenango, Guatemala. "This 400-year-old church is fascinating because of the bustling market on its front steps and the nature of the services, which are as traditional Maya as they are Catholic. The church itself was built on a Mayan platform." Dr. Crit Minster, Rochester, New York, U.S.A.

6. Igreja do Senhor do Bonfim, Salvador, Brazil. "This smallish church, set on the top of a hill overlooking Salvador, is notable for several reasons. Locals consider it very special, and go there to purchase special lucky ribbons, ask for medical miracles, or even to have their cars blessed by the priests. It is considered holy not only by Catholics but by those who practice Candomble as well. It also offers a good view of the city." Shelley Wallis, U.K.

7. Catedral Basilica Menor de Santa Maria, Santo Domingo, Dominican Republic. "The oldest church in the Americas. Supposedly, Christopher Columbus was originally buried there." Mark Smith, Bedford, England.

# SAMAIPATA

By Kelley Coyner, Texas, U.S.A.

Samaipata—Quechua for a "rest in a higher place"—is a jumping off point for a visit to El Fuerte, the easternmost of several pre-Inca fortifications. From here you can head to Las Cuevas, where natural swimming holes flanked by gorgeous waterfalls give way to a variety of walking trails. The area is perfect for short and long hikes and horseback riding, or just having a pleasant break to poke around and explore the old Spanish Colonial route from Santa Cruz to Sucre and Cochabamba.

The area is a great launching point for treks into the Amboró National Park and—further on eastern route—to the Noel Kempff National Park and the Jesuit Missions. Hardy hikers and trekkers can also use this as a starting point for a four day trip retracing the old trade route to Sucre via Vallegrande, Río Grande, Villa Serrano, Zudañez and Tarabuco. Hiking boots aside, this place houses the enigmatic El Fuerte ruins. Despite years of investigation and excavation, little is known about this World Heritage site. It is thought to have first served as a lookout and ceremonial center for Amazonian tribes before a brief stint as an Inca fortification. Carved from a solid slab of sandstone, El Fuerte is sadly suffering from erosion. At one time, the stones carried distinct images of jaguar and puma, but the serpentine marks near the water canal are quickly fading.

Until 1998, visitors were free to walk around the carvings up-close, but in the name of preservation, they must now view the structure from walkways built above and around the site. Erosion notwithstanding, the site is striking due to its unexplained animal and geometric markings, and its mummy and icon niches. The chikana (Quechua for labyrinth) located nearby is also a visitor magnet. This maze-like structure winds underground, and begins at the foot of a deep hole, where excavators located a tunnel entrance. Vultures and condors may also be spotted from the walkways.

Described as having a Never-Never Land feel (minus Peter Pan), Amboró Park also features cloud covered fern forest seemingly pulled right from a fairytale. The whole region is a bird watcher's paradise. Whether you choose to hike and trek, bird watch, or visit La Fuerte, this place is sure to keep you busy.

*"I forgive the people in the White House for their numerous humiliations and accusations. I forgive them because we must embark, through dialogue, on the search for peace and social justice."*
-Juan "Evo" Morales, President of Bolivia (1959-)

## BOLIVIA FACTOIDS

By Dr. Crit Minster

Bolivia is the only completely landlocked country in South America (Paraguay has a navigable river to the Atlantic).

Bolivia and Peru share Lake Titicaca, the highest navigable lake in the world.

Bolivia is one of the poorest countries in Latin America: 64% of the population lives below the poverty line.

Bolivia is the world's third-largest producer of coca, the plant from which cocaine is made.

During the Spanish colonial period, millions of tons of silver were mined from Cerro Rico, near Potosí, Bolivia, making it one of the richest mines in history.

The famous Spanish "pieces of eight," or silver coins worth eight reales, were minted in Bolivia before being shipped to Spain.

In the 19th and 20th centuries, Bolivia lost significant chunks of national territory in wars with Chile (1884) and Paraguay (1935). They also lost some land in 1903 when one of their territories seceded and was subsequently annexed by Brazil

While in Bolivia, try an *empanada salteña*, a sort of fried turnover filled with meat.

Back in the 1930s, a president of Bolivia ordered the construction of a Bavarian-style castle along the road from Chulumani to La Paz. It was built with convict labor, and is reported to be haunted by the ghost of one of the workers. Today, "El Castillo" is a run-down but charming hotel.

# CAL ORKO

## By Kelley Coyner, Texas, U.S.A.

At a cement quarry near Sucre, Bolivia, one can come close to traveling through Jurassic Park on the Dino Truck. You can follow in the footsteps of the monstrous dinosaurs that walked the land eons ago. When visitors arrive from the main plaza in Sucre, they are handed bright orange hard hats and herded outdoors to the sandy area outside the park's small headquarters.

After entering the park, a guide with a basket of plastic dinosaurs describes how workers found the first footprints in 1998 and how shortly afterwards a German led expedition arrived to study the site. Each different plastic dinosaur illustrates a different species of dinosaur that roamed through this former swamp and lake bed.

The prints are found in an upended lake bed near Cal Orko outside of Sucre. The theory is that dinosaurs left their prints in the muddy bottom of the lake and surrounding wetlands. After the footprints fossilized, the earth's plate moved, leaving the lake bottom nearly perpendicular to the earth and forming a wall of sorts. Month to month and week to week the shale continues to peel off, both naturally and due to the workers who continue to mine the quarry for construction purposes. As each layer crumbles at the hands of both man and nature, new layers appear.

After the orientation, guide and guest scramble through the sand and along a broad ledge below the wall. Without assistance, one can easily see the hundreds of gigantic dino-prints across the wall. Just walk up to the wall and look closely at the tracks, which range in size from small to very large. The depth and breadth of the tracks provides visitors with a sense of the size and the weight of these dinosaurs. With the help of the guide's laser pointer, visitors can follow the claw prints of a tyrannosaur chasing its prey and trace the trail of more than 150 different kinds of dinosaurs.

Scrutinize this site with a scientific eye and observe that some dinosaurs are limping and others seem to meandering and still others running. You can discern this by looking at the depth of the tracks, smudge marks where an animal seems to be dragging a foot, and the distance between the tracks. With more than 2000 different prints, paleontologists consider this to be the richest find of tracks in the entire world.

The town of Cal Orko is creating a new museum, funded in large measure by the Inter American Development Bank. The museum will preserve the fossil record, tell the story, and advance research on the site.

## EARLY ORIGIN THEORIES

By Dr. Crit Minster

Before the New World was fully explored, the Spanish and Portuguese who conquered and colonized it wondered where the New World natives had come from. In the sixteenth century, faith in the Bible was quite literal, so the Europeans believed that everyone in the world was descended from Noah and his sons—and therefore had to reach their present locations from Armenia, where the Ark allegedly came to rest.

Theories about the origins of the New World natives abounded. Many theories were biblical in nature: one theory posited that the New World was Ophir, the source of King Solomon's wealth. Another popular theory was that the New World natives were descended from Jews: it was believed by many that they were the descendants of the Ten Lost Tribes of Israel, exiled during biblical times.

One of the most interesting theories was the Atlantis theory. Based upon Plato's description of Atlantis, many believed that there had once been a mighty continent between Europe and the Americas. Atlantis was believed to have been home to fabulous kingdoms: in 1571, Spanish historian Pedro Sarmiento de Gamboa wrote:

> *The lineage of Atlas extended in grand succession of generations, and his kingdom was ruled in succession by the firstborns ...That Island produced all things in great profusion. In ancient times it was sacred, beautiful, admirable and fertile, as well as of vast extent. In it were extensive kingdoms, sumptuous temples, palaces calling forth great admiration, as is seen from the relation of Plato respecting the metropolis of the island which exceeded Babylon, Troy, or Rome, with all their rich buildings, curious and well-constructed forts, and even the Seven Wonders of the World concerning which the ancients sing so much.*

With the advent of sciences such as ethnography, archaeology, linguistics and anthropology in the 18th and 19th centuries, origin theories based on the bible and ancient sources such as Plato became untenable. Eventually they were forgotten, replaced with migration models that generally have the ancestors of the peoples of the New World crossing into North America from Eastern Asia millennia ago.

# TARABUCO

## By Kelley Coyner, Texas, U.S.A.

An hour or so from Sucre, on the road towards Potosí, lies the market town of Tarbuco. Thirty minutes further down the road you'll find the Hacienda La Candelaria. The market in Tarabuco is a Sunday-only experience but La Candelaria is always an experience a la *One Hundred Years of Solitude*. Founded in the 17th century, Candelaria somehow escaped total nationalization by the Bolivian government in 1952. Credit is given to the young doña who struck an agreement with the campesinos in residence.

Today visitors can stay in recently constructed bedrooms equipped with electricity and water, although on a somewhat irregular basis. Even a short stay overnight provides a glimpse into hacienda life and its history. Food is prepared in the original wood-fired stove in large ollas or kettles. The courtyard is often filled with local residents selling handcrafted items. A handy pamphlet provided by the management will lead you on a walk through the main house, granary, and family chapel, as well as to the homes of the campesinos who continue to work the land and weave in their courtyards as they have for centuries. The traditional weaving, which was in danger of becoming a lost art, has seen a resurgence in recent years, in part because of support from international development organizations. There are several local textile styles. One of the more striking patterns features bands of white, black and purple with zoomorphic and human figures woven into the fabric. The figures tell a story, or often represent a dream or vision of the weaver. When in residence, the dueña or someone else will offer weavings and other handicrafts for viewing and sale.

The traditional hats are also noteworthy. The hats of Bolivia differ from region to region and frequently signal marital status. In the case of Tarabuco, a single woman wears a stiff cap of sorts decorated with beads that dangle before the eyes.

In a country filled with lively, colorful, and character-filled markets, Tarabuco may be one of the best. The mounds of produce, spices, and talismanic arrangements of llama imprinted sugar rival any other colorful Andean local market. Regional textiles are found on every corner. Inevitably, a visit reveals that textiles are not just for the tourists. The striped ponchos and poncho dresses are worn by many, as are the hats by married and single alike.

---

TARABUCO FACTOID:

The inhabitants of Tarabuco are known as *soncko mikus*, Quechua for "heart-eaters." During the time of the Spanish invasion, two men living in the town are said to have ate the raw hearts of Spanish soldiers to vindicate the rape of the native women. Two statues stand in the plaza today to commemorate the brutish locals.

---

# BOLIVIAN COCA

By Leigh Gower

For centuries Bolivians have chewed on coca leaves and brewed its tea to repress hunger, illness and fatigue; its advocates claim it contains essential minerals and nutrients and could even help combat obesity. But since the explosion of the illegal cocaine market in the 1980s (drawing between $600 million and $1 billion annually) the plant has come under fire from anti-narcotics agencies and countries of which the US has been its most vehement enemy.

Since the 1961 U.N. Single Convention on Narcotic Drugs, coca itself has been classified an illegal substance as harmful as cocaine or heroin. Today, anti-narcotic forces destroy up to seven ditches filled with coca leaves a day in the Chapare region of Bolivia, primary harvesting area in the country.

Bolivian President Evo Morales and many others see this classification as a historical error that needs to be corrected. He endorses the slogan "coca is not cocaine" and hopes to change coca's status within the U.N. narcotics and crime agency by 2008. A long-time leader of the *cocaleros* (coca farmers), Morales realizes that farming coca plants provides an enormous source of employment and income to Bolivian families who cannot make nearly as much money harvesting oranges or coffee. Bolivia's economy is one of the poorest in the Americas, second only to Haiti. The coca plant as the source for cocaine has become the cash crop of the country, bringing in millions of dollars to the economy's informal sector.

U.S. officials are insistent on coca eradication however, skeptical that coca plants can be grown in Bolivia without increasing the manufacture of its cocaine by-product. Officials from other countries in the Americas also have expressed concerns that Morales' plans will lead to increased gun-related violence fueled by the cocaine trade on their own streets.

# POTOSÍ

By Chris Sacco, Hamilton, New York, U.S.A.

Looking down upon Potosí from the barren heights of Cerro Rico, it's hard to believe that it was once the largest urban center in South America and one of the richest metropolises in the world.

From 1545 through the mid 18th century, the Spanish empire extracted millions of tons of silver from the hills around Potosí, so much that colonists bragged that they had mined enough ore to build a silver bridge that could span from Potosí to Madrid. By the time Bolivia won its independence in 1825, the vast majority of the area's mineral wealth had been shipped to Europe and the seemingly inexhaustible mines were in sharp decline.

Today, though, Potosí has little in the way of modern services and infrastructure to show for its age of affluence. Nevertheless, the old mines and the hopelessly friendly present-day miners tell a captivating yet sad tale.

Participating in a guided tour of Cerro Rico, once the most productive of all Potosí's silver mines, is the highlight of any visit to Potosí and, for many, the most memorable experience they have of Bolivia. Tours, which are led by current and former miners, begin with a trip to the market where workers stock up on dynamite, blasting caps and other tools of the trade, as well as the coca leaf and cigarettes that help them tolerate the brutal conditions. Afterwards, you will climb down several levels into the mine, making your way through cramped tunnels to catch a glimpse of miners extracting silver ore much as they did during the colonial era.

If you don't like the idea of slithering your way through narrow tunnels while miners hack and blast sections of rock away in search of the bits and pieces of a once vast silver vein, then you can cut out of the tour after the market and head over to the Royal Mint—a massive museum that once served as Spain's first colonial mint and later as the headquarters of the Bolivian Army during the Chaco War—or take a stroll through the narrow streets of older neighborhoods to observe the city's unique architecture.

Whether you brave the mines or are content to visit museums and the remnants of this once thriving mining hub, you will surely leave Potosí with a new appreciation for the bountiful human spirit that has enabled working-class potoseños to endure centuries of oppression and poverty.

---

FACTOID:

The Cerro Rico miners have a complex relationship with God—and the Devil. Although devout Catholics, each day when they enter the "Devil's Mountain" to work, they leave those beliefs behind them and honor the devil whom they call "Tio." They believe he rules this underworld and will protect them against any harm. To show their affection for him, the miners have constructed hundreds of chambers enshrined to Tio in his image. The shrines consist of bull horns, shattered glass, and teeth. The workers make daily offerings of alcohol, coca leaves, and cigarettes to the underworld ruler in hopes he will bring them wealth and safety.

---

*Climbing in the Potosi tunnels. Photo by Freyja Ellis.*

# TUPIZA

### By Lorraine Caputo, Columbia, Missouri, U.S.A.

Traveling for days across the blinding salares of Uyuni, brilliant white, ruby and sapphire, a cold that seeps to the marrow of one's soul ... to another land of worn, warm earthen colors.

Or one can arrive to Tupiza along the Wara-Wara del Sur train line, which winds through the narrow slice of the Bolivian highlands where Butch Cassidy and the Sundance Kid assaulted their last train. Some say the two famous bandits grew tired of living in quiet exile in Argentine Patagonia—others say they were broke and needed the money. They came to southern Bolivia to try their luck—working in the mines, or better yet, robbing paycars. Some say their spirits still can be glimpsed walking beneath the porticos of the town center.

Tupiza had already been here several centuries by the time Butch Cassidy and the Sundance Kid arrived. Founded in 1574 by Captain Don Luís Fuentes y Vega, the town got its name from the Chango indigenous word "Topejsa," meaning "red earth."

The beauty of this town lies in its Wild West landscapes. Located between the Uyuni salt flats and the Humahuaca canyon of northern Argentina, the cragged rocks change colors all day. The mountains, with its catacomb of mines, turn blood-red in the dying light of day. A hush falls over the earth. If one listens closely, one can hear the voices of the ghosts of workers echoing through the valleys.

On the opposite bank of the river is the former country villa of the Aramayo family, one of the most powerful mining barons of the late 19th and early 20th centuries. A statue of its founder, Victor Carlos Aramayo, stands in the main plaza. On a hill to the west, there is a large statue of Christ from which views of the countryside and sunsets are spectacular. Just off the main plaza is a small museum.

Hikes take the visitor along the rocky river or into the hills, through small settlements of present-day miners scraping a survival from this soil, through the semi-desert forests. Hikes are only one way to explore the Tupiza area: you can also rent a bicycle or go on a horseback riding tour.

Agencies in Tupiza offer other excursions: a three-day trip through the Uyuni salt flats, or to San Vicente, where Butch and Sundance allegedly were gunned down by Bolivian lawmen: some believe that one or both may have escaped. Despite rumors, their graves are there, in the local cemetery.

A place where the earth speaks in colors that touch the soul, where tales of miners and bandits echo through the mountains: Tupiza is this place, enchanting its visitors into staying for just a few days more, just to listen.

> *"If he'd just pay me what he's paying them to stop me robbing him, I'd stop robbing him."*
> -Butch Cassidy, U.S. Train Robber (1866-1908?)

## LATIN AMERICAN MYSTERIES # 5: WAS BUTCH CASSIDY REALLY KILLED IN BOLIVIA?

San Vicente, Bolivia: November 6, 1908

Everyone who has seen the movie knows that Butch Cassidy and the Sundance Kid were killed by the Bolivian police in 1908, a few days after robbing the payroll of the Aramayo mining company. Right?

Not so fast. Police reports from the incident report clearly that two English-speaking men who were wanted for the robbery were killed in a shootout on the night of November 6, 1908. It is also true that infamous bandits Robert Leroy Parker (who went by "Butch Cassidy") and Henry Alonzo Longabaugh ("The Sundance Kid") were in the region, having left the United States for South America in 1901 in an effort to escape the high price on their heads. Most people, then and now, believe that the two dead Americans were, in fact, Butch Cassidy and the Sundance Kid (the people of the Bolivian town of San Vicente certainly do: they'll take you to see the graveyard!).

But doubts about the identity of the two men began right away. Although the thieves had allegedly stolen a lot of money, there was little on the two after the shootout. The Pinkerton Detective Agency, which had been on the trail of Butch and Sundance, wasn't convinced and didn't call off its search for them. Some think the second man was not Butch Cassidy but Harvey Logan, aka "Kid Curry," a bandit who had worked with Cassidy and Sundance before in the American west.

Butch Cassidy's sister, Lulu Parker Betenson, claimed that he returned and visited her in 1925. She always maintained that he died in Spokane in 1937 (oddly, her son disputed her claim, saying that his grandfather, Butch's father, had told him that Butch had never returned from South America). Some believe that Butch Cassidy changed his name again, this time to William T. Phillips, and moved back to the west.

In 1991, the graves were dug up and forensic tests were done on the remains. The results were inconclusive.

# SALAR DE UYUNI

## By Martin Li, London, England

Active volcanoes, hot springs and a palette of colour-splashed lakes populated by hardy flamingos punctuate surreal, high altitude landscapes of blindingly bright salt plains and deserts, considered by many to be one of the most extraordinary sights in all Bolivia.

Uyuni is the gateway to Bolivia's remote southwestern corner. The town itself isn't noted for much apart from its train cemetery, where rusting hulks of steam engines and railway carriages slowly decay—victims of Bolivia's shortage of intact railways. Not far outside Uyuni, the terrain soon becomes engulfed by the blinding whiteness of the 12,000 sq. km. (about three million acres) Salar de Uyuni salt flats. Miles and miles of dazzling white nothingness are bizarrely punctuated by two "islands": sports stadium-sized mounds of rock and earth upon which flourish cactuses and a population of marooned viscachas (large Andean rabbits).

The Salar formed from two evaporated lakes. The salt is the result of minerals leeched from surrounding mountains and deposited at the lowest point in the region. The ramshackle Colchani factory is the only plant to commercially exploit the estimated 10 billion tonnes of Uyuni salt. Workers hack out raw material with picks and shovels and heap it into long rows of conical piles. With supply greatly outstripping demand, there is understandably no hurry.

To the south of the great Salar, the terrain turns higher and wilder as the Altiplano meets the Andes: a harsh desert landscape dotted with snow-capped pink-brown mountains, active volcanoes and isolated, serene lakes. The fiery red Laguna Colorada (4,278 m, or about 14,000 feet) never fails to astound, its incredible coloration caused by micro-organisms and a high ochre level. Several species of hardy, brightly plumed flamingos somehow manage to prosper along its ice-lined shores.

More sensational still is Laguna Verde, isolated in Bolivia's southwestern corner (over the next pass is Chile) at 4,260 m (13,976 feet), with Volcán Licancábur rising 5,960 m (19,500 feet) behind its turquoise, borax-lined surface. The lake's green-blue colour derives from a high cobalt concentration and is particularly striking when the frequent winds whip the surface into froth. When the winds calm, the vista assumes a dreamy, otherworldly quality you will never forget.

Temperatures plummet as fast as the setting sun, although the single great advantage of this remote, rarefied location is the astonishing clarity of the night sky. Above this high altitude wilderness, even a full moon struggles to outshine a night sky as spellbindingly clear and starry as anywhere this side of outer space. Nights can be freezing cold and visitor facilities very basic, but you will never forget the Milky Way or the jaw-dropping salvos of shooting stars.

Salar de Uyuni. Photo by Maximilian Hirschfeld.

Geyser Sol de Mañana, Uyuni. Photo by Maximilian Hirschfeld.

# CHILE

## Snow and Sand, Fire and Ice

Chile is not for the faint of heart; it never has been. The first European to see present-day Chile was Ferdinand Magellan in 1520, who landed on Chiloé Island on his way around the world. He and his men had gone through the rugged Strait of Magellan, one of the world's most treacherous waterways. In 1534, Diego de Almagro led a troop of Spanish conquistadores onto Chile looking for wealth and glory: they only found the Atacama Desert and the indomitable Araucanians, an indigenous tribe who fought the invaders every step of the way. Almagro lost almost all of his men and returned to Peru empty-handed and disgraced. Later, in 1584, Pedro Sarmiento de Gamboa founded the city Rey don Felipe in southern Patagonia: within two years all of those settlers who didn't desert either froze or starved to death: the British named the site "Port Famine."

Chile is still a rugged, tough land, wedged on a narrow strip of land between the majestic Andes and the icy blue waters of the Pacific. From the parched Atacama Desert in the north to the windy plains and stark mountains of Patagonia in the south, Chile offers exhilarating extremes for those bold enough to follow in the footsteps of Almagro and Sarmiento de Gamboa. Fortunately for modern visitors, Chile's infrastructure and services have improved greatly since the days of the intrepid first explorers. The country which also gave the world such internationally renowned writers and artists as Isabel Allende, Pablo Neruda, and Victor Jara is the most economically stable in Latin America. You can tour Chile's unforgettable vistas, modern cities, rugged islands and sapphire lakes in comfort and style, roughing it only when you want to.

The travelogues that follow capture Chile at its rugged, starkly beautiful best. Our writers will take you from Easter Island and its famous pagan statues to the high peaks of the Andes, from the incomparable Chilean vineyards to the unparalleled beauty of the Torres del Paine National Park. You'll see this narrow slice of heaven through their eyes, and it's a sight you'll never forget.

# SAJAMA TO ARICA

By Kelley Coyner, Texas, U.S.A.

One could say that the trip from landlocked Bolivia to the beach in Arica, Chile is a real downer: a 5,000 meter (16,404 feet) downer to be exact. Despite the huge drop in altitude though, the emotional value of this amazing road trip makes it an incredible upper.

The trip typically begins in La Paz, the seat of the Bolivian government and the world's highest capital at 3,600 meters (11,811 feet). After several hours of travel across the great Andean plateau of the *Altiplano*, the road scoots along the border of Sajama National Park, home to its namesake, Bolivia's highest peak. Make sure to stop for thorough discussion and photo documentation of Sajama, and enjoy a jaunt around Inca Chulpas or the burial chambers that dot the plain in front of Sajama. This part of the trip alone is worthy in its own right.

Fifteen minutes past Sajama, you will hit the border crossing into Chile at Tambo Quemado, or rather, the border will hit you.

*Tambo* is a Quechua word for old Inca travel lodges or rest stops. In contemporary Spanish, *quemado* means burnt. The immigration line surges as bus loads of travelers attempt to cross before everything closes for a couple of hours in the afternoon. Almost two hours and nearly 20 forms later, you will pass into Parque Nacional Lauca with its Parinacota volcano, one of Chile's highest peaks at 6,330 meters (20,767 feet). This peak is decorated with miniature volcanic peaks that are sometimes dusted with powdery fresh snow.

The park is home to various members of the camelid family, including the domesticated llama and the endangered vicuña. The vicuña is smaller, softer, and more uniform in color than the llama (something like a deer-shaped llama). The vicuñas

> *The vicuñas of Lauca seem comfortable with the human presence of road builders and tourists. Visitors often walk within a few feet of these lithe animals at the only official rest stop.*

of Lauca seem comfortable with the human presence of road builders and tourists. Visitors often walk within a few feet of these lithe animals at the only official rest stop. One can also spot dozens of flamingo—known as *parinacota* in Aymará, the indigenous language of this area—as they hunt for fish in the various lakes along the edge of the park.

Once through the park, the highway passes through Putre, home to the only sizable human population between Tambo Quemado and Arica. The next edifice is a *pukara*, or Incan fort. Its location on a huge promontory no doubt made it easy to defend. A modern day fortification, Taki Posado, comes into view on the right. Advertised as an alternative camping and renewable energy center, Taki Posado is an eclectic assemblage of passenger railroad cars, driftwood, and awnings. About 12 km (7.5 miles) further, you can glimpse pre-Columbian Socoroma poking out from a patch of trees. Socoramo hosts a restored 16th century church and staggered terraces used for growing oregano. There are virtually no more signs of human habitation until the Lluta Valley at the end of the trip.

Though much of trip is through the Atacama, the world's driest desert, there is some startling plant life along the way. Most notable are the storybook candelabra cacti marking the rocky, sandy mountain sides.

After an hour or two in the desert, stone cliffs yield to mammoth sand dunes and the road twists to the coast. By craning your neck to look straight up you can see huge petroglyphs known as the *los gigantes*, or the giants. Suddenly, the valley floor turns shockingly green. This oasis with palm trees is the Lluta Valley. Finally, the road ends, leaving you with a long stretch of beach and the sparkling waters of the Pacific Ocean.

---

**ARICA TRAVEL TIP:**
After a long drive, the cool water of the Pacific Ocean will undoubtedly be a welcome relief. The beaches of Arica are a perfect place to jump in. The water is warm enough to not shock the system, but cool enough to be refreshing. Head south of the city along Avenida Commandante San Martín and stop at Playa El Laucho, Arenillas Negras, Playa Corazones, or Playa La Lisera.

---

## CHILE LOS GÉISERES DEL TATIO

By Mariana Cotlear

Situated 4,200 meters (13,780 feet) above sea level, the El Tatio Geysers in the Antofagasta region of Chile are a truly amazing sight. The third largest geyser field in the world, this spectacle of nature features 80 active geysers.

Arrive pre-dawn, between 5:00 and 7:30 a.m., to see the geysers in peak action; you might want to make arrangements to camp somewhere near the geyser field. Alternatively, a very early wake-up call might be in order, and you can hire transportation (or a guide) to get you there.

# PUTRE

By Pete Nelson, Chester, Maryland, U.S.A.

Clinging precariously to the dizzying Andean heights of the northernmost region of Chile's slender 4,300 kilometer-long mainland, the pueblo of Putre (POOH'-tray), 140 kilometers east of oceanside Arica, is one of Chile's gems, albeit a raw one. Ramshackle and unkempt, it quietly proclaims its status as Chile's northernmost town—although a handful of miniscule hamlets and military outposts might challenge that claim. Above all, it is the gateway to the stunning Parque Nacional Lauca (LAO'-kah).

Putre and Parque Nacional Lauca bask in air that is cool and clean—and thin. Climbing steadily into the mountains directly from sea level in a well-maintained vehicle along Ruta 11 from the coast into Bolivia seems effortless, but high altitudes reached swiftly can be treacherous for many. Putre sits at 3,500 meters (11,480 feet) above sea level; the nearly 138,000 hectares of Parque Nacional Lauca lie between 3,000 meters (9,800 feet) and over 6,000 meters (19,600 feet) above sea level.

The focal point of Parque Nacional Lauca, now a World Biosphere Reserve, is the dazzling Lago Chungará (choon-gah-RAH'). At 4,500 meters (14,750 feet) above sea level it is one of the highest lakes in the world. On a clear day, the sight of the snow-covered cone of still-active Volcán Parinacota reflected in the mirror-like surface of Lago Chungará, vicuñas like four-legged ballerinas feeding along its shoreline, is worth a trip to Chile from anywhere. This is also the realm of the vizcacha (chinchilla); the ñandú, a flightless, ostrich-like bird; and the majestic condor. Small herds of domesticated alpacas and llamas meander everywhere.

Tucked deep in the highest altitudes of the Parque Nacional Lauca, a few kilometers west of Lago Chungará, is the almost-deserted altiplano indigenous village of Parinacota (pah-ree-nah-COH'-tah). The 17th century Iglesia de Parinacota—rebuilt in the late 19th century—is another sobering reminder of the long religious arm of the early conquistadores.

Busloads of passengers off cruise ships calling into Arica routinely visit Lago Chungará on single day trips. The tour operators carry oxygen as a matter of course, but unwary visitors are regularly afflicted by altitude sickness, known locally as *soroche*. For your head, an overnight in Putre is highly recommended. Quickie tours from Arica into Parque Nacional Lauca (via Putre) are not very rewarding, "windshield tourism" at its worst. True travelers to the area too often return with the nagging feeling that their visit was interrupted. You're best to spend some time on your own, ambling about and exploring this remarkable area.

## SIDE TRIPS FROM PUTRE

By Pete Nelson

En route from Arica, about 35 kilometers (22 miles) out, a *carabinero* (checkpoint) is a good landmark for Poconchile, a pre-Incan-era pueblo, with its Iglesia de San Gerónimo, one of the oldest in Chile (1605), although it may appear more recent because of its 19th century reconstruction.

Some kilometers farther along, the Aymara hamlet of Socorama, hugs a steep hillside about five kilometers (3.1 miles) down a rough, barely driveable switchback trail, a pre-colonial-era pack route, off the highway. If you're lucky, you'll get stuck behind a flock of sheep being herded along ahead of you, waddling along so slowly you'll have ample time to snap a number of photos

Villages like Socorama, virtually untainted by modernity, are common throughout the mountainsides and valleys of northern Chile, southern Peru and western Bolivia. Few are as easily accessible as Socorama, with its single story adobe buildings enclosing narrow dirt streets that converge at the central plaza with its 17th century Iglesia de San Francisco.

Brightly colored flowers tumble over age-old walls and cover patches of steep hillsides beyond. Behind the church, a rickety park bench faces out over the plunging valley adjacent; below, a pair of bright green portable toilets. The population is elderly. A dilapidated dust-covered swing set in an unkempt yard silently yields the reality of migration by younger generations to the urban centers below. Stop and visit for a spell before Socorama follows its young into the thin mountain air.

About two thirds of the way from Arica to Putre, the most incongruous collection of brightly colored structures suddenly materializes on the northern side of the road. The most startling is an early 20th century railroad passenger car. Hand-lettered signs welcome you for mate de coca and German küchen. Slender antennae bristle everywhere, bending in the breeze. A group of solar panels glints in the sun. A never-been-washed Toyota Land Cruiser of indeterminate color sits to one side.

This is Maellke (may-EHL'-kay), the homestead of Andréa and Alexis—she of German descent, he Italian—and their four children are all home-schooled by cultured, fluently multi-lingual Mom, who was once a pre-med student. Originally squatters, the land on which they live year-round is now legally their own. The rainwater they collect is supplemented by water delivered by truck and their electricity is solar generated. Take a break here to enjoy the healthful and wholesome, mostly prepared from scratch food they sell to visitors.

# SAN PEDRO DE ATACAMA

## By Michelle Hopey, New Hampshire, U.S.A.

Breathing in fresh sharp air and gazing at the voluptuous red rock formations set against a crisp blue sky, one has to wonder why many guide books say to skip the northern Chilean desert.

The notion is that northern Chile is just a desert without any great, unusual attraction. However, this red sandstone desert is home to pools of natural hot springs, islands of towering curvaceous rocks—that look as if they were made for climbing—and the 10,000 year-old tiny, but funky village of San Pedro de Atacama, which might as well have birthed the concept of relaxation.

Tucked in the northeast corner of the Antofagasta region of the Chilean Altiplano, San Pedro de Atacama is home to just over 2,500 people. Just miles from the Bolivian border, and a 10-hour drive west of Salta, Argentina, San Pedro doubles as an indigenous village and modern hippie town. This meshing of cultures guarantees that any experience in San Pedro is authentic, adventurous, cultural and relaxing.

Once a farmer's town, the village is now a refuge for backpackers either departing for or arriving from the southern Bolivian salt flats. Of the many travelers who end a salt flat tour in San Pedro, most try to hitch the next bus out of town. But those continuing on to Argentina usually find themselves stuck since the only bus to Argentina departs just two to three times a week. From lounging around in the town square to hiking in the nearby Altiplano, what starts as an inconvenience soon becomes a gift.

Enough to soothe any outdoor junkie, one can venture into the 4,000 meter high altiplano which is composed mostly of ash from the collapse of a volcano nearly a million years ago. Rent a bicycle and set out for the stark, but amazing moon-like scenery of Valle de la Luna (Moon Valley), climb several exquisite rock formations, horseback ride to the sandy, but mountainous Valle de la Muerte, also known as Mars Valley, and of course indulge in the warm waters (60 C°) of the desert's natural hot springs and geysers.

Spectacular turquoise blue, high altitude lakes and massive salt flats sit along the border of Chile, Argentina and Bolivia. The region is also home to Aymara llamas and alpaca herders. This unique ecological zone with extreme climates, including gusting winds, hot sun and low temperatures creates the unique colors and formation of the desert and also separates the Atacama Desert from the Amazon Basin.

Back in town, you can stroll through the Plaza de Armas where a few silver artisan vendors set-up shop daily. Local civil offices such as the post and tourism offices are found here as well, along with a few shops and restaurants. Iglesia San Pedro faces the edge of the square, while Chile's premier archeological museum, Museo Arqueológico Padre Gustavo Le Paige—which houses over 400,000 items collected by Gustavo Le Paige, a Belgian priest and archeologist who made this his collection zone—skirts the other side.

Small orange and pink adobe houses line the streets and there are also a wealth of restaurants-come-bars in the late night. Also found here are a number of tour agencies who will create a tour just for you, or if you want them to simply be your driver, pitch a price and you'll likely get what you wish.

While camping has become more popular, (it's cheap, and guaranteed to be dry) in recent years beautifully structured adobe-made hotels and spas have sprung up, catering to Chileans and international travelers seeking pampering and relaxation. While they are on the pricier side, these upscale hotels have all managed to maintain consistency with the original laid back and raw style of San Pedro, the reason so many have come to love the town.

With all that San Pedro has to offer, it might be easy to mistake it for a tourist town, but the term "tourist town" should be clearly identified here—dial-up internet connection is still considered a new concept, there are no medical facilities within a two hour radius and it wasn't until late 2005 that one ATM was finally installed, which only on occasion operates properly. San Pedro and its surrounding red-rock dessert is an oasis in the desert.

## ATACAMA DESERT

### By Peter Anderson

It's the highest and driest desert in the world. The Atacama Desert of Chile and Peru is a virtually rainless plateau, extending from the Andes Mountains to the Pacific Ocean. The average width is less than 160 kilometres (100 miles) but it extends from the Peruvian border 1,000 kilometres (620 miles) south to the Bolivian Altiplano.

At first glance, the barrenness of the scenery might give one the feeling that there is nothing of interest in this inhospitable area, but this part of the world contains spectacular and varied scenery; majestic mountains, volcanoes, geysers, salt lakes, salt basins (salars), sand and lava flows. The landscape has been compared to that of Mars, and the sheer austerity of the desert makes a trip to this locale truly awe-inspiring.

Because of the lack of rain, (Antofagasta once went 40 years without a drop) the land is virtually sterile. The hypolithic algae, lichens and sparse cacti found in this region survive on the meagre drops of moisture they can eke out of the occasional marine fog. For photographers, the early morning and evening light drapes dramatic shadows over Atacama's otherworldly landscapes. Astronomers also flock to the desert: dry, clear nights far away from civilization make for ideal star-gazing. The views of the heavens from the Atacama desert are among the best on the whole continent.

# PAKANA'S SENTINELS

## By Carol Ann, Rhynie, Scotland

The Altiplano, or high plateau, lies at an altitude of over 4,000 metres (13,000 feet) to the east of San Pedro de Atacama, in the remote border region shared by Chile, Bolivia and Argentina. It is a stark landscape of visual feasts created by extreme conditions; of volcanoes, salt flats and shallow lakes; where high winds, low temperatures and erosion create a colourful panorama. The nights are crisp and clear: the Milky Way stretches across the black sky and millions of stars gaze down upon weary but content hikers.

By day, temperatures rarely rise above 6° C, despite the almost constant clear, blue skies. Intrepid travellers who venture here need warm clothes, sunglasses, sunblock and plenty of water. The area has an annual rainfall of only 65 to 70 millimetres (2.5 inches). December to March is the "rainy" season, but unseasonal snowfalls can block the solitary road for days, adding crisp white to the startling palette of nature's colours. This remote landscape was wrought in fire over four million years ago when a huge volcanic dome collapsed, spreading around 1600 cubic kilometres of volcanic debris over thousands of hectares. Dotted across the caldera floor and surrounded by rust-coloured hills, the weird shapes and isolated formations called Pakana's Sentinels rise up six metres (20 feet) or more into the sky—the solitary remains of volcanic rocks that have been densely welded together by extreme heat. Up close, their surfaces are pitted with holes caused by the constant peppering of windblown sand, until they shatter into fragments to join the accumulated debris on the ground below. This may be a stark, even desolate landscape, but it is not empty. There are places where small, scrubby plants and mosses grow, tinting the hillsides with greens, reds and yellows.

Towards the Argentinean border, in Reserva Nacional de los Flamencos, the light blue waters of the Tara lagoon and the expansive Tara salt flats are a popular playground for flamingos and vicuña. The vicuña is the smallest, most delicate of the camelids, with soft fine wool, almost as thin as a thread of silk. It's not unusual to see a small group foraging in the shallow waters, with the single male leading his harem of four to five females and their young. Early in the morning, you might even catch a glimpse of a grey vizcacha (a large, nocturnal rodent) on the side of the road, or sitting on a rock, warming itself in the sun to bring its lowered, night-time metabolic rate back to normal.

The Altiplano is a magnificent natural landscape, with plenty to enthrall those with a passion for trekking, hiking, horseback riding, cycling or volcano climbing, as well as those who prefer to explore from the comfort of a 4x4. Use San Pedro de Atacama as your base and come lose yourself in this unforgettable wilderness.

The Hand. Photo by Freyja Ellis.

# LA SERENA

*By David Brown, Glasgow, Scotland*

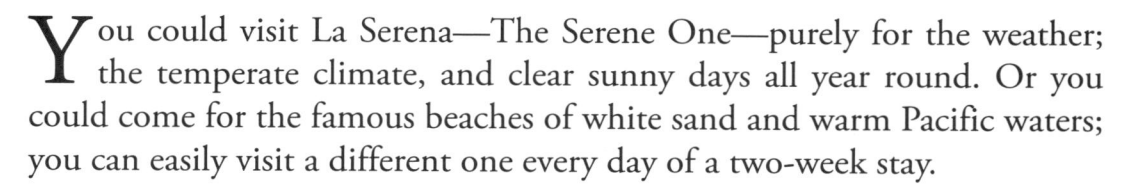

You could visit La Serena—The Serene One—purely for the weather; the temperate climate, and clear sunny days all year round. Or you could come for the famous beaches of white sand and warm Pacific waters; you can easily visit a different one every day of a two-week stay.

Chile's second oldest city, founded in 1544 as a sea link between Santiago and Lima, also offers a strategic link inland. It is an ideal base for exploring the scenic Elqui valley. It is here amongst the lush, fertile hillsides and tiny villages, that Chile's national drink, Pisco, is produced against the glorious backdrop of the mighty Andes.

From La Serena, the valley town of Vicuña is just an hour away. Here, thanks to those cloudless skies, you'll find the highest concentration of astronomical observatories anywhere in the world and the Cerro Mamalluca Municipal Observatory offers nightly star gazing and theories on the beginning of the universe.

Back in La Serena, a less intellectually challenging day can be passed strolling along the avenues, shopping, or just lazing about the main square, Plazas de Armas, with its impressive "Colonial Renaissance" architecture on all sides.

Come evening there is something else on offer. Something more exciting, dramatic and outright chaotic than everything else. There is soccer.

Nothing in Latin America invokes more passion and pride, noise and colour than soccer, and La Serena is no different. Tickets for the local team—Club Deportes La Serena—can be purchased from the club shop, just off the main square, for $6. The stadium is easily spotted and can be reached on foot from just about anywhere in town.

At the stadium, the tranquility of day belies the cauldron of noise at night. Although not much by Latin American standards, each home game sees 14,000 fans packed tightly into the Estadio La Portada. Charismatic fans sing and chant with gusto, waving banners, flags, scarves, shirts off their own backs and anything else that comes to hand.

Fireworks and flares are ignited and thrown and drums pound constantly. The noise is particularly remarkable considering the stadium has no roof to trap the din. And what makes this all the more enjoyable is that, in Chile, soccer matches are attended by men and women, the young and old. The atmosphere may be volatile but it certainly isn't hostile.

The arrival of the officials to start the match is greeted by whistling, jeering and coin throwing. Wisely, they are ushered in by riot police! By the time the players make an entrance the crowd is frenzied. The frantic pace of the 90 minute match mirrors the conspiring crowds, seen scaling the security fences in vain and futile attempts to get on the pitch themselves. And when a goal is scored ... chaos ensues.

With its frenzied energy and fury of fans, La Serena's stadium is a great spot to soak up some of Latin America's notorious soccer culture, and after a night here you'll surely be ready to kick back on its beaches with a cold drink or two.

A full-time architect and freelance writing in his spare time, David Brown is an experienced traveller. If he had the money, he would be an eternal backpacker.

The most bizarre cultural experience Brown had abroad was being stranded in the Ecuadorian countryside. He eventually managed to flag down a passing bus to find the passengers totally engrossed in the playing video of *Braveheart*.

# FIESTA INTERNACIONAL DE LA CANCIÓN DE VIÑA DEL MAR

By Mariana Cotlear

Every year during the third week of February, a huge musical event takes over Chile and Latin America. This is the Fiesta Internacional de la Canción ("International Song Festival"): a six-night performance and competition that takes place in the seaside town of Viña del Mar, Chile.

The festival, "the most important event in the Chilean summer," has become an international music extravaganza. Fifteen thousand spectators gather in Viña del Mar's open-air amphitheater, Quinta Vergara, to watch huge stars from around the world attempt to win them over with their song and dance.

Performing at the Viña festival is a huge honor, but it's not always easy. The crowd—affectionately known as *el monstruo* ("the monster")—is ruthless with both criticism and praise. Their cheers and shouts of "encore, encore!" for a great performance can quickly become hisses and boos for the following act. The monster also plays a decisive role in which artists get to take home one of the festival's four coveted prizes: the Golden and Silver Torches and the Golden and Silver Seagulls.

The festival is a spectacle not to be missed, as Chilean group La Ley proved when they opted to perform in Viña rather than fly to the States to accept their Grammy award.

# VALPARAÍSO

## By Pete Nelson, Chester, Maryland, U.S.A.

You don't have to be in great physical shape to explore Valparaíso to the fullest, but it helps. Micros and *colectivos* (diesel-belching buses and "group" taxis) and creaking *ascensores* (funiculars, a type of cable railway used on steep inclines) notwithstanding, "Valpo," as it is known, affectionately or derisively, depending on who's using it, is a walking town and the most intriguing neighborhoods—and jaw-dropping vistas—are "up there" on the steep hillsides.

Facing west over the not-very-passive Pacific, Chile's principal port city curves around its maritime stage like a massive amphitheater, hugging a bustling *bahía* (bay) of the same name. Sturdy wooden fishing boats with melodic names like Reina Elena vie for anchorage among hulking freighters flying flags of nations representing six continents—and the odd ice-breaker capable of visiting the seventh. Most of these ships can readily face the sobering challenges of the southern oceans; others are bereft of even paint, unabashedly exhibiting vast orange patches of ominous rust. Beyond the inner harbor, the gray silhouettes of Chilean (once British) naval vessels lie sheltered by the southern curve of the bay.

The broad Avenida Errázuriz—named for an accomplished Chilean citizen of the mid-19th century—sweeps along the waterfront, this *costanera* (coastal road) the aged port's definitive border between the dockside activity and city's sea-level structures. Unenlightened architecture of the latter half of the 20th century towers arrogantly over squat English and Spanish rococo of the 19th century, their incompatible façades permanently darkened by the ravages of the Pacific's fickle weather. Behind them, eastward, the rest of Valpo clings to its mountainsides. Indeed, the first sunlight of the day doesn't begin to brighten most of its narrow, meandering streets until late morning. Tired, dour villas of the once-wealthy and the brightly painted ramshackle homes of the modern poor sprawl with blind faith in their foundations on the ridges and in the shallow valleys of this uncommon urban labyrinth.

Stepped sidewalks, slippery footpaths and impossibly narrow streets zigzag everywhere (Valpo men extol their women as having the best legs in Chile. Well muscled, surely, but most shapely is debatable). Entryways to homes and shops, churches and eateries are located at every imaginable level of the structure. To enter the front door of one tidily maintained home, you must cross a short, sturdy scaffold to a tiny porch hovering over a drop of a hundred meters or more. Adventuresome visitors who do not get lost at least twice a day among the 28 or so *cerros* (hills) of Valpo are not true urban explorers.

More than a dozen ascensores—literally "elevators," actually "funiculars" dating to the late 19th and early 20th centuries—climb the steep slopes of the various cerros from the city's centers up into a myriad of neighborhoods. Local legend has it that there was widespread suspicion of devilry in the clattering, rickety contraptions, much of the unsophisticated populace regarding them as some kind of un-godly route between hell and heaven. This fear was dispelled when wives of local officials were persuaded to board the dark wooden cabins, one at the top of the short route and another at the bottom. As they passed one another mid-way, the motors were stopped and the ladies enjoyed tea together, exchanging prerequisite gossip through the tiny windows. The naysayers were duly hushed.

During the heady years of early independence, Valpo was transformed into the young nation's commercial and financial center in which English expatriates played an integral role. Spurred by obscene wealth flowing from the northern nitrate mines, Chile's first banks were established here—among them A. Edwards and Co. and the Bank of London—as was its first stock market. The obvious legacies of Spain notwithstanding, the influence of 19th century England emerges throughout this singular city on the cerros.

Plaza Victoria, the "nucleus of elegance" at the turn of the last century, is today one of its commercial and social hubs and Paseo Atkinson, a narrow plaza on Cerro Concepción, is a popular gathering place for young people. The imposing Iglesia Anglicana Saint Paul, by engineer and architect William Lloyd, still holds services as it has since 1858. Once-grand mansions of the city's long-departed elite grace Avenida Gran Bretaña that curves around the flanks of Cerro Playa Ancha, Valpo's easternmost hillside. And perched prominently overlooking the docks, the Hotel/Restaurant/Pub Brighton reigns with premier accommodations.

All along Valpo's narrow waterfront "downtown," the past is omnipresent, not only visible in its eclectic architecture, but evident among its enduring enterprises, most of them highly revered, a few huddled in shadows of ill repute. Among the former are the venerated restaurants: the Bar Cinzano, the Café Riquet, the Café Turri, the Casino J. Cruz M., all half a century old or more. When the breeze is right, the dishes of the day are revealed by their aromas that waft out onto the sidewalks to mingle with the salty smell of the ocean.

Late into the night, alluring strains of the bolero and the tango serenade patrons who may sit for hours undisturbed, whether savoring a multi-course dinner or simply sipping a tiny *cortado* (coffee). The musicians and singers may be almost as old as the establishment in which they play, but their passion for the melodies and lyrics is quietly exhilarating.

Incongruously, perhaps, Valpo is rife with post-secondary school institutions, particularly for the arts. Young people appear everywhere, gathered in doorways along narrow streets or around park benches in shaded plazas. They listen to a promising musician or sing along, draw or paint an obscure building, scribble lines of poetry in a well-worn notebook. Indeed, renowned Chilean poet Pablo Neruda found inspiration in Valpo for several years.

As the sun sets behind the horizon of the southern Pacific, the panorama to the east is one of its reflections in 10,000 windows shimmering across a vast mosaic of brightly colored facades of toy-like buildings terraced high into the evening mist.

*"Love is a road that suddenly appears and from so much walking upon it, it is lost."*
-Víctor Jara, Chilean Musician, from "Love is a Road" (1932-1973)

# SANTIAGO

### By Pete Nelson, Chester, Maryland, U.S.A.

Santiago (San-tee-AH'-goh) is 2305 km south of Arica, 3141 km north of Punta Arenas, 100 km from the Pacific coast, and 40 km from the Andean Cordillera border with Argentina with a population of six million (2004).

Looking at a map of Chile's extraordinary dimensions, it becomes clear why defining a national character for the country seems an impossible task. Conversely, to appreciate the complexity of its capital city, Santiago de Chile, it is best not to look at a map that depicts its entirety in one glance for this *región metropolitana* of 155 square kilometers can appear quite overwhelming when it's not.

Despite its size, Santiago exudes an aura of energy comparable only to a handful of cosmopolitan cities beyond South America: New York, London or Johannesburg, for example. One explanation for this is that this capital city, the center of the Chilean universe, is one of barrios—loosely defined as residential neighborhoods—spread along the valley of the Río Mapocho and into the Andean foothills. Any given block off either side of the bustling avenidas reveals a commercial and residential community comprised of aging villas and modern apartment blocks, venerable small business ventures and up-start, low-rise office buildings. Yet somehow it all blends comfortably.

This urban center is at once well-liked and disparaged by both residents and visitors. They celebrate its collection of eclectic characters and varied personalities but lament the challenges created by them. They praise its world-class amenities and laud its access to leisure activities but moan about heavy traffic and air pollution. Few recognize nor acknowledge its greatest and most visible asset, the Santiaguinos themselves.

With a predominantly Hispanic history, the people have developed a heritage of indigenous roots blended with immigration from Europe. Today, while Chileans recognize their geographical isolation, they remain unrelentingly connected to the rest of the world. They are savvy and sophisticated, educated and urbane, wealthy and poor, rabidly socialist and arrogantly elitist and everything in between.

Days in Santiago are long because while Chileans are hard-working, they also savor life. Midday meals are lengthy and evening meals are late. Evenings last far into the night; sleep is an annoying interference and mornings begin again slowly.

Above all, the people of Santiago—and by and large of Chile everywhere—are innately hospitable. This is a city that welcomes exploration and discovery. These are people with whom you can safely discuss politics, religion, or even fútbol.

Like every major world-class city, Santiago has a handful of "must-see" sites. If you are short of time, visit them by night, since the city is one of South America's safest. They include: the two *cerros* (hills)—Cerro San Cristóbal, adjacent to Barrio Bellavista and Cerro Santa Lucía, on Avenida O'Higgins; historic el Centro, with its surviving buildings and plazas; la Moneda, the presidential offices; and the Mercado Central.

With limited daytime on hand, make sure to do the Museo Chileno de Arte Precolombino. If shopping is your mandate, budget an hour—and some pesos—for Los Domínicos. Time permitting, stroll Avenida Providencia between Avenida M. Montt, and Avenida Los Leones.

Long regarded as merely the base for adventure travelers heading elsewhere in Chile, Santiago today is a destination unto itself. Chileans welcome visitors with a broad range of accommodation ranging from charming hostales, hosterías, and residenciales to five-star multi-national hotels; and with restaurants catering to all tastebuds, they certainly aim to rival some of the finest establishments across the globe.

View over Santiago from Cerro. Photo by Freyja Ellis.

# MERCADO CENTRAL

## By Peter Anderson, Christchurch, New Zealand

All photographers and seafood lovers visiting Santiago, Chile should head along Calle Puente to the Mercado Central (Central Market). This market is not only a culinary feast, but also a sight and sound fiesta.

A striking wrought-iron building, built in England and assembled in Chile, houses the city's principal food market. The seafood is shipped in every morning. With 4,300 kilometres of coastline, Chile offers an impressive variety of seafood from which to choose, and every day this treasure trove of fresh seafare makes its way to the Mercado Central. So varied is the selection that you can even find 10 different types of clams.

The pack of hawkers and fishmongers vying for your attention can at times overwhelm the senses, but the noise and the colours are part of the market atmosphere; be sure to bring your bargaining skills. In the morning hours the market overflows with Chileans shopping for the fresh daily catch of fish and local produce. A number of places also double as restaurants, so you can choose your fish, then sit down and take a bite right out of the ocean. Just remember to order your fish *a la plancha* (grilled)—otherwise the waiter will assume you want it fried. The market is also a great place to sample some of the country's national dishes. *Erizo* (sea urchins) and *loco* (abalone) are popular, as are fried *congrio* (an eel-like fish with thick white meat) and *corvina* (sea bass).

Originally built as an exhibition hall for Chilean painters and craftsman, Mercado Central was artfully constructed and offers its own unique architectural edge. Its life as an artists' market was short lived, however, and the government soon determined the building would better serve the community as a central market place for the hodgepodge of vendors and sellers scattered throughout the city's streets and plazas.

Not far from Mercado Central, and just across from the Plaza de Armas, via Ahumada and Huérfanos, is a pedestrian-friendly district packed with dozens of small shops, restaurants and, of course, the city's famous "coffee with legs" establishments, so called because the waitresses wear eye-catching mini-skirted uniforms and serve coffee to locals on lunch breaks. Most coffee stands do not have chairs, so patrons simply stand, sip and watch the world go by (or at least watch the waitresses go by). If you visit one establishment regularly, you will be surprised that the charming, mini-skirted girls will take time to have a friendly chat and offer advice on where to eat and what to see.

A cosmopolitan city, equipped with enough museums, restaurants, and artists' haunts to rival any other world class metropolis, Santiago also plays host to a number of slightly more understated, but certainly no less interesting sites and sounds. The hectic Mercado Central is one such place, and a visit here is best savoured with an early morning stroll, mid-day side of fresh seafood, and perhaps, a late afternoon cup of java-with-legs.

## U.S. STUDY ABROAD IN LATIN AMERICA By Michelle Hopey

Typically U.S. college students have flown over the pond to Europe, and particularly England to study abroad, but in the past few years, while still not as popular as Europe, Latin America has become a region of choice. In fact, in 2003/04 Latin America saw a nine percent increase in the number of study abroad students over the 2002/03 school year, according to a 2005 report by the Institute for International Education.

Open Doors 2005, the yearly report by the Institute for International Education reported that nearly all Latin American countries have experienced significant growth in the number foreign students entering their country to study, whether it was for a year, semester, summer or winter break. Several Latin countries such as Chile and Cuba grew by over 50 percent from 2002/03. Open Doors, released every November, tracks the mobility of academic students from the past school year. The report said trends often have to do with potential career and job prospects or downfalls.

Mexico and Costa Rica are among the top 10 countries around the world, where U.S. students studied in 2003/2004. About 9,293 American students studied in Mexico, a six percent increase over the previous year and 4,510 college students went abroad to Costa Rica, up five percent. The other lead countries attracting study abroad students included the United Kingdom, Italy, Spain, France, Australia, Germany and China. China and India saw the most growth percentage wise.

But destinations throughout the developing world on a whole saw a marked increase. Notably, Argentina went from 868 to 1,315 students, a 52 percent rise, while Bolivia went from 159 students to 234 equaling out a 47 percent increase. Cuba was up 46 percent over the previous year from 1,474 to 2,148 students.

Other countries that fared well: Chile enrolled 2,135 students, a 10 percent increase over the following year. Ecuador hosted 1,678 students with only a seven percent hike and Brazil saw a 16 percent increase with 1,554 visiting academics. In total, 29,053 students studied in Latin America or about 15 percent of all study abroad students chose a developing country for study. Honduras and Belize were the only two Latin Countries that saw a decline in the number of students studying in their homelands. The Netherlands and Austria also saw a decline. The report gave no indication as to why this might have occurred.

# CARMENÈRE

### By Peter Anderson, Christchurch, New Zealand

It may not be the most recognized wine in the world, but Carmenère is the emblematic grape of Chile and, given a few years, it may begin to take its rightful place among the better known wine varieties.

A number of tour companies offer wine tours from Santiago, and a day tour to three vineyards offers stunning views of the Andes, as most vineyards are east of the city. Usually included in the tour are Concha y Toro, which is Chile's largest producer of export wines, Undurraga and Cousiño Macul.

Chile has carved itself an impressive standing in the world wine market. Its reds are regarded as some of the best available, and in 2003, Casa Lapostolle Clos Apalta Raphael Valley 2000 finished third in *Wine Spectator*'s Top 100. Concha y Toro's Cabernet Sauvignon Puente Alto Don Melchor 2000 would top this impressive feat in 2004, finishing 26th with 94 points; Viña Almaviva's Puente Alto 2001 coming in 16th with 95 points, and Clos Apalta Colchagua 2001 achieving number two with 95 points.

Carmenère actually originated in Bordeaux. In 1860, a *phylloxera* outbreak devastated the French vineyards. French winegrowers replanted, adapting their varieties to a phylloxera resistant American rootstock, but Carmenère performed poorly. In the Bordeaux climate, Carmenère proved sensitive to the cold spring weather, reducing yields, and because this grape variety has to be harvested so late, the region's early autumnal rains impaired the grape's quality. As such Carmenère was overlooked

> *Well-made Carmenère is a big, soft, plum-like, spicy red with mouth filling flavours that blow Merlot off the table.*

and forgotten; not for being of poor quality but rather for its precarious natural requirements.

In Chile, however, the variety came to be interplanted with Merlot. Growers fell into the casual habit of calling it Merlot and harvesting the grapes together. In the 1980s, when Chile began releasing a mixture of wines instead of merely Vino Tinto and Vino Blanco, the Merlot wines usually included a lot of Carmenère.

This was unfortunate, because Merlot is ripe about a month earlier than Carmenère. Unless the wineries were fastidious and waited until Carmenère was ripe to be picked, the resulting wines often consisted of unripe, vegetal flavours.

Ten years ago, several of the big Chilean wineries hired some grape experts from France to unscramble their vineyards. DNA testing was used and the Carmenère was separated from the Merlot.

Once Chile realized it had the world's largest planting of this variety, the wineries began growing the grapes to their full ripeness. This resulted in two things: First, the Merlot improved tremendously and began featuring a ripe taste which now means that most Chilean Merlots are delicious. Second, many wineries began releasing Carmenère as a unique variety of its own. And what a wine it has become! Well-made Carmenère is a big, soft, plum-like, spicy red with mouth filling flavours that blow Merlot off the table.

Visiting Chile without tasting Carmenère is akin to going to Paris and not seeing the Eiffel Tower.

---

WINE TIPS:

Because of its heartier flavor, winter is a good time to sip Carmenère. Also consider wines that contain the grape in blends with varieties like Cabernet Sauvignon.

If you decide to enjoy a nice Carmenère, here are foods that complement the wine best: medium-rare steak, rack of lamb, duck, pastas with meat sauces, and ripe cheeses like Gouda.

---

Grapes. Photo by Freyja Ellis.

# EASTER ISLAND

## By Will Gray, Kettering, England

This mysterious place, home to a lost tribe and their unique carved statues, is the most remote island in the world and is well worth the five-hour flight from Santiago to experience its unique wonders.

Located 3,700 km (2,299 miles) from mainland Chile, the island has three names—Easter Island, Isla de Pascua or Rapa Nui—depending on where you come from, but it has only one town, called Hanga Roa, where you will be greeted on arrival at the airport in true hula-hula style by a few of the 3,000 inhabitants, believed to be of Polynesian descent.

Exploring Easter Island is easy, as the whole place is just 15 km (nine miles) wide and 25 km (15 miles) long, and there are plenty of folk happy to hire out a jeep for you to get around. It is thought by some that the giant statues were all knocked over by the ancient tribes, the Long Ears and the Short Ears, but they are slowly being resurrected and put onto their plinths to reveal how the place would have looked all those years ago.

A visit to the restored clifftop Ahu Tahai Moai site outside Hanga Roa puts you right in front of five of the high statues which face inland with their backs to the deep blue Pacific. Then, on the other side of the town, there is a road up a hill, winding through trees and bushes, to reach the spectacular Rano Kau volcano crater from which the island was made.

The view from the edge of the crater rim is beautiful and it is possible to walk the circle, staring down at the direct drop into the Pacific and Moto Nui, the three rocks of the "Bird Man" cult, on one side and the unique puddle-filled mossy bowl on the other. Don't forget to stop at the ancient petroglyphs en-route. The rugged rocky coastline welcomes the crashing Pacific waves as the road heads out of town to the other Moai locations, passing many cave sites that may have been homes to the tribal people in ancient times. The biggest Moai site is Ahu Tongariki, a platform of 15 statues, some with their original red-stone top-knots, while there are many others with fallen or partially restored statues all along the journey.

At the other end of the island to Hanga Roa is Ranu Raraku, the second volcano crater and a fascinating place where the statues were carved in the rock before being cut out and carried to their Ahus around the island. That method is clear to see as there are still many half-carved stones laying in the rock or buried in the ground up to their necks. The most picturesque site on the island can be found by the Anakena beach, where seven Moai stand on a platform in the shade of the palm trees by the white and yellow sand, and where the tranquil sound of the lapping sea can make a spectacular sunbathing spot.

The town itself is pretty, with cobbled streets and a small fishing harbour with a handful of boats, and it makes a nice place to base yourself, staying in the welcoming homestays, eating in the beautiful restaurants overlooking an endless Pacific Ocean and taking in the abundance of local culture and dancing. In fact, the atmosphere of the place is so easygoing that many people arrive for as little as a few days and find it easy to stay for months.

### EASTER ISLAND TRAVEL TIPS:

• Getting to this out of the way island is no easy task. By plane, the island is accessible by only two destinations: Tahiti and Santiago, and each one has flights twice a week, so planning ahead is essential. LAN Chile is the only air carrier that flies to Easter Island. Travelers departing from the U.S. or Canada and landing in Santiago can add Easter Island as an extra leg of their journey relatively inexpensively.

• When you vistit the Ahu site, a word of caution: do not walk on the platform. It is considered completely disrespectful.

• For a more rugged way to get around the island, rent a horse and really feel as if you have stepped back in time.

Easter Island. Photo by Will Gray.

# PUCÓN AND VOLCÁN VILLARRICA

## By Will Gray, Kettering, England

The lakeside town of Pucón sits at the centre of a mini world of adventure, where snowshoeing, volcano climbing, cycling and swimming are all on the menu.

The friendly and welcoming town is made up of a couple of streets packed with restaurants, hotels and activity shops. Lying on the edge of the large and very picturesque forest-fringed Lake Villarrica, which unfolds in the shadow of the perfectly conical (and currently active) Volcán Villarrica, Pucón makes the perfect base to relax and enjoy the activities that surround it.

One of the easiest trips to make is the cycle ride out to Los Ojos del Caburga, a beautiful set of waterfalls that tumbles into a circular pool. Bikes can be picked up, with a map, from one of the hire companies in town and the ride heads out through villages and over a suspension bridge into the mountains, where the terrain becomes tougher and bikes occasionally have to be carried over the bumpy bits before arriving at the picturesque plunge pool area. A stop-off for an apple strudel on the way back is well earned.

Slightly further out of town is the national park of Huerquehue, but the local tour companies can easily arrange transport out to the entrance with a pick-up later in the day. The walk, which for much of the year is snow-covered, heads up a steep switchback path past a refuge cabin and, after around two hours, arrives at a lake surrounded by monkey puzzle trees (Araucaria araucana, a type of pine tree native to Chile and Argentina). The trail then splits and heads towards two different lakes, both easily accessed and both offering picture-perfect postcard views, before an about turn takes you back to the drop-off point.

Another nice trek can be had in Reserva Forestal Cañi, the private park of Hostel Ecole, which incidentally houses perhaps one of the most comfortable lounge areas in Chile and operates as an informal tour company. A very steep climb takes you high up with fantastic views over the Villarrica area. In winter, snow shoes are the order of the day, and with them strapped on, it is easy going across a wide expanse of snow to a couple of lakes and past a 2,000-year-old monkey puzzle tree before a climb up to a spectacular viewpoint that offers views right out to the Argentine border.

Last but not least is the climb of Villarrica itself, a gruelling and often snow-bound ascent but one only open if the volcano is not on alert. At the foot of the mountain lies a ski field, so it is possible to get a bus up to the station, then save a few paces by taking one of the chair lifts higher up the mountain. From there it is a tough but not technical climb to reach the summit, where you are offered spectacular views across the area and down into bubbling lava in the cone.

www.vivatravelguides.com/106473

# VILLARRICA

## By Kelley Coyner, Texas, U.S.A.

Rainy days can test the spirit of the hardiest traveler, especially when a locale is best known for outdoor adventures.

Located in the northern end of the Chilean Lake District, the area around Volcán Villarrica and the lake by the same name traditionally take until mid summer (in this case February) to warm up and dry out. Rain or shine, Pucón and Villarrica are both popular travel and holiday hubs, each offering its own twist on tourism. Pucón is upscale with high end gear stores, snazzy boutiques, cute cafés and plenty of condos and high-end hotels. Twenty minutes away, Villarica is a slightly less glamorous version of its high-heeled neighbor, with cheaper, more basic accommodation.

If it's pouring when you visit, don't despair: both towns offer five perfect things to do in the rain: head to the hot springs, visit the Mapuche Museum in Pucón, enjoy a küchen or the local version of cheesecake, take a horseback riding lesson indoors, or visit a wildlife refuge.

Where there are (active) volcanoes there are bound to be hot springs. The area around Villarica is no exception. A soak in the springs is a perfect antidote to drizzle.

After a dip in the restorative waters, there are numerous opportunities to sample German and Swiss cakes and other pastries. A snack of küchen and hot chocolate or coffee is bound to hit the spot. Most proprietors welcome lingerers, whether they are a family with feisty kids or a solo traveler who wishes to catch up on postcards or dive into a good book.

Both Pucón and Villarica have museums dedicated to Mapuche culture, who call this part of southern Chile home. The museum in Villarica is located above the town's library and adjacent to a group of kiosks featuring Mapuche crafts and a replica of a ruca or traditional Mapuche house. Pucón's brand new museum, although small, packs quite a punch per square foot. Ornate silver work adorns the entry. A wall of masks demonstrates the range of Mapuche imagination. Beautiful textiles, ceramics and musical instruments fill, but do not crowd the glass cases.

Taking advantage of two other rainy day highlights requires you to make the acquaintance of Dagmar and Ralf Gamper, the proprietors of Parque Natural Dos Rios. Their property is located outside of Villarica in the opposite direction of Pucón. In addition to the trails, zip lines, and rafting, Dos Rios offers trips to temperate rainforest, fly fishing, a cup of red wine in the evening and fully equipped cabins. Rain or shine, Dagmar offers world class riding lessons in a fully outfitted indoor riding hall (some guests come from Europe, the U.S. and South Africa to study with her for months).

To visit the private wildlife rescue center, you will need Dagmar's introduction. Another perfect rainy day activity, the wildlife center's owner shows a darker side to adventure travel. This is the world where exotic animals have been captured and often harmed. One really wonders what someone was thinking when they tried to turn a puma or mountain lion into a house cat.

Back at Dos Rios, Dagmar promises kids (and any interested adults) enchanted forest walks and the run of the farm animals, from rabbits to llamas. On overcast days, both make pacts with the weather gods and promise the clouds will lift. And sure enough they do, revealing a postcard-perfect view of the volcano, a fitting backdrop for the enchanted forest.

# VALDIVIA

By Pete Nelson, Chester, Maryland, U.S.A.

Long a vital river port and crucial military garrison, both for Spain as a colonial power and for Chile as a young nation, Valdivia is today one of Chile's most favored, albeit under-sung, cities. It lies a little over 30 kilometers to the west of the Panamericana Highway and less than 20 kilometers from the Pacific coast.

The narrow Río Cau Cau flows into the broad Río Calle Calle just above the northern edge of the city to create the Río Valdivia, which continues for barely more than ten kilometers to its wide mouth at the Pacific, joined along the way by the robust Río Cruces and any number of smaller tributaries.

Isla Teja (TAY'-hah), site of the Universidad de Austral de Chile, is an integral part of the city, linked to the downtown area by the Puente Pedro de Valdivia.

As elsewhere throughout southern Chile, Valdivia's German heritage is readily apparent, in the architecture of its older buildings as well as in its cuisine, such as that offered at Café Hausmann, and above all, in its uncommonly fine beer, brewed and served with artery-blocking *wursts* at the nationally-renowned Cervecería Kunstmann. Accommodations—*hostales, hosterías,* and full-service hotels—abound.

Valdivia's easy access to the Pacific ensures fresh seafood daily, distributed to the public and to restaurateurs alike directly from fishing boats moored against the city's outdoor riverside marketplace. Obese sea lions wait nearby, hopeful for a free mouthful of freshly caught fish.

Where the mouth of Río Valdivia empties into the Pacific Ocean, Spain constructed one of its most formidable maritime defense complexes. The hamlet of Niebla (NEEYAY'-blah), 19 kilometers southwest of Valdivia, is perched on the eastern promontory, facing across the water to Corral. Isla Mancera rises strategically just inside the extensive mouth of the Río Valdivia. Each has its own remarkably well-preserved and/or partially renovated complex of fortifications. The Castillo de la Pura y Limpia Concepción de Monforte de Lemus, with its Batería del Piojo Niebla, is the pride of Niebla, overlooking Isla Mancera toward Corral. The Castillo San Pedro de Alcántara dominates Isla Mancera. Adjacent to Corral, the Castillo San Sebastián de la Cruz offers tours by guides in period costume.

Together, these three sites comprised the formidable defense of colonial Valdivia. The drive along the northern riverbank to Niebla from Valdivia is short and easy. The drive to Corral from Valdivia is long, circuitous and much of it is unpaved. A collection of small launches ply back and forth between Niebla and Corral, some via Isla Mancera.

Birding is as big in Chile's central regions as it is in the far north and south. The Santuario de la Naturaleza Carlos Andwandter on the Río Las Cruces to the north of Valdivia is one of Chile's most sublime. It is readily accessible by road and by water, the latter route a much shorter one.

Located north of Valdivia on the Río Las Cruces, within the boundaries of the Santuario de la Naturaleza Carlos Andwandter, the Hualamo ("Between Great Grebes" or "Between Waterbirds") Bird Sanctuary, is one of the most expertly operated enterprises of its kind in Chile. The sanctuary shares an early 20th century German colonial homestead with a small commercial nursery which serves to attract wildlife to the area.

Birders—experienced and beginner alike—may visit from Valdivia for the day, or they may stay for a night or more. The Hualamo complex, surrounded by impressively landscaped gardens, includes the Santa María Lodge, comprised of the immaculately maintained main house and tastefully appointed guest cottages. Room décor is enhanced by paintings of indigenous birds by Hualamo's director and principal guide, Jorge Ruiz, also a licensed veterinarian and published writer. Food and hospitality are quintessentially Chilean.

Surprisingly undervalued, Valdivia and its environs offer visitors an intriguing insight into southern Chile's European heritage, pre- and post-colonial history, and unique ecosystem.

## THE PISCO CONTROVERSY
By Mariana Cotlear and Michelle Hopey

Want to see the gloves come off? Gather a Peruvian and a Chilean, then ask them where the best Pisco comes from. Make sure you stand far back, because the fight could get dirty; a huge controversy surrounds this grape brandy.

The history of Pisco production dates back to the beginning of the colonial era and the early wine-producers in what would become southern Peru. In order to supplement their income, these viticulturists produced a stronger, cheaper drink, which they sold at the port of Pisco. Today, Peruvian Pisco production is highly sophisticated and heavily regulated. The spirit comes in several varieties, including Pisco puro, made from a single grape (usually Quebranta or Italia), and Pisco acholado, made from a blend of several grapes. Pisco can be found throughout the Andean region in the form of Pisco Sour, a cocktail made with Pisco, lime juice, sugar, egg whites, and angostura bitters. This delicious drink, an excellent accompaniment to ceviche, is deceptively mild and famous for sneaking up on the unwary.

A veritable war is now being fought between Peru and Chile over the rights to claim Pisco as their respective national drink. While Peru claims its historic origin, Chile was the first to expand its production and create a massive export market. Chileans argue that foreign taste buds recognize their product as the "authentic" version. Peruvians counter that the Chilean version, which allows additives and is yellow in color as opposed to clear, is not "authentic" because it deviates from the traditional method of production. The Pisco battle is not likely to be settled anytime soon. In the meantime perhaps each side could try to kick back, and have a strong Pisco Sour—made with Pisco from their origin of choice.

Ingredients: 2 oz. Pisco; ¾ oz. lime juice; ½ oz. simple syrup (granulated sugar melted in water); 1 egg white; 3 oz. ice or enough to fill a cocktail shaker; a few dashes of Angostura bitters

First make the simple syrup then blend together Pisco, lime juice, simple syrup, and egg white with ice. Take an old-fashioned or highball glass, dip the rim in egg white and then sugar. Strain the drink into the glass and sprinkle with a few drops of Angostura bitters. Salud.

# LAKE LLANQUIHUE

### By Teresa Colomer, Madrid, Spain

Lake Llanquihue is one of the largest lakes in South America (the second largest in Chile) and also one of the most beautiful, due to the kaleidoscope of colours you can find around it: the shimmering blue water; the unfolding green landscape; the blossoming flowers; and undoubtedly the blinding white of soaring snow-capped volcanoes.

It is possible to wander around the lake in one day. Besides lofty landscapes, the trip boasts fascinating attractions: wooden German churches and watermills, built in the 19th century with the arrival of German emigrants; a very interesting ethnographic museum, located in a cozy little town called Frutillar; and the "must" in this tour, the Petrohué Falls. The falls came about as the result of the eruption of Osorno Volcano: as the molten lava hit the river, it changed its course, creating a split-level landscape over which the turquoise water flows. There are trails to visit the river downstream and the woods beside it.

Very close to the falls, you will encounter Lake Todos los Santos (All Saints' Lake), where it is almost possible to "touch" the Osorno Volcano, its perfectly symmetrical cone covered in snow. The lake reflects the green foothills of the magnificent volcano. On the horizon, other snow-capped volcanoes valiantly reach skyward.

Both lakes are excellent for recreation: fishing, kayaking, swimming, windsurfing and sailing are some of the more common activities. Todos Santos Lake is on the Chilean side of the legendary Chile-Argentina lake crossing. If you decide to do the crossing—and it's breath-taking—you'll either begin or end your trip there. Active visitors may want to climb Osorno Volcano, or visit one of the many National Parks in the region.

For those who do not like to fish or sail, there are many more laid-back activities in which to participate, especially in the summer time. Check out the week-long run of classical concerts at the end of January or the handicraft exhibition in Frutillar.

There are all kinds of hotels, hostels and cabins along the shores of the lake and in the towns. There are also many restaurants to enjoy lake fish, lamb and traditional pastries based on German recipes (küchens), as well as traditional Chilean fare.

In short, the Lake Llanquihue region has something for everyone, from nature lovers to adventure travellers, shoppers and fans of fine dining. Bring a camera and your sense of adventure, and don't forget to send postcards home to make your friends jealous!

Born in Valencia, but a resident of Madrid her entire life, Teresa Colomer studied Psychology at university and has a Master's in Industrial Psychology and Human Resources. She works in HR, and her job allows her the opportunity to travel frequently in Latin America.

One of her dream destinations is New Zealand—she visited the country previously and fell in love with it.

## TOP LIST: BEST PLACES TO SWOON YOUR SWEETHEART

Looking for a good spot for a romantic getaway with someone special? Try one of these places, pre-approved by our readers. Guaranteed romantic or your money back!

1. Antigua, Guatemala (p.152).
Casa Madeleine, "Romantic getaway in the charming city of Antigua, Guatemala." Sergio Rimola, Virginia, U.S.A.

2. Torres del Paine, Chile (p. 341).
"The splendour of its landscape makes it a very romantic place." Teresa Colomer, Spain.

3. Baños, Ecuador (p. 254).
"Best, most exciting horseback riding and bicycle sightseeing of the breathtaking waterfalls I've ever done, and totally complete with the hot springs after an exhausting and fantastic day! Unfortunately I wasn't with my lover, but it would have been a great place to be together at!" Annina Riikonen, Sweden.

4. Tango Shows, Argentina.
"Watching the professional dancers do the tango is one of the most romantic things you can do in South America." Mike Adams, Omaha, NE, U.S.A.

Runners-up:

Hacienda Cusín, Ecuador. Matilda Skipp, Romford, London, England. Nahuel Huapi Lake, Argentina. "A beautiful lake with snow-capped mountains around." Teresa Colomer, Spain.

# PUERTO MONTT TO PUERTO NATALES

By Will Gray, Kettering, England

This three-day ferry ride is one of the most spectacular sea journeys in the world as it takes you right into the heart of Patagonia.

From the pretty town of Puerto Montt, the route takes you through a wide gulf and into a rocky island-filled paradise of mountains and snow, where whales and dolphins swim and where the non-seafarer cannot reach.

This is as remote as it gets: a bleak and often damp and cloudy world with scenery appearing and disappearing through the mist and low clouds as the gentle drone of the ship's engines power you through.

On board, the vessel is surprisingly comfortable. A nice lounge area is available with comfy cushions to relax while the canteen, where included meals are served, turns into a disco area at night. The cabins come in all sizes and have all the expected facilities, and there is plenty of deck space to move around and, most importantly, find the perfect position for the countless photos you end up taking during the daylight hours.

The ferry leaves port around midnight and heads into the night and, if the weather gods are on your side, you awake in a different world, surrounded by round-topped mountains and expansive scenery. The sun sets spectacularly and, with clear skies, the stars come out brighter than you have ever seen them before. Clear skies or no, seas tend to roughen up on the passage through the gulf on the second night. Dolphins and seals play in the bow waves as the ship continues to head through the mountainous and increasingly snowy scenery. Regardless of where you stand, there is plenty to see as the ship is very open, allowing travellers to visit the bridge and study the navigation charts as they prepare for one of the trickiest parts of the journey, the narrow English Passage.

Squeeze through the Passage and a town appears out of nowhere, a place called Puerto Eden, where the ship drops anchor and meets a small boat of townfolk who collect their post and provisions, some boarding to join the ship on its route down to true civilisation. Then the route flows past a rusty shipwreck, just to prove how dangerous it can be out here, as the passage narrows and the mountains become steeper, with waterfalls flowing through the tree-lined slopes and into the fjord.

Overnight and into the third day, the scenery takes on another dramatic change, with trees making way for barren moss-covered rocks and tall rugged, snow-covered peaks and rock towers.

Patagonia is truly upon you as you head through an archipelago of islands and through a narrowing just 100 meters wide before slowing right down to navigate the three-meter-deep shallows on the other side and on to the final destination at Puerto Natales.

*"Someday, somewhere, you will, without fail, come face to face with yourself. That, and only that will be the happiest or the bitterest of your hours."*
*-Pablo Neruda, Chilean Poet (1904-1973)*

## SKIING IN CHILE

By Katie Hale

While your friends are slurping daiquiris by the pool side back home, you could be sitting by the fireplace sipping a nice Chilean wine after a long day of skiing on the Andean slopes.

Chile's location in the southern hemisphere promises skiing all summer (or winter, depending on your viewpoint) long—the season officially begins June 15th and ends in early October. The country has 15 ski resorts, world renowned for the quality of their trails and amenities.

Portillo is by far the premiere ski resort of Chile. A self-contained town situated two hours northeast of Santiago, the resort offers some of the best runs in all of South America, Portillo has a distinctive structure where guests stay from Saturday to Sunday, much like a camp. The Grand Hotel Portillo offers pricey but plush accommodation, complete with stunning lake views, disco, heated outdoor pool, and cinema.

Termas de Chillán, located near the city of Chillán in central Chile, is another popular spot for the more adventurous snow bunny. This resort, perched at the base of a steaming volcano, boasts great skiing and hot springs to soak in after a grueling day on the mountain. Termas' backcountry acreage provides heliskiing opportunities for advanced riders and skiers.

Reserva Nacional Magallanes, located a mere eight km from Puerto Arenas, offers a place to escape the high season skiing crowds. With only a few thousand visitors annually, this is the perfect place to hear no more than the swish of your skis gliding through freshly fallen snow.

# THE WHEELS ON THE BUS GO ROUND AND ROUND

By Kelley Coyner, Texas, U.S.A.

Andrew, age two, may not have much sense of place, but he was delighted to rely on city buses, local buses and long distance buses to travel around Southern Chile. As far as this young adventurer is concerned, the principal purpose of travel is to ride buses.

For older travelers, nothing could be finer than a lovely bus liner for traveling around from Chiloé to Santiago. Chilean buses beat renting a car or traveling by air. No cars to park. No turnoffs to find. More time to read, play Go-Fish, sleep and look at the scenery. With so much to see and do, travel-by-bus is almost an end in itself. It is a terrific way to see Chiloé and the Lake District of Chile.

You can start from any point in Chile, but Puerto Montt serves as an air, land and sea hub. There are dozens of travel options; trips to Puerto Varas, Chiloé, and Santiago to name just a few. Take a 15-seater from Puerto Montt to Puerto Varas and study the two huge volcanoes that grace the horizon. On arrival, ask the driver to drop you at his favorite restaurant along the lake shore, and chow down on *curanto*, a local version of New England's clam bucket. After poking along the black sand beach, walk or take a bus to zip line rides high above the temperate rainforest canopy. The canopy and the lookout point provide a sweeping 360-degree view of the lake.

If you are not ready to hop aboard the bus and board a ferry to Bariloche, then flag down a mini bus and head back to Puerto Montt. A longer trip which takes two to four hours will bring you from Puerto Montt to Chiloé and its archipelagos. The bus drives right up on the ferry, which chugs on through to the middle and southern venues of the island. From the ferry deck, you can spot black necked swans paddling ferry-side. Once in Chiloé, stop in Ancud for the Humboldt and Magellanaic penguins, early Spanish colonial fort and an interesting modern art museum.

> *Somewhere on route from Southern Chile to Santiago our kids started singing the "Gilligan's Island" theme song and changed the lyrics from a three-hour tour to a 10-hour trip.*

Use Ancud as a stepping-off point for the northern sector of the National Seashore park or keep riding the bus to Castro and beyond. Along the way there is kayaking, dozens of striking wooden churches, the second half of the national seashore, trekking, and local markets of all varieties. A bus may be your best option to return from Southern Chile and catch a flight out through Santiago. It is a long ride, but then again, so is flying back. Travel by night and you can ride on a deluxe sleeper bus where the seats fold out to flat, sheet covered beds. Travel by day and you will see a string of volcanoes, wetlands, seaside, ranches, and vineyards.

Somewhere on route from southern Chile to Santiago our kids started singing the "Gilligan's Island" theme song and changed the lyrics from a three-hour tour to a 10-hour trip. (Tiresome yes, but it was singing, not whining.)

Whether you choose to sing, sleep, or eat your way across the great stretch of country that is Chile, a bus is a great way to see the sights it has to offer.

*"Write what should not be forgotten."*
-Isabel Allende Llona, Chilean Novelist (1942-)

# GET ON THE BUS

By Michelle Hopey

Unless you are renting a car, or are on an organized tour traveling in Latin America, your travels are likely to involve public transportation, and inevitably, a bus. Cheap, but often time-consuming and anxiety-inducing, riding the bus is just a way of life in Latin countries.

Bus travel in any country can be overwhelming, but in Latin America, whether you are cramped into a chicken bus, medium-sized coach, or air-conditioned *ejecutivo* for five minutes, five hours or five days, you're likely to encounter thieves, roads that make your stomach heave, and distractions ranging from C-movies to vendors that walk the aisles advertising their goods like auctioneers, making sleep an impossibility. At times, you'll feel like a sardine—the prime moment for thieves to spring into action.

With a few precautions, riding the bus is quite easy and remains on of the best ways to experience true, everyday Latin culture and to witness some fabulous landscapes. Read the Bus Travel Tips box on page 349 to get you going on your way safely and efficiently.

# CHILLING IN CHILOÉ

## By Will Gray, Kettering, England

The tranquil island of Chiloé has few true attractions but it is the ideal place to kick-back for a few days and enjoy the open spaces and the long, long beaches.

Reached from the busy town of Puerto Montt by a combination of bus and ferry, Chiloé is South America's largest island, more than 180 km long and 50 km wide, but its village atmosphere makes it seem much smaller. It is renowned for its cool damp weather and its warm-hearted people, who make their living in salmon farming or fishing.

The main settlements are Ancud, Castro and Quellón, spread out down the long and bumpy central island road, but if you are looking for a bit of peace and quiet then one of the nicest places to stay is in the community of Chonchi, just down the road from the island's capital of Castro on the east side of the island, where fresh salmon is served up by the plateful at the Hostel La Esmeralda.

Heading in, the road soon reveals scenery of rolling hills and fenced fields. The colourful town of Castro is well worth a stop en-route, with its church, Inglesia San Francisco, sparkling in bright pink and purple, and its famous stilted palafito houses reflecting their vibrant colours in the still creek water below them. Chonchi allows easy access to the more natural and totally uninhabited west coast, which reveals the island's wild side in the Parque Nacional Chiloé, an isolated area of forested hills and never-ending sandy beaches that is home to more than 100 species of birds and offers forest trails, a climb to a viewpoint overlooking the massive Lake Hullinco, and a long meandering trek along the deserted beach.

A sea tour is a must in this area. There are several local small motor-powered boats that will take you out past the salmon farms to chase dolphins, which are often seen playing in the wake of the fishing trawlers, then back to the coast to visit the colony of sea lions that take up residence on the rocks nearby. The island of Lemuy is another place to visit for a wander and Chonchi offers the easiest route here as the ferry terminal is just a short walk down the road. Arguably this is one of the safest places in the world to hitchhike, so while on the five-minute ride across to the island it is usually possible to secure a lift all the way to the main town, from where you can just walk the roads and take in the curvaceous hills and views of distant volcanoes before heading back to the beach for some more rest and relaxation.

## LATIN AMERICAN MYSTERIES # 7: WHAT IS THE MEANING OF THE EASTER ISLAND STONES?

Easter Island, Chile: dates unknown

When Dutch ship captain Jakob Roggeveen discovered Easter Island on Easter Sunday, 1722 (hence the name), he found a population of 2,000 to 3,000 humans and 900 statues. The people had apparently stopped carving them, and the stones, which had all been carved out of a central quarry, were located in different places around the island. No one could tell how the statues got to their respective locations after being carved. Ever since, people have asked questions about Easter Island: what do the statues mean? How did they get to their locations? Why did they stop carving them?

The statues are called moai and are of stylized human heads and torsos. They are solid stone and weigh several tons each. One statue, half-finished in the quarry, would have stood almost seventy feet tall and weighed over 200 tons had it been completed.

There are many theories about the island and the statues. The statues may have been intended as a way for kings to "channel" their energy and rule the whole island at once, or they may have been offerings to the legendary first king of the island. They may also have been intended as a way of asking the Gods for favor.

If they were intended as a way to ask for favor from the Gods, then it is ironic that many believe that the decline in the population of Easter Island—known as Rapa Nui to the locals, who had no idea that they would someday be "discovered" on Easter Sunday—was due to the enormous costs in resources that the statues demanded. One popular theory is that there was a vicious circle of sorts: first, the inhabitants decided to build a statue to please the Gods. Once the stature had been carved, they would cut trees to use as rollers, deforesting the island and destroying bird habitat (birds were a major source of food for the islanders). As a result, food and firewood became scarce, resulting in hard times for the people—who immediately decided to build another statue to please the Gods, thus starting the cycle all over again.

# COIHAIQUE

## By Pete Nelson, Chester, Maryland, U.S.A.

The Carretera Austral stretches several hundred kilometers southward from Chile's major port city of Puerto Montt into the country's "final frontier." It is more than 200 kilometers—plus two ferry links totaling several hours—from there to Chaitén, then another 420 kilometers to an archetypal modern frontier outpost, Coyhaique (or Coihaique, Coy-HIGH'-kay), the last community of any consequence in Chile's southern realm before the mainland farther south begins to crumble into a maze of sounds and straits, channels and fjords.

Nestled at the confluence of two rivers, the Simpson and the Coyhaique, this remote capital city, only officially established in 1929, is hilly, but conducive to walking. With its eclectic collection of accommodations, eateries and welcoming enterprises such as cyber-cafés, vehicle rental firms and shops, Coyhaique is a quintessential adventure travel base: accustomed to visitors both Chilean and foreign, its infrastructure is strong and residents eminently hospitable, eager to help and inform.

Perhaps Chile's most awe-inspiring national park, Parque Nacional Laguna San Rafael, approximately 1.74 million hectares sprawling southwest of Coyhaique, is comprised of two linked ice fields, El Monte San Valentín and Campo de Hielo Norte, surrounded by almost perpetually cloud-capped mountains. The Pacific pounds its western edge; Argentina encroaches from the east; the Carretera Austral snakes along in between, from Coyhaique to Cochrane and beyond. Created in 1959 primarily to protect its pristine state in the interests of national heritage, the park is vast and almost impossible to visit easily or comfortably.

However, Laguna San Rafael, for which the park is named, has emerged as one of Chile's elite travel destinations, accessible most readily by ferry from Coyhaique, but also from Puerto Montt, both via Puerto Chacabuco. Also, the deluxe resort, Termas de Puyuhuapi, to the north, operates its own 70-passenger high-speed catamaran as the highlight of its packaged lodging.

The allure of Laguna San Rafael is the 70-meter high Ventisquero San Rafael glacier at the southern end of the lake. From an altitude of 3,000 meters (9,840 feet) above sea level, it flows out of the northwest corner of the Campo de Hielo Norte at the rate of 17 meters a day, making it one of the world's fastest moving.

Among the several other opportunities to travel this area rife with glaciers is an incomparable white-knuckle tour by air. Several small firms in Coyhaique operate fixed-wing aircraft or helicopters piloted by experienced, knowledgeable professionals. By plane it is about an hour's flight to a strip on the northern side of the glacier. Helicopters land regularly at pre-determined spots on the solid surface of the (moving) glacier. The downside to these trips is that weather conditions often preclude this tour and prospective passengers too often must wait for several days to travel.

For many Chileans and visitors both, the rugged maritime outposts of Puerto Aisén (ice-EN') and Puerto Chacabuco (chah-kah-BOO'-koh), about 65 and 70 kilometers, respectively, west of Coyhaique, hold a certain mystique as they are the last links of any consequence between the country's northern regions and its far south. In recent years Puerto Chacabuco has replaced Puerto Aisén as a viable port. Indeed, they are tucked into a largely pristine area of remote hanging glaciers and cascading waterfalls inhabited only by extensive colonies of waterfowl. Offshore, perpetually mist-shrouded islands appear and vanish, defined only by a maze of fjords.

Chilean Woman. Photo courtesy of Corporación de Promoción Turística de Chile.

### GLACIER FACTOID:

Most glaciers in the Parques Nacionales are called *glaciares*, while others are called *ventisqueros* (vehn-tee-SKAY'-rohs). The terms are often used interchangeably. Glaciers which end at the edge of a cliff—as opposed to ending in a body of water—dropping their bergs onto dry land, are *colgante* (cohl-GAHN'-tay, hanging). Most of these are called ventiqueros. This imprecise terminology is simply another part of the enigmatic charm of Chilean Spanish.

# CARRETERA AUSTRAL

By Scott Ferree, McPherson, Kansas, U.S.A.

The idea of the sublime has something to do with a beauty that is so awe-inspiring that it quite nearly inspires terror. If that's the definition, then there are certainly occasions during a trip on southern Chile's Carretera Austral that call for use of the word.

After several years splitting his time between Europe and the U.S., Scott Ferree is currently living in Buenos Aires, Argentina, where he is a translator and short story writer. Ferree has undergraduate degrees in English and French literature from the University of Kansas and a Master's degree (MPhil) in Comparative Literature from the University of London, Goldsmiths College. He is at work on his first novel.

The craziest place Ferree has ever visited is his home town—when the plane comes down over the wheat fields in Wichita, Kansas, it never fails to feel like the strangest place in the world to the world traveler.

His dream destination is Madagascar for its crazy animals, plants and micro-climates. He would have already visited the island nation if it weren't on the other side of the world, with a plane ticket priced to match.

One that comes to mind, from a recent trip that my girlfriend and I took on Chile's southern highway, happened on the last day of our trip. We were heading towards the Argentine border on a route which had us spending the greater part of the day circumnavigating the banks of the Lago Carrera—an immense, intensely turquoise glacial lake. The sun was already setting as we were finishing the last bit of road leading in to the town of Chile Chico. Sailing through town, we emerged on the other side and were shocked by the sight before us: the highway had spit us out on the other side, in the face of soaring peaks, rising and falling beside a ribbon of road carving a precarious route into the abrupt turns and jagged cliffs. And that's where the sublime came into play.

The hairpin curves, steep rises, and sudden descents were certainly terrifying—and the terror was intensified by the fact that we were on the side of a mountain with 90-degree cliffs; on a road surface of unpaved gravel. But the beauty of the place was as overwhelming as the drops were fear-provoking. On the opposite shore of the lake, the snow covered Andean peaks turned orange and then purple with the dying light, and at every sharp curve in the road—as we held our breath and sometimes gasped—we were treated to a new, stunning vista.

As the hotel clerk in Chile Chico told us later: "If anyone asks you if you've ever piloted an airplane, you can say, 'No, but I've come pretty close.'"

The Carretera Austral is a long, mostly gravel highway which serves as Patagonian Chile's only land link to the more populated northern part of the country. Its north to south route parallels that of the mythic Highway 40 on the Argentine side of the border, but where the 40 only gives you a glimpse of the Andes in the faraway distance, Chile's Carretera Austral traces a route right through the heart of the mountain chain—circumnavigating the northern and southern ice caps and the snow blanketed peaks which surround the ice fields—passing high mountain glaciers, waterfalls, fjords, and national parks with dense Pacific forests. Along the way, in the port cities, there's fresh salmon on offer, probably some of the very best in the world.

We took the Carretera only as an afterthought, a way to break up the monotony of a 1,500 kilometer trip south from Bariloche to the glaciers in Argentina's southern Santa Cruz province. But our unplanned detour turned out to be one of the most memorable parts of the trip. After all, as we were told in the hotel: it's the closest you can get to flying without leaving the ground.

Carretera Austral. Photo by Scott Ferree.

# TORRES DEL PAINE NATIONAL PARK

By David Vincent, Lenox, Massachusetts, U.S.A.

The name Patagonia evokes mystical images of towering peaks and sky-blue glaciers. It is therefore surprising to learn that most of the vast region covering southern portions of Argentina and Chile consists of relatively flat, desert-like prairie and is not particularly spectacular. However, it is along the spiny Andean border between the two countries where Patagonia derives its mythic reputation. Widely considered to be the star attraction of the region is the Torres del Paine National Park, located in southern Chile.

Thrusting dramatically upward from the flat pampas (prairie) is a range of chiseled, jagged, snow-covered peaks. Principal among them are the three Paine Towers, monolithic spires sculpted thousands of years ago by a sea of glacial ice. "Paine" (pronounced "pie-nay") means blue in the native Tehuelche language, though the rock is primarily pink granite. The Central Tower, highest of the three at about 3,400 meters (roughly 11,000 feet), draws some of the best mountaineers in the world. Equally awesome are the Cuernos del Paine (Horns of Paine), knobby, two-colored mountains that appear like a turreted castle.

The national park (about 2,400 sq. km) was declared a UNESCO Biosphere Reserve in 1978 and is one of *National Geographic*'s 50 places to visit in your lifetime. The park's varied terrain includes Magellenic forest, muddy bogs, alpine meadows, glacial lakes and rushing rivers. Visitors can make a day hike up to the towers, trek the popular "W" route in about five days, or go for the full circuit, spending about eight or nine days. One can also take a short cruise across Lago Grey up to base of Glacier Grey, an extension of the third-largest ice-field in the world. The crack and boom of calving glacial ice is an unforgettable experience.

Torres del Paine is a fantastic destination for wildlife viewing as well. One can spot the guanaco, a more lithesome member of the llama family, endangered from years of over-hunting for its delicate fur. The Patagonian Gray Fox, the Huemul (Andean Deer) and the elusive Puma also occupy the park. The diverse microclimates support over 120 species of bird, including Black-necked swans, Patagonian Woodpeckers, Austral Parakeets and even Chilean Flamingos in the salt lagoons. It's not uncommon to glimpse the majestic Andean Condor with its ten-foot wingspan. The Lesser Rhea is a rare and rather awkward-looking ostrich-like bird also found in the park.

Visitors to Torres del Paine must be prepared for Mother Nature's less hospitable side. The weather is notoriously unpredictable, and can include pummeling winds, rain, sleet or snow, even during the best season for visits (December to March). The iconic towers may be shrouded in clouds upon arrival. Rain or shine though, Torres del Paine is Patagonia at its most spectacular and grandiose.

Torres del Paine. Photo by Freyja Ellis.

# PUNTA ARENAS

## By Dr. Crit Minster, Rochester, New York, U.S.A.

Punta Arenas is easy to locate: it's at the end of the world.

One of the southernmost cities in the world, Punta Arenas sits on the Strait of Magellan, a treacherous channel between the Atlantic and Pacific Oceans. This choppy route passes by the rocky islands of southern Chile and Argentina, between the mainland and the large island of Tierra del Fuego. The strait was discovered by Ferdinand Magellan in 1520, and has been used ever since as a major trade route by those seeking to avoid the more dangerous Drake Passage to the south. Until the construction of the Panama Canal, the Strait of Magellan was the best way to ship goods.

The city of Punta Arenas marks the third crack at establishing a base in the region. In 1584, the colorful Spanish historian and explorer Pedro Sarmiento de Gamboa established the first settlement, which he named Rey Don Felipe after the king of Spain. The conditions were very harsh, however, and all 300 settlers eventually deserted or perished: when British pirate Thomas Cavendish visited the site in 1587 no one was left alive. Cavendish renamed the site Puerto Hambre, or Port Famine, and it later became a British naval base. Charles Darwin visited the base during his voyage with the HMS Beagle. The second settlement was sponsored by the Chilean government and was named Fort Bulnes. It, too, was abandoned: a reconstruction is now on the site for interested visitors.

The history of Punta Arenas consists of a series of boom-and-bust cycles. Punta Arenas was established in 1849 and reaped the benefits of the California Gold Rush, as it was often easier to ship supplies around South America than it was to send them overland. The next boom followed in the late 1800s, when it was discovered that sheep thrive in the chilly climate. Wool merchants made vast fortunes: their legacy is still visible today in the grand mansions lining the streets of Punta Arenas. The wool boom fizzled around World War II, but two more booms were waiting in the wings: oil was discovered on the island of Tierra del Fuego and the fishing industry took off.

Since the late 1980s, tourism has been a huge industry in Punta Arenas as well. There's much to do in this unique area at the end of the world. The city itself is worth a visit: some of the homes of the old wool barons have been converted into museums. The most notable is the Palacio Sara Braun, built between 1894 and 1905. Today it houses the elegant if pricey José Nogueira Hotel as well as a museum: stop in for a coffee or a snack at the restaurant even if you can't afford the hotel itself.

Punta Arenas is also very close to one of the most beautiful vistas in the world: Torres de Paine national park. These majestic mountains are breathtakingly beautiful, and visitors come from around the globe to gaze upon them. There are penguin habitats in the nearby Otway inlet which are relatively easy to visit, and Magdalena and Marta islands are home to penguins as well as other marine birds.

---

PUNTA ARENAS TRAVEL TIP:

Located just eight km (five miles) from Punta Arenas, is Cerro Mirador Ski Center, where you can hit the slopes and simultaneously get a fabulous view of the Strait and Tierra del Fuego. Ski season is from June to September, where you can slide down 11 different runs for every skill level.

---

## MAGELLANIC PENGUINS

By Will Gray

Just an hour outside the spartan port town of Punta Arenas lives a colony of Magellanic penguins, where hidden viewing stations offer the unique sight of these creatures in their natural habitat.

The Magellanic penguin is distinguished from the Humboldt and African penguins by the two bands that cross its front, one a wide black strip under the chin and the other a horseshoe shape on the stomach. The penguins are naturally shy and nest in deep burrows, many of which can be spotted as you follow the roped-out area around the site. The penguins often hide if approached, but keep quiet and you will not be disappointed.

The park is well laid out with three viewing zones, each mapped out at the small entrance area and each having a concealed viewing hut where you can stand and stare out of the gaps without disturbing the penguins. If you time it right, the penguins, some of the only black and white breeds you will see outside Antarctica, can be observed chasing between the beach and their nests.

The 60 cm tall animals, which feed on a diet of squid and small schooling fish, nest all around the southern part of Chile and Argentina but this location gives you a rare opportunity to get a close-up view as they come in from feeding time, and it is very easy to spend a good two hours just watching the amusing antics of these lovable birds.

The best time to see these waddling creatures is during the breeding season from late September to early February, when adults spend much of their time on the beach constructing the nesting sites. It takes five to six weeks for the eggs to hatch and spotting chicks is rare as they usually hide out in the burrow for a month or so before being prepared for the sea and taking their first icy plunge sometime around April.

# PUERTO WILLIAMS

## By Pete Nelson, Chester, Maryland, U.S.A.

Setting the record straight. Long renowned as the southernmost town in the world, Ushuaia, Argentina is not. Puerto Williams, Chile, is.

There are only three reasons to budget the time and funds to visit Puerto Williams on barren, mountainous Isla Navarino, all relatively irrational: one, for a brief encounter with the only known remaining Yámana (also Yagán and Yaghan), several of who are mestizos; two, for a visit to the world's southernmost—and, not surprisingly, one of the world's smallest—yacht clubs; three, simply for the "been there" boast.

Isla Navarino lies opposite the southern flank of Tierra del Fuego, southeast of Ushuaia, Argentina, on the shore of what is today called the Beagle Channel (after Captain Fitzroy's ship, the HMS Beagle, whose illustrious early 19th century passenger was Charles Darwin). The native Yámana called the island Uspashum.

Wild-eyed European immigrants attracted by the much-hyped—and short-lived—gold rush to Tierra del Fuego just prior to the turn of the last century created an informal settlement here. It was known as Puerto Luisa until 1956 when its name was changed in honor of Juan Williams who laid formal claim to the Estrechos de Magallanes (Straits of Magellan) in 1843 and established Fuerte Bulnes to the south of present-day Punta Arenas. Today Puerto Williams is a Chilean naval base, home to some 2,000 sailors, officers and their families; civilian residents number about 500.

Directly south of Isla Navarino are the treacherous Islas Wollaston, tipped by the notorious Cape Horn. Beyond that, Antarctica.

A short walk to the east of Puerto Williams, a tiny cluster of wooden houses comprise the community of Ukika, home to the last of the Yámana. The men eek out their living as fisherfolk. It is unclear just how many of these inhabitants are pure descendants of the original Yámanas, but there is little doubt that they are friendly and hospitable and do not mind the occasional stranger wandering into their enclave.

A small protected inlet on the western edge of Puerto Williams shelters the southernmost yacht club in the world, Club de Yates Micalvi, named after the rusting hulk of a small, between-World-Wars-era Swiss freighter, the Micalvi, listing to port, permanently moored to the shoreline. Her tilted pilothouse (or bridge) is the clubhouse, welcoming the world's most intrepid sailors with comfortably worn seating of every description, an unimaginably well-stocked bar, and a small fireplace in one corner. It is open to all visitors, its irregular hours notwithstanding.

The Punta Arenas-based airline, DAP, operates a twin-engine aircraft a few days a week, weather permitting, from Punta Arenas, a flight of a little over an hour provides spectacular vistas over the glacier-strewn Cordillera de Darwin and the fjords. There is also a weekly ferry from Punta Arenas, southward through the Canal Cockburn into the Pacific, then into the western extremity of the Canal Beagle, a trip lasting up to a day and a half.

North American "Captain Ben" sails the 75-foot schooner Victory around Cabo de Hornos (Cape Horn) from his home in Puerto Williams on the Canal Beagle. In addition, he is the representative for some 17 vessels available for visiting Antarctica under sail, private yachts for charter and "tall ships".

Captain Ben's extraordinary website (www.victory-crusies.com) contains "1,400 graphics and 450 pages of information on culture, history, fauna, flora, anthropology, geography, archaeology, Chile and Antarctic facts, kayaking, whale watching, trekking". It meanders a bit, but click on the "Cape Horn" patch to the left for more or less of an index. It's well worth a visit. Creating an extensive website might be the 21st-century equivalent to carving scrimshaw for whiling away the long winter months.

Puerto Williams. Photo by Will Gray.

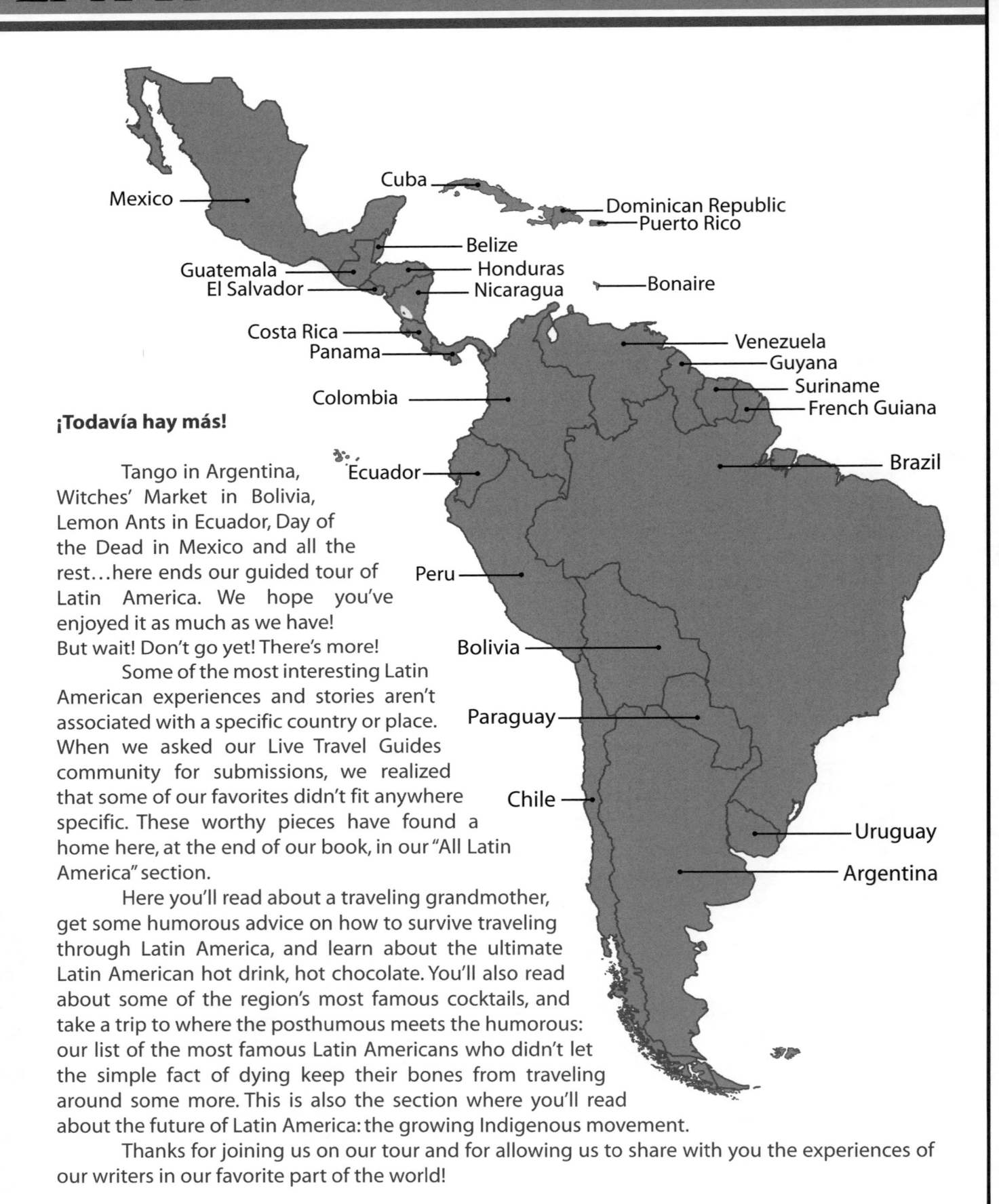

# LATIN AMERICA

**¡Todavía hay más!**

Tango in Argentina, Witches' Market in Bolivia, Lemon Ants in Ecuador, Day of the Dead in Mexico and all the rest…here ends our guided tour of Latin America. We hope you've enjoyed it as much as we have! But wait! Don't go yet! There's more!

Some of the most interesting Latin American experiences and stories aren't associated with a specific country or place. When we asked our Live Travel Guides community for submissions, we realized that some of our favorites didn't fit anywhere specific. These worthy pieces have found a home here, at the end of our book, in our "All Latin America" section.

Here you'll read about a traveling grandmother, get some humorous advice on how to survive traveling through Latin America, and learn about the ultimate Latin American hot drink, hot chocolate. You'll also read about some of the region's most famous cocktails, and take a trip to where the posthumous meets the humorous: our list of the most famous Latin Americans who didn't let the simple fact of dying keep their bones from traveling around some more. This is also the section where you'll read about the future of Latin America: the growing Indigenous movement.

Thanks for joining us on our tour and for allowing us to share with you the experiences of our writers in our favorite part of the world!

# HOT CHOCOLATE IN LATIN AMERICA

## By Michelle Hopey, New Hampshire, U.S.A.

It began as a hot potion sipped only by noble Mayans in ancient Latin America, but today hot chocolate is a common beverage found around the world in homes, cafés and supermarkets. However, as its popularity soared and its birthplace was lost in commerce, its native land never forgot how to make a perfect, decadently rich hot chocolate.

After all, the seed responsible for making mouths melt—whether as a liquid or as a solid bar—hails from Latin America. Found in most tropical climates in Latin America, the cacao plant is the root of all chocolate treats. Cacao has been mashed, ground, shaved, sipped, baked and frozen for centuries.

The white seeds—yes, white—are nested inside a yellow, squash-like fruit which grows from the lanky cacao plant. Picked fresh from the tree and cracked open, you can suck on the large seeds which have a somewhat bitter taste.

The white seeds are usually roasted over fire, turning dark brown, and then peeled. Once bare, the seeds are reheated and with little effort they melt into a brown, heavenly smelling liquid. With a dash of milk, honey, vanilla or cinnamon, the rich, delectable treat which people of the world call chocolate comes to be.

Over 2,000 years ago, the cacao bean was considered like gold and used as a form of currency by the Mayans. Whether it was Hernando Cortez or Christopher Columbus who brought the cacao beans to Spain has been the subject of debate. Most reports say that somewhere between 1517 and 1519, Hernando Cortez was offered a drink, in a golden goblet, by Montezuma II. Cortez tasted the drink made by the Aztecs and declared it a treasure. Apparently Montezuma II called it "chocolatl," meaning warm liquid, and he consumed up to 50 goblets a day. Aside from that, chocolatl was reportedly drunk only during special ceremonies.

Cortez is said to then have brought the beans back to Spain where the chocolate drink was made, heated and sweetened. It was an aristocratic beverage, to be sipped only by the upper class. By the mid-1600s, word got out. The drink became took hold among the French and the first official hot chocolate parlor was opened in London.

Currently, hot chocolate is celebrated in Latin America, primarily because of its rich, full-bodied flavor. In many parts of the world hot chocolate is blended with boiling water, but in Latin American warm milk is used, making it just that much more creamy and smooth (if also fattening) in consistency. While still retaining its power as a special drink, Latin Americans typically sip hot chocolate after dinner or as a treat. Needless to say, special goblets are no longer used—regular ol' mugs or tea cups suffice.

It is also common for different countries to give the drink a special twist. In Colombia and Ecuador for example, it is common to have chocolate caliente con queso, essentially hot chocolate with a slab of fresh cheese, on the top and left to melt. It might sound bizarre but the salty flavor of the cheese mixes perfectly with the sweet chocolate flavor. Possibly an acquired taste, but most who try it are pleasantly surprised. Peruvians tend to put in a little extra chocolate syrup to their warm chocolate milk, the enhanced sweetness making it a dessert, but a very good one at that.

In Argentina, hot chocolate is served up in many fashions, the most popular being the *submarino*, consisting of steamed milk in a mug with a chocolate bar on the side. The bar should be submerged into the milk and will quickly disappear, melting into the liquid. A quick stir and a dash of sugar make it extra creamy, but the best part is that it tastes, and is, freshly made.

Whichever way you take your hot chocolate, make sure you sip some in Latin America. If you feel the guilt of chocolate over-indulgence come on after consuming two or three cups, remember this is special stuff was once reserved for kings and queens. So sit back and treat yourself royally.

Café Tortoni, Buenos Aires. Photo by Christian Denes.

# TALES OF A 57-YEAR-OLD GRANDMOTHER TRAVELLING ALONE IN LATIN AMERICA

By Carol Ann, Rhynie, Scotland

With its tales of spectacular waterfalls, lush jungles, harsh deserts, remnants of long lost cultures and man-made wonders, South America has always beckoned to me.

But it wasn't until 2005, as a 57-year-old grandmother, that I managed to spend six weeks travelling independently in South America. Like many travellers, I had a "shopping list" of places I wanted to visit: Iguaçu Falls in Brazil, Chile's Easter Island and Atacama Desert, Sun Island and Lake Titicaca in Bolivia, Cusco, Machu Picchu and Nasca in Peru, the Avenue of Volcanoes in Ecuador and finally the beautiful, volcanic islands of the Galápagos—a long list to do in a very short time.

In most locations, I arranged for a local, knowledgeable guide and driver to take me around. Although places like Machu Picchu, are very popular, I was hoping to be surprised—I wanted to see and experience places tourists don't normally go to, as well as explore by myself.

Travel guide publications always warn of "dangers and annoyances," but the best advice often comes from unexpected sources. I learned that this is key. Fellow travellers can teach you a lot.

Friends in Rio showed me how to pay for things without making open displays of money, how to keep small amounts in different places and to move around without attracting too much attention. In northern Chile, I met a man in the Calama airport who gave me priceless information on how to avoid altitude sickness: don't exert yourself, eat little and often, drink plenty of water and rub Mentholatum under your nose at night—it helps breathing when asleep.

The departure for each new location was like the start of another adventure. Locals can teach you a wealth of knowledge. On Easter Island, a lovely Rapa Nui woman named Edith took me to visit her favourite places, including old lava tubes, caves and other sites which most tourists never see.

Patricia, my guide in San Pedro de Atacama, shared insights about ancient Andean Indian beliefs, which provided an excellent foundation for the rest of my trip. I learned about the condor (representing the freedom of the skies), the puma (the ground world) and the snake (water and the underworld)—symbols which I was to see over and over again, expressed in paintings, on pottery, in sculpture and legends.

On Sun Island, Lake Titicaca, I was privileged to watch the local Kallawuaya (fortune teller and native doctor of the northern highlands) as he conducted an offering ceremony to bless Pachamama (Earth Mother) for bringing fertility and prosperity to the lake and its people.

Even in Cusco, I was able to explore off the beaten path and stay safe. On the outskirts of Cusco, I explored the rarely visited Temple of the Moon, built around and inside a natural rock formation. Long before the Inca, these rocky outcrops were considered sacred (or Huaca) and used as places of worship—they are still in use today.

In the Nasca desert I learned of a culture totally built around water, or the lack of it. As well as the famous Nasca Lines, there are mummy cemeteries filled with the remains of women and children sacrificed to bring rain; ancient stone aqueducts that still bring water from the mountains to the parched plains; and pyramids buried in giant mud slides.

On the Galápagos Islands, I learned to swim with turtles, seals and penguins. On land I came face to face with giant wild tortoises, mating and cavorting in a natural mud bath.

Five countries, eleven islands, nineteen planes, three trains, six boats and numerous cars and buses later I landed back in Aberdeen, Scotland, safe and sound. My journey and experiences in South America were priceless and now I have a further list of places that I know I will definitely return to one day as a young, ripe 60 or 70-something.

Niña on the way to Colca Canyon. Photo by Maximilian Hirschfeld.

# TOP TEN LATIN AMERICANS WHO COULDN'T KEEP STILL—EVEN AFTER THEY DIED!

By Dr. Crit Minster, Rochester, New York, U.S.A.

**Pancho Villa:** Gunned down on July 20, 1923, Villa was buried at the local cemetery in Hidalgo del Parral. He was dug up several times, however, and some say his skull is in the possession of the Skull and Bones Society at Yale University. The mayor ordered his body relocated to an unmarked grave. Later, he was dug up and entombed at the Revolution Monument in Mexico City.

**Christopher Columbus:** The man we all learn about in history class moved multiple times after passing to the other side. DNA results have proved that he lies in Seville, Spain, but the Dominican Republic also claims to have some of his remains. Since Dominican authorities won't let testing be done on the supposed explorer's bones, his death, like his life, remains legendary.

**Evita Perón:** After death, her husband, President Juan Perón, ordered her body preserved (think taxidermy). After Perón lost power, the opposition sent Evita's body to be buried in Milan, Italy, under another name. In 1971 Perón, living in exile in Spain, took possession of the body and kept it in his home until his return to Argentina in 1973. When he died in 1974, their bodies were displayed side-by-side for a while. Evita Peron was moved to her present location, Recoleta Cemetery in Buenos Aires, in 1974. There is no word on her future travel plans.

**Ché Guevara:** In October 1967, Ché Guevara was captured and executed by Bolivian forces working in concert with the CIA. He was buried near an airstrip near Vallegrande. In 1997, his remains were exhumed, identified with DNA, and returned to Cuba. His remains currently rest in a special mausoleum dedicated to him in Santa Clara, where he won an important battle of the Cuban Revolution in 1958.

**Simón Bolívar:** The great Liberator of South America died of tuberculosis in Santa Marta, Colombia, in 1830. He was buried there for a while, but was moved to Caracas, Venezuela in 1842, where he currently resides in a mausoleum built in his honor.

**General Santa Anna's leg:** In 1838, two years after losing Texas, General José Antonio de Santa Anna, president of Mexico, lost one of his legs below the knee fighting the French, who had invaded in order to recoup certain debts. The leg was initially buried at the Hacienda Manga del Clavo, one of Santa Anna's own properties. Later, he had it dug up and buried in a solemn military ceremony at the Santa Paula Cemetery. Later still, locals angry with Santa Anna's politics dug up the leg and dragged it through town. Meanwhile, in 1847, Santa Anna, fighting the U.S. – Mexican war, was surprised while eating dinner by a regiment of Illinoisans, who carried off his wooden leg. In spite of repeated requests for its return by the Mexican government, the wooden leg still can be seen at the Illinois National Guard Museum, Camp Lincoln, Springfield, Illinois.

**Emperor Maximilian of Mexico:** On June 19, 1867, Maximilian of Austria, Emperor of Mexico, was executed by firing squad. His body was displayed in Mexico for about a year before being returned to Austria, where it resides in the Imperial Crypt.

**Eliza Lynch:** In 1855, Francisco Solano López, the son of Paraguayan president Carlos Antonio López, came back to Paraguay from a trip to Europe with a surprise: Irish prostitute Eliza Lynch, who he had met in Paris. Before long, Eliza had turned Paraguayan society upside-down, ordering the construction of lavish buildings and confiscating the jewelry of Paraguay's elite in the name of "the war effort." After López died, she returned to Europe where she died in 1884. Over a hundred years later, her body was exhumed and returned to Paraguay, where it was reburied with honor in the national cemetery.

**José de San Martín:** (1778-1850) General San Martín liberated much of southern South America from Spanish rule, including his native Argentina. After independence, he refused to take part in the civil wars that were tearing his young country apart and moved to France where he lived from 1824 until his death in 1850. In 1880, his remains were returned to Argentina: they're still in the Buenos Aires Cathedral.

**Carlos Gardel:** Carlos Gardel was a famous tango singer. Originally from Uruguay, he was killed tragically in a plane crash in 1935 in Medellín, Colombia. Such was the outpouring of grief that his body was sent to New York, Rio de Janeiro and Uruguay before finally being laid to rest in Buenos Aires, Argentina.

Evita's grave. Photo by Ara Armstrong.

# LATIN AMERICAN COCKTAILS

## By Michelle Hopey, New Hampshire, U.S.A.

You can sip them, or you can slurp 'em, chug them or even gulp 'em, but one things is for sure: Latin Cocktails are one of Latin America's most defining qualities and well-deserved at that. Not that Latinos are consumed by alcohol, no they just like to consume alcohol, but not every day. And while *cerveza* is the number one thirst quencher, Latin cocktails, from the famous Margarita to the lesser known Canelazo, are second to none.

The Latin cocktail sums up the Latino culture in one, complete full sip: smooth, exotic, sultry, fresh, and colorful. Latin drinks should be a state of mind. It's an adventure to satisfaction. So, if you're looking for a little sizzle with a traditional drink, its likely that a Latin Cocktail will do you right. So to experience this intrepid genre of cocktails, raid your nearest liquor cabinet and go on a Latin adventure of your own. Here are a few for the journey:

The M*ojito*, a classic, minty drink from Cuba, has grown quite popular amongst bar flies in the United States and Europe. Reportedly the Mojito was Ernest Hemmingway's drink of choice. Refreshingly sweet and cool on your lips, a Mojito makes you feel as if you deserve to be sitting on a beach relaxing. Mix-up clear rum, a muddled concoction of fresh lime and mint leaves, simple syrup (sugar and water melted) and club soda with ice.

The oh-so-sophisticated Brazilian *Caipirinha* is another chart climber. As national drink of Brazil, the Caipirinha is a sassy drink designed for those who are sweet and sour. The prime ingredient, cachaca (distilled from sugarcane), tastes a bit like rum and with fresh lime, sugar and ice tossed in there, you'll be left wondering where you can stock-up on cachcaca. (Psst..your local liquor store or on the web).

Then on your adventure you'll stumble upon the *Pisco sour*. This drink spawns so much controversy that it must be good—and luckily it is. For decades, both Chile and Peru have fought over the birthrights to the Pisco sour, the sweet, Margarita-like drink. Both claim it as their national drink, but no one can actually settle on who really birthed this fantastic, sour baby. You see, Pisco is a type of brandy that is distilled from Muscat grapes in South America—grown in both Peru and Chile. To make a sour, first make a simple syrup then blend together with two shots of Pisco, lime juice, one teaspoon of egg white and ice. Take an old-fashioned or highball glass, dip the rim in egg white, then sugar and you'll know why no one would want to let this one get away.

For a little kick, go for the Mexican *Michelada*, a shandy, or prepared beer. While there are many variations, sometimes its similar to a Bloody Mary, only containing beer instead of vodka. Other times a Michelada is a Mexican beer mixed with sauces and lime juice added. It origins date back to the 1940s, when mixing beer with hot sauce or salsa became the rage in Mexico. Of course, though you could always give a shot of tequila a try, being as it is Mexico's national liquor and might go down a bit smoother than salsa and XX Dos Equis.

More than likely you've heard of the *Pina Colada*, but did you know that it is known as the official beverage of Puerto Rico? In case you haven't tried one, give it a shot, and if you have, well, have another because this tropical creamy, rum-based pineapple smoothie is a delight. It's a mix of light rum, coconut cream and pineapple juice blended with crushed ice.

So why we're on the less exotic, a *Cuba Libre* (Spanish for Free Cuba) is your standard rum and cola except for one twist: lime. Mixed with lime juice, this Cuban-invented concoction is so refreshing and typically strong, that you're likely to feel free all night long.

For a more unique, lesser known drink, try one of these peculiar concoctions:

A traditional drink served-up warm, Ecuador's *Canelazo* is made with aguardiente, sugar, cinnamon and naranjilla and tastes a little like spiced hot apple cider, minus the apple. It's combo that will not only knock you down and back up again, but taste spicy and sweet all the while.

For something a bit easy, but still an obscure blend, mix-up some red wine with cola, and then picture yourself on the coast of that skinny little country called, Chile, where this drink called the *Jote*, originated from.

*Caju Amigo* is a Brazilian drink or often, shot made of cachaca and cashew juice. You chew-up a cashew, don't swallow wait until you take a shot of straight cachaça, swallowing the nut and the liquor in the same gulp.

## CANELAZO  By Paula Newton and Katie Hale

Canelazo provides a warm, comforting feeling on a cold night, high in the Ecuadorian Andes. It is popularly served on Chiva buses with the accompaniment of a *banda del pueblo* (town band), and it is more potent than at first it seems . . .

Ingredients for 6 portions:

3 cups water
1.5 cups light brown sugar
6 cinnamon sticks
1 cup aguardiente
1 tbsp lime juice

Combine the water, sugar and cinnamon sticks in a saucepan and bring to the boil. Pour the aguardiente into the mixture and maintain the mix simmering. Once it is very hot remove from the heat and add the lime juice. Serve very hot in short and thick glasses. Accompany with fresh cinnamon sticks. Total preparation time: thirty minutes.

# GETTING AROUND IN LATIN AMERICA

### By Dr. Crit Minster, Rochester, New York, U.S.A.

Looking for adventure, and possibly some great stories? Road-tripping across Latin America could provide some of your most lasting memories—from a taxi ride with a zealous soccer fanatic to a five hour bus ride with a pig in your lap.

Of course, the most comfortable option for traveling around is with a tour. If you spend any time in Latin America, you'll see immaculate tour buses full of mostly elderly travelers sporting Tilley hats and fancy walking sticks riding, staring wide-eyed out into the Third World while their guide—who may or may not have been a military commando in a previous life—describes the local flora, fauna and culture.

Tours are great if you've got extra cash to spare. If you can't spring for a tour, or if you simply don't want to be an owl-eyed passenger traveling in sterilized comfort, you might prefer a local bus. In general, there are two kinds of buses in Central and South America: The first sort is the common ones used by most of the people, often to go to market. In Guatemala, they're known as "chicken buses" because chances are you'll be sharing a seat with a chicken, pig, goat, sheep or a dog for some or all of the way. The other human passengers are friendly and outgoing if occasionally unwashed and toothless.

The nickname "chicken bus" may be Guatemalan, but you can expect to find variations of it anywhere you go. In some cases, you may find yourself on top of the bus, balancing on a sack of potatoes, dodging oncoming power lines and trying not to think about what it is that is moving about inside an oddly-shaped sack tied to a nearby roof rack. At other times, you may find yourself standing for several hours, one passenger out of 175 or so on a bus intended for about 40. Local bus rides are always memorable, whether it's for a friendly conversation, a chance meeting with a fellow traveler, or the unbearable trauma of ten hours listening to tinny ranchera music blaring through the bus speakers (funny how those seem to be the only part of the bus that consistently works). It should be noted that local buses do occasionally break down, catch on fire, explode or plunge off cliffs, but not necessarily on the same trip. Oh, and there's no bathroom on board, so try to refrain from drinking liquids for about two days before taking a local bus.

If you want to have a trip that is relatively free of chickens, explosions, toothless locals and stuff falling off of the ceiling rack onto your head, you may want to upgrade to a first-class bus. Generally, most places in Latin America have first-class bus services between major cities. These buses often have assigned seats, which is nice, and some even have a cabin steward who passes out Coca-Cola and very dry cookies. Best of all, they generally have a bathroom in the back (remember that when buying your reserved seat: the bathrooms can be smelly). They'll often have a TV with DVD player and will occasionally pop in pirated copies of Hollywood movies. This may sound like a good thing, but the bus assistant is usually a male teenager, which means you'll be watching such screen gems as *Leprechaun 3* and *Kung Fu Fists of Death*. Still, it's easier to sleep through a screen leprechaun running around with a cleaver than it is to sleep with a duck on your lap. Believe me on this.

Once you reach your destination, you have the problem of getting around within the town. City buses are the most common and cheapest way to see an unfamiliar city, but these come with complications.

Take the city of Quito, Ecuador, for example. There are numerous city buses which link every possible corner of the city, and the buses are clearly numbered. But this is where the problems start. The numbers on the front of the buses don't actually mean anything. Hop on a #41 bus two days in a row and you'll go two different places. What you're supposed to actually do is read the signs in the front bus window, because they'll accurately tell you where the bus is headed, most of the time. So, to summarize, if you want to catch a bus somewhere in Quito, you need to stand on the sidewalk as close to the street as possible, squinting through black clouds of exhaust, peering at the windows of buses as they zoom past. If you see a sign that indicates the bus is going your way, wave your arms madly. The bus will slow but never stop: some long-time Quito visitors theorize that every bus in the city has a bomb in it that will go off if the bus ever comes to a complete stop. Jump on, find a seat and pray to the Transportation Gods that you made the right choice.

Difficult buses may make you want to take a taxi. This may or may not be a good idea. Hailing the wrong cab on the streets of Mexico City may get you mugged, kidnapped, raped, murdered, ransomed, kidney-harvested and/or sold to Tunisian sex slave dealers, not necessarily in that order. Many other cities in Latin America have perfectly safe cabs where the most you have to worry about is whether the cabbie is going to charge you twice or three times what he would charge a local. According to my informal research, in several Latin American cities it is necessary to be a raging soccer fanatic if you want to get a cabbie's license. Cabs are often decorated in the dazzling colors of the local team, and if you ask the cabbie about local fútbol, he will start ranting and raving so much, he may even forget to overcharge you.

Whether it's by chicken bus, first class bus or soccer taxi, getting around in Latin America is an unforgettable experience. You're looking for excitement, right? So grab the nearest chicken and hop on the bus!

## BUS TRAVEL TIPS By Michelle Hopey

1. Turn your backpack around so it sits on your front instead of back, especially while you are getting on and off buses because it is easy to become distracted and get pick-pocketed.

2. Sometimes people stand in the aisle for seven hours straight when there are no available seats. This is considered to be perfectly acceptable, and don't be surprised if you have to do the same.

3. If possible, wear your money belt, or keep money and documents in your shoes, socks or under your clothes.

4. Get up a few minutes before your stop to get past all the people in the aisles, if need be.

5. Don't be afraid to sit next to the driver, often this is considered a purchased seat and is actually quite comfortable, since you get a great view and don't have to worry about pick-pocketers so much.

6. When you get on or off the bus do a quick leap on or off the bus. Often the bus never fully stops.

# THE MODERN INDIGENOUS MOVEMENT IN LATIN AMERICA

By Ricardo Segreda, Quito, Ecuador

Of Costa Rican and Ecuadorian heritage, Ricardo Segreda was born in Washington, D.C., and grew up just outside of New York City. He graduated with Departmental Honors from Manhattanville College in Purchase, New York, earning a B.A. in Religious Studies and Literature. Segreda managed a hostel for Hostelling International in Washington State, and also served on its Board of Directors before moving to Quito, Ecuador in 2004. He is currently the film critic for Ecuador's largest daily, *La Hora*, and President of Ecuador's Society of Film Critics. He has written features articles and investigative pieces for Ecuador's *Revista Diners*, *Arte y Movimiento*, and, in Washington State, the *Bellingham Weekly*. He also teaches and lectures on the subject of film and journalism throughout Ecuador.

Segreda wouldn't leave for his travels without all of the right vaccinations. The craziest place he has visited is "my head," while his most bizarre experience was getting a haircut in New Zealand; the Maori barber was livid when he asked her to cut some more after her initial trim while only wanting to pay for one cut. His dream destination is Mongolia, but he is not planning any trips in the near future.

Before a crowd of thousands, Evo Morales was sworn as President of Boliva in January of 2006, not in the capital city of La Paz, but at the historic archeological site, Tiawanaku. Morales, a socialist who overcame all the racial and social obstacles of his culture to become one of the very few *indigenas* to become a national leader, was sending a very clear signal not just to Bolivia, but to the world: for the indigenous peoples of Latin America, their time had come. Indeed, representatives from progressive social movements across Latin America were in attendance as Morales stated that 500 years of colonialism had come to an end.

In a sense, this also signaled the dawn of a new era in the struggle for Latin America's preponderantly indigenous and mestizo, but economically marginalized population: the use of the ballot box to become a notable political force.

Fourteen years earlier, in fact, during the quincentennial anniversary of Columbus' arrival to the Western Hemisphere, the Nobel Prize for Peace was awarded to Rigoberta Menchu of Guatemala, whose acclaimed biography, "I, Rigoberta," detailed her personal experiences of the genocidal violence perpetuated by Guatemala's military government, with American assistance, against the indigenous peoples of Guatemala, supposedly in the service of "anti-communism."

The legacy of horror and violence against native people in Menchu's testimony was symptomatic of the struggle of indigenous people throughout Central and South America for most of the 20th century. Communism, whether real or perceived, often served as an excuse for Latin America's military governments, with American backing, to resort to Machiavellian measures to suppress any attempt by the descendents of the original inhabitants of the Americas to assert their rights and calls for economic justice.

During the 1990s, partly due to the fall of communism, and partly due to peace negotiations brokered in Latin American states, often with the help of the United Nations, a new movement on behalf of indigenous peoples has emerged, bringing attention to such issues as land reform, cultural recognition, greater participation in the political process and increased sovereignty over the natural resources in their territories.

The degree of advancement has varied from country to country. The three most notable advances for indigenous rights have been in Mexico, Ecuador and Bolivia, though the indigenous in Chile, Brazil, and Colombia have mobilized for their rights as well. The situation varies according to the population numbers, the ideology of leaders and to the degree of unification amongst communities within a nation.

In Ecuador, for example, the native movement originally concentrated on the timely return of land. President Rodrigo Borja gave them over two million hectares in eastern Ecuador. They also agitated for their own local governments, and their success with a town called Cotacachi resulted in its being declared by UNESCO the first illiteracy-free territory in Ecuador. Ecuador's indigenous population has the advantage of a shared language—Quechua—as a unifying factor. In Guatemala, by contrast, progress has struggled against a more fragmented community with 22 separate linguistic groups. But even there, peaceful, democratic elections are providing the means for the needs of Guatemala's indigenous to be addressed.

Many challenges lie ahead for all of the America's indigenous, but a lack of momentum is not one of them.

Bolivian man. Photo by Martin Li.

# Index

## A

Actun Tunichil Muknal 166
Agran, Hannah Fairlie 193, 206, 207, 210
Aguas Calientes 286
Álamos 113
Alandaluz Resort 262
Amazon Ecopark Lodge 75
Ambergris Caye 169
Amboró National Park 312
A Natural Obsession 158
Anderson, Peter 23, 82, 325, 330, 331
Angel Falls 80
Ann, Carol 265, 302, 326, 346
Antigua 152
Araya Peninsula 90
Arequipa 294
Arghiris, Richard 110, 117, 132, 162
Armstrong, Ara 31, 347
Asunción 49
Atacama Desert 325
Aventuras Sobre Rieles 108
Aztec Sun Stone, The 125

## B

B'omb'il Pek and Jul iq' 157
Bahia de Solimán 140
Baker, Terence 148, 222, 231
Balkus, Brad 272
Banana Republic of Guatemala 154
Baños 254
Baracoa 105
Bariloche to Puerto Varas 15
Barra 71
Barto, Anna L. 105
Bartolomé de Las Casas & the Verapaz Experiment 162
Basilica del Voto Nacional 240
Batopilas 111
Bay of Pigs, The 104
Beef it Up in Buenos Aires 36
Beley, Degan 170, 188, 199
Belize's Baboon Sanctuary 171
Bellavista 259
Bennett, Caroline 145, 153, 159
Bennett, Jessica 34, 37, 65, 97
Bennett, Will 19
Bernales, Cia 215
Berns, Maria 36
Biddle, Ellery 16, 102
Bike Riding in Buenos Aires 32
Bike Trip in Antigua 154
Birdwatching in Iquitos 274
Birdwatching in the Pantanal 58
Black Sheep Inn 250
Blake, Laura Watilo 273
Bocas del Toro 215
Bolivia Factoids 315
Bolivian Coca 317
Boquillas 109
Botero, Fernando 231
Bower, Douglas 118
Brass, Cyril 196, 202, 208
Breaking Eggs or Knocking Over Chairs 54
Breaking the Bank 269
Brown, David 327
Buenos Aires 30
Buenos Aires After dark 32
Bullfighting at the Festivities of Quito 242
Burke, Denis 158
Bus Travel Tips 349

## C

Cabañas Copal 142
Cabo San Lucas 114
Cahal Pech 167
Caipirinha 62
Cal Orko 316
Canaima 81
Cancuén 156
Cancún 139
Candela Music and Art Festival 94
Candelaria Caves 161
Cann, Erika 96, 195
Caputo, Lorraine 9, 84, 86, 89, 90, 91, 108, 112, 126, 129, 134, 146, 160, 176, 183, 190, 219, 227, 247, 319
Caracas City Tours, 91
Caracol 165
Caraz 275
Carmelo 41
Carmenère 331
Carnaval in Puno 298
Caro Pepe 21
Carretera Austral 340
Cartagena 226
Casabindo 27
Casablanca on the Río Paraguay 50
Casas Particulares 103
Cassidy, Steven 62, 64, 71
Catemaco 129
Cementerio de Chauchilla 282
Ceviche 271
Chaco Road Warrior 54
Chan, Sharon 93
Chariatte, Alpana Varma 217, 218, 220
Cheng, JenFu 204, 213
Chiapas 132
Chicha 303
Chicken Buses 161
Chiclayo 273
Chile Los Géiseres del Tatio 323
Chilling in Chiloé 338
Chirripó 207
Chiva Party Bus 226
Choquequirao 289
Christiano, Richard 205
Christie, Andy 187
Ciullo, John 27
Classic Cars 105
Coast to Coast 73
Cobá 141
Coble, Melynda 167, 168, 170, 216
Cocos Island Diving 213
Coihaique 339
Colca Canyon 293
Colmer, Teresa 335
Colombia's Turn to Tourism 229
Colonia del Sacramento 42
Colonial Heart of Rio, The 64
Copán Ruins 175
Coppelia Ice Cream Park 102
Copper Canyon 110
Cordillera Vilcabamba 283
Coro 87
Coroico 305
Cotlear, Mariana 20, 252, 271, 277, 283, 297, 323, 327, 334
Cotopaxi 248
Cox, Allen 113, 136, 137, 138, 141
Coyner, Kelley 8, 17, 38, 44, 50, 51, 52, 53, 54, 303, 308, 310, 311, 312, 315, 316, 317, 323, 333, 337
Crossland, Martin 151, 154, 155
Cuarenta 242
Cuban Cigars 100
Cuenca 257
Cueva de las Manos 20
Cuillo, John 11
Culebra 95
Cult of the Afro-Venezuelan Saints 86
Curitiba 60
Cusco 290

## D

Damm, Patricia 74
Darwin, Charles 267
Davies, Michael 295, 298
Deep Sea Fishing 138
DeGrazier, Dominic 228
Denes, Christian 13, 14, 39, 345
Devil's Island 77
Devil's Nose, The 256
Devlin, Kieron 81
Diving in Bonaire 93
Diving in Salvador 70
Diving the Blue Hole 170
Dominican Republic Baseball 99
Don't Drink the Kool Aid 77
Doyle, Grant 101
Driving La Ruta del Sol 260

## E

Early Origin Theories 316
Easter Island 332
Eating Lemon Ants in the Rainforest 246
Eaton, Scott 151
Edwards, John 177
El Bolsón 12
El Cajón 283
El Chalten and Cerro Torre 7
El Drugstore Restaurant 44
El Habanero 121
Ellis, Freyja 3, 8, 49, 51, 55, 59, 67, 68, 71, 73, 80, 81, 82, 84, 91, 225, 226, 227, 232, 233, 235, 256, 259, 271, 294, 296, 318, 326, 329, 331, 341
El Mirador 162
El Museo del Oro 233
El Oriente and the Waorani 245
El Rosario Monarch Reserve 117
El Valle 217
Embera Drua Village 221
Estelí 183
Esteros del Iberá 29
Evita Museum 35
Evo Morales' Jumper 312

## F

Fantastic Flora 52
Fernando de Noronha 72
Ferree, Scott 25, 28, 340
Festivales de Misiones de Chiquitos 314
Fierro, Martín 9
Fiesta Internacional de la Canción de la Viña Mar 327
Fisher, Kathleen 240, 245
Fiske-Chow, Denise 115, 119, 121
Fitzgerald, Darren 68, 104, 116, 120, 135, 225, 228
Flynn, Brenda 269
Fonseca, Mauricio 211
Foz Tropicana Bird Park 59
Frías, Hugo Rafael Chávez 86
From Ground to Grande: Costa Rican Coffee 209
Fry, Kip 61
Furlong, Melanie 103

## G

Galápagos Islands, The 264
Gallo Pinto 191
Gamboa, Pedro Sarmiento de 272
Garcia, Albert 156, 157, 282, 297, 309
Gardel, Carlos 45
Gay Bogotá 234
Gentille, Michelle 287
Get on the Bus 337
Getting Around in Latin America 349
Getting Fíjased in Guatemala 146
Get Your Mojo On 287
Gibson, Craig 123
Gilbert, Rona 95, 171
Gower, Leigh 22, 42, 45, 66, 83, 88, 104, 169, 171, 195, 197, 203, 206, 207, 209, 210, 221, 303, 312, 317
Graf Spee Museum 44
Granada 188
Grave of William Walker, The 178
Gray, Will 3, 4, 7, 15, 101, 116, 133, 160, 175, 181, 189, 258, 274, 276, 286, 290, 293, 332, 333, 336, 338, 342, 343
Greater Colombia 89
Groesbeck, Geoff 313, 314
Guanajuato—Land of Frogs 118
Guaro 209
Guy, Sandy 57, 72
Guzmán, Abimael 278

## H

Hacienda Pinsaquí 238
Hacienda San AgustÍn de Callo 249
Hagenbuch, Brian 25, 29
Hale, Katie 37, 43, 79, 98, 100, 105, 109, 121, 122, 123, 124, 134, 135, 137, 138, 147, 148, 154, 158, 161, 201, 209, 217, 219, 220, 237, 254, 269, 309, 336, 348
Hall, Kerrie 153
Hannah, Louise 12
Hartwell, Cat 200, 203, 204
Haunted Museum, The 241
Havana 101
Havers, Nic 132, 143
Hedlund, Kyle 60
Here's the Beef: Where to Eat Typical/Atypical Cuisine 50
Hidalgo del Parral 112
Hiking el Misti Volcano 295
Hiking in the Cajas National Park 258
Hirschfeld, Maximilian 243, 276, 280, 285, 293, 298, 299, 320, 321, 346
Hoedt, Claire den 280
Homegrown Saints 89
Homestay at Flamingo Beach 210
Hopey, Michelle 17, 20, 21, 23, 30, 31, 32, 36, 37, 38, 42, 62, 97, 130, 131, 197, 251, 253, 264, 277, 278, 284, 287, 289, 291, 296, 311, 325, 330, 334, 337, 345, 348, 349
Horseback Riding: A Family Affair 203
Hot Chocolate in Latin America 345
Hotel Mono Azul 203
Huaca Rajada 273
Huang, Carol 109, 230
Huaraz and the Cordillera Blanca 276
Huayna Picchu Climb 286
Humitas 255
Huntley, Katrina 186
Hurling, Chris 234

## I

Ica Desert 279
Ice Cream 38
Iguassu Falls—A Brazilian Perspective 59
Iguazú falls 28
Iguazú Grand Hotel 28
Ilha de Silves 74
Ilha Grande 62
Imbessi, Paul 223
Inca Trail, The 284
Iquitos and the Jungle 274
Isla de Margarita 88
Isla de Ometepe 190
Isla Grande 220
Isla Mujeres 138
Iximché 151

## J

Jacó 201
Jerrigan, Bonnie L. 286, 292
Jinotega 185
Jurassic Park—Neuquén 17

## K

Kadey, Matthew 165, 166
Kass, Amanda 98, 99
Keeling, Stephen 35, 61
Khimm, Suzy 65
Kilo Bars 68
Kimer, Stan 273
Kirchner, Liz 142
Koppel, Julie 289
Korn, Allison 267
Kunas of San Blas 222

## L

La Boca 37
La Casa del Mundo and Café 148
La Casa de Mama Hilda's 251
La Ciudad Perdida Ruins 228
La Finca de Mariposas 207
La Gran Chiquitania 313
La Gruta Hotsprings 119
Laguna del Altar 255
Lake Atitlán 148, 149
Lake Crossing Into Chile 14
Lake Llanquihue 335
Lake Titicaca and the Island of the Sun 301
Lake Titicaca Homestay 296
La Mansion Inn 202
Lambing at the Estancia 51
Language Lesson 147
Lapa: The People's Theatre 65
La Paz 306
La Quinceañera 109
La Serena 327
La Sierra Horse Riding 124
Las Olas Surf Camp 115
Latin American Cocktails 348
La Trochita 11
La U Versus Alianza: Fierce Fútbol Rivalry 277
Lavendar Farm 16
La Virgen de Guadalupe 124
Learning to Dive in San Pedro 169
Leatherback Turtles at Playa Grande 199
Leslie, Fiona 10, 58, 73, 274
Leslie, Robyn 127
Li, Martin 79, 80, 222, 283, 288, 301, 304, 305, 306, 320, 351
Lievano, Wilson 67, 226, 229, 232, 233
Lima 277
Linde, Warren 262
Little Corn Island 187
Llao Llao Hotel and Resort, The 16
Local Emerging Artists 291
Los Altos and Chocolate 198
Los Calabazos 99
Los Llanos 83
Los Nevados 85
Los Roques 88
Lucha Libre 137
Lúcuma 297
Lynch, Madame 53

## M

Macas 247
Machu Picchu 285
Madidi 303
Madre de Dios River 292
Magellanic Penguins 342
Mahoney, Jenna 41, 115, 140, 200, 201
Making Tamales: A Christmas Tradition 134
Malbec Wine 23
Mal País 200
Máncora and Punta Sal 271
Manuel Antonio National Park 202
Maracanã Stadium 67
Mariscos 160
Markets of Masaya 189
Markets of Mexico City 127
Márquez, Gabriel García 227
Marsh-MacNeil, Neruda 149, 150, 161
Masewal Forest Garden 168
Massello, Amanda 43
Mbaracayú Reserve 53
McGlynn, Daniel 189, 191
Medellín 230
Meeting of Waters 73
Mendoza 20

Mercado Central  330
Merengue  97
Merida  137
Mérida  84
Mexican Jumping Beans  113
Mexico City Aztec Tour  125
Michael, Caroline  186
Miller, Josey  169
Minster, Dr. Crit  6, 9, 13, 14, 16, 28, 30, 60, 69, 70, 77, 86, 89, 93, 99, 107, 113, 125, 130, 131, 133, 136, 139, 145, 146, 150, 152, 159, 162, 163, 175, 177, 178, 227, 231, 237, 238, 241, 243, 246, 249, 252, 255, 257, 264, 266, 267, 268, 269, 272, 279, 281, 285, 290, 307, 315, 316, 347, 349
Mismaloya  123
Modern Indigenous Movement in Latin America, The  350
Montañita  263
Monteverde  197
Monteverde Dairy Factory  206
Monteverde Ziplining  197
Montevideo  43
Monument to the Bandierantes  61
Morelia  119
Mothers of the Disappeared  33
Mountain Biking and Tea in the Andes  19
Mountain Biking the World's Most Dangerous Road  305
Mount Roraima  79
Muela del Diablo  308
Music and Dance of Santería at Casa Elba  102
Mystery Remains, The  98

## N
Nasca Lines  281
Nebaj and the Ixil Triangle  146
Nelson, Pete  85, 88, 324, 328, 329, 334, 339, 343
Newton, Diane  249
Newton, Paula  239, 242, 243, 244, 258, 259, 260, 348
Nicaraguan Dance  186
Noriega, Manuel  219
Nowlan, John and Sandra  77

## O
O'Connor, Dennis  149
Oaxaca  130
Offerings to Pachamama  302
Off the Beaten Track in and Around La Paz  308
Ollantaytambo  288
Orosí  206
Osa Peninsula  211
Otavalo  237
Oyacachi  244

## P
Pakana's Sentinels  326
Palenque  133
Palermo  34
Panajachel  150
Panama Canal, The  219
Panama City  218
Panamanian-Chinese, The  220
Pantanal Wetlands, The  57
Papallacta  244
Paria Peninsula  91
Parque Nacional Corcovado  212

Parque Nacional del Café  229
Parque Nacional Montebello  134
Pátzcuaro: Day of the Dead  120
Peace of Mind  204
Peltier, Claire  275
Perito Moreno Glacier  6
Perquín  181
Petrified Forest of Puyango, The  268
Piñar del Río  100
Pisco Controversy, The  334
Placencia  172
Playa Blanca  225
Playa Bonita Resort  223
Playa Rincón  98
Playa Zancudo  210
Plaza de Toros  42
Plunkett, Thomas  211
Polga-Hecimovich, John  5, 18, 43, 83, 87, 90, 244, 253, 255, 261
Polyforum Cultural Siqueiros  126
Posada de Santiago  149
Potosí  318
Potter, Natalie  276
Proyecto Ecológico Quetzal  158
Pucón and Volcán Villarrica  333
Puerto Diaz  191
Puerto Montt to Puerto Natales  336
Puerto Williams  343
Puff Puff: A Ride on Guatemala Choo-Choo  155
Punta Arenas  342
Punta del Este  45
Punta de Mita  115
Punta Prieta Guesthouse  261
Putre  324

## Q
Quebrada de Humahuaca  26
Quechua Words  296
Querétaro  122
Quesillo—Oaxacan Cheese  131
Quetzaltenango  147
Quilombos  60
Quinoa  311
Quiriguá  159
Quito Cleats  241
Quito Homestay  240

## R
Rafting in the Ecuadorian Amazon  247
Rafting the Coyolate  155
Recoleta  35
Reef Madness  177
Reggaeton  252
Rincón de la Vieja  193
Rio Chiriquí Rafting  216
Rio de Janeiro  63
Rio Favelas  66
Rio Muchacho Organic Farm  262
Rio Orinoco  82
Río Pacuare Rafting  208
Road Tripping Along the Michoacan Coast  123
Roatán  177
Rocha  46
Ross, Dustin  94
Ruins of Monte Albán, The  131
Ruottinen, Jussi  284
Ruta Nacional 3, Patagonia  18

## S
Sabatiuk, E. Elizabeth  46
Sacco, Chris  247, 248, 256, 257, 305, 318
Saenz, Manuela  268
Sailing the Beagle Channel  4
Sajama to Arica  323
Salar de Uyuni  320
Salasaca: Day of the Dead  253
Salta  25
Salvador da Bahia  69
Samaipata  315
San Antonio Oeste  9
San Carlos de Bariloche  13
San Cristobal de las Casas  132
Sandboarding Around Ica  280
San Joaquín de Flores Heredia  195
San Juan Chamula  135
San Pedro: Isla Bonita  169
San Pedro de Atacama  325
San Pedro Prison  309
Santa Anna, Antonio López de  136
Santa Marta  227
Santa Teresa's Soda  201
San Telmo  31
Santiago  329
Santo Domingo and Cabarete  97
São Paulo  61
Saquisilí Market  252
Saraguro  267
Saucy, Seductive Salsa  253
Schwartz, Penny E.  262
Scott, Sandra  28, 35, 44, 47, 64, 75, 184, 198, 202, 223
Segreda, Ricardo  229, 350
Sehrt, Marc  26
Selva Negra  184
Shank, Kevin  173, 176, 179
Sian Ka'an Biosphere Reserve  143
Side Trips from Putre  324
Sillustani  297
Simmons, Martha  172
Singer, Paola  45
Sing it ... Latin Style  291
Skiing in Chile  336
Slaughter, Stephany  107, 117, 119, 120, 125, 128, 139, 140, 141, 142
Smith, Kerry L.  63, 114
Snorkeling in the Galápagos  266
Sosa, Kena  122, 125, 128
Spence, Kimberly Nelson  84
Splurging in Palermo  34
Stanford, Joanne  124
Statue to Statue in Cusco  290
Staying at an Estancia  22
Studying Spanish in Quito  239
Surf's Up! Pico Alto and Chicama  272
Surfing in Mal País  200
Surviving the Sambadrome  64
Swallow Caye Wildlife Sanctuary  170
Swimming Waiters  71

## T
Tabacón Spa  195
Taborcillo  221
Tales of a 57-Year-Old Grandmother Travelling Alone in Latin America  346

Tango 37
Tarabuco 317
Taxco Silver City 128
Taste of a Soccer Game, A 36
Tayrona National Park 225
Tela 176
Telefériqo 243
Tepoztlán 122
Tequila—A Way of Life 116
The Peoples of Lake Titicaca 302
Tibbetts, Katie 240, 241, 254, 263
Tijuana 107
Tikal 163
Tiwanaku 309
Tiwanaku Off the Beaten Track 310
Tlayudas 130
Tobacco Caye 171
Todos Santos 145
Tolhuin, Tierra del Fuego 5
Tomás' Sapo Falls 79
Tonner, Sarah 24, 33
Too Tired to Tango 38
Top Football Stadiums 66
Top Ten Latin Americans Who Couldn't Keep Still—Even After They Died! 347
Torres del Paine National Park 341
Tortuguero 196
Traditional Crafts and Shopping 278
Trekking Condoriri to Huayna Potosí 311
Trekking the Cordillera Apolobamba 304
Trinidad 104
Tropical Hotel and Resort, Manaus 75
Tropic Star Lodge 223
Tupiza 319

## U
U.S. Study Abroad in Latin America 330
Uruapan 121
Ushuaia 3
Uxmal 136

## V
Valdez Peninsula 8
Valdivia 334
Valparaíso 328
Vapor Cué 52
Vieques 96
Vilcabamba 269
Villa de Leyva 231
Villarrica 333
Vincent, David 59, 100, 294, 341
Virgin of Quito, The 243
Viteri, Suco 239, 248, 295
Volcán Arenal 194
Volcán Barú 217
Volcán Pacaya 153
Volunteering Adventure in Costa Rica 205
Volunteer in Peru 289

## W
Walker, Kim 110, 111, 221
Walli, Carla 250
Walsh, Gary 66
War of the Triple Alliance, The 69
Weberling, Brooke 147
Welsh Tea in Patagonia 10
Weston, Wes 49, 194, 212, 215

Wheels on the Bus Go Round and Round, The 337
Wild Albatross Mating 265
Wild Tortoises on Santa Cruz Island 265
Willka T'ika Eco-Lodge 287
Winding Your Way Through the Andes 24
Winston, Ben 66
Witches' Market 307
Wopperer, Suzanne 185
World Record Ice Cream 84
World's Highest Cable Car, The 83

## X
Xunantunich 168

## Y
Yerba Mate 17

## Z
Zapatista Women 135
Zipaquirá 232

# Revolutionizing the travel guide...
## Written for Travelers, By Travelers

# V!VA
## TRAVEL GUIDES

- **Unbiased**
- **Up-to-Date**
- **Created by Travelers**

All V!VA Travel Guides' books begin on the VivaTravelGuides.com website, collecting reviews, comments, rants and raves, suggestions, and updates from travelers like you.

The community´s favorites are then compiled into a book. Most guide books rely on the opinions and research of one single person who may or may not share your tastes.

V!VA Guides, on the other hand, rely on unbiased first-hand accounts from fellow travelers. This process guarantees that you have the most up-to-date, accurate information available for planning your travels.

## Other V!VA Titles:
- Ecuador Travel Guide
- Peru Travel Guide
- Living and Working in Peru, Ecuador and Bolivia

## Available in 2008:
- V!VA List World
- Ecuador Climbing and Hiking Guide
- Argentina Travel Guide
- And More!

**buy them at: shop.vivatravelguides.com or amazon.com**